D0072678

CLASSICAL MUSIC

In the same series:

Medieval Music by Richard H. Hoppin
Romantic Music by Leon Plantinga
Twentieth-Century Music by Robert P. Morgan

The Norton Introduction to Music History

CLASSICAL MUSIC

The Era of Haydn, Mozart, and Beethoven

PHILIP G. DOWNS
The University of Western Ontario

W·W·NORTON & COMPANY
New York · London

Jacket art attributed to François André Vincent (Paris, 1746–1816), *Un concert,* from the Collection E. and O. Lavalard, donated to the Musée de Picardie, Amiens, France, in 1890; with permission of the Musée de Picardie, Amiens (Photo Bulloz).

Printed in the United States of America

First Edition

The text of this book is composed in Bembo.
Composition and manufacturing by The Maple-Vail Book Manufacturing Group.

Library of Congress Cataloging-in-Publication Data
Downs, Philip G.
Classical music: the era of Haydn, Mozart, and Beethoven / Philip G Downs.
p. cm.—(The Norton introduction to music history)
Includes bibliographical references and index. 1. Music—18th century—History and criticism. 2. Music—19th century—History and criticism. 3. Haydn, Joseph, 1732–1809. 4. Mozart, Wolfgang Amadeus, 1756–1791. 5. Beethoven, Ludwig van, 1770–1827. I. Title II. Series.
ML195.D68 1992
780'.9'033—dc20 92–5037

ISBN 0–393–95191–X

W. W. Norton & Company, Inc., 500 Fifth Avenue, New York, N.Y. 10110
W. W. Norton & Company Ltd., 10 Coptic Street, London WC1A 1PU
2 3 4 5 6 7 8 9 0

CONTENTS

PART NINE. THE EIGHTEENTH-CENTURY HERITAGE AT WORK IN THE EARLY NINETEENTH CENTURY

List of Illustrations

Preface

Any attempt to pin a label onto a period of history springs from the observation that society changes, and from the wish to group together things that are alike. It is undeniably handy to be able to refer to "The Renaissance" or "The Period of the Bustle" or "The Age of the Virtuoso." The obvious danger in their use lies in the assumption that other people will understand the same things from the label that we ourselves do. The more remote we are from the period under discussion, the easier it is to lump hundreds—even thousands—of years together, while the closer we are, the more our knowledge of detail prevents us from putting it into any one pigeonhole. Evidence of this process is to be found in the titles of the books in this *Norton Introduction to Music History* series. Thus, the first four volumes carry titles connoting a kind of quality: Medieval; Renaissance; Baroque; Classical. The fifth volume appears to follow the same idea, with its title of *Romantic Music,* but its subtitle connects it inexorably with nineteenth-century Europe; while the last volume, *Twentieth-Century Music,* carries the further explanatory subtitle, "A History of Musical Style in Modern Europe and America."

I feel uneasy about applying the term "classical" to music, because its widespread use has caused it to mean distinctly different things to different people. No attempt to define the term and the qualities it connotes can remove its inherent ambiguity. Moreover, the last fifty years have witnessed such an expansion of studies into all aspects of the artistic life of the eighteenth century that we now possess a knowledge of this time unparalleled by that of any period. Even the eighteenth century did not know itself as well as we know it. What we may lack in knowledge of fact and detail we more than make up for by our perspective over the whole span of the time and our synoptic vision of the unity underlying its processes. The more we come to know, the less useful the term becomes, and scholars have tried to assauge their feelings of guilt over the misconceptions that terminology was perpetuating by speaking about "Rococo" and "Pre-Classical" and referring to the *style galant,* distinguishing each from the simply "Classical." Such subdivisions, while they are not soiled with overuse, have only a limited utility since they are either too restrictive or too inclusive. Yet we cannot refer simply to eighteenth-century music, for such a title would obscure one of the biggest, most important, most epoch-making events of the last half-millennium of music: the widespread change in musical ideals that occurred between the Classical period and what came before it.

The shape of the present volume is the outcome of this quandary: how can one recognize that a period of approximately one hundred years has a certain unity, beyond geography and beyond time, without obscuring the fact that the rate of change of the arts within that period is both rapid and constant? The first outcome of this question is the recognition that almost any statement about music in this book or any other, needs to be qualified by some date or point to which it can be attached. In other words, a means had to be found of separating discussion of the music of 1740 from that of 1780, so that some impression of stylistic development could be recognized by the reader. Hence there arose the decision to divide the book into fairly arbitrary twenty-year periods, and I tried to make sure that in each general history section only musical artworks of that time would be discussed. This consideration has inevitably created difficulties in dating works but I believe the principle to be sound. In those chapters dealing with the great composers whose names figure so prominently in the subtitle of the volume, the temptation to stray from arbitrary periodization into one based upon epochs has proven irresistible: Mozart's going to Vienna in 1781, and the death of Haydn's favorite Prince in 1790 were such important breaks in the continuity of these men's lives that they could not be ignored.

Within the sections of general history, I have attempted to follow a consistent pattern in the treatment of materials, recognizing that a book such as this needs to be useful in a variety of ways. It is hoped, therefore, that the reader will be able to trace, let us say, the history of the piano sonata, or the development of chamber music, or the growth of philosophical response to music, or the development of music publishing, by referring successively to the relevant chapters. At the same time, the book can be used as a "great composer" study, not only for Haydn, Mozart and Beethoven but also for a lesser "great" such as C. P. E. Bach. Such a plan necessarily entails a certain amount of repetition, which, it is hoped, will not be obtrusive.

From early in the conception of the book it was accepted that the fundamental attitude to the music of the time had to take into account not only the great composers, whose names are household words and whose music has formed both the basis of taste and the foundation upon which later composers have built, but also the host of lesser composers, those *Kleinmeister* who may have enjoyed fame in their lifetime but towards whom posterity has been less kind. There can be no doubt that a knowledge of the broader fabric of music in any society will help to define those ways in which the greater composer's art is superior to that of his lesser contemporaries. It is not the work of a Haydn or of a

Beethoven that defines the particular greatness of a Mozart; that kind of comparison points up differences. Nor can any answer be obtained to that eternal, nagging question: "Why did their contemporaries not appreciate the quality of Mozart (or of Haydn) since their superiority is so self-evident to us?" It is only through knowledge of works such as *L'Arbore di Diana,* or *Una Cosa Rara* of Martìn y Soler, or *Il Matrimonio Segreto* of Cimarosa that one can see how far removed was Mozart from the taste of many of the Viennese, particularly those of the Court milieu. Put the other way round: in those places where Cimarosa and Martìn represent the taste of the time, how can mature Mozart seem anything other than perversely complex and turgid? We are so fortunate in that the taste of *our* time has revived an interest in the art of the eighteenth century in a way that seemed impossible fifty years ago. This history has had to take into account the work of many minor masters, and we are now in a position to see how enormously rich in variety, both temporal and geographic, was the musical life of eighteenth-century society.

The structure of the book was planned to fulfil what I perceived to be the author's responsibility to satisfy the needs of a wide variety of readers. Unfortunately, no amount of historical scholarship can answer the questions we would most like to ask, and tell us precisely how Mozart's stated ideals of piano playing were translated into actual sound, or how the Mannheim orchestra articulated the notes of the score under Johann Stamitz's direction. The world of authentic performance practise has developed so rapidly, has been so subject to revision, and has become so specialized, even personal, that I judged it wiser not to venture into these troubled waters. The most important contemporary sources of such scholarship are, of course, referred to.

The investigation of individual compositions has clearly not been intended to either follow or cultivate a particular method or analytical stance. Rather, in dealing with an age where the composer often tried to embody unique features in each work, I have attempted to isolate those aspects of the composition in which concentrated efforts at individuation may be found.

The opportunity to write a book such as this appeared at first to be a dream. The actuality, like so many other things in life, was often less gratifying, since the process of formulating a generalization inevitably involves a sacrifice of important detail, and because the written word is such an inadequate approach to the artwork. The path through the inferno was made easier by many friends who were prepared to play Virgil to my Dante, and from whose wisdom and kindly responses I profitted on many occasions through the years, while their work was in preparation. Among these guides must be numbered Elaine Adair, Jane Baldwin, Jeffrey Stokes, James Whitby and most particularly Dillon Parmer and John Glofcheskie, who read the entire manuscript. Barry Brook,

Lewis Lockwood, and Bruce MacIntyre are each owed a great debt of gratitude for their penetrating and invaluable advice, which both fleshed out parts of the work that were too skeletal and slimmed down others that were too exuberant, but most of all for their encouragement. Colleagues whose help and support has been unstinted, and gratefully accepted, even when they did not know that they were helping, include Terence Bailey, Sandra Mangsen, Don Neville, Richard Semmens, and Robert Toft.

What thanks can be conveyed to Claire Brook, my editor, that others have not already conveyed more eloquently? What careful compliment can be offered her that has not become stale through repetition? Perhaps it is best simply to state that I cannot imagine any person as busy and energetic as she is, being more tolerant, more patient, more kindly, more helpful, more encouraging than she has been over the many years this book has been in preparation. She is a rare person indeed!

Finally, I want to thank Fred and Jeff, without whom this book would not exist and my family—Anne, Robin, Dorothy, and Margaret—who give meaning to it all.

Philip G. Downs
London, Ontario

PART I

The Transition from Baroque: Music to 1760

CHAPTER I

The Background to Eighteenth-Century Thought

The predominant patterns of eighteenth-century thought grew out of the legacy of seventeenth-century achievement in science, mathematics, and philosophy. In the early 1600s, society had experienced great difficulty in accepting the new scientific approach to the world and to God, and had shown its resistance by persecuting one of the greatest scientists of the day, Galileo Galilei (1564–1642), during the last twenty-eight years of his life. By the early years of the eighteenth century, however, the work of René Descartes (1596–1650), Isaac Newton (1643–1727), and many others had been sympathetically received and completely accepted by a broad-based intellectual community.

It is impossible to overestimate the effect upon men's minds wrought by this new approach to science: it was as if a burden had been lifted, quite comparable to that change which historians note when the Middle Ages blossom into the Renaissance. The poet Alexander Pope (1688–1744), in many ways representative of the ideal intellect of the day, proposed the following epitaph for Newton in 1728:

> Nature and Nature's laws lay hid in night:
> God said, *Let Newton be!* and all was light.

The couplet demonstrates the difference between seventeenth- and eighteenth-century thought, and the way in which it was recognized at the time. The poet John Milton (1608–1674) summed up the older attitude when he wished that his epic poem *Paradise Lost* (1667) might "justify the ways of God to Men." The newer attitude, epitomized in the Newtonian Light, led to the conception of a rational universe—a mechanism in which the earth and the other planets revolving around the sun were held in their elliptical orbits by the universal laws of physics. The idea of an earth-centered universe was put aside forever, and with it

The Greenwich Observatory in the late 17th century. When Haydn visited here, a hundred years later, Herschel's telescope was forty feet long with an aperture of four feet. (Science Museum, London)

went much of the power of the conception of God that had dominated earlier ages.[1]

In its place, there arose an overall feeling of confidence in the future. The basis of such confidence rested upon the expansive colonization of the "uncivilized" world, which supported the conviction that there were riches out there simply waiting to be picked up and upon a growing determination that people were in control of their own destiny. The immediate result of this complex of thought was the development of religious skepticism and atheism among intellectuals and the new commercial classes, as well as a universal questioning of political institutions.

The seventeenth century witnessed the growth of scientific inquiry and the broadening of knowledge in many areas. But by the end of that century the reforming ideas of Luther and Calvin had been worked into a body of dogma as formidable as that of the Church of Rome, and the new Light of Reason spared no orthodoxy from close scrutiny. Indeed,

1. Newton believed that the place of God in the universe was as the rectifier of the small irregularities which he (Newton) perceived in the motion of the heavenly bodies, i.e., as a kind of engineer looking after a complex piece of machinery. The French scientist Pierre-Simon de Laplace (1749–1827), whose work demonstrates the mathematical certainty of what Newton had perceived as irregular, when taken to task by Napoleon for having neglected anywhere to mention the place of God as the creator of everything, replied: "I had no need of that hypothesis, Sire."

faith in the brightness of that light was such that philosophical theologians could maintain that reason is the reflection of the divine in the soul of man. Even matters of conscience were to be tested by it. And whereas philosophy had formerly been honored for the support it gave to religion,[2] now it became an active and potentially subversive force, free to move in whichever direction Truth seemed to beckon.

There were several signs that marked the progress of thought along the road from superstition[3] to Rationalism. The realization that the earth was a minute part of the universe rather than the center of Creation has already been mentioned. The growth of religious tolerance was a much longer process—indeed, it is still incomplete—but humanity has certainly progressed from the time when the burning stake was the answer to any heresy. Belief in the power of witchcraft—that age-old explanation for misfortune and illness, which the medieval Church had cod-

2. One of the strongest supporters of Catholicism, Thomas Aquinas (1225–74), succeeded in reconciling the philosophy of Aristotle with the teachings of the church.

3. The word "superstition" connotes the irrational and is the word commonly used in the free-thinking eighteenth century as a synonym for religion. The great historian Edward Gibbon (1737–94), in identifying the reasons for Christianity's spread in his *History of the Decline and Fall of the Roman Empire* (1776–88), wrote in a manner that typifies the eighteenth-century approach to religion. Two passages will suffice, both from Chapter 15 of his *History,* the second of which is one of the supreme examples of irony.

> So urgent on the vulgar is the necessity of believing that the fall of any system of mythology will most probably be succeeded by the introduction of some other mode of superstition.
>
> But how shall we excuse the supine inattention of the Pagan and philosophic world to those evidences which were presented by the hand of Omnipotence, not to their reason, but to their senses? During the age of Christ, of his apostles, and of their first disciples, the doctrine which they preached was confirmed by innumerable prodigies. The lame walked, the blind saw, the sick were healed, the dead were raised, daemons were expelled, and the laws of Nature were frequently suspended for the benefit of the church. But the sages of Greece and Rome turned aside from the awful spectacle, and, pursuing the ordinary occupations of life and study, appeared unconscious of any alterations in the moral or physical government of the world. Under the reign of Tiberius, the whole earth, or at least a celebrated province of the Roman empire, was involved in a praeternatural darkness of three hours [after the death of Jesus]. Even this miraculous event, which ought to have excited the wonder, the curiosity, and the devotion of mankind, passed without notice in an age of science and history. It happened during the lifetime of Seneca and the elder Pliny, who must have experienced the immediate effects, or received the earliest intelligence, of the prodigy. Each of these philosophers, in a laborious work, has recorded all the great phenomena of Nature, earthquakes, meteors, comets, and eclipses, which his indefatigable curiosity could collect. Both the one and the other have omitted to mention the greatest phenomenon to which mortal eye has been witness since the creation of the globe. A distinct chapter of Pliny is designed for eclipses of an extraordinary nature and unusual duration; but he contents himself with describing the singular defect of light which followed the murder of Caesar, when, during the greatest part of the year, the orb of the sun appeared pale and without splendour. This season of obscurity, which cannot surely be compared with the praeternatural darkness of the Passion, had been already celebrated by most of the poets and historians of that memorable age.

ified into a body of demonology—declined rapidly in this period, and the literal conception of Hell as a sulphurous pit of everlasting fire also lost much of its vivid power, being replaced by more spiritual ideas.

While rationalism made its appeal to the intellect and the process of reason in human affairs, the opposite side of human nature, which operates on emotion and feeling and upon the need to do good works, was fulfilled by the Pietistic movement in Germany and by the growth of Methodism and the teachings of John Wesley (1703–91) in Britain. In the industrial areas of Britain, where the established church had failed to keep up with the pace of social change, Methodism and other types of nonconformism made their mark.

The outcome of all these changes was, as the Catholic establishment had always feared, the loss of a solid foundation in faith. Along with questioning the nature of God, and the relationship of God, man, and Bible, came the questioning of those human beings previously thought of as appointed by God and, inevitably, the challenging of the whole social order. The last gasps of absolute monarchy were heard in a number of places. In England the argument for the divine right of kings was lost when, in 1647, Parliament executed Charles I. It was lost in France in 1789 with the Declaration of the Rights of Man. Elsewhere monarchical power was whittled away during the nineteenth century, and today virtually nothing is left of the old unwritten contract between sovereign lord—God on earth—and his people. In this climate of constant and radical change the expression of faith becomes of necessity a personal thing, since the formal rites of a religion can serve as much to conceal disbelief as they serve to demonstrate conformity.

There developed among the people a new understanding of their environment—knowledge that modified social attitudes to a marked degree. This was a growing perception of a coherent system which seemed to reconcile all observable phenomena into a harmonious whole. In other words, the mysteries of Creation seemed to be better explained by the rational thought processes of humans than by divine revelation or myth. Much of the spirit of optimism that pervades eighteenth-century thought is based upon the belief that scientific inquiry was opening doors to knowledge, wealth, and power. Implicit is the conviction that this process could, if put to the test, answer all questions.

From this attitude arises the tone of Pope's couplet, confident in its refusal to be overawed by the Deity and prepared to face large issues with the kind of humor that deflates pomposity. It also speaks of another of the crucial changes in outlook between the centuries. The seventeenth century had loved the idea of artifice and the artificial (since nature's laws were hidden, either deliberately or through mischance) and had seen in the park and palace of Versailles, for example, a marvelous demonstration of man's ability to set his environment in order. Indeed, this great seventeenth-century accomplishment succeeded in pushing

The Palace of Versailles. When Louis XIV died, the formal gardens covered 135 acres, the "Small Park," 4,200 acres, and the wall around the "Hunting Park" was 27 miles long.

untouched landscape beyond the horizon; everything in sight had to be modified by man, thus putting into practice God's sanction to "replenish the earth, and subdue it."

Quite different from this attitude was the easy sense of comprehending their surroundings which gave to people of the eighteenth century a new approach to their environment, enabling them to live with nature and the natural. In landscaping they did away with the straight alleys and formal *parterres* of the previous generation, and allowed grass and trees, in artfully casual design, almost up to their front doors. The concept of the "natural" became the touchstone for what was proper, not only in the art of landscape gardening but in the other arts, as well as in religion and social life. Whereas earlier ages had tended to visualize God in human form, as the orderer of the social hierarchy—the power above even kings and popes—the eighteenth century began to see Him in the world around, for example, in the grandeur of untamed mountain scenery. The sublime in nature came to be a kind of synonym for the divine.

Despite these changes, the momentum of seventeenth-century institutions and manners preserved the appearance of continuity. Events such as the death of Queen Anne of Great Britain (1665–1714) and of Louis XIV of France (1638–1715), while they involved enormous shifts of power from one party to another, were glossed over, in the first case through the will of Parliament, and in the other by monarchical succession. *"Le Roi est mort!"* said the grand chamberlain, the Duc de Bouillon, wearing a black feather as he announced the close of an era with the death of the great French king. A moment later, having replaced his black feather with a white one, he proclaimed the accession of the five-year-old Louis XV (1710–74), the late king's great-grandson, with the words *"Vive le Roi!"* .

But the clock cannot be stopped. Throughout western Europe, the spirit of rational inquiry into the nature of institutions was widespread, and these last representatives of seventeenth-century monarchy were confronted by the artists and thinkers around them with questions and attitudes keener and more critical than those current earlier in their reigns. The French writer Jean de La Bruyère (1645–96) was able to demonstrate to the public and to Louis XIV how far short of the ideal his monarchy had become, and how the pursuit of glory had reduced the king's subjects to beggary, by the simple means of asking questions such as the following, taken from his *Caractères* (1688):

> Is the flock made for the shepherd or the shepherd for the flock?
>
> If men can feel no joy on earth more natural, more grateful, and more rewarding than that of knowing they are loved, and if kings are men, can they pay too high a price for the hearts of their people?[4]

This example of seventeenth-century free-thinking stands out in its time as exceptional. By the eighteenth century, however, the expression of such ideas had become commonplace, and one senses the new style of the time from the way Alexander Pope, in his poem *The Rape of the Lock* (1714), deals with his monarch, Queen Anne, and her habits, particularly her love of drinks stronger than tea. Speaking of the royal palace of Hampton Court, where the ultimate power of the state resides, he wrote:

> Here Britain's statesmen oft the fall foredoom
> Of foreign tyrants, and of nymphs at home;
> Here, thou, great ANNA! whom three realms obey,
> Dost sometimes counsel take—and sometimes tea.[5]

The anticlimax in these lines pricks the bubble; the great are but human, and share the weaknesses of the flesh with other mortals. What chance has the doctrine of the divine right of kings[6] against such an attack?

4. Jean de la Bruyère, *Du souverain ou de la république* (Paris, 1858)
5. Alexander Pope, *The Rape of the Lock,* canto 3, lines 5–8.
6. King Charles I of England lost his head through his belief that kings were accountable only to God, i.e., that they ruled by "divine right." The American Revolution of 1776 was a revolt against colonial status, not against monarchical rule, since Britain had been a constitutional monarchy governed by a Parliament since 1688. France, on the other hand, like most other European states, remained an absolute monarchy until the Revolution of 1789.

ART AND THE PHILOSOPHER

This was a period when people were interested in gathering together all the knowledge of the world: it was the age of the encyclopedia, designed to accomplish this task, with Chambers' *Cyclopaedia* appearing in 1728, and the eagerly awaited French *Encyclopédie* from 1751. In their efforts to define their subject matter, the writers of these comprehensive works were forced to carry the process of inquiry still further. Just as artists caused society to ask reasonable questions about its institutions, and as scientists applied the same methods to problems of physics and mathematics, so philosophers attempted to approach problems of aesthetics—that is to say, the way in which art is experienced. As never before, tome after tome appeared, in which the various arts were dissected and attempts were made to establish their proper function and their distinctions, one from another.

There were two fundamental premises common to almost all the philosophical treatises that attempted to deal with art. One, which proved very difficult to accept by those committed to religious orthodoxy, was that the mind is not born with any innate knowledge of morality or of God, but is formed only by that evidence carried to it through the senses.[7] The other is the strongly and frequently-voiced adherence to the dictum of Aristotle that Art imitates Nature. So widely is this notion accepted that the premise is never questioned, but instead the ways in which the arts can be seen to fulfill its truth are examined.

The English philosopher and philologist James Harris (1709–80) wrote *A Discourse on Music, Painting and Poetry* in 1744, in which he set out "to consider in what they agree and in what they differ; and which, upon the whole, is more excellent than the other two."[8] He states the following as the premises for his argument:

> . . . the Mind is made conscious of the *natural World* and its Affections, and of other *Minds* and their Affections, by the several *Organs of the Senses.* By the same *Organs,* these Arts exhibit to the Mind *Imitations,* and imitate either Parts or Affections of this *natural World,* or else the passions, energies, and other Affections of *Minds.* There is this Difference, however, between these *Arts* and *Nature;* that Nature passes to the Percipient thro' *all* the Senses; whereas these Arts use *only two* of them, that of Seeing and that of Hearing.

Painting, therefore, says Harris, can properly imitate color and figure, since it passes through the eye: music, entering by the ear, can properly imitate only motion and sound. He goes on to say that poetry, like

7. This statement defines a philosophical position popular at the time and referred to as "empiricism."

8. James Harris, *Three Treatises, The Second Concerning Music, Painting and Poetry* (2nd. ed. London, 1765); facsimile reprint, Garland, New York, 1970. All quotations are from the first chapter.

music, can only imitate motion and sound, since it is perceived through the ear. It is conventionally agreed, however, that the sounds it uses correspond to ideas; hence, poetry can imitate "as far as language can express." Harris's immediate conclusion, before he proceeds to examine each art in detail, is that all three arts "agree, by being mimetic or imitative. They differ as they imitate by different media."

The French writer Abbé Charles Batteux (1713–80) published a work in 1747 entitled *Traité sur les Beaux-Arts réduits à un même principe* (Treatise on the Single Underlying Principle of the Fine Arts),[9] which proved to be one of the most influential works on asthetics of the time, particularly in Germany, and he makes many interesting points that shed light on the way the cultivated eighteenth-century person approached art. He seems not to have known about earlier thoughts on the same subject, such as those of Harris, for he writes as though he were the first to perceive the all-embracing force of the Aristotelian doctrine that Art imitates Nature, and the first to expose its treasures to mankind. It is hard to take him completely at his word, however, since many of his ideas were in the wind at the time and his work and Harris's have several points of planning and detail in common.

Like Harris, Batteux believes we are the result of what our senses have perceived. Thus, "we cannot come out of ourselves, nor can we characterize the imaginary other than with the features that we know from reality." Even the genius ought not to attempt to overcome this limitation: "His function consists not in imagining what might be but in finding what is." Man's perennial search is for the true, the good, and the beautiful, all of which are to be found in nature. Batteux argues that the goal of the sciences is the true, whereas the goal of the fine arts is the beautiful and the good, thus establishing what was then commonly accepted as the connection between the arts and morals. In one of the most significant phrases, central to the understanding of the period, Batteux asserts the eighteenth-century doctrine that the substance of the arts "is not the True but the appearance of truth . . . The masterpieces of Art are those which imitate Nature so well that one takes them for Nature herself." It is paradoxical in a work which so often appeals to "feeling" rather than to reason that Batteux's assertion is one of intellectual supremacy over emotional credulity.

The scope of this study is defined by the speculation that primitive man had three means of expressing himself: through tone of voice, through word, and through gesture (i.e., dance). Hence, Batteux's conclusions tend to confirm the unity of his single principle of imitation. He says:

9. All quotations from Batteux are taken from the first edition. They can be found on pages 11, 14, 299, 30, 267, 268, 279, and 282 respectively. The translations are by the author.

The Pleasures of the Dance. Watteau's engraving shows dancing as an exercise in poise and grace: two dancers perform while the rest look on. (Musée du Louvre, Paris)

> Although poetry, music and dance sometimes are separated in order to conform to the will of men, yet Nature created them to be united and to move together towards a single goal.

Nevertheless, he has some interesting things to say about music. Because of his acceptance of a primal expressive purpose in art, Batteux has to believe that music must express something. Independent of words, music is lessened, to be sure, but "music without words is still music." In addition to holding to the conventional wisdom that "the principal objective of Music ought to be the imitation of the passions. . ." Batteux is prepared to carry his historical speculation still further. He says:

> . . . if the tone of voice and gesture had a meaning before they came to be measured, they must surely keep that meaning in music and dance, just as words preserve their meaning when they are set in verse; and consequently, all music and all dance music must have meaning. . . . Everything that Art adds to tone of voice and to gesture must help to increase this meaning and to make its expression more pointed.

He is even prepared to elaborate his speculation to the point where he transforms it into a rule:

> If I were to say that I cannot take pleasure in an argument that I do not

> understand, my confession would be unexceptionable. But let me dare to say the same thing about a piece of music . . .

and having defended himself against an anticipated attack by another appeal to "feeling" rather than to reason, he continues:

> Music speaks to me through Tones: the language is natural to me: if I do not understand it, then Art has corrupted Nature rather than adding a perfection to it.

In other words, any music that Batteux, a cultivated man of taste, does not understand cannot be good music. He relates that whenever he has asked a composer to indicate to him those parts of his compositions which have pleased him most, the composer has invariably pointed out those passages or compositions which have the most clearly defined expressive character. The author concludes from this that "the worst of all music is that which has no characteristic affection."

Batteux's ideas had considerable influence on the way people thought about art in the eighteenth century, but they were not universally accepted. His fellow country-man and the moving spirit behind the *Encyclopédie,* Denis Diderot (1713–84), took him to task in a long letter published in 1751, although he was generally concerned with matters other than music.[10]

It is worth pausing to observe that the preceding thoughts were expressed by men whose first concern was not music but philosophy and letters. Indeed, as men of letters, Harris and Batteux reach a similar and hardly surprising conclusion about the supremacy of poetry over music and the other arts.

THE MUSICIAN AS PHILOSOPHER

Many musicians as well, took up their pens to formulate and propagate their ideas in this period. As is to be expected, the majority of their treatises are concerned with matters of musical technique rather than aesthetics alone, and this kind of work will be considered in due course. The writing of two independent and forward-looking musicians, Johann Mattheson (1681–1764) and Charles Avison (1709–70), will demon-

10. In his *Dictionnaire de Musique* (Sonate: Paris, 1768), Jean-Jacques Rousseau writes the following on this subject of music and meaning: "Instrumental music gives life to Song and adds to its expression, but in no way supplants it. In order to know the meaning of this jumble of sonatas we are loaded down with, one would have to do what the crude painter did who wrote under the things he painted: 'This is a tree,' 'This is a man,' 'This is a horse.' I shall never forget the witticism of the famous Fontenelle [Bernard de, 1657–1757], who, becoming exasperated with these never-ending instrumental pieces, cried out aloud in a transport of impatience: 'Sonata, what do you want from me?' " Rousseau makes it clear that music without words is, in his view, sound, more or less pleasant, without meaning. Author's translation.

strate how many composers thought about the philosophical basis of their art.

Mattheson more properly belonged to an earlier age, but his most comprehensive treatise, entitled *Der volkommene Capellmeister* (The Complete Music Director), dates from 1739 and was widely used until the end of the century. Indeed, Ludwig van Beethoven (1770–1827) is known to have possessed a copy of this work and is believed to have based many of his ideas about word-setting on its precepts. Avison's work, entitled *An Essay on Musical Expression,* is much less comprehensive and his influence is not as great as Mattheson's. Yet he is one of the earliest writers on this subject in English, and he makes some important points.

Both musicians agree with the philosophers on the moral basis of music: its business is to make listeners love the good, the beautiful, and the virtuous, and to hate evil. Mattheson says:

> It is an aspect of moral teaching which the complete master of sound must adopt as his own, so that he may properly represent virtue and vice with his tones in order to inspire his listeners with love for one and hatred for the other. For this is the proper purpose of music, to be, above all, a moral lesson.[11]

Avison's expression of the same idea is less dogmatic:

> We may venture to assert, that it is the peculiar Quality of Music to raise the *sociable* and happy Passions and to *subdue* the *contrary ones.*[12]

They also agree that art imitates nature, but they become quite explicit in denying the value of simple imitation. Thus Avison says "Music as an imitative Art has very confined Powers"[13] and adds that to make imitation the most important aspect of the art is to reduce it to the lowest levels. He goes so far as to suggest the existence of a "peculiar and internal Sense . . . of a much more refined Nature than the external Senses,"[14] with which those endowed with the capacity can enjoy melody and harmony. He observes as proof that stimulation of this peculiar sense does not result in boredom or disgust, as sometimes occurs with the five senses we recognize. When the effect of musical expression is added to melody and harmony, then the passions or feelings are brought into play and the full power of music is experienced.

Between these two authors, Mattheson and Avison, one can see just how attitudes toward music are changing at this point in the eighteenth century. Mattheson, as a late representative of the Baroque, still clings

11. Johann Mattheson, *Der volkommene Capellmeister,* revised trans. with Critical Commentary by Ernest C. Harriss (Ann Arbor, 1981), p.123.

12. Charles Avison, *An Essay on Musical Expression* (London, 1753; facsimile edition New York, 1967), p.4.

13. *Ibid.,* p. 60.

14. *Ibid.,* p. 2.

to the idea that a composer's business lies in arousing a wide variety of passions or feelings, ranging from tender emotions such as love, pity, and melancholy, to hatred, obstinacy, and fickleness. He believes this can be accomplished by the use of specific keys, tempos, dynamics, and musical figures. This idea is generally referred to as the Doctrine of Affections in English, or *Affektenlehre* in German. Moreover, he propagates the idea that a dance, for example, a *passepied,* should express a generalized feeling or characteristic throughout. He says:

> *Le Passepied,* either in a sinfonia or for dancing . . . Its nature comes close to frivolity: for, with all its disquiet and inconstancy, such a Passepied, has by no means the zeal, passion or ardor which one comes across with a volatile *gigue.* Meanwhile it is still a kind of frivolity which does not have anything detestable or unpleasant about it, but rather something pleasant: just as a little inconstancy in womankind does not take away their charm.[15]

Avison, on the other hand, denies music the power of raising negative emotional states, such as hatred, jealousy, anger, and revenge. While he alludes to the variety of means that the composer has at his disposal, ". . . the *Sharp* or *flat* key; slow or lively Movements; the *Staccato;* the *Sostenute,* [sic], or smooth-drawn Bow . . ."[16] etc., he does not clearly link these causes with a specific expressive effect.

Although Mattheson, a man belonging to the same generation as Johann Sebastian Bach (1685–1750), has one foot in the past, it must also be recognized that, like Avison, he reflects the attitudes of the 1740s. Both composers argue the necessity for variety within a composition: Mattheson advises his readers that the sonata, whether for one instrument or for several, should contain something for everyone, whatever their taste or frame of mind; Avison advises key change, both within a single movement and between the movements of a single work.

One cannot read these authors without acknowledging their differences and their similarities. Mattheson's work places him squarely in the tradition of the Enlightenment.[17] Everything in music can be reasonably explained since the art is conceived as a logical, albeit enormously complex, chain of cause and effect. For the modern reader, his innumerable categories of feeling and his preparedness—for example, to state that the emotion of jealousy is made up of "seven passions" and then to name them—excites wonder at his diligence and prompts a tolerant smile at such a mechanistic conception of human emotion. The same reader finds it equally difficult to accept the totality of Avison's

15. Mattheson, *op. cit.,* p. 460.
16. Avison, *op. cit.,* p. 74.
17. The term "Enlightenment" is synonymous with the term "The Age of Reason" and refers to that period in which the redefining of many social responsibilities and attitudes came about through rational questioning of everything.

thought. His idea of the special sense of music is appealing, although it is not taken up again until much later in the century, but too often Avison, like Batteux, is obliged to resort to an appeal to feeling where his readers look for reason. Although his work is called *An Essay on Musical Expression,* he is forced tacitly to admit defeat when he says:

> After all that has been, or can be said, the Energy and Grace of *Musical Expression* is of too delicate a Nature to be fixed by Words: it is a Matter of Taste, rather than of Reasoning, and is, therefore, much better understood by Example than by Precept.[18]

The questions which the aesthetics of music poses then, whether treated by philosophers, such as Harris and Batteux, or by practicing musicians, such as Mattheson or Avison, were not answered with complete success, at least for the modern reader. However, there can be no question about their success in their own time.

THE IMPORTANCE OF "TASTE" IN THE EIGHTEENTH CENTURY

We observe in all of these thinkers a common faith in a few premises which they share with the greater part of their society. They do not question those premises, but seek to reconcile the fact of music with them. One of the reasons they were successful in their own time may be the acceptance of their belief that the cultivated, educated society of their day ought to respond to an artistic stimulus in like manner. It is not so much that people of the eighteenth century believe in universal responses to the artwork, as their belief in the correctness of the response of a certain part of society, and their belief that *all* society, given the proper and necessary education, can share that correct response. In this age, which saw the birth of egalitarian ideals, all are not equal by birth, but they have the power to make themselves equal. For this reason, the eighteenth century took delight in the growth of movements such as Freemasonry, which recognizes the unity and universality of like minds. The eighteenth century appears to be a time of rules and regulations—a time when propriety was the ultimate arbiter and "taste" counted above all. For this reason, later ages have thought of this period as one in which form was more important than content, in which manner was more important than matter. Eighteenth-century society never saw itself in this light.

Perhaps what all our authors exhibit most strikingly is a common faith in the process of reason, which nevertheless has to take into account an opposing principle of sentiment or feeling. This is no more than

18. Avison, *op. cit.,* p. 81.

William Hogarth's satire shows the trend-setting Lord Burlington climbing a ladder to help Alexander Pope with his whitewashing. Hogarth saw Pope as Burlington's propagandist.

another kind of statement of the constant polarities of human nature, but the tension of this polarity lies at the heart of a period in the history of music usually referred to as The Classical Period. Further exploration of the eighteenth century will show how much of the vitality of the art of this time, as well as its social life, is dependent upon the recognition of the constant adjustment that is required to evolve a balance between intellect and emotion, logic and feeling—between head and heart.

CHAPTER II

The Musician in Society

In his play *Le Barbier de Séville* (1775), Pierre-Augustin Caron de Beaumarchais (1732–99) describes the character Don Basilio—a music teacher by trade—as "*à genoux devant un écu*" (on his knees at the sight of money).[1] This description represents the prevalent opinion of the ordinary musician who eked out a living from his art in whatever way he could, for money was hard to come by for the vast majority, whether talented or not. Indeed, the cynic might well point out how little the situation has changed. Then, as now, one finds repeatedly that original creative genius was overlooked, and large financial rewards were often given to performers of ephemeral talent. Yet the gathering momentum of change that characterized all aspects of eighteenth-century life affected the social status of the artist slowly but surely—for the better in some ways and for the worse in others.

Earlier ages had conceived the artist as someone with a strong bent or a pronounced talent for an art, which could be refined and polished by application and study. This conception makes the creative artist hardly distinguishable from the tailor who cuts the cloth and sews the clothes that adorn society: in their own way, painters or musicians produce adornments for society. Around the middle of the century, however, the word "genius" begins to take on new significance and is applied to the artist of transcendent imagination and exalted intellectual powers—the kind of artist who is born, not made. We have already seen how the eighteenth century came to a conception of God through the sublime in nature. The new connotation of the word "genius" is evidence of a revised notion of God in man. From it arises the idea of inspiration—a divine breath upon the soul—as the stimulus to artistic production. Artists are viewed differently from the way they had been until, in the nineteenth century, they come to be looked upon as priestlike revealers of divine truth.

1. Act I, Scene 6.

THE SYSTEM OF PATRONAGE

Although this change in the status of the artist is not obvious until the example of Beethoven reveals it in full force, the idea affects the way some philosophers and historians see the relationship of the artist and his society. Its practical results must be examined, since they affect the various means by which the musician earned a living. The ancient system of patronage, under which the artist depended upon a protector to ensure the necessities of life, persisted, either during the production of a single work or over the longer term. On the other hand, the growth of the publishing industry and the development of the public concert have much more tenuous links with the past, and they are, arguably, among the most important contributions to eighteenth-century musical life.

Perhaps the most pressing issue in a mid-eighteenth-century musician's life was finding a position, for the kind of position would frequently determine the nature of his creative output and the extent of his productivity. The system under which a rich man supports a needy artist and, in return, exercises a measure of control over what that artist produces is more repugnant to twentieth-century sensibilities than to those of the eighteenth. Enough of the feudal, hierarchical aspects of social structure and responsibility remained so that the musician could generally accept the notion of service to the king or nobleman as a suitable goal in life. The eighteenth-century composer, from François Couperin (1688–1733) to Wolfgang Mozart (1756–91), aimed to please an audience, and saw nothing degrading in matching their creative impulses to a perceived taste.

The nature and size of musical establishments varied greatly. Around 1750 a wealthy, music-loving prince might maintain a theater for operas and plays, with an orchestra of perhaps eight to ten strings and half a dozen winds; a military band for his regiment, suitable members of which would be used to fill out the theater orchestra on occasion; and an organist and choir connected with his chapel. In addition, there might be as many as six highly paid Italian singers, whose duty it was to take the principal roles in opera productions, as well as the solo parts in music for his chapel. An example of unusually large orchestral forces is found in the musical establishment at Mannheim of the Elector Karl Theodor (reigned 1742–78), deservedly the most famous orchestra of the day, which, around the middle of the century, regularly numbered about fifty players (thirty-four strings plus winds).

In smaller establishments, where the nobleman neither maintained a theater nor provided for the organization of church music, but nevertheless loved music and perhaps played an instrument, a large measure of versatility might be expected of his employees. The man who powdered his master's wig during the day might be expected to take up an instrument on a couple of evenings a week and fit into a musical ensem-

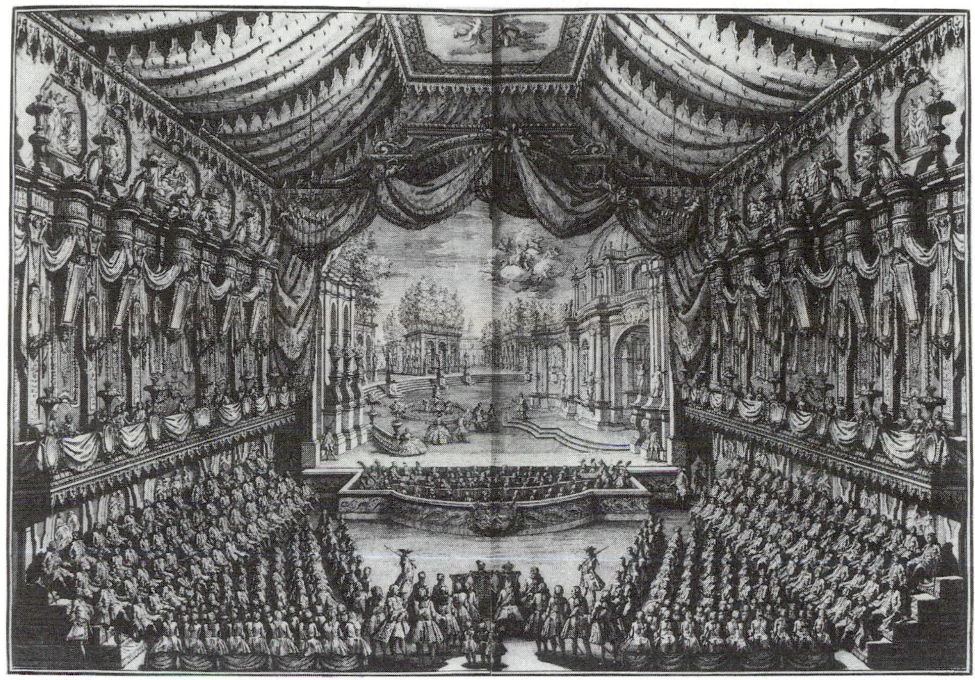

The royal theater of Naples in 1747, during the performance of a serenata *Il Sogno di Olimpia* by Giuseppe de Maso. Note the orderly seating arrangement and the ample space between the royalty, the orchestra, and the armed guards. An engraving by Vincenzo Ré.

ble—indeed, his ability and his willingness to do this at times assured him a job, when to be musical was a desirable qualification in a servant. An inverse example of this kind of thing is to be found in the life of Joseph Haydn (1732–1809) who, when he was in his twenties, was taken on by the composer and singer Nicola Porpora (1686–1768) as accompanist for his pupils. To keep his job, Haydn also had to perform a variety of menial valeting services for Porpora.

Even composers with established reputations and with permanent positions occupied themselves with other activities, such as teaching, writing books, and free-lancing in various ways, in order to achieve fame and fortune and to spread their name beyond their own immediate circle. It was not general practice for a patron to hire a composer, as such, for his staff. The composition of music was regarded as only one of a number of duties. It is all too easy for us to lose sight of the fact that a composer may be remembered today for reasons quite different from those for which he was hired. From the accounts of expenditures on music made by Frederick the Great (1712–86) during 1744–45 we learn that one Italian singer was paid ten times more than Johann Sebastian's second son, Carl Philipp Emanuel Bach (1714–88; henceforth referred to as Emanuel), and that eight or nine singers and dancers, all of whose names are forgotten, enjoyed salaries many times higher than those of musicians for whose existence posterity is ever grateful. For us, Emanuel Bach is primarily a composer-teacher. But for Frederick he was a *continuo* player, and a somewhat troublesome one at that.

The important points of a contract between artist and patron were the specification of duties and rewards, and the conditions under which that contract could be terminated. Typically, they were made with a long-term relationship in mind, and the patron assumed something of the feudal relationship of lord to vassal. Thus, in addition to some specific amount of cash, there might well be provision for lodging, as well as stated amounts of firewood, wine, salt, etc., together with meals taken at a certain position at the household table (young Mozart objected to sitting among the servants) and a variety of uniforms for different occasions.[2] In return for these various compensations, the musical duties of the employee were spelled out, together with instructions about cleanliness, sobriety, punctuality, and other virtues necessary for the smooth running of an organization involving many people. From our point of view it is interesting to note that if the musician's duties included the provision of compositions when required, then the ownership of these compositions was often vested in the employer, and the composer was enjoined to use all possible discretion in having his material copied, lest it leak out to an unauthorized public. On the other hand, if the musician was to be paid for playing the violin, and if, in addition to that duty, he happened to compose, then he might well be free to sell his compositions on the open market, and to publicize them in whatever way might seem suitable.

The benefits of such a system are clear. The patron gains in that an aspect of his pleasure is looked after, and his prestige is enhanced. When the Empress Maria Theresa of Austria (1717–80) said that if she wanted to hear good opera she had to go to Esterháza, Haydn's prince was flattered and his connoisseurship vindicated. From his bondage, the musician gained security and a chance to continue doing what he was best fitted to do. If he gave good service he could confidently hope to be looked after in sickness and adequately pensioned in old age.

There are, of course, less agreeable aspects to the system of patronage, of which many in the eighteenth century were fully aware. Mozart's annoyance at being seated with the lackeys at table has been mentioned,

2. It must be remembered that all classes in the eighteenth century loved uniforms. When Mme. de Pompadour, Louis XV's mistress, organized a weekend party for the king and a few hand-picked guests, every man found a specially designed uniform waiting for him upon his arrival. For someone of the lower classes to wear a uniform meant the achievement of a certain status, related to that of his or her employer. The uniform of a soldier was designed to be colorful and attractive, and the wearer of it was not only seen to be in the highest service—that of king and country—but also the possessor of an undeniable glamour.

but this can only be seen as a minor affront. A more serious illustration will be helpful. When Emanuel Bach took up his appointment with Frederick the Great in 1740, he was a 26–year-old bachelor. He married and had a family in due course. When service with Frederick became too irksome and he wished to leave, he found he was free to go at any time, but since his wife and family were born Prussian subjects, the king could—and did—prevent them from leaving his realm. In order to further his career, Bach had to choose between forsaking his family or submitting to the king's pleasure.

The qualms about patronage expressed in the mid-eighteenth century tended to arise, however, not so much from a resentment of an injustice suffered in individual cases as from a concern for the reconciliation of individual liberty with the needs of society[3] A philosopher like Denis Diderot, who, as much as anyone, verbalized the problems of patronage, saw the artist needing solitude for reflection and introspection, but also requiring the approval of society for his work. For the artist to create optimally he must possess a measure of self-esteem. The creation of a work of art for a single patron is most damaging, since it breeds a sense of futility in the creator; he is denied the breadth of recognition needed to foster his self-esteem, which, for Diderot, is more important than material security. Further, the control which the patron may wish to impose upon the work of art is seen as an attack upon the professional authority of the artist, since the creative act must be the statement of the self-directed creator, freely expressing his own nature. Thus, Diderot writes in 1763:

> One should order nothing from an artist, and when one wants a picture from him one ought to say: "Paint me a picture and choose whatever subject suits you." It would be even safer and quicker to choose one from his stock.[4]

It is interesting to see an attitude that we tend to associate with the nineteenth century surfacing so close to the middle of the eighteenth, and it clearly demonstrates the insufficiency of any attempt to define a period as complex and fluid as this with the clichés of classicism—at best, partial truths. Despite Diderot and others who wrote against the system of patronage, it worked well for composers, for the most part,and throughout the century it continued to offer protection from the harsh realities of the world of buying and selling.

3. The word "liberty" is another of the catchwords of the time, to be placed in the same category as"nature" or "taste." One meets it repeatedly, not only in philosophy but in novels, plays, and even opera. It is not to be interpreted necessarily as expressing a desire to subvert political institutions—in general, the period did not see itself as particularly oppressed—but rather as an expression of the belief that all questions and all actions should be permissible, within reason.

4. Denis Diderot, *Salon de 1763, Oeuvres Complètes* (Assézat-Tourneux, Paris,1875–79) X, p. 204. Author's translation.

PRINTING AND PUBLISHING

The growth of the publishing industry during the eighteenth century had the greatest effect on the composer and the writer. Authors, in particular, were able to make very substantial sums from the sale of their work, in some cases achieving complete financial independence. Because of the somewhat lesser demand for printed music, composers took much longer to reach this position, and to live off the publication of one's compositions did not really become feasible until the nineteenth century. As the publishing industry grew, one gradual effect of its growth was to lessen the importance of the individual patron, while making the composer more dependent upon the support and favor of the public—a master devoid of any sense of responsibility and more difficult to satisfy.

There was a great deal of money to be made in the business of music during this age of economic expansion, when the growth of commerce and the dawning industrial age put more money into more hands than ever before. For the most part it was not the composer who made the money, but the businessman engaged in the entrepreneurial activities of providing entertainment in the theaters or concert halls, and in publishing. The career of George Frederick Handel (1685–1759) is proof that when a composer had the energy, the willpower, and the business sense he could become wealthy. But Handel, together with some other composers of opera, remains an exception, and for the majority, the experience of the marketplace must have been more often disappointing than enriching.

The law afforded the composer precious little protection against the rapacity of the world around him. The old organization of trades into guilds, which had worked to guarantee the quality of products and to protect the tradesman against unauthorized intrusion, was falling into disuse throughout Europe, and the various licensing acts of the time were largely ineffectual. England made an effort to protect the creators of works of the imagination or intellect with the Copyright Act of 1709, which attempted to protect the publisher and the writer for a period of fourteen years from the date of publication, but generally the law was slow to move in this direction, and on the Continent there was even less impetus toward legislation of this kind.

The major difficulty lay in the law's inability to prevent unauthorized copying. Piracy in publishing yielded profits as great as those from legitimate business, and many respectable publishing houses turned to it from time to time when it suited their interest to do so. An important publisher like the London firm of John Walsh (in business from 1695 to 1766 and perhaps the most successful of its time in all of Europe) kept in close touch with musical taste on the Continent, and tapped the lucrative English market for works originating there without paying the composers a penny. Obviously, since there was no legal basis for

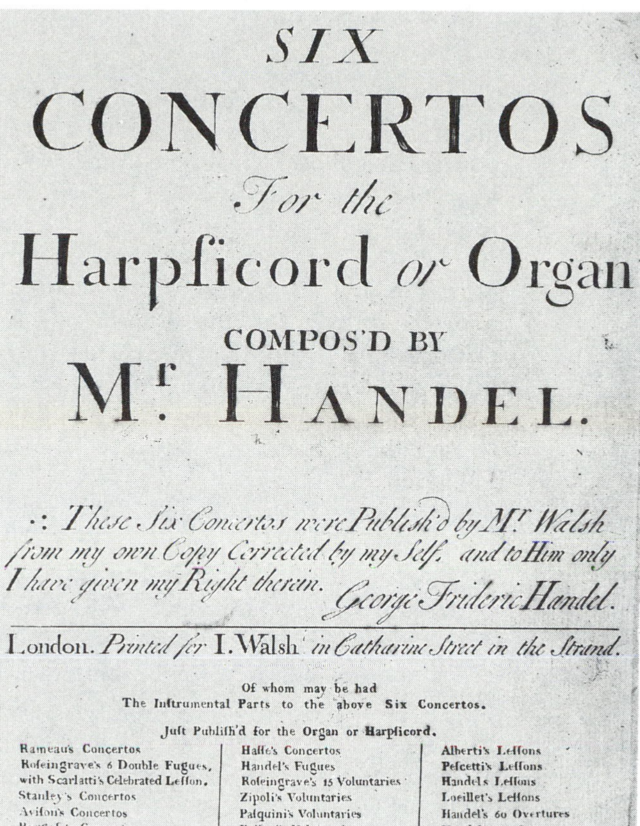

SIX

CONCERTOS

For the

Harpſicord or Organ

COMPOS'D BY

Mr. HANDEL.

These Six Concertos were Publish'd by Mr. Walsh from my own Copy Corrected by my Self, and to Him only I have given my Right therein. George Frideric Handel.

London. Printed for I. Walsh in Catharine Street in the Strand.

Of whom may be had
The Inſtrumental Parts to the above Six Concertos.

Juſt Publiſh'd for the Organ or Harpſicord.

Rameau's Concertos	Haſſe's Concertos	Alberti's Leſſons
Roſeingrave's 6 Double Fugues, with Scarlatti's Celebrated Leſſon.	Handel's Fugues	Peſcetti's Leſſons
Stanley's Concertos	Roſeingrave's 15 Voluntaries	Handel's Leſſons
Aviſon's Concertos	Zipoli's Voluntaries	Loeillet's Leſſons
Burgeſs's Concertos	Paſquini's Voluntaries	Handel's 60 Overtures
	Baſſani's Voluntaries	Handel's 80 Songs

This extremely plain and inexpensive title page is interesting for the composer's statement combatting piracy and for the advertisements of other John Walsh publications.

international monitoring of this kind of activity, the pirating of foreign works could be freely carried on. All that was necessary was to obtain a copy of a work, however imperfect and by whatever means, and hurry it into print. This process was equally effective with domestic works, provided there was a market and the copy was not directly traceable to a source. Many copies were printed in England bearing, instead of the publisher's name and address, the words "Sold at the Music Shops."

The composer had little recourse: if the demand for his work was great and pirated editions were appearing, he could either advertise that only a certain edition was authorized and correct, or he could change his work by adding new parts or modifying it in some way. Having taken these steps, he would have to rely upon the public's desire to possess the work in its most recent, most accurate form.

The essence of piracy was the speed with which a market could be seized in a society eager for novelty, and those businessmen who practiced it were typical products of the age that invented the term *laissez-faire*. Of course, it must not be inferred that all publishers were pirates. The main centers for music printing were Amsterdam, London, and Paris, and most businesses, small family concerns, were conducted honestly. With few exceptions, the life of a business coincided with the life of its founder. Upon his death his widow might carry on until she remarried, and occasionally a business was handed on to a child. It often happened that the widow would eventually marry her late husband's foreman—a practical turn of events to keep the business functioning—who would then carry it on, but usually under his own name. The other possibility, and that which occurred most frequently, was that upon the founder's death the business was put on the block, its stock-in-trade—plates, printing press, etc.—purchased by some other publisher and its name forgotten. Many such establishments in London and Paris arose, flourished, and died in this manner during the century, leaving almost no trace except for one or two copies of works they had published.

Most businessmen came into music publishing indirectly, since it did not initially yield a sufficient livelihood by itself. They tended to start out as sellers of musical instruments (John Walsh of London), as engravers (Artaria of Vienna), as printers and booksellers (Breitkopf of Leipzig), or as composers (Hoffmeister of Vienna, etc.), and most operated out of their homes. The term "publishing" would seem to imply circulation in printed form, and in Amsterdam, London, and Paris printing had been done mainly from engraved plates since very early in the century. But most of the music trade in Italy, Germany, and Austria was carried on in manuscript copies, and the bulk of music in circulation until the 1770s never went through a printing press. Although labor was relatively cheap, hand-copying a score was a slow process and therefore its cost was considerable. Its advantage was that, like other developing industries of the time, it could be done at home since it needed no complex machinery. By the beginning of the eighteenth century, the printing of music had a long history extending back over 200 years. Many processes had been tried: printing from carved wood blocks or engraved metal plates; printing from movable type; printing the staves and adding the notes by hand; printing the notes and adding the staves by hand; and printing with multiple impressions. By the early 1700s, the printing of music from copper plates engraved by specialists had become the most common of all methods. With the constant urge to save money and time, the metal used for the plates was changed from copper to zinc, pewter, or other alloys, and the slow process of engraving was partially bypassed by the punching of noteheads onto the plate. Just as some publishers allowed the quality of the printed page to fall from the ideal in the interests of saving time and making money, so others maintained the highest standards and employed the finest craftsmen. Some of the elaborate title pages of publications exhibit the most refined taste in layout and show the highest achievements of the engraver's art. On the other hand, many title pages were standardized so that they could be used over and over again for different works simply by changing the title of the work and the composer's name. These are called *passe-partout* pages—like a master key, they fit anywhere.

The composer could expect, at best, a small financial reward from the publication of his works. At worst there might be no reward but some expense, since publishers frequently required that the costs of engraving and printing be covered, offering in return only the marketing of the work. And yet the composer persisted, weighing the frustration of seeing the publisher make whatever profits there might be against the gratification of seeing his name in print, of knowing that his reputation was being spread to the world at large. If his compositions met with success, then his hand was strengthened for his next round of bargaining with the publisher.

THE BEGINNINGS OF THE PUBLIC CONCERT

During the eighteenth century the public concert grew from its infant beginnings to affect the cultural life of the whole of society and the status of the composer in that society. The reasons why concerts gained favor at this particular time differ from place to place, but the fact that across the face of Europe and North America the practice of giving and attending concerts became much more common attests to the growth of public demand.

To France belongs the honor of having established the first public concert organization with sufficient longevity to establish a tradition. The *Concert Spirituel* (note the singular form) was begun in 1725. The name, which means "Concert of Sacred Music," indicates the nature of the programs performed at the outset, and it persisted, even when the programs had become largely secular. The reasons for the name reach back into the seventeenth century when, as early as 1673, all the public music of Paris had been assigned to the composer Jean-Baptiste Lully (1632–87). His successors were able to ensure the continuance of the monopoly into the eighteenth century. This meant, in effect, that nothing musical was allowed to take place in public that might possibly diminish the profits of the *Académie royale de musique*—that is to say, the monopoly of the Opéra. In 1725, Anne Danican Philidor (1681–1728) was granted a privilege for three years to hold concerts of sacred music on those days when the opera was not allowed to open, i.e., religious holidays. The king, Louis XV, made available a suitable hall in the Tuileries palace. In return for this privilege, Philidor was to pay 1000 *livres per annum* to the holder of the monopoly. When three years were up, Philidor's privilege was renewed, but six months into his second term, deeply in debt, he had to resign his license, which was taken over by a partnership. At the outset of this second term, however, he had succeeded in modifying the terms of the contract, enlarging the concert season beyond religious holidays and establishing a format of program somewhat different from the original idea. He thus set a style of programming which lasted until 1790, when the Revolution forced the discontinuance of the series. In addition to sacred works, Philidor introduced French and Italian secular works as well as symphonies and concertos. A comparison of programs from three different Ascension days before 1760 is interesting, since they show how the programs were modified, even on holy days.[5]

1725 10 May	*Cum invocarem*	Bernier (1665–1734)
	Miserere mei Deus quoniam	Bernier
	O dulcis Jesus	Destouches (1672–1749)
1728 6 May	Two Motets	Lalande (1657–1726)
	Two Violin sonatas (played by Leclair and presumably composed by him also)	Leclair (1697–1764)
1755 8 May	Symphony	Croes (1705–86)
	Nisi dominus	Mondonville (1711–72)
	Violin Concerto, played by	Dupont (?)
	Two Italian arias	Giardini (1716–96)
	Overture *Pygmalion*	Rameau (1683–1764)
	Dominus regnavit	Mondonville

By 1750, symphonies or overtures by German composers such as Georg Philipp Telemann (1681–1767), Carl Heinrich Graun (1703/4–59), and Johann Adolf Hasse (1699–1783) appear on the programs, and Parisian receptivity to such compositions is shown by the following program, honoring the arrival in Paris of Johann Wenzel Stamitz (1717–57) in September 1754:

New Symphony, with horns and oboes	Stamitz
Domine in virtute	Cordelet
Nubes et Caligo	Lalande
Concerto for Violin, composed and played by	Stamitz
Two Italian arias	
Sonata for viola d'amore, composed and played by	Stamitz
Coeli enarrant	Mondonville

For the first twenty-five years of its existence, this concert series was under an evil star, and the various entrepreneurs who took it on made little, if any, profit. By the 1750s, however, its position was more firmly established, its excellence more widely appreciated, and its continuance assured.

In addition to the public *Concert Spirituel,* private concerts gained in importance in the musical life of Paris since they afforded an obvious

5. The various programs of the *Concert Spirituel* are drawn from Constant Pierre, *Histoire du Concert Spirituel, 1725–1790* (Paris, 1975).

way around the monopoly situation. Of particular note were the concerts at the home of the wealthy tax farmer,[6] Jean le Riche de la Pouplinière, directed from 1731–53 by Jean-Philippe Rameau (1683–1764), during 1754–55 by Johann Stamitz, and from 1755–63 by François-Joseph Gossec (1734–1829).

The public concert life of London initially developed in small private houses, in taverns, or in rooms specifically built for the holding of concerts, balls, etc., and, since there was no monopoly of music in London, the commercial concert developed earlier there than elsewhere. Private individuals were able to do very well from the giving of concerts, and a series organized by Jean Baptiste Loeillet (1680–1730) was successfully continued for many years at his own house. A society called the Academy of Ancient Music met at the Crown and Anchor tavern, and gave concerts from around 1710 until 1792. Another series called the *Castle Concerts,* after the tavern where they took place, carried that name even after the concerts were moved to another location. Occasional programs were given in Mr. Hickford's Room from about 1714–79. Mr. Hickford was a dancing master, and the large, multipurpose

6. In France the collection of taxes was assigned to individuals who undertook to raise a certain amount for the king from a certain geographic area, for which privilege the tax "farmer" would pay a fee, also to the king.

A ticket of admission to a concert in Hickford's Rooms. The inscription reads: CONCERT / OF / ANCIENT VOCAL / AND / INSTRUMENTAL / MUSIC and the banner in Latin reads: "They shall rise again who are now fallen."

hall was where he gave lessons. At other times it was available for hire and many concerts, organized by individual artists for their own benefit, took place there, including one by young Mozart in 1765. It is remarkable that no really important or long-lasting series, comparable to the *Concert Spirituel,* came into being in London during the first half of the eighteenth century, despite the many organizations in which the aristocracy and the bourgeoisie collaborated. Perhaps London society saw no need for such an enterprise, since the great variety of concert fare that was available at all times ensured that all tastes were catered to.

Germany in the eighteenth century lacked a real center comparable to London or Paris, and yet its contribution to the growth of the concert tradition is distinct and different. Whereas the French concert was completely professional, and was organized for the purpose of making money, the German concert, with its origin in the *collegium musicum,* developed as an occasion for actual music-making, rather than a performance for a group of passive listeners. Leipzig is a typical example of a city with an outstanding concert tradition; in 1743 the *Grosses Concert* was established in a private house, with a small orchestra of 16 players. This series carried on until 1756, when the Seven Years' War (1756–63) caused it to be discontinued.

The development of the concert was important to the eighteenth-century musician and composer, since it brought him into immediate contact with a paying public in a way that had been available before only at the opera house. The concert was responsible for the development of a preference for specific repertoire and the popularity of the symphony or overture independent of its opera, and the solo concerto was an outgrowth of it. In estimating the taste of an audience, the power of attraction possessed by a famous soloist had to be balanced with the popularity of the works performed, and favorite pieces came to be repeated because the public enjoyed them. Thus the composer's emancipation from the private patron progressed and the public concert offered him an important alternative to a life in service.

INSTRUCTIONAL LITERATURE

Many musicians have felt the need to pass on their technique and their perception of the basis of their art as strongly as the desire to have an audience appreciate their performance or their composition. During the course of the eighteenth century, many works were printed as basic instruction on an instrument; these often consisted of a collection of well-known tunes or even suites and sonatas (very often described as "lessons") which the beginner could use both to gain proficiency and for recreation. Three substantial books were published in the period immediately before 1760 describing the technique of the flute, the keyboard, and the violin: the *Versuch einer Anweisung die Flöte traversière zu spielen* (Essay toward a Method for Playing the Transverse Flute) published in 1752 by Johann Joachim Quantz (1697–1773); the *Versuch über die wahre Art das Clavier zu spielen* (Essay on the True Art of Playing Keyboard Instruments) published in two parts, the first in 1753 and the second in 1762, by Emanuel Bach; and the *Versuch einer gründlichen Violinschule* (A Treatise on the Fundamental Principles of Violin Playing) which Leopold Mozart (1719–87) published in 1756. After nearly 200 years of comparative neglect, they have all become invaluable source material for historically accurate performance of eighteenth-century music, in all its aspects. It is interesting to see in these works of Quantz, Emanuel Bach, and Leopold Mozart a musical reflection of the urge to encompass all knowledge, discussed earlier and exemplified in the underlying ideals of the encyclopedia. While they certainly describe an orderly progress from the basic technique of the instrument to its complete mastery, they also look at the whole art of music through the window of that instrument. In describing their ideals, they prescribe an immense number of different things: they tell us how a concerto should be written; how a *continuo* should be extemporized; how an *Adagio* can be ornamented; and how to structure a fantasia—in other words, they give us a picture of what was expected of the complete musician, both as performer and composer.

The distance that separates the philosophers and the musicians of the period is not great. It can generally be defined as that which divides the speculative and theoretical from the practical. Jean-Philippe Rameau, alone among composers of the highest order, has occupied a place on both the speculative and the practical sides of the line. Even before his fame as a composer was well established, his *Traité de l'harmonie réduite à ses principes naturels* (Treatise on Harmony reduced to its Natural Principles; 1722) won for him the reputation of a musical scientist. His chief concern was to establish the relationship of music to nature, and thus to give music its rightful place in the unity of all things. His specific goal was to demonstrate the natural acoustical basis of the primary consonances of music—the octave, the fifth, and the major third—as upper partials of a fundamental tone. Deriving the major triad from these upper partials, Rameau considered this chord, followed by the minor triad, as the source of all consonant harmony, deriving the 1st and 2nd inversions of the triads from them. This in turn led to a theory of roots of chords and to the idea of a fundamental bass, as opposed to the thoroughbass, or *basso continuo*. Rameau's speculative work has been of enormous influence in the history of music and has made him perhaps the most significant theorist of the century, as well as one of its most important composers.

On the other hand, Rameau unites with Quantz and Emanuel Bach and Mozart in the belief that music must move the listeners and move them in a manner that relates closely to other kinds of experience. Leopold Mozart is more concerned than the others with technical, violinistic matters, but in his last chapter, even he says:

> The good performance of a composition according to modern taste is not as easy as many imagine, who believe themselves to be doing well if they embellish and befrill a piece right foolishly out of their own heads, and who have no sensitiveness whatever for the affect which is to be expressed in the piece.[7]

Quantz has many references to the same matter which add yet another dimension, the most succinct of which is:

> the passions change frequently in the Allegro, just as in the Adagio. The performer must therefore seek to transport himself into each of these passions, and to express it suitably.[8]

In his essay, Emanuel Bach defines performance as "the ability through singing or playing to make the ear conscious of the true content and affect of a composition." He sums up his creed in a famous passage from his Autobiography, in which he writes

> I believe music must, first and foremost, stir the heart. This cannot be achieved through mere rattling, drumming or arpeggiation, at least not by me.[9]

Of the three, only Quantz attempts to assess those physical and spiritual qualities which he deems necessary for success as a musician. The whole of the first section of his book is devoted to this topic, during which he reassures his reader in this way:

> Whoever has a healthy body, with well-disposed and healthy limbs, and yet is not stupid or of unsound mind can, with much industry, learn what is called the mechanics of music.
>
> Music seldom procures the same advantages as the other arts, and even if some prosper in it, this prosperity is most often subject to inconstancy. Changes of taste, the weakening of bodily powers, vanishing youth, the loss of a patron—upon whom the entire fortune of many a musician depends—are all capable of hindering the progress of music. [10]

His list of qualifications and cautions seems endless. The fact remains that although patronage continued to offer a shelter for many musicians

7. Leopold Mozart, *A Treatise on the Fundamental Principles of Violin Playing* trans. Editha Knocker (Oxford, 1951) p.215.
8. Johann J. Quantz, *Essay toward a Method for Playing the Transverse Flute,* trans. and ed. Edward R. Reilly (London, 1966) p.133.
9. C. P. E. Bach, *Essay on the True Art of Playing Keyboard Instruments,* trans. and ed. William J. Mitchell (New York,1949), p. 148.
10. Quantz, *op. cit.,* pp. 14–15.

unable or unwilling to face the vicissitudes of the free-enterprise system, the eighteenth-century composer/performer, more than any other artist, had to develop his capacities in both performance and business. Like the actor and unlike the painter or the writer, he had to excel in the peculiar demands made by performance—he had to convince the public through his vivid projection of states of mind, through his instrument, and he had to appeal to his audience in a conventionally approved manner ("good taste"). As a creator he had also to avoid any abstruseness in technique or manner and be simple and accessible ("natural"). Increasingly he had to deal with the marketplace, where goods, including his own wares, were bought and sold. It is hardly surprising that so few musicians were able to conquer both worlds, when to succeed in even one was so difficult.

CHAPTER III

Music for Private Performance

The part played by music in the complex machinery of society—for example, in the worship of God or in theatrical entertainments—has long been acknowledged, explored, and documented, and historians have attempted to assemble a complete record of its use. This study, not simply of what music was used, but of how it was used and how listeners responded to it, is possible because written records of the rituals, traditions, and organized activities involving large companies of participants exist in the form of instructions to performers, accounts of production costs, or observers' reports. Almost all those conditions are lacking, however, when it comes to that music which enables players to commune with each other or with a few friends, for these activities are not prescribed by rite or tradition, nor do they necessarily involve anyone else as audience or spectator. It is indeed a rare occasion when an opera is rehearsed and staged purely for the pleasure of those taking part, yet playing a string quartet or a keyboard sonata has always been recognized as its own reward.

Nevertheless, private performance of music is documented in a number of ways. There are some records in the diaries of those who took part, or of one who happened to be a privileged listener, and in the paintings of such events. But the most important record is in the notated music that survives, and a vast quantity of music has been left to us from the eighteenth century. In part, this legacy is attributable to the growth in the practice of printing music and its wider circulation as the population of the major European and American cities grew by leaps and bounds. But we must also recognize that the practice of making music privately in the home changed as it grew.

Masked balls were a popular evening pastime. Here, in 1754, at the Castle of Brühl, two orchestras spell each other from either side of the ballroom. The disguises of the dancers afford a degree of anonymity and excitement. (Rheinisches Amt für Denkmalpflege, Abteil Brauweiler, Lieven)

The detail of the left and right foreground shows the different makeup of the orchestras, and, in particular, the various masks and dresses of the dancers.

THE *STYLE GALANT*

In the late seventeenth and early eighteenth centuries there were two easily distinguishable national styles of music—the French and the Italian. By the middle of the eighteenth century the distinction, although still a call to arms in the world of opera, had largely ceased to be an issue in instrumental music—a cooling-off considerably hastened by the strong emergence of German music. The predominant ideal of instrumental music, whether German, English, or Italian, embodied a style described by the French word *galant.* Like the term "good taste," *style galant* is a conventionally approved phrase which is nowhere clearly defined but which has a number of connotations. In general it is used to refer to that which is modern, current, in fashion, contemporary, of the latest style, as opposed to the old-fashioned, the outmoded, and the *passé.* The term was invented during the reign of Louis XIV, but it was most used in a later age, often called "rococo" after the French style of decoration in architecture and all manner of artifacts, from teapots to hairbrushes, and from candlesticks to fabric design.

The style associated with Louis XIV had been elaborate, heavy, ornate, formal, and despite the amount of ornamentation, symmetrical. It was designed to be imposing, and it can be thought of as ecclesiastical, courtly, and larger than life. It was a theatrical style, particularly appropriate for surrounding a king whose whole life was lived in the public eye, whose every action, from getting up to going to bed, was watched by a host of courtiers, some taking part in the ceremonies and others dreaming of being singled out by the Sun King to hold a candle or some article of apparel. Thirty years after Louis XIV's death, rococo style, which had its roots in the seventeenth century, was dominant. Although it could be seen throughout the royal palaces, its mood is more intimate than formal, and its prevalence affords an interesting insight into the thinking of the new king. Louis XV carried on the traditions established by his great-grandfather, Louis XIV, but did not relish the public life of a monarch; his taste ran rather to deer hunting in the forest. It was he who had the small private apartments built in the vastness of Versailles, where he would entertain small parties of close friends, for whom he would make and serve coffee. The public image of Louis XV was only a part of the man. The style that is called *Louis Quinze* (or rococo) aims to be light where the earlier style was heavy, asymmetrical as opposed to symmetrical, and witty and amusing instead of imposing.

Rococo is a style of fantasy—it is a state of mind that aims to charm. That its name derives from the French word *rocaille,* meaning rockwork as used in the grottoes and rockeries that were a feature of contemporary gardens and houses, is of little significance. The word "picturesque" was more commonly used at that time. The new, picturesque

Les Tendres Accords or Sweet Harmonies, an engraving by Jean Mondon le fils. The flute, a man's instrument, is accompanied by a guitar or lute, traditionally played by a woman. The swirling, vertiginous curves of the rococo are here applied to imaginary and fanciful architecture.

style completely rejects straight lines and loves flowing "C" and "S" curves in opposition. Using these means, it defies reality and works a kind of alchemy upon heavy substances, making them seem insubstantial: buildings become lighter and seem to float on their foundations as pillars become more slender; silver and bronze cease to be heavy metal and become liquid, frozen in a moment of turbulence. In addition to these abstract shapes, the picturesque style makes use of elements from nature, copied with complete realism but often placed in fantastic conjunction. Many of the silver or ceramic artifacts of the time are decorated with lifelike vegetables, fruit, flowers, shellfish, crabs, crayfish, animals, and birds, as well as figures of men, women and particularly children. The result is a rich combination of fantasy built upon a strong underlying structure in an art that is designed to be lived with on intimate terms.

The *style galant* in music aimed to do very much what the picturesque was doing in applied art and architecture. Its primary objective was to appeal to the widest audience, and hence music had to be simple and natural for both listener and performer. That simplicity cannot be attributed solely to the growing amateur public in need of music that matched their abilities. Rather the lack of technical demands in the music should be seen as an artistic goal, deliberately sought for universal appeal. Many of the staple compositional practices of the previous period were either rejected entirely or modified beyond recognition. Polyphony was largely discarded, to the point where accompanying parts were completely subordinated to the principal melodic line. A number of devices were used to split up a chord of supporting harmony (Example III–1), many of which were novel at the time, and have proved most useful and durable. Patterns (a) and (b) are frequently called an "Alberti" bass, after the composer Domenico Alberti (*c.*1710–*c.*40), in whose sonatas for harpsichord the melody is supported with this kind of rhythmically active yet undemanding and completely subservient accompaniment. Alberti was among the earliest to use these patterns, but he was neither the first nor the only one; they quickly became a commonplace and are found in the work of Mozart and many of the lesser Italian composers. Most idiomatic to keyboard music are (a) and (b), although (b) is to be found in string music quite early and (a) follows shortly after. Pattern (c) was used by J. S. Bach in his *Italian Concerto* (1735) as a deliberate modernism—proof that Bach was up-to-date. By the middle of the century this pattern is used widely and indiscriminately. Pattern (d) is also found in music for strings or keyboard. It is frequently used in duets for two string instruments, where a melody in one instrument is supported by an extremely sparse yet lively accompaniment in the other. The four patterns are only a sampling of the many possibilities which composers of the period explored and used with great success to replace a polyphonic texture.

Example III–1: Four typical figural-bass patterns

Imitative counterpoint was abandoned since it was looked upon as a learned or "artificial" device, the consistent use of which anywhere outside the Church showed a deplorable lack of taste. Instead, part of the effect of such counterpoint—the audible repetition of the head motive of a melody—became incorporated into the single melodic line. The following theme by Tomaso Albinoni (1671–1751), which J. S. Bach used as a fugue subject, is a typical, finely curved example of a spun-out tune. Once the melody has begun its course, it describes its shape in one long-breathed movement. It does not define a meter but a tempo; it does not identify a phrase length in any way that might cause the listener to expect a balancing, complementary phrase; it does not create a harmonic scheme by itself but is open to a number of possibilities; the rhythmic relationship of notes is flexible and is not defined by a sequence of motives.

Example III–2: Example of Baroque melody, ALBINONI (from Bach)

On the other hand, the following example from the slow movement of a symphony by Johann Stamitz, the first of a set entitled *La Melodia Germanica* that was published in Paris around the middle of the century, shows many of the ways in which the new style steered clear of the old. The differences are obvious: meter, tempo, phrase length, and motivic relationships are clear, while an obvious harmonic scheme brings about a general reduction in harmonic activity. Most interesting is a comparison of the way the two melodies of Albinoni and Stamitz balance the relationship between steps and leaps: Albinoni covers a wide range in the first few notes and then glides slowly down to his final note; Stamitz defines the harmony with leaps, while the steps create affective opposition to the leaps. In the example by Stamitz, the strong motivic connections within the melody create lateral relationships, comparable in some ways to the diagonal relationships found between different voices in imitative counterpoint.

Example III–3: Melody by J. STAMITZ. *La Melodia Germanica* No.1, *Andante*

Perhaps the greatest change was made in the nature of the melodic line, in which all interest now tended to concentrate. Composers in the new style began to condition their listeners to expect a regularity of phrasing, generally into 2– or 4–bar periods, quite different from the practice of Baroque composers. Not only were phrases regular, but they tended to be short and separated from each other by rests, and cadential affirmations of key were used frequently, in effect separating the material. Textures were made thinner, even to the point of sacrificing the contrapuntal relationship of the bass with the melodic line, which the Baroque had enjoyed. More and more, the bass line acts as a simple harmonic support for the upper part. Inner parts, too, tend to lose the independence they had possessed in the *Brandenburg Concertos* of J. S. Bach, for example. It should be said, however, that the use of the *basso continuo* had never granted full equality to the middle parts, although it had allowed them to work toward it. Such a large sacrifice of the integrity of parts was compensated for, in mid-century, by an increased concentration of rapid textural changes, more varied than Baroque composers had dreamed of.

The *style galant* represented, in many ways, a radical change of style. Its deliberate simplification certainly made it popular with the public, and it bred into its listeners very different expectations, upon which Haydn, Mozart, and Beethoven built some of their greatest effects. But in this age of rapid change its failure to give lasting satisfaction to its audience can be seen in the sudden profusion of compositions for new and different combinations of instruments. Whereas private music had heretofore been written either for solo instruments or for instruments with *basso continuo,* around the middle of the century one sees the emergence of the accompanied solo keyboard sonata and the string quartet. The prevalence of the *style galant* was also counterbalanced by the development of a mannered style of composition, often referred to as the *empfindsamer Stil*, or the "Style of Sensibility," which we will explore shortly.

SOLO SONATA WITH *BASSO CONTINUO*

The practice of *basso continuo,* or thoroughbass, continued throughout the whole of the century, but by 1750 it showed unmistakable signs of decline. It had been one of the most important compositional principles as well as performance practices of the seventeenth century, and one of the major characteristics of the whole Baroque period. As a compositional device it allowed the composer to indicate the harmonic substance of an accompaniment by the addition of figures to a complete bass line. The figures indicated the most important intervals to be played above the bass note, superposed figures indicating chords, while successive figures showed voice leading. A system of figures was evolved that allowed for the shorthand notation of every conceivable harmonic circumstance. Methods of thoroughbass occupied teachers, in practice and in print,throughout the seventeenth and eighteenth centuries, and the ability to fill in harmonies tastefully and inventively was an impor-

Dame au klavier by Charles Knight illustrates why ladies of the time favored keyboard instruments: it allowed them to maintain their poise, serenity, and grace. (Graphische Sammlung Albertina, Vienna)

tant qualification for a professional keyboard player as well as a necessary skill for the amateur music maker. Hence, the *basso continuo* has important implications for performance practice in modern times, since so much of the effect of a composition in which it is used must depend upon the skill with which its figures are interpreted.

The chief merit of *basso continuo* lies in the way the one or two solo voices may be supported by a strong bass line that is usually uninvolved with the melodic material of the upper part or parts. The wide appeal of this textural quality, together with the attraction provided by the ever-fresh challenge of the quasi-improvisational harmonization, did not disappear as soon as the popularity of polyphony receded.

The solo sonata with *continuo* accompaniment flourished before 1760 and indeed well into the 1780s, mainly in the hands of Italian violin composers such as Giovanni Battista Somis (1686–1763), Pietro Locatelli (1695–1764), Francesco Maria Veracini (1690–1768), Giuseppe Tartini (1692–1770), and Pietro Nardini (1722–93); it was also used with distinction by the great French violinists Jean-Marie Leclair (1697–1764), Pierre Gaviniès (1728–1800), and as late as Rodolphe Kreutzer (1766–1831). Many of these violinist-composers properly belong to the Baroque period, but they lived in an age of transition, and their style embodies much that was new in melody and structure.

Giuseppe Tartini, the most celebrated Italian violin virtuoso of the mid-century, was from a wealthy family. He seems to have had no great teacher and, despite pressing offers from London and Paris, seems not to have traveled outside Italy after 1726. He composed voluminously, chiefly concertos and sonatas, and he was also interested in the science of music, writing a speculative treatise on harmony, which was published in his home city of Padua in 1754.

The structure of the Italian violin sonata in this period is variable. In his Op. 1 (1721), Veracini mixes dance and non-titled movements freely, adhering to a four-movement scheme, arranged, like the typical Baroque sonata, slow/fast/slow/fast (S/F/S/F). Yet in the first of this group he starts with a French overture, followed by a slow Aria and then three fast dances. A group of sonatas by Antonio Vivaldi (1678–1744) from 1722 uniformly follows a three-movement arrangement, S/F/S, in which the fast movements are most often entitled *Allemanda* or *Corrente*. Another collection of sonatas, composed before 1720 by Somis, seems to turn away from both suite and *sonata da camera,* utilizing the three-movement scheme, S/F/S, but not indicating any connection with the dance.

Tartini's sonatas are more closely connected to the *sonata da chiesa* and the *sonata da camera* than any of those mentioned above. His Op. 1, published in 1734 by Le Cène of Amsterdam, is a collection of twelve sonatas, the first six of which clearly stem from the *sonata da chiesa* and the last six from the *sonata da camera* ; all are in three movements. In the first six there is a short cantabile first movement, marked either *Grave, Largo,* or *Adagio* and in 4/4 time, allowing for the extempore ornamentation which was such a feature of the Italian style. The second movement is invariably a free fugue marked *Allegro,* in the same key as the opening movement. In five of these six fugues an *Adagio* section brings the movement to a close; in one case this section is considerably extended and set in the key of the relative minor, becoming in effect a slow movement connected to the fugue and springing from it. The final movement is fast, marked *Allegro, Allegro assai,* or *Presto,* and in binary form. (The first movement of the Sonata Op. 1, No. 4, is reproduced in facsimile in the *Anthology of Classical Music [ACM]* as No. 1)

One of the most interesting features of the first six sonatas is that in each one the last two movements have a clear and obvious thematic connection through the contour and tessitura of their head motives. Sometimes the opening slow movement is independent of the other two, but invariably it, too, shares common material. All three movements of Op. 1, No. 4, while they develop independently, start from common material, as shown in Example III–4. This procedure is not unusual for Tartini, who, more than most of his contemporaries, appears to be fond of connecting independent movements, thus giving many of his works a kind of unity. In Op. 1, he amalgamates the old with the new: the unity of key and the unifying head motive link these sonatas with the variation *canzona* of the seventeenth century. The "new" may be found in the second group of six sonatas, in which binary forms appear in all movements with the repeat signs commonly used in dances; no single movement is based on fugue. The derivation from the *sonata da camera*[1] is clear.

Example III–4: G. TARTINI, Sonata Op .1, No. 4, head motives

The *style galant* requires a certain piquancy and vivacity in *Allegro* and a certain affectedness of manner or sentiment in the *Adagio*. Tartini goes beyond the *style galant* in that the melody of the *Grave* first movement of Op. 1, No. 4 is majestic, serious, and extended in its flow, creating a completely Baroque feeling, and yet its techniques are almost all modern. In Example III–5 note the strength of the harmonic structure in which the first phrase establishes the tonic and leads to the dominant (mm. 1–5); the second phrase (mm. 5–9) is in the dominant; the third phrase (mm. 9–13) is in a state of sequential flux leading back to the tonic; the fourth phrase (mm. 13–17) is in the tonic and is reinforced by a fifth, coda-like phrase (mm. 17–20). The excerpt also shows the compositional craft of the composer, who, starting with a group of four notes in a fixed rhythmic relationship, proceeds to develop that motive, not by the Baroque process of *Fortspinnung* but by repetition in a manner that creates all kinds of inner relationships and shapes. These appear to have been thoughtfully built and purposefully juxtaposed—one senses a progress in the resultant symmetries that leads inexorably from a beginning to a conclusion. The resulting shape is comparable to a stanza form or a sonnet in poetry. Thus the arrows in the example below, which schematically indicate the melodic direction of the rhythmic head motive within each phrase, show a beautiful balance between the first two phrases and a progressive increase in the downward melodic

1. It is worth noting that Corelli's Op. 5 consists likewise of 12 solo sonatas, arranged in the same manner—six *sonate da chiesa* and six *sonate da camera*.

Example III–5: G. TARTINI, Sonata Op. 1, No. 4, first-movement melody.

direction—a progress inseparably linked to the affective purpose and content of the movement. The second half of each of the first four phrases stands in an **abab** relationship. The final phrase is different, effectively reinforcing the tonic cadence by emphasizing the motion from F♯ to G and the downward scale from the dominant, D, to the tonic, G.

This movement is particularly rich in relationships of this kind, and it demonstrates the unity which composers of the *style galant* worked to obtain. In a single melodic line, all elements of rhythm, phrasing, motive, harmony, and large-scale structure become one. Few violinists of the time were Tartini's equal as players and still fewer were his equal as composers.

The other genre left over from the Baroque, which still maintained a considerable currency, was the sonata for two melody instruments and *basso continuo,* usually called the trio sonata. In the years before 1760, many composers wrote for this combination in the time-honored style, which postulated an equality between the upper two voices through the sharing of common material and through the use of imitative counterpoint. It proved to be adaptable to the changing tastes of the public, and modifications were gradually made which, while keeping the instrumentation intact, allowed the trio sonata to sever its connection with the Baroque *sonata da chiesa* and *sonata da camera* and become a uniquely eighteenth-century creation.

THE TRIO SONATA

In accordance with the *style galant,* the trio sonata drew away from the idea of suite and fugue and became more closely allied with the solo instrumental sonata. Four-movement trio sonatas still existed, written by such conservatives as Quantz and Hasse, and these tend to consist of a freely structured, slow first movement; a fast second movement in which the modulatory scheme and imitative counterpoint resemble that of a Baroque fugue; a slow third movement, often a *Siciliano;* and a fast final movement in some kind of binary form. More and more frequently, however, the trio sonata is in three movements, F/S/F, with the middle movement most usually in the key of the dominant, subdominant, or the relative minor. The structure of movements is liable to much greater variation, and while those sonatas composed in Italy or Vienna show a certain uniformity based upon the use of rounded binary form in first and last movements, those composed in Berlin, particularly by Emanuel Bach, demonstrate an amazing fertility of formal invention schooled by rigorous compositional craft. The Sonata in D, H.575 (W.151)[2] for example, has a first movement based on a ritornello, concerto-like structure using a drawn-out melodic substance that recurs in a variety of keys—D, B minor, G—reminiscent of the tonal structure of fugue. The Sonata in A minor, H. 572 (W. 148) written in 1735 and extensively revised in 1747 when H. 575 (W. 151) was composed, is written in a clear, terse sonata form.

The Sonata in B♭, H. 578 (W. 161; *ACM* 2) is a further example of Emanuel's experimentation with structure. This trio sonata for flute and violin was written in 1751, together with another for two violins (which the composer describes in his foreword to the printed edition as "representing a conversation between a Sanguine person and a Melancholy person"). Both works can be performed as trio sonatas by three or four players, or, as Bach says, the keyboard player can take the bass with his left hand and the upper melody part with his right hand, thus creating a real sonata for violin and keyboard. The first movement is a hybrid kind of structure, demonstrating the varied origins of the sonata form. It is a binary structure since it has a strong cadence in the dominant in m. 61, followed by a repeat sign, and the second part wends its way back to the tonic, but it carries many marks of ritornello structure as well.

This is a sonata whose essence is melody, and the first ten bars contain the material upon which the entire movement is built. Where earlier works had set out a two-bar melody as a fugue subject with the second voice answering in orthodox manner, here the melodic rhetoric is such that the answer in the dominant does not convince either the player or the listener that the composer has fugue in mind, although it is in fugue that its origins are to be found. There is an avoidance of

2. There are two thematic catalogues in use for the works of Emanuel Bach. The letter "W" refers to the catalogue compiled by Alfred Wotquenne in 1905. The letter "H" refers to the catalogue compiled by Eugene Helm published in 1989. Helm numbers are in the process of superseding Wotquenne numbers.

tonal issues, despite a clear first part or exposition (mm. 1–61), second part (mm. 62–115), and third part or recapitulation (mm. 116–142). Instead, its structure seems to be defined by the manner in which the melodic material is shaped and reshaped.

The fine flow of the ten-measure subject involves a complex balance within itself and repays careful examination. Example III–6 shows a possible division of the melody into its components. The exposition of this melody and its answer and extension to m. 26 constitutes the first of three sections which make up the structure to the double bar. At m. 27, **a** in an ornamented version is joined to **d,** which then separates and develops a still smaller fragment **d**^{1}. The last section begins in m. 45, where once again **a** provides the opening which is used sequentially, much as in **d,** and followed by **b** and **c** worked into a strong cadential function.

Example III–6: C. P. E. BACH, Trio Sonata, H. 578 (W. 161), opening melody.

The manner in which Bach treats his material after the double bar really merits the term "development." Beginning conventionally with the opening material **a** in the dominant, the composer takes motivic fragments, such as the syncopated rhythm from m. 9 which becomes the substance of mm. 82–87, and makes them into something different and greater than they were.

The last part of the structure, beginning in m. 116, seems like a truncated recapitulation. The opening material appears to be intact until we notice that **d** is omitted. The entry of the second voice in what we expect to be the position of the "fugal answer" begins with the head motive in the tonic and proceeds to recapitulate, with small but significant differences, the third and closing material from the first part of the movement.

It is clear that whatever points the composer intends to make are not primarily dependent either upon a play of tonality, or a departure and a return, or an exploration of novel relationships, although it is tempting to see a purpose in the way Bach sets out his material, separates and resynthesizes it. What is certain, however, is that this is a composer for whom the smallest element of melody has a significance beyond the normal, and that the music, while it speaks to the spirit and is filled with expressive power, absorbs the intellect to the same degree.

The trio sonata fills more musical and social needs than any other form in the period before 1760. During the discussion of the Bach sonata above, it was noted that that particular work was playable by harpsichord and one instrument or harpsichord and two instruments. There are, of course, the usual *continuo* options available—with or without cello, and, if the cello is present, with or without harpsichord. There is also plenty of evidence to show that the trio sonata could equally serve as a symphony for small orchestra. The most famous example of this practice is the first publication by Johann Stamitz, the *Six Sonates à trois ou avec tout l'orchestre* Op. 1 (1755; *ACM* 3). Written on three staves these works can serve as string trios, trio sonatas with *continuo,* or orchestral symphonies with violas and wind instruments added *ad libitum.* The surprising amount of contrapuntal play between the voices in no way adversely affects the piquancy of rhythm or the modernity of the *style galant* melody. The Stamitz usage was not unique, and a further stage in the development of the trio sonata is reached when a separate voice is freely added to the single line of the *basso continuo,* labeled clearly "viola." The addition of such an independent voice shows that the trio sonata of the mid-eighteenth century is well on the way to becoming one of the tributaries of the string quartet.

THE SOLO KEYBOARD SONATA

The development of the solo keyboard sonata paralleled that of the symphony-overture in magnitude and importance. Just as the rhythmic verve and *élan* of the symphony swept all before it (see p. 73 and following), so, in the 1730s, the composer who wished to make his name and to see his music in print wrote sonatas. While it is true that the term "sonata" covers an immense variety of forms and styles, the formal implications of the term which obtained in the eighteenth and at the beginning of the nineteenth centuries, and which are generally exemplified in the works of the Viennese masters Haydn, Mozart, and Beethoven, are established in many works composed during the 1730s and 1740s.

The sonata in the eighteenth century is characterized by certain features which can be perceived as "oppositions" or as "creators of tension" but which are probably better viewed as elements of musical contrast. Whereas the Baroque composer had moved easily, constantly, and generally uneventfully from one tonality to another, the sonata composer emphasized the process of modulation and sought to establish contrast between areas of tonal stability and areas of tonal flux; of lesser importance, because it is less frequently used, is the contrast between one area of tonal stability and another area of tonal stability.[3]

The Baroque composer sought a flow of rhythm from the beginning to the end of a composition of such momentum that a considerable slowing was necessary to bring about a successful conclusion; on the other hand, the sonata composer around 1750 attempts to segment his composition in any of the following ways: by separating one part or function from another by cadence, thus producing an effect of stopping and starting; by creating balanced, periodic structures; or by repeating melodic fragments or rhythmic motives.

Variety within unity is a sound artistic principle, but the balance between the two has always fluctuated. The Baroque suite grouped disparate dances together and unified them by key, by structure, and often by the use of common head motives or by aspects of variation. When the *style galant* elevated discontinuity and contrast to the status of a dominant aesthetic principle, the balance with the principle of unity had to be struck in another way, and composers of the period made perhaps the most far-reaching discovery in the whole of Western music. They wanted variety in their compositions above all, and the ternary structure (used in minuets and trios, in the *da capo* aria, and in the rondo) provided a certain amount of variety together with a measure of unity. But these ternary structures afford at best only a limited sense of unity, and composers realized that maximum variety can only be perceived when it is set against a larger oneness. Hence they took the binary structure, used in countless dances, which may be visualized as a large single arch, and proceeded to expand and extend it. The feat is to be compared with that of the medieval master masons, who, working by trial and error, without mathematics, pushed the Gothic arches of their cathedrals higher and higher, making a functional roof into an artistic

3. Tonal movement as such—for example, the movement from a tonic to its dominant—does not distinguish the eighteenth-century composer's work from that of earlier masters, where such modulation is equally prevalent and equally important. It is a truism that such modulation brings about movement, dimension, or span and necessitates a return to the original key. On the other hand, it is an unwise exaggeration to regard such modulation as creating "tension" or "opposition." Such an observation is likely to obscure the real contrast sought by the careful composer, whose search for novelty and forceful expression is not likely to be satisfied with the modulatory scheme routinely used at that time, as it had been for many years and as it was to be until well into the nineteenth century. It is not until the last quarter of the eighteenth century that the dominant pedal before a recapitulation in a symphonic movement creates an emotional climax in a structural-tonal area where none had previously existed.

expression of humanity's eternal aspiration. In the same way the expansion of the binary arch takes a functional (dance) periodic structure and gives it the potential to encompass a world of musical expression, as in the first movement of Beethoven's Ninth Symphony.

There are several types of binary structure prevalent by the beginning of the eighteenth century:

a. The simplest kind shows a balance in the length of both parts, with the tonal scheme I–V :][: V–I, and with no obvious repetition of material from the first part in the second part.

b. The asymmetrical binary structure has, of course, the same tonal movement away from a tonic and back to it, but it allows the second part to expand in order to accommodate greater tonal movement before returning.

c. A further stage is reached when either the tonic key or the secondary tonal area is identified by specific melodic-rhythmic material which recurs in the second half. This so-called rounded binary form is only a short step away from sonata form.

These differences can perhaps best be summed up in diagrammatic form:

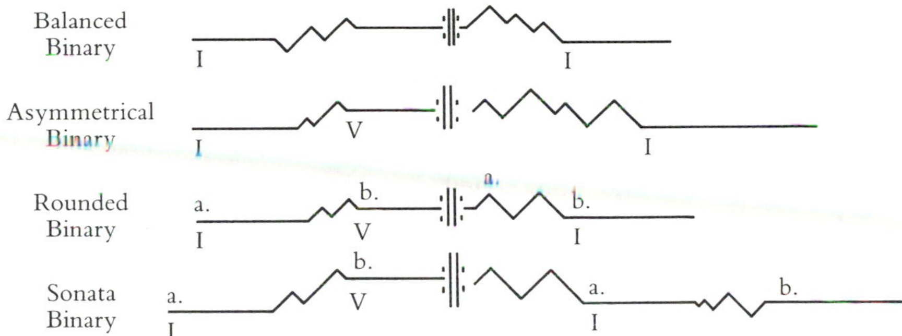

Roman numerals indicate harmonic area.
Letters indicate melodic material, themes or groups of themes
Zig-zag lines indicate areas of tonal flux

There is a danger of seeing a progression from good to better, or from naive to sophisticated, in the sequence of these structures. The rounded binary and sonata form, in particular, coexisted for many years, and although their relationship is demonstrated by their overall tonal structure, their differences are outstanding. The rounded binary offers the composer who cares for symmetry the possibility of creating a balance, with the necessary repetition of melodic material yet at the same time preserving a sense of freshness. Material is not heard the same way in both halves. Thus, what you hear initially in the tonic key will probably be heard in the dominant at the beginning of the second half of the piece, before it is moved through a number of keys or sequences. Likewise, what you hear in the dominant in the first half, most commonly reiterated intact in the second half, is repeated in the tonic key.

a in I, **b** in V :||: **a** in V with sequential treatment, **b** in I

It is clear that the ear perceives a two-part structure of inverse relationships in this form which appealed to many extremely sophisticated ears, including those of the young Mozart in his first symphonies and his early sonatas.

The sonata kind of binary arch, featuring a more or less complete repeat of material from the first half, also involves a direct repeat in the tonic of material first heard in the tonic. But while it retains its right to the binary name, since it makes a single tonal arch, it also becomes a structure which sounds tripartite, or three-part. (It is advisable not to call it "ternary" since that term has certain tonal connotations.) This type of structure allows the composer the possibility of wider tonal digression and gives him the opportunity to make a far greater expressive, emotional effect of the return to the tonic key and to the melodic material associated with it. History has proven that the sonata form offered more aesthetic satisfaction to composer and listener than did the rounded binary, but we must keep in mind the particular attributes of both kinds of structure.

No one can say that the work of Domenico Scarlatti (1685–1757) lacks sophistication, yet it is squarely based upon the rounded binary form. Scarlatti was born in the same year, the *annus mirabilis,* as Bach and Handel. It is interesting to note how differently the careers of these men developed. Handel, born in the little German town of Halle, traveled all over Europe and became the celebrated, cosmopolitan musician-entrepreneur, who knew all music at first hand; Bach, also born in a little German town, Eisenach, did not travel beyond his own locale but observed the world at arm's length, digesting and making his own those parts he approved and rejecting the others. Domenico Scarlatti, on the other hand, was born in Naples, one of the great centers of music and the very cradle of the new and the progressive. His father, Alessandro (1660–1725), a Sicilian by birth, was one of the most famous composers of his time, supreme in the composition of Baroque opera and the cantata in the Neapolitan style, and many of his relatives were musicians. Domenico's first attempts at opera were produced in 1703 and they were followed by others. It is, however, as a player and composer of music for the harpsichord that Domenico is best remembered. Concerning his playing, Handel's earliest biographer tells one of the most oft-quoted anecdotes:

> Here also he (Handel) became known to Dominico *[sic]* Scarlatti, now living in Spain, and author of the celebrated lessons. As he was an exquisite player on the harpsichord, the Cardinal was resolved to bring him and

> Handel together for a trial of skill. The issue of the trial on the harpsichord has been differently reported. It has been said that some gave the preference to Scarlatti. However, when they came to the Organ there was not the least pretence for doubting to which of them it belonged. Scarlatti himself declared the superiority of his antagonist, and owned ingenuously, that till he had heard him upon this instrument, he had no conception of its powers.[4]

This encounter probably took place in 1709, in Rome, where Scarlatti had a post in the Vatican. Approximately ten years later, he left that center of power to take up a post as master of the chapel to the king of Portugal. Thereafter, he was relatively removed from the musical world, his life confined to the periphery of Europe in the courts of Portugal and later of Spain, when his pupil the Princess Maria Barbara of Portugal married the crown prince of that country.

Many, perhaps most, of Scarlatti's compositions are lost and we know him almost entirely from the 555 sonatas for harpsichord that survive. Only a small part of this enormous body of work appeared in print in Scarlatti's lifetime. The first and most important publication was a collection of thirty sonatas, or *Essercizi,* first printed in 1738, almost certainly in London, where a small Scarlatti cult flourished and where his works were more influential than anywhere outside Spain. Only a few additional sonatas were actually published during the eighteenth century. While there is no way of knowing accurately when any of these sonatas were written, taking into account the circumstantial evidence, we can accept the view expressed by Ralph Kirkpatrick that "for the moment we are forced to assume that what looks like the development of a lifetime actually took place after Scarlatti was fifty, and largely after his sixty-seventh year."

Along with Bach and Chopin, Scarlatti belongs to the small group of composers who systematically advanced the technique of their instrument. His compositions belong to the harpsichord and embody its peculiarities to the extent that they make their effect properly on no other instrument. Insofar as the sonatas were written for Scarlatti's pupil the queen of Spain, we can assume that they were designed to exemplify and develop those aspects of technique which the composer valued above all. He was not writing for an amateur audience, or for wide circulation, and hence he produced music unmatched in its individuality.

Perhaps the most remarkable thing about these keyboard works is the way in which they use the whole register of the instrument. Whereas in Bach or Rameau the fingers take the arm where they want it to go, Scarlatti constantly requires movement from the arm which drops the

4. John Mainwaring, *Memoirs of the life of the late George Frederic Handel* (London, 1760), pp. 59–60.

Example III–7: D. SCARLATTI, Typical figurations using the entire keyboard

fingers where they are needed. The four examples on pp. 50–51 demonstrate the delight which the composer took in this kind of arm movement, with all its attendant thrills and spills for the player, and they also show how Scarlatti created a unique kind of texture which covers far more of the keyboard than is usual. In the fourth example, the arm movement required for hand-crossing becomes an end in itself. In addition to this kind of leaping and hand-crossing, Scarlatti required velocity and facility in consecutive thirds, sixths, and octaves much more frequently and consistently than did his contemporaries.

The Scarlatti sonata is almost invariably a one-movement work and only occasionally does it contain a number of different tempos or movements. In the large collections of manuscript sonatas, probably put together for Scarlatti's royal pupil, each work is separately headed "Sonata" with a tempo indication. Yet it is noteworthy that many of these works appear side by side with another sonata in the same key. Such pairs of works are frequently placed in complementary relationships of tempo or meter, and may have been intended to be grouped together in performance. Most of the single-movement sonatas consist of various dances, fugues, toccatas, etc., but the majority of them are written in a balanced binary structure with a variable amount of repetition.

In his preface to the *Essercizi,* Scarlatti addresses the reader in the following terms:

> Whether you are an amateur or a professional, do not expect to find profound learning in these compositions, but rather, ingenious jesting with the art in order to train you towards your freedom of the harpsichord.[5]

Scarlatti always wears his learning lightly: had he not done so he could hardly have appealed to anyone for whom the *style galant* represented good taste. His textures are predominantly two-part with occasional passages of lush, idiosyncratic harmonic progression, thickly chorded with grinding acciaccaturas. He frequently opens his sonatas with one voice leading, to be imitated at the fifth bar by a second voice. Usually the fugato effect breaks down after the second voice enters. Not infrequently, Scarlatti's quasi-fugal openings imitate at the unison and fall into that category of *galant* writing where one man's imitation becomes another man's repetition.

5. Domenico Scarlatti, *Essercizi per Gravicembalo* (London? 1738?, facsimile ed., Florence, 1985). Author's translation.

The Sonata in G, K.2[6] (*ACM* 4) is the second piece in the *Essercizi* of 1738. It exemplifies the incisive, aphoristic nature of the early Scarlatti sonata, without any of the idiosyncrasies that later characterized his work. The two halves of the structure are of very nearly equal weight (**a** = 37 mm., **b** = 41 mm.) and of equal material. The first 12 measures and the last 17 measures of **a** correspond with the first 12 and the last 17 measures of **b.** The differences between the two parts occur at the point where the modulation has to take place, as is to be expected.

Of especial significance is the manner in which the sonata hangs together. Repetition is the means by which Scarlatti creates a sense of coherence, phrasing, and color. The first four measures present a figuration of the tonic triad, from which a rhythm, ♫♪ ♩. , and the strict imitation between the parts emerges most prominently. As has been mentioned, the canon is a familiar opening effect. The rhythm, on the other hand, is pervasive. The initial textures seem to divide the four bars into 2 + 2 and the metrical unit appears to be, not the 3/8 of the time signature but 6/8. There is no closer complement to the opening four measures than the three measures closing the first part, in which the original arpeggio figuration and static harmonic rhythm are echoed.

The next four measures are made up of 2 + 2, which both conclude on strong tonic cadences but which otherwise have different rhythmic profiles and textures, ♫♪ ♩ ♪ + ♫♪ ♫♪. This four-bar unit of dissimilar halves is then repeated exactly in mm. 9–12. There follows a group of four 4–measure units in which both halves are identical and which are all based upon the opening rhythm, ♫♪ ♩ . M. 29 to the end of the half consists of three groups of 3 measures which, unlike all other groupings, elide with each other and move quickly to the conclusion. We can now see why Scarlatti did not wish to make the first part of this sonata 38 mm. in length, which he could easily have done by repeating m. 37. He evidently wanted an unsettling asymmetry, an incongruence which makes the opening of the sonata different from the conclusion of the first half.

A tabulation of the structure of the whole sonata, using the bar groupings as indicated above, yields the following results:

m.	
1	3 x 4 m. (2+2) unlike halves (no.1 group unique, 2 and 3 identical)
13	4 x 4 m. (2+2) like halves
29	3 x 3 m. (2+1) unlike halves (no.1 and 2 identical, 3 unique)

6. In referring to Scarlatti sonatas, the "K" number stands for the name of Ralph Kirkpatrick, whose numbering of the works is generally accepted as authoritative. Occasionally a number preceded by the letter "L" is found. This refers to the numbering of the first complete edition of Scarlatti's sonatas, edited by Alessandro Longo, who compiled the sonatas, arbitrarily, by key into suites—hence, the "L" numbers have limited value, since they only identify sonatas from this particular Ricordi edition. Kirkpatrick's numbering, it is believed, places the sonatas roughly in chronological order of composition.

Double bar

38	3 x 4 m. (2+2) unlike halves (first unique, 2 and 3 identical)
50	2 x 4 m. (2+2) like halves
58	1 x 4 m. (2+2) unlike halves
62	2 x 4 m. (2+2) like halves
70	3 x 3 m. (2+1) unlike halves (1 and 2 nearly identical, 3 unique)

There is an attractive symmetry about this table which makes it seem as though the composer had written in a calculated, intellectual way. When the single group of four measures in the second half is compared with the first of the groupings of three measures in the same half, Scarlatti's achievement is highlighted. Here is the core of the sonata's peculiar ambiguity: the creation of an easy expectation of a regular 6/8 meter which is contradicted by the 3 x 3 bars, whose only adequate metrical orthography is 3/8.

The Sonata in D, K.492 (*ACM* 5), shows Scarlatti extending himself to a much larger symmetrical rounded binary structure, incorporating a wider variety of harmonic and textural color, keyboard technique, and Spanish guitar flavor, while retaining the tightest logic of flow from one bar to the next. Although there is a strong emphasis on cadential articulation there is also a deliberate obscuring and elision of phrases, which makes this composer's works vital and challenging. In the preface to the *Essercizi,* Scarlatti had assured his readers not to expect profound art. This was not a facetious warning, for his readers did not want the profundity of a J. S. Bach. His English and Spanish admirers prized his ability to create so artfully that he concealed art.

It is surprising that Scarlatti did not have a greater influence on those who followed. In Spain, his pupil Antonio Soler (1729–83) wrote numerous sonatas bearing remarkable points of comparison with those of his master. In England, the *VIII Sonatas or Lessons for the Harpsichord* which Thomas Augustine Arne (1710–78) published in 1756 seem to show the occasional touch of a Scarlattian flavor, as in the cadential passage (Example III–8) from the Third Sonata in G, but otherwise this set of lessons is distinguished by formal variety, a feeling more antique than forward-looking and a happy eclecticism. Most movements are in a rounded binary structure with leanings toward full sonata form.

Example III–8: T. A. ARNE, Cadence from Sonata in G

Perhaps Scarlatti's most worthy successor outside the Italian mainstream is Pietro Domenico Paradies (or Paradisi; 1710?-91). At first a composer of operas which, according to Burney, were lacking in charm, Paradies established himself as a teacher of singing and harpsichord in London in 1746, where he remained until late in his life. He taught a number of successful pupils, but his most important legacy is in his collection of 12 Sonatas, first published in London in 1754. These works are each in two movements in no fixed tempo relationship: four have first movements faster than the second, e.g. *Moderato/Andante;* seven consist of two fast movements, e.g. *Allegro/Presto*. The tonality is the same in each of the two movements although the modality may be different: Nos. 4 and 9 have first movements in minor mode and the second in major; No.10 has a first movement in D major and a second movement in D minor. Paradies and Scarlatti share the same concern for using the whole range of the instrument, particularly the lower range, and arpeggios and hand-crossings abound. Paradies is much more likely than Scarlatti to use a three-part structure, however, so that the **b** part of the binary structure after the the double bar is much extended.

In Italy a number of celebrated harpsichordists and composers kept keyboard music flourishing, although posterity has tended to view their efforts far less favorably than those of the expatriate Scarlatti. Venice proved as natural a center for instrumental music as for opera. By the eighteenth century, its days of political power were long past. During the fourteenth, fifteenth, and sixteenth centuries the trading power and wealth of the city-state was enormous and out of all proportion to the size of its territory. Its power was based upon its ability to finance the rulers of much larger territories and upon a grimly efficient, not to say inhuman, organization of great families, whose justice was severe and far-reaching. With the growth of the great kingdoms of western Europe, Venice's might declined, although many of the trappings of power—the pomp and ceremony—remained, and the city gradually retreated into a dreamlike state of unreality, which, today, has become something of a nightmare of decay. The memoirs of the famous Venetian Giovanni Casanova (1725–98) give a vivid picture of the life of pleasure in his home town, the masked balls, the amorous encounters with novices and nuns in the little *casini* owned by foreign ambassadors and fitted out in the highest luxury for the lowest debauchery. The eighteenth century had few lessons to learn from the twentieth in the arts and crafts of self-indulgence.

A style of keyboard artistry associated with Venice and its composers had wide currency and considerable influence; in it, brilliance of technique is juxtaposed with smoothly affective melodic lines and harmonic coloring. The kind of unifying devices already noticed in the work of Tartini were not used. Within individual movements different melodic material is associated with different key centers. Occasionally, a motto-like phrase, heard at the outset of a movement may be used again to reinforce the beginning of a new tonal area, but in general one looks in vain for the derivation of new material from old. Harmonic coloring tends to be confined to a tasteful and well-placed reliance upon the chord of the flattened sixth in major-mode works and the use of the augmented sixth chord built upon the same scale degree. Baroque-like sequences are subjected to increased chromatic color. Much of the appeal of this smoothly *galant* music is to be found in the concentration of individual affects in small passages, such as the following:

Example III-9: Affective passages from Venetian keyboard music

A set of eight sonatas by Domenico Alberti was published by Walsh in 1748 and these works must have been well received since they have survived in numerous copies and were later republished in Paris and Amsterdam. They are all in two movements with a predominance of rounded binary structure.

The most important Venetian composer of keyboard music of the mid-eighteenth century is undoubtedly Baldassare Galuppi (1706–85), whose success as an opera composer took him all over Europe, from London to St. Petersburg. His work combines attractive melody, ranging from the melancholy, through the sprightly to the flashy, with textures which contain pseudo-polyphonic references, echoes of thoroughbass techniques, and pure keyboard figuration. He composed throughout his long life and the dating of much of his work is problematic. Before 1760 the invaluable firm of John Walsh comes to our assistance, for in 1756 they published a set of six sonatas by Galuppi. These works show a very wide range of styles and binary structures, ranging from the simple symmetrical binary to the fully developed sonata structure. One sonata (No.3) even shows a clear relationship of head motives between movements, not only in the material associated with the main key area but with the secondary key area also. The second sonata is in one movement; Nos. 3, 5, and 6 are in two movements, in each case showing a relationship of slow/fast with the second movement having a more complex formal organization than the first. The first sonata of the set is in three movements *(Adagio, Andantino, Allegro)* and the fourth has four movements *(Adagio, Allegro, Spiritoso e Staccato,* and *Giga, Allegro).*

The second sonata from this set (*ACM* 6), referred to in the English style as a "lesson," is found in other eighteenth-century copies labelled "Toccata." It is very different from other works in the collection, not simply because it is in one movement but because of its exceptional length (181 mm.) and its unusual textures. The piece has a clear three-part structure with a first part of 68 bars. An orthodox continuation (63 mm.) after the double bar sets the opening material in the relative major key while the secondary material recurs in the minor dominant. In the return, or third part (50 mm.), all the main material is recapitulated in the tonic key. Within this overall structure there are many subtleties that repay observation, but perhaps the most striking is the way that the keyboard textures differ from those in other sonatas and seem to cry out for an orchestral setting (see particularly mm. 49–63). The spaciousness of the harmonic rhythm also seems to require more color than the keyboard can give. Is it possible that here is a symphony or overture movement transcribed for harpsichord?

Twice during the set Galuppi uses an attractive setting in three parts of a sequence involving a dotted rhythm and a bass descending through a tetrachord. (Example III–10 shows the two examples from his sonatas.) Graceful and charming as the passages are, their precise likeness cannot be found elsewhere in Galuppi sonatas, hence this cannot be considered a cliché.

Example III–10: B. GALUPPI, Walsh sonatas (1756)

a. Sonata No.4

b. Sonata No.1

Eight months after the Galuppi sonatas were issued, in November of 1756, Walsh printed the *Eight Lessons* of Arne, whose second sonata opens as follows:

Example III–11: T. A. ARNE, Sonata No.2

Is Arne imitating Galuppi? Even if he were, no one in the 1750s would have raised an eyebrow.

The keyboard works by composers of southern Germany and Austria, in the orbit of northern Italy in so many ways, differed hardly at all from those of the expatriate Italians, such as Giovanni Benedetti Platti (1690–1763), living in that part of the world. Georg Christoph Wagenseil (1715–77) is among that generation of composers at the height of their careers when Mozart and Haydn were beginning theirs, and because of the similarities between his mature work and their early work, it may be pre-sumed that he was influential. His sonatas for keyboard—called *Divertimentos,* as Haydn so often named his—do not show any of those qualities of keyboard virtuosity which made him a famous performer and teacher to the Empress Maria Theresa. They are short, simple works in three movements, structurally unadventurous, relying upon a fairly regular use of the balanced binary principle, with a return to the tonic key at the point where the secondary melodic material returns. Textures are varied only slightly, so that the music lacks a strong profile, seeming to be designed more expressly for amateur pleasure than for professional display.

THE *EMPFINDSAMER STIL*

Further north, however, and centered around the court of Frederick the Great at Potsdam (Berlin), there arose a manner of composition which has come to be called the *empfindsamer Stil.* The term can be translated as the "Sensitive Style" or the "Style of Sensibility," but however translated it must be interpreted as a style in which emotion is valued above all, and in which a more than usual susceptibility to a wide range of emotional response is required in both performer and listener. Since its chief practitioner was Emanuel Bach, one of the most notable composers of the century, the style provided an effective contrast with the works emanating from the south, and ultimately had a significant effect on Haydn and Beethoven.

The sensitive style has been looked upon as a localized variation—a North German branch office—of the *style galant,* but while it shares certain ideals characteristic of the time, the differences in practice are so great and the gap between the two aesthetics so wide as to merit its being considered a separate phenomenon. Insofar as its characteristics emanate from a certain exaggeration of the elements of music considered normal at the time, we may be justified in thinking of it as a "mannerist" style.

Two quotations from the contemporary critic, writer, and composer Friedrich Wilhelm Marpurg (1718–95) will serve to isolate the aesthetic of the Berlin composers. In *Des critischen Musicus an der Spree* (The Critical Musician on the Banks of the Spree) of 1749, he writes:

> The rapidity with which the emotions change is common knowledge, for they are nothing but motion and restlessness. All musical expression has as its basis an affect or feeling. A philosopher who explains or demonstrates seeks to bring light to our understanding, to bring clarity and order to it. But the orator, poet, musician seek more to inflame than to enlighten. With the philosopher there are combustible materials which merely glow or give off a modest, restrained warmth. Here, however, there is but the distilled essence of this material, the finest of it, which gives off thousands of the most beautiful flames, but always with great speed, often with violence. The musician must therefore play a thousand different roles; he must assume a thousand characters as dictated by the composer. To what unusual undertakings the passions lead us! He who is fortunate, in any respect, to capture the enthusiasm that makes great people out of poets, orators, artists will know how precipitately and variously our soul reacts when it is abandoned to the emotions. A musician must therefore possess the greatest sensitivity and the happiest powers of divination to execute correctly every piece that is placed before him.[7]

In the same periodical, Marpurg asserts the independence of the Berlin composers from the source of all *galanterie,* France, when he later writes:

> A special distinction of Berlin music is that it makes very sparing use of manners and embellishments; but those that are used are the more select and the more finely and clearly performed. The performances of the Grauns, Quantz, Benda, Bach, etc., are never characterized by masses of embellishments. Impressive, rhetorical, and moving qualities spring from entirely different things, which do not create as much stir, but touch the heart more directly.[8]

Emanuel Bach adds to these important points on the subject of embellishment in his essay. Cautioning against the need for profuse ornamentation, he says:

7. Friedrich Marpurg, *Des critischen Musicus an der Spree* (Sept.2, 1749), Cited by William J. Mitchell, ed. C. P. E. Bach, *op. cit.,* p. 81.

8. *Ibid.*

> . . . the portrayal of simplicity or sadness suffers fewer ornaments than other emotions. He who observes such principles . . . will know how to pass skillfully from the singing style to the startling and fiery (in which instruments surpass the voice) and with his constant changing rouse and hold the listener's attention. . . . Notes of no great moment and those sufficiently brilliant by themselves should remain free of them.[9]

The sensitive style never aimed at the fashionable, broad audience of the *style galant*. For its fullest expression it needed composers of exceptional talent and schooling, while its appreciation required a certain level of connoisseurship. It was a personal, subjective, eccentric style of angular melodies in which appoggiaturas stuck out like knobby protuberances, in which rhythmic hiatuses catch the breath, in which metrical oddities subject similar phrases to different emphases—in which the only expectation is the unexpected. Because of these qualities, the style did not lend itself equally to any medium or any function. That music associated with social occasion, the opera and the symphony, or the church, although flavored with the style from time to time, rarely allowed for the exclusive concentration upon musical content which the sensitive style required. Since it speaks so personally, its fullest expression is to be found in the sonata and other forms for keyboard solo. Since it speaks so forcefully, its influence is best to be seen in the works of the Viennese masters later in the century, where, purged of idiosyncrasy and eccentricity, its strength—founded upon the exploitation of the force inherent in the most basic elements of music together with the new formal and tonal structures of the time—is multiplied to the highest power.

One of the few outstanding masters of the style of *Empfindsamkeit* is Jiři (Georg) Benda (1722–95), whose Sonata in B♭ (1757; *ACM* 7) serves as an exemplar of many of its most significant traits. Benda came from a family of Bohemian musicians brought to Berlin by Frederick the Great. His elder brother František (Franz; 1706–86) became a favorite violinist of Frederick's and a celebrated composer. Jiři was also employed as a violinist in the king's orchestra for a few years from 1742 to 1749, and in 1750 he went to Gotha as Kapellmeister. As a composer he gained the admiration and respect of no less an authority than Mozart, and he will be mentioned later in connection with his invention of the vocal melodrama.

In 1757 Benda published a set of six sonatas for keyboard, described by Charles Burney (1726–1814) as "very elegant," as well as "in the style of Emanuel Bach." This set is perhaps the smallest yet most comprehensive compendium of the sensitive style. In order to establish the features of the style, the first four measures of this sonata will be subjected to a succession of alterations which will strip off different stylistic layers. Example III–12a shows the original opening of the sonata.

9. C. P. E. Bach, *op. cit.*, p. 81.

Example III–12: J. BENDA, Sonata in B♭, I

a. Opening

b. Harmonic simplification

c. Melodic simplification

d. Metrical and rhythmic simplification

e. Recreation of opening in *style galant*

Example III–12b aims to simplify the harmony by removing Benda's chromaticism and making the whole passage clearly diatonic in B♭. The accidentals in mm. 1, 2, and 4 all conform to the primary harmonies accompanying them.

Example III–12c deals with those aspects of melody that separate the sensitive style from the *style galant*. Benda uses the acciaccatura in the first measure to accent the progression F to E♮ and since there is no shock in the progression F to E♭, it can be dispensed with. While the rest is a common feature of the *style galant,* standing for a breathing space or a separation of like elements, the hiatus or gaping void (not necessarily longer in time, only different in effect) is not. Here, Benda's short rest followed by six disproportionately short notes forms a gap between two dissimilar elements—the opening of the first measure and the opening of the second. In the *galant* style this effect is changed to a steady breath and an affective yet gentle leap. The startling (*cf.* Emanuel Bach quotation earlier) runs of m. 2 are replaced by a scale in the arch, dotted rhythm which the *style galant* took over from the French taste and notated literally. In m. 3, conjunct motion replaces the leaps on beat three and the non-harmonic tones are replaced with unaccented passing tones, while the final bar remains untouched.

In Example III–12d the metrical and rhythmic aspects of the piece are reconciled with the *galant* style. Benda's breathless accompaniment is here replaced by a steady Alberti-bass pattern, which adds continuity throughout. The left hand absorbs any free voicing from the right hand, and in the fourth bar creates a steadier harmonic rhythm than heretofore; the throw-away cadence is replaced with an orthodox perfect cadence on a strong beat.

The last example, III-12e, is a fanciful attempt to show why Benda's music is so different from *galanterie* and how radical the means required to make it consonant with that style. Here, some of Benda's material is arranged in a manner completely congruous with the prevalent style. The emphasis is placed upon the syncopated motive of the first two beats and the following motive, , of which much is made. The most striking feature of Benda's music becomes subordinate detail: the sixteenth-note rest in m.1 is doubled in length and yet, paradoxically, its effect is changed from that of hiatus, a wrenching break, to that of a breathing space. A balancing rest is introduced into the second measure. The second half of m. 2, which is perhaps Benda's most telling point, now becomes a scale whose function is obviously only to connect the first two measures with the second two.

Of course, this examination of four measures cannot be expected to provide a complete catalogue of the sensitive style, and some further generalized points can be made. The composers in the style do not turn their backs on their Baroque heritage. They are apt to use contrapuntal devices, such as imitation, inversion, etc., extensively and completely unselfconsciously. Example III–13 from Emanuel Bach shows the incipit of a slow movement in which imitation is used throughout, as in the opening bars. The composers using this style preserve complete flexibility in the creation of phrase structure, for while they occasionally resort to the short-breathed utterances of the *style galant,* they more frequently enjoy binding together longer melodies, often extending to six bars, sometimes to eight, as in Example III–14:

Example III–13: C. P. E. BACH, Sonata in F minor, H. 40

Example III–14: J. BENDA, Sonata in G (1757)

They delight in connecting odd lengths of note groupings to create asymmetry in which a phrase of six quarter notes is balanced by a phrase of eight:

Example III–15: C. P. E. BACH, Sonata in B minor, H.32.5

They preserve the Baroque use of hemiola (three in the time of two):

Example III–16: J. BENDA, Sonata in D (1757)

and even extend a penchant for metrical contrast, as in the next example, in which the first four bars of a phrase, while written in triple time sound like six measures of duple time, whereas the last four measures are quite unambiguous.

Example III–17: C. P. E. BACH, Sonata in B minor, H. 32.5

They tend to write angular melodies in which there is greater than usual predominance of leaps over steps, and yet they frequently embody the vocal style in sonatas, occasionally even using instrumental recitative.

Example III–18: C. P. E. BACH, Sonata in F, H. 24

Add to the characteristics described above a fondness for the use of the minor mode in an affective manner, the non-avoidance of extreme key signatures, a harmony conditioned by frequent chromaticism, and a preparedness for remote modulation, and the list, while not exhaustive, is at least indicative of the wide range of expressive possibilities inherent in the *empfindsamer Stil*.

The *style galant* aimed at a quality of grace that would complement the mannered world of the eighteenth century. It remained an art of surface—of appearance—and its polish reflected light, preventing penetration. Because the stuff of music was still the emotions, it could not avoid emotional content, but the range of that content was limited to those emotions which could readily be displayed in public and which were fashionable. From the quietly melancholic to the witty and the brilliantly showy, this range was effective, but of necessity *galanterie* avoided the tragic, the uncouth, the shocking, and the humorous. The adherents of *Empfindsamkeit* possessed, and at times restricted themselves to, all the refinements of *galanterie,* but their inclination lay in the expansion of music's means, and thus, in the development of music's power of expression. In the moody art of *Empfindsamkeit* is the musical counterpart of those intimations of literary Romanticism, such as Macpherson's *Ossian* and Bishop Percy's *Reliques* (see pp. 115–17). A local art it certainly is, but its echoes resound through the century, reemerging around 1770 under the guise of *Sturm und Drang* in the Viennese composers, and again in the last years of the century, when its aesthetic goals of the untrammeled expression of emotion became the slogans on those banners behind which all progressive young artists marched.

Wilhelm Friedemann Bach (1710–84) is the third of the most important masters of the sensitive style, along with his brother Emanuel and Jiří Benda. It is no accident that these two sons of Bach should play such an important role in this stylistic development. Johann Sebastian certainly lavished the efforts of his systematic mind upon the training of his eldest and most promising son, Friedemann, and Emanuel himself acknowledged that he had had no teacher other than his father. Despite his reputation and early success, Friedemann had few pupils of note. Emanuel, on the other hand, exerted a most profound influence upon Haydn, Mozart, and Beethoven.

Friedemann Bach could hardly have had a better start to his life. Born three years after his parents' marriage, his systematic instruction began at the age of ten, when his father gave him the *Clavier-Büchlein vor Wilhelm Friedemann Bach*. Numbers of other works were written with this son in mind and out of the hope that his father placed in him *(Two-Part Inventions, Three-part Sinfonias, Little Preludes, The Well-Tempered Clavier)*. In fact, one of the factors that impelled father Bach to leave Cöthen for Leipzig was the thought that his sons might be better educated and attend the university there.

Friedemann's first appointment, in 1733, was to the Sophienkirche in the royal city of Dresden, but despite the advantages of the situation, he resigned in 1746 and moved to the Liebfrauenkirche in Halle. He hoped for an appointment as Kapellmeister in Darmstadt and there is some uncertainty about how far negotiations may have proceeded before falling through. At any rate, he resigned his Halle post in 1764 and from that point eked out a living in declining circumstances without a fixed position. His age worked against him in those positions for which he competed, and he lived through the embittering experience of seeing himself overlooked in favor of less talented but younger men. In 1774 he moved to Berlin, where he remained until his death in 1784.

In 1744 Friedemann began what was intended to be a set of six sonatas that he hoped to publish by subscription. The first Sonata in D met with little success when it appeared and the series was not continued. In many ways this sonata typifies Friedemann's style: traditional in the constant use of imitation and canon and in the three-part writing (although some sections are freely voiced). Nowhere does he use a *continuo*-like left hand. Old-fashioned in some ways, this sonata reflects the fashions of its time in its modulatory freedom, its sectionalization, and its strongly unified disparities. The slow movement reads like a curiously distorted trio sonata by Bach père: the chromaticism and the melodic angularity are not his, but the devices of inversion, imitation, and stretto would meet with his approval. The third movement is a complex, gigue-like structure, not fugal but constantly contrapuntal, preserving from the gigue only the element of inversion at the beginning of the second half.

Quite different is one of a collection of Polonaises (*ACM* 8) which demonstrates the composer's chromatic and harmonic sophistication. Friedemann uses this kind of technique to infuse a poignant, introspective quality that permeates much of the music of this minor master.

Four years younger than his brother, Emanuel Bach was baptized under the best auspices, having as one of his godparents the celebrated Georg Philipp Telemann, whose death in 1767 was to affect Emanuel's life profoundly. His early education was carried out entirely under his father's eye at the Thomasschule in Leipzig. Later he went to the university at Frankfurt on the Oder, where he studied law. His earliest compositions, such as the first movement from the 1732 Sonata in D minor (H. 5; *ACM* 9), antedate his university studies. Its superficial likeness to a number of preludes by his father is apparent, but by the third measure the differences become clear. The chromatic movement of the inner voices, the resultant chords, and the interrupted cadences all speak of the new style espoused by the 18–year-old composer. Interesting also is the very clear articulation of the piece—an articulation carried out by the opening statement of the first two bars and the repetition of this statement in the keys of F, A and D minor in mm. 14, 20, and 30 respectively. The compelling sense of structure is heightened by the harmonic activity of mm. 34 and 35 and the static harmonic rhythm of the last seven measures, which give the listener the feeling of conclusion. It is this sense of timing, by which an unexpected melodic

In 1852, Adolph von Menzel created a fanciful interpretation of life a hundred years earlier. Here the subject is Frederick the Great playing the flute at Sans-Souci, his Potsdam palace, accompanied by Emanuel Bach and a small orchestra. (Nationalgalerie, Berlin)

event coincides with a strong tonal event, that makes this piece a prominent milestone on the road to the sonata.

In 1740, Emanuel Bach was appointed cembalo player to the newly crowned king of Prussia, Frederick II. It was his duty to play the *continuo* part in the concerts at which the king played; these were held every night of the week except Mondays and Fridays—the opera nights. The king was in many ways an excellent flute player, but his relationship with Emanuel, which must have started off reasonably well, slowly deteriorated. Emanuel's caustic wit, for which he had a reputation, may well have contributed to this worsening. Frederick may have looked upon himself as an "enlightened" despot, but after all he had engaged a *continuo* player, not a jester to remind him of his human failings.

Emanuel's first keyboard publication, six sonatas dedicated to Frederick and therefore called the *Prussian* Sonatas, was printed in 1742. These works are written in a judicious mixture of styles calculated to please without descending to the trivial. A clear, generous melodic line is never allowed to step over the mark into the idiosyncratic style of *Empfindsamkeit*. Counterpoint is never pedantic but assimilated easily into a modern texture. Emanuel even duplicates a device from one of the king's own compositions, when in the slow movement of the first sonata, he mingles instrumental recitative with composed *arioso*. The left hand alternates between reiterated bass notes on the beat, sounding like a *basso continuo* and having a purely harmonic function, and more melodic substance. Overall, the sonatas contain a wide variety of structural and textural innovation designed to impress the thoughtful listener with the thorough musicianship of the composer.

The "infinite riches in a little room" which Emanuel reveals to his audience may be seen in the exposition of the first of the *Prussian* Sonatas (see in Example III–19). Despite the imitation, and in accord with Emanuel's practice, most of the action takes place in the right hand. The melody is made up of a profusion of ornamented repetitions,

Example III–19: C. P. E. BACH, Sonata in F, H. 24

sequences, and allusions, and the result is a line in which the vast number of interrelationships create a kind of cohesiveness, concentration, and variety without parallel in the music of the time. Observe, for example, the way in which the relationship of the interval from B♭ to A (mm. 2 and 4) creates a weak cadence, and the same interval in a different rhythmic position (between mm. 5 and 6) concludes the phrase on a strong cadence. Observe the way in which the material in the dominant tonality (m. 15) relates as a free inversion to the opening bar, and the way in which its repetition, developing into the minor mode, allows for a brief, colorful harmonic excursion.

Emanuel's second set of sonatas was printed in 1744 and dedicated to the Duke of Württemberg, to whom he had given some instruction in Berlin. The *Württemberg* Sonatas require greater technical ability, and they are more fantastic,[10] melodically and harmonically. In these works, Emanuel most clearly establishes one of the important features of the later sonata, when, in the first of the set, he sets out contrasting material which he later reconciles in a synthesis that Beethoven might have been proud of.

During the years between 1732 and 1760, Emanuel composed many sonatas, which, in their experimentation with procedures of all kinds, make the twelve published works pale by comparison. Historians often remember Friedemann and Emanuel Bach's disparaging remarks about their father as "the old wig" and Emanuel's damning of counterpoint, as reported by Burney. But among the various sonatas that Emanuel wrote there are a substantial number in which counterpoint is used ostentatiously and re-conciled with sonata structure, seemingly based upon the two- and three-part invention style of his father, as well as movements that incorporate elements of fantasia. The fertility of his formal inventiveness and the unceasing experimentation that resulted from his inquiring intellect shocked many of his listeners while delighting others.

The Sonata in C (H. 46; first and second movements, *ACM* 10) of 1746 exemplifies the *empfindsamer Stil*. Curiously bound to *continuo* style in the left hand, as are many of Emanuel's works of this time (it is unthinkable that he did not elaborate the left hand in performance), the sonata shows the rhythmic hiatuses of the style and creates, in the section immediately following the first double bar, an amazing and unprecedented confluence of metrical, rhythmic, and tonal outlandishness. Note, however, how the tonal excursion is prepared and justified in mm. 13–16 and in the similar position in the recapitulation, mm. 74–79. Perhaps the most remarkable thing about this work is the middle

10. The Italian word *fantasia* and the English adjectival form "fantastic" refer to products of the imagination (fantasy). As applied to music, the term *fantasia* signifies a musical composition which obeys no set formal procedures but which is designed to evoke the free expression of a succession of emotional states.

section, or slow movement, mm. 92–123. Here the composer creates a strange rhetoric from the repeated juxtaposition of a strong quotation from the first-movement opening figure with an *Adagio* in triplets and dotted rhythms, thereby evoking a vocal, recitative style. The main body of the movement is in *Andante* tempo and proceeds for 13 measures until it is interrupted by the *Allegro-Adagio* pair, and thereafter, in its process of fragmentation, the movement involves ten tempo changes in nineteen bars. The last section emerges from the middle section with only a notated break as separation. It is an early example of this composer's method of working, in which a calm and formal dance rhythm—here the minuet—is combined with a graceful melody so that the movement may have all the greater effect. A careful examination of this work will reveal the composer's scrupulous attention to formal organization combined with the greatest imagination in the compression of disparate or unexpected material.

In this same period, the sonata structure, with its possibilities of infinite variety, became the basis for composition in a number of performance mediums. Whereas much Baroque practice had featured a solo or trio sonata accompanied by the *basso continuo,* the opposite now became very popular and a keyboard sonata might well have optional parts for violin and cello. In these cases the string instruments might have almost no integrity, simply doubling the keyboard melody in unisons, thirds, and sixths, filling in the gaps at the ends of phrases with some kind of articulating figure, or echoing small motives from the main melody. The value of this kind of work was great in an age in which musical products were tailored to fit the abilities of the amateur performer. These sonatas, like many concertos of the time, were readily playable with minimal rehearsal by the group, which was only required to follow and to support the solo player unobtrusively. It is significant that works in this medium tend, without exception, to the *galant* style. They form a bridge between private and public music.

OTHER KEYBOARD FORMS

At the same time, although sonata structure was most frequently used, it was not the only means of giving delight to the amateur. Pieces with fanciful titles *à la Couperin* and dances in binary form were also popular. The minuet and the polonaise were perhaps the most common. The minuet,[11] most usually a free-standing piece, is the short, danceable kind, with a first strain of 8 or 12 bars and a second strain in 8, 12, 16, or 20 bars, and is not to be confused with the *Tempo di Minuetto,* often found

11. The word is spelled variously: minuet (Eng.); menuet (Fr.); Menuett (Ger.); minuetto (It.).

as the last movement of a sonata, which may follow the phrase length of the dancing minuet, but is generally much more complex. The polonaise in the eighteenth century is vastly different from the dance of the same name in the nineteenth century. Whereas minuet phrases are usually assembled in multiples of four, the polonaise has no necessary phrase length dictated by the dance steps. In practice, its measures are grouped in multiples of two in a moderate to slow triple time. The left hand does not usually emphasize any particular rhythmic figure but is neutral and supportive, while the melody in the upper part tends toward triple repetitions of short motives. The polonaise's most abiding characteristic is its move to final cadence on the weak beat of the bar.

In the age of the amateur, the fantasia appears to have suffered a temporary setback. Emanuel Bach writes about it in both the first part of his *Essay* (1753) as well as in the second part (1762). Of the fantasia he writes that it requires "only a thorough understanding of harmony and acquaintance with a few rules of construction" and that "it consists of varied harmonic progressions which can be expressed in all manner of figuration and motives." That this is an art of performance is vouched for when he says that "it is principally in improvisation of fantasias that the keyboardist can best master the feelings of his audience."

THE SONG

The final medium to be touched upon here, that of voice and accompaniment, also occupies a middle ground between private and public music. Before 1760 the song had almost been supplanted by the popularity of operatic arias, collections of which, published as "Favourite Airs in the Opera . . . ," sold in great numbers. In France and England the development of the song was hindered by this concentration upon works for the theater, although many works for voice entered the national repertoire of both countries. Arne's Shakespeare songs or William Boyce's (1710–79) "Hearts of Oak" had wide circulation and are the equivalent of the French *ariettes* which had been the rage for some time and the *romances* which were coming to be so. On the other hand, a pronounced interest in folksong can be documented from early in the century, antedating the literary revival of the ballad, already mentioned, by many years.

In Germany, however, foundations were laid which led to the astounding proliferation of the song in the last years of the eighteenth century and the beginning of the nineteenth. On 1 October 1753, a group of composers anonymously issued a collection entitled *Oden mit Melodien,* (Odes with Melodies), thereby inaugurating what has since been called the first Berlin Song School. The composers, later acknowledged, comprised Johann Friedrich Agricola (1720–74), Emanuel Bach,

František Benda, Carl Heinrich Graun and his brother, Johann Gottlieb Graun (1703–71), Gottfried Krause (1719–70), Christoph Nichelmann (1717–61/2), and Georg Philipp Telemann. The charm of many of the songs has been noted as well as the strong motivic structure of many of them. What is also clear is that the collaboration was one of like minds, and that there was a shared ideal of song, expressed in a foreword by Krause, a lawyer by profession, as follows:

> Nowadays, we Germans are everywhere studying music and yet in many large towns people want to hear nothing save operatic arias. Song is not the ruling element in these arias—that song principle which is to be found in the unpretentious, amusing little tune which issues easily from every mouth and which can be sung without piano or other accompaniment. If only our German composers would compose, singing their songs, without needing a keyboard to hand, or even thinking of one, so that only a mere bass line need be placed under the melody, then would the taste for singing become widespread and bring joy and happiness everywhere.[12]

The activities of this Berlin-based group led to the production of a large number of collections of songs, together with an outpouring of discussion of theoretical aspects about song in musical periodicals. The verses of C. F. Gellert (1715–69), with their religious, moralizing tone, matched many of the ideals of the group, and achieved an immense popularity which lasted well into the nineteenth century. In 1758 Emanuel Bach published a collection of 54 songs entitled *Geistliche Oden und Lieder* (Spiritual Odes and Songs) to verses by Gellert, while Beethoven published a set of six songs, Opus 48, to his words almost fifty years later.

The Berlin group saw the song as a means for culture and education, but in championing the importance of melody, the significance of the accompaniment was denied. As is so frequently the case, however, the purity of the theory was weakened in practice, and composers were quick to sense the degree to which the accompaniment could heighten the expressive intention of the words and melody. In the ferment of discussion about song in the 1760s we can clearly see the emergence of considerations which were to lead to the definition of nineteenth-century song.

12. Gottfried Krause, cited in Hermann Kretschmar, *Geschichte des neuen Deutschen Liedes* (Leipzig, 1911; reprinted Hildesheim, 1966), p. 235. Author's translation.

CHAPTER IV

Music for Public Performance

The various functions of music in fashionable society during the 1730s and 1740s remained as they had been earlier, in many ways: the opera house, the Church, and the private chamber used music as they had always done. But the emergence of the public concert created a demand for a kind of music that could be perceived not through several senses but through the ears alone. This music absorbed the popular features of chamber music and opera so successfully that the concerto and symphony have maintained their appeal and their central position in concert programs from that day to this. It was possible to make the transfer from one milieu to another because most orchestras and performing bodies were small and the practice of *basso continuo* was universal, pervading all music. Thus, the early symphony, which has its strongest roots in the Italian and the French opera overtures and in the *ripieno* concerto, never-theless can still take the texture of the trio sonata, a chamber music medium, as one of its fundamental means. The solo concerto, on the other hand, brings many reminiscences of the opera to the concert stage, as the solo instrument presents, within the framework of an aria-like structure, a virtuosity destined later in the century to outstrip the capacity even of those masters of technique, the *castrati*.

THE SYMPHONY

No genre in the history of music enjoyed greater vogue than did the symphony during the eighteenth century. Considerably more than 12,000 such works have survived from the years 1720–1810; their actual total may well have been in excess of that number. The symphony was in such demand, and its function in society was so widely appreciated, that the existence of an orchestral body of whatever size or efficiency seems to have been enough to set composers busy producing them.

The basis of the orchestra is provided by the strings, frequently without winds. Early symphonies, in particular, are often scored for two violins and bass, like a trio sonata, although the majority use violas as well. In a larger orchestra oboes and horns were added (the presence of bassoons was taken for granted). In some scores the wind orchestration differs from movement to movement: the second movement might use flute instead of the oboes of the first movement, an exchange which is found at times in Haydn and Mozart. This indicates that the player is expected to double on flute/oboe, and does not mean that the flute player has been sitting idly during the first movement. When orchestras were small the player often doubled on a variety of instruments. Finally, for the largest ceremonial occasions, trumpets and drums might further broaden the orchestral spectrum.

The production of symphonies was widespread, but some centers became outstandingly important. Milan was the home of a group of composers who comprised the earliest school of symphonic production, the most famous of their number being Giovanni Battista Sammartini (1700/1–75), whose activity in all fields of music was remarkable. Celebrated as a composer of church music, chamber music, and theater music, as well as for his skill as organist and as teacher (Christoph Willibald Gluck [1714–87] was his most famous pupil), Sammartini is best remembered for his chamber works and symphonies. In addition to the wide circulation of his works in manuscript, printings of his music by several publishers became popular in Paris and London from the 1740s to the 1760s, more than 25 being recorded in London and more than 20 in Paris. It is thought that his music spread to Germany in the 1740s, and to Vienna later in the same decade.

Much of Sammartini's posthumous fame resulted from a remark by the Bohemian composer Joseph Mysliveček (1737–81), who, upon hearing symphonies by Sammartini, said, "I have found the father of Haydn's style." When Haydn heard of this comment he replied that he owed nothing to Sammartini, whom he looked upon as a "scribbler." The truth lies between these extreme positions: while Sammartini was no Haydn, yet he was a better composer than Haydn's opinion indicates. His work falls into three stylistic periods: from *c.*1724 to *c.*1739, during which Baroque and Classical elements are mixed; from *c.*1740 to *c.*1758, when the early Classical style appears; and from *c.*1759 to *c.*1774, when the features of a mature Classical style can be perceived.

The nineteen symphonies from the early period show a variety of structure and texture within small dimensions, surprising in a 'scribbler." They are written, with one exception, for strings only, on three or four staves. In his scoring Sammartini tends to link the viola with the bass, both instruments moving together either in unison or in chords. When the viola part is written on the middle stave, first and second violins unite on the top stave, creating a strong solo line with subordinate accompaniment. However, in those symphonies scored for first violin, second violin, and basso, the composer generally created a trio sonata texture with motivic imitation between the upper voices. The symphonies are in three movements, F/S/F. The majority contain a strong minor-mode flavor: three of them have minor-mode tonics, and eleven of the remainder have slow movements set in either the tonic minor or the relative minor. First movements tend to be binary structures, with textural and thematic variety. Imitation is not uncommon in both three- and four-stave works.

The first movement of Sammartini's Symphony No. 13 (*ACM* 11), an example of the composer's early symphonic style, uses a complex, polythematic structure worked out in tripartite form with full recapitulation. The music is the embodiment of the *style galant* in its textural changes, its sprightly rhythms, its orchestral effects, the balance of the three sections, and the distinction between those sections, emphasized by the identity of the beginning and the ending of the exposition and the recapitulation. The slow movement offers a chord sequence of six measures with a minor-mode coloring and a Phrygian cadence reminiscent of the Baroque. It is possible that the fermatas may have been used to allow the insertion of cadenzas for solo instruments. The last movement demonstrates Sammartini's frequent use of monothematicism, in that the main material (mm. 1–12) and the material in the dominant (mm. 25–37) are identical. The effect of this arrangement leads to a different kind of structural emphasis. Instead of pursuing balance and symmetry, as in the first movement, after an exposition of 38 measures, Sammartini begins his 50–measure development in orthodox fashion with a repeat of the opening material in the dominant, but then extends his modulation over a relatively long period into remote keys. The small recapitulation of the opening theme (12 measures) is extended by a coda of seven measures to reach a satisfying conclusion—so satisfying that Haydn's remark increasingly appears to be bilious and uncharacteristically petulant.

The connections between Vienna and northern Italy were close throughout the eighteenth century, especially in opera, but the growth of the Viennese symphony was possibly inhibited by the strength of the late-Baroque tradition in that city. Outstanding among its composers were Wagenseil and Matthias Georg Monn (1717–50), whose symphonic works reflect the range from the *sinfonia a tre,* in which the two upper violin parts share material imitatively, to the fully orchestrated *sinfonia a otto,* (2 oboes, 2 horns, 2 violins, viola, and bass), relying as it does upon mass orchestral effects. Typical of the Viennese style is the use made of all the instruments: no single line predominates, and much of the interest of the music lies in the tossing back and forth of short motives (see Example IV–1). At this period, the Viennese symphony, like the Italian, tends to be a three-movement work, although Monn

Example IV–1: M. G. MONN, Symphonie in D, I

was for many years credited with being the first to introduce a fourth movement, the minuet. The slow movement is usually either in the tonic, the tonic minor, the relative minor, or the subdominant, while the minuet—where there is one—will be in the tonic with its trio in the tonic minor. Mention must also be made of the composer Carlo d'Ordonez (1734–86), whose work will be discussed later. One of his symphonies with a slow introduction—a device with which Haydn later became so strongly identified—survives in a copy dated 1756.

The city of Mannheim was the seat of the most brilliant court of Germany during much of the eighteenth century. The Elector Karl Theodor, who came to the title in 1742, was keenly interested in the arts and sciences, and played several instruments. He spared no expense to gratify his interest, and he assembled a notable group of musicians in his establishment, which became the best-trained musical organization in Europe. The fame of his music director, Johann Stamitz,[1] both as composer and orchestra trainer, was such that the musical style of Mannheim took root in France, and Paris fell under the spell of his collection of symphonies entitled *La Melodia Germanica*. The famous traveler and commentator Charles Burney, upon visiting Mannheim in 1772, experienced the prolific second generation of composers there at first hand: the first generation, some of whom had died by that time, was a notable group. Franz Xaver Richter (1709–89) was the oldest and his music exemplified, more than that of any other member of the Mannheim group, residual Baroque elements. Ignaz Holzbauer (1711–83) settled in Mannheim in 1753 as Kapellmeister, after firmly establishing himself in Vienna as a composer of opera and music for the church. Anton Filtz (1733–60), employed as a cellist, was considerably younger than the others, yet is accounted one of the first generation of Mannheim composers. These men and others, together with Johann Stamitz, established a style of orchestral playing based upon a uniformly excellent band of musicians, carefully drilled and prepared for each performance. Burney commented in a famous passage: "There are more solo players and good composers in this than perhaps in any other orchestra in Europe; it is an army of generals, equally fit to plan a battle as to fight it."

Dynamic effects, made possible by the discipline, are probably the single most important aspect of the Mannheim style. The contemporary writer Schubart, writing around 1784–5, says:

> Its forte is like thunder, its Crescendo like a waterfall, its Diminuendo is like a distant plashing brook, its Piano is like a breath of Spring.[2]

Nicknames have been given to the various clichés of the Mannheim style that have passed into the folklore of music history.[3] The collective style of the Mannheim composers, however, perhaps better than any other, exemplifies the *style galant* in orchestral writing: full of verve and spirit yet tender, the music is built from many scraps of melody and texture, each differentiated from the other, most lasting for only two measures and repeated; it is highly sectionalized, and moves over a generally slow harmonic rhythm based on primary triads. This is music

1. Many of the best musicians in the Mannheim establishment, as well as in Vienna, came from Bohemia or Moravia, and Czechs today still like to see Stamitz's name spelled Stamič.
2. Christian Friedrich Daniel Schubart, *Ideen zu einer Aesthetik der Tonkunst,* cited by Roland Würtz in *The New Grove Dictionary of Music and Musicians* (London, 1980) XI, p. 625.
3. It had been customary to refer to a theme using an upward arpeggio over an extended range as a "Mannheim rocket," or a melodic appoggiatura as a "Mannheim sigh," or a crescendo passage building over several measures as a "Mannheim steamroller," etc. More modern research has shown that many of these effects did not originate in Mannheim, and the use of the nicknames has diminished.

whose essence is color, not line, whose effect is irresistibly bound up with its medium of performance—the orchestra.

Johann Stamitz was the leader and music director of the Mannheim orchestra from 1745 to his death in 1757. He was a virtuoso violinist and it was undoubtedly because of his disciplined training that the orchestral bowing was so uniform, that phrase articulation was so precise, and that dynamics were so unanimously executed. Twice Stamitz visited Paris: once in 1751 and again, for a longer period, from late 1754 to August 1755. His Symphony in D (*ACM* 12, movements 1 and 2), a four-movement work, was published in France by Bayard in 1761. The first movement resembles an Italian opera overture in its tempo indication *Presto,* in its lack of a repeat sign after the exposition, and in its clear structure. A unison *forte* gesture, followed by a melodic gesture *piano* is repeated (mm. 1–8). A *crescendo* (mm. 9–16) leads to a climactic piece of passagework, which comes to a *fortissimo* on the dominant (mm. 17–24). A *piano* melody for strings alone establishes the dominant key (mm. 24–32), which is followed by another *forte* climax of sequential passagework, leading to a strong cadence on V of V. A third *piano* melody, this time for the winds accompanied by the strings (mm. 38–50), is again followed by similar *forte* passagework to a conclusion of the exposition in m. 58.

The middle section is 24 measures long. It remains in the dominant key for the first 12 measures, then uses the second theme on three sequential steps, V of IV, V of V, V of VI, returning to the tonic key in m. 81 by a reverse process, V of III, V of II, V of I.

The recapitulation is not complete, since the composer reiterates only the *forte* chords of the opening gesture, and then omits all subsequent material from the exposition until the second theme, now restated in the tonic. The articulating passagework is longer than expected because the composer now brings back the material from mm. 17–23 and juxtaposes the passage mm. 32–37 (mm. 90–101). The conclusion (mm. 114 to the end) brings back the material from mm. 9–16, and repeats it to strengthen the ending.

Typical of Johann Stamitz is the combination of naiveté and sophistication. The *forte* passagework, overworked as it is by later composers, cannot be construed simply as filler material, for its repetition shows it to be an integral part of the structure; and the melodic material, while simple to the point of banality, is subtly interrelated and its effect, terse and compact. Habitually, he takes a texture or a melody and arbitrarily moves it into some other part of the composition; in fact, one can visualize him handling the elements of his symphonies as a mosaic designer might handle pieces of colored glass or stone. These elements are articulated in the clearest manner imaginable, with passages, rests, and fermatas; yet the rearrangement of material in the tonal return defeats complete predictability. This music is the embodiment of the *style gal-*

ant; its fundamental divisions of the musical texture into melodic and dynamic material had an enormous effect on subsequent French music, and on the nineteenth-century conception of a concerto.

Paris was perhaps the most important center for the publication and performance of symphonic music—indeed, of instrumental music in general—and in the years before 1760 public and private concert giving flourished as never before, both in the capital and in numerous provincial cities. Despite the existence of works entitled "symphonie" by native Frenchmen, such as François Martin (1727?-57), Charles-Henri Blainville (1711–77), *et al.,* as well as certain stylistic determinants of the form current in the capital before Stamitz's visits to Paris, the effect of his work with the orchestra of La Pouplinière and of his compositions made a lasting impression upon the musical taste of the city, and established Germany as the preeminent source of instrumental music. François-Joseph Gossec, a composer whose longevity made him an active musical force in the *ancien régime,* the Revolution, the Napoleonic era, and the restored Bourbon monarchy, was born in Belgium and went to Paris in 1751. There, owing to Rameau's influence, he obtained a post in the orchestra of La Pouplinière (see p. 27). He issued his first collection of six symphonies as Opus 3 around 1756. They follow the Italian model, in three movements, and are orchestrated for strings and *basso continuo.* Gossec probably came to know the work of the Mannheim School through direct contact with Johann Stamitz, and in his next group of symphonies, Opus 4 of 1758, turned to the four-movement variety with minuet. The orchestration of these works calls for horns, and in one case, horns and oboes.

THE CONCERTO

The concerto was second only to the symphony as the most popular form of public concert music, and, like the symphony, it was equally at home in the chamber. In his *Essay* (1752), Quantz gives a description of the style and the structure of the medium that includes both the solo concerto and the *concerto grosso.* He says:

> . . . the *concerto grosso* . . . in which two or more instruments, the number sometimes extending as high as eight and more, play together in turns. In the *chamber concerto* . . . only a single concertante instrument is present.
>
> The character of the *concerto grosso* requires the following features in each movement. . . At the beginning a majestic ritornello must appear which is more harmonic than melodic, more serious than jocular, and which is interspersed with unison passages. . . There must be a skillful mixture of imitations among the concertante parts, so that the ear is surprised now by this instrument, now by that. . . . The inner tutti sections must be short. . . . The last tutti must conclude with the most forceful and majestic ideas

of the first ritornello. A concerto of this kind requires a large accompanying body, a large place to perform it, a serious performance and a moderate tempo.

Concertos with one concertante instrument, or so-called *chamber concertos,* are also of two classes. Some demand a large accompanying body, like *concerti grossi,* others demand a small one. . . The class to which a concerto belongs may be perceived from the first ritornello. . . . A ritornello which consists of fleeting, jocular, gay, or singing melodies, and has quick changes of harmony, produces a better effect with a small accompanying body.[4]

The heyday of the *concerto grosso* was past by 1740, although they continued to appear in some countries until the 1760s (e.g., Britain, where the strength of the Corelli/Handel tradition kept them in vogue). In taking its place, the concert symphony from time to time incorporated *concertante*[5] elements, thus perpetuating the enjoyment of tonal variety—the surprising of the ear—that Quantz had talked about. Indeed, the amalgamation of the symphony with the aural variety of the concerto was a process which continued through the rest of the century. But it was the three-movement, solo concerto that most immediately replaced the *concerto grosso* in the public ear,[6] and by 1760 it was generally dominant. Where the symphony flourished so did the concerto and many composers famous for their symphonies, e.g., the Mannheimers, Stamitz, Filtz, etc., or the Viennese, Monn, Wagenseil, etc., or the Milanese Sammartini, were also celebrated for their concertos.

In this period of the solo concerto, composers like Leclair in Paris, and Locatelli and Tartini in Italy—as well as a host of others—produced a vast number of concertos for violin. The most important solo keyboard concertos, as well as the greatest number, were produced in Johann Sebastian Bach's immediate circle. It is interesting to note that the elder Bach's violin concertos date from *c.*1720 and were written for court use, whereas the harpsichord concertos date from *c.*1735–40 (by which time his elder sons had already written their own first keyboard concertos) and were, presumably, for family use. By far the greatest number of concertos were composed by Emanuel, 35 of whose 50 or so were written before 1760. These works display a sophistication of musical means, a development of keyboard idiom and of formal structure without parallel at the time. Normally couched in the three-movement form,

4. Quantz, *op. cit.,* pp. 310–311.

5. The term *concertante* implies a soloistic or virtuosic quality in the music—as in a concerto.

6. The tradition established by Corelli has the *concerto grosso* most closely related to the four-movement trio sonata, from which it developed by the simple expedient of adding instruments to create tuttis, whereas the solo concerto, from the Venetian tradition established by Torelli, has three movements. In addition, by the middle of the eighteenth century, both types of concerto use the same kind of structure, depending upon ritornellos played by the whole body, alternating with solo passages.

F/S/F, his concertos reveal the same kind of key relationship found in the sonata. Quantz describes that relationship as follows:

> If the [first] Allegro is written in a major tonality, for example, in C major, the Adagio may be set, at one's discretion, in C minor, E minor, A minor, F major, G major, or G minor. If, however, the first Allegro is written in a minor key, for example, C minor, the Adagio may be set in E-flat major, F minor, G minor, or A-flat major. These sequences of keys are the most natural ones. The ear will never be offended by them, and the relationships are acceptable for all keys, whatever their names.[7]

The first movement is the most developed and demanding; the second movement is usually free in form, most idiosyncratic and filled with *Empfindsamkeit;* and the last tends toward the greatest simplicity.

In his precepts for the first movement, Quantz requires that:

> A majestic ritornello must be carefully elaborated in all the parts.
>
> The melodies must be pleasing and intelligible.
>
> The best ideas of the ritornello must be dismembered, and intermingled during or between the solo passages.
>
> The ritornello must be of suitable length. It must have at least two principal sections. The second, since it is repeated at the end of the movement, and concludes it, must be provided with the most beautiful and majestic ideas.
>
> If the opening idea of the ritornello is not sufficiently singing or is not appropriate for the solo, a new idea quite unlike it must be introduced, and must be joined to the opening materials . . .
>
> At times the solo sections must be singing, and at times these flattering sections must be interspersed with brilliant melodic and harmonic passagework appropriate to the instrument . . .
>
> . . . In general, light and shadow must be maintained at all times. If it is possible, a good effect is produced if the passagework is invented in such a way that the accompanying parts are able to introduce a recognizable portion of the ritornello simultaneously . . .
>
> The end of the piece must not be hurried or cut short; it must be clearly confirmed. The piece must not conclude with entirely new ideas; in the last solo section the most pleasing of the ideas previously heard must be repeated.
>
> Finally, the Allegro must be concluded as briefly as possible in the last tutti with the second part of the first ritornello.[8]

Our authority writes extensively on the "serious solo concerto," and all the precepts quoted above refer to that kind of work. The concerto,

7. Quantz, *op. cit.*, p. 313.
8. *Ibid.*, pp. 311–312.

however, is not defined solely by these terms: like other forms of composition, it too has a range of possible shapes and sizes. Dealing with the opposite extreme from the large concerto, Quantz writes:

> Anybody who knows how to write a concerto of this kind [the serious solo concerto] will find it easy to fashion a jocular and playful *little chamber concerto*. Thus it would be superfluous to deal with it separately here.[9]

The "little chamber concerto" is a kind of unpretentious work that continues to be composed well into the 1780s. Elements of virtuosity are almost absent, and the solo keyboard part seems to be designed for the amateur. Like the sonata, this kind of work, used for social music-making, is typically entitled "Divertimento" as often as "Concerto" or "Concertino."[10] In its small dimensions, in its simple melodic and harmonic style, and in its avoidance of virtuosic demands, such a work shows the distance that the Concerto was to travel in the next thirty years.

9. *Ibid.*, p.315.

10. Around 1760 Haydn wrote a number of small works "for beginners," as he himself describes them, entitled either "Divertimento" or "Concertino." They bear little resemblance to Quantz's prescription but consist rather of three movements, the two outer in rounded binary structure separated by a slow movement.

CHAPTER V

Words and Music on the Stage

More books have been written about the theory, the practice, the criticism, and the evolution of opera than about any other genre in the history of music. Perhaps this is to be expected since opera itself arose among a group of intellectuals for whom words were the most natural medium. Even as the new art form gathered around itself all the trappings of staging, scene painting, design, and acting, it also lent itself readily to discussion by both amateurs and professionals, by philosophers as well as musicians. During the whole of the eighteenth century, the central conception of opera—the idea that an acted drama can be entirely set to music and that the greatest emotional validity can be added to the words by the music—managed to adapt itself marvelously well to almost all society's needs and functions. On court occasions, such as coronations, weddings, or birthdays, the extravagant displays of opulent costumes and stage sets, the bringing together of miracle-working machinery to astonish the eye and technically polished voices to charm the ear, and the use of all the devices of language to flatter the absolute monarch and his family, all made opera the obvious choice for a memorable, regal entertainment. With modifications, it could work equally well as social satire and comedy in the popular theater, dependent upon a paying public for its existence.

THE THEATER AS A SOCIAL CENTER

In the eighteenth century, the theater offered perhaps the most convenient setting for carrying on one's social activities while enjoying an entertainment. The public concert could not yet be compared in popularity with the theater, nor did the public ballroom rival the private gathering in prominence. But the common factor in all these social phenomena (among which the church might also be included) is that they all offered participants the opportunity to see and be seen. Like many

A performance at the Teatro Reggio, Turin, in 1741. The costumes are typical of an *opera seria*. The audience may be seen buying oranges, turning round in conversation, reading their librettos, drinking coffee, etc. (Turin, Museo Civico)

other complex social structures, the opera theater made a wide gamut of activities available to its audiences, providing them with a place to meet friends, to eat meals, to make lovers' assignations, or to transact business while at the very center of things. Many authors have commented on the social history of the opera, but few have described the commercial theater of Italy better than the impresario Count Giacomo Durazzo (1717–94), the supposed author of the anonymous *Lettre sur le méchanisme de l'opéra italien* (Letter on the workings of Italian opera). His anonymity allowed him to write as if he were a Frenchman, comparing the operatic scene in France and in Italy. About Italian opera, he said:

> Habitually, people get together about one hour after sunset. When the theater is playing, private parties do not take place: people meet in the theater. The theater boxes are, so to speak, rooms for receiving company; indeed, gentlemen go from box to box to pay court to the ladies, and the ladies visit with one another. . . . It is part of good manners to step regularly into each box every evening. The corridors resemble streets; moreover, people play cards in the boxes, eat their evening meal, and the noise . . . is such that one can hardly hear the orchestra.
>
> The attention of the audience, while distracted in so many ways, can nevertheless be attracted, and the star singer performing a big aria will be able to instill silence.[1]

THE SINGERS

Italian opera belongs to its singers and the voice that dominated the eighteenth century was the soprano, both the natural female and the male *castrato*. The conception and composition of heroic roles for male soprano constitutes one of the several stumbling blocks to our full apprecation of the *opera seria* (serious opera) today. Another comparison between French and Italian opera, of an earlier date, 1702, by François Raguenet (1660–1722?), gives a fine account of this voice type. Raguenet writes:

> I observed in the beginning of this Parallel how much we had the Advantage over the Italians in our Basses, so common with us, and so rare to be found in Italy; but how small is this in comparison to the Benefit their Operas receive from their Castrati, who abound without Number among them, whereas there is not one to be found in all France. Our Women's Voices are indeed as soft and agreeable as are those of their Castrati, but then they are far from being either so strong, or lively. No Man or Woman in the World can boast of a Voice like Theirs, they are clear, they are moving, and affect the Soul itself.
>
> Sometimes you hear a Symphony so charming, that you think nothing in Musick can exceed it, 'till on a sudden you perceive it was design'd only to accompany a more charming Air, Sung by one of these Castrati, who with a voice the most clear, and at the same time equally soft, pierces the Symphony, and tops all the Instruments with an agreeableness which they that hear it may conceive, but will never be able to describe.
>
> These Pipes of Theirs, resemble that of the Nightingale; Their long-winded Throats draw you in a manner out of your Depth, and make you lose your Breath: They'll execute Passages of I know not how many Bars together, they'll have Echo's on the same Passages and Swellings of a prodigious Length, and then with a chuckle in the Throat exactly like that of a Night-

1. Giacomo Durazzo, *Lettre sur le méchanisme de l'opéra italien* (Florence, 1756), pp. 64–65. Translation by the author.

> ingale, they'll conclude with Cadences of an equal Length, and all this in the same Breath.
>
> . . . Besides, the Italian Voices being equally strong as they are soft, we hear all they Sing very distinctly, whereas half of it is lost upon our Theatre unless we sit close to the Stage, or have the Spirit of Divination. Our Upper Parts are usually Perform'd by Girls, that have neither Lungs nor Wind; whereas the same Parts in Italy are always Perform'd by Men, whose firm piercing Voices are to be heard clearly in the largest Theatres without losing a Syllable, sit where you will.[2]

Of course, the idea of a *castrato* singing heroic male roles with his high voice attracted a great deal of ridicule, then as now. But it speaks highly of the voice's power to suspend audience disbelief that the names of famous *castrati* resounded through the eighteenth century as household words. In an art form governed by the "star system" the *castrato* commanded the highest salary of any musician, and those who were at the top lived like princes. Just as audiences marveled at their vocal powers, so the cognoscenti notated their florid cadenzas, and there are many records of their achievements in the pages of Burney and his contemporaries. The most famous *castrato* was Carlo Broschi(1705–82), called Farinelli, who, in the second third of the century, conquered the whole of Europe (except England) with his voice. Unlike many of his fellows,

2. François Raguenet, *A Comparison between the French and Italian Musick and Operas* (London, 1709), pp. 36–39.

The castrato Carlo Broschi, known as Farinelli, painted by Jacopo Arrigoni in 1752.

who seemed to want to exact revenge for their emasculated state by petty meanness, Farinelli was, by and large, generous and wise. He found favor at the Spanish court, and there achieved large financial rewards, a noble title, and a generous pension, which was continued when he retired in princely splendor to Italy.[3]

THE DRAMATIC CONVENTIONS

The earliest operas were serious works, intended to appeal to a small audience of like-minded intellectuals. This unity of mood and purpose was soon abandoned as opera became dependent upon a paying audience, whose desire for variety and entertainment necessitated the introduction of comic scenes. By the end of the seventeenth century two distinctly different styles of opera coexisted: the Italian and the French. The Italian style had developed, in the last third of the century, into a conventionalized art form, not dependent upon the continuous unfolding of narrative events in a dramatic sequence, but upon the alternation of recitative and aria according to voice types. While the French style tended toward the development of dramatic content, it also contained elements from the ballet and the masque which worked against the developing drama.

It is a tribute to the centrality of French manners and thought in seventeenth- and eighteenth-century Europe that at the heart of eighteenth-century Italian opera lie ideals developed from French drama in the seventeenth. It must also be observed that English-speaking playgoers, brought up as they are on the dramas of Shakespeare and more recent playwrights, may find it difficult to appreciate these ideals from which Italian *opera seria* took its nourishment.

During the seventeenth century, people came to revere the rational processes of the human mind and the scientific method. The most celebrated practitioners of French classical tragedy, Pierre Corneille (1606–84) and Jean Racine (1639–99), sought to bring the theater closer to real life and to overcome the problem of dramatic convention—that the audience agree for a time to suspend their disbelief and accept what is happening on stage as real—by following the so-called Aristotelian unities of time, space, and plot. In brief, it was argued that in order to accept a drama as true to life, the plot must unfold over a reasonable amount of time, i.e., the action cannot stretch over years when the audience is seated in front of the stage for three hours (unity of time). The action of the drama must take place in one location, since the stage is fixed in one place and the audience knows that it cannot be one moment

3. Charles Burney's *General History of Music* (1776–1789) contains biographies and descriptions of the vocal excellence of many of these famous singers.

a ship at sea and the next the throne room of a palace (unity of place). The drama must revolve around one plot dependent upon a limited number of characters, since, given the other unities, it would be stretching convention too far to expect an audience to swallow several plots involving many characters unfolding in this single location (unity of plot). Whether observation of these unities actually achieves the desired effect is not easy to determine, but history shows that in some periods it was more successful than in others.

ITALIAN *OPERA SERIA*

Under the influence of seventeenth-century French ideals, a series of attempts were made in the early eighteenth century to rid Italian opera of the theatrical devices it had accumulated during its transformation from an intellectual exercise into a popular urban entertainment. The single most important practical force was the work of Apostolo Zeno (1668–1750). His librettos, which embodied the reforming zeal of the Arcadian Academy in Rome, constituted a serious attempt to refashion the libretto into an admirable literary form. His remedies included the pruning away of any distractions from the central theme of the drama; the excision of any comic episodes; and the reduction in the number of characters. In order to fulfill the didactic function of art, characters are simplified and become symbols of specific human virtues or vices; for the same reason, plots tend to revolve around noble characters faced by Fate with the necessity of making an impossible choice between love and duty, or between patriotism and sedition, or between loyalty and personal ambition. Since the purpose of the artwork is to teach, and since drama teaches by encouraging the audience to emulate what is admirable and reject what is foolish, the main characters, with whom the audience is to identify, are noble (kings, princes) or heroic (warriors). Naturally, the stratum of society immediately below the highest provides the main protagonists with servants as well as friends and confidants.

This, then, is the stuff of the Italian *opera seria* as it was conceived by Zeno, and indeed, the patterns set by him endured until the middle of the eighteenth century. Even more influential than Zeno, however, was his younger contemporary Pietro Metastasio (1698–1782), who, arguably, is the most important librettist in the history of opera. During the eighteenth century his theatrical writings—full-length *drammi per musica* as well as shorter pieces—were set to music over a thousand times. The most popular of his librettos were set as many as seventy times, and many composers used certain favorite librettos more than once.

The Metastasian libretto offered a standardization of procedure that made those of earlier times appear confused and shapeless. Opera was already made up of recitative (that part of the music in which the char-

Typical costumes of the male and female principals in an *opera seria*. (Museo della Scala, Milan)

acters utter text which forwards the dramatic action) and aria (that part of the music which crystallizes or dwells on a particular emotional situation). The structure of the scene is defined not by place but by numbers of characters on stage: if one person leaves the stage, for example, the remaining complement of characters makes a new scene, which, in turn, lasts only until a new character either enters or leaves. This structure assumes, in Metastasian practice, a uniform shape—a progress from dramatic action to emotional reflection, a heightening of language from blank verse to rhymed verse, and a heightening of music from speech rhythms, declaimed to a sparse accompaniment of *continuo,* to the full apparatus of melody, harmony, and orchestration. The singer/actor within this structure steps on and off the stage. Initially interacting with other characters in recitative, in the aria, as the character expands on the emotional reaction to the dramatic situation, and as the other characters recede, it is clear that the audience itself is being addressed. At the aria's conclusion, the resultant and hoped-for applause provides a release of the tension created by this kind of dramatic crescendo, and the character leaves the stage; arias that come at the close of scenes are called "exit" arias.

RECITATIVE AND ARIA

Of course, the aria and the recitative became almost infinitely varied, and the skill of the librettist and the composer can be measured by the way variety of plot situation evokes variety of emotional response, which in turn allows the composer to vary tempos, modes, orchestration, meters, etc. John Brown (1752–87), a Scotsman who lived in Italy for ten years, wrote a series of "Letters upon the Poetry and Music of the Italian Operas" which was published two years after his death. He is chiefly remembered for his succinct account of aria types, but what he has to say casts light in a number of directions. In his first letter he justifies the distinction between recitative and aria and describes simple (or "dry") recitative *(recitativo semplice* or *recitativo secco):*

> The Italians have, with great propriety, considered, that the speeches in the drama, whether in dialogue or soliloquy, must be either such as are expressive of passion and sentiment, or such as are not so. On this real distinction, and not, as with us, on the mere caprice of the composer, is founded their first great division of vocal music into *recitative* and *air*. It is evident . . . many passages must necessarily occur, such as simple narration of facts, directions given . . . none of which, as they contain nothing of passion or sentiment, can ever become the subject of musical expression. Simply to have spoken these passages, however, and then abruptly to have set up a singing, when any pathetic part presented itself, would have produced exactly that barbarous jumble of prose and poetry, of music and dissonance which characterizes the English comic opera. To avoid this . . . the Italians have invented that species of singing termed by them *simple recitative*. Its name almost sufficiently explains its nature: It is a succession of notes so arranged as to coincide with the laws of harmony, tho' never accompanied but by a single instrument, whose office is merely to support the voice, and to direct it in its modulations. Though for the sake of this accompanyment, recitative is, like other music, divided into bars, yet are not these bars, as in other music, necessarily of equal lengths; the notes of which they are composed being subjected to no precise musical measure, but regulated in this respect, almost wholly by the natural prosody of the language. . . and, being music itself, the transition from it to the higher and more interesting parts is perfectly natural, and agreeable to the ear.[4]

In his second letter, Brown describes another kind of recitative:

4. John Brown, *Letters upon the Poetry and Music of the Italian Opera; addressed to a Friend* (Edinburgh, 1789), pp. 2–5.

> They [the Italians] . . . have observed, that all those passages in which the mind of the speaker is agitated by a rapid succession of various emotions, are, from their nature, incompatible with any particular strain, or length of melody; for that which constitutes such particular strain is the relation of several parts to one whole. . . Air they think even inadmissible in those passages, in which, though the emotions be not various, yet the sentences are broken and incoherent . . . such passages, however, . . . were of all others the most proper subject for musical expression. . . . It is to them they adapt that species of recitative termed *recitativo istrumentato* or *recitativo obbligato—accompanied recitative.* In this kind of recitative the singer is, in a more special manner, left to the dictates of his own feelings and judgment with respect to the measure . . . he may give to particular syllables what length he pleases, and precipitate considerably the pronunciation of others, just as he thinks the expression requires. . . It is in this species of song that the finest effects of the chromatic . . . are peculiarly felt; and it is here also that the powers of modulation are most happily, because most properly, employed, by changes of tone analogous to the variety of the matter, in a wonderful manner enforcing and characterizing the transitions which are made from one subject or emotion to another . . . nor are the instruments limited to the simple duty of supporting and directing the voice. In this high species of recitative it is the peculiar province of the instrumental parts . . . to awake in the audience sensations and emotions similar to those which are supposed to agitate the speaker.[5]

In his third letter, in which he opens the discussion of aria types, Brown, having said that recitative and air may be considered as *genera* in music and the different types as *species,* puts the distinction between them in a nutshell:

> All those passages where the transition from one emotion to another is sudden and violent, and which, therefore, can neither, on account of their brevity, make each a whole of itself, nor, by reason of their variety, be made parts of the same whole, are expressed in Recitative. Those, on the other hand, in which one sentiment pervades a whole sentence composed of different parts, become proper subjects for Air; and, indeed, every complete musical strain may, with great justness, be termed a sentence or period in melody.[6]

The aria was the vehicle for the star singer. It alone had the power to quiet the audience and seize its attention; for this reason variety in the sequence of arias was vital. Therefore, a number of "species" of aria were created which mirrored the emotional/expressive situation of the character on stage and displayed the vocal excellence of the soloist. Brown lists five types and two forms in his third letter.

> *Aria Cantabile* . . . gives the singer an opportunity of displaying at once, and in the highest degree, all his powers, of whatever description they be. The proper subjects for this Air are sentiments of tenderness.

5. *Ibid.,* pp. 12–17.
6. *Ibid.,* pp. 29–30.

> *Aria di Portamento* . . . This kind of Air is chiefly composed of long notes, such as the singer can dwell on . . . or the beauty of sound itself, and of voice in particular, as being the finest of all sounds, is held, by the Italians, to be one of the chief sources of the pleasure we derive from music. The subjects proper for this Air are sentiments of dignity.
>
> *Aria di mezzo carattere* . . . is a species of Air, which, though expressive neither of the dignity of this last, nor of the pathos of the former, is, however, serious and pleasing.
>
> *Aria parlante* . . . speaking Air, is that which, from the nature of its subject, admits neither of long notes in the composition, nor of many ornaments in the execution. The rapidity of the motion of this Air is proportioned to the violence of the passion which is expressed by it. This species of Air goes sometimes by the name of *aria di nota e parola,* and likewise of *aria agitata*.
>
> *Aria di bravura, aria di agilita* . . . composed *chiefly,* indeed, too often, *merely* to indulge the singer in the display of certain powers in the execution . . . in general the means are here confounded with the end.[7]

Brown here adds a short description of the forms of aria called *Rondò* and *Cavatina*. In a subsequent letter he also describes an aria type which he calls Airs of Imitation, in which the subject is a simile. (Perhaps the most famous example of this class of eighteenth-century aria is "Come scoglio" (Like a rock) sung by Fiordiligi in Mozart's *Così fan tutte*). Further, he adds extensive discussion of each aria type together with examples of representative texts.

Some of the conventions governing the use of the aria originated from dramatic considerations; for example, an exit aria shall not be followed directly by an entrance aria; or no two arias of the same type shall follow one another, even though separated by recitative. In both cases the reason is loss of *chiaroscuro,* or contrast. On the other hand, those conventions which dictated that almost all arias should be in *da capo* form; that the main characters should have at least one aria in each act; that arias for the same voice type should not follow one another; that the lesser characters should have fewer arias than the main characters and that they should be less impressive—all reflected the fact that it was the singer who attracted the paying audience and who, therefore, exercised great control over the *opera seria.*

PASTICHE

The extent to which the system accommodated the "star" must be pursued further, since it affected the composition of the opera so greatly. Durazzo (already quoted on p. 85), describes the practice of singers

7. *Ibid.*, pp. 36–39.

substituting favorite old arias for those newly composed and untried. He says:

> It often happens that the Virtuosi, i.e. the principal actor and the principal actress, who take all the decisions over the heads of their fellows, the composer, the impresario and even the public, bring arias with them from other operas which they have sung to great acclaim, and force the composer to insert them, come Hell or high water, into their roles . . . "to ensure the success of the opera" as they say.[8]

The paying audience for the Italian *opera seria* was so little concerned with the unity of the composition and so much concerned with the effect of the vocalization that the habit of inserting arias was accepted without demur. Indeed, whole operas were cobbled together using compositions chosen from a variety of composers whose works were meeting with success at the time. Such works were called *pastiches* or *pasticii,* and this kind of composition remained popular until well into the nineteenth century.

Much of the character of Italian opera is dictated by the constant need for new works, for as Durazzo says: "The Italian is as indifferent to last year's music as the Frenchman is attached to it." The demand for novelty may appear to be at odds with the insertion of old arias and the popularity of pastiches, but both practices grew out of the audience's order of priorities, in which the voice took precedence above every other consideration. At any rate, the enormous demand for new operas was matched by the increased number of theaters in small and large Italian towns. Durazzo tells us that in the Carnival season, over 50 serious operas were staged, and if comic operas are added the number exceeds one hundred. He also describes how those operas were put together:

> An individual or a group of people undertake to mount an opera for Carnival season. They bring together from different towns in Italy singers and dancers, who, coming together from all directions, find themselves in a company without ever having seen or known each other before. A composer from Naples or Bologna, the two best schools of music in Italy, is commissioned. He arrives about a month before the 26th December, when the opera is to open. He is told which play has been chosen, he composes twenty-five or twenty-six arias with accompaniments, and there is the opera—done. The recitative takes only as much trouble as its writing costs. As the arias are finished they are given to the singers, who learn them easily since most of them are excellent musicians. As for the Recitative, they do not take the trouble to study it but merely glance at it. They are satisfied to repeat what the Prompter utters more loudly than they, and the harpsichord keeps them on key. There are five or six rehearsals and *voilà* your opera is staged in less than a month.

He goes on to say:

8. Durazzo, *op. cit.*, pp. 46–47.

> A composer arrives with forty or fifty arias already composed, written during moments of inspiration, and which he adjusts to the words as much as he can. And when they absolutely will not fit with the music destined for them, the composer has new words made, which may fit better or worse. Whether or not they (the words) have any relationship with the subject matter is, as I have told you, immaterial; the composer's one worry is to make the aria suitable to the taste and the voice of the person who will have to sing it.[9]

ITALIAN *OPERA BUFFA*

As described above, Italian eighteenth-century *opera seria* reflected the dominance of the voice. But the situation was somewhat different with comic opera. From the earliest introduction of elements of comedy into Italian opera, the characters connected with those elements belonged to the lower orders of society. Servants, countryfolk, the bourgeois, or the physically disabled were the butt of general humor. As the *opera seria* increasingly divested itself of elements of comedy the genre of comic opera developed. Although the earliest comic operas sprang out of aristocratic patronage, the rapid growth of a popular audience made it possible for the new genre to survive. In 1709 the first season of comic opera was mounted in Naples, where a substantial tradition of works in Neapolitan dialect developed. Perhaps because of its special dialect, the Neapolitan comic opera remained local. But in Naples as well as the rest of Italy the loss of comedy within the body of the *opera seria* was gradually compensated for by the interpolation of another kind of dramatic work between the acts: the *intermezzo*. As its name implies, the *intermezzo* was inserted in the middle of the opera; usually the opera was in three acts, and hence the *intermezzo* was divided into two parts, one for each interval.

The point has often been made that the *intermezzo* is, in its own way, just as much of a stereotype as the *opera seria* for its characters are stereotypes and do not resemble fully-fleshed human beings. But this view ignores the central dramatic means of both comedy and tragedy. It has already been noted that the *opera seria* teaches through identification: the tragic character is noble and the audience identifies with that character. Comedy, on the other hand, teaches through rejection: the audience laughs at the comic character and only upon sober reflection recognizes the character's faults in themselves. The comic *intermezzo* of the 1720s and 1730s, like later eighteenth-century forms of comic opera, uses stock figures largely derived from the improvised folk art of the *commedia dell'arte,* and its weapons are ridicule, parody, and satire. Neither the serious nor the comic genres of this time attempt to portray

9. *Ibid.*, pp. 43–44.

Two typical *Commedia dell'Arte* characters, complete with humps and bellies, performing a comic dance. On the left is Pulcinello. (Engraving by Johann Georg Puschner, 1705–50)

real people: their purpose is rather to illustrate universal human characteristics. Thanks to their folk origins, the figures from the *commedia dell'arte* are taken from life. Pantalone or Dr. Graziano is almost always a lecherous old man, a parent or guardian figure, a member of the legal or medical profession, and is meant to be deceived and ultimately defeated by young love. Capitano or Scaramouche is invariably a boastful, lying, and utterly cowardly soldier who is ultimately exposed for what he is. Brighella is a vivacious, resourceful, and clever servant-girl who is maid to a lovesick mistress, Columbina. Arlecchino is Brighella's male counterpart and also a young lover. Pulcinello is a short, fat, stupid, and deformed servant who beats his wife. An enormous number of dramas have been created throughout the history of the theater on these few characters and what they represent .

Like the *opera seria,* the *intermezzo* was made up of recitatives and arias. However, there were usually only two characters and they sang in natural voices. Since the star singers of the *opera seria* did not take part in the *intermezzo,* there was no need for the vocal paraphernalia that went along with the heavier genre: coloratura, cadenzas, improvised ornamentation, aria types, and exit arias. Music and plot bore no relationship to that of the opera which it accompanied, and frequently it was the work of a different composer. Most important, the best *intermezzi* quickly were detached from their "parent" *opera seria,* and were performed separately, or with other *opere serie.*

FRENCH OPERA

It is no accident that the last years of the seventeenth century and the first half of the eighteenth saw the publication of numerous essays and philosophical tracts by Frenchmen, calling attention to the deficiencies of French opera by writing enthusiastically about the musical theater in Italy. But neither wishful thinking nor rational argument could bridge the gulf between the French and Italian opera, despite their common origin.

As has been said, France was by far the largest, wealthiest, and most powerful country in Europe during the seventeenth and most of the eighteenth centuries, due perhaps to the degree of authority wielded by the government of the country. Everything in France emanated from the king and had to bear his stamp of approval. The opera was no exception. In 1672, Louis XIV had granted to Jean-Baptiste Lully the right to found an *Académie royale de musique* (see p.25)—in effect giving him a monopoly over the production of opera in Paris—and the operas that both met with the king's approval and matched the public's taste tended to involve the eye as much as the ear. The French already had a long tradition of ballet, and it was almost unthinkable that opera in Paris could thrive without the visual entertainment provided by the dance. But also the intellectual strength and dramatic force of the French poetic tragedy of the seventeenth century was bound to leave its mark upon the opera.

The presence of the ballet within the opera worked against the drama. It was said at this time that operatic plots should be constructed to allow for the interpolation of scenes of revelry, etc., that would justify the introduction of balletic *divertissements;* by these means the drama could alternate between tension and relaxation. But in the majority of cases the introduction of ballet weakened the continuity of the drama and entertained the eye without engaging the spirit.

The influence of the poetic tragedy is felt in several ways, and perhaps Lully's greatest legacy to the eighteenth century is his adaptation of the early seventeenth-century recitative style of Caccini to the French language. He studied the conventionalized style of delivery of one of the greatest tragic actresses of the day and attempted to mirror her subtle inflections and shifts of accent in his melodic line. The resulting recitative is more deliberate than *recitativo secco;* the written note values are so strictly observed that metrical shifts in the words are reflected by changing time signatures. The increased importance of the melodic line demands a *continuo* of greater melodic and harmonic interest that mirrors the greater emotional content. Clearly, not only is this type of recitative more demanding of the listener and of the musician, but it also has a more significant role in the opera.

The aria, on the other hand, never catering solely to the demands of the voice, remained much closer to the simplicity of the popular air.

Indeed, the singability of the aria and the ease with which it could be committed to memory contributed greatly to the success of an opera. Given then a recitative that constantly pushes toward *arioso* and an aria that tends to brevity and simplicity, it can be seen that the characteristic alternation of musical means in Italian opera is avoided in its French counterpart, and that in its place a homogeneous web of music gives continuity to the fluctuating dramatic tension.

The frequent use of the chorus served to emphasize dramatic contrast. French tragedy, unlike its Greek progenitor, did not use the chorus to comment on the drama—a representative of Everyman, as it were, and a very real element in the dramatic tissue. Rather, the operatic chorus is rarely intimately involved with the action but appears as a balletic, choreographic interlude, presenting stately or energetic movement with fitting harmony and rhythm, as the occasion demands, yet ultimately distracting attention from the drama.

Lully's legacy of opera-ballet and *tragédie lyrique* was powerful and composers in the first half of the eighteenth century were inevitably compared to him. The style he had perfected echoed the taste of the ruling monarch and his court, and was, accordingly, widely popular. Such enduring popularity inevitably becomes a conservative element in society, and its effect was to insulate France and French music from the wide-spread changes that were taking place in the rest of Europe.

OPERA IN ITALY

Politically, much of Italy belonged to the Holy Roman Empire during the eighteenth and early nineteenth centuries (in effect these parts of Italy were colonies of Austria), yet there can be no question that the whole of Europe, with the partial exception of France, was the musical colony of the Italians, who went abroad to make a living and then retired home on the lavish proceeds. In the century since its birth, opera had become so important in the cultural life of Italy that it was of consuming interest to all levels of society. The most important centers were Venice, Rome, and Naples, but Milan, Parma, Genoa, Verona, Bologna, Turin, Florence, and several other cities also had active opera seasons.

Italy led the way in developing commercial opera, just as England led the way in developing a commercial concert life. The first public opera house had been opened in Venice in 1637, and by the end of the seventeenth century the city boasted ten houses at which more than 350 operas had been presented by 1700. By the close of the eighteenth century that number had increased to close to 1600. While no other city could rival Venice in its profusion of opera houses, many of even the smaller centers had at least two theaters.

Venice, Rome, and Naples each performed a repertoire which included newly commissioned works, but for the most part the works were several years old. When a new work was successful, it was usually mounted elsewhere within a couple of years. Thus Hasse's *Artaserse,* first produced in Venice in February of 1730, was staged in Genoa in the spring and in Lucca in the fall of the same year, while Pergolesi's *Olimpiade,* first produced at Rome in January 1735 without success, was nevertheless staged in Venice in 1738. Despite local differences, there was an overall homogeneity in the Italian opera season.

VENICE Before 1749 it is clear that the Venetian opera directors favored the *opera seria* , and Vivaldi, Hasse, Gluck, and Niccolò Jommelli (1714–74), among others, were asked to write in that style. After 1749 Venice seemed much less interested in commissioning new works on Metastasian librettos than in restaging old ones. The most favored librettist for new works was Carlo Goldoni (1707–93), and in the period between 1748 and 1759, of the twenty new operas staged in Venice, seventeen were written to his texts.[10] His librettos, more sophisticated than the old Neapolitan dialect comedies from earlier in the century, and of greater interest than the *intermezzo,* laid the groundwork for a new genre of Venetian comic opera.

The collaboration of Goldoni with Baldassare Galuppi, both Venetians and at the height of their powers in mid-century, brought about some notable results. Galuppi, after a sojourn in England, acquired a position in the Cathedral of St. Mark's in 1748, and a year later began composing a series of comic operas to Goldoni texts, including the most famous of all Venetian *opere buffe, Il filosofo di campagna* (1754). In all, he set twenty librettos of Goldoni between 1740 and 1766. His operas are remarkable for their use of short aria forms, allowing for a more incisive insight into character than the more cumbersome *da capo* form. He also made a contribution to the development of the operatic finale: instead of merely bringing the characters together in an ensemble number, he ended some acts with a chain of sections, unrelated in melody and tempo, through which a sequence of dramatic events is brought to a climax, a device Mozart was to raise to unequaled heights.

NAPLES Opera did not become prominent in Naples until the late seventeenth century, when Alessandro Scarlatti (1660–1725) went there from Rome. Naples was a secular state and there were none of the restrictions on opera that obtained in Rome. Comic opera and opera in the local dialect flourished, but although dialect opera was popular for a long time, it had, by and large, only a local currency. The *intermezzo* is closely associated with this city since the most famous of them all,

10. Goldoni, born in Venice, wrote more than 250 plays, as well as librettos for numerous operas. He is credited with replacing the old *commedia dell'arte* with modern, realistic comedy.

The ordinary, everyday dress of the characters in an *intermezzo* reflect the occupations and voices of the protagonists, as well as the nature of the plot. (Museo della Scala, Milan)

La serva padrona (1733) by the Neapolitan composer Giovanni Battista Pergolesi (1710–36), was first performed there. This epoch-making little work in two parts requires two singers and one actor in a silent clown's role. The plot involves the successful plan of a servant girl (Serpina, soprano) to marry her elderly bachelor master (Uberto, bass-baritone). Each part consists of a couple of arias separated by recitatives and concludes with a duet, the second part being slightly shorter than the first. Of the seven musical numbers, five fall into *da capo* forms. The style is extremely simple, with frequent use of unisons:

Example V–1: G. B. PERGOLESI, *La serva padrona,* No. 1

Short scraps and tags of melody are repeated *ad infinitum:*

Example V–2: G. B. PERGOLESI, *La serva padrona,* No. 3

and the harmonic formula of the perfect cadence, I for two beats, then IV and V for one beat each is repeated (see Example V–3). In an age in which the natural and the simple were equated, this style was very easily perceived as a most "natural" style.

It should be remembered, however, that the *intermezzo* resulted primarily from the exclusion of comic elements from the reform opera of Zeno and Metastasio; they were composed all over Italy, not only in Naples. Since these small comic operas were in standard Italian rather

Example V–3: G. B. PERGOLESI, *La serva padrona,* No. 6

than dialect, they traveled well throughout Europe, and, together with the fine examples of *opera seria* emanating from Naples, contributed greatly to the popularization of the so-called Neapolitan style. Indeed, so highly were they esteemed that Pergolesi became a legend after his untimely death, and his reputation grew out of all proportion to his actual musical legacy, so that he became everybody's favorite composer—an eighteenth-century "hit."

ROME Opera in Rome flourished as private entertainment during the seventeenth century, but public opera had difficulties in establishing itself after the death of Pope Clement IX, himself the author of opera librettos. Later popes, in their concern for public morality, tended to frown on opera in public places. Hence, for the first half of the eighteenth century, Roman theaters, which included two of the largest in Europe, were restricted to the production of *opera seria* when they were allowed to operate at all. In the period 1730–59, seventeen operas were given first performances in Rome, of which fifteen were *opere serie,* eleven to librettos of either Zeno or Metastasio. The Neapolitan composer, Niccolò Jommelli, found great favor with his operas in Rome in the 1740s before his appointment to Stuttgart. His works, as well as those of Tommaso Traetta (1727–79), will be discussed in Part Two.

OPERA IN GERMAN-SPEAKING COUNTRIES

By the eighteenth century the Holy Roman Empire, governed by the Habsburg dynasty from Vienna, had spread in a haphazard way across Europe, and modern boundaries within that continent bear only a slight relationship to what existed then. It seems appropriate, therefore, to discuss the development of opera during this period within that entire linguistic area.

As in Italy, opera was adopted eagerly in German-speaking countries, and theaters for their performance sprang up everywhere. Unlike Italy, however, middle-Europe was divided into many small states, almost all with a ruler of some kind: prince, count, bishop, etc. Hence, opera developed in the courts, like the private, aristocratic, and intellectual phenomenon it had been earlier in Italy; commercial opera, however, was slower in coming. Indeed, the tradition of centralized control and of state subsidy for opera is even today much stronger in German-speaking countries than elsewhere.

VIENNA The imperial city of Vienna boasted the most musical royal family of Europe. The Habsburgs had been players and composers and patrons of music for centuries. During the reign of Empress Maria Theresa, however, political problems and the shortage of money caused music to decline in importance, and power and position accumulated in the hands of the court Kapellmeister, Georg Reutter (1708–72), a highly regarded but self-serving man. In 1749 Count Durazzo was appointed Genoan ambassador to Vienna, and because of strong intercession on his behalf by Prince Kaunitz, Maria Theresa's most trusted statesman, he eventually became the director of theater productions for the city of Vienna.

Durazzo was determined to end the dominance of the *opera seria* in the city where Metastasio lived, occupying the position of court poet, and Chancellor Kaunitz wanted to strengthen ties between Austria and France in order to oppose Prussian expansion. Both men shared a community of interest in promoting things French: they worked together, Kaunitz abetting Durazzo, in bringing French actors to Vienna to present French *vaudevilles*. Durazzo supported a number of like-minded poets and musicians who fostered a new kind of opera based on a union of Italian and French styles; and Kauntiz's policy brought about the marriage between the Austrian Archduchess Marie-Antoinette and the Dauphin of France. Intrigue forced Durazzo to leave Vienna in 1764, but his efforts to bring a rational to the drama in opera were vindicated by his protégés, the composer Gluck and the poet/librettist Raniero Calzabigi (1714–95).

BERLIN The seat of the militaristic kingdom of Prussia, Berlin, had no opera until the accession of Frederick the Great, in 1740. This king, it will be remembered, had had to keep all his intellectual and artistic aspirations as secret as possible before coming to the throne, but upon the death of his father, he immediately set about making Berlin into a cultural center. Since he aspired, personally, to be a flutist, a composer, a writer, and a philosopher, he gathered around him musicians, authors, and philosophers. One of these was Francesco Algarotti (1712–64), who was invited to be Frederick's consultant and translator of Italian operas in 1740. Today Algarotti is most famous for his small book on opera entitled *Saggio sopra l'opera in musica* (*Essay on Opera;* 1755). Like Durazzo in Vienna, Algarotti was an Italian who found much to criticize in the *opera seria,* and there can be no doubt that he must have discussed with his patron the points he makes in his book. His fundamental points are simple and depend upon the exercise of reason. First and foremost, the poem is the most important aspect of the opera and must be chosen with great care:

> The two operas of *Dido* and *Achille in Sciros,* written by the celebrated Metastasio, come very near to the mark proposed here. The subjects of these dramatic poems are simple, and taken from very remote antiquity, but without being too farfetched. In the midst of their most impassioned scenes, there is an opportunity of introducing splendid banquets, magnificent embassies, embarkations, choruses, battles, conflagrations,etc., so as to give a farther extension to the sovereignty of the musical drama, and makes its rightfulness be more ascertained than has been hitherto allowed.[11]

He urges poets to collect subjects from mythology and ancient history that fulfill these conditions, and from this idea springs the repeated use of favorite librettos by the same or different composers. He also inveighs against modern music which has corrupted opera:

> For, as if music were yet unrudimented, and in its infancy, the mistaken professors spare no pains to trick out their art with every species of grotesque imagination and fantastical combination, which they think can be executed by sounds. . . . It is almost impossible to persuade him, [the composer] that he ought to be in a subordinate station; that music derives its greatest merit from being no more than an auxiliary, the handmaid to poetry. [12]

Algarotti's conclusions echo the ridicule which Durazzo's anonymous letter had tried to convey. Algarotti writes:

> . . . we should behold the theatre no longer as a place destined for the reception of a tumultuous assembly, but as the meeting of a solemn audience; where an Addison, Dryden, a Dacier, a Muratori, a Gravina, a Marcelli, might be spectators, without the least disparagement to their judgements. . . .

11. Francesco Algarotti, *An Essay on the Opera,* trans.(Glasgow, 1768), pp. 25–26.
12. *Ibid.,* p. 30–31.

> Then would the Opera be no longer called an irrational, monstrous, and grotesque composition: on the contrary, it would display a lively image of the Grecian tragedy, in which, architecture, poetry, music, dancing, and every kind of theatrical apparatus united their efforts to create an illusion of such resistless power over the human mind, that from the combination of a thousand pleasures, formed so extraordinary a one, as in our world has nothing to equal it.[13]

Algarotti's praise for the idea of writing an opera on the subject of Montezuma comes as no surprise, since an opera by that name was first staged in Berlin in 1755, the same year as his *Saggio* was published. The music was by Carl Heinrich Graun, while the words were translated from Italian into French by Frederick the Great.

OPERA IN LONDON

Perhaps the richest and most vital center of Italian opera in 1720 was London. There, satire was a popular mode of expression. In poetry or in prose, the style afforded amusement to its readers, and to its writers unlimited opportunities for attacking personal enemies or social evils. Prose satire of Italian opera in London reached new heights in the hands of Addison[14] and there was plenty to mock, yet it flourished for a few years. With the support of King George I and members of the nobility, the high point of Italian opera in London was reached during the 1720s with the company assembled by Handel at the King's Theatre. Included were the composers Giovanni Bononcini (1670–1747) and Attilio Ariosti (1666–1729), the female sopranos and rivals Francesca Cuzzoni (1698–1770) and Faustina [Bordoni] (1700–81), and the *castrato* Senesino (Francesco Bernardi, died 1759). The salary paid to Senesino (2,000 pounds sterling for a season) was enormous and rivals what is paid to stars today. Handel's opera production at this time was of high quality, and for most years of the decade he produced two operas a season.

In 1728, the most potent satire of the Italian opera exploded upon the scene. *The Beggar's Opera,* with text by John Gay (1685–1732; also author of *Acis and Galatea,* set wonderfully by Handel) and music assembled by Christopher Pepusch (1667–1752), used every means to attack the foreign enemy. Its characters are not heroes but the scum of society; it retains the sententiousness of Italian opera, giving lip service to a kind of morality, but its morality is that of buying and selling, of betrayal for profit—the law of the human jungle; its characters speak English, and when they sing, they sing the popular tunes of the day with new English words; and, best of all, *The Beggar's Opera* attacks the government of the day, thus serving a complex social function.

13. *Ibid,* p.110.
14. See the excerpts from *The Spectator,* quoted in Strunk, *Source Readings,* p. 511.

The wild success of *The Beggar's Opera* resulted in "the longest run of any play on the English stage before 1822," and gave rise to a number of works, similar in that they were compilations of musical materials from a variety of sources. These pastiches, which lacked the polemical and realistic thrust of the original model, were called ballad operas. Thus, *The Beggar's Opera* was followed the next year by *The Gentle Shepherd* and *The Contrivance,* while in 1731 *The Devil to Pay,* with text by Charles Coffey (d. 1745), was so well received it was translated into German and became the basis of a *Singspiel,* the popular form of German musical theater.

There is no doubt that the Italian opera suffered a great reverse because of the success of *The Beggar's Opera* and the genre it established. But a large part of the English theater-going public had always disliked Italian opera, with its long, dull, incomprehensible recitatives, and that disenchanted group grew in number. On the other hand, those who were prepared to support Italian opera found themselves split into two camps. Handel's opera company, backed by the king, was to suffer the rivalry of the "Opera of the Nobility," founded in 1733 and endorsed by the Prince of Wales.[15] By 1737 both opera companies were ruined and Handel was a sick, though not broken, man. Powerful in physique, optimistic by nature, and strong in his artistic convictions, he was still not convinced that the cause of Italian opera in London was lost. It was not until 1741 that he produced his last opera and finally turned to oratorio.

Continuous attempts had been made to establish opera in English. Aaron Hill wrote a letter to Handel in 1732, asking his help and saying: "My meaning is, that you would be resolute enough, to deliver us from our *Italian bondage;* and demonstrate that *English* is soft enough for Opera . . ."[16] Handel could certainly have helped, but did not. Instead, English opera, at its most popular, turned to the burlesque—a peculiarly English form of this period, created to parody a particular opera.

A burlesque opera entitled *The Dragon of Wantley,* satirizing Handel's opera *Giustino,* was very successfully staged in 1731 with sixty-seven performances in its first season. (During the first five months of that year Handel staged three new operas for a total number of nineteen performances.) The *Dragon,* composed by John Lampe (1703–51) with all the ingredients of the Italian opera, was a setting of a libretto by Henry Carey (1687–1743) derived from an earlier popular ballad. Carey retained much of the language of the ballad while cutting out some of the more extreme vulgarity. What remained, combined with the ridiculousness of the language, appealed to a universal aspect of English

15. During the eighteenth century it became a tradition of the Hanoverian kings of England that their sons, titled Princes of Wales, should oppose and annoy them publicly and violently in every conceivable way.

16. Aaron Hill, Letter dated 5 December 1752 to G. F. Handel, quoted in *Handel, A Documentary Biography,* ed. Otto Erich Deutsch (London, 1955), p. 299.

humor. The serious opera in the English language that Aaron Hill hoped for failed to materialize, as did subsequent attempts until the twentieth century.

OPERA IN PARIS

The importance of Lully to opera in Paris is impossible to underestimate. For over half a century after his death in 1687, a number of his operas were still being staged, despite all the changes in the style of music and musical theater. Lully's strength was rooted in his thoughtful and deferential setting of the French language as well as his strong melodic gift. The French have historically been more concerned about safeguarding the purity and the quality of their language than any other nation. From the very beginnings, when it was suggested that Louis XIV found a French opera, one of the bases upon which the structure rested was nationalistic spirit. Indeed, Lully, born an Italian, fostered this nationalism in opera, and proved himself more French than the French by urging the king to get rid of foreign musicians. And at the heart of the French opera lay the principle that the vocal line, whether in recitative or in air, should be built upon the accentuation of the word. Whereas Italian opera had sprung from a linguistic group with little or no sense of nationhood, France was the greatest state in Europe, and thus French opera was, from its origins, exclusive and nationalistic, in a way that Italian opera never was.

After the death of Lully there was no one of sufficient stature to carry on his work, and in the early years of the eighteenth century the serious *tragédie lyrique* began to give way to the *opera-ballet* and more frivolous entertainments. This all changed with the appearance of Rameau in 1733, with his *Hippolyte et Aricie (tragédie lyrique),* followed by *Les Indes galantes (opera-ballet)* in 1735, and by *Castor et Pollux (tragédie lyrique)* in 1737 and *Dardanus (tragédie lyrique)* in 1739. These works met with growing acceptance from a broad public, provoking a strong reaction from those who still looked back to Lullian opera as the ideal. Rameau was at first hampered by his reputation as a "scientist" of music. (His *Traité de l'harmonie* had appeared in 1722 followed by a number of other writings.) Whereas Lully had been praised for his naturalness, Rameau was attacked for his over-complexity, his lack of melody, his unnaturalness. Yet Rameau wrote in the preface to *Les Indes galantes:*

> Always bearing in mind the beautiful declamation and the fine turn of melody which reigns in the recitative of the great Lully, I try to imitate him, not as a servile copyist, but, like him, taking beautiful and simple Nature as my model.[17]

17. Jean-Philippe Rameau, *Préface aux Indes Galantes. Oeuvres complètes.* (Paris, 1902; reprinted New York, 1968) VII, p. xxxv. Author's translation.

Certainly, his scores contain pages that are marvels of complexity and variety in orchestration when compared with Lully's; Rameau himself wrote his scores, employing all his sophisticated knowledge of harmony and all the devices of imaginative and thoughtful orchestration suggested by the variety of instrument at his disposal, whereas many of Lully's were completed by assistants. Rameau tends to use his inventive power in the notation of pages in which the orchestra imitates—and thereby arouses the feelings of—thunderstorms or raging seas. These pages are, however, exceptional, and in his merging of recitative into *air* and *air* into recitative, and his avoidance of anything that smacks of Italian opera, it is clear to us, as it was not clear to the *Lullistes* of 1735, that Rameau is a complete disciple of Lully in more modern dress.[18]

In 1752, when Rameau was sixty-nine, the constantly simmering opposition between Italian and French music came to the boil, and there arose what is called the *Querelle des Bouffons* or the *Guerre des Bouffons* (The Quarrel [or War] of the Comedians). It began in February 1752 when a pamphlet was published using a performance of the opera *Omphale* by André Cardinal Destouches (1672–1749) to attack the very principles of French opera. This pamphlet by the German Baron Friedrich Grimm (1723–1807), entitled *Lettre sur Omphale,* was designed to be provocative, and, politely, to needle French music, the French idea of singing, and French recitative, setting up the Italian as an ideal. Early in the pamphlet Grimm makes the following point:

> Italian music promises and gives pleasure to everyone with ears, and it requires nothing more than that. [As opposed to French music which can only be understood in the national context] If all the nations of Europe have adopted it, despite language differences, it is because they have put their pleasure ahead of their snobberies.[19]

The attack is keen and well mounted, and a parry came quickly, dated 17 March 1752. Grimm made his riposte with a short letter on 2 April, receiving strong support from another quarter when, later that month, Jean-Jacques Rousseau entered the fray. Perhaps the whole storm in a teacup might have calmed at that point and made no mark on history but for another event.

A troupe called *Les Bouffons* (The Comedians) came to Paris in 1729 and met with considerable success. They were, however, speedily forgotten. A second venture, in 1746, saw the production of Pergolesi's *La serva padrona,* which, at that time, made no particular impact. In August of 1752, on the third visit of the *Bouffons, La serva padrona* was presented again, this time successfully, along with two other works, *Il giocatore (The Gambler),* at the time thought to be by Pergolesi, and his

18. It is ironic that the public found most fault with those parts of *Les Indes galantes* where Rameau had deliberately tried to imitate Lully's style.

19. Friedrich Grimm, *Lettre sur Omphale* in *La Querelle des Bouffons,* ed. Denise Launay (Geneva, 1973) I, p. 3. Author's translation.

Il maestro di musica (The Music Master). Thereafter, beginning in November, the rivalry between the Italian imports and French opera raged, fast and furious, for eighteen months. The king, as might be expected, favored French opera, as did Mme. de Pompadour, his mistress; therefore, the queen naturally went over to the side of the Italians, and the intellectuals, led by Rousseau, who was both convinced of the rightness of the cause and delighted to oppose the establishment in any possible way, went the same way. And so nationalism, sexual politics, aesthetics, and music were intertwined and it was almost impossible not to take sides. One's position in the *Querelle* determined where one sat at the theater.

The broad mass of the public, captivated by the *Bouffons* and finally tiring of the large apparatus of gods and shepherds of the *tragédie lyrique* and the *opéra-ballet,* turned increasingly to the popular entertainments parodying the opera, provided by the *vaudeville.* Performed in the Théâtres de la Foire and with a long history of social satire, like the ballad opera, the *vaudeville* was an entertainment which used popular tunes set with new words. As it merged into *opéra comique* the term came to signify melodies of a popular cast.

As the quarrel raged, the old subject of the unmusicality of the French language and the impossiblity of setting it decently to music was put forth by Rousseau. This attitude did not, however, prevent him from setting his own musical composition in French. *Le devin du village* (The Village Fortune Teller), with both words and music by Rousseau, was first produced in 1752, and was immediately successful, being repeated forty-one times between 1 March, 1753 (its first performance in Paris) and 27 December, 1753. The music has a pleasant melodic simplicity and naiveté which matches the story admirably, and it was praised as the kind of music that might result if the French could only shake off their past.[20]

The operatic scene in Europe in the years immediately preceding 1760 presents a confusing picture. Performances in the Italian centers seem to reflect a growing public affection for *opera buffa* at the expense of *opera seria,* with some courts, notably Parma, tending toward aspects of French opera. Currents in Vienna ran in that direction, too. Londoners seemed to want to abandon foreign opera altogether, and in Paris, French intellectuals pleaded the case for Italian comic opera against the French style. The one constant that emerges is the universal desire for change according to the prevailing thought of the time. For behind the preference for Italian comic opera lies the impulse toward "The Natural" and "Nature," while behind the impulse to change serious opera lies the preference for "The Reasonable" and "Reason."

20. For an example, see the *Norton Anthology of Western Music,* 2nd ed. (1988), ed. Claude V. Palisca, p. 170.

PART II

Embracing the New Style: Music 1760–80

CHAPTER VI

The Social and Philosophical Milieu

The fruit of seventeenth- and eighteenth-century scientific inquiry is to be found not only in a broadening basis of knowledge of the world and its inhabitants but also in the application of that knowledge to practical situations. Increasingly, men pondered the problem of how to lessen the effect of the biblical curse ("In the sweat of thy face shalt thou eat bread." Genesis 3:19) and to make one person, using mechanically harnessed energy, do the work of several. While it is not possible to see the beginnings of the Industrial Revolution in any one invention or idea, there is general agreement that by 1760, the process that was to change man from an agricultural laborer into a repairer and tender of machines had begun in earnest. During the two decades 1760–80, immense ingenuity was applied to the development of machinery activated by water power, and the productive capacity of a single individual was multiplied many times. In 1769, James Watt, the inventor of the modern steam engine, took out his first patents. Indeed, the process of innovation gained such momentum that in 1779 workers in the cotton mills of Lancashire, England, wrecked several mills in an effort to destroy the machinery which they believed was putting numbers of them out of work.

Although the process of industrialization did not spread to continental Europe from Britain until the nineteenth century, the awareness of the potential to control vast sources of power began to change man's vision of himself across the whole of the Western world. Over thousands of years he had developed sophisticated means of protecting himself against external forces over which he had no control, e.g., wind and weather, and over internal forces over which, likewise, he had no control, e.g., greed, lust for power, etc. Roofs, fireplaces, and clothing protected against the first, and laws and armies protected against the second. Now he began to see that with knowledge of physics and chemistry came also knowledge of the life process and of technology, and with these means came unprecedented power over the environment: man would become God. The development of technology was justified in two ways: it served to free labor by enabling one to do the work of many, and it created wealth. It did not really matter that those men, women, and children who operated the machines became slaves to them, for clearly the thousands who flocked to the growing cities from the countryside were going freely and were seeking to better their lot. At the beginning of the century the solar system had been perceived as an arrangement of forces and counterforces; now, gradually, there arose a tendency to view human society in similar, mechanistic terms, and it is to this dehumanizing tendency, which created a longing for lost peace and security, that many of the attributes of later romanticism must be ascribed.

THE BEAUTIFUL AND THE SUBLIME

Writers on aesthetics at this time shared with those of earlier years the belief that the function of music was to "express" the passions, but they were less likely than their predecessors to seek in art some kind of imitation of nature. Already the beginnings of a "proto-Romanticism" can be observed, springing from the eighteenth-century battle cry "Back to nature," yet different in effect. The idea that civilization corrupts, and that true, natural nobility is to be found among societies otherwise primitive—the idea of the "noble savage"—has its roots in the seventeenth century and persists at least until the end of the eighteenth. One can sense the growth of a stronger emphasis on goodness as the outcome of the enjoyment and practice of the arts, and one can also notice a strong upsurge of faith in the intuitive, the inborn, and even the irrational, together with a distrust of the rational and the civilizing.

Jaucourt writes in the *Encyclopédie* on the subject of sensibility, which we might define as the capacity to respond, as if instinctively, to the emotional and the pathetic, as follows:

> . . . sensibility of the soul leads to a kind of wisdom in honourable matters that goes deeper than purely intellectual comprehension. Sensible souls may fall into error that calculating man would never commit, simply because they are so responsive. However, they do infinitely more good. . . . Contemplation can make a man upright, but sensibility makes him virtuous.[1]

Here, feeling has become not simply the subject matter of the arts in general, but something that lies at the foundation of the proper life.

Since man was coming to understand nature and how to harness natural forces, artists and philosophers of art now begin to concentrate their attention on those aspects of nature which can still terrify, over-

1. Louis, Chevalier de Jaucourt, *Sensibilité,* cited in *Music and Aesthetics in the Eighteenth and early-Nineteenth Centuries,* Peter le Huray and James Day, eds. (Cambridge, 1981), p. 106.

Jane, Countess of Harrington by Sir Joshua Reynolds. In portrait painting it was fashionable to enhance the beauty of the sitter with the awe-inspiring sublimity of a storm. (Henry E. Huntington Library and Art Gallery, San Marino, Ca.)

awe, or impress beyond the power of reason. Here they found aspects of the beautiful which could not be seen to conform, in either structure or effect, to any preconceived rules, such as those which had been thought to govern "good taste." One of the most important works exemplifying the newer thinking is Edmund Burke's (1729–97) *A Philosophical Enquiry into the Origins of our Ideas of the Sublime and Beautiful*. This book proved to be one of the most influential of the century, undergoing many printings after its first publication in 1757, and being translated into French (1765) and German (1773). For Burke, the difference between the sublime and the beautiful opens up a new world of artistic possibilities, and prefigures many of the tenets of Romanticism long before the fact. He says:

> . . . sublime objects are vast in their dimensions, beautiful ones comparatively small: beauty should be smooth and polished; the great, rugged and negligent; beauty should shun the right line yet deviate from it insensibly; the great in many cases loves the right line, and when it deviates, it often makes a strong deviation: beauty should not be obscure; the great ought to

> be dark and gloomy: beauty should be light and delicate; the great ought to be solid and even massive. They are indeed ideas of a very different nature, one being founded on pain, the other on pleasure.[2]

Unlike some writers, who reason that ". . . no disagreeable combination of sounds is entitled to the name of music: for all music is resolvable into melody and harmony which imply agreeableness in their very conception,"[3] Burke is prepared to accept that music is capable of both beautiful and sublime utterance. In his description of these qualities in music, he might almost be speaking of the *style galant,* as opposed to the *empfindsamer Stil.*

> . . . the beautiful in music will not bear that harshness and strength of sounds which may be used to raise other passions, nor notes which are shrill or harsh or deep; it agrees best with such as are clear, even, smooth and weak. The second is that great variety and quick transitions from one measure or tone to another are contrary to the genius of the beautiful in music.[4]

Access to the sublime is either through the observation of the great in nature, or through the mediation of a genius, who is a genius through his possession of extreme sensibility. The genius creates his own rules, and feels restricted by generally accepted ideas of taste. Jaucourt, in the article on "Genius" in the *Encyclopédie,* writes that:

> Taste is often remote from genius. Genius is is a simple gift of Nature; what it produces is the work of a moment; good taste is the outcome of study and time; it depends upon knowledge of a multiplicity of rules, either real or fabricated, and it produces a conventional beauty. For something to be beautiful according to the rules of taste, it must be elegant, polished, full of art without appearing artful. For it to be a imbued with genius it must sometimes appear negligent, irregular, rugged, wild. Genius and the sublime shines in Shakespeare, like bolts of lightning in a long night—Racine is always beautiful: Homer is full of genius, while Virgil is elegant.[5]

The effect of experiencing the sublime, either in nature or in art, is, according to Burke:

> . . . astonishment; and astonishment is that state of the soul in which all its motions are suspended with some degree of horror. In this case the mind is so entirely filled with its object that it cannot entertain any other, nor by consequence reason on that object which employs it. Hence arises the great

2. Edmund Burke, *A Philosophical Enquiry into the Origins of our Ideas of the Sublime and Beautiful* (London, 1739; facsimile reprint, New York, 1972) pp. 237–38.
3. Henry Home, Lord Kames, *Elements of Criticism,* (Edinburgh, 1785; facsimile reprint, New York, 1972) I, p. 137.
4. Burke, *op. cit.,* p. 234.
5. Jaucourt, "Génie" in the *Encyclopédie, ou Dictionnaire des Sciences, des Arts, et des Métiers*(Paris, 1751–66) Tome 7. Author's translation.

> power of the sublime, that far from being produced by them, it anticipates our reasonings and hurries us on by an irresistible force.[6]

According to these ideas, examples of which could be multiplied many times, the genius from whom the realization of the highest ideals of art flowed naturally, without the intervention of the civilizing processes of study or reflection, was a natural person—not made but born, and, unlike the lesser artist who offered only mildly melancholic pleasure, the genius gave both pleasure and pain, together with the godlike humor called jollity, the attribute of Jove, or Jupiter.

Within this definition of natural genius is to be found the seed of almost every development in nineteenth-century art. The canons of taste were acknowledged to be conventional, that is to say, something upon which there was common agreement for a time. It followed, then, that the art whose value depended upon "good taste" must be both a contemporary and a temporary art; it could have little lasting value, but must disappear as the rules of taste changed. On the other hand, the natural genius created his work independent of "taste" or even in spite of it; therefore, his art could come to have a value beyond its own time, and it ought to speak equally strongly to the present, whether it was created in 1760, 1660, or earlier.

Upon this train of thought depends the whole developing current of historicism, which seeks to discover and reestablish the works of genius from the past, which contemporary taste had caused to be forgotten. It is an important part of late eighteenth-century thought that becomes even more pronounced in the nineteenth and twentieth centuries. Similarly, since the creations of the natural genius are the outcome of an innate and acute sensibility, and are not dependent upon formal education, it follows that while "taste" may be the prerogative of the educated classes, genius may be found at any level of human society. From this idea springs the consciously inclusive aim of much eighteenth-century art, which often attempts to speak to "connoisseurs and amateurs" of all classes.

LITERARY ANTIQUARIANISM

The work which perhaps most effectively capitalizes on the progressive thinking of the time, and which had an immense influence on the development of lyric poetry in England and Germany, and on music in Germany, was a collection of old verse, compiled by Bishop Thomas Percy (1729–1811), entitled *Reliques of Ancient English Poetry* and first published in 1765. This was not by any means the first attempt to form a collection of old ballads and popular verse: large collections survive

6. Burke, *op. cit.*, pp. 95–96.

from the seventeenth century, which were well known to scholars. Percy, however, gathered a selection of verse ranging from the ancient to hardly more than a hundred years old and whose authors were well known. Many of the old ballads were selected because they had been quoted by Shakespeare, whose work was beginning to be acclaimed after having been despised as barbaric for the better part of a century. Other traditional poems satisfied a taste for the primitive, the savage, the gory, in a way that no contemporary verse was able to do. A single example will serve to demonstrate the simple yet vivid language and the typical narrative style in ballad meter.[7]

At last the Duglas and the Perse met
Lyk to captayns of might and mayne;
The swapte togethar tyll the both swat
With swordes, that were of fyn myllan.

Thes worthe freckys for to fyght
Ther-to the wear full fayne,
Tyll the bloode owte off thear basnetes sprente,
As ever dyd heal or rayne.

Which may be rendered as:

At last, Chief Douglas and Lord Percy met
Like captains, of might and main;
They exchanged blows 'til both did sweat
With swords made of fine Milan steel.

These worthy fighting fellows
Went at it enthusiastically
Till the blood sprinkled out of their helmets
Just like hail or rain.

It is of the greatest interest to note that in the preliminary remarks to this ballad, Percy writes:

> Those genuine strokes of nature and artless passion which have endeared it to the most simple readers, have recommended it to the most refined; and it has equally been the amusement of our childhood, and the favourite of our riper years.[8]

The archaic language became an end in itself, and it has been imitated by a host of writers during the subsequent two hundred years.

At the same time, another publication appeared which struck a similarly responsive chord in public taste. Between 1760 and 1763, James Macpherson (1736–96) published a number of fragmentary, prose effu-

7. Thomas Percy, "The ancient ballad of Chevy Chace" in *Reliques of Ancient English Poetry* (London, 1906) I, pp. 70–71.

8. *Ibid.*, p. 65.

sions under the title *The Poems of Ossian,* which he claimed were translations of old manuscripts of Gaelic poetry dating from the third century and later. The authenticity of the work is not in question here. Rather, it must be observed that, like Bishop Percy's *Reliques, Ossian* was, for at least sixty years after its first appearance, one of the universal works of its time, carried by Napoleon on his campaigns, and a daily companion for countless others. The effect of these books was widely felt in Europe, and the development of German lyric poetry, which achieved such a rapid flowering, owes much to their influence.

STURM UND DRANG

The idea that sensibility or feeling makes for virtue, together with the accompanying idea of natural genius, has been shown to have practical and far-reaching results in the new popularity of old, folk, or pseudo-folk poetry. The quality of this poetry is that it conveys in the simplest, most unaffected language powerful feelings of sympathy and horror, without the least trace of sentimentality. In this context, sentimentality may perhaps be defined as that kind of insincerity which self-indulgently gets pleasure from the expression of misery. This poetry retains a directness, a severity of simplicity which is at the opposite pole from self-indulgence and sentimentality, while the literary products of the

J. H. Fuseli's *The Nightmare* (1780) shows how strongly people in the last years of the century needed to experience feelings of pity and horror. (Freies Deutsches Hochstift, Goethe Museum, Frankfurt am Main)

time tend to fall into mawkishness. The English and the German novel, and the drama, provide numerous examples of plots and characters designed on the principle that if feeling equals virtue, and if tears equal feeling, then the best way to demonstrate virtue is through bursting into tears whenever possible. In Germany, the term *Sturm und Drang* (Storm and Stress), after a play of that name by Maximilian Klinger (1752–1831), was applied to the literary movement which operated on this principle. The best known, most representative work of this movement is the novel by Johann Wolfgang von Goethe (1749–1832) *Die Leiden des jungen Werthers* (The Sorrows of the Young Werther), published in 1774, a story of frustrated true love. The lover, Werther of the title, a young poet, shoots himself inefficiently and lingers on long enough to make the loved one, Charlotte, realize the extent of her love for him, while knowing the inevitability of his death. Countless tears have been shed by the readers of this romantic tale. At the same time, writers were quick to perceive that nothing was easier to counterfeit than the external attributes of a "man of feeling," and characters abound in plays and novels who hypocritically mask their base intentions under the guise of tears and moralizing and all the trappings of virtue: Joseph Surface in Sheridan's comedy, *School for Scandal* (1777) is a prime example from the time, but the fashion continues well into the nineteenth century, with characters like Mr. Pecksniff, from Dickens's novel *Martin Chuzzlewit* (1843), just as it antedates the eighteenth century in Molière's play *Tartuffe* (1664). Indeed, hypocrisy of this kind is universal: it fell to the second half of the eighteenth century to make its externals acceptable on a broad scale—at least in theory.

THE CONCEPT OF THE "CLASSICAL" AND ITS OPPOSITES

Around the middle of the eighteenth century, another important train of thought began with the discoveries of the ancient world of Greece and Rome by the German archaeologist Johann Winckelmann (1717–68), whose *Geschichte der Kunst des Altertums* (History of the Art of the Ancient World) was published in 1764. The immediate effect of Winckelmann's work was manifest in the applied arts: furniture and silverware, for example, bore the swirling "C" and "S" curves of the rococo style; these gave way, during the 1760s, to the straight lines, the oval and circular shapes, typical of the surface designs of Roman art. From the widespread influence of Roman art was taken the notion of the "Classical," and, by extension, the term was generally applied to the art of the last third of the eighteenth century, by a generation that was, for the most part, unborn in 1760.

It is important to note that the term "Classical," which has such widespread use, has tended to undermine our understanding of the music

Giovanni Battista Piranesi's romanticized version of the Arch of Constantine in Rome sets that great block of orderly beauty against squalid dwellings and rough boulders.

of the time, by contributing to the belief that the way a thing is said was more important to the artist and to the public than what was said—that balance of structure, i.e. form—was more important than content. That this is a fiction, or at least an unsympathetic reaction to the art of an earlier generation assiduously spread by the articulate generation of young Romantics of the 1820s, must now be obvious, for the creative artists of the period 1760–80, like those before 1760, aimed to move their readers, their viewers, or their listeners through the force of their expression. Indeed, every writer on the subject of the musical art speaks of its task of moving or expressing, while relatively few mention large-scale musical structure as an element of any importance.

It must be recognized that those elements in the art of 1760–80 which appear to justify the term "Classical," while of great importance, nevertheless constitute only a small part of the whole scene. Architecture and the applied arts that adorn architecture may be seen to undergo a classical vogue during the 1760s, but it is of short duration. The straight line, the rectangle or square, the circle, those elements which recall the Greece and Rome of classical times, begin to give way, and to yield pride of place during the 1770s to the pointed arch and the vertical thrust of the Gothic influence. Architecture and the applied arts felt the force of the Gothic quite as fully as they experienced the Classical and the reason for this is largely to be found in the eighteenth-century conception of "the sublime." Burke makes the contrast between the beautiful and the sublime when he said: Beauty should not be obscure; the great ought to be dark and gloomy." Insofar as the Classical in architecture emanates from Greece and Rome it is an art of sunlight and clear

Wealthy William Beckford, cousin of Clementi's protector, built a Gothic mansion called Fonthill Abbey. Unfortunately, its 260-foot tower collapsed and destroyed the house.

blue skies; insofar as the Gothic emanates from northern Europe and is associated with old churches and ruined abbeys it is an art of gloom, mystery, and horror. The utilization of horror was brought back into art during this period and it has preserved its attraction ever since. The Gothic novel came into existence around the same time as the German *Sturm und Drang* movement and was the outcome of a similar need to feel deeply and violently, to react instinctively and even irrationally, and to acknowledge that side of human existence which is not accessible to the light of reason. These characteristics are typical of eighteenth-century proto-Romanticism, but the capacity for viewing the world realistically—so well developed in eighteenth-century writers—caused the popular Gothic novel to be satirized as incisively as the "man of feeling" had been. In this period the distinction between life and art is still preserved, a distinction later artists were to surrender.

The pace of inquiry into the nature of the arts quickened noticeably during these two decades, yet there is no discernible shift in thought. Rather, writers tended to become more systematic in their investigations and more elaborate in their descriptions. Johann Georg Sulzer (1720–79) is remembered for his *Allgemeine Theorie der schönen Künste* (General Theory of the Fine Arts), a kind of dictionary in which articles on a variety of subjects are arranged alphabetically. Considerable space is devoted to music. Although old-fashioned in his devotion to the idea of art as an imitation of nature, he treats the ideas of genius or of the sublime in a very modern manner. Particularly interesting is his article on inspiration, which could stand as a nineteenth-century definition of the subject. The article begins:

> All artists of any genius claim that from time to time they experience a state of extraordinary psychic intensity which makes work unusually easy, images arising without great effort and the best ideas flowing in such profusion as if they were the gift of some higher power. This is without doubt what is called inspiration . . .[9]

At the same time as the mimetic, or imitative, theory of the arts was compelling adherents, it was coming under severe attack in other quarters. Sir William Jones (1746–94) wrote an essay entitled "On the Arts, commonly called Imitative" (1772) in which several ideas stand out. He mentions Batteux and the mimetic theory and says:

> . . . whatever be said of painting, it is probable that poetry and music had a nobler origin . . . their greatest effect is not produced by imitation but by a very different principle, which must be sought for in the deepest recesses of the human mind.[10]

In his conclusion, having ridiculed and belittled that art which is mere imitation, he says:

> Thus will each artist gain his end, not by imitating the works of nature but by assuming her power and causing the same effect upon the imagination which her charms produce to the senses.[11]

No longer can it be thought that the excellence of poetry or music can be judged from the accuracy of its imitation, but in its power to move in a way analogous to, but different from, the natural.

Also one notices in the writers of the 1770s, and later, a persistent tendency to regard painting as largely imitative, as opposed to the non-imitative arts, which, because they open up vast fields of imagination, are more highly regarded. With all the talk of the sublime, the genius, and the power of music to affect the imagination, there is still a strong philosophic and practical basis for believing that music must abide by the rules of harmony and consonance, and that the artist, genius though he may be, cannot be as free in practice as he might seem in theory.

9. Johann Georg Sulzer, *Allgemeine Theorie der schönen Künste* (Leipzig, 1792; facsimile reprint, Hildesheim, 1970) I, p.349. The translation is taken from Le Huray and Day, eds., *op. cit.*, p. 130.

10. Sir William Jones, *Essay II. On the Arts, commonly called Imitative* (London, 1777), p. 192.

11. *Ibid.*, p.206.

CHAPTER VII

The Musician's Livelihood

In painting a picture of the eighteenth-century musician's means of making a living, we have already looked at the system of patronage, which offered the best possibilities for long-term security. Yet while finding a good position with a good patron was normally a matter of the highest priority, there were a number of avenues available to the independent musician, which, as the century progressed, overtook the patronage system in importance.

For a number of years the opera had offered the composer the surest road to fame and fortune, particularly in Italy. Commercial operatic activity was more widespread there than in any other country in Europe, and the public appetite for new works was insatiable. The result was that in Carnival season—that time from Christmas to Ash Wednesday, the beginning of Lent—there might be as many as a hundred operas staged in various Italian cities, as we have already learned. Many of these operas were commissioned by an individual or a group for performance during Carnival. Often the subject was specified by the commissioner, who offered the composer a lump sum in payment for the work, which, it was expected, would take a little over a month to complete. The success or failure of the opera was of little immediate concern to the composer, who would only rarely see any additional recompense. But the successful composer, of course, received more commissions.

Achieved in this way, operatic fame frequently led to more permanent posts, particularly when an Italian composer, having made his name at home, left his native land to work for a royal or noble patron. Such a career was enjoyed by Niccolò Jommelli, who wrote for most of the important operatic centers in Italy. However, after his works were performed in Vienna and London, he was offered posts in Mannheim and Lisbon. He finally became *Ober-Kapellmeister* to the Duke of Württemberg in Stuttgart, where he remained until his last years, when he returned home to Naples.

CONCERT ORGANIZATIONS

The growth in the popularity of the public concert was perhaps the most significant occurrence in musical life during the second half of the eighteenth century, for from its success arose not only the dominant forms of the symphony and the solo concerto but also the spectacular ascent of the virtuoso. As a result of the proliferation of the public concert it finally became possible for a musician to make a good living as a traveling performer, independent of a single patron.

LONDON There had been no dominant concert-giving organization in London, so the series jointly organized by Johann Christian Bach (1735–82) and Carl Friedrich Abel (1723–87), which ran from 1765 to 1781, was of the greatest significance. The first of these concerts took place on 23 January 1765 in Carlisle House, Soho, as part of the entertainment managed there by a Mrs. Cornelys. This woman, whose exploits are described in the memoirs of Casanova, by whom she had two children, was a typical eighteenth-century adventuress, who settled in London in 1759 after traveling around Europe as a singer. In 1760 she rented Carlisle House in Soho, where she offered cards, dancing, and music to the upper classes of society and enjoyed considerable success until, some years later, she was charged with keeping a disorderly house and bankrupted. In 1764 she added a larger concert on Wednesday evenings, the management of which was taken over by Bach and Abel the following year. These concerts were very profitable, and in 1768 Bach and Abel moved them to larger quarters under their own auspices. The concerts were so popular that the enterprising composers built the Hanover Square Rooms, which remained one of the most

A concert in Hanover Square Rooms. This 1840 engraving shows us that the stage, roomy enough for Bach and Abel's orchestra, had become overcrowded with the larger forces used in the early nineteenth century.

important concert halls in London for almost a hundred years. The programs introduced the best musicians from France, Germany, and Italy to London audiences, and placed the finest native artists before their refined and discriminating clientèle. It is probable that the concerts fell from favor when the composer-managers overplayed their own compositions at the expense of a more varied fare. Burney wrote succinctly about this series, the most successful private enterprise in the history of concert giving in the century, saying that since they initially brought in the best performers and since their compositions were new and excellent

> . . . the concert was better patronized and longer supported than perhaps any one had ever been in this country. The same concert now subsists in a still more flourishing way than ever under the denomination of the PROFESSIONAL CONCERT, with the advantage of a greater variety of composition than during the regency of Bach and Abel, to whose sole productions the whole performance of each winter was chiefly confined.[1]

The pleasure gardens at Ranelagh, Vauxhall, and elsewhere continued to flourish during this period, drawing much of their success from the growing appetite of the bourgeoisie for entertainment during the summer, when the concert-giving organizations were inactive.

An interesting anomaly in the London concert scene was the Concert of Antient [*sic*] Music, which was founded in 1776 with the object of preserving, through performance, the great works of earlier composers, going so far as to adopt a rule that no composition less than twenty years old should be performed. This series, organized by a committee of noblemen and patronized by the king, continued well into the nineteenth century, when it became clear that older music was in no danger of being forgotten. It remains of sociological interest precisely because of its antiquarian concerns, although it affected the musician and his livelihood very little.

PARIS The Parisian scene during this period is comparable in many ways to that of London. The *Concert Spirituel* continued to adapt its programs to modern taste, while adhering to the practice of including religious works, thus reinforcing the notion that music in general and concert-going in particular was a force for moral uplift.[2] The concert programs of the time demonstrate the popularity of the symphony and the *symphonie concertante,* which, together with motets and chamber works, made up a very mixed bag. Most important, however, they

1. Charles Burney, A General History of Music (London, 1776–89; reprint New York, 1957) II, pp. 1017–1018.
2. All the information about the *Concert Spirituel* and its programs has been obtained from Constant Pierre, *Histoire du Concert Spirituel, 1725–1790* (Paris, 1975).

enable us to see the preeminent position of the solo concerto, one, two, three, or more examples of which are to be found on almost every concert. The programs also reveal that many of the soloists played the same repertoire from place to place. Two typical programs, chosen from the beginning and the end of the period under discussion, show the ways in which the format was changing and the ways it was remaining the same:

8 Sept. 1760

Symphony	?
Cantate Domino	Lalande
Petit Motet	?
Organ Concerto	Balbastre
Petit Motet in the Italian Style	?
Nisi Dominus	Mondonville

8 Sept. 1779

New Symphony	Haydn
Motet	Moreau
Violin Concerto	Jarnovichi
New Aria	Sacchini
Symphonie Concertante (pedal keyboard, harp and violin)	Adam
Motet	Gossec
New Clarinet Concerto	Baer
Italian Rondo	J.C. Bach

While French music still held an honored position on concert programs and concertos are predominant, the penetration of German instrumental music and Italian vocal music continued to grow.

The impresarios for the *Concert Spirituel,* having a legal monopoly on concert-giving as holders of the old royal privilege granted to the *Académie royale de musique,* exercised every ingenuity to impede anything that might lessen their profits. Of course, they could do nothing about the innumerable private performances in the homes of many wealthy amateurs. In 1772, however, they took the organizers of the *Concert d'Amis* to court on the grounds that they were making money by selling tickets.

The *Concert des Amateurs,* founded in 1769, was as important in Paris as the Bach-Abel series in London. They assembled what was possibly the largest and best-trained orchestra in the whole of Europe for their performances, numbering 40 violins, 12 cellos, 8 basses, and winds in proportion. The concerts operated on the basis of subscriptions to the series, a method of financing which kept this organization out of the reach of the monopolistic *Concert Spirituel,* since the funds were not coming from the ticket-buying public. There were many professionals involved, and the orchestra included some of the most important names among the French nobility. Their music director until 1773 was Gossec, whom Mozart described as "a very good friend and a very dull fellow,"(*Letters,* 5 April 1778)[3] and he was succeeded by the Chevalier de Saint-Georges (1739–99). This multitalented man, born in Guadeloupe of a black mother and a French father, spent all of his adult life in Paris. Small in stature, he was particularly gifted in athletic pursuits, excelling in swimming, skating, shooting, riding, and dancing, and was recognized as one of the finest swordsmen in the whole of Europe. He united a generous, sensitive, and gentle disposition with exceptional talents as a violinist, composer, and conductor. The *Concert des Amateurs* ceased to exist as such when, at the end of 1780, the financial embarrassment of some of its most influential members caused the withdrawal of their support.

LEIPZIG The *Grosses Concert* of Leipzig, which had been abandoned during the Seven Years' War (1756–63), was taken up again in 1763 under the directorship of the composer Johann Adam Hiller (1728–1804), but the series was finally dissolved in 1778 when the standard of performance had declined under Hiller's successors.

VIENNA Perhaps because of the city's relatively small size and the high proportion of music-loving nobility, the concert life of Vienna at this time was largely restricted to performances held in private homes, and there was no public concert series comparable to those noted elsewhere. Concerts mounted by individual artists for their own profit were, of course, standard.

MUSIC PUBLISHING

During this period the music publishing business expanded in response to the growing demand for music in the home and concert hall, and certain changes can be noted. The London business of John Walsh, so important up to this point, ceased to exist in 1766 with the death of John Walsh the younger. Although it was carried on under other names, it lost its pre-eminence as other firms flourished. The old-established Leipzig publishing and music-copying house of Breitkopf continued to

3. There are many references to Mozart's letters and those of his family throughout this book. In each case, the date of the letter will be indicated but the citation will not otherwise be footnoted. The reader is referred to the fine collection of Mozart's letters translated by Emily Anderson and published in a revised edition in 1985 by W. W. Norton or to the complete edition of the letters in German, collected and edited by Wilhelm Bauer and Otto Erich Deutsch (Kassel, Bärenreiter. 1962–63). The translations used here are either by Anderson or by the author.

thrive and between 1762 and 1787 issued an important series of catalogues of music available from them. These catalogues are of the greatest historical interest, not only because they are the first of their kind but also because they contain incipits of approximately 14,000 works, thereby aiding in the dating and identification of compositions from this time. In some cases the Breitkopf incipits are apparently all that is left of otherwise lost works.

Two important publishing houses were founded during this period. In Vienna, whose reliance upon hand-copied music, and whose late coming to the field of music printing seems strange in a city so central to the development of Western music, the firm of Artaria and Co. established themselves as dealers in copper engravings in 1766. Ten years later they began to sell music imported from London, Paris, and Amsterdam (a well-known Parisian publisher, Huberty, worked for them as an engraver) and two years later still, they issued their first publication. In Offenbach the composer Johann André (1741–99) founded the house that carried his name through the nineteenth century. Originally intended for the family's silk business, André had some slight musical training, but it was not until 1773 that he composed a successful stage work and saw the financial success to be gained from publishing it. In the following year he left the family business to set up his own.

WRITINGS ABOUT MUSIC

During the years 1760–80 there were no comprehensive or important publications on the nature of the music at that time, or on the playing of instruments comparable to the treatises of Emanuel Bach, Quantz, and Leopold Mozart that were discussed earlier. However, the *Dictionnaire de musique* (1768) by Rousseau and *Die Kunst des reinen Satzes in der Musik* (The Art of Strict Musical Composition; 1771–79) by Johann Philipp Kirnberger (1721–83), filled an important place in the education of the public, and they are of great historical importance for us today. Rousseau's work enjoyed a wide circulation, and Kirnberger preserves for us much of the teaching of his old master, Johann Sebastian Bach. It was during this time that the first biography of a musician was published: John Mainwaring's *Memoirs of the life of the late G.F.Handel* (London, 1760).

Perhaps the most important books of these decades were the histories that appeared in Italian, English, and French. The noted composer, teacher, and contrapuntal theorist, Padre Giovanni Battista Martini (1706–84), wrote three volumes entitled *Storia della Musica* (1761–81), but they did not reach beyond ancient times. In London, Sir John Hawkins (1719–89), a lawyer, published all five volumes of his *A General History of the Science and Practice of Music* in 1776, and Dr. Charles Burney, a composer and teacher of music, began publication of his frequently cited work *A General History of Music* in the same year, bringing out the last volume in 1789. Of the last two works, the chief merit for us lies in the extensive coverage of the eighteenth century which Burney gives, and in his broad knowledge of the state of musical affairs, gained during his extensive travels preparatory to the writing of his *History*. The French contribution to this stream of historiography is best represented by the *Essai sur la musique ancienne et moderne* of J. B. de la Borde (1734–94) published in Paris in 1780.

This impressive trend toward a scholarly assessment of the whole history of music must be seen as an important indicator of the growth of a movement in the direction of historical studies in general—a movement which the following century was to raise to a pinnacle of ideals and achievement. The constant interaction between the revival, study, and performance of old music and the study of the history of the art provides the historian, from this period on, with a chicken-and-egg problem—it is impossible to say which was the more important in the development of future trends. But it can be said with assurance that the antiquarianism of the eighteenth century, beginning with the study and revival of folk poetry, and moving from there into the ballad with music and into the developing form of the novel, provided a fertile intellectual and spiritual atmosphere for growth. The folk culture strengthened its roots in the past and, in growing, renewed and shaped the art culture of the nineteenth century as well as the study of the history of art.

CHAPTER VIII

Music in the Home

Based upon the evidence of the music printed and sold during this period, it would appear that the practice of musicmaking in the home continued to increase and the medium of performance continued to change. The use of the *basso continuo* began to decline in the concert hall, the opera theater, and the church, and disappeared almost entirely from private music, where two dominant mediums are seen to emerge, both of which become central to chamber music to the extent that other combinations tend to be seen as offshoots of them: the sonata for solo keyboard and the string quartet.

The greatest decline in *basso continuo* compositions is observable in the trio sonata for two melody instruments and bass. Baroque practice does not change overnight, and between 1760 and 1770 many composers of the older generation continued to produce trio sonatas, but with very few exceptions the stream dries up shortly after 1770. Long before this, however, the central principle of two independent melody voices in contrapuntal relationship had been violated, and the first part had become the melodic voice while the second part had been reduced to the role of accompaniment. Thus, in addition to its connection with the symphony (see pp. 73–74), the trio sonata developed in three directions: toward the accompanied solo sonata, toward the string trio for two violins and cello (a very popular combination of instruments at that time), and toward the less common combination of violin, viola, and cello.

FURTHER EVOLUTION OF THE SONATA WITH *CONTINUO*

The solo sonata accompanied by *basso continuo* pursues its course with its vigor only slightly impaired by other developments. Indeed, with the increased popularity of the virtuoso professional performer and the

Johann Eleazer Zeissig's 18th-century watercolor further illustrates the predilection of female amateurs for instruments that allowed them to display a neat wrist or a beautiful hand. (Bildarchiv Foto Marburg)

gradual dissemination of the virtuoso ideal to sections of the amateur public, the solo with *basso* accompaniment fulfilled an important function. For the virtuoso, such a performance vehicle allowed all technical and artistic accomplishment to be demonstrated with nothing musically obtrusive to detract from it; for the amateur of some accomplishment it allowed for an accompaniment played by a performer of much more limited capabilities. It must also be remembered that the guitar and the harp were instruments that enjoyed a vogue at this time, and they too might be used to play the bass, as in the sets of sonatas for violin with guitar by Paganini some years later.

More than any other, this combination allowed for even more display of string virtuosity than the contemporary concerto, and the works of many lesser composers, particularly those from France and Italy, reveal a technical command of the instrument (usually the violin) that is of a very high order. Typical of the Italian composers who followed in the footsteps of their teacher, Tartini, is Pietro Nardini, whose playing was described in superlatives by all who heard him, including Leopold Mozart. Among his compositions are several sets of sonatas for violin and bass which date from the 1760s. By happy accident the anthology by Jean Baptiste Cartier (1765–1841) entitled *L'art du violon* (The Art of the Violin) published in Paris in 1798, contains an edition of six sonatas by Nardini which Cartier says was printed in Venice in 1760, and which survives in no other source. The beauty of this particular edition is that it contains examples of ornamented *Adagio* movements printed on three staves, allowing for direct comparison of the unornamented composition with the performance they might receive. From earlier discussion it will be recalled that the performance of *Adagio* movements was itself a specialized art upon which performers were judged. In this kind of performance the artist was expected to bring to bear an entire vocabulary of the affective, emotive apparatus of music and apply it in an improvisatory fashion. Nardini was famous throughout the civilized world for his performance of slow movements, which, in his sonatas and those of his master, Tartini, stand in first position, to be followed by two *Allegro* movements.

In the embroidered or ornamented *Adagio (Adagio brodé)* from Nardini's Second Sonata in D (*ACM* 13), the absence of figures in the bass should be noted; while it does not imply the abandonment of the *basso continuo,* there is certainly the implication that the cello alone may carry the bass line. The composed melody, printed on the middle stave, shows both the fragmentation of line typical of the *style galant,* and the harmonic basis of the melody, with its slow harmonic rhythm and its regular placement of affective, appoggiatura-like notes. The ornamentation of this skeleton is obviously the main business of the player. Because of the number of notes it is clear that the tempo must be extremely slow, and although the violinist has to cover the fingerboard more rapidly than in many an *Allegro,* the feeling must be restfully *Adagio.* This is a fine example of the kind of ornamentation practiced by virtuosos on melody instruments, such as the violin or the flute, and even on the keyboard.

THE KEYBOARD SONATA

The sonata for solo keyboard becomes increasingly popular, but at the same time, tends to greater uniformity of form and texture. The image of the keyboard as an instrument for lady amateurs is undoubtedly responsible for the appearance of sonata sets described as *"à l'usage des Dames ,"* which subordinate technical and musical demands to the perceived need for an innocuous, milk-and-watery kind of music. However, there are exceptions, and the end of the period sees the emergence of a virtuosity in the keyboard sonata comparable to that of the violin in the solo sonata with *continuo.*

Antonio Soler is without doubt the most important Spanish composer and theorist of his generation. Like Scarlatti (his probable master), he is best known for his keyboard sonatas, twenty-seven of which were published in London. These were the only works of Soler to appear in print in the eighteenth century. His sonatas survive not in the composer's autograph but in contemporary manuscript copies which differ considerably from each other. As a result, there is as yet no complete edition of these works to enable us to grasp the whole picture. The more than one hundred sonatas that survive from an output that has been estimated to exceed two hundred reveal a composer who superficially resembles Scarlatti but who is definitely of a younger generation.

Soler was born in Catalonia in northern Spain and was taught by a pupil of the great seventeenth-century organist, Juan Cabanilles. He became a monk when he was twenty-three and went to Madrid to serve as organist and choirmaster at the Escorial, that mixture of monastery and royal palace, the seat of the kings of Spain. At the same time, Domenico Scarlatti was serving the queen of Spain and going through his very productive final period. The two men must have known each other well during the last five years of Scarlatti's life.

Soler's keyboard technique included all the devices that Scarlatti used: leaps, arpeggio figurations, chains of thirds, sixths, and octaves, hand-crossings, etc., and it may well be that these similarities recommended his sonatas to the London publisher, Birchall, who hoped to capitalize on the English vogue for Scarlatti. Example VIII–1, taken from what is perhaps the most Scarlattiesque of Soler's sonatas, shows a cadence very like that master's; it also features hand-crossing *ad nauseam*.

The differences, however, are even more striking. Soler's sonatas, written, it is believed, between 1760 and 1783, are usually in two, three, or four movements. In addition to the typical rounded binary structure, which is perhaps the prevalent form, Soler at times writes complete recapitulations, making complete sonata forms. Ternary structures with repeated material are not uncommon. A number of Soler's sonatas carry titles or descriptions, such as *Rondon* (Rondo), *Pastoril* (Pastorale), *In modo dorico* (In the Dorian mode), *Minué* (Minuet), and *Intento (Tiento)*. The last title offers one of the most interesting insights into this composer, for it is nothing more than the sixteenth- and seventeenth-century Spanish version of the Italian *ricercare* brought up to date. In Soler's hands, the *Intento* is a long, contrapuntal movement which serves as the final movement of some multi-movement sonatas. The integrity of the voices is maintained (to an extent that Scarlatti's fugues do not) despite an abundance of movement in thirds and sixths. In using this old style, Soler is certainly making a statement about the Spanish musical heritage that very few of his contemporaries (Kirnberger is a noted exception) are able to make for their respective countries. Perhaps he was also giving a history lesson to his pupil, the Infante. Yet at the level of mel-

Example VIII–1: A. SOLER, Sonata No. 10 in B minor

ody, meter, and texture, Soler reflects his own period and is capable of writing long, *cantabile* lines which speak far more of 1780 than of 1740, belonging to Mozart's world rather than Scarlatti's. He also writes sonata-form movements that seem as though they might have been directly influenced by Haydn in the 1770s.

Example VIII–2. A. SOLER, Sonata in B♭, II

No composer writing sonatas for solo keyboard in Italy during this period meets the standard of interest and variety set by Galuppi, but of the others, the most important is the prolific Giovanni Marco Placido Rutini (1723–97). Born in Florence, Rutini worked at various times in Germany, Russia, and in many Italian centers. His sonatas, produced between 1748 and 1786, were all published in Florence or Nuremberg, and they found praise, even in the critical Mozart family. Writing from Verona in 1771, Leopold Mozart asked his daughter to pick out "some good sonatas by Rutini, for instance, in E♭, in D, and so on."(*Letters,* 18 Aug. 1771) It is clear from what he writes that the Mozarts had several of Rutini's works and even more than one copy of some of them. Many of his sonatas are written in two movements, with a large first movement (in form ranging from rounded binary with incomplete recapitulation to complete sonata structures) in an extremely unbalanced relationship with a short, lightweight second movement in ternary structure, often a minuet. There is, however, considerable variety in the music, and Rutini is resourceful in avoiding monotony. Occasional *cantabile* melodies extend well beyond the norm and cry out for the singing voice, and there are movements which seem to attempt the reconciliation of a contrapuntal style with *galant* feeling.

Example VIII–3: G. RUTINI, Sonata in D, Op. 6, No. 2, I

As might be expected in a creative life lasting forty years, there is considerable change in Rutini's style, and even in the period 1760–80 a compositional development that is discernible. This is the opening of the Sonata in D, Op.6 No.2. published in 1760. It may well be one of the sonatas described by Leopold Mozart as "good." Its compositional quality can be seen in the drawing of much of its substance from the rhythmically vital opening. However, the Scarlatti-like repetitions make it readily identifiable as a work of pre-Classic *galanterie.* The first movement of a sonata from Opus 8, which dates from no later than 1774,

(*ACM* 14), is shown on page 136 in a facsimile of its original printing.[1] The structure of both these works (the Sonata in D mentioned earlier and this Sonata in F) is broadly identical, yet the melodic and rhythmic components of each are very different. The first theme of the Opus 8 sonata is made up of twelve bars, 4+4+4, in which the identity of the first two four-bar groupings is very similar: antecedent/consequent relationship, 2+2 bars and then, as it were, an ornamented repetition of the same process. The final four-bar grouping shares a similar melodic, harmonic, and textural identity with the preceding, but its move to cadence gives it an overall different cast: it is not made up of antecedent/ consequent relationships, and thus it brings the whole to a satisfying conclusion. It will be noticed that the opening 12 bars do not lean at any point toward V except at the final cadence. The business of modulation is left until the succeeding short period of passagework (four bars) which eventually leads to the second tonal area. The whole movement is worth inspection, with its long pedal (m. 21), its material in the new key area (m. 27) which, with its start on IV sounds like the old tonic, and finally, its closing theme, deliberately different from anything else, with its Alberti bass and its rustic close (m. 43).

The work of Rutini has a certain vitality and it can serve as a worthy contemporary comparison with the work of early Haydn and Mozart. But it must also stand as one of the last Italian efforts in the solo keyboard sonata, for beside the examples of the genre in Germany, Austria, and France, the sonatas composed in Italy appear slight and uninteresting.

In Paris perhaps the most important solo keyboard sonatas of the period 1760–80 were those by expatriate Germans. Johann Schobert (c. 1735–67)—about whose life very little is known, but whose spectacular death, along with wife, one child, servant, and friends, was brought about by his obstinate insistence that certain poisonous mushrooms were edible—was harpsichordist to the Prince de Conti and a celebrated figure in the musical life of the French capital.[2] He is chiefly famous for sonatas with optional violin accompaniment (see *AMC* 15), but in all his keyboard works one can sense a desire to transform the symphonic/ orchestral style, which we associate with the Mannheim composers, and which was most popular in Paris, into an idiomatic keyboard style. His skill on the harpsichord was pronounced and his compositions were enthusiastically received in Paris and London, where almost all his works were reprinted. Burney makes some of the most astute criticism of Schobert which can still hardly be bettered when he says:

1. A comparison of this example with its counterpart in the anthology demonstrates the editorial method which has been used in the preparation of a modern edition.

2. The French Mozart scholar Théodore de Wyzéwa asserted that Schobert was perhaps the single most important influence upon the development of the young Mozart, and he downplays the influence of Christian Bach. More modern scholarship has tended to reverse that judgment and weaken Wyzéwa's point, while not nullifying it.

Example VIII–4: G. RUTINI, Sonata in F, Op. 8, No. 1, facsimile

> In 1766, I was the first who brought his works to England from Paris. His style never pleased in Germany so much as in England and France. Those of Emanuel Bach's party allowed him to be a man of genius, but spoiled by his affectation of a new and extraordinary style, accusing him of too frequently repeating himself. The truth is, the spirit and fire of his pieces require not only a strong hand but a *harpsichord,* to give them all their force and effect. They are too rapid, and have too many notes for clavichords or piano fortes, which supply the place of harpsichords in Germany. The novelty and merit of Schobert's compositions seem to consist in the introduction of the symphonic, or modern overture style, upon the harpsichord, and by light and shade, alternate agitation and tranquillity, imitating the effects of an orchestra. The general use of piano fortes, for which the present compositions for keyed instruments are chiefly written, has more contributed to lessen the favour of Schobert's pieces, than their want of merit.[3]

Normally Schobert's sonatas are in three movements, F/S/F, with key variety in the middle movement. The chief interest of these works lies in their textures, which are unique for their time and obviously influenced Mozart's mature keyboard style. Schobert the harpsichordist clearly enjoys the rattling volume of sound produced by the use of all stops with thick textures in low register:

Example VIII–5: J. SCHOBERT, Sonata Op. 2, No. 1

3. Burney, *op. cit.*, pp. 956–957.

In fact, the lowest notes of the instrument are frequently used and pedals in all registers are common. In Example VIII–6 the harpsichord creates a kind of textural polyphony which Mozart imitated in variations and sonatas composed in Paris in 1778. Indeed, it is because the style can be considered a kind of pianistic orchestration that it appears to be a reduction of an orchestral score.

Example VIII–6: J. SCHOBERT, Sonata Op. 4, No. 2, *Andante*

Contemporaries considered Johann Gottfried Eckard (1735–1809) less talented than Schobert, but recognized in his music a greater complexity. Eckard, who was born in Augsburg and went to Paris in 1758, admitted to learning much of his craft from reading Emanuel Bach's *Essay*. He published the first six of his sonatas for solo keyboard in 1763 and the remaining two in 1764. The style here is very different from that of Schobert, who has few points of contact with the North German idiom, but at the same time it cannot be confused with Emanuel Bach's. Eckard uses certain effects reminiscent of the *empfindsamer Stil,* effects dependent upon harmonic surprise, and textural contrast. However, he is apt to repeat passages literally and is prone to use the Alberti bass, which makes his music sound far more like a highly spiced version of Viennese or Italian music than like North German *Empfindsamkeit*.

It is interesting that even when we move out of the top rank of *clavecinistes* in Paris, German names still predominate. Leontzi Honauer (*c.*1730–*c.*90) and Hermann Friedrich Raupach (1728–78) were both important figures of the time, although not in the same class as Schobert and Eckard, either as composers or instrumentalists. Sonata movements by these men, as well as by Emanuel Bach, found their way into the four pastiche concertos for keyboard that young Mozart arranged in 1768 and which were his first attempts in a genre he was eventually to dominate.

During the 1760s and 1770s Emanuel Bach demonstrated most fully the two sides of his musical character: the fantastic eccentric and the conformist. His third set of *Six Sonates pour le Clavecin avec des Reprises*

Variées (Six Sonatas for keyboard with varied repeats)[4] were composed in 1758 and 1759 and published a year later. In a preface to the edition he says:

> Since people repeat themselves these days and say the same thing twice, it is necessary to make changes in performance. It is expected of anyone who is to perform a work. One person goes to no end of trouble to play a piece exactly as it is written and according to all the rules; should one deny him this pleasure? Another, often forced by necessity, makes up for his lack of expression of the written notes by the boldness of his modifications, and the public does not applaud him any the less. It seems that any kind of thought should suffer alteration upon repetition, regardless whether the nature of the piece or the capacity of the player permit it. Modification by itself, and even more when followed by a long and ornate cadenza, will draw a "Bravo" from most listeners. What abuses result from these two adornments of performance? At the first playing through the performer has not the patience to perform the notes as they are written; he cannot wait for the "Bravos". Most frequently the modifications are out-of-place, and negate the spirit of the composition, its emotional content, and the flow of its ideas: nothing could be more infuriating for the composer. Even when the work is performed by someone with all the abilities to make proper changes in it, will it follow that he will always be in the right mood to do so? Will not new pieces create new difficulties? Is not the chief aim of any modification to reflect well on the piece and on its performer? And consequently is not the performer duty-bound to produce on repetition ideas at least as good as those that were heard the first time? Nevertheless, despite abuses and difficulties, well-executed modifications are worthwhile. I refer the reader to what I have said on the subject at the end of the first volume of my *Essay*.
>
> In composing these sonatas, I kept in mind those beginners and Amateurs, who, because of their age, or their occupation have neither the time nor the patience to tackle difficult exercises. I hoped to provide them with something easy and to give them the satisfaction of varying the pieces that they play without them needing to invent the modifications themselves, or resorting to others who might prescribe things that they would be able to learn only with great difficulty. I have therefore written down explicitly everything which might make the performance of these pieces most effective, so that beginners and amateurs may play them with freedom, even when they are not so disposed.
>
> It is, for me, a pleasure to be the first, as far as I know, to have worked in this way for the use and pleasure of my patrons and my friends. How happy I shall be if this effort gives complete evidence of the strength of my zeal and my readiness to be of service.[5]

4. The previously published sets of sonatas were the *Prussian* (1742) and the *Württemberg* (1744).
5. Translation by the author.

It is impossible to know why Emanuel did not publish any sonatas between 1744 and 1760. During this time he was still in the service of Frederick the Great and was chafing under the treatment he was receiving. We know he wrote a great many sonatas, many of which, in their extremely personal means of expression, perhaps comprise the kind of private utterance which is not for publication but which serves to sublimate feelings otherwise frustrated.

This third set of sonatas openly addresses an old problem: what recourse do composers have who see their carefully considered work mutilated by inappropriate ornamentation. And although Emanuel Bach never again published a set of sonatas of this kind, yet the principle of repeating the two sections of the sonata (the exposition, or **A** section before the repeat sign, and the development/recapitulation, or **B** part, after it) and introducing ornamental variation into the repeats is useful, and he continued to employ it sporadically to the end of his life.

It does, however, create problems. During the 1760s, Emanuel continued writing sonatas on the grand scale, as he had done earlier. One can see in some works clear evidence that he wished some of his sonatas to impress by their size as well as by the richness of their textures and harmonic content. In this context he was not at all deterred by the "varied repeat" format, where everything is written twice, spreading over a long period of time and a large number of pages. One obvious disadvantage from a commercial point of view was that it took twice as long to engrave the plates and that increased the cost considerably. But Emanuel, who was otherwise very apt to think in commercial terms, cannot have worried about this publication, for whether due to the novelty of the idea or the excellence of the music, the sonatas were very popular and were reprinted no less than five times during the composer's lifetime.

Addressed to amateurs, the *Sonatas with varied Repeats* are a beautiful combination of the *galant* and the *empfindsamer* styles. Every phrase is polished; *Allegros* are sprightly and energetic; *Andantes* and *Largos* are *cantabile* and imbued with melancholy. Yet the chromaticism in the slow movements is perhaps a little too sophisticated and the changes of texture in the *Allegros* perhaps a little too extreme. Whatever the case, after bringing out two more sets of six sonatas with the same publisher, in 1761 and 1763, Emanuel made a determined effort to woo the public with a set of *Six Easy Keyboard Sonatas,* published by Breitkopf in 1766.

It should be remembered that in 1767 Emanuel finally gained his freedom from Frederick and from Prussia on the pretext of ill health, and he immediately took on the very demanding position of music director and Cantor of the five most important churches in Hamburg, a position which had been occupied by Emanuel's godfather, Georg Philipp Telemann, until his death. On his departure from Prussia the king's sister, Princess Amalia, named him her honorary court Kapellmeister with no duties attached. Perhaps in return for the compliment, Emanuel dedicated his next and seventh set of sonatas (1770) to the princess, to whom the sonatas with varied repeats had been dedicated ten years earlier. In these works the music, while forceful and interesting, is stripped of everything resembling the sensitive style, as the textures are unvaried and the harmonies conventional. Only in those linking passages which modulate freely between first and second movements does anything like *Empfindsamkeit* appear.

Emanuel's fires were not yet burned out, however, and in 1779 he issued the first of his most important legacy for the keyboard, the six collections of sonatas for Connoisseurs and Amateurs *(für Kenner und Liebhaber)*. Only the first of these collections properly falls under consideration here since it came out in 1779; the other five will be examined in a later chapter. In these volumes, Emanuel, who was sixty-five years old when the first one appeared, attempted to display the full range of his expressive power to his public, and he kept to this objective despite the fact that the healthy subscription list of 519 for the first issue dwindled to 288 subscribers for the last.

The first collection, from 1779, although not dignified with an opus number, was assembled exactly as a composer might bring together previously composed works to make a publishable opus. There are few collections, however, that contain such a range of forms and styles. The following tabulation allows comparison of some basic facts:

No.1 in C. Composed in 1773.
I: Prestissimo, 3/4 (69m). II: Andante in E minor, 3/4 (39m). III: Allegretto, 2/4 (44m).

No.2 in F. Composed in 1758.
I: Andante, 2/4 (79m). 4m. modulating link to II: Larghetto in F minor, 9/8 (49m). III: Allegro assai, 2/4 (160m).

No.3 in B minor. Composed in 1774.
I: Allegretto, 2/4 (42m). II: Andante in G minor, modulating (25m). III: Cantabile, 2/4 (69m).

No.4 in A. Composed in 1765.
I: Allegro assai, C (121m). 7m. modulating link to II: Poco Adagio in F♯ minor, C (32m). III: Allegro, 2/4 (136m).

No.5 in F. Composed in 1772.
I: Allegro, C (29m). II: Adagio maestoso in D minor, 3/8 (30m). III: Allegretto, 2/4 (37m).

No.6 in G. Composed in 1765.
I: Allegretto moderato, C (66m.). II: Andante in G minor, C (30m). III: Allegro di molto, 3/4 (122m).

There are a number of interesting points to be noted about this set. Emanuel has not worried unduly about overall tonal variety since he has included two sonatas in the key of F. Only one sonata has a minor mode tonic, which is a small proportion for this composer, but every slow movement opens in the minor mode. Two of the sonatas use the device of joining the first and second movements through the insertion of a modulatory linking passage. The set contains some of Emanuel's shortest, most aphoristic sonata first movements in Nos. 3 and 5; his most "Classical" composition as determined by the balance of phrase structure (No. 4); his largest, most expansive structure, apart from the sonatas with varied repeats, No. 4; his richest textural contrasts (No. 6). The list of superlatives could be continued.

The first movement of the first sonata may be compared with Emanuel's Sonata in D minor (H.5; *ACM* 9). Here, however, the main elements of sonata structure can easily be found beneath the uniform texture provided by the *prestissimo* sequence of sixteenth notes. The use of a single *moto perpetuo* texture within a sonata structure is never a common procedure, since sonatas depend on contrast, but there are other examples in Emanuel's works.

The second sonata of the set opens with a movement that is as full of turns, mordents, ornaments of all kinds and dotted rhythms, chromaticism, etc., as the first is plain.

The third sonata (*ACM* 16) in B minor is looked upon as one of this composer's most famous examples of *empfindsamer Stil*. Its harmonic deception and dynamic and textural contrasts make it a textbook of the style. In addition, it exemplifies the tendency to make the sonata more and more terse and epigrammatic, a tendency that Emanuel gave in to increasingly with advancing age. The structure is condensed, and the statements made within it become compressed, so that there are many significant musical events within a very short space. The slow movement, which opens in G minor, never really defines the key. Twice, in m. 4 and m. 9, the cadence to G minor is interrupted, moving to E♭ and B♭, and thereafter the music continues discursively to form a link with the tonality of the final movement. The last movement is most unusual in the prominence of a recurring bass pattern, almost like a ground bass, with a sensuous and melancholy melody of the utmost introspection above it.

The fourth sonata is unlike any other in Emanuel's output. It is long, its monothematic material laid out in a manner so aggressive that the interrelationship between the parts cannot fail to be observed. The remaining two movements of this sonata are also rich in material and workmanship.

The fifth sonata resembles the third in its compression and *Empfindsamkeit,* while the sixth is extensive and prodigal in its richness and inventiveness.

It can be seen that the ideals of Emanuel's art in the sonata seem to have changed very little, even by 1780, from the earlier *empfindsamer Stil,* and his instrument remains, by and large, the clavichord rather than the newer piano.

Perhaps the most significant developments in the keyboard sonata during this twenty-year period took place in London, where, by 1780, the beginnings of what has been called the London Pianoforte School were well established. In the 1760s, however, this development was hardly in sight, and the period was dominated by the figures of Johann Christian Bach and Abel.

Christian Bach had arrived in London in 1762 in his late twenties. He was the last son of Anna Magdalena and Johann Sebastian Bach. Upon his father's death in 1750 the fifteen-year-old boy moved to Berlin to live with his half brother, Emanuel, whose pupil and assistant he became. Between 1754 and 1756 he went to Italy, where he was able to establish a firm student/teacher relationship with Padre Giovanni Battista Martini and lay the foundation of his own solid reputation as a composer for the church and the theater. He was known as the "Milanese" Bach before he became the "London" Bach. Appointed organist at the cathedral in Milan in mid-1760, Christian's duties were light, and in the following year he composed his first opera, *Artaserse,* for Turin. The same year saw his second opera, *Catone in Utica,* performed in Naples, and its success was such that he was invited to produce yet another the following year. Moreover, his popularity in Italy spread his name and reputation abroad, and we next meet him in London in the summer of 1762. By early 1764 he was appointed music master to Queen Charlotte, wife of George III, and it is clear that before this date he was a familiar figure in the royal household. Early in 1763 he dedicated six keyboard concertos to the queen, and in the same year published his first set of keyboard sonatas with the optional accompaniment of violin or flute and cello. In December of 1763 he obtained a royal privilege for the publication of his works.

His first set of six sonatas, Opus 5, for "le Clavecin ou le Piano Forte"[6] was published about 1766, but some of them were undoubtedly written earlier. Three sonatas from this set (Nos. 2, 3, and 4) were turned into piano concertos by the young Mozart. It is interesting to recall that the Mozart family arrived in London in April of 1764 and stayed there for fifteen months, i.e., just at the time when Christian was establishing his reputation. The relationship between the little boy of eight and the young man twenty years older has always been numbered among the anecdotes in the life of Mozart. It may well be that Mozart came to

6. At a public performance on 2 June 1768, Christian Bach played a "Solo on the Piano Forte." This was probably the first time that the instrument was used in public in London.

know the London Bach's sonatas at this time and may have taken manuscript copies of them with him. The second set of six sonatas, Opus 17, was published in Paris in 1774 and in London in 1779. The ingratiating melodies, the regular phrasing, and the slow harmonic rhythm make so much of Christian Bach's work appear typically "Classical." The repetition of material cannot be divorced from the frequent cadences, and the strength of the cadences emphasizes the fact that this style belongs to the *style galant.*

A comparison of this sonata with others by this composer shows how difficult it is to make an accurate generalization about the formal procedures of first-movement structure. Christian Bach appears to be most concerned with surface polish and to compose easily in the most fashionable vein. He is said to have compared himself to his brother Emanuel, wittily saying: "He lives to compose; I compose to live." It can be shown, however, that in the sonatas of Christian Bach, substantial importance is generally given to the middle or "development" section, comprising from one-quarter to one-third of the whole. The effect of the rounded binary structure (in which half his sonatas are written, the other half being in sonata form) is to increase further the sense of the importance of development. All his first movements are spacious, leisurely, even stately structures, as are the slow movements of his three-movement works. Fast final movements, by contrast, seem almost perfunctory. It can also be said that *cantabile* melody, as opposed to motivic or instrumental melody is, at some point, a feature of each work. Not infrequently the middle sections emphasize their quality as free fantasias by employing new material, and Christian seems to enjoy introducing new melodic material in his recapitulations. Leopold Mozart paid tribute to Christian Bach by holding him up as a model for Wolfgang to follow.

It is hard to believe that while Christian Bach was composing his stately sonatas, each gesture of which is the reflection of a fashionable man moving easily in society, the young Muzio Clementi (1752–1832) was writing works for the same medium in the same milieu, but with a totally different effect. Clementi was born in Rome, where he underwent a thorough musical training. He was appointed to an organist's post and had large-scale compositions performed in public before he was fourteen; at that time his father placed him under the guardianship of a wealthy Englishman, Peter Beckford, so that his musical education might be furthered and he might benefit from the musical life of London. From 1766 to 1773 he lived in Beckford's house and practiced, it is said, for eight hours a day, the works of the Bachs, father and sons, Handel, and Scarlatti. Upon these foundations Clementi built a formidable pianistic technique which, from his earliest compositions, shared very little with his famous European contemporaries Haydn and Mozart. Taking his lead from the Scarlatti compositions that he had learned,

Clementi did not seem to want his works played by a broad amateur public. Rather, in order to play Clementi's works it was necessary to match him in technique.

The rondo of an early sonata in A major, Op. 2, No. 4 (*AMC* 17) which was published in 1779 and hence may well have been written still earlier, shows off aspects of the pianistic technique that made the composer famous. Included in the rondo theme, which typically presents a simple balanced structure of 2+2+2+2 measures, are the chains of thirds basic to the style. These are followed by the double broken octaves in mm. 24–25 and 30–31. The first episode of the rondo uses three common Scarlattian devices: the rapid scale passage which covers the whole range of the keyboard (mm. 42–43); the rapid repetition of notes using changing fingers (mm. 52–56); and the wide-ranging arpeggio in one hand (m. 71). In addition, prominence is given to a novel figure in mm. 44–48 and mm. 56–59 which requires a degree of finger strength and independence far beyond that required by Scarlatti. To these devices the second rondo episode adds chains of rapid octave scales and broken chords, together with wide leaps, making the whole movement a virtual compendium of modern pianistic technique.

THE KEYBOARD SONATA WITH OPTIONAL ACCOMPANIMENT

The sonata with optional accompaniment for either one treble instrument (usually a violin) or for a treble and a bass instrument (usually a cello) reached a pinnacle of popularity during 1760–80. Virtually all composers interested in writing for the keyboard wrote for this kind of combination. The reasons for its popularity are not hard to find, for it was looked upon as sociable music, archetypically "galant." Indeed, many composers are careful to make stylistic distinctions between the solo keyboard sonata, intended either for display or for serious musical thought, and the accompanied sonata, usually less demanding, technically and musically. Thus, such sonatas by Emanuel Bach are less interesting than his solo sonatas from our point of view, since in these he is consciously writing for a large audience, whereas many of the solo sonatas are written for himself. On the other hand, the accompanied sonatas of Rutini or Christian Bach differ very little from their solo keyboard sonatas, since their aim and their audience were the same in both cases.

During this period, the accompanied sonata took definite steps towards the violin and piano sonata and the piano trio by following an observable tendency to increase the roles of the *ad libitum* instruments. At its least essential, the role of the accompanying instrument was simply to double at the 3rd, 6th, or 8ve, or to add rhythmic point to the lines of the keyboard. On the other hand, an interesting reversal of roles from the old and still vital *continuo* sonata can be seen: the *continuo* player might insert into his part some motivic figuration drawn from the melody instrument. Precisely the same situation is seen in the accompanied sonata, although here it is the string instrument which either repeats or anticipates motives in the keyboard part, not, however, *ad libitum,* but as determined by the composer.

Example VIII–7: J. C. BACH, Sonata in A ,Op. 18, No.1

Even the famous set of six sonatas for harpsichord with accompanying violin, Opus 5, composed in 1768 by Luigi Boccherini (1743–1805) shows only slightly greater interaction between the instruments, and it is not comparable to Mozart's set of Mannheim sonatas (1778) from the point of view of shared material. The characteristic of the G-major Sonata from this set by Mozart is that the violin, far from accompanying the keyboard, asserts itself at the outset by exposing the melodic material against a keyboard backdrop. No wonder those works were greeted upon their appearance as representatives of a new genre.

Sonatas accompanied by violin and cello share some of the characteristics of sonatas accompanied by one treble instrument. It must be noted, however, that composers at this time treated the cello very differently: some treated it simply as a reinforcement for coloring the left hand of the keyboard; others employed considerable ingenuity to give it a separate and distinct rhythmic life.

THE STRING TRIO

The 1760s witnessed the development of the truly modern kind of chamber music combinations without keyboard. The string duet, string trio, string quartet, and quintet, although they may have been used before 1760, come to form a major part of the active life of the cultivated amateur musician as never before. The duet for two violins remained the most popular of the string-duet types, closely followed by the duet for two cellos, while that pairing for which the most famous string duets of all were written—the duets for violin and viola of Mozart—was least popular. Of the string trios the combination of two violins and cello was clearly the most frequently employed, probably because of its relationship to the old trio sonata combination of two violins and *continuo*. Composers all over Europe used the three instruments to great effect. In most examples the use of the cello departs very little from the role of the *continuo,* performing a harmonic and rhythmic role, rather than a melodic one. In the trios of Luigi Boccherini, the first set of which he entered in his own catalogue of his works with the date 1760, the cello oscillates between its expected bass function and a prominent *concertante* function, which this cellist/composer enjoyed writing and obviously enjoyed playing. There is no doubt about the historical trend toward the combination of violin, viola, and cello, but it is not strongly demonstrated at this time.

THE STRING QUARTET

The composition and the publishing of string quartets for two violins, viola and cello increased to such proportions in London and Paris between 1760 and 1780, that it can be viewed as the single most important change taking place in instrumental music. Well over 500 new quartets were printed in Paris alone, where there were more publishers than anywhere else, together with an equivalent quantity of reprints.

From the outset, many works which the composer may have conceived for quartet were sold by publishers and accepted by the playing public either as symphonies (to be played with more than one player per part) or chamber music (with one player per part), and *vice versa.* Boccherini's quartets, Op. 2 (which were composed probably during 1760–61, since they were listed by the composer in his own catalogue under the date 1761) were first published in 1767 and described on the title page as "six symphonies," and then in much smaller letters, "or quartets." The edition is addressed in eighteenth-century fashion "to real Amateurs and Connoisseurs of Music." The publisher's catalogue which follows the title page in this edition does not even list quartets as a separate medium but lumps them together with symphonies, since many of the symphonies have wind instruments only as optional parts in the score.

The beautifully engraved title page for Abel's Op. 8 quartets is the work of two artists: G. B. Cipriani, who painted the picture and F. Bartolozzi, who engraved it.

Closely contemporary with Haydn's first quartets, this set by Boccherini is among the earliest examples of the genre. It is interesting to observe how many of the characteristics of the later quartet are present in these works and in the early repertoire of string quartets. Op. 2, No. 2 of Boccherini (*ACM* 18) is far from the *quatuor dialogué* or dialogue quartet, in which the players toss musical motives back and forth among themselves. This was to become the most important aspect of the mature quartet writing of Haydn and Mozart, but it is hardly in evidence in the Boccherini. Only in mm. 8–10, where the motive beginning with the distinctive falling sixth appears in close imitation between the cello and the violins, does this style appear. Boccherini's writing is far more closely related to the concerto and particularly to the *symphonie concertante.* Indeed, if this work were played with several instruments to a part it would be a *symphonie concertante,* with the solo parts carefully indicated by the publisher. There is an obvious effort to distribute soloistic passagework or melodic material among all four parts, but within a hierarchy of importance. Least favored, although not disregarded, is the "violetta," or modern viola, which is allotted more prolonged pedals than any other instrument. This treatment of the viola is perhaps partially explained by the peculiar virtuosity of the cello, Boccherini's own instrument, which is constantly in the tessitura usually occupied by the viola. One of the characteristic sonorities of Boccherini's music throughout his career is to place all instruments in close position around middle C, with the cello in a melodic role while the viola provides the bass. The violins, true to their ancestry in the trio sonata, retain much more equality than is often to be found in the later quartet; thus, the material of the second tonal area (from m. 11 on) is displayed by the first violin and then repeated, in all its brilliance, by the second. The sharing of soloistic, even virtuosic material, as well as the sharing of melodic substance, is characteristic of the *concertante* quartet, which was to retain its popularity well into the nineteenth century.

The structure of the quartet is perhaps of less interest than the disposition of material among the instruments, but it may be noted that this symphony/quartet, like the others in this opus, is a three-movement work, invariably arranged F/S/F. In this particular work the slow movement is a *Largo* in the subdominant, and the final movement is a fast fugue. The first movement, the most complex of all, is cast in a sonata-binary form with a complete recapitulation which includes a radical modification of the transitional material. It is a feature of these symphony/quartets of Boccherini that none of the players is required to engage in anything like the virtuoso activity that Haydn's early quartets or Boccherini's later quartets require, yet all parts offer rewards to the players—they are "grateful" to play.

The number of quartet compositions circulating during this period is amazing since the medium is so new, and the publishing centers of Paris and London printed works from all over Europe as well as those of native composers. Thus in Paris, Gossec's quartets and the first quartet collection by Pierre Vachon (1731–1803) appeared in print in 1770; the first collection by the Chevalier de Saint-Georges appeared in 1773; Jean-Baptiste Bréval (1753–1823), a noted cellist and the author of a celebrated tutor for that instrument (1804), issued his first collection in 1776, as did Etienne Bernard Joseph Barrière (1748–1816?). Among the foreign-born composers working in Paris, Giuseppe Cambini (*c.*1746–1825?) must be mentioned. He came to Paris from Italy *c.*1773 and in the next 35 years or so wrote voluminously, achieving his greatest success with his instrumental music, and particularly the 174 string quartets and over 80 *symphonies concertantes*. At the outset, Cambini wrote in four movements, but three quickly became the norm. After 1776 the quartet in two movements gained in popularity throughout western Europe. However, in the later years of his productive life, Cambini reverted to his earliest practice, and three and four movements once again prevailed. The quartets are mostly written in *concertante* style, which demanded a fairly high degree of virtuosity from all instruments, particularly the violins—perhaps because this was what Cambini himself played.

In London the situation was similar in that there was a large and growing market for chamber music. The field, however, was dominated by the foreign-born musicians Christian Bach and Abel, and while native composers, such as Thomas Arne, were active in the composition of works for solo keyboard and for trio sonata they seem hardly to have touched the more complicated instrumental combinations. Bach's quartets and quintets usually combined strings with a wind instrument, and they are frequently, like his sonatas, in two movements. Undoubtedly the finest chamber works composed in London during this period are the quartets of Abel, which rank with anything being produced in the London/Paris orbit for craftsmanship and melodic charm.

Abel's Op.12 quartets, unlike the Boccherini set just discussed, are not quartet/symphonies but were written for the chamber. Uniformly in three movements with a tripartite sonata-form first movement, a short, *cantabile,* slow movement, and a fast or moderato rondo or *Tempo di Menuetto* finale, they rely not so much on the principle of dialoguing motives as upon the statement of a melody or a passage which is then passed into another voice—i.e., the *concertante* principle. The texture is traditional, usually consisting of two or three upper parts in a melodic/imitative relationship supported by the bass. The writing of the lowest part shows the influence of the *basso continuo* much of the time—in contemporary editions several of the Abel quartets were printed with figures added to the cello part—yet the cello is also given rapid solo passagework. The viola part shows greater independence and is often used in three-part points of imitation, or in passages paired in thirds or sixths with the first or second violin. The two violins carry most of the melodic and passage material, sharing the burden almost equally, and sounding brilliantly effective, even when they are not being taxed with great virtuosic demands.

Abel's melodic style is typical of his time in that the use of rhythmic motives gives a degree of tautness to the melody, and yet the line expands not by repetition or development of the motives, but discursively. The result is a *cantabile* line which gives the impression of great elegance and variety, demanded by the fashion of the time. His textures display an effective, occasional admixture of learning amongst the contrasting *cantabile* and rapid, scalic passages. His structures have an inevitability that springs not from an inner artistic necessity, but from the orthodoxy of 1770, which eventually fell from favor and was superseded.

There can be no doubt that the practice of playing string quartets flourished in Vienna as early as anywhere else in Europe and Haydn's Quartets Opp. 1 and 2 (*c.* 1759), discussed in Part Three, are among the very first surviving compositions for this medium. Viennese quartets during this period show surprising differences from those originating in London or Paris—differences that reflect, among other things, the prevalent treatment of instruments in the symphony, in which Viennese practice was at variance with that of, say, Mannheim. One of Haydn's interesting contemporaries provides an illustration. Little is known of Carlo d'Ordonez except that he was active during the 1760s and 1770s in Vienna, and led the second violins during the first performance of Haydn's oratorio *Il ritorno di Tobia*. He is known to have composed many orchestral symphonies, much chamber music, and two operas. The six Quartets Op. 1, are thought to have been composed in the mid-1760s and their writing demonstrates, perhaps better than the Paris or London quartets, the way in which old techniques were adapted and made new. All six quartets are composed in the church-sonata format of movements following the order S/F/Minuet/F, with the opening slow movement practically a long introduction to the second, fast movement, the subjects of which are often of a severe, fugal cast. The imitation between the three upper voices over the walking bass shows how closely this style resembles the Baroque trio sonata or *sonata a quattro*. The first movement of the first quartet of this set, Op. 1, No. 1 (*ACM* 19), has moved one giant step beyond the Baroque into a style dominated by the rhythmic pattern . The pattern becomes detached from the larger melody and assumes a life of its own as it wanders from instrument to instrument over a pleasing harmonic background. This technique lies at the heart of Viennese chamber music, not only from Haydn through Mozart to Beethoven but also from Ordonez to Schubert and Spohr.

Florian Leopold Gassmann (1729–74), a composer much more highly regarded by his contemporaries than Ordonez, was educated in Italy. His quartets are generally less contrapuntal and motivic than those of Ordonez, but they still show the kind of sensitivity to the interplay of instruments that distinguishes the Viennese style, which was capable, as we shall see, of moving Leopold Mozart to tears when he encountered it in his son's work.

Most of the quartets of Johann Baptist Vanhal (1739–1813) date from this period and are written in a fluent and more modern style than those of Ordonez, placing rather less emphasis upon the technique of motivic imitation than upon graceful melody and sprightly rhythm. The manner of the quartets varies from set to set, presumably depending upon the desires of the dedicatee, One set is clearly dominated by the first violin, while another is written in dialogued fashion and another includes a lengthy cadenza for all instruments in each slow movement. Haydn, Mozart, and Dittersdorf would not have scorned these charming works when they played quartets with Vanhal.

During this period many quartets for mixed combinations of instruments were published in Paris and London. The most usual substitutions for the first violin were the flute or the oboe and numbers of publications are advertised as "quartets for flute or oboe, violin, viola, and cello." The quartet for mixed instrumentation came into being slightly later than the string quartet, and it flourished primarily during the 1770s and 1780s, with notable compositions by Friedrich Schwindl (1737–86) and Vanhal.

THE STRING QUINTET

Works for larger combinations of instruments belonged to the kind of music that has a public face, because the distinction between an orchestra and a chamber group is not defined strictly by size. An important literature exists for larger groups, particularly quintets made up of a string quartet plus another instrument, often of another kind. Most numerous are the quintets for two violins, viola, and two cellos by Luigi Boccherini, the first group of which was published in 1771. These were written for Boccherini's own use, and the first cello part is often set off as if it were a solo instrument, moving in excessively high register. The immense range of the cello provides the composer with a textural possibility in which any one of the four upper parts may dominate at any time, giving a sonorous effect of great rarity and beauty. Boccherini's style is extremely varied and cannot easily be reduced to a couple of phrases, but perhaps his most salient characteristics are to be found in his slower movements, where simple harmonies are embroidered with fanciful ornaments, trills, and arpeggios in all parts. He frequently pairs instruments in thirds and sixths, and he is apt to extend a single harmony to the breaking point. The effects of his years in Spain are to be felt in the numerous movements containing dance elements, either overtly by title, e.g., *Fandango,* or simply in rhythmic or harmonic color. In his earlier period, i.e., before 1780, Boccherini worked within orthodox proportions, but his later writing produced some of the most unusual structures.

VOCAL MUSIC

We cannot leave this discussion of private music in this period without a few words about vocal music. Whether in Vienna, Berlin, or London, whether written for the middle-class *salon,* the court, or for actual public performance in Vauxhall Gardens, the song at this time is a far simpler thing than it was shortly to become. It is still composed on two staves, with the lower stave either explicitly for *continuo* realization or for the left hand of a keyboard player. Just as the verse chosen for setting is conventional in its imagery and often written by amateur poetasters, so the musical realization is usually of extreme simplicity, with little more than a pleasing melody and an apt harmony in a simple structure. The Viennese songs of Leopold Hofmann, Josef Anton Stef-

Music figured largely in the upbringing of every young woman of wealth and class. Entitled *Le Chant,* this 1782 Bartolozzi engraving probably depicts a singing lesson.

fan (1726–97), Carl Friberth (1736–1812), or those that Christian Bach wrote for the pleasure gardens at Vauxhall, although conceived as public music, all give gentle pleasure to the singer. As far as the audience is concerned, the song was still aiming at the broadest possible cross-section of the public, and hence its means were deliberately kept simple.

Far from simple are the settings of ballad verses that begin to be popular at this time. The long, strophic poems that constitute the old ballad may well have been sung, originally, to a repeated strain of music, but the composers in this period were more readily influenced by staged opera than by historical considerations. They sought to echo, in their music, the various moods of the narrative, and, if possible, to heighten them. The resulting work is often through-composed, using tempo, mode, meter, texture, and key changes to increase the emotional impact of the drama inherent in the word. Indeed, composers considered the verbal drama so important that in the last quarter of the eighteenth century, they even began to use a kind of progressive tonality—for example, ending the composition in a different key from that in which it began, in order to call attention to the distance traveled by the narrative from opening to conclusion. It is clear, in such compositions, that the fine line between public and private music is, at most, tenuous, and at the least, impossible to discern, for just as it was when ballad singing was part of the minstrel's entertainment for those crowding the hall of a medieval castle, in the late eighteenth century the song has become more and more a public art.

CHAPTER IX

Concert and Church Music

In the years before 1760, certain regional features were discernible in the symphony as well as traits of its ancestry in the sonata, the concerto, and the opera overture. After 1760 these differences diminish: orchestration tends to become more standardized, consisting usually of four parts for strings, plus two oboes and two horns; slow movements feature strings alone, with no winds; the short-breathed, motivically based melodies of the *style galant* give way to longer, smoother lines with less fussy figuration; sonata structures become clearer as composers place more emphasis on the audibility of the structure. For example, the point of recapitulation becomes a point of structural emphasis rather than the tonal hiatus that it often had been. Of course, in 1760 many composers in their prime had their musical roots firmly fixed in Baroque practice and many traces of the past can still be found. But this is the period in which almost all remaining signs of the Baroque disappear, and the "Classical" symphony approaches full maturity.

THE EMERGENCE OF THE "CLASSICAL" SYMPHONY

VIENNA The Viennese school of symphonic composition began to dominate the musical world in a way that could hardly have been predicted twenty years earlier. Wagenseil is one of the older composers who wrote most of his symphonies in the preceding period, but who produced his most mature works in the 1760s. These demonstrate, as might be expected, a devotion to the *style galant* in their profusion of small, rhythmically defined melodic cells. As a rule, his symphonies contain three movements, and in many cases, the last movement is either a Menuet and Trio or a *Tempo de Menuet,* as has been noted in his divertimentos for solo keyboard. His orchestration does not change greatly: he preserves a violin-dominated texture with rudimentary accompanying figures for the other instruments. Occasionally a trio-sonata kind of relationship is to be found between the upper strings. But in this period there is a tendency to free the viola from the inevitable pairing with the bass, and it is occasionally allowed to serve as the bass on its own, or even to enunciate an articulating figure between phrases.

It is with a group of composers born in the ten years between 1729 and 1739 that Vienna's position in the vanguard of symphonic music is assured. Florian Gassmann, Joseph Haydn, Carlo d'Ordonez, Johann Georg Albrechtsberger (1736–1809), Michael Haydn (1737–1806), Leopold Hofmann, Carl Dittersdorf (1739–99), and Johann Vanhal, the most important composers active in Vienna and its immediate surroundings, form a constellation of the greatest magnitude. Their style of writing shows a noticeable change from that of Wagenseil, and indeed, from the majority of the previous generation of symphony composers. This change is observable not so much in broad structure or orchestration as in the way individual phrases relate to one another, giving a new breadth and balance to melodies as well as forward thrust. The following example shows the opening melodic material of two symphonies by Wagenseil, whose music was a dominant force in the court of Vienna from 1750–70.

Example IX–1: G. C. WAGENSEIL,

a. Symphony in C (C 3)

b. Symphony in B♭ (B♭ 4)

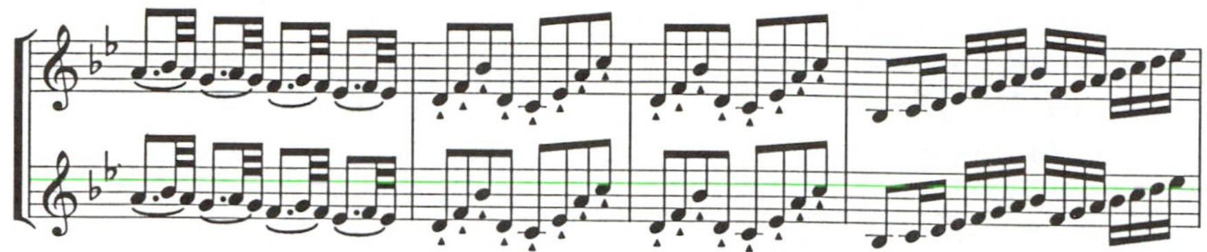

The constant, small-scale contrast gives a high level of variety, but its effect is lessened by the amount of direct repetition of material. By contrast, here are three examples of symphonic openings by composers of the newer generation:

Example IX–2

a. C. DITTERSDORF, Symphony in C

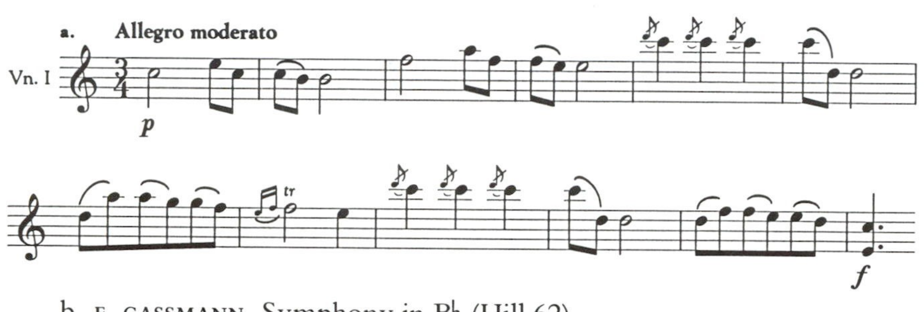

b. F. GASSMANN, Symphony in B♭ (Hill 62)

c. J. G. ALBRECHTSBERGER, Symphony in C

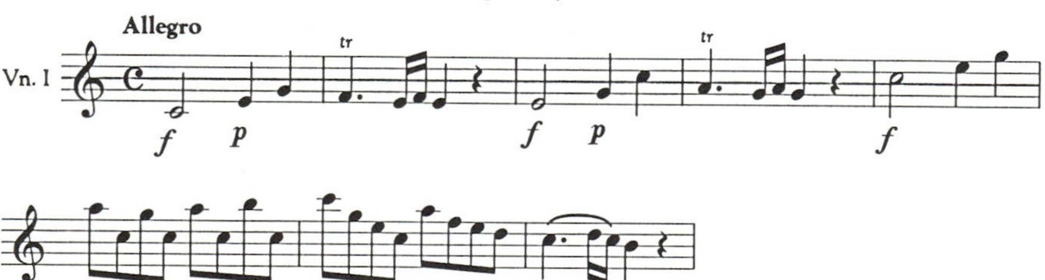

The attractive melody that opens the Dittersdorf consists of three equal phrases of four measures, each of which is made up of 2+2 measures. In the first four measures the repetition of the melodic shape is differentiated and made significant by its antecedent/consequent relationship. The next two four-bar phrases are identical, except for the cadence—the conclusion to the first is V to VI while the second is V to

I. Such sentences, consisting of three phrases, **a-b-b,** were dear to Emanuel Bach, even in his earliest published works (see Example IX–3). Clearly, the Dittersdorf example is both longer and more obviously divided by cadence and repetition. Yet its sense of drive through to the conclusion is even greater than that of the Bach because its melodic substance is symphonic in style and therefore simpler; its tonal implications are not deflected by the lurches of Emanuel Bach's personal idiom; and it dramatizes its cadence by holding it off for so long. The *empfindsamer Stil* had used the device of postponing the cadence (see also Example III-14, p. 63) but there the postponement was effected by opening the door to several tonalities, rather than by moving within a single tonality and strengthening it.

Example IX–3: C. P. E. BACH, *Prussian* Sonata No. 2, I

The Gassmann and Albrechtsberger examples resemble each other in their cumulative phrasing, 2+2+4, and half-close endings, but Gassmann's elegant variations and well-defined climax give it a much greater sense of melodic flow. Each of these three examples illustrates a greater concern for equal balance among the various components of the musical texture than had generally obtained in the earlier symphony: rhythmic vitality balancing motivic repetition; faster harmonic rhythm offering greater chord variety. In short, what was prized in the earlier symphony—rhythmic verve—has now begun to lose its primacy. The Viennese composer of the period has introduced into the symphony *cantabile* song-like melodies that resemble, in their phrase structure, the stanzaic forms of verse rather than the periodic structures deriving from the steps of particular dances, such as the minuet.

The Albrechtsberger example is useful since its melodic material recalls the earlier style, in that the motive is "closed" (i.e., it does not require a continuation) and its rising contour is typical. Where this excerpt shows its provenance is in the sudden flowering into the concluding four-bar phrase from the comparative sterility of the 2 x 2 bar phrases.

MANNHEIM As a center of symphonic production, Mannheim continued to be important during this period, maintaining and even improving upon the standards set by Johann Stamitz. Of the first generation of composers in what came to be known as the Mannheim School, Johann Stamitz had died in 1757, Filtz, in 1760. Richter, always the most resistant to adopting the style that prevailed in the court of the Elector Palatine, left Mannheim in 1769 to take up the position of Kapellmeister at Strasbourg Cathedral. Holzbauer, who was Kapellmeister for the theater, was nevertheless active as a composer of symphonies during the 1760s and into the 1770s.

The Mannheim composers of the second generation reflect, in their output of symphonies, the continued and growing importance of the genre. Christian Cannabich (1731–98) was director of instrumental music at the Mannheim court from 1774. While still quite young he had attracted the attention of the Elector, who sent him to Rome to study under the famous Jommelli from 1750 to 1753. Like his predecessor, Johann Stamitz, Cannabich went to Paris on several occasions in the 1760s and early 1770s and established himself there as a popular composer and performer. During Mozart's sojourn in Mannheim in 1778, the Cannabich family were helpful, friendly, and hospitable. In one of his keyboard sonatas of that period, Mozart included a musical portrait of Cannabich's daughter, Rosa, to whom he had given some piano lessons. But despite Cannabich's strong position and his influence at court, Mozart never made any headway in his search for a position in Mannheim, and it is possible that Cannabich simply did not wish to make an enemy of someone whom he did not wish to help.

Cannabich composed voluminously in all forms, including opera and ballet, but the majority of his surviving works are instrumental—symphonies and chamber works. The Mozarts, who were often unkind critics, did not hesitate to condemn his compositions while acknowledging his genius as a conductor. Writing an "I told you so" letter to his son, Leopold calls Cannabich "a wretched scribbler of symphonies"(*Letters,* 6 Apr. 1778) and says, "I never liked the Mannheim compositions. The orchestra there is good . . . but the interpretation is not in that true and delicate style which moves the hearer." (*Letters,* 8 Nov. 1780) Wolfgang, however, calls him "the best conductor I have ever heard," (*Letters,* 9 July 1778) and by 1780 indicates that his opinion of Cannabich's compositions is rising. The symphonies of the early 1760s are in four movements, but around the time of his first visits to Paris (1764) the three-movement symphony became the rule. Like others by the Mannheim composers, these early works are not distinguished for the quality of their melodic writing. They tend to open with a call to attention by the *premier coup d'archet,* the attack of the strings, just as in so many works of Johann Stamitz, but in the handling of the orchestra Cannabich shows himself closer to Haydn and Mozart. The melodic style is still based upon the use of motive, but Cannabich uses motives in a kind of counterpoint—to fill gaps in the texture and against one another—to great effect (Example IX- 4). The string writing, while

Example IX–4: C. CANNABICH, Symphony No. 22, I

less reliant upon continuity of string textures, leans towards virtuosity at times. Thus, the arpeggio passages in the first and second violins of Symphony No. 22 spring not only from an easy familiarity with string idiom but also from a desire to exploit the sonorous effect of arpeggiated chords over three strings (see Example IX–5, p. 160). In short, his use of the orchestra is resourceful and effective, and even though critics other than the Mozarts found his work uninspired, his compositions from the early 1760s show us some of the seeds of the future. None of the other composers at Mannheim—Carl Joseph Toeschi (1732–88), Ernst Eichner (1740–77), Franz Beck (1730–1809) or Carl Stamitz (1745–1801), to name but a few—demonstrate a sense of color as advanced as his.

PARIS The connections between Mannheim and Paris were, from the middle of the century, close and cross-fertilizing. Almost all Mannheim artists spent periods in Paris, where they reaped fame and money as performers and as composers. Many Mannheim composers arranged to have their works published in Paris. Others, like Richter and Beck, settled in France to work and teach, further disseminating the "Mann-

Example IX–5: C. CANNABICH, Symphony No. 22, I

heim" style. It is hardly surprising, then, that Paris, during this period, offered the most flourishing milieu for the symphony.

François-Joseph Gossec, without doubt the most important of instrumental composers in France during this period, enjoyed a very long and productive life. As mentioned earlier (see p. 79), Gossec's Opp. 3 and 4 symphonies were published in 1756 and 1758 respectively. The six symphonies of Op. 5, dating from the early 1760s, continue to include the minuet as part of the symphonic cycle. The orchestra in all six works requires at least two flutes and two horns, as well as strings. The next set, Op. 6, also dates from the early 1760s, but is quite different: the first three are symphonies with a mix of obligatory and optional winds, while 4, 5, and 6 are *sinfonie a quattro,* or quartet symphonies for strings alone with *basso continuo*. They alternate between three and four movements and even make use of fugue. Gossec also expands his harmonic vocabulary in passages such as the following (Example IX–6), highly unusual in 1762. In the slow movement of this same work, Gossec's

Example IX–6: F.-J. GOSSEC, Symphony Op. 6, No. 2, I

A concert at the home of the Comtesse de Saint Brisson. The artist, Augustin de Saint Aubin, has clearly shown that many in the elegant audience do not particularly wish to listen to the music being performed.

use of dissonance within an *ostinato* accompaniment forms a clear link between the Baroque techniques of Corelli and Vivaldi and those of the young Mozart (Symphony No.1 in E♭, slow movement; 1765), who may well have heard this very work by Gossec on his Grand Tour through Paris to London in 1764–5 (see p. 183, fn. 2.).

Gossec's other symphonies from this period include three works for orchestra, Op. 8 (1765); three orchestral trios, Op. 9 (1766); and six symphonies for orchestra, Op. 12 (1769). He published a number of other symphonies without opus number or in collections with other composers' works. Even though Gossec uses counterpoint and fugue quite freely in his compositions, it is interesting to observe that the orchestral-trio symphonies are quite homophonic, showing no sign of the Stamitz influence so widespread in other works by this composer.

While no other composer achieved Gossec's prominence, Simon Le Duc (1742–77) deserves to be singled out of the large number of *petits maîtres* who were active in France at this time. Unlike Gossec, his symphonic production was small and his life short, but his work demonstrates the high quality of the Parisian symphony in the late 1770s. By that time, the influence of Mannheim, as represented in the work of Johann Stamitz, had been absorbed and changed beyond recognition. The orchestral devices and the short melodic motives, even the use of the instruments, had all changed. Orchestral discipline and the *premier coup d'archet* were still a point of pride for the Parisians, and dynamic graduations are made much of in Le Duc's scores. The rapid passages for the strings give a great effect of virtuosity, and the textures within the orchestra are enriched by simple contrapuntal relationships among the parts. Textural change is, of course, still one of the most important aspects of composition, but the changes become less frequent as one texture persists for a longer time, thus losing the impression of fussiness and creating, instead, one of grandeur and majesty.

The first six symphonies of Luigi Boccherini were published in Paris by La Chevardière in 1771. Written in Spain, their style was largely determined by the local conditions, for Boccherini's orchestra was much smaller than those of Mannheim, Paris, or London, often allowing him no more than one instrument to a part; hence there is a much closer relationship between these symphonies and his chamber music than is usually the case. Soloistic passages were common for all instruments, and the demands made upon the players' technique were greater than in any other works discussed in this chapter. The scoring of the works vary: the largest (No. 2) requiring 2 principal violins, 2 ripieno violins, viola, 2 cellos, double bass, 2 oboes, and 2 French horns. In the separation of the bass and cello parts, Boccherini was far ahead of his time.

LONDON The symphony in London at this time is largely in the hands of the two foreigners Abel and Christian Bach. Their spectacular success caused the work of such masters as William Boyce, Thomas Arne, and Thomas Erskine, Earl of Kelly (1732–81), to be quickly forgotten, although all five men wrote a great many symphonies between 1760 and 1780. Boyce and Arne were strongly influenced by the dominant figure of Handel, who died in 1759, as well as by the Italian composers of the time, and both interchanged the idea of overture and symphony. (Both the French and the Italian overture were still very popular in England.) Thomas Erskine, more than any other British composer, was directly influenced by the Mannheim style, having been a pupil of Johann Stamitz in both violin and composition. When he returned to Scotland from Germany in 1756, some of the forward-looking practices he brought with him separated his work from that of many composers at the center of things in London. Nevertheless, despite the excellence, originality, and strength of many compositions by native composers, it was in the works of Bach and Abel that fashionable London found its definition of satisfying music. Depending as they do upon their suaveness of melodic line, the easy, assured grace of their movement, whether at slow or fast tempo, and the occasional glitter of the virtuosic, fast, scale passages, these works demonstrate the proximity of London and Paris taste at the time.

In the first of his symphonies, dating from 1761 at the latest, Abel shows complete command of that maximally contrasted yet totally balanced opening, which has always seemed such a Mozartian characteristic. Here, *forte,* unison, upward-moving arpeggios contrast with *piano,* downward-moving scalic melody harmonized over a pedal, the whole effect happening twice. In m. 3 the moving arpeggio is a third higher and that change is answered by the descending melody a third lower; such is the composerly sense of balance in operation here. Indeed, the composer's intellectual control over the elemental forces that music offers him (the upward and downward melodic tendencies) creates an effect of restrained power out of which the whole symphonic structure emerges. Simple to the point of being ordinary, understated and utterly without bombast, if ever there was "Classicism" as it is usually defined in music, these four measure exemplify it.

Example IX–7: C. F. ABEL, Symphony, Op. 1, No. 1, I

In his symphonies, Christian Bach illustrates the change that took place during this twenty-year period, when the Mannheim style, with an admixture of the Italian, gave way to the newer "Classical" style. The Symphony in E♭, Op. 6, No. 3 (*ACM* 20) was written before Bach moved from Italy to London in 1762. Its three-movement structure reflects an adherence to Italian models, while the mosaic-like profusion of the melodic and motivic material in the first movement shows that fluid approach to structure more characteristic of Mannheim than of

Sammartini, for example. Like many of the earlier symphonies of Christian Bach, this is a work full of invention in which successive ideas resemble one another, but there is very little exact repetition even between exposition and recapitulation: the fanfare of the opening two bars is repeated at the recapitulation (mm. 77–78); mm. 20–24 reappear in mm. 87–91; and mm. 36–38 are echoed in mm. 97–99. Literal repetition is more a matter of decor than of structure—e.g., mm. 3–4 are repeated in mm. 5–6, though never heard again. This is a style which develops material through changed repeats and allusions. Thus, after the double bar, the "new" melodic material which begins the second half (a common characteristic of Christian Bach's sonata-form compositions, which his disciple, Mozart, not infrequently uses) begins with a phrase which has no precedent, yet the consequent phrase bears a close relationship to material from the opening of the second group. Likewise, the material of mm. 60–63 has no precedent in the exposition, but it is followed by other material which is closely related. In recapitulation, Christian Bach shows his power of invention, for almost nothing follows in routine sequence but everything bears signs of an active imagination and the sure hand of the thoughtful master.

The later years of the eighteenth century saw the production of a number of works for multiple orchestras, for audiences delighted in echo effects, just as their seventeenth-century predecessors had. Christian Bach wrote three symphonies for two orchestras which must be mentioned since they are among his finest and most popular works. In these compositions, the two orchestras oppose and combine in the presentation of the music—an eighteenth-century *concertato* style—but the basic structure is not affected by this interaction.

Unique among the symphonies of the period are those of Emanuel Bach, whose musical language has already been shown to differ markedly from that of most of his contemporaries. The symphony genre was not the most congenial to Emanuel, if we judge by the number he composed: before 1760 he wrote seven and between 1760 and 1776 another eleven. Indeed, his most fertile period for symphonic composition was 1773–76, when he wrote ten, six for strings and four for twelve *obbligato* instruments.

One can make a broad generalization about Emanuel's symphonies: as in his sonatas, he is devoted to the three-movement work, F/S/F, the first movement of which is in some variety of sonata form, and is the longest and most complex of the three; the slow movement tends to be rhapsodic, and leads to a lighthearted, short finale; the movements are not infrequently linked by transitional passages, and some of these works proceed without a break. The fashionable devices, such as the "call to order" of the loud, reiterated, chordal opening followed by a triadic theme, or the easy tonal hierarchy with its respective primary triads ranged in order, or the repeat signs at the end of the exposition—none of these are to be found. In their place, Emanuel gives us a translation into public terms of the private, self-communicating style of *Empfindsamkeit* which becomes ever more personal, original, and idiosyncratic as he gets older. The first of the last four symphonies (*ACM* 21) was written in 1775/6 and published in 1780 with a dedication to Frederick William, nephew of his old master, Frederick the Great, who would become king of Prussia upon the death of his uncle (1786). Every page of this work is a lesson in style, in composition as well as orchestration, and there is hardly a measure that can be considered routine. The opening in the first violin, in which the whole note D diminishes erratically against the beat down to an eighth note, is a superbly original translation of the routine fanfare of the symphonic introduction, during which the D moves from the tonic to the fifth of the chord. The second statement appears to duplicate the first a major third higher, but although the rhythm is the same, the functions differ melodically and harmonically. The third statement might have begun on the A but instead begins on the subdominant chord with the third, B, in the top. Through an extravagant chromatic passage the first area of tonal stability is reached in m. 27, where a trio-sonata texture leads to a cadence on the dominant in m. 34. A solo woodwind section between oboes and bassoon begins a sequence, which sounds as though it ought to be diatonic in A, but which quickly takes harmonic turns in many directions before settling on V of V. The sequence in mm. 49–56 might have been expected to follow an orthodox harmonic scheme, $A^{7,}$ $D^{7,}$ $G^{7,}$ $C^{7,}$ F, but it is more arresting and old-fashioned in sound, as Emanuel returns to the trio-sonata texture. In m. 56, the solid tonal plateau which emphasizes the key of the dominant begins, continuing to the end of the exposition. The remainder of the movement repays close attention. Having composed an exposition containing so many irregularities and surprises, Emanuel clearly felt the need to create balances, and the rest of the movement, the middle section and the recapitulation, stands in a straightforward relationship with the exposition. Material follows in due order and the reshaping and reinstrumentation are subtle and easily overlooked. Perhaps most artful in this movement is the way the composer makes the opening rhythmic gesture by the first violins all-pervasive, even when the foreground material is of a quite different kind (see oboes in mm. 27ff.; oboes in mm. 35ff.; violins in mm. 44ff.).

The coda also works as transition. It is worth noting that initially, the B♭ in the bass is the lower member of an anticipated augmented 6th. In the transition it becomes the root of a $B\flat^{7,}$ thus establishing E♭, the flattened second, as the key of the slow movement.

In the slow movement the flutes carry the melody doubled by violas and cellos, two octaves lower. The idiosyncratic sound of Emanuel's orchestra here is a long way from the deliberately sparse texture often encountered at this time, but it is also very far from the lush sonorities of slow movements to come.

In the years 1760–80 the symphony is the single most important form of public music throughout Europe. It had become self-sufficient; complexity had begun to replace simplicity, sophistication to replace naiveté, searching, expressive melodic content had interposed itself upon rhythmic vitality, and a subtle need for orchestral color had modified the previous broad washes of relative monochrome.

Many writers have testified to seeing evidence of a "romantic crisis" in the music of this period, generally referred to as *Sturm und Drang,* or "storm and stress." As proof of this phenomenon the symphonies in the minor mode by Haydn are usually cited, and the distant rumblings of revolutionary storm are inferred by those who are attached to this idea. But in the arts there is constant need for change, and in searching for the new the artist periodically resorts to the exotic, without revolutionary intent. Similarly, adherents to the *Sturm und Drang* theory have emphasized the role of the minor mode, failing to see it simply as part of a greater urge to deepen the expressivity of music. As such, it must be considered in combination with the refinements of orchestration, the development of a strophic structure of melody, and all the other distinguishing facets of music at this time, which lead not to revolution and the destruction of the *ancien régime* but to the most refined utterances of the late eighteenth-century symphony at the hands of Haydn, Mozart, and Beethoven.

THE *SYMPHONIE CONCERTANTE*

One of the most interesting developments resulting from the public's affection for expressive, orchestral coloring was the programmatic symphony, such as Haydn's Nos. 6, 7, and 8, *Le Matin, Le Midi,* and *Le Soir,* and Boccherini's Op. 12, into which elements of the *concerto grosso* had been hybridized. The *symphonie concertante* was another kind of hybridization in which the concert symphony is crossed with a variety of other forms, the resulting work resembling a concerto more than a symphony. Since, at this time, cross-fertilization of genres and the interchangeability of compositions from one instrumental combination to another is a dominant principle, the antecedents of the *symphonie concertante* can be identified at least twenty years before the term and the composition became popular. From 1770 many works of this kind were written all over Europe. However, its greatest vogue was in Paris, where more *symphonies concertantes* were composed than in all the rest of the continent, with the possible exception of Mannheim.

At the outset, the *symphonie concertante* was composed for two violins with orchestra (in this, resembling its ancestor, the *concerto grosso*). Shortly afterward, other instruments such as the viola, cello, and flute began to make their way into the solo body. The other woodwinds quickly followed, and by 1778 the *symphonie concertante* had become a work very closely associated with wind soloists, or with mixed orchestration. Mozart's *Symphonie concertante* for flute, oboe, bassoon, and horn, written for Paris in 1778 and never performed because of the intrigues of Cambini, is typical of the period. The other extant *Symphonie concertante* for oboe, clarinet, horn, and bassoon, K. App. 9, may well be a nineteenth-century arrangement, or, as some believe, not by Mozart at all.

Many of these works are written in two movements, but a number are in the more customary three movements. The first movement tends to be considerably longer than the first movement of a symphony. In part, this is due to the double exposition for, like the solo concerto, the *symphonie concertante* opens with an orchestral exposition before the entry of the soloists. While the melodic material may resemble that of a symphony, the *symphonie concertante* will feature the *cantabile* qualities of the solo instrument, and melodies of considerable spaciousness and deliberateness are often used. In the two-movement *symphonie concertante* the second movement is usually a lighthearted rondeau, much shorter and less demanding for the audience than the first movement. In the three-movement version the second and third movements follow the orthodox pattern of the solo concerto.

THE SOLO CONCERTO

Perhaps because of the variety of ways in which the increasing public appetite for virtuosity could be gratified, the solo concerto continues to be as popular in this period as it had been earlier. Still the most successful concerto features an orchestral instrument in the solo role. The choice of instrument was usually determined by what the composer himself played, especially when his reputation was based primarily on his performances. Thus the violinists François-Hippolyte Barthélemon (1741–1808), Gaviniès, Felice Giardini (1716–96), Antonin Kammel (1730–87), and Le Duc, wrote concertos for violin only, while others, such as Albrechtsberger, Dittersdorf, Eichner, Joseph Haydn, etc., wrote for a wide variety of solo instruments.

The history of the *Concert Spirituel* in Paris affords a complete record of concert programs during this time and we can see the important part played by the solo concerto. Many concerts contained two or three solo concertos and the featured instruments included violin (by far the most popular), viola, cello, flute, oboe, clarinet, French horn, and harp. The solo organ was also frequently heard, but there is no mention of either the *clavecin* (harpsichord) or pianoforte in a solo role until the year 1778, when a harpsichord concerto by Christian Bach was performed by a girl of thirteen. The first appearances of a solo pianoforte concerto in this series date from 1779, 15 August and 24 December. Clearly, harpsichord solos were not very popular, and many concertos written for this instrument were performed on the organ or harp.

Despite the evidence of the *Concert Spirituel* programs, Paris must have adopted the harpsichord as a solo concerto instrument just as it was adopted in London, Vienna, and Berlin, for Schobert and Eckardt, two distinguished keyboard players, established themselves in Paris (1760 and 1758 respectively) and composed concertos for their instrument. (Unfortunately, those by Schobert cannot be dated and those by Eckardt have not survived.) Indeed, from the first of his few publications (1763) Eckardt made it clear that he was not writing for harpsichord alone but also for fortepiano, and the name of that instrument figures on the title page of his next opus (1764):*Deux Sonates pour le clavecin ou le piano forte . . .*

In London, Christian Bach had his first collection of six harpsichord concertos, Op. 1, printed in 1763. A further set, Op. 7, appeared in 1770 and another, Op. 13, in 1777. His colleague, Abel, also produced a set of six in 1774. Like Mozart, Christian Bach undoubtedly produced these works for his own use, but the technical demands are such that they are readily accessible to amateur musicians. The orchestration does nothing to take these works out of the chamber music category for they are scored for two violins and bass. The third set, Op. 13, includes optional parts for winds, which are not intended to impede private performance.

For Christian Bach, the concerto, like the sonata, may be in two or three movements. The ritornello form of the first movement persists in Op. 1, Nos. 4 and 6. In the remaining works and in subsequent concertos the prototype of the Classical concerto is roughly analyzable as:

Orchestral exposition	I
Solo exposition	I - V
Orchestral transition	V
2nd Solo	Various
Recapitulation	I
Solo Cadenza	I
Concluding orchestral passage	I

From time to time, the composer departs from the typical format outlined above. We have already noticed that Christian Bach habitually introduces new material into his development sections, and he often follows that principle in the concerto.

Emanuel Bach's concertos for keyboard add woodwinds to what had earlier been a small string orchestra. In moving toward the large orchestra, the solo keyboard concerto finally departs from the ideals of the earlier chamber concerto (or divertimento, as Haydn called it), but it has not yet succumbed to the cult of instrumental virtuosity that is to dominate the concerto of the next period, 1780–1800.

MUSIC IN THE SERVICE OF GOD

The changes taking place in music itself also mitigated against the creation of an appropriate style for use in church. The stylistic gulf between the archetypes of Baroque music and the *style galant* was as great as the differences between the archetypes of Renaissance and early Baroque music. But whereas the earlier stylistic change had at its roots the desire to make music more responsive to the expressive quality of a text, at the heart of the *style galant* was the notion that music should correspond to the ideals of a secular society. The problems inherent in the creation of religious music for a secular society were solved by composers of the time in two wildly different ways: certain sections of the Mass were set in the modern, operatic manner and others in a fugal style (considered "science" in music, although in any other circumstance the use of fugue would have been considered unacceptably pedantic).

These fundamental differences, combined with the emancipation of philosophical thought, resulted in an attitude reported by Burney after a meeting in 1772 with the Berlin composer J. F. Agricola:

> He shewed me some of his compositions for the church, in score, which were very masterly; but he said that it was a style of writing which was but little cultivated, at Berlin, as the King will not hear it. Indeed, I had been told before my arrival that his Prussian majesty carries his prejudice against this kind of music so far, that when he hears of any composer having written an anthem, or oratorio, he fancies his taste is contaminated by it, and says, of his other productions, every moment, *Oh! this smells of the church.*[1]

The nature of the opposition to church music by adherents of the *style galant* is further clarified by Burney in the same account of his travels when he is in Vienna. He writes:

> To aim at equal perfection in both [church and theater music], is trying to serve God and Mammon. . . .I do not call every modern oratorio, mass, or motet, *church music;* as the same compositions to different words would do equally well, indeed often better, for the stage. But by *Musica di Chiesa,* properly so called, I mean grave and scientific compositions for voices only, of which the excellence consists more in good harmony, learned modulation, and fugues upon ingenious and sober subjects, than in light airs and turbulent accompaniments.[2]

Burney's definition of church music is, in essence, a definition of everything that the *style galant,* and indeed, all late eighteenth-century music, is not. Many eighteenth-century writers, like Burney, recognized the possibility of an ideal music for the church. But in attempting

1. Charles Burney, *The Present State of Music in Germany, the Netherlands and United Provinces* (London, 1773) II, p. 91.
2. *Ibid,* I, pp. 329–30.

This engraving by J. E. Mansfeld (1784) entitled *A Musical Offering in a Church* shows the celebrant and servers at the altar being ignored by the congregation. More attention is paid to the singer here than in the *opera seria* illustration (see p. 84).

to describe that ideal they appear to run into significant problems, shown by their invariable preference for the vague over the specific, the evocative over the prescriptive. Thus Mattheson describes a number of styles proper to church music, but two of them are historical and no longer used, even in Mattheson's day; the others are used in both the theater and the chamber, and hence they can only be distinguished by a certain suitability for worship. Having attempted to describe these categories, he draws this conclusion:

> Now in so far as the instrumental style belongs in the church style (though, like the previous madrigal style, it is also amply present in the theater and chamber) to that extent it requires, in sonatas, sonatinas, sinfonias, preludes, interludes, and postludes used in religious affairs, its special solemnity and a serious quality directly based on the proceedings; lest it smack of a loosely-united overture; therefore, in sacred matters, this style of writing must be respectable, well considered and strong; not jesting, destitute and feeble, inasmuch as to this day this style has been ejected from the papal chapel on this account, where nothing else is permitted but the most

> indispensable organ and bass instruments for strengthening the fundamental voices.
>
> Yet one should not on this account indiscriminately abandon all vivacity in the sacred service, especially since the style of writing under discussion often naturally requires more joyousness and cheerfulness than any other . . . A cheerful disposition is best disposed for devotion . . . Only the appropriate discretion and moderation with the joyful sounds of the clarino trumpets, trombones, violins, flutes, etc., must never be lost sight of, nor be to the slightest detriment of the familiar commandment, which says: **Be joyous; yet in fear of God.**[3]

More than ten years later, Quantz attempts to lay down principles about composition, and on the subject of church music commits himself as follows:

> Music is either vocal or instrumental. . . .Vocal music is intended for the church, the theatre, or the chamber. Instrumental music is likewise performed in all these places.
>
> *Church music* is of two kinds, namely *Roman Catholic,* and *Protestant* . . . each piece must accord with its purpose and with its words, so that a Requiem or Miserere does not resemble a Te Deum or a composition for Easter . . . or a motet a gay opera aria. An *oratorio* or dramatically treated sacred history is ordinarily distinguished from a theatrical composition only by its content and, to a certain extent, by its recitative.
>
> In general a serious and devout style of composition and performance is required in church music of any type. The style must be different from that of an opera.
>
> You should not believe that church music must consist exclusively of pedantries. Although the object of the passions is different, they must be excited here with as much or even more care than in the theatre. Devoutness simply imposes some limits. But if a composer is not able to move you in the church, where stricter limits are imposed, he will be even less capable of doing so in the theatre, where he has more freedom. One who knows how to move you in spite of constraints promises to do much more when he has greater freedom. Likewise the poor performance of church music at many places does not provide sufficient grounds for rejecting all church music as something disagreeable.[4]

This last paragraph is particularly revealing, not only for the curious logic in the sentence "But if . . . " but also for the description of a general state of affairs at that time. Clearly Mattheson and Quantz find this portion of their task difficult. Burney, writing twenty or so years after Quantz, has no such problem and says quite specifically that church music should be "grave and scientific," etc. But it was not until the last two decades of the century, when, building upon the work of numbers

3. Mattheson, *op cit.,* p. 209.
4. Quantz, *op cit.,* pp.305–307.

of lesser masters working in churches large and small, as well as upon the newly created instrumental style—a style capable of such deep seriousness that it could serve as a basis for a style of church music congruent both with an atmosphere of worship and with emotional depth and sincerity—that Haydn and Mozart were able to create their greatest achivements in music for the church.

We may assume that Frederick the Great, as quoted by Agricola above, was not alone among the multitude of rulers—kings, princes, counts, bishops—to be bored by music tainted with the musty atmosphere of the church. Where his patron expressed boredom with the service, a composer, naturally enough, imported more of the style of the theater or the chamber into the church, and tried to make time spent in church as much like a fashionable situation as he decently could.[5] Some rulers wanted Masses to be short, and composers as great as Haydn occasionally superposed texts in the *Gloria* and *Credo* and made liturgical nonsense in order to save time. Others required all the color resources that a full orchestra could give, whenever possible. Yet another facet of the disinterest in orthodox belief and practice evident in some quarters was the abolition of the Christian Church in France in 1794 and the establishment of the cult of Reason and worship of a non-denominational "Supreme Being."

But it was not only the skeptics and disbelievers who were seen to work against organized religion. Far and wide in Germany, Austria, France, and England people were attempting to diminish the influence of the church and thereby to strengthen the state. Even the devout were suspected of working against the Church when they tried to effect social change.

In Austria, the Empress of the Holy Roman Empire, Maria Theresa, lived through turbulent times of war and distress, her accession to the throne being followed first by the War of the Austrian Succession (1740–48) and then by the Seven Years' War (1756–63). With the return of peace in 1763 and a growing measure of prosperity, she and her son, Joseph II (who ruled jointly with her until her death in 1780), worked tirelessly to instill in their disparate peoples a sense of unity and loyalty to Vienna. An instrument of this policy was the weakening of the influence of the Church of Rome. While Maria Theresa hesitated to enact some of the logical conclusions of the new relationship between the state and the Church, Joseph II did not feel the same constraints, and upon his mother's death he effectively isolated the Austrian church from Rome. Although devout, he was also a broad-minded and progressive liberalizing reformer with a strong streak of the dogmatic about him. An edict of toleration (1781) enabled Freemasonry, as well as the Prot-

5. In some essential ways the situation recalls Luther's use of popular songs with new words, and the remark "Why should the devil have all the best tunes?"

estant sects, to flourish more than had been possible during his mother's lifetime. With the broad aim of decreasing the power of the clergy, he worked toward simplicity and intelligibility in the service, and an effort was made to strip superstition and meaningless ritual from religious practices. He proposed the inclusion of hymns with texts in the vernacular, in order to increase the significance of the service for the people, and to restrict the use of instruments during the service to High Mass on Sundays and certain holidays.

Such proposals met with enthusiastic support in some places, most notably in Salzburg, where Mozart's oppressive Archbishop Colloredo assumed office in 1772. Colloredo went much further than Joseph in 1783 when he decreed that, in his state, Kohlbrenner's collection of hymns, which had been praised by the Pope, should alone be used in churches and that no other vocal or instrumental music should be used. These reforms were short-lived, but had they prospered they would have brought the Roman church close to the Wesleyan in working with a hymnody which took the place of the vast and time-honored quantity of music that had been attached to the liturgy.

RELIGIOUS MUSIC IN ROMAN CATHOLIC EUROPE

By the middle of the eighteenth century the large majority of compositions for the Mass comprised a judicious mixture of styles, ranging from the fugal to the homophonic, and of mediums, ranging from the chorus accompanied by full orchestra to the solo aria with keyboard accompaniment. While each composer tried to make a personal statement through his treatment of the liturgical words, the tradition of setting certain parts of the text in certain ways—e.g., the setting of *Cum Sancto Spiritu* fugally—persisted. A chorus, or a soloist, or a group of soloists in ensemble split the text into sections, and the contrast between homophony and counterpoint further emphasized the variety within the uneasy amalgam. This kind of Mass, in which a phrase or two of liturgy is used as the basis of a large musical movement, has often been referred to as a "Cantata" Mass. It is perhaps more accurate to call it a *missa longa,* since a cantata normally includes recitative, while this version does not. Such Masses abound in the work of Haydn and Mozart, as well as in the music of lesser masters, such as Michael Haydn, Antonio Salieri, Leopold Gassmann, Georg Albrechtsberger, Carl Dittersdorf, and Leopold Hofmann (1738–93), among others.

The oratorio in Catholic Europe resembled, in both words and music, the *opera seria.* Its text was a mix of metrically arranged words for aria or recitative, and its subject matter usually Bible stories or the lives of the saints; it differed from opera in that it was not intended to be staged and acted, but was to be performed in a church or chapel, in educational institutions, and in private houses. During Advent and Lent it was also performed in theaters. After the middle of the eighteenth century there is evidence that oratorios were even performed in costume and acted from memory, thus drawing the form still closer to opera. Significantly, the poet whose work was used most often in these oratorios is Pietro Metastasio. (For further discussion of this type of oratorio, see the section on Haydn's *Il ritorno di Tobia*, p. 257).

CHURCH MUSIC IN NON-CATHOLIC EUROPE

After the middle of the century, the quality of Protestant church music suffered. Unlike the service of the Roman church, which had often relied as much upon the emotional response of the uneducated to the awe-inspiring visual and aural ritual as it had appealed to needs of the intellectuals and the sophisticated in the flock through the liturgy, the Protestant churches based their appeal on the word, and hence the Sermon was the center of the service. Often music was allowed in the service only during the hymns, of which the reformed church had a rich and extensive heritage.

Protestant countries, with their emphasis on the personal nature of God and of worship in the home, developed and cherished the sacred song, i.e., a song comparable to the Lieder already described, but written to devotional poems by such noted poets as Christian Gellert and Friedrich Gottlieb Klopstock (1724–1803). Such poems were set by some reputable composers, and fine examples survive from Emanuel Bach, J. Benda, Hiller, and others. These songs were intended for amateur use in the home, in order to mingle worship with recreation at the family hearth.

The Church Cantata continued to excite composers for some time, particularly among Bach's sons and pupils, but after the middle of the century it began to diminish in importance. As in Catholic countries, the oratorio enjoyed great favor in the Protestant world, with texts taken particularly from the story of the Passion. Carl Heinrich Graun's *Der Tod Jesu* (The Death of Jesus; 1755) uses a typical subject made into a typical libretto, and the work achieved great and enduring success. The text is by Carl Wilhelm Rammler (1725–98), a respected man of letters in Berlin in mid-century. Not a poet of genius, he attempts, in the best traditions of Pietism, to make an immediate emotional impact through the use of melodramatic imagery. Thus, the scene of Jesus dying on the cross is evoked by

> . . . suddenly the suppressed pain furiously strikes the soul of the hero; his heart pounds in his tortured breast. A dagger turns in every vein . . ."

And when it is all over the closing chorus is set to the words:

> Here we lie, agitated sinners, O Jesus, bowed down low, to dampen with tears the dust that drank your life's blood.

Graun was Frederick the Great's favorite Kapellmeister and operatic collaborator. He used four-part chorale settings, contrapuntal and homophonic writing, accompanied and *secco* recitative, and arias for solo voice, as well as a duet for two voices. The thorough contrapuntal technique in the choruses comes as a surprise in the light of what Frederick's attitude is supposed to have been to anything that "smelt of the church." Equally surprising are the chorale settings, which proceed almost entirely note against note, with very little attempt made to paint the word by voice-leading or harmonization, as in Bach's Passion settings. Instead, there is the occasional use of attractive orchestral color, of musical figures, and of affecting melodic lines, all of which amply demonstrate why Graun's oratorio maintained its hold on a public when the same text set by greater composers, such as Telemann, did not.

Emanuel Bach's setting of another text by Rammler, the *Auferstehung und Himmelfahrt Jesu* (The Resurrection and Ascension of Jesus) from 1777, differs from the Graun in that it consists solely of choruses and solo numbers separated by accompanied recitatives. There are no chorales, and the participation of the congregation is here limited to their contemplation and reflection on the subject matter and the music. Bach's score is rich where Graun's is thin, and imaginative where Graun's is pedestrian. Bach's introduction to the work is below. Without harmony, and with virtually no dynamics, these nineteen measures are unlike anything written before Wagner in mid-nineteenth century; they make their effect through melodic direction and through the bleak sparseness of the violas, cellos, and basses in unison. The text of the

Example IX–8: C. P. E. BACH, *Auferstehung. . .* , Introduction

chorus that follows, "For thou, O God, wilt not leave his soul in Hell . . ." leads the reflective listener to conclude that the opening is a depiction of the Hell to which Jesus has descended. These repetitive bars of music bear study, since they involve a descent (to the grave) and the consequent change of direction. The great paradox of death and resurrection is here preached, briefly and in great music. Bach uses extended counterpoint to end both parts of his oratorio, which is certainly a nod in the direction of the established church style, but the interlocking of material in his homophonic "Triumph" choruses spaced throughout the oratorio and the way he builds the long and complex final chorus are unique.

Fine though Emanuel Bach's oratorios are, they have not made a place for themselves in the great repertoire. He himself knew very well how much labor and thought he had put into them, and he was confident, as he wrote to Breitkopf, that they would eventually enjoy success equal to Graun's *Der Tod Jesu*. The result has not been what he hoped for. Very little sacred music composed by minor masters in the second half of the eighteenth century is performed today. It survives only as part of the history of music, providing evidence that many composers preserved their faith in an age of skepticism and were prepared to devote their imagination and skill to the service of the church.

CHAPTER X

Opera

SERIOUS OPERA IN ITALY

The Italian *opera seria* has been characterized as a singer's opera, consisting largely of arias connected by recitatives. While this may be an acceptable generalization, exceptions could be found in Italy before 1760. After that date, however, the exceptions become the rule, affecting the entire complection of the genre.

Italy itself resisted the kind of modifications that were being made to the *opera seria* by Italians in foreign lands. For example, when Jommelli returned home to Naples after working in Germany for fifteen years, his reputation and that of the theater he had directed were such that he was looked upon as the greatest of all opera composers at that time. Yet his last operas, written in and for Naples, were not successful there, since his compatriots found them too complicated, too Germanic. Nevertheless, popular operas traveled freely across borders and from city to city, despite differing tastes. It is reported that when one of Galuppi's *opere serie,* which had been first performed in Vienna, was to be played in Italy, the composer had to substitute arias in place of a quintet that forwarded the action of the opera.

An *opera seria* at this time was not a fixed thing. An opera composed for a certain theater and conducted by the composer might well be substantially different at each performance, as singers demanded that their arias be changed or that arias by other composers replace those originally in the score. The practice of tailoring an opera to suit local conditions became inviolate when a new production of an old opera was mounted in a new location.[1] In the middle of the century the *opera seria*

1. The impossibility of achieving a definitive score, even of an opera of the stature of *Don Giovanni,* provides a useful illustration. After its premiere in Prague in October 1787, Mozart added three numbers for its first performance in Vienna in May 1788. Thus, an opera from the eighteenth century surviving in holograph, one of our main criteria for authenticity, could conceivably convey a false impression since the opera may never have been staged as the holograph preserves it.

was not yet an art form identified by its overall structure, but was, rather, a background for gratification by momentary effects, whether musical or visual.

The great opera composers in this period worked to increase its dramatic content, and demanded that the audience stretch its attention span beyond the momentary effect toward a greater artistic unity. To that end modifications were made. The *da capo* aria was shortened to become a *dal segno* aria. This process involved, at the least, the omission of the introductory ritornello, and frequently reduced the **a** section by half. A change of this sort did not please the singers since the repeat of the first half of the aria was the place where they could most successfully demonstrate their technique, their skill in improvised ornamentation, and their superiority over other singers. Aria forms became more varied. The distinction between the **A** and the **B** section of the *da capo* aria, which was originally emphasized by change of tempo, meter, mode, and key, became less important by 1780; and the **b** section began to resemble the middle (or development) section of an instrumental sonata, often using the same rhythmic motives and tempo as the **a** section. The two-tempo aria, which began with a slow section followed by a fast one, became more popular. The number of ensembles increased ever so slightly. There was also more action taking place in *recitativo stromentato,* as opposed to the *recitativo semplice,* in which the music reinforced the emotive words to move the plot of the opera forward; hence it identified music with the drama. And finally, the treatment of the orchestra moved away from the *ad libitum* traditions of the *continuo* to the *obbligato* orchestration of four staves of strings and winds when required.

In all of Italy, only at the court of Parma was serious opera subjected to an extraordinary force of change. As in Vienna, where political events created a climate in which French influence on theater and opera could develop, so too in Parma under the reign of a Spanish Bourbon. The appointment of a Frenchman as intendant of the royal theaters as well as the prevailing political alignments encouraged artistic inquiry and exploration. Duke Philip appointed Tommaso Traetta as head of his musical establishment in 1758. Present at the court in Parma for many years was the poet Carlo Frugoni (1692–1768), and he and Traetta, under the leadership of the French theater intendant, du Tillet, attempted to amalgamate the respective virtues of the French and the Italian opera. Frugoni translated the text of Rameau's opera *Hippolyte et Aricie* and Traetta set it, using Rameau's music and ideas from time to time. The result was presented in 1759, and it was followed by other adaptations of French *tragédies lyriques* during the early 1760s. The success of Traetta's work in Parma caused his fame to spread, and although he remained in the duke's service until 1765, his new works were created with increasing frequency for centers in the German-speaking world.

Metastasian *opera seria,* adapted to suit the time, the place, and the occasion, remained a strong force in Italy during this period, with important settings of *Alessandro nell'Indie* by Christian Bach (Naples, 1762) and Niccolò Piccinni (1728–1800)(Naples, 1774), *Armida abbandonata* (Naples, 1770) by Jommelli, Hasse's *Ruggiero,* (Milan, 1771), and many more. Indeed, *opera seria* maintained a hold on the stage, increasingly becoming the stuff of court occasions rather than of commercial theater. Attached to high ceremonies, such as coronations, royal weddings, etc., its didactic function could be absorbed within the duties imposed upon the royal actors by the occasion.

THE CHANGING ITALIAN *OPERA BUFFA*

The performance of *La buona figliuola* (The Virtuous Maiden) by Niccolò Piccinni in 1760 in Rome provides a clear line of demarcation between epochs. It demonstrated that the comic opera had superseded the *opera seria,* and that even in conservative Rome old ideals were giving way to new. However, a change in the nature and the subject matter of the *opera buffa* must be noted to account for its universal acceptance.

In the years immediately preceding 1760 a new literary genre had emerged in the novel and the drama. This genre has been called *comédie larmoyante*, or "tearful comedy," and the basis of its popularity was its ability to move the audience to tears one minute and to laughter the next. *La buona figliuola* was written to a libretto by Goldoni, which he himself created based on his adaptation for the theater of a novel by the English author Samuel Richardson (1689–1761) entitled *Pamela, or Virtue Rewarded* (1741). The novel itself had broken new ground in a number of ways: its technique of narrative was conducted through a series of letters written between a maidservant and her father. This technique allowed the main character to develop from the inside, rather than through the eyes of an all-seeing narrator, as was most usual at the time; further, Richardson's characters reveal depths of motivation beyond the event-strewn, picaresque novels of Fielding and Defoe. The virtuous maid is of humble birth and in service, and is pursued by her master; she, however, will not yield and he eventually marries her. Although this summary reduces the novel to absurdity, Richardson's deeply felt, staunchly lived, almost puritanical morality was criticized as promoting licentiousness. But in fact Richardson wanted virtue to be rewarded, in part because Pamela is a "natural" heroine, and in part because through her actions she can cut through class barriers and demonstrate the universality of an ideal humanity. Goldoni's adaptation of this subject into a libretto weakens the didactic purpose of the original by bringing in an external event to solve the operatic problem: Pamela, now turned into Mariandel, is discovered to be the long-lost daughter of a German baron, and therefore she can marry her aristocratic suitor without giving offense to his family.

Example X–1: N. PICCINNI, *La buona figliuola,* Recitative

Piccinni's score made apparent certain attitudes about the kind of music appropriate to the modern, sentimental comedy. First, the movement toward the use of *recitativo stromentato,* which has been observed in the *opera seria,* does not affect *opera buffa,* where *recitativo semplice* or "dry" recitative is used almost exclusively. Moreover, the *recitativo semplice* takes on the tone of a much more rapid conversational interchange than formerly, so that characters can inject humor and acting into their roles. Where accompanied recitative is used, an element of parody is often intended—and indeed, parodying of *opera seria* is constant in the eighteenth-century *opera buffa.* In Example X–2, a peasant, Mengotto, bemoans the apparent loss of his love, Mariandel, to his master. The musical language is that of serious opera and of sincere desperation, but the incongruity between the vulgar earthiness of his metaphor, "Mi ha levato il boccon quasi di bocca" (The dainty morsel has been snatched

Example X–2: N. PICCINNI, *La buona figliuola,* Parody

out of my mouth), and the elevated musical style makes the parodistic intent quite apparent.

The same element is again found in the full *da capo* aria by the Marchesa, who is determined to prevent the marriage between her brother and a servant. This aria has all the characteristics and the coloratura of offended majesty, and it recalls the *aria di bravura* described on p. 92.

The development of the finales at the conclusion of this opera is remarkable. Here there is no question of a simple ending, but clearly the concluding ensemble both mirrors the action and carries it forward, while at the same time the recurrence of material creates a rondo-like effect. This combination of the discursive, continuous movement of the drama and the deliberately repetitive character of the musical material is of the greatest significance for future developments.

Example X–3: N. PICCINNI, *La buona figliuola,* Melody

The basic musical language is revealed in the three-part overture/ symphony, in which the simplest melodic fragment is repeated over drawn-out, basic harmonies. Example X–3 illustrates this melodic characteristic in Mengotto's first aria.

Piccinni's command of melody and accompaniment is shown in a much more sophisticated light in Act II, scene 12 from *La buona figliuola* (*ACM* 22). The heroine, who undergoes severe trials during the course of the opera, sings an apostrophe to Sleep.[2] While she sleeps, her lover and a German soldier appear. The lover leaves the soldier to guard her while she sleeps and he goes to arrange the marriage. In her dream, the heroine imagines the soldier to be her father, and they are observed by two characters who misinterpret what they see. This is the stuff of comedy, of course, but it holds the seeds of further trials for the heroine before all ends happily.

By the end of this period a number of composers were writing *opera*

2. This aria and its connection with sleep and later with dreaming probably had a profound influence on Mozart. From the slow movement of his first symphony, through the G-major Violin Concerto, K.218, to the Piano Concerto in C, K.467, a sequence of great slow movements has been described by Eric Blom as "dream" *Andantes*. Piccinni's heroine may well be the source of the Mozartian dream as well as of Gossec's symphonic slow movement, Op. 6, No. 2, mentioned in the previous chapter.

buffa, but the genre did not enjoy its greatest success until after 1780. However, in the decade of the seventies the early works of Giovanni Paisiello (1740–1816), Pasquale Anfossi (1727–97), Domenico Cimarosa (1749–1801), and Giuseppe Gazzaniga (1743–1818) were gathering increasing popularity that would carry the *opera buffa* triumphantly into the next century.

SERIOUS OPERA OUTSIDE ITALY

VIENNA In the years before 1760, many composers looked with new eyes upon the *opera seria,* imagining how it might be made to accord more closely with modern taste. In no place was the struggle against Metastasian opera more vigorous than in the city where the poet himself lived—Vienna. There, under the influence of Count Giacomo Durazzo a movement to make Italian opera more serious had begun in the 1750s. The first sign of Durazzo's tampering with texts is in the little opera by Gluck entitled *L'innocenza giustificata* (Innocence Justified) of 1755, in which the recitative texts are by Durazzo and the aria texts by Metastasio. This piece has been described as "no longer a conventional spectacle . . . but a musical drama" and "In reality . . . a declaration of war against Metastasio whose operatic ideals it defies at every turn."[3]

In 1761, Traetta's opera *Armida,* to a text which Durazzo had adapted from Quinault's libretto for Lully's *Armide* (1686), was first performed in Vienna. In the same year, the poet Raniero Calzabigi (1714–95), who was to be the librettist of two of Gluck's celebrated reform operas, came to Vienna. He was a typical, classically educated, morally unscrupulous adventurer, who, like his friend Casanova, was ready to turn his hand to anything, and the operas on which he and Gluck collaborated did more to demolish the omnipotence of Metastasian opera than any other single factor.

Christoph Willibald Gluck came of country stock—his father was a forester who achieved a position of some responsibility. Young Gluck made his way to Vienna in 1736 as chamber musician to Prince Lobkowitz. With the permission of his patron, he went to Milan, where he studied with Giovanni Battista Sammartini, composer of symphonies and instrumental music. As has been suggested, the purveyors of the novel, fluent style of the 1730s and 1740s had their own brand of subtlety, unburdened by a profound knowledge of counterpoint or harmony, and Gluck and Sammartini belonged to this new age. Gluck spent the next few years in Italy composing his first operas, which met with some success.[4] In 1745, with his patron, Lobkowitz, he visited

3. Alfred Einstein, *Gluck* (London, 1964), pp. 41–42.

4. His first opera, *Artaserse,* to a libretto by Metastasio, was produced in Milan in 1741.

The Austrian royal family (all in uniform) at a performance of Gluck's *Il Parnasso* in the palace opera theater at Schönbrunn, 1765. The Archduke Leopold may be glimpsed at the harpsichord. (Kunsthistorisches Museum, Vienna)

England, where he produced two operas and evoked from Handel the famous comment that "Gluck knows no more about counterpoint than my cook, Waltz."[5] After further travels in Germany, in 1750 Gluck married a woman who not only brought him happiness but also a sufficient dowry to make him financially independent. Four years after his marriage he was appointed by Durazzo to the court in Vienna "for the composition of theater and concert music," at a generous salary.

It is obvious that Durazzo recognized Gluck's qualities, but not until the appearance of Calzabigi did Gluck find his ideal librettist. Their first work together was the serious Italian opera *Orfeo ed Euridice,* first performed in Vienna in 1762 to immediate acclaim. The opera opens with a surprise—for us although not for Gluck's audience—in that the overture in no way matches the subject of the opera. Like any opera overture of an earlier time, this is a simple *sinfonia avanti l'opera,* but it has only one movement. Also surprising to a modern audience is the fact that the libretto maintains the old tradition of the *lieto fine,* the happy ending of the *opera seria,* despite the fact that so much operatic polemic of the time had inveighed against it. Here, the *deus ex machina* is Cupid,

5. Gustavus Waltz (dates unknown) was a bass singer attached to Handel's household.

who, at the end, descends to make the lovers happy, despite all the force of myth. As soon as the curtain rises upon the funeral rites of Euridice, we, the audience, know that we are in a country only visited before in the imagination. (See *AMC* 23).

As soon as the last notes of the C-major overture have died, the orchestral color is modified by a change to C minor and the introduction of trombones, which symbolically imbue the scene with overtones of death. The chorus expresses restrained grief, and against this sad backdrop the periodic interjections of Orfeo's cries of "Euridice!" form as profound a depiction of human grief as is to be found in the whole of music. The balletic element of this conception is further defined in the short accompanied recitative in which Orfeo asks his friends to sprinkle their flowers on the marble tomb and to leave him alone with his grief. The *Ballo* following requires sensitive choreography, and the effect of solemn rite is further enhanced. The repetition of the opening chorus reinforces the structure and properly concludes the ceremony that we have just witnessed. All has been measured and restrained with no element of the discursive to distract the attention. What then follows is a three-part lament by Orfeo, broken by interspersed recitative. The shaping of the melodic line according to the words and their meaning, and the use of a second orchestra to throw back an echo, emphasizing Orfeo's aloneness, show the difference between the older *opera seria* and the reformed opera: on one hand, the hasty composition of arias designed as much to feature the singers' *ad libitum* ornamentation as the overall emotional impact of the text, and on the other, the careful calculation that matches each dramatic situation with the uniquely appropriate musical setting. The whole score abounds with imaginative felicities in the use of instruments and, *mutatis mutandis,* seems closer to Boccherini and his sense of color than to anyone else.[6]

Gluck and Calzabigi collaborated twice more: in 1767 they produced the opera *Alceste* and in 1770 *Paride ed Elena. Alceste* was published in 1769, and to the printed score was added a dedication which has become one of the most celebrated documents of the eighteenth-century movement of operatic reform. Gluck wrote as follows:

> Royal Highness!
>
> When I began to write the music for *Alceste,* I resolved to free it from all the abuses which have crept in either through ill-advised vanity on the part of the singers or through excessive complaisance on the part of composers, with the result that for some time Italian opera has been disfigured and from being the most splendid and most beautiful of all stage performances has been made the most ridiculous and the most wearisome. I sought to restrict the music to its true purpose of serving to give expression to the

6. The year before *Orfeo* Gluck had produced a ballet on the subject of Don Juan and hence had already experimented with relating his music to a visual effect.

poetry and to strengthen the dramatic situations, without interrupting the action or hampering it with unnecessary and superfluous ornamentations. I believed that it should achieve the same effect as lively colors and a well-balanced contrast of light and shade on a very correct and well-disposed painting, so animating the figures without altering their contours. So I have tried to avoid interrupting an actor in the warmth of dialogue with a boring intermezzo or stopping him in the midst of his discourse, merely so that the flexibility of his voice might show to advantage in a long passage, or that the orchestra might give him time to collect his breath for a cadenza. I did not think I should hurry quickly through the second part of an air, which is perhaps the most passionate and most important, in order to have room to repeat the words of the first part regularly four times or to end the aria quite regardless of its meaning, in order to give the singer an opportunity of showing how he can render a passage with so-and-so many variations at will; in short, I have sought to eliminate all these abuses, against which sound common sense and reason have so long protested in vain.

I imagined that the overture should prepare the spectators for the action, which is to be presented, and give an indication of its subject; that the instrumental music should vary according to the interest and passion aroused, and that between the aria and the recitative there should not be too great a disparity, lest the flow of the period be spoiled and rendered meaningless, the movement be interrupted inopportunely, or the warmth of the action be dissipated. I believed further that I should devote my greatest effort to seeking to achieve a noble simplicity; and I have avoided parading difficulties at the expense of clarity. I have not placed any value on novelty, if it did not emerge naturally from the situation and the expression; and there is no rule I would not have felt in duty bound to break in order to achieve the desired effect.

These are my principles. Happily all my intentions fitted admirably with the libretto, in which the famous author [Calzabigi], having devised a new plan for the lyrical drama, had replaced florid descriptions, superfluous comparisons, sententious and frigid moralisation with the language of the heart, with strong passions, interesting situations and an ever-varied spectacle. My maxims have been vindicated by success, and the universal approval expressed in such an enlightened city [Vienna] has convinced me that simplicity, truth and lack of affectation are the sole principles of beauty in all artistic creations. None the less, in spite of repeated demands by the most respectable persons that I should decide to publish this opera of mine in print, I have realized how much danger lies in fighting against such widespread and deep-rooted prejudices, and I have found it necessary to avail myself in advance of the powerful protection of Your Royal Highness by imploring the favor of prefixing my opera with His August Name, which so justly carries with it the approval of all enlightened Europe. The great protector of the fine arts, who rules over a nation which is famed for having freed them from universal oppression and for having set in each of them the finest examples, in a city which has always been the first to break the yoke of vulgar prejudice and pave the way to perfection, can alone

> undertake the reform of this noble spectacle, in which all the fine arts play such a large part. When this has been accomplished, I shall have the glory of having moved the first stone, and this public testimony of Your Highness's protection, for which I have the honor to declare myself with the most humble respect
>
> Your Royal Highness's
> Most humble, most devoted,
> Most dutiful servant
> Christoph Gluck[7]

In Vienna the career of Antonio Salieri (1750–1825) was beginning to gather momentum. A pupil of Gassmann, he met Gluck in 1769 and gained that man's friendship and patronage. When Gassmann died in 1774, Salieri succeeded to his post and at the age of twenty-four found himself in charge of the Italian opera at the court of Vienna. His own earliest operas were comic, but in 1771 he wrote his first serious opera, *Armida,* to a libretto of Marco Coltellini (1719–99). In this work he acknowledged his heritage from his musical father, Gluck: choruses are active and recitative is explicit in its notation and full orchestration, i.e., it is *recitativo stromentato.*

STUTTGART One other German center is of particular importance in the growth of serious opera. At the same time as Gluck, Durazzo, and Calzabigi were working in Vienna, opera was being created at the court of Karl-Eugen, Duke of Württemberg, in Stuttgart to rival any in Europe The duke had lived in Berlin in the early years of Frederick the Great's reign and had taken lessons from Emanuel Bach. He determined to make Stuttgart the home of Europe's finest talents, and appointed Niccolò Jommelli his *Ober-Kapellmeister* in 1754, and Jean-Georges Noverre (1727–1810) master of his ballet in 1760. Following the trend to incorporate techniques drawn from French opera, Jommelli used choruses, ensembles, and accompanied recitative to build complex structures, and with the encouragement of the duke, he enlarged the orchestra at his disposal and used it to such notable effect that it is reported he overwhelmed the audience.

In this period a strong movement to encourage and develop serious opera in German arose, with the courts of Weimar and Gotha in the lead. The composer Anton Schweitzer (1735–87) and the poet Christoph Wieland (1733–1813), both resident in Weimar under the patronage of the grand duke, produced an opera on the subject of *Alceste.* Its success, despite trenchant criticism, led to the writing of *Günther von Schwarzburg* (1777) by Ignaz Holzbauer, the court conductor in Mann-

7. This translation of the Preface is by Stewart Thomson and is to be found in Christoph Willibald Gluck, *The Collected Correspondence and Papers of C. W.Gluck,* ed. Hedwig and E. H. Mueller von Asow (London, 1962), pp. 22–24.

heim. This work reflects Holzbauer's wide experience as a composer in all fields of chamber, theater and church music, and as an opera conductor as well. Using all devices of the *opera seria,* he creates a rich score which mirrors the drama in its expression and in its forms. That keen critic Mozart wrote to his father:

> Now for the opera, but quite briefly. Holzbauer's music is very beautiful. The poetry doesn't deserve such music. What surprises me most of all is that a man as old as Holzbauer [he was 66] should still possess so much spirit; for you can't imagine what fire there is in that music. (*Letters,* 14 Nov. 1777)

One development related to serious opera in German must be noted, although it has to do with the speaking rather than the singing voice. In 1770, Rousseau had experimented with a combination of music and the spoken word in a *scène lyrique* entitled *Pygmalion.* The experiment was eagerly taken up and called "melodrama," its chief exponent being Jiri Benda, at this time Kapellmeister to the court at Gotha. His first melodrama, entitled *Ariadne auf Naxos* (1775), and several subsequent works set the musical world talking. Even Mozart was enthralled by the idea that the music could flow along its own course, pausing from time to time to allow the spoken word to penetrate, or provide a backdrop for it, recognizing in this technique an extension of accompanied recitative.[8] (See *ACM* 24)

Benda's excellent work was emulated by a number of minor masters and the principle behind melodrama—that of obtaining ever more vivid representation and communication of the idea—remains fundamental to all serious opera of the nineteenth century.

LONDON In London, where forty years earlier the *opera seria* had been all the rage, the years 1760–80 saw Metastasian opera stage some-

8. On 12 November 1778, Mozart wrote to his father from Mannheim: [Herr von Dalberg] refuses to let me go until I have composed a duodrama for him; and indeed it did not take me long to make up my mind, for I have always wanted to write a drama of this kind. I cannot remember whether I told you anything about this type of drama the first time I was here? On that occasion I saw a piece of this kind performed twice and was absolutely delighted. Indeed, nothing has ever surprised me so much, for I had always imagined that such a piece would be quite ineffective! You know, of course, that there is no singing in it, only recitation, to which the music is like a sort of obbligato accompaniment to a recitative. Now and then words are spoken while the music goes on, and this produces the finest effect. The piece I saw was Benda's *Medea.* He has composed another one, *Ariadne auf Naxos,* and both are really excellent. You know that of all the Lutheran Kapellmeisters Benda has always been my favorite, and I like those two works of his so much that I carry them about with me. Well, imagine my joy at having to compose just the kind of work I have so much desired! Do you know what I think? I think that most operatic recitatives should be treated in this way—and only sung occasionally, when the words can be perfectly expressed by the music."
The following year he experimented with the technique in his unfinished opera, *Zaide* (1779). Having tried it once, he never touched it again.

The opera theater occasionally provided unexpected entertainment. In 1763, the audience at Covent Garden in London rioted during a performance of Arne's *Artaxerxes,* when the manager of the theater refused to admit some of the public at half price.

thing of a comeback. The urge to have a serious opera in English bore fruit not in the works of Handel, as Aaron Hill had suggested it might, but in the works of Thomas Augustine Arne, who in 1762 produced *Artaxerxes* at Covent Garden. The composer translated Metastasio's famous libretto of 1729 into English for this opera. The work achieved considerable success and some of the numbers from it survived in the vocal repertoire long after the opera was quite forgotten; of these "Water parted from the Sea" is the most notable. Arne lavished careful attention on this opera, but its popularity was not sufficient inducement to commit himself similarly again. Although there were a few attempts to travel the same path, they met with no success, and the Englishing of Italian opera ceased to have any attraction. Instead, Arne next composed a setting of Metastasio's *Olimpiade* in Italian. But any Italian opera not written by an Italian could not succeed, and even Christian Bach, whose Italian operas were highly successful in Italy, found himself having to turn to instrumental rather than operatic composition when he settled in London. Much better received was Antonio Sacchini (1730–86), an Italian trained in Naples whose career had already taken him throughout Italy and thence to Germany. In 1772 he moved to London and established himself as an opera composer, despite difficulties reported by Burney as follows:

> Millico [a *castrato* and composer who had just appeared in London] . . . found the musical part of our nation in no favourable disposition towards him. The admirers of Tenducci and Guadagni, as well as the Cocchi, Gug-

> lielmi, Giardini, Vento and Bach parties, however hostile in other particulars, all agreed in decrying every part of that opera in which their favourite had no concern. SACCHINI, who arrived here soon after, was involved in their cabals. None of the friends of their predecessors would allow that Millico could sing or the new master compose. Violent and virulent means were used to poison, or at least to shut the ears of the unprejudiced public, but not with much success . . . at length, Sacchini's compositions were generally allowed to be admirable . . . and at the end of the next season, several who had boldly pronounced that neither Sacchini could compose nor Millico sing, would have given a hundred pounds if they could have recalled their words, or made their acquaintance forget they had been guilty of such manifest injustice and absurdity.[9]

Sacchini worked with great success during his ten years in England. So firmly established was his reputation that the arrival of Traetta in 1776 made no impression. Again in the words of Burney:

> In 1776, a new Neapolitan composer was engaged for the opera, Signor TOMMASO TRAETTA; but, though an able master of great reputation, he arrived here too late: for Sacchini had already taken possession of our hearts, and so firmly established himself in the public favour, that he was not to be supplanted by a composer in the same style, neither so young, so graceful, or so fanciful as himself.[10]

But in 1781 Sacchini's debts forced him to flee to France, where he enjoyed the favor of Marie-Antoinette and where he played a minor part in the battle between Piccinni and Gluck.

PARIS Serious opera in Paris was not really at issue in 1752 in the *Querelle des Bouffons,* when the rivalry between Italian comic opera and the old French *tragédie lyrique* began. At the time, there seemed to be no real issues at stake, but gradually, Rousseau's polemic against the French language as a poor medium for setting to music gained an increasing number of converts. The influence upon Parisian musical life of the German instrumental composers, especially Johann Stamitz, has already been noted, and it would appear that the City of Light was ripe to receive the kinds of reform that Durazzo, Calzabigi, and Gluck had introduced in Vienna. An attaché to the French Embassy in Vienna, François du Roullet (1716–86), determined to prove Rousseau wrong, made an adaptation of Racine's tragedy *Iphigénie en Aulide,* and interested Gluck in setting it. As Gluck had attacked Metastasio in Vienna, he now proposed to attack Rousseau in Paris, and he made his preparations with care. Through a correspondence in the *Mercure de France,* a situation was created in which the direction of the Paris Opéra could not refuse to stage the opera which Gluck had written without seeming unpatriotic. The reply from the Opéra was clever. Knowing that Gluck

9. Burney, *op. cit.,* pp. 877–78.
10. *Ibid.,* p. 883.

Design by Boquet (or his school) of a costume for the first performance of Gluck's *Iphigénie en Aulide* in 1774. (Paris: Bibliothèque de l'Opéra)

was of an advanced age, they replied that since the opera was so good that it would sweep all others from the stage, they could accept it only if the composer promised to compose six more in the same style. Gluck accepted the challenge. And he did so knowing, as he said, that it "is assuredly a bold undertaking and there will be serious obstacles, for we must face up to the national prejudice against which reason is of no avail."[11] There is no doubt that Gluck and du Roullet were also relying on help from the dauphine, Marie-Antoinette, who had known Gluck in the old days in Vienna.

Iphigénie en Aulide was first presented at the Opéra on 19 April 1774, and was well received, but the death of Louis XV three weeks later brought about a period of mourning which prevented further performances. It also meant that Gluck's protectress was now queen of France. During this period of enforced idleness, Gluck worked on a French version of *Orfeo ed Euridice,* without *castrati.* This was presented in August

11. For a full acount of the intrigue surrounding Gluck in Paris, see *The Collected Correspondence and Papers . . .* cited in footnote 7 above.

and was very successful. Gluck consolidated his position in Paris by dedicating these two works to the new king and queen respectively.

A pair of operas were planned on the related subjects of *Armida* and *Roland* to librettos by Quinault that had first been set by Lully in 1685 and 1686. But by this time intrigues against Gluck had begun to arise, and undoubtedly the queen's support became a liability in some quarters, since she was unjustly identified with the unpopular alliance between Austria and France. Without Gluck's knowledge, the libretto for *Roland,* which he had been working on, was given to Niccolò Piccinni. Here would have been the perfect scenario for the most virulent artistic war Paris had ever seen: the Italian, Piccinni, and the international German, Gluck, both famous and of equal status, having set the same libretto. Gluck, however, was no fool, and as soon as he learned that Piccinni had the libretto for *Roland* he destroyed what he had done, for, as he wrote to du Roullet in 1776, Piccinni, personal merit aside, "would have the advantage of novelty, for Paris has already had from me four operas—whether good or bad matters not." The war over the comparative merits of Gluck and Piccinni raged in Paris for a while, but neither of the principals did anything to fuel it since they behaved to each other with generosity and humanity.

Gluck wrote two more operas for Paris, *Iphigénie en Tauride* (1779) and *Echo et Narcisse* (1779), the final products of his creative life. *Echo et Narcisse* failed, but with *Iphigénie* he achieved his greatest dramatic success, and although Piccinni produced an opera on the same subject to a different libretto, Gluck's popularity was not affected. After suffering several strokes, Gluck returned to Vienna, where he contemplated writing a new opera for Naples. He may even have started work on *Les Danaïdes* to a libretto by Calzabigi, but after the work's twelfth successful performance he announced to the public that the music was entirely that of Salieri, thus virtually naming the younger composer his creative heir.

Gluck's achievement can best be measured by pointing out that his operas of the 1770s are the direct forerunners of Wagner's works of the 1850s. Even the arch-Romantic, Hector Berlioz, was fanatical in his worship of this immortal master of the musical theater.

COMIC OPERA IN FRANCE

In the aftermath of the *Querelle des Bouffons* in Paris several things became apparent. First, the nature of drama had changed all over Europe, and it was now no longer deemed necessary for a drama to have a historical or mythological subject. Human characters in natural situations were seen to have not only the power to generate dramatic situations and human sympathy but also the capacity for social criticism consonant with that being carried on in other areas of society. The comic opera, like the pictures of Chardin, was perceived to be something at the heart of the political and intellectual ferment of the time. As the comic opera moved away from its humbler origins in the Théâtres de la Foire, its substance moved away from farce and slapstick to take on the bitter-sweet taste of a mixed genre—a comedy with deeper shades and serious characters who excite pathos, admiration, and empathy as well as laughter and ridicule.

These works were simple structures lightly scored and primarily for solo voices. Ensembles, which are not essential to the style, are only sometimes included. Around 1760 the works of three composers dominated the stage of the *opéra comique* in Paris. The Italian Romualdo Egidio Duni (1708–75), who, before coming to Paris had been *maestro di capella* to the court at Parma, where he had been thoroughly exposed to the French influence, was the first to combine elements of Italian musical style with a French libretto in order to popularize the new genre; he also adapted Goldoni to the French stage. He was joined by François André Danican Philidor, a member of the important French family of musicians and a distinguished chess player, still remembered in the game by a defensive move named after him. Philidor produced a steady stream of *opéras comiques* during the 1760s. His *Tom Jones,* adapted from Fielding's novel, was staged in 1765 and is a good model. It is in three acts, each containing approximately seven numbers separated by spoken dialogue. Of twenty-two numbers, four are duets and there is a septet at the end of the second act in which the various characters express different responses to the situation. A concluding ensemble is preceded by a "vaudeville" in which successive characters sing a verse of the text set to a simple and catchy tune. The atypical "Drunkards' Quartet" is a kind of glee sung by four unaccompanied voices. The piece is a late eighteenth-century parallel to Purcell's catches, and is undoubtedly intended to poke fun at the English. More important, it is the first time an ensemble for unaccompanied voices has been introduced into an opera.

Pierre Alexandre Monsigny (1729–1817) came onto the scene in 1761 with two works, *Le Cadi dupé,* which Gluck was also to set in the same year, and *On ne s'avise jamais de tout* (You can never think of everything). His most important work was *Le Déserteur* (1769), which, for a comic opera, presented an unusually strong dramatic situation.

In the late 1760s André Grétry (1741–1813) arrived in Paris and rapidly became the most important figure on the French musical stage, displacing both Philidor and Monsigny in public favor. What propelled him to these unexpected heights was a rare melodic gift through which, as has been said, "he catches the expression, the tone, the pace, and the weight of a character to perfection." He produced a series of popular works during the 1770s and 1780s and then was largely forgotten as public demand required music of greater inventiveness and complexity.

COMIC OPERA IN LONDON

The Beggar's Opera continued to hold the stage in London, but following Italian fashion, the newer works were populated by ordinary characters with ordinary voices. It is noteworthy, however, that in adapting both Galuppi's *Il filosofo di campagna* and Piccinni's *La buona figliuola* for the English stage, spoken dialogue was substituted for the sung recitative, and English opera has ever since had a predilection for the mixture of the sung and the spoken word. Despite the everyday characters on stage, plots tended to fall back on happy endings, as in *La buona figliuola*.

On the London stage at this time it was customary to present a full-length play or opera and to follow it with a short, one-act "afterpiece." This afterpiece may be considered the English counterpart to the Italian *intermezzo,* placed at the end rather than between the acts, and the custom is responsible for the large numbers of short theatrical pieces that were written during this period, the most famous of which is Arne's *Thomas and Sally* (1760).

In 1762 Thomas Arne and Isaac Bickerstaffe (1735–?), perhaps the most important English librettist of the second half of the century, produced an opera called *Love in a Village.* A full-length work in three acts, it was a pastiche—a "ballad" opera—but with some differences. While some of the songs were of the ballad type—strophic with slight accompaniments—the majority were fully orchestrated, taken from other works together with their instrumental preludes and postludes. Arne and Bickerstaffe put the work together from a variety of sources. Six numbers by Arne were new and twelve were taken from works he had previously composed. The works in the other half of the opera were taken from several other composers, with Abel writing a new, specially commissioned overture for the show.

This opera had an immense success, and has been revived in the present century. It also spawned a host of imitations. Two of these, *Love in the City* (1767), which failed, and *Lionel and Clarissa* (1768), which succeeded, were also Bickerstaffe's work, this time in collaboration with Charles Dibdin (1745–1814), whose melodic gifts and sense of the dramatic made him a dominant figure in English musical theater during the whole of the second half of the century.

COMIC OPERA IN GERMANY

The Devil to Pay, a ballad opera (already referred to on p. 105) with text by Charles Coffey, first staged in London in 1731, was such a success that it was translated into German and staged in Berlin in 1743, probably with the original music assembled from various sources. An adaptation of this work, with text by Christian Felix Weisse (1726–1804) and music by Johann C. Standfuss (died after 1759) was staged in Leipzig in 1752, and although the original music is lost, the work survives in a version which J. A. Hiller presented in Leipzig in 1766. Hiller, conductor of the Leipzig *Gewandhaus* concerts, was also a composer. Indeed, his opera *Die Jagd* (The Hunt; 1770) was received as an ideal by a public eager for German theater works, and it retained its great popularity until it was displaced by Weber's *Der Freischütz* (1821). Hiller's style consisted of a mixture in which simple strophic songs of folklike character predominate in a score that includes many fine ensembles. His major achievement was in elevating the German *Singspiel* from the lowest level of popular entertainment to the point where good singers could find musical rewards in the score, and cultivated bourgeois might feel comfortable taking their daughters to the theater. He achieved this primarily through his simple and pure melodic style, which so often harks back to national folksong. The following example is the melody of one of the songs, which, like Papageno's music in Mozart's *Zauberflöte,* lends itself to whistling:

Example X–4: J. A. HILLER, *Die Jagd,* folklike melody

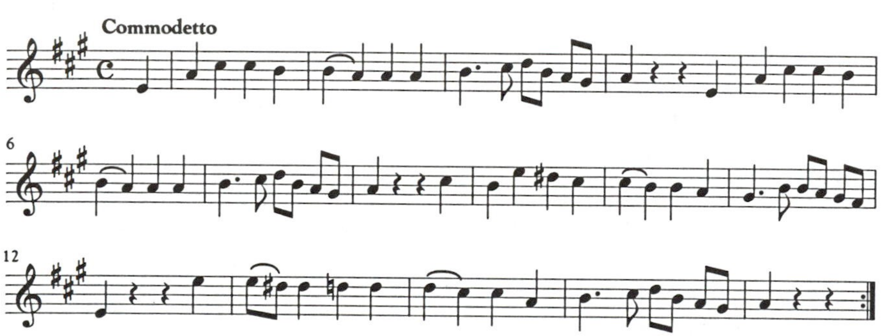

In the southern German-speaking lands, the Emperor Joseph II founded a national opera in 1778 at the Burgtheater in Vienna. Although this endeavor was short-lived, lasting barely five years, it nevertheless provided an enormous stimulus to German opera composers, and led eventually to the main developments of Viennese *Singspiel* in the last two decades of the century.

PART III

Haydn, the Developing Master

CHAPTER XI

The Early Years: 1732–60

Looking back, Bach and Handel seem to have dominated the world of music in the first half of the eighteenth century, while Haydn and Mozart towered over the second half. This view has not always obtained, however, and few connoisseurs in the eighteenth century would have included either Bach or Mozart among the immortals. Although today we are acutely aware of the similarities between these pairs, their contemporaries saw only their differences, and acknowledged those differences by appreciating one and ignoring the other. As we come to understand Haydn and Mozart better, we can more readily perceive that they actually had little in common except contemporaneity, surpassing excellence, and the highest mutual regard.

It is a striking testimony to the egalitarian ideals of the time that Franz Joseph Haydn, who embodied in his melodies and rhythms so much from folksong and peasant dance, should nevertheless become the darling of high society wherever he encountered it. For the folksong and the popular dance tune, not the sonata or the fugue, were the substance of his earliest musical experience, and Haydn carried those memories with him into old age. Indeed, when he could have claimed to be the most honored and best-known composer in Europe, he often reflected on his humble beginnings, setting them into clearer focus with justifiable pride, for he is reported as saying, "Young people can see from my example that something still may come from nothing. What I am today, moreover, is the product of utmost poverty."[1]

His fame was such that during the last years of his life, no less than three writers began to question Haydn closely and to collect his reminiscences with a view to writing his biography. Characteristically, Haydn could not be brought to believe that his life story might be of interest to anyone. The first aspiring biographer, Giuseppe Carpani (1752–1825), was an Italian who moved to Vienna in 1796 and came to know Haydn at that time. In 1812 he published his account of the late composer in

1. Dies, *Biographische Nachrichten von Joseph Haydn,* pp. 80–81.

the form of a series of letters entitled *Le Haydine*. The next, Georg August Griesinger (d. 1828), was sent to Haydn in 1799 by the publishing firm of Breitkopf und Härtel to consolidate a business relationship between the company and the composer. His *Biographische Notizen über Joseph Haydn* (Biographical Notes on Joseph Haydn) was published in 1810. And lastly, Albert Christoph Dies (1755–1822), alone among the three, was introduced to Haydn in 1805 for the express purpose of writing his biography. He carried out his task conscientiously, and his *Biographische Nachrichten von Joseph Haydn* (Biographical Information on Joseph Haydn) was also published in 1810.[2] It is a pity that by the time Dies met Haydn, the composer had become infirm and was often subject to periods of lethargy and apathy from which he had to be roused. Dies developed a rare ability to help the old man on, but at times even he failed.

EARLY LIFE

Most subsequent biographies have depended on the work of these three men for the wealth of anecdote that surrounds the composer. Griesinger wrote:

> Joseph Haydn was born on March 31, 1732, at Rohrau, a village in Lower Austria, in the district of Unter Wiener Wald near the Hungarian border, not far from the town of Bruck an der Leitha. Of the twenty children from two marriages of his father Mathias, a cartwright by profession, Joseph was the eldest. The father had seen a bit of the world, as was customary in his trade, and during his stay in Frankfurt am Main had learned to strum the harp. As a master craftsman in Rohrau he continued to practice this instrument for pleasure after work. Nature, moreover, had endowed him with a good tenor voice, and his wife, Anne Marie, used to sing to the harp. The melodies of these songs were so deeply stamped in Joseph Haydn's memory that he could still recall them in advanced old age.[3]

Dies's account of the composer's beginnings is so nearly identical that one can only wonder how many times the old man must have repeated the story.

The composer's mother was deeply religious and when little Joseph showed precocious signs of intelligence, she conceived the hope that he might make a career in the Church, and indeed his unswerving faith remained a fundamental aspect of his character throughout his life. His musical talent showed itself in so pronounced a manner that his parents were persuaded to allow the child to lodge in the house of a cousin,

2. Good translations of both Griesinger and Dies are to be found in: Vernon Gotwals, *Joseph Haydn: Eighteenth-Century Gentleman and Genius* (Madison, Wis., 1963), and it is to this edition and translation that all references are made.

3. Griesinger, *op. cit.*, pp. 8–9.

who was schoolmaster and precentor of the church in the larger town of Hainburg. So, before reaching the age of six,[4] the future composer left his parents' house forever to face the world, and develop the independence of spirit, the adaptability, the tact, and diplomacy that would characterize his future.

In Hainburg, young Haydn received instruction in reading, writing, and catechism, as well as singing and many string and wind instruments. Looking back on these three hard years spent with cousin Franck, old Haydn was not bitter at his lot. Griesinger reports that he often repeated: "I shall owe it to this man, even in my grave, that he set me so many different things, although I received in the process more thrashings than food."

At the age of eight, he was moved to the choir school of St. Stephen's Cathedral, the major church of the Austrian capital city of Vienna, where he was to remain until his voice broke. The choirmaster of St. Stephen's, Georg Reutter, himself a successful composer, taught Haydn little except how to live with hunger and that in his own talent lay the solution to that problem. For the first five years the boy was more and more in demand as soloist, but in 1745 his position was taken over by his younger brother, Michael, who, when he went to St. Stephen's, appeared to be the more promising of the two. With the onset of puberty Joseph's voice deteriorated and he was no longer allowed to sing solo. Dies reports that the Empress Maria Theresa complained: "Joseph Haydn doesn't sing any more; he crows."[5] The blow fell in 1749, when, at the age of 17, the boy was caught in a silly practical joke and was expelled: "helpless, without money, outfitted with three miserable shirts and a worn-out coat . . ."[6] The month was November and winters in Vienna are cold.

Chance put a roof over his head, and for a while he shared the garret of a young married couple and their baby, earning whatever he could by giving lessons and playing in serenades.[7] When circumstances improved some time later, Haydn moved into his own garret, where ". . . the rain of summer or the snow of winter drove through the chinks in his attic and he awoke soaked through or covered with snow."[8] However, in his own words, "when I was sitting at my old worm-eaten clavier, I envied no king his lot."[9] All his spare time was spent

4. The actual date of Haydn's departure for Hainburg is not known. Griesinger says it was in his sixth year, and Dies says that he had passed the age of six.

5. Dies, *op.cit.*, p. 88.

6. *Ibid.*, p. 89.

7. "Serenade" is a term that was used to signify (a) the open-air concert performed in the evening in front of a house belonging to someone to whom a compliment is being paid; (b) the group of musicians employed for such a purpose; or (c) the actual composition written to be played in such circumstances.

8. Dies, *op. cit.*, p. 91.

9. Griesinger, *op. cit.*, p. 12.

studying. He was self-taught and never received more than the most perfunctory training in the theory of music. We are told that among the works he used were *Gradus ad Parnassum* (Steps to Parnassus; 1725) of Johann Joseph Fux (1660–1741), and *Der volkommene Capellmeister* (1739) of Johann Mattheson. He also obtained Emanuel Bach's *Essay* (Part I; 1753) shortly after it was published and held it in the highest esteem. Perhaps most important of all was his exploration of the early published sonatas of Emanuel Bach. It is always assumed that he knew only the *Prussian* sonatas of 1742, but he may have been familiar with the *Württemberg* set of 1744 as well. Haydn said to Griesinger:

> I did not come away from my clavier till I had played through them, and whoever knows me thoroughly must discover that I owe a great deal to Emanuel Bach, that I understood him, and have studied him diligently. Emanuel Bach once made me a compliment on this score himself.[10]

Around this time, Haydn was engaged to give piano lessons to a young protégée of Metastasio. Through this association, Haydn came to know Nicola Porpora, the teacher of some of the greatest singers in history and a renowned composer. He recognized that he had much to learn from Porpora, so he persuaded that bad-tempered old man to employ him as accompanist for his pupils. The job brought him many insults, little money, much musical experience, and fluency in Italian. In addition, he met many of the most important musical figures of Vienna.

COMPOSITIONS

It is not known exactly when Haydn began to compose, but it is probable that his expulsion from the choir of St. Stephen's in 1749 provided a strong stimulus in that direction. In an autobiographical sketch written in 1776, he says that after St. Stephen's he "eked out a wretched existence for eight whole years [until *c.*1757] by teaching young pupils." He adds that in his zeal for composition during this time he would write "well into the night." Although his first datable compositions come from the mid-1750s, it is most likely that his reputation as a composer began to build earlier in the decade. Gradually the conditions of Haydn's life improved as he became better known and as his compositions circulated. His first string quartets were received with as much enthusiasm by amateur musicians as they were criticized by pedantic theoreticians. His earliest attempt at opera, *Der krumme Teufel* (The Crooked Devil), now unfortunately lost, was also very successful. Finally, in 1759, Haydn received his first professional appointment: he was named music director to one Count Morzin, at a salary of 200 gulden plus free room and

10. *Ibid.*, p. 12.

board. The count had a small orchestra of about sixteen musicians, for which Haydn composed his first symphony.[11] At its first performance the symphony created a particularly favorable impression on one member of the audience, Prince Anton Esterházy. It was not long before Count Morzin had to disband his orchestra for lack of money, and Haydn found himself once again out of a job after only twelve months of secure employment. The year 1760 was such an important watershed in Haydn's creative life that it is well to interrupt the narrative here in order to inspect his output up to this point.[12]

KEYBOARD SONATAS There are perhaps eighteen complete keyboard sonatas remaining in their entirety from this early period up to 1760. None can be dated with any more certainty than "before 1766" though we may conjecture that most of them date from before 1760, when most of Haydn's income came from the piano lessons he gave. The autographs have disappeared because Haydn gave away his manuscripts to his friends and pupils, without keeping records of their existence. We are fortunate that so many have survived in handwritten copies,

11. Griesinger, on Haydn's authority, quotes the opening of the symphony generally called No.1. Some doubt has been expressed whether this work is actually the first symphony that Haydn ever wrote.

12. There is still no complete Haydn edition. One was first begun in 1907 but only ten volumes were issued. Another attempt was made by the Boston Haydn edition of the 1950s, which issued four volumes of scores and a number of recordings. Now, a third attempt by the Haydn Institute of Cologne looks as though it will eventually achieve its goal—nearly 200 years after the composer's death. Anthony van Hoboken (1887–1983) completed the formidable task of compiling a catalogue of Haydn's works, and his scheme of numbering is now generally used to identify each composition. The number consists of two parts: a Roman numeral which refers to a category of work (symphony, quartet, concerto, etc.) and an Arabic numeral which identifies, when possible, a chronological ordering within a category. Thus, Hob. XVI:49 identifies the 49th work in the sixteenth series, the piano sonatas, of the Hoboken catalogue.

Why should the essential task of cataloguing this composer's work be so difficult, and why should the achievement of a complete edition be so delayed? The quick answer is that Haydn's compositions were so popular that authentic compositions have come down to us in a number of copyists' hands, or in a range of printed sources embodying variant readings, and autograph manuscripts have not often survived; in addition, the last quarter of the eighteenth century saw an enormous number of works by other composers put into print under Haydn's name. The composer himself occasionally made the situation still more complicated by selling the same work to different publishers, and was not above some sharp practice, as the following story makes clear. In 1787, a certain prince requested three symphonies for his own exclusive use; Haydn accepted the commission, making it clear that he was very busy. Later in that year, he wrote a letter explaining that he had such eye troubles that the symphonies were not in his own hand, but in the hands of a number of copyists. The prince sent Haydn a gold snuff box stuffed full of gold ducats, little suspecting that he had received, most probably, works that the composer had already sent to Paris in fulfillment of another commission. It can therefore be seen that there are problems in determining the authenticity of many works and still further problems in deciding which edition of the clearly authentic works is the most trustworthy. The Hoboken catalogue, imperfect though it is in certain respects, has laid a solid foundation upon which subsequent research can be based.

for we know of at least seven other keyboard sonatas that Haydn listed in his own catalogue with their incipits, which appear to have disappeared forever, unless some happy accident brings them to light.

Some of the surviving sonatas are extended works in which a great variety of forms and textures are employed; some call upon almost as much keyboard technique as Haydn ever acquired—he was no virtuoso on any instrument although a competent keyboard player and an excellent violinist—and some are short and deliberately simple. These small sonatas are written in the "easy" keys of F, C, G and D whereas most of the bigger, more complex works are written in B♭, E♭, A, and E, further strengthening the theory that the degree of complexity is more closely related to the proficiency of Haydn's pupils than to the exact date of their composition. Most are in three movements, a fast first movement, followed by a Minuet and Trio, concluding with a *Presto* or an *Allegro*. In four cases a slow middle movement marked *Largo* or *Andante* is followed by a concluding Minuet and Trio. Two sonatas have two movements—a fast movement followed by a Minuet—and two sonatas have four movements in the order F/Minuet/S/F.

These works reflected the stylistic influence of Haydn's Viennese contemporaries, such as Wagenseil, more clearly than that of Emanuel Bach. Haydn avoided the minor mode as tonic, like Wagenseil and unlike Bach. Haydn and Wagenseil tended, with few exceptions, to set all movements in the same key like a suite, while Bach invariably wrote the outer movements in the same key and changed either the tonic or the mode for the middle movement. Haydn invariably inserted a minuet with a trio in tonic minor (occasionally in relative minor) like Wagenseil; on the other hand, Bach never used the minuet in a sonata or made overt reference to the dance, apart from the *Siciliano*. Like Wagenseil, Haydn notated the C-minor Trios to his C-major Minuets with two flats in the key signature instead of three.[13] Finally, Haydn tended to use of sonata form in last movements as well as first movements, whereas Bach used simpler, more balanced binary structures for his last movements.

Most of Haydn's first movements show a tripartite sonata form, although Hob. XVI:5, 6, 1, and 3 may be perceived as rounded binary structures. It is clear that within these movements, Haydn was experimenting with a variety of ideas, some of which are never repeated. In Hob. XVI:13, he emphasized the tonic key (E) seven bars into a development which opens with six bars of dominant pedal. Only after 14 bars does he move to the relative minor (C♯ minor) for three bars before preparing the tonic for a complete recapitulation. This relatively rare

13. This practice, common in minor-mode works of the seventeenth and early eighteenth centuries, represents a survival of the major sixth degree from the Dorian mode.

device of an early return to the tonic is a stylistic feature which inevitably indicates, in Haydn's work, an early date of composition.

Hob. XVI:G1 (*ACM* 25) is an early illustration of the strong feeling of cohesiveness—of all the parts belonging to the whole—that is so characteristic of Haydn's work. The powerful downward impulse of the opening motivic gesture is reiterated at the beginning of the second tonal area (m. 13) after which balance is achieved in the opposite motion of the conclusion. In the middle section (mm. 29–57), the opening material is conventionally set in the dominant tonality, reflecting the balanced motion of mm. 17–21, while moving upward by step from C through D to E. The return is effected by the opening motive moving through the circle of fifths, E, A, D to G.

ACCOMPANIED SONATAS Haydn's output before 1760 also included chamber works for more than one player. Several trios for violin or flute, cello, and cembalo date most probably from these years. They are three-movement works which, like the keyboard sonatas, are derived from the suite and carry the title *Partita* or *Divertimento*. As is to be expected, the movements all have the same tonic, with some variety provided by the trios of the minuets, which are either in the tonic minor or the relative minor. The Trio in E♭ (Hob. XV:36) has a middle movement called *Polones,* or polonaise, which is exceptional in its C-minor tonality.

Taken from the title page of Artaria's printing of a Haydn Trio, this tiny vignette confirms the importance of women keyboardists at this time, while the men play the "unladylike" instruments.

Perhaps the most interesting aspect of the trios is the relationship between the instruments. Haydn conceives his trios as *continuo* works, and he ties the cello part to the left hand of the cembalo. The only difference between them occurs when the cello part is written down an octave or simplified (evidence of the way the *continuo* part could be modified). The violin or flute, on the other hand, is treated much as if it were one of two melody voices in a trio sonata, alternating with the right hand of the keyboard or playing along with it in thirds or sixths. In Chapter III the variety of performance combinations possible for the trio sonata are discussed.

QUARTETS Haydn earned part of his living before 1760 playing in serenades and he composed a number of divertimentos for two violins and cello and for larger, mixed combinations of instruments at this time, possibly for his own use. But it is the early string quartet which must now engage our attention. Once again, we have no way of knowing exactly when Haydn first ventured into the field he was to make so peculiarly his own—later generations have called him the father of the string quartet.[14] Griesinger reports that Haydn was eighteen years old (1750) when he wrote his first quartet for an amateur, Baron Fürnberg, with whom Haydn played quartets from time to time. On the other hand, Carpani talks about the same quartet parties but says that they took place when Haydn was a little over twenty. Both these men had the story from Haydn's own mouth, but clearly the old man's failing memory caused him to make small variations on a favorite theme. Recent research has tended to place Haydn's acquaintance with Baron Fürnberg still later and hence to date his early quartets between 1757 and 1759.

These works are hybrids, as might be expected, showing something of the diverse origins of their structure. In the extant copies they are called variously: *Quartetto, Cassatio, Divertimento, Notturno, Sonata a quattro, Parthia,* and even *Symphony*. They are invariably in five movements arranged symmetrically for the most part as follows: 1. Fast; 2. Minuet and Trio; 3. Slow; 4. Minuet and Trio; 5. Fast. In two cases we find instead: 1. Adagio; 2. Minuet and Trio; 3. Scherzo, Presto; 4. Minuet and Trio; 5. Fast. The outer movements and the first minuets of movements two and four are invariably in the tonic key. The middle movements are generally in the dominant or subdominant, with one in the tonic and another in the tonic minor. The same choice of related tonalities is used for the trios of the minuets. A few of the quartets preserve the texture of the trio sonata, using the two lower strings to provide a rhythmic-harmonic background to the melodic material equally

14. Long before Hoboken, the quartets were familiar to music lovers by opus numbers, and their use has persisted. Here, the quartets will be identified by both opus and Hoboken numbers to avoid confusion.

Example XI–1: J. HAYDN, Quartet Op. 1, No. 3 (Hob. III:3), I

shared between the violins (Example XI–1) The slow movement generally consists of an impassioned melody for the first violin accompanied by the lower strings in reiterated chords.

Haydn himself played the viola in Baron Fürnberg's quartet, and there, seated in the middle of the quartet texture, it is possible that he gained his exquisite perception of the ways in which the players found their rewards. The tossing back and forth of a small figure between violin and viola at the same pitch; the trio of a minuet in which the three lower strings play in unison (three in one) opposed by a solitary first violin playing three-note chordal harmony (one in three); a slow movement in trio-sonata texture in which the muted second violin repeats the conclusion of each first-violin phrase, giving an effect of distant echo; such devices attest to the fertility of Haydn's melodic wit and creative imagination. The early quartets abound in novel effects and instrumental combinations that can only be the result of humorous intent. Hob. III:3 in D has a *Ländler*-like trio to the first minuet in which the first violin accompanies its bowed melody with its own pizzicato. The friendly, light-hearted atmosphere which these quartets generate contrasts strikingly with the almost Baroque gravity of many movements of the trios, an observation further supported by the fact that five of the quartets in Op. 1 (Hob. III:1, 2, 3, 4, and 6) have first or last movements in either 3/8 or 6/8. These meters were judged by the times as lively yet gentle, and not particularly appropriate for conveying of serious sentiments.

Example XI–2: J. HAYDN, Quartet Op. 1, No. 3 (Hob. III:3), III

SYMPHONY From the string quartet to the symphony was a short step in the 1750s. All that was necessary was to strengthen the string parts by doubling and to add winds, which was easily done according to common convention, by having oboes or flutes doubling the violin parts from time to time and the bassoon doubling the bass line. It is now generally agreed that Haydn had written several symphonies before he composed what is usually called No. 1 (Hob. I:1) for Count Morzin. That work consists of three movements: *Presto* in D; *Andante* in G; and *Finale, Presto* in D. Not until his third symphony does Haydn include a minuet. Two oboes and two horns are added to the strings, but the wind parts show nothing unexpected: the oboes double the strings from time to time and the horns are restricted to playing fanfare-like figures. The melodic material is divided between the violins, which are often treated as if the work were a trio sonata, although in many places they play in unison. The lower strings are bound together almost entirely. Their function is to provide harmony (the harpsichord *continuo* is not indicated but possibly would have been used) and, with their reiterated, scrubbing eighth-notes, provide a forward-driving rhythm. It is interesting to note how frequently the viola plays the same material as the cello an octave higher, and how, occasionally, the violas are the highest in the string texture. If we can also imagine the bass line doubled an octave lower by the string basses, perhaps with bassoons added, we can see what importance Haydn placed on it in the overall texture.

STAGE WORKS Haydn's first composition for the stage is lost. Griesinger and Dies both relate how Haydn came to compose the work, which was a success and earned the composer a fair sum of money. This is what Dies says about it:

> Haydn, when he was about twenty-one years old, [Griesinger says he was nineteen], set to music a comic opera in German. This first piece for the stage bore the title *Der krumme Teufel* (The Crooked Devil), and came about in an odd way. Kurz, a genius of the German theater, performing at that time in the old Kärnthnerthor Theater was delighting the public in the role of Bernadon. He had heard a great deal spoken in praise of the young Haydn; this drew him to seek an introduction. A happy chance soon created an opportunity for him to satisfy his wish. Kurz had a beautiful wife who was kind enough to receive serenades from the young musicians. Now young Haydn brought her a serenade, which Kurz took to honor himself as well as his wife. He sought a better acquaintance with Haydn. The two came together; Haydn must go home with Kurz. "You sit down at the piano and accompany the pantomime I will act out for you with some suitable music. Imagine now that Bernadon has fallen in the water and is trying to save himself by swimming." Then he calls his servant, throws himself flat on the stomach across a chair, makes the servant pull the chair to and fro across the room, and kicks his arms and legs like a swimmer, while Haydn expresses in six-eight time the play of waves and swimming. Suddenly Bernadon springs up, embraces Haydn, and practically smothers him in kisses. "Haydn, you're the man for me! You must write me an opera!" So began *Der kumme Teufel*. Haydn received twenty-five ducats for it and counted himself rich indeed.

> The opera was performed twice to great acclaim, and then was forbidden because of offensive remarks in the text.[15]

RELIGIOUS WORKS Throughout his life, Haydn's religious faith was steadfast. When composing, it was his habit to preface each large composition with the words *In nomine Domini* (in the name of the Lord) and to conclude his manuscript with *Laus Deo* (praise be to God) or *Soli Deo gloria* (to God alone, the glory). The earliest religious work extant, dating from the early 1750s, is a *Missa bevis* (Hob. XXII:1) written for two boy-soprano soloists, four-part choir, and an orchestra consisting of two violins and *basso continuo,* i.e., organ, cellos, and basses. These orchestral forces are typical for less than full, ceremonial Masses and were commonly used by Mozart in Salzburg, not only in masses but also in his so-called *Epistle* sonatas. The melodic writing for the strings shows a florid quality similar to that in many of the trios.

No section of this little Mass is allowed to last long. There are no orchestral preludes or postludes and in the *Gloria* and *Credo* the soloists and choir sing as many as three different texts simultaneously. Only in the *Benedictus* is any musical expansion allowed, and the sopranos and orchestra perform a fine little duet. The conclusion, *Dona nobis pacem,* uses the same material as the opening *Kyrie,* symbolizing Haydn's child-like faith and confidence that prayers will be answered.

Was Haydn the child father to the man? The question must be answered in the affirmative. Little music of the 1750s survives in today's concert repertoire, and Haydn's early work is neglected except for "complete" recordings of symphonies, keyboard sonatas, trios, and quartets, primarily historical in intent. Yet the seeds of the future are there, along with much that one may enjoy. The Baroquish melodies will soon disappear forever and the tunes in a more popular style, already slipping into last movements of the trios and throughout the quartets, will survive and proliferate. The acuteness of the composer's ear for orchestration will also grow. Most of all, his genius in the creation of large, incredibly varied, and ever-fresh structures, already very much in evidence, will continue to expand and develop in unique ways to the end of his life. It is no wonder that young Haydn readily achieved popularity within the limited circle in which he moved, for his earliest works already exhibit a richness and profusion of material, and a disciplined yet varied expression, unexcelled by his older contemporaries in Vienna.

15. Dies, *op. cit.,* pp. 97–98.

CHAPTER XII

The First Esterházy Years: to 1770

THE BEGINNINGS OF RECOGNITION

The decade of the 1760s began with two important events in Haydn's life, one which at the time looked like a curse but became a blessing, while the other looked like a blessing and became a curse. The latter was Haydn's marriage. He is neither the first nor the last to make this kind of mistake, but why he committed such a blunder is hard to imagine. Griesinger puts the affair succinctly and delicately:

> Haydn had oftentimes received help in the house of a hairdresser in Vienna (in the Landstrasse) named Keller; he also gave music lessons to the eldest daughter, and his preference for her grew with closer acquaintance. But she went into a convent, and Haydn then decided, since his future was somewhat secured by a fixed salary and the hairdresser, to whom he felt grateful, kept urging it, that he would marry the second daughter.
>
> Haydn had no children by this marriage. "My wife was unable to bear children, and I was therefore less indifferent to the charms of other ladies." His choice did not turn out very well in general, for his wife was a domineering, unfriendly character. He had to be careful to conceal his income from her, because she loved to spend, was bigoted on the subject [of religion], was continually inviting the clergy to dinner, had many masses said, and was freer with charitable contributions than her situation warranted. Once when I was obliged to inquire of Haydn how a favor he had shown, and for which he would take nothing, could be repaid to his wife, he answered me: "She does not deserve anything, and it is all the same to her if her husband is a shoemaker or an artist." She died in the summer of 1800 near Vienna.[1]

Apart from the fact that Griesinger, like Haydn, had the wrong woman—Haydn loved the *younger* sister, who went into a convent, but married the *elder,* who was nearly three years his senior—his description is chilling. The anecdotes about Haydn's wife are legion for she has carried a

1. Griesinger, *op. cit.,* pp. 15–16.

greater load of opprobrium for her relationship to her husband than almost any other wife in history, with the possible exception of Socrates' Xantippe. Griesinger's last sentence makes its inexorable point: she lived a long time.

Haydn probably felt considerable dismay when Count Morzin's musical establishment was disbanded, taking with it the short-lived security of a regular salary. But the advantage of having his professional freedom must have been exhilarating and it may also be possible that Haydn had already been cultivating a relationship with the princely house of Esterházy, for it did not take him long to find the patron and the family who claimed his allegiance for the rest of his life.

Prince Paul Anton Esterházy (1711–62) was the head of one of the wealthiest families in eastern Europe and owned immense estates in Hungary as well as in Austria and Bavaria. For Haydn to have been taken into the household of such a potentate implies that the composer's reputation was already secure and his superiority established. Prince Paul Anton could afford to buy the best of anything he liked. He liked music but probably little suspected that, in appointing Haydn to be Vice-Kapellmeister, he was purchasing a place in history.

When Paul Anton came into his inheritance in 1734, his musical establishment was headed by one Gregor Joseph Werner (1693–1766), a prolific composer of church and instrumental music, some of whose works still survive in modern editions. Since the prince was in the empress's service abroad, he did not settle on his estates until the late 1750s. It speaks much for the quality of the man and of the patronage system at its best that in appointing the bright new star Haydn, Prince Paul Anton did not displace his old servant, Werner, whose dignity was protected in the contract to which Haydn agreed. This contract, the signing of which gave Haydn's father "the joy of seeing his son in the uniform of that family, blue, trimmed with gold, and of hearing from the Prince many eulogies of the talent of his son,"[2] is a famous document, here reproduced in full.

> This day (according to the date hereto appended) Joseph Heyden, native of Rohrau in Austria, is accepted and appointed Vice-Capellmeister in the service of his Serene Highness Paul Anton, Prince of the Holy Roman Empire, of Esterhaza and Galantha, etc., subject to conditions here following:
>
> 1. Whereas the Capellmeister at Eisenstadt, namely Gregorious Werner, having devoted many years of true and faithful service to the princely house, is now, on account of his great age and infirmities, unfit to perform the duties incumbent on him, it is hereby declared that the said Gregorious Werner, in consideration of his long services, shall retain the post of Capellmeister, and the said Joseph Heyden as

2. *Ibid.*, p. 16.

Vice-Capellmeister shall, so far as regards the music of the choir, be subordinate to the Capellmeister and receive his instructions. But in everything else relating to musical performances, and in all that concerns the orchestra, the Vice-Capellmeister shall have the sole direction.

2. The said Joseph Heyden shall be considered and treated as a member of the household. Therefore his Serene Highness is graciously pleased to place confidence in his conducting himself as becomes an honorable official of a princely house. He must be temperate, not showing himself overbearing toward his musicians, but mild and lenient, straightforward and composed. It is especially to be observed that when the orchestra shall be summoned to perform before company, the Vice-Capellmeister and all the musicians shall appear in uniform, and the said Joseph Heyden shall take care that he and all the members of his orchestra follow the instructions given, and appear in white stockings, white linen, powdered, and with either a queue or a tiewig.

3. Whereas the other musicians are referred for directions to the said Vice-Capellmeister, he shall therefore take the more care to conduct himself in an exemplary manner, abstaining from undue familiarity and from vulgarity in eating, drinking, and conversation, not dispensing with the respect due to him, but acting uprightly and influencing his subordinates to preserve such harmony as is becoming in them, remembering how displeasing the consequences of any discord or dispute would be to his Serene Highness.

4. The said Vice-Capellmeister shall be under obligation to compose such music as his Serene Highness may command, and neither to communicate such compositions to any other person, nor to allow them to be copied, but he shall retain them for the absolute use of his Highness, and not compose for any other person without the knowledge and permission of his Highness.

5. The said Joseph Heyden shall appear daily in the antechamber before and after midday, and inquire whether his Highness is pleased to order a performance of the orchestra. On receipt of his orders he shall communicate them to the other musicians, and take care to be punctual at the appointed time, and to ensure punctuality in his subordinates, making a note of those who arrive late or absent themselves altogether.

6. Should any quarrel or cause of complaint arise, the Vice-Capellmeister shall endeavor to arrange it in order that his Serene Highness may not be incommoded with trifling disputes; but should any more serious difficulty occur, which the said Joseph Heyden is unable to set right, his Serene Highness must then be respectfully called upon to decide the matter.

7. The said Vice-Capellmeister shall take careful charge of all music and musical instruments, and be responsible for any injury that may occur to them from carelessness or neglect.

8. The said Joseph Heyden shall be obliged to instruct the female vocalists, in order that they may not forget in the country what they have been taught with much trouble and expense in Vienna, and, as the said Vice-Capellmeister is proficient on various instruments, he shall take care himself to practice on all that he is acquainted with.

9. A copy of this agreement and instructions shall be given to the said Vice-Capellmeister and his subordinates, in order that he may be able to hold them to their obligations therein laid down.

10. It is considered unnecessary to detail the services required of the said Joseph Heyden, more particularly since his Serene Highness is pleased to hope that he will of his own free will strictly observe not only these regulations, but all others that may from time to time be made by his Highness, and that he will place the orchestra on such a footing, and in such good order, that he may bring honor upon himself and deserve the further favor of the prince his master, who thus confides in his zeal and discretion.

11. A yearly salary of four hundred florins to be received in quarterly payments is hereby bestowed by his Serene Highness upon the said Vice-Capellmeister.

12. In addition, the said Joseph Heyden shall board at the officers' table, or receive a half-gulden per day in lieu thereof.

13. Finally, this agreement shall hold good for at least three years from May 1, 1761, with the further condition that if at the conclusion of this term the said Joseph Heyden shall desire to leave the service, he shall give his Highness six months' previous notice of his intention.

14. His Serene Highness undertakes to keep Joseph Heyden in his service during this time, and should he be satisfied with him, he may look forward to being appointed Capellmeister. This, however, must not be understood to deprive his Serene Highness of the right to dismiss the said Joseph Heyden at the expiration of the term, should he see fit to do so.

Duplicate copies of this document shall be executed and exchanged.
Given at Vienna this first day of May, 1761.

Ad mandatum Celsissimi Principis;

Johann Stifftell, Secretary[3]

The terms of the contract make interesting reading. Haydn's duties were never-ending, and it would have been so easy for him to fail in some aspect of them. To look after instrumental repairs, to train the orchestra, to appoint and manage the personnel, to adjudicate grievances, to set an example at all times, and, in addition, to compose is surely more than one man could be expected to accomplish. Yet Haydn succeeded and filled every role with distinction. Prince Paul Anton had indeed found a treasure.

3. The translation of this document is by Karl Geiringer.

At about this time, Prince Paul Anton was in the process of expanding his musical establishment, and while he added nine new musicians, some others were released. It is not known whether Haydn was involved in these changes which both enlarged and revitalized the orchestra, but it seems very likely that he would have been consulted. Although the orchestra never grew large, in modern terms, Haydn was able to engage players who could double on a number of instruments, and hence he had a wide variety of timbres available and could experiment with all kinds of combinations. It is assumed that at times Haydn played keyboard *continuo* and conducted from that position and at times played first violin in the concertmaster's position, giving the beat with his bow and leading the orchestra in that manner. From the lists of his orchestral players we can see that one of his violins also sang bass while another doubled on viola; most of his horn players doubled on violin; his bassoonists also played the violone (an instrument that resembles today's double bass), viola, and flute, and his oboe players doubled on flute and *cor anglais*.

As the contract shows, the music for the church remained under the supervision of Kapellmeister Werner, and the court and chamber music was under Haydn's control. This arrangement lasted until 1766, when Werner died and Haydn became Kapellmeister. From the beginning of his service, Haydn obviously knew how to manage his subordinates and rapidly learned to gain the trust of his superiors. When any of his musicians (he called them his "children") got into trouble or difficulty of any kind, Haydn could be relied upon to know the best way to direct his prince toward the right frame of mind, and to the right solution to the problem. He could yield gracefully when the occasion demanded and he could also argue a case forcefully. Not only was he a good man to work for, but it is clear that Esterházy appreciated him fully: one year after signing the contract above, his salary was increased by 50%, from 400 to 600 florins—considerably more than Werner had been making.

In 1762, at the age of fifty-two, Prince Paul Anton died, and was succeeded by his younger brother, Prince Nikolaus "the Magnificent" (1714–90). This was the prince whom Haydn was destined to serve for twenty-eight years, and to whom he felt bound by such ties of loyalty that he rejected all offers of travel and other employment.

Prince Nikolaus himself did everything to merit the sobriquet "the Magnificent." His most superb accomplishment was the construction of the palace and park of Esterháza, which he began almost as soon as he succeeded to the title. He had inherited many castles, among which the palace of Eisenstadt remained the principal family seat, and it was there that Haydn spent the first six years of his service. Nikolaus wanted to live in a palace of his own creation, so he looked about him for a place to build. His eye lit on the most unpromising territory imagin-

The Palace and Park of Esterháza. The plan of the park, made some time after 1762, shows the projected palace at the bottom, with the main avenues and allées radiating from it. (Österreichische National bibliothek)

able, and, in Baroque fashion, he resolved to subdue Nature to his own desires. He chose an area of flat marshland, teeming with wildfowl and game, and also with mosquitoes and fever. It was ideal hunting country, where Haydn was to develop into a first-rate marksman—he once had the distinction of bringing down with one shot three grouse, which were later served to the empress. Nikolaus already had a lodge there, so just as Louis XIV had converted a hunting lodge into the palace of Versailles, he set out to do the same. It cost him an immense amount of money but he succeeded, and from the waterlogged wilderness there emerged something like an eighteenth-century version of Kubla Khan's "stately pleasure dome" described by Coleridge.

The palace itself was nominally completed in 1784, after being under construction nearly a quarter of a century. In the park there was an opera house and a marionette theater as well as temples to various mythological figures, including one to Diana (goddess of virginity) and one to Venus (goddess of love). Prince Nikolaus spared no effort in order to give pleasure to his friends and visitors to his fairytale world. This was his favorite toy and he played with it unceasingly until his death in 1790.

He was a master worthy of Haydn. By rank an aristocrat, he was by nature intelligent and kindly. His financial good sense enabled him to carry out his grandiose schemes of building and entertaining without impoverishing his estate, and he controlled all his expenses carefully. He was avid in his appetite for music, and he accepted everything that Haydn created for him eagerly and gratefully. In Haydn's own words:

> My prince was content with all my works, I received approval, I could, as head of an orchestra, make experiments, observe what enhanced an effect, and what weakened it, thus improving, adding to, cutting away, and running risks. I was set apart from the world, there was nobody in my vicinity to confuse and annoy me in my course, and so I had to be original.[4]

Nikolaus played the baryton, a bowed instrument now obsolete related to the viola da gamba; its sound quality is largely determined by two separate sets of strings, one which is bowed and fingered normally, and the other which vibrates sympathetically with the bowed strings; the second set can also be sounded by plucking through the carved-out neck with the thumb of the left hand. The instrument had little currency, yet composing for it cost him precious time. He also spent countless hours learning to play it, in the hope of pleasing his prince. When he displayed his hard-earned skill, he was received coldly. Haydn's response was remarkably positive, and significant of the composer's state of mind:

> "I understood the Prince perfectly," Haydn told me, "and although at first I was hurt by his indifference, still I owe it to his curt reminder that I

4. Griesinger, *op. cit.,* p. 17.

> suddenly gave up the intention of being a good barytonist. I remembered that I had already gained some note as a Kapellmeister and not as a practicing virtuoso, reproached myself for half a year's neglect of composition, and returned to it with zeal renewed."[5]

Prince Nikolaus and Haydn reached a relationship of mutual confidence and even friendship, which, in the early days, had its trials. In 1765, old Kapellmeister Werner wrote a malicious letter accusing Haydn of dereliction of duty in a number of ways: instruments damaged; music lost or even sold; singers missing rehearsals, etc. It may be that there was some truth in the allegations. Haydn was probably not a stern disciplinarian and obviously enjoyed the affection of his staff. In the event, he received a reprimand which also included the injunction to compose more diligently, a command which we might find it difficult to justify, but to which Haydn responded with such alacrity that when Werner died there was no question whatsoever of Haydn's fitness to succeed to the post of Kapellmeister.

COMPOSITIONS

Haydn's compositions of the 1760s can be placed more accurately within the decade than was the case in the previous chapter. Also, his genius was in full flower, and he operated with equal ease in the chamber, the church, and the theater. It was during this decade that his reputation started to spread, not only to Vienna but also to North Germany. Late in 1766, the *Wiener Diarium* published an article entitled "On the Viennese Taste in Music," in which Haydn was compared with other composers active in Vienna, as follows:

> Herr Joseph Hayden, the darling of our nation, whose gentle character impresses itself on each of his pieces. His movements have beauty, order, clarity, a fine and noble expression which will be felt sooner than the listener is prepared for it. In his cassatios, quartets and trios he is a pure and clean water, over which a southerly wind occasionally ripples, and sometimes rises to waves without, however, losing its bed and course. The art of writing the outer parts in parallel octaves is his invention, and one cannot deny that this is attractive, even if it appears rarely and in a Haydenish fashion. In symphonies he is as masculinely strong as he is inventive. In cantatas charming, fetching, flattering; and in minuets natural, playful, alluring.[6]

This attitude contrasts strongly with the critical approach of the North Germans. From earlier in the same year, a German critic writes:

> A Hayden *[sic]* is pleasant, witty and full of inventiveness . . . Whether, however, his minuets in octaves are to everyman's taste is something I will

5. Dies, *op cit.*, p. 107.
6. Cited by Landon, *Haydn: Chronicle and Works*, (London, 1976–) II, p. 130.

> leave undecided. They are good for amusement; but one easily gets the idea that one is hearing father and son begging by singing octaves: and that is a bad object for musical imitation.[7]

In 1768, J.A. Hiller writes:

> It is true that one does find well written, magnificent and affecting movements in them [the symphonies] . . . but is not the curious mixture of the noble and the common, the serious and the comic, which so often occurs in one and the same movement, sometimes of a bad effect? Not to speak of those repellent octaves . . .[8]

How the Austrians reacted to such fundamental rejection is not known, but it is perhaps significant that around this time there occurs that upsurge of emotionalism in Austrian music, that prototype of Romanticism, which was explored earlier, and which is usually called *Sturm und Drang*. Far from remaining aloof from the movement, Haydn was one of those composers whose works provided the most important examples of the style.

KEYBOARD SONATAS The keyboard sonatas of the 1760s show a remarkable growth in cohesiveness and expressive power. The sonatas Hob. XVI:18, 19, 44, 45, 46, all of which probably date from the years 1766–70, are expanded in structure and communicate intense seriousness in their first movements, because the tempo has been slowed to a stately *Moderato* or *Allegro moderato*. Two of the five sonatas are in two movements and the others in three. It is also noteworthy that the Minuet and Trio is abandoned, although Hob. XVI:18 and 44, both two-movement works, conclude with *Tempo di Minuetto*.

In the G-minor Sonata, Hob. XVI:44 (*ACM* 26) written around 1768, Haydn unites his finest compositional craft with the emotional power of the minor-mode works of the period, producing a pattern of cause and effect that forces the player and listener to perceive the music as both the end and the means to an expressive statement beyond music. This composition, with its roots in the fertile soil of Emanuel Bach, is different from anything produced by any other composers of the 1760s, and points directly toward Beethoven. Its uniqueness is not to be simply explained in its affective use of the minor mode, far different from Baroque practice though this is, for many composers were writing *Sturm und Drang* works in which the minor mode is part of the stock-in-trade of powerful expression. Rather it is to be found in the peculiar significance which Haydn gives to commonplace musical material, and his use of the sonata form to point up the changes that this material undergoes.

The opening four notes of the right hand provide Haydn with the

7. *Ibid.*, p. 132.
8. *Ibid.*, p. 154.

motive which he will work and rework throughout the sonata, and the vicissitudes of the melodic line allow him to develop the expressive power of the sonata. The first four bars contain a clipped and balanced repetition of a melody whose antecedent cadences on a weak beat and whose consequent cadences on a strong beat.

The important addition of a free third voice on B♭ in m. 3 does not obscure the progress of the main melodic line, now become an inner voice, down to the cadential G in m. 4. No sooner is this strong and complex statement made than development starts, creating a transition to the relative major and a new shape from the opening material. At the end of m. 7, the composer chooses to develop the initial upper neighbor figure of the piece over seven measures. The thirteenth measure sees the beginning of the second tonal area in the relative major (B♭) and the radically new texture obscures the fact that the developmental process has continued. To be sure, the A-B♭ oscillation, the new tonic and its leading tone, is not the D-E♭ of the opening notes, but the relationship is clarified through the B♭-A in the upper voice in m. 3.

At the start of m. 15 Haydn turns his attention to the interval of the fourth, taken from the opening four-note figure. The manner in which the notes are written (its orthography) makes the compositional process clear. The left hand could equally well have been written as follows:

Example XII–1: J. HAYDN, Sonata (Hob. XVI:44, I)

In performance, this passage would probably have sounded the way Haydn wrote it, and hence the reason cannot simply be a direction to the player. Haydn's orthography makes his intellectual process apparent: he has turned his attention from the first three notes to the third and fourth notes of the opening motive. The second element of the B♭-major material, beginning in m. 21, turns out to be a development of the substance of m. 5, which itself effected the transition to the major. Here it is further developed sequentially and texturally, up to the concluding two measures of the exposition.

This cursory examination of the exposition of the sonata will demonstrate the rationale of the entire movement, and the thoughtful manner in which the problem of the cohesiveness of the whole is attacked. Now to attempt to approach Haydn's expressive content, which is, after all, his artistic goal.

It is clear that the notes of the scale generate varying degrees of tension and the basis of tonal music is to be found in this dictum. It is equally clear that Haydn is concerned with rising melodic lines contrasted with falling melodic lines, not only in this work but in all works of expressive purpose. His opening gesture engages the energy required to change the downward pull of the first note, D, which has the tendency to fall five notes to the tonic, into an upward force that will carry the line to the higher G. If this were a cadence, the affective force of this upward movement would be assertive, positive, and energetic and would counter the *Affekt* of the minor mode. Conversely, had the D fallen to the lower G the *Affekt* would have been more of introversion, of resignation to the inevitable, and would have reinforced the minor modality. The following four bars make a complete statement, presenting a marvelous line of stresses in which upward and downward forces, appoggiaturas, suspensions, and leaps move to a conclusion in which, as was initially implied, the opening D reaches its affective goal on the lower G.

The first development of the opening (m. 5) begins an octave lower, and changes the direction of the downward movement from the G in m.1 into an upward movement, G, A, B♭ (m. 5) and A, B♭, C (m. 6). The impression is inescapable that the opening figure in m.1, which turns on itself and is a veritable image of introversion, has now been modified into something with a sense of direction—upward—and that modification has been achieved through effort and resolve. The immediate result of the effort is seen in the lighter tessitura of mm. 7–12, and in the arrival at the relative major. The second tonal area opens (m. 13) with a development that may have shocked the North German critics, for the comic effect is undeniable amidst the surrounding deep seriousness. The light tessitura is maintained, the harmonic rhythm is quickened, and, perhaps most significant, the opening triplet figure is changed into a trill whenever it occurs on D (second half of mm. 13 and 14)—a trill, moreover, in which the upper note, E♭, sounds against an E♮ in the bass. Thereafter, beginning in m. 15, a new development features the leap of the fourth from the opening, which was followed there by a stepwise descent, proceeding upward by step from G to D in the inner, tenor voice. When this grand assertion is complete there follows a statement of the descending tetrachord (m. 18) in its original shape as in m. 1, which is combined with the upward tendency of E♮-F in the left hand, and the downward tendency, E♭-D (right hand, mm.18 and 19), and emphasized by an unusual left-hand figure. In m. 21 the melodic line abandons its triplet anacrusis and moves upward through a three-part sequence which cadences in one of the most significant gestures of reconciliation that Haydn can make. The second half of m. 23 contains the descending tetrachord, G-D, doubled at the lower third and balanced by an ascending tetrachord of F-B♭. The figure also contains the ornamented progression A-B♭. From this point to the end of the exposition, this atmosphere of synthesis and differences resolved continues until the last two measures, where syncopated rhythm and the G-D tetrachord, now in the middle voice, prepare for the return of the affective minor mode.

Starting atypically in the minor mode instead of continuing in the relative major, the development repeats the opening four measures of the work in C minor, with some significant changes: the left hand accompaniment of the upward leaping octave is omitted and the second half of the phrase is transposed down an octave, with immediate consequences. The appoggiaturas, first met in m. 3, now become extended to Wagnerian length as the listener waits for their resolution. In m. 33, E♭ is extended to three beats against the two-beat F♯, and while the F♯ resolves normally to G, the sense of downward resolution to D of the E♭ is almost lost in an upward rush of sixteenth notes to high B♭. At the same time as these opposing tendency tones (E♭ and F♯) are placed together as a chord, the left-hand arpeggios remind us of the only other place in the movement where they occur (mm. 17–18), combined in a single melodic line. The process of mm. 33–34 is repeated in mm. 35–36, but a tone lower.

Now follows the first of the three expressive climaxes of the movement. The anacrusis to m. 37 is the same kind of triplet as at the start of the sonata and it carries the same implication of a *tendency* to fall to F in minor mode, V, ♭VI, V, I. Instead, it leaps to the higher octave, C, and then in 32nd notes repeatedly falls to F until, as if in a desperate access of energy, it attains high E♭ which seems about to bring back the tonic G minor. However, emotional respite is offered by the major-mode harmonization, as the oscillating G-A♭ are placed in the context of B♭ major. Haydn writes no dynamic marks, nor does he need to, for both the expressive content of the music and the accompanying figures dictate a solid *forte* in mm. 37–38 and a *piano* in mm. 39–40. There follow two bars of the whimsical material from the second group, but this time in C minor and built upon the oscillation of C and B♮, the leading tone. In the exposition this material had been followed by the upward movement of fourths; here it is followed by a rapid upward scale which leads to the pivotal note, C, followed not by B♮ but B♭. The effect of this is to drop the tessitura to its lowest level in the entire movement, and to lead up to the second climax, which heralds the recapitulation. Mm. 46–49 build a most unusual stretto effect in which the opening four notes of the sonata are used pseudo-contrapuntally to give the impression of five or six voices, creating a massive expression of energetic outburst, which quickly fades away as soon as the lines have once again reached high E♭.

The recapitulation (m. 52) is noteworthy for the changes it makes in the material of the exposition. The register of the first phrase is set an octave lower than at its first appearance, and the left-hand leap is omitted, as at the opening of the development. The second phrase (mm. 54–57) begins as it does in the exposition; instead of moving to its emphatic conclusion (m. 4), it dissolves into a downward chain of dissonant non-harmonic tones over a framework of upward fourths in rapid downward sequence (m. 56) closing on a half cadence. Mm. 5–12 of the exposition are omitted and the second group material is presented, now in G minor. Apart from the modal change and a subtle, Baroquish difference in barring, the arrangement of the notes is literally repeated for five bars, but then the sequence continues upward for two more steps to the cadence in m. 63. The cadence is, however, reached by a downward scale which runs directly to its goal, through twelve notes.

The third and last climax of the movement occurs over mm. 66–70. From m. 64 to m. 66 the material of the exposition has been repeated in the tonic, G minor; but in m. 66 there occurs something which has no precedent within the composition. Haydn could equally well have followed the plan of his exposition and written the following:

Example XII–2: J. HAYDN, Sonata (Hob. XVI:44), recomposition, omitting cadenza

It is clear that what he wrote is far removed from the reconciliatory conjunction of opposites that took place in the exposition (m. 23). Here the right hand breaks free of the figuration conditioned by its derivation from earlier material, and on the last beat of m. 66 it simply becomes an upward gesture culminating in high E♭—as in mm. 38 and 49—from which it drops away quietly and with increasing lassitude. For expressive reasons, Haydn chose to place this climax on the flattened sixth degree of the scale, a strongly affective degree, rather than on the highest note of the keyboard. The note F♯ does not stop the fall to E♭ but simply delays it, and the left hand stands still while the whole right-hand gesture is repeated until it, too, is still.

It is in this context that the concluding material of the sonata is now heard quite differently from the same music from the exposition in the relative major. The concluding measures of exposition and recapitulation now have the same upper melodic voice, E♭ falling to B♭, and how different their *Affekt* is when harmonized in the keys of B♭ major and G minor. Indeed, this might seem to be the argument of the work; to demonstrate the affective difference between E♭ falling to D as a major scale's fourth degree falling to the third, and as a minor scale's sixth degree falling to the fifth. Finally, observe the connection between Haydn's first and last statements:

Example XII–3: J. HAYDN, Sonata (Hob. XVI:44), opening and closing juxtaposed.

The first notes in the left hand are not repeated during the course of the musical argument. Their peculiar conformation is that of a minor third repeated an octave higher on two successive beats. The last notes in the left hand describe a falling octave in the lowest register. Certainly the particular aptness of the deep reverberation cannot be denied at the conclusion of a sonata movement which started with a demonstration of optimism but which saw that optimism fade away into introspection and passivity. But as well as the affective consistency there is what may be called the "law of complementary opposites," which is a principle of melodic style in the late eighteenth century according to which an upward figure must be counterbalanced by a downward figure. Here, at the conclusion, is the counterbalance, the complementary opposite to the beginning, which rounds off the whole structure. The beginning and the end are one: the wheel has come full circle.

That Haydn could write a movement of such concentrated force as this is cause enough for wonderment. That he should have confided such a movement to a piano sonata, where it is much less conspicuous than it would have been in either symphony or string quartet, is less cause for amazement. For here is yet another proof of the proposition, already put forward in the discussion of the *empfindsamer Stil,* that a profound statement in a personal style is most suited to the means of the solo sonata. For this is music which, in its own time as in ours, would challenge a player's musical perception perhaps more than his technique, and would reward repeated playing and close examination of the score. No symphony or quartet—indeed, no other kind of composition—is made to be used thus in 1768.

The complete assimilation of Emanuel Bach's influence is to be seen in the slow movement of the A♭ Sonata, Hob. XVI:46 (*ACM* 27). A striking similarity between Haydn's recapitulation in the G-minor Sonata, just examined, and that of Emanuel's A-minor Sonata (H.30), the first of the *Württemberg* set, has been noted. Now we observe a family resemblance between this slow movement in D♭ major and the slow movement of Emanuel's second *Württemberg* Sonata (H.31), in A♭.

The point of the movement, however, is not to be found in its similarity to an earlier work. The twenty years that separate the Bach and the Haydn inevitably witnessed such a degree of stylistic change as to obscure resemblance. In the A♭ Sonata, Haydn creates one of his most thoughtful and rich slow movements, far removed in sound from any trace of Baroque influence and the *basso continuo*. Perhaps the only element that survives from the past is to be found in the rather self-conscious (and perhaps not very successful) evocation of a repeating bass pattern in the first four bars, and it is interesting that Haydn uses it only once again. The work is in three and four voices interspersed with homophonic passages, and the mixture is purest Haydn. The abstruse handling of the harmony, enharmonically, is another aspect of Haydn's music in which the enriching influence of North Germany and of J.S. Bach is seen to be reaching the composer through Emanuel Bach.

Strangely enough, the question of the latter's influence on Haydn was raised during the composer's lifetime. In 1784 an English periodical stated that the Piano Sonata Hob. XVI:19 in D was an intentional parody of Emanuel Bach's style, and imputed revenge as a motive. Bach himself replied that the charges were unfounded since Haydn and he were the best of friends. From our vantage point we can only wonder at the basis for the anonymous writer's statement, for this G-major Sonata appears to be a typically Haydnesque work, and we have so much musical evidence that there was no place for parody or malice in the relationship between Bach and Haydn; not imitation but assimilation was the sincerest form of flattery that Haydn could pay to his revered older contemporary.

BARYTON TRIOS During the 1760s, the most important contributions that Haydn made to the chamber music repertoire—at least in sheer number—were his trios for baryton, viola, and cello, of which he produced at least 126, turning them out at the rate of perhaps two a month for several years. Between 1765 and 1769 he composed six dozen. This enthusiastic production was the direct result of Prince Nikolaus's injunction of 1765 that Haydn should compose more diligently, and it was the foundation upon which Haydn built his strong relationship with the prince. The compositions are of the highest interest to the historian, both for what they show of the composer's ingenuity and invention, and for the unique way in which they match the taste and needs of an educated eighteenth-century patron. For this corpus is the epitome of music written for a single patron rather than for a large audience. Indeed, when Haydn later expressed some regret at having spent so much time writing for the baryton, he must have meant that these works did not enhance his reputation in any way, since they were for solitary consumption. This comment is one of his few expressions of resentment at the system under which he worked and prospered.

The trios are almost all cast in the familiar, three-movement configuration of the Viennese divertimento, with a minuet in either second or

Haydn's own baryton on which he practiced to become as skilled as his Prince. The illustration clearly shows two sets of strings: one bowed, the other sympathetically vibrating.

third place. Among the seventy-two trios probably composed in the years 1765–69, the most usual first movement is a slow *arioso* in binary form. (There is one that is an arrangement of Gluck's famous aria "Che faro" from his opera *Orfeo ed Euridice.*) Fast binary forms are the next most frequently used, with rudimentary sonata forms and themes with variations trailing behind. The sonata structures are small and bear no relationship to the extended and serious keyboard works of the period. On the other hand, the final movements of a number of the trios, from the very earliest, exhibit a leaning toward the old-fashioned and the traditional. Written in *alla brève* time, they are full of trio-sonata-like devices, such as steadily moving basses, and chains of suspensions in the upper voices. The thematic material of many Finales sound as if they came from ecclesiastical polyphony, and while several Finales are actually called fugues, many more use all the devices of the learned style, albeit with a very different effect.

In these trios Haydn, as always, worked within self-imposed limits and accomplished the well-nigh impossible. He accommodated his princely soloist with a texture that flattered him and his playing abilities, yet in no way sacrificed the integrity of the viola and cello; within the constraints of the fashionable *style galant,* Haydn introduced an immense variety of material with echoes of the church, the opera theater, and the ballroom into the private chamber. Almost every trio has some particular delight, and moreover, they seem to get better the more Haydn writes.

STRING QUARTETS Haydn continued to produce string quartets in the early 1760s, and a number of them, published together as Opus 2, greatly resemble those of Opus 1. It is clear that both sets are random gatherings written without any thought that they might eventually be put together. Modern scholarship has rejected the Op. 3 quartets from the Haydn canon, attributing them to an obscure monk, Roman Hofstetter (1742–1815); hence, a gap of seven or eight years separates the Op. 2 quartets from those of Opus 9, composed probably around 1769. Haydn's life had changed radically in the years between 1759 and 1769 and so had his music; the differences between these quartets and the earlier ones are great.

The Op. 9 quartets are in four, not five, movements, with the minuet in second position, and an *Adagio* or *Largo* in third. Of particular interest is the fact that four of the six first movements are marked *Moderato* in "common" time, a marking which Haydn regularly used in keyboard sonatas and chamber music at this time, but which he avoided in symphonies, preferring *Allegro*. The reason for this may well be that *Moderato*—in modern terms really a slow tempo—allows the composer to use a wide variety of note values and a wide range of emotional affect, often including the kind of seriousness inappropriate in the first movement of a symphony, where high spirits were the rule. It is equally interesting that of the five final movements marked *Presto,* four are in 2/4 meter. Perhaps Kirnberger helps us to perceive something of Haydn's artistic aims when he says, "Lively sentiments generally require a fast tempo" and that 2/4 meter is to be "performed much more lightly."[9] Haydn seems to want the greatest possible contrast between successive movements, and hence the placing of the minuet as second movement (an option generally available to the string quartet in the eighteenth century) is desirable, since such a stately pace for a first movement can hardly be followed by another, still slower, movement. Thus, although variety of keys and tempos is obviously desired, a certain structural uniformity is tolerated.

Throughout these quartets—indeed, throughout his life—Haydn required more virtuoso technique from the first violin than from the other instruments. He played the violin as well as he played any instrument, and in the Op. 9 quartets he had the added incentive of writing for a fine violinst, Luigi Tomasini, of whom he was particularly fond. In no sense can any of the quartets be looked upon as "solo" quartets for violin with accompaniment of string trio: the integrity of all instruments is guarded carefully. But concerto influences make themselves felt from time to time in cadenzas, double-stopped passages, flights into the highest register of the instrument, and aria-like slow movements in which the violin becomes an operatic heroine. By the middle of the

9. Johann Philipp Kirnberger, *The Art of Strict Musical Composition,* trans. David Beach and Jürgen Thym (New Haven, 1982), pp. 380, 386–87.

following decade, Haydn's quartet writing is largely purged of this kind of virtuosic demand, yet to the end he continues to think like a violinist.

SYMPHONIES The decade is particularly rich in the production of symphonies (approximately forty), and while the piano sonata and the string quartet exemplify chamber music ideals, and the baryton music personifies Prince Nikolaus's musical tastes, no other single genre in Haydn's output brings the past and the present together more effectively. As might be expected, the four-movement symphony, opening and concluding with fast movements which enclose an *Adagio* or *Andante* as second movement and a Minuet and Trio in third place, accounts for more than half the total. The next most common format is the three-movement configuration in which a fast first movement is followed by a slow one, concluding with another fast movement or a Minuet and Trio. Throughout the decade, he also wrote symphonies in church-sonata form, S/F/Minuet and Trio/F, with all movements in the same key. Very occasionally, a Minuet and Trio will be used as second movement, or you will encounter a slow introduction to a fast first movement. There is even an example, in Symphony No. 15, of a slow introduction which recurs at the end of the first movement.

First movements, except for those in the church-sonata symphonies, are invariably brisk, and carry the marking *Allegro* or *Presto* or *Vivace*. The material is fundamentally different from that which Haydn finds suitable for sonatas or quartets. Unison passages, the alternation of tonic and dominant harmony, cadential figures, and simple melodic motives all help create a sense of verve and motion in a texture in which musical events are spread very thin, in contrast to the compression, concentration, and pregnant density of the average sonata or quartet. The typical symphonic gesture can perhaps be compared to the broad brush strokes used by the painter of stage scenery: both must make their mark clearly, without ambiguity or subtlety, and are not designed to bear close scrutiny. Indeed, it is impossible to separate the early eighteenth-century symphony from its performing force since its musical material tends to be so slight and its structures so simple. Its very lifeblood depends upon the varied timbres of the orchestra and when reduced for the keyboard alone, it seems to disappear. The following examples illustrate typical symphonic openings. Symphony No. 13 was composed around 1763. Here are the first eight bars of the first-violin part; all the strings are in unison and the flute, 2 oboes, and 4 horns sustain chords:

Example XII–4: J. HAYDN, Symphony No. 13, I

The following string parts are from the opening eight bars of Symphony No. 35 (1767). The relationship of each two-bar motive is simplicity itself, yet even greater simplicity follows, for the next eight bars alternate tonic and dominant harmony with all the strings in unison.

Example XII–5: J. HAYDN, Symphony No. 35, I

Beyond the opening, the structure of the fast first movements is almost invariably tripartite, with exposition, development, and recapitulation clearly defined. While there is something like parity between the large sections, the exposition is usually the longest section, and two-thirds of the first movements have recapitulations somewhat longer than the developments. Within that broad structural outline, however, the small-scale variations, the exploration of novel relationships between different parts of the melodic material, the variety and the extent of contrast, all these exceed in invention and workmanship anything else in symphonic music at this time. Indeed, in building the fast first movements of his symphonies, Haydn brings to mind a medieval mason working on a cathedral. The broad outlines of the work and its proportions can be appreciated by everyone, yet hidden in places where few will ever see them are the gargoyles, those fantastic figments of the artist's imagination, and the finely crafted details whose purpose is to speak to the greater glory of God. *In nomine Domini* and *Laus Deo,* says Haydn.

On the other hand, the first movements of the church-sonata symphonies bespeak a mood of deep seriousness from the outset. Symphony No. 22 in E♭, which carried the title *The Philosopher* even in Haydn's day, uses a rudimentary kind of *cantus firmus* technique, setting an ecclesiastical-sounding melody in half notes played by English horn and French horn alternately, against a bass line in even eighth notes on the strings. The first movement of most church-sonata symphonies is in binary form, divided in the middle by a strong cadence in a new key, with both sections repeated. Symphony No. 21 in A (*ACM* 28) is written in a free form that exemplifies the sonata principle excellently without adhering to the usual structure. The movement presents a duality, the first part of which is introduced by the strings in mm. 1–3, and the second by the winds in mm. 4–7. The progress of the movement, which explores the potential of the first three measures of string material in a series of thoughtful and searching developments, is marked by the progressive assimilation of the opposing material of the opening, until, in the last cadence, one could argue a complete reversal of roles by strings and wind and the simultaneity of these role reversals—a real sonata synthesis.

The events which called the early symphonies into being are, for the most part, unknown. We can be fairly certain, however, that Haydn's appointment to the Esterházy family engendered the richest response to the symphony genre of the decade. Symphonies Nos. 6, 7, and 8, which carry the programmatic titles *Le Matin, Le Midi,* and *Le Soir,* were written, it is said, at the suggestion of Prince Anton, and in them Haydn united a variety of stylistic influences. Perhaps the most evident quality of these works is their sonorous richness, which arises not from the use of novel or unexpected instruments, but from utilizing the concerto principle within the symphonic framework. In some movements the strings are scored as *ripieno* with a *concertino* of two violins and cello. In almost all movements the wind players depart from their customary role of sustaining harmonies to become soloists—a striking compliment to the prince on the quality of his musicians, and a diplomatic way for Haydn to ensure his popularity with the players. In all three symphonies, the trio of the minuet movement contains a prominent solo part for the double bass recalling Baroque practices in the *concerto grosso;* yet Haydn, using the standard combination of flutes, oboes, bassoons, horns, and strings, creates a modern orchestration, many of the features of which are retained and used by him in his later symphonies.

Programmatic elements, on the model of Vivaldi's *Seasons,* might be expected to abound, since the eighteenth-century audience loved music that painted pictures as directly—even naïvely—as possible. They are not abundant here, however. *Le Matin* opens with a short sunrise, a slow introduction to the *Allegro* movement, and *Le Soir* closes with a storm movement, entitled *La Tempesta.* Two slow movements cry out for explanation, however: that of *Le Matin* is a three-part structure, **A B A,** in which the *Adagio* opening and closing offer what has been described as an "amusing parody of a solmization class,"[10] while the middle section is an *Andante* concerto movement for solo violin and cello. The slow movement of Symphony No.7, *Le Midi* consists of an accompanied recitative and a sensitively orchestrated aria, in which the

10. Karl Geiringer, *Haydn, A Creative Life in Music* (Berkeley, CA 1982), p. 236.

solo violin once again acts the tragic operatic heroine, declaiming a variety of emotions. (This is the first of Haydn's many transcriptions of the operatic idiom into instrumental terms.) Beyond these examples, the more typical slow movement of Symphony No. 38 in a simple binary form and orchestrated without winds, relies upon a special effect to make its mark. In this case it is echo, and the fact that this particular echo has a variable time lag and repeats selectively did not worry the eighteenth-century audience at all. It allowed for the lavish use of orchestral color, and thus rewarded composer, connoisseur, and inexperienced listener alike. Moreover, it was an improvement on nature.

The Minuets and Trios, usually the third movement, require very little explanation. They involve the whole orchestra again after the generally restricted orchestration of the slow movement, and Haydn frequently makes his trios a sonorous contrast to the minuets by some orchestral device. The first minuet is invariably written in the tonic key of the symphony, and that tonic is maintained in the trio, although Haydn is quite prepared to change the mode. A small number of trios are in the subdominant, but the dominant is very uncommon.

The majority of finale movements carry tempo markings such as *Presto, Allegro di molto,* etc., and a couple have *alla breve* time signatures. One is even a *Fuga,* as in the baryton trios. Most are small sonata structures, even simpler in extent and nature than the first movements. Ternary movements and rondos are not common.

This, then, is the Haydn symphony during the decade when he wrote more of them than at any other time in his life. His instinctive sense of those qualities appropriate to a symphony results in works substantially different from any other instrumental compositions. For the most part, they are brilliant in color, exuberant, and more humorous and detached than emotionally searching. This general description must always be qualified in the light of the few exceptional works in the minor mode, such as Symphonies Nos. 26, 39, and 48. In these, simplicity of form does not prevent Haydn from moving away from the restraints of the *style galant* into a world of broad, expressive power undreamed of by earlier composers. Perhaps these works can only to be truly savored by the real connoisseur.

OPERAS Haydn's works for the theater from this fruitful decade are lost, although fragments of *La marchesa Nespola,* an Italian *commedia* which he wrote around the time of Nikolaus's accession to the title, and *Acide,* composed in 1762 for the wedding of Nikolaus's son, have survived. *La canterina* (1766) is the first of his operatic works preserved in its entirety. It is an intermezzo designed to be performed in the two intervals of a three-act *opera seria.* There are four characters instead of the more customary two in this little work, which has, as its subject, the scheming of a pretended mother-daughter team (the relationship is somewhat that of genteel procuress and harlot) to exploit a pair of lovers. All ends happily as the men philosophically accept the mercenariness of the women, since it brings its rewards. Haydn uses his quartet of characters to excellent effect throughout the work. Much has been made of the parody of *opera seria* style that Haydn writes into the score, and certainly the endless accompanied recitative and aria that the singing teacher (one of the lovers) prepares to teach is humorous in its long-windedness. Thirty bars of fine, boisterous music precede the phrase "What must I do?" which is followed by a further seven bars before the single word "husband." Other parody effects abound, such as the C-minor aria (No.10) with English horn which, together with the *recitativo accompagnato* that follows, mimics the accents of true emotion. But the length is part of Haydn's ordinary procedure in his operas, and the emotionalism is certainly no more strongly pronounced than that which any skilled opera composer could readily produce on demand. Perhaps the largest element of humor is to be found in the story itself and in the fact that Haydn's first-performance cast had Appolonia, the pretended mother, sung by a man in falsetto, while the younger of the lovers was sung by a woman in pants. Much of the stage business lends itself to comedy, and altogether this little intermezzo stands up well enough to have been successfully revived in modern times.

Haydn's next opera, *Lo speziale* (The Apothecary), was composed in 1768 to a play by Carlo Goldoni, probably for the opening of the Esterháza opera theater. The designation of the opera as a *dramma giocoso,* which seems to link it with later masterpieces such as Mozart's *Don Giovanni,* is relatively insignificant, for this work is pure *commedia dell'arte.* In adapting Goldoni's play for the Esterháza cast of players, the serious characters were dropped and only the *partie buffe* were kept, with the result that the opera has not a serious thought in it. The plot concerns Sempronio, an old apothecary, who wishes to marry his ward, Grilletta, for her money. She has two other suitors, however: Mengone, who has gone into the apothecary's service to be close to Grilletta, and Volpino, a poor rival. Like *La canterina,* this opera survives only in incomplete form, since some music for the third act is missing. But what remains shows that Haydn is developing a complete command of his own style of Finale. At the conclusion of the first and second acts, Haydn writes music which completely reinforces the developing situation of the comedy. In his arias, however successful they may be on other counts, he allows the drama to stagnate, and events which are comical at first hearing are repeated, perhaps in response to an instinct for musical symmetry. Unfortunately, the result is that their return is anticipated and all humor is lost. An example is No. 5, in which vulgar comedy is made from Mengone's graphic description of what happens to costive bowels after a dose of his rhubarb prescription. Yes, Haydn's musical language can cope with this situation, as his orchestration hints at actions to be demonstrated by the singer. Scatology was considered appropriate material for comedy by all levels of eighteenth-century society, and the byword "Nature" had many ramifications. Similarly, Volpino's aria (No. 9), set in the minor mode, has the coward threatening death and destruction to his rivals in love, but then he has second thoughts whether or not he might survive in hand-to-hand combat. These second thoughts are comically expressed by Haydn, but when the symmetry of his aria has him repeat the idea, its effect is one of prolixity. Totally successful is the evocation of Turkish music in Volpino's third-act aria (No. 20; *ACM* 29) in which he masquerades as a wealthy Turk in order to buy Grilletta from her guardian. In this aria Haydn succeeds in supporting the verbal comedy with highly colored, exotic music that matches the text in every way and fulfills the dramatic needs of the situation with not one note too many.

Haydn's last opera of the decade was also written to a play by Goldoni. *Le pescatrici* (The Fisherwomen) was composed in 1769 and first performed in 1770 at the wedding celebrations of a niece of the prince. It comes down to us in a fragmentary state, but it is still the largest and most impressive work for the stage to this point. Haydn wrote for a larger force of soloists and chorus, as well as for a larger orchestra, and the work is a *dramma giocoso* in that it has two comic pairs of lovers and one serious pair. In this work Haydn wrote his longest and most formulaic arias, regardless of the dramatic situation. For example, the opening aria for one of the comic fishermen (167 measures in length—as long as many a symphonic movement) has a 25–measure orchestral introduction, during which the singer must do something—but what? The words of the aria are high-flown and supported by the following kinds of extravagant coloratura:

Example XII–6: J. HAYDN, *Le Pescatrici*

It is possible to argue that Haydn is here parodying the style of the current Neapolitan *opera seria,* but this argument is weakened by the observation that such extended and formal coloratura arias are given indiscriminately to all characters, not only in this work but in the others mentioned above. A better explanation for this seemingly undramatic usage is that at this stage Haydn, quite uncritically, used the forms and mannerisms that were most popular with theater audiences.

MUSIC FOR THE CHURCH After 1766, Haydn's position as Kapellmeister required him to produce music for religious occasions, and two Masses survive from this period together with a quantity of other church music. The *Missa Cellensis in honorem B.V.M.* (Hob. XXII:5) may well have been a show of gratitude to Prince Nikolaus when Haydn succeeded Werner, for it is a long "number" Mass. In it, the various phrases of the text of the *Credo* and *Gloria* are set as separate musical movements, and Haydn was able to compose in a variety of styles, from the learned *Gratias* fugue to the *Laudamus Te* for soprano, indistinguishable from an operatic aria except in text. So broad is the stylistic spectrum and so profound the craft that until some dated autograph fragments were discovered, scholars believed that this work was composed much later in Haydn's career.

As Haydn's reputation grew he began to receive requests for compositions from outside his own court. In 1768 he was asked to compose a cantata on the Latin text *Applausus* in celebration of the 50th anniversary of the Abbot of Zwettl's taking his vows after his novitiate. The work itself is of limited musical interest here, since it consists of elaborate arias and recitatives in the long-winded style of the most formal opera or oratorio. What is of great interest, however, is that Haydn was not able to prepare the first performance himself, sending a letter to the monks instead, in which he enumerated the specific details of correct performance practice, which are obviously of great value today. Here is the letter in its entirety:

> (Letter to an unnamed Austrian monastery, probably Zwettl in Lower Austria . . . 1768)
>
> > Since I cannot be present myself at this *Applaus* [*us*], I have found it necessary to provide one or two explanations concerning its execution, *viz.:*
> >
> > First, I would ask you to observe strictly the tempi of all the arias and recitatives, and since the whole text applauds, I would rather have the allegros taken a bit more quickly than usual, especially in the very first ritornello and in one or two of the recitatives; but no less in the two bass arias.
> >
> > Second: for the overture all you need play is an allegro and an andante, for the opening ritornello takes the place of the final allegro. If I knew

"A mighty fortress is our God," wrote Luther. The position of the Abbey of Melk overlooking the Danube River is that of a fortress, but it has no fortifications. Instead, it symbolizes the power of the church, its wealth, and its civilizing beauty.

the day of the performance, I might perhaps send you a new overture by that time.

Third: in the accompanied recitatives, you must observe that the accompaniment should not enter until the singer has quite finished his text, even though the score often shows the contrary. For instance, at the beginning where the word "metamorphosis" is repeated, and the orchestra comes in at "-phosis", you must nevertheless wait until the last syllable is finished and then enter quickly; for it would be ridiculous if you would fiddle away the word from the singer's mouth, and understand only the words "quae metamo . . ." But I leave this to the harpsichord player, and all the others must follow him. N.B.: our scholars in Eisenstadt—and there are very few—disputed a great deal over the word "metamorphosis"; one wanted the penultimate syllable short, the other long; and despite the fact that in Italian one says "metamòrfosi", I have always heard it pronounced "metamorphòsis" in Latin; should I have made a mistake, the error can be easily corrected.

Fourth: that the fortes and pianos are written correctly throughout, and should be observed exactly; for there is a very great difference between *piano* and *pianissimo, forte* and *fortiss[imo],* between *crescendo* and *forzando,* and so forth. It should be noted, too, when in the score the one or the other *forte* or *piano* is not marked throughout all the parts, that the copyists should rectify this when preparing the performance material.

Fifth: I have often been annoyed at certain violinists in various concerts, who absolutely ruined the so-called ties—which are among the most beautiful things in music—in that they bounce the bows off the tied note, which should have been joined to the preceding note. And so I would point out to the first violinist that it would be silly to play the following (as found in bar 47)

—in which the first two notes are to be taken on one bow—in such a disagreeable and mistaken way as

all staccato, and as if there were no ties present.

Sixth: I would ask you to use two players on the viola part throughout, for the inner parts sometimes need to be heard more than the upper parts, and you will find in all my compositions that the viola rarely doubles the bass.

Seventh: if you have to copy two sets of violin parts, the copyist should see that they do not have to turn their pages at the same time, because this takes away a great deal of strength from an orchestra with only a few musicians. The copyist should also see that the *da capo* signs are written out in one of the violin parts as in the score, but in the other he can put the *da capo* a couple of bars after the sign v and then write the sign in its proper place.

Eighth: I suggest that the two boys [soloists] in particular have a clear pronunciation, singing slowly in recitatives so that one can understand every syllable; and likewise they should follow the method of singing the recitation whereby, for example

must be sung

and not

The penultimate note "g" drops out entirely, and this applies to all similar cases. I rely on the skill of the tenor, who will explain such things to the boys.

Ninth: I hope for at least three or four rehearsals for the entire work.

Tenth: in the soprano aria the bassoon can be omitted if absolutely necessary, but I would rather have it present, at least when the bass is *obbligato* throughout. And I prefer a band with 3 bass instruments—'cello, bassoon and double bass—to one with 6 double basses and 3 'celli, because certain passages stand out better that way.

Finally I ask everyone, and especially the musicians, for the sake of my reputation as well as their own, to be as diligent as possible: if I have perhaps not guessed the taste of these gentlemen, I am not to be blamed for it, for I know neither the persons nor the place, and the fact that they were concealed from me really made my work very difficult. For the rest, I hope that this *Applausus* will please the poet, the worthy musicians, and the honorable reverend *Auditorio,* all of whom I greet with profound respect, and for whom I remain

Your most obedient servant, Giuseppe Haydn[11]

By the early 1760s Haydn had effected the transition from apprentice to journeyman and from journeyman to master musician. Leaving behind his humble origins and memories of grinding poverty and frequent hunger, he became the indispensable Kapellmeister to one of the most powerful men in eastern Europe. He quickly learned his place in the hierarchy around the prince. He controlled his staff humanely and generously and his prince relied upon him. His music accorded completely with his employer's taste and was written for those singers and instrumentalists whom his prince was pleased to employ. During this decade, through inner discipline and devotion to his art, Haydn was able to interest himself in the process of composition, whether it was of commissioned works or those written in answer to some internal, personal necessity. His mental absorption and delight in detail enabled him to create vital, logical structures from unpromising scraps of common musical property. Haydn's instinctive ability to distinguish between works designed to be heard and those designed to be played developed significantly during this decade. Indeed, there is a greater difference between the first movement of a quartet from Op. 9 and a symphony of the same period than between the quartets Op. 76 and the *London* symphonies. The stuff of the symphonies in the 1760s is quite comparable to that of the operatic overture or the aria ritornello. Perhaps most significant of all is the way in which Haydn used the minor mode, not solely for the half-serious, half-affected despair of the operatic *scena,* nor its translation into instrumental terms, but to broaden the whole gamut of musical experience. Haydn's moves in this direction were not entirely unique, for many composers of the time felt the need to revitalize their art with deeper, more passionate emotions. But he alone, through his genius, was able to create music that could be measured against the best in all recorded history.

11. Joseph Haydn, *The Collected Correspondence and London Notebooks of Joseph Haydn,* ed. H. C. Robbins Landon (London, 1959), pp. 9–11.

CHAPTER XIII

The Great Stylistic Break: 1770–79

HAYDN'S DUTIES AT ESTERHÁZA

The entire Esterháza establishment was dedicated to the pursuit of pleasure—a perfectly respectable eighteenth-century goal—and as one of the most important purveyors of pleasure to Prince Nikolaus and his guests, Haydn had little leisure time. The constant entertainments that the prince provided for his guests were elaborate and, when that guest was particularly important, enormously complex. The spectacular events that were scheduled for the visit of the Archduke Ferdinand and his lady in 1775, for example, will indicate the lavishness of the amusements, and the amount of labor involved in organizing such a celebration.

> 28 August. Guests arrive at 8:00 p.m. Elaborate reception followed by a short play. Illumination of the castle and concluding banquet.
>
> 29 August. Guests wakened by wind-band music. Inspection of Castle and Theater. Luncheon. Tour of park and gardens ending at the opera-house, where Haydn's newly composed opera *L'incontro Improvviso* was performed. A "*souper*" followed the opera and the evening concluded with a masked ball for 1300 guests.
>
> 30 August. Morning of rest. In the afternoon a drive to the park where a village market had been set up with stalls from which guests could purchase gold jewellery. Then, after the high personages had examined the various merchants' stalls, they came to a great open clearing, which reminded one of the great boulevards in Paris. Here one saw: (1) a Punch and Judy theater; (2) a hawker's stall; (3) a female singer who sang pictures; (4) a dentist's stand; (5) a dance platform with peasant music; (6) two musician's stands. As soon as you entered this section, you were invited to some special pleasantry. Three characters of well-known farcical roles displayed their art, Harlequin, Pierrot and Balliazo, just as in Paris. Thereafter a dentist, mounted on a horse, arrived, with his assistants mounted on mechanical horses; then a hawker, seated on a wagon drawn by six oxen; the wagon was accompanied by monkeys, lions and tigers. The hawker had on a large sheet a list of all his cures in pictorial form, which he humorously explained. Then each one took his place and displayed his abilities.

> Monsieur Bienfait, who is in the actual service of the Prince, showed the artful tricks of his marionettes; the cobbler from Paris played his little farce; the hawker hawked his wares; the dentist showed his abilities strutting on stilts eighteen feet high, and how he drew teeth; the 'picture singer' explained her painted murder scene in a French song. Then back to the marionette theatre, where an opera by d'Ordonez was presented. This was followed by fireworks, a "souper" and another masked ball.
>
> 31st Aug. A deer hunt in the morning. A play with incidental music by Haydn in the afternoon. After the evening meal, the company, with the princely *Feldharmonie* [wind band] went to the great oval clearing in the park, to see the gala illumination. . . . A cannon salute brought a swarm of 2000 Hungarian and Croatian peasants who filled the clearing in an instant and, swinging banners, danced to their own music and filled the air with shouts of joy. This *Volksfest* went on until the early hours of the morning, and as the day dawned on the exhausted folk dancers and the sleepy guests, who were also participants in a final masked ball, the park was softly illuminated by innumerable green lampions.[1]

The condition of the visitors when they left can only be guessed at!

The circumstances of Haydn's life and duties underwent little change during this decade. He looked after his staff, patching-up their quarrels, standing as godfather to their children, and pleading their case with the prince. In 1776, the prince decided that instead of maintaining an opera theater solely for visiting troupes of actors and for occasional musical theatrics, there should be, on the premises, a full-blown, well-rounded opera season each year. This decision resulted in an immense amount of additional work for Haydn, since the operas presented invariably had to be adapted in some way for the Esterháza stage or for their singers. In compensation, however, the prince's interest in playing the baryton declined as his interest in opera increased.

In 1779, the great ballroom and the opera theater burned down, and amidst all the destruction, the performing parts and scores of many of Haydn's works were entirely lost. That we still have fragments of *Lo speziale, Le pescatrici,* and a few other works is due only to a happy accident, for Haydn had parts of the manuscripts at home at the time of the fire. It is typical of the imperturbable and monolithic organization that despite the immense loss and disruption, a new marionette opera was presented hardly twenty-four hours after the ruins stopped smoking, for there were guests in residence.

On 1 January 1779 Haydn had signed a new contract of service with Prince Esterházy which superseded the one made almost twenty years earlier. Under the new terms Haydn's salary rose from 600 to 782 florins, with a number of other provisions for payment in kind. More important, however, is the reduction of the original fourteen conditions

1. Cited in Landon, *op. cit.,* II, pp. 218–223, here paraphrased and shortened.

For a long time, this picture was thought to be of an opera performance in the theater at Esterháza, and that the man playing keyboard continuo was Haydn. Although this is now in doubt, the illustration does give us a good idea of the dimensions of a private theater, the size of the stage, and the seating plan of the orchestra. (Deutsches Theatermuseum, Munich)

to six, summarized as follows:

1. Haydn shall lead a Christian life.
2. He shall behave decently to his subordinates.
3. He shall be available at the Prince's pleasure.
4. He shall not absent himself without permission.
5. Both parties can give termination notice of three months.
6. The Kapellmeister shall have a new winter and summer uniform every two years, or cash in lieu.

A comparison of this summary with Haydn's original contract (see p. 212) will demonstrate the difference which eighteen years of exemplary service had made, and Haydn must have been gratified by the relative independence and artistic self-sufficiency which he was now accorded.

On the other hand, although Haydn's reputation was growing apace, he had a number of powerful enemies in Vienna who consistently frustrated his attempts to gain a foothold there. There can be little doubt that the Italian clique in that city worked against Haydn as they also worked against Mozart, and moreover, they had the ear of the emperor, Joseph II. This enmity persisted to the very last years of the century.

COMPOSITIONS

The music Haydn wrote during this decade reveals a mastery of materials, a subtlety of craftsmanship, and a fertility of invention that the composer was never to surpass. But it must also be acknowledged that there were occasional lapses when the works he wrote were purely routine, at best.

The early 1770s were particularly rich in instrumental music, and Haydn produced masterpieces in the fields of sonata, string quartet, and symphony. Owing to Prince Nikolaus's growing interest in opera, however, Haydn composed more operas at this time than in all the remaining years of his life. At least four were lost entirely in the fire, but five big operas survive as well as one marionette opera.

KEYBOARD SONATAS He wrote at least eighteen keyboard sonatas in this period, the majority of which are works of genius. The works were published in sets of six: the first in 1774, dedicated to Prince Esterházy; the second in 1776; and the third, dedicated to the Misses Auenbrugger, in 1780. The last collection contains one of the most famous of Haydn's sonatas, written very early in the decade. The C-minor Sonata (Hob. XVI:20) is always singled out as the best of the *Sturm und Drang* works, although many consider the first movement of the G-minor Sonata (Hob. XVI:44), already discussed, a better example of the style. It is certain, however, that the development and particularly the recapitulation of the C-minor's last movement are among Haydn's most thoughtful and expressive pages. Overall, the consistently mature sonatas are in the set dedicated to Esterházy (Hob. XVI:21–26), although critical opinion has judged them somewhat conventional. In fact, they were an ideal set to dedicate to this particular connoisseur, who, as we know, was quite prepared to object to anything that did not suit his taste. Each is very different from the others, and they are all filled with novelty, *galanterie,* humor, learned effects, and originality. In putting the set together, Haydn placed at the outset the sonata with the most orthodox opening movement, full of insistent *galant* dotted rhythm (the Austrian notated equivalent of the French *notes inégales*), and regularity of phrase structure. The entire sonata (Hob. XVI:21) might seem conservative were it not for its aggressively monothematic last movement, sparkling with wit and almost bursting with compressed energy. The short development section is packed with incident, moving rapidly, and leaning strongly, at first, to the flat side of tonic, then as strongly to the sharp side, returning to the tonic only after further rhythmic and tonal sleight of hand.

The second sonata (Hob. XVI:22) speaks to connoisseurs. The opening eight bars display material that is deceptively simple. Nothing quite balances, however, and relationships between figures are always a little off center. The cadence in m. 8 betrays its origins in the *empfindsamer Stil* of North Germany. The recapitulation of this opening material points up Haydn's response to the throwaway, off-beat cadence, for the first four bars are identical with the opening, but where the dominant chord initially occupied the space of one eighth note, in the recapitulation it takes up six and a half bars. Perhaps the most significant moment of the work takes place after this event, when the small figure in m. 15 is developed over six bars (mm. 61–66), uncovering a moment of seriousness seemingly out of place in a work of such polished humor.

It is noteworthy that of the four three-movement sonatas in this set, three have slow middle movements in the minor mode. The E-minor slow movement of the second sonata holds no surprises comparable to those in the first movement. It is a melodic movement, full of sentiment and with a mixture of antique and modern flavor—antique in its echoes of the trio textures with Corellian suspensions, and modern in the vehemence of its pre-cadential textures. The D-minor slow movement of the fourth sonata (Hob. XVI:24) runs into the last movement without a break—a device that Haydn never overuses although it has considerable precedent. The Haydn Finale reaches full maturity in these six sonatas, ranging from binary sonata forms to the hybrid, ternary rondo, and variation structures. The two-movement Sonata in E♭ (Hob. XVI:25) concludes with a *Tempo di Menuet* written in strict canon. The final movement of the E-major sonata is a variation/rondo hybrid in *Tempo di Menuet*. The binary theme in E is subject to repeats, then is followed by an episode in E minor. At the return of the main theme in the major it is played again with a varied reprise. The first episode is then repeated in variation, followed by a final appearance of the main theme, again with varied reprises. The complex resultant form can be pictured as follows:

<table>
<tr><th>A</th><th>B</th><th>A</th><th>B</th><th>A</th></tr>
<tr><td>a:||:b</td><td>c:||:c'</td><td>a a' b b'</td><td>c~:||:c'~</td><td>a a² b b²</td></tr>
<tr><td>E major</td><td>E minor</td><td>E major</td><td>E minor</td><td>E major</td></tr>
</table>

At the opposite pole is the last Sonata in A (Hob. XVI:26), which has a long, rich first movement, followed by a short Minuet and Trio (a further aspect of Haydn's humor—the minuet and trio are both to be played *al rovescio,* i.e., first forward and then backward). It ends with a tiny Finale, marked *Presto,* which is only 26 bars long (*ACM* 30). This incredibly flippant conclusion to a set of six works, although rare, is not unique. It is the image of the last movement of the Op. 9 quartets (coincidentally in the same key), which has always caused critics such a problem when they try to explain its brevity by alleging that Haydn must have become tired, or that he lost interest. This set of sonatas alone is sufficient to immortalize Esterházy's name, since it affords enjoyment to the amateur and delight to the connoisseur. The other sets of the period contain many features of note, and some of them, in particular Hob. XVI:36, are among the finest that Haydn ever wrote.

The sonata for piano with accompaniment of strings seems not to have attracted Haydn during this time, and the couple that are tentatively dated in this decade differ in no way from earlier works for the same combination. However, the production of trios for baryton, viola, and cello continued unabated until approximately 1775, when, as stated above, the prince's interest in the baryton mercifully waned.

STRING QUARTETS The six String Quartets Op. 9 (Hob. III:19–24; 1771) were composed as a group, as were the six Quartets Op. 17 (Hob. III:25–30; 1772) and the six of Op. 20 (Hob. III:31–36; 1772) and were not gathered together by publishers, as Op.1 and Op.2 had been. We cannot be entirely certain of the order of quartets within each opus. Different publishers issued them in different order, and whether Haydn suggested the order or simply agreed is not known (he was not above rearranging the order of works within an opus so that he could sell them to different publishers at the same time). All eighteen works of the three publications were probably composed within the space of three or four years at most, and hence it is not surprising that they show similarities. Rather the wonder is the evidence of difference and development. Like Op. 9, the six quartets of Op.17 include one in the minor mode, which is fourth in the set; four of the six open with *Moderato* movements in common time; of the remaining two, one opens with a *Presto* movement in 6/8 and one with a slow theme with four variations; the Menuet is invariably placed as second movement, with an *Adagio* or *Largo* movement in third place; a Finale movement in simple or compound duple time concludes five of these six quartets. The Op.17 set also embodies some differences which seem to indicate developmental change. The minor-mode work (No.4; Hob. III:28) uses a coda to round off its first movement—a practice that is carried forward into Op.20. One Menuet (No. 4; Hob. III:28) differs in mode from the fundamental tonality of the work, and four of the trios are in the minor mode, as opposed to two in Op. 9. Similarly, two of the Op. 17 slow movements are in the relative minor.

The overall differences become more pronounced with Op.20, despite the fact that very little time can have elapsed between the writing of the last quartet of Op.17 and the first of Op.20. Two quartets are set in the minor mode (No. 3; Hob. III:33 and No.5: Hob. III:35) and the first movements of both have coda conclusions. Instead of all Menuets in second-movement position, three appear as second movements and three in the symphonic configuration as third (both minor-mode works have a second-movement Menuet). The slow movements also show greater variety than previously. There is only one example of the aria-like slow movement (No.6; Hob. III:36). Instead, No.4 (Hob. III:34) has a theme with variations and coda, and No. 2 (Hob. III:32) has a free-form *Capriccio,* a fantasia-like piece which opens with an emphatic unison melody broken by declamatory passages and pauses, moving into an affective melody with accompaniment. The slow movement of No.1 (Hob. III:31) is one of the most singular in all of Haydn's production. It proceeds mostly in even notes in all parts, and the melodic initiative quietly and subtly shifts from part to part. In addition, the emotional atmosphere breathes more of the spiritual than the theatrical, the deeply serious rather than the affected.

The Op. 20 quartets have always been considered exceptional because three of the six have fugal finales. Today we are in a better position than ever before to see that Haydn's use of "learned" devices is not unique to these quartets, nor is it simply a manifestation of historicism on his part. It is clear that Prince Nikolaus enjoyed a touch of fugue and believed it a proper part of a connoisseur's equipment to be able to appreciate it, without losing his claim to be a *galant,* fashionable man (fugue was, by nature, serious, and the *galant* man was never too serious). However, Haydn's seriousness is not manifested in fugue; on the contrary, it is characteristic of his use of learned devices in instrumental music that they are to be found only where they cannot be taken seriously. The use of canon, the strictest of the learned devices, was observed in a dance movement, a minuet, as was the use of *al rovescio,* or retrograde motion, and fugal finales have been noted in the baryton trios—those *galant* works *par excellence.* Eighteenth-century manners, whether at Versailles or Esterháza, required that skills acquired through hard work be played down, and matters of life and death be treated lightly—how else could dueling have flourished? The man of fashion could be serious, witty, sentimental or lighthearted; he could never be pedantic or dull. In these Op. 20 Quartets, as traditionally arranged for publication, fugal finales appear in numbers 2, 5, and 6. In Haydn's own catalogue, the quartets are organized into two sub-groups: 5, 6, 2 and 3, 4, 1, i.e., those with fugues and those without fugues.

The fugues themselves are all fast in tempo and each carries the injunction "*sempre sotto voce*" (quiet throughout).The fugal subjects warrant inspection. The first is called *Fuga a 2 soggetti* and has a main subject of archaic or traditional flavor, to be expected perhaps from the *alla breve* time signature.

Example XIII–1: J. HAYDN, Quartet Op. 20, No. 5 (Hob. III:35), subject

The second fugal finale is headed *Fuga con 3 soggetti* with a tempo marking of *Allegro.* The time signature here is common, which covers

Example XIII–2: J. HAYDN, Quartet Op. 20, No. 6 (Hob. III:36), subject

a variety of expressive aims from the serious to the sprightly. The main subject has nothing archaic about it, but clearly belongs to its own time.

The third finale is entitled *Fuga a 4 soggetti,* the main subject of which, with its octave leaps, sliding chromaticism, and lurching falling fifths, seems more appropriate for peasants' merrymaking than for the Esterházy court.

Example XIII–3: J. HAYDN, Quartet Op. 20, No. 2 (Hob. III:32), subject

While the remaining finales do not set out to be fugues, a certain amount of contrapuntal usage is assimilated, perhaps more than was in evidence in earlier finales.

Many writers have praised Haydn for reviving Baroque techniques, but this is not really the case. Baroque techniques of counterpoint never died but were always a vital part of eighteenth-century practice, particularly in compositions for the church. Haydn's real achievement, in so much of his work of the early seventies, was to reconcile counterpoint and fugue and all the other learned devices with the *galant* ideals of wit and deftness that denigrate expertise and try to make every accomplishment seem easy.

Haydn thought so highly of the last-composed quartet of Op.20 (*ACM* 31) that he placed it first in the published set. The unique slow movement has already been mentioned and its virtues speak for themselves. In the first movement there is a new lightness in the way the instruments are handled. The sonorous possibilities resulting from the division of the quartets into different groupings, setting three of the four instruments of the group against another three, of using duets, of placing the viola in the bass and giving the melody to the cello, of using groupings antiphonally—Haydn had never realized all these ideas as fully as he did in this quartet. Above all, the integrity of each instrumental part within the texture is novel. This is particularly noticeable in the first fifteen measures of the movement. In the overall structure there is a total absence of padding or anything that resembles passagework; hence the movement is as lean as its lines are taut.

Quartet players, amateur and professional, have tended to disregard the quartets of Opp. 9, 17, and 20 as "early" quartets, hardly worthy of attention, despite the fact that Haydn wrote them between the ages of thirty-six and forty. Since his quartet corpus is so large the loss of these works was hardly felt. Today, however, there is little excuse for failing to acknowledge these as masterpieces. Tovey says:

> With op.20 the historical development of Haydn's quartets reaches its goal, and further progress is not progress in any historical sense, but simply the difference between one masterpiece and the next . . . not even op.76, is, on its own plane, so uniformly weighty and so varied in substance as op.20.[2]

SYMPHONIES Haydn's symphonic production in the seventies is only slightly smaller than in the sixties. The twenty-odd works from this decade tend to be more uniform in structure. The church-sonata symphony disappears, and its most important feature, the slow first movement, is perpetuated by Haydn as the slow introduction to the first *Allegro* movement, a practice which reached its peak in the last symphonies. The uniformity of key of the church sonata is not entirely given up, and three symphonies, Nos. 44, 46, and 52, preserve the idea of a single tonic for all four movements, varying only the mode. In this period there are only a couple of exceptions to the Menuet as third movement.

The pervasive uniformity tends to make Haydn's exceptional procedures, his experiments with form, the more striking. The so-called *Sturm und Drang* symphonies, Nos. 44 in E minor, 45 in F♯ minor, and 52 in C minor are each distinguished by thematic material of unusual potency. The Symphony No. 46 in B incorporates a repeat of the Menuet (3rd mvt.) within the body of the last movement. No. 67 in F (1778) uses a three-part, **A B A** form with an unusual balance; in the midst of the *Allegro di molto* finale, Haydn inserts an *Adagio e cantabile* section of considerable length, which opens with two violins and cello solo. After this, the tutti, dominated by the winds, continues the material until what has seemed like an interpolated slow movement gives way to a return of the opening material. The single most exceptional symphony is perhaps No. 60 in C of 1774, subtitled *Il distratto* (The Absent-minded Man) since it is based on music Haydn wrote for a play by Regnard, called *Le Distrait*. It is in six distinct movements, not counting the extended slow introduction to the first movement, and is built like an ordinary symphony with an extra *Adagio* and *Presto* tacked onto the end. The additional two movements allow the composer a broader key scheme than normal, as follows:

2. Donald Francis Tovey, "Haydn" in *Cobbett's Cyclopedic Survey of Chamber Music* (London, 1963) I, pp. 537–38.

Movement	Key	Time signature	Tempo
I	C	2/4	Adagio
	C	3/4	Allegro di molto
II	G	2/4	Andante
III	C	3/4	Menuetto
	C minor	3/4	Trio
	C	3/4	Menuetto
IV	C minor	2/4	Presto
V	F	2/4	Adagio (di lamentatione)
VI	C	2/4	Finale prestissimo

Because of the nature of the play, Haydn used a wide variety of rhythmic and harmonic devices, and the expressive effect ranges from seriousness to out-and-out buffoonery, from art music to folk music.

Most curious in this decade is the apparent difference between the symphonies of the early seventies, which speak eloquently of total concentration and involvement, and many of those from the late seventies and early eighties, which appear disinterested and routine. The Symphony No. 61 in D (1776) is a typical example. Reference has been made to the use of ordinary material in earlier symphonies to make striking gestures and large effects. The work in question, throughout its first movement, relies on simple forms matched by melodic triteness. Success or failure is often in the ear of the listener as well as in the function of the music, and it seems to the author that only Haydn's inimitable orchestration saves the day for this symphony.

Perhaps this is neither the time nor the place to speculate on why Haydn's inspiration did not match his industry, but other writers have dealt with the problem so we must try to place the matter in perspective. What exactly do we know? The elements of *Sturm und Drang* had been present in Haydn's work for many years, and had been enjoyed by his patron. Those compositions either dedicated to Nikolaus (the six piano sonatas of 1774) or designed by Haydn to influence him (the *Farewell* Symphony No. 45 in F♯ minor of 1772) embody the richest development of the emotional style. Hence it is difficult to accept the hypothesis that Haydn might have fallen from favor or had been instructed to write differently. He himself may have wanted to change his style, however. Criticized in North Germany and by his own emperor in Austria for the complexity of his music, Haydn undoubtedly saw that the undemanding, naive style of the Italians was successful everywhere and resolved to purge his own music of some of its pungent idiosyncrasy and humor in order to speak more directly to an international audience. And why should he wish to make this contact? Apart from the natural ambition of a man who knew his own worth, there was little to hold him back: he had no family life or childen; his days at Esterháza from

1775 were increasingly taken up with the production of operas by other composers, leaving him less and less time for the work which interested him most; in short, life was passing him by. Publishers' contracts and popularity on a broader scale would lead to emancipation from his superior kind of slavery. Whatever the roots, we know that Haydn's symphonies written in this lighter style were destined to carry his name further abroad than any of his earlier works.

THE *FAREWELL* SYMPHONY The most individual, the most important, and the most artistically successful of the symphonies of the seventies is No. 45 in F♯ minor, known as the the *Farewell*. How it came by that title is related in an anecdote, best recorded in the words of Haydn himself:

> Prince Nikolaus Esterhazy spent the whole summer at Esterhaza in a new palace that he was then building and that later became his favorite residence. His court had to attend him there. The palace, only partly built and furnished, was not yet roomy enough for such numbers; so a selection was made and the musicians who had to accompany the Prince to Esterhaza found themselves obliged to do without the companionship of their wives for six months. They were all spirited young men who looked longingly toward the last month, the day, the hour of departure, and filled the palace with lovelorn sighs. "I was then young and gay and consequently no better than the rest," said Haydn with a smile.
>
> Prince Nikolaus must long since have guessed the secret wishes of his musicians. The comic goings on must even have amused him. Otherwise how could he have taken it into his head this time to lengthen by two months the usual six months' residence?
>
> This unexpected order threw the ardent young husbands into despair. They stormed Kapellmeister Haydn, they begged, they implored: he must, he should do something!
>
> On an evening soon after, Prince Nikolaus was surprised in the most wonderful way with this music. Right in the middle of the most passionate music, one voice ends; the player silently closes his part, takes his instrument, puts out the lights, and goes off. Soon after, a second voice ends; the player behaves the same as the first, and withdraws. Now a third ends; a fourth voice; all put out their lights and take their instruments away with them. The orchestra grows dark and increasingly deserted. The Prince and all the audience maintain a wondering silence. Finally, the last man but one, Haydn himself, puts out the lights, takes his music and withdraws. A single violinist is left. Haydn had picked him to be last on purpose, because his solo playing pleased the Prince greatly, and he would be almost forced by the art of this player to wait for the end. The end came, the last lights were put out, and Tomasini also went off.—The Prince now stood up and said, "If they all go off, we must go too."
>
> The musicians had meanwhile collected in the antechamber, where the Prince found them and smiling said, "I understand, Haydn; tomorrow the

> men may all leave," whereupon he gave the necessary orders to have the princely horses and carriages ready for the journey.[3]

The *Farewell* symphony (*ACM* 32) stands as evidence of the way Haydn chose to make a point with his patron. The opening sixteen bars constitute an exquisite blend of formal structure with urgency and determination. The balanced four-bar phrases each conclude on a strong beat; the fourth phrase, no longer in harmony but in string unison, has the same rhythmic shape but is melodically contorted. The texture of the whole also presents a complex balance of forces, since the oboes and horns sing a melancholy melody which rises a minor third and then falls a step, while the first violins' avoidance of stepwise motion and determined masculine endings is supported by the urgency of the syncopations and reiterated bass notes.

In most works which have a minor-mode tonality, it was customary to modulate to the relative major as quickly as possible after the opening statement. Haydn's *Farewell* proceeds to construct an exposition in which the relative-major mode (A) is heard for a moment in the stormy ocean of rhythmic development, but at the first sign of a sustained tonal plateau (m. 38) the tonic turns to A minor and the opening material is heard again, to be followed by a rising sequence conditioned by the bass (mm. 43–49) whose material extends the rising minor third and falling step of the winds' opening. The sequence also moves the tonality to its goal of C# minor. Grinding suspensions (mm. 50–53) lead to a hiatus (m. 55), always a creator of uncertainty and tension. A unison passage in the lower strings and oboe against a high pedal Gs which has all the expressive power of an instrumental *de profundis clamavi,* recalls the unison phrase of the opening measures. Here, however, the contortions are exaggerated further by the pleading, feminine rhythm and by the augmented second interval, heard melodically in mm. 56 and 58, and then harmonically, with repeated *sforzando* stabs in mm. 60, 62, 66, and 68, as the exposition closes in C♯ minor.

The second part of the movement opens in orthodox fashion with the opening material in the relative major, A, but a series of interrupted cadences lead to a repeat of the unison passage with the augmented second, this time on the dominant of B minor, followed by a hiatus of two beats with a fermata. Critics and writers, obsessed with ideas of formal necessity, have thought to find in what follows (mm. 108–140) a displaced "second subject" from the exposition. Nothing could be further from Haydn's formal and expressive intention, although had he been intent to create a large and leisured structure he might have recapitulated this material in a coda, as Beethoven was to do in his *Eroica,* the *Farewell* Symphony's close formal descendant in this regard. After this fermata, which stands for an infinity of time, and after the human

3. Dies, *op. cit.,* pp. 100–102.

cry of despair that precedes it, Haydn takes a leaf out of the opera, for here is the only place in this movement where vocal melody is to be heard. A fragment of operatic heroine's music, lightly orchestrated on first violins accompanied by second violins and violas, pleading in its feminine cadences yet completely proper and controlled in its phrasing, comes from a distance. It is set in D, the subdominant of the relative major we have been wanting for so long, an archetypally feminine tonal relationship which Haydn was to reiterate in writing the music for the feminine moon as opposed to the masculine sun in *The Creation*. This vision of imploring femininity fades away, as the angels fade from the sight of Handel's shepherds abiding in the field in *Messiah,* in high tessitura on the first violin (mm. 139–140) to be followed by a long break which leads back to the recapitulation. Here the formal restraint of the opening is lost, and impassioned arpeggio follows arpeggio in a harmonic development of great abstruseness. In m. 150 Haydn writes the Latin tag *sapienti pauca,* a phrase which has been variously interpreted, from calling attention to the modulation to instructions to a copyist to watch the bar count. It seems much more likely that here, Haydn, who, like Mahler, was apt to write remarks on his scores that were personal prayers[4] was fervently praying that his musical message might reach its mark, for now he has done all that he can through music alone.

The finale of the symphony makes its effect primarily through the actions of the players departing, and without the visual effect, beautiful though the music may be, Haydn could not expect to succeed in his attempt. The first movement, on the other hand, must work purely as music, and hence Haydn's figurative crossing of his fingers. *Sapienti pauca* may be translated as "a word to the wise" and Haydn is expressing his confident hope that his wise prince may perceive the meaning of the few words that Haydn has addressed to him. Why did Haydn write the words in the middle of the score rather than at the end as he usually does? Probably because that was where the idea of the Latin tag occurred to him, and because beyond this point in the music there is nothing more to be said except the formal repeat of material recapitulated.

The rest of the work can speak for itself. With all their richness of key scheme, in the middle movements the entertainment value of the music takes precedence over the transmission of powerful emotional messages, as is customary. The finale is, of course, unique. The whole work has a kind of idiosyncratic fervor which must have offended and alienated many critics. While this is not Haydn the comic, it is clearly Haydn the man who knows the rules so well he can bend them when

4. The Quartets Op. 20 are sprinkled with a greater variety of Latin tags than any other set of works of Haydn, ranging from the usual to the unique "sic fugit amicus amicum" (thus friend runs from friend).

he wishes. When so many listeners, two hundred years after the event, cannot reconcile the restraints imposed by form and the license inherent in expression and refuse to see the inseparability of the two in the *Farewell* Symphony, how much more puzzling it must have seemed to Haydn's contemporaries. And how much it speaks for Esterházy's connoisseurship that he understood it at first hearing!

OPERAS The list of operas that survived the fire at Esterhaza amply demon-strates Haydn's impressive operatic activity at this time:

Title	Genre	Date	Librettist
Le pescatrici (The Fisherwomen)	Dramma giocoso	Comp.1769 Perf.1770	Goldoni
L'infedeltà delusa (Infidelity Deceived)	Burletta per musica	C.1773 P.1773	Coltellini
Philemon und Baucis	Marionette opera *Singspiel* type	C.1773 P.1773	C.G.Peffel
L'incontro improvviso (The Chance Meeting)	Dramma giocoso	C.1775 P.1775	Friberth
Die Feuersbrunst (The Conflagration)	Marionette opera *Singspiel* type	C.1775–8? P.1774–5?	unknown
Il mondo della luna (The World on the Moon)	Dramma giocoso	C.1777	Goldoni
La vera costanza (Real Constancy)	Dramma giocoso	C.1778–9	Puttini & Travaglia
L'isola disabitata (The Uninhabited Island)	Azione teatrale	C.1779	Metastasio

The summary table shows that the extant works for marionettes are of the *Singspiel* type with spoken dialogue in German, and smaller, song-like, even strophic, arias. The Italian operas are of two types: the *burletta* or *dramma giocoso,* both of which are essentially *opera buffa,* and the single *azione teatrale,* which is more closely related to the *opera seria.*

Perhaps Haydn's greatest progress as a theater composer was made in the short period between *Le pescatrici* and *L'infedeltà delusa.* The later work, which was chosen for performance during the famous visit to Esterháza of the Empress Maria Theresa in 1773, conforms much more closely to modern ideals of eighteenth-century opera than does the earlier, and fully justifies the empress's memorable remark, "When I want to hear good opera I go to Esterháza." In this opera, Haydn shows more insight into characterization by musical means and a greater sense of musical theater. There is a noticeable enriching of the melodic materials and the orchestral textures as well, all of which broaden and deepen Haydn's power to express the drama through the music. He begins to use vocal color as effectively as he has hitherto used the orchestra. Following the overture, the opera opens with a quartet of soloists with orchestra (there was no opera chorus available) which celebrates the beauty of the cool evening with a sensuousness that anticipates parts of Mozart's *Così*. In addition to its outstanding musical quality, this number also works well dramatically since it represents the calm before the storm, and serves as a foil to the troubles that are to follow so quickly.

Repeatedly throughout the score one finds foretastes of a sound that we have come to call Mozartian. The following example with its change of mode from major to minor and back again, and with its dissonant sequential structure, shows Haydn a master of what is so admired in Mozart—the ability to mirror rapidly changing emotions within a single aria, and even more, within a few measures of music (Example

Example XIII–4: J. HAYDN, *L'infedeltà delusa,* No. 1, Quartet (vocal parts only)

Example XIII–5: J. HAYDN, *L'infedeltà delusa,* No.6

XIII–5). Rapid modal change, stabbing *fortes,* and plangent dissonance all function metaphorically, standing for the anxiety of a character subject to conflicting emotion.

Whether Mozart ever saw this score by Haydn cannot be known, but it is unlikely. Yet there are places where similarities are so pronounced as to make one wonder at the power of coincidence. One of the characters, Nanni, learns that he has a rival in love and that his sweetheart, Sandrina, is being compelled by her father to marry a rich man. He sings an aria remarkably similar to "Se vuol ballare " from *The Marriage of Figaro,* which Figaro sings in a similar dramatic situation. The burden of the texts is similar: Nanni, furious, says that it shall not happen and they will be sorry for their interference; Figaro, also furious, says that if the Count wants to dance, he, Figaro, will play the tune. Both composers use F as the tonality, but in keeping with Figaro's character, his song is in major, while Nanni's is in minor turning to major. The poetic meter chosen by the librettists is the same, which leads to a melodic/rhythmic similarity. Nanni's aria is sectional, that is to say it concludes in a different meter and mode from its beginning, a procedure common in Haydn, and somewhat less so in Mozart; there is even some resemblance in the orchestral use of trills and turns. This comparison is not made to assert Haydn's influence over Mozart—influence is far too subtle a thing to be proved by a few similarities—but to show that Haydn, in 1773, has already achieved a certain modernity of operatic technique in the few years since 1769.

Example XIII–6

a. W. A. MOZART, *The Marriage of Figaro,* No. 3, "Se vuol ballare"

b. J. HAYDN, *L'infedeltà delusa,* No. 8, "Non v'e rimedio"

Striking effects in word painting abound; perhaps the most notable is to be found in a serenade-type aria sung by Nencio. The dissonance on the word "guai" (woe) and the quite unexpected move toward the key of C♭ at the words "ch'hanno posticcio il cor" (who have false hearts) are shown in the following example:

Example XIII–7: J. HAYDN, *L'infedeltà delusa,* No. 12

The libretto for this fine opera was adapted from the work of Marco Coltellini by someone close to Haydn. Coltellini was court poet in Vienna after Metastasio and a man thoroughly versed in the ideals of operatic reform held by Gluck and Calzabigi. In common with the *opera buffa* tradition, the characters are ordinary people and the aristocratic audience would have enjoyed seeing an ordinary character masquerading as "His Lordship." The two-act structure of the opera avoids the problem that plagued much Italian opera at the time—a weak, even superfluous third act—and the tonal structure allows each act the greatest tonal variety (E♭ to E), while bound to the tonic C. While Haydn has not entirely forsaken the lengthy formal structure of aria (Haydn told Dies "nothing was too lengthy for my prince"), and while incredible demands are made on the voice (Haydn's tenors sang as high as high C with ease and his basses had wide range) the kind of virtuosity that has been noted in *Le pescatrici* is less visible. This opera also provides a striking example of how Haydn began an operatic finale (for a general description, look ahead to the discussion of *La vera costanza*).

L'incontro improvviso of 1775 allowed Haydn to further develop the "Turkish" music that he had first exploited in *Lo speziale*. This mildly bizarre style was popular around Vienna in the late eighteenth century, when memories of Turkish invasion were not yet dead but were remote enough to be laughed at. In addition to inviting the use of exotic percussion instruments, cymbals and triangles, and nonsense syllables for comic effect, the music sanctioned all kinds of awkwardness not allowed in art music—consecutive fifths, fourths, and octaves, in particular.

Despite shorter arias and a shorter introductory ritornello, the pace of this opera is not as brisk as *L'infedeltà* and it was not as successful. It does contain, however, some of the most glorious music ever to come from Haydn's pen: the terzetto for three sopranos, "Mi sembra un sogno" from Act I, a set piece in which dramatic action is suspended, is almost unique in the world of opera and worthy to be set beside *Der Rosenkavalier* in its sensuous exploitation of the three female voices accompanied by two English horns, two horns, and strings.

Il mondo della luna (1777) and *La vera costanza* (1778?) are both further examples of the *opera buffa* style. *Il mondo* is Haydn's third and last opera to a Goldoni text, full of wit and moralizing, which is set to music of great humor. When Lisetta, the maid, in a tongue-in-cheek aria to her foolish master says, "Sometimes I say no, whenever I can I say yes—but never at the expense of my virtue," Haydn responds with music compelling in its *sous-entendre*. He shows more flexibility in his use of aria structure than ever before; when the arias are formal and virtuosic, the opening ritornellos are long, but on the other hand he does not hesitate to abandon the opening ritornello altogether. This in itself is a clear demonstration of his growing sense of characterization. and the dramatic.

La vera costanza is a glance backward from the modernity of Goldoni, and Haydn is often accused of showing a lack of discrimination in his choice of this libretto. As in *Le pescatrici,* the characters represent a cross-section of the social classes, with the heroine a fisherwoman secretly married to an aristocrat. (Was Haydn's preoccupation with fisherfolk the result of living in land-locked Austro-Hungary, and a reflection of his desire for travel?) It adds little new to Haydn's profile as opera composer. The Finale to the second act, however, is one of the most complex that he ever wrote: 651 measures long and in eight sections of contrasting tempos, the keys range from the initial D, through G, E minor, and B♭ back to D. The opening *Moderato* section (*ACM* 33) is a fine example of an effect also found in *Lo speziale* and *L'infedeltà delusa.* It is a type of ensemble that Rossini later featured in which the characters use a *parlando,* or speaking, style, while the orchestra carries attractive melodies, sufficiently insubstantial and repetitive to remain in the background and allow the words to be of prime importance. The action on stage at the beginning of this kind of finale is usually either static or quiet, and serves as a foil to the turmoil and tension to come as the action unfolds.

L'isola disabitata (1779), to a libretto by Metastasio first set in 1752, is styled an *azione teatrale.* As one authority has rightly said, it is "more of an oratorio than an opera," and it constitutes a return to a type that had formerly been able to hold the stage with less action than opera in 1780 required. The music is a finely wrought sequence of arias and accompanied recitatives. *Recitativo secco* is abandoned entirely. Haydn's mistress, Luigia Polzelli, played the part of Silvia in this opera, and although the score was composed with love it stands outside the mainstream of Haydn's work and of opera in general.

ORATORIO During this decade Haydn was to enter the field which, perhaps more than any other, would carry his fame through the wilderness of the nineteenth century: the oratorio. Unfortunately, *Il ritorno di Tobia* (1775) was completely in the Metastasian libretto tradition, reducing action in favor of moralizing, and placing whatever action there was in accompanied recitative. The Italian oratorio tradition dictated that the work consist of a sequence of arias and recitatives, with a chorus to open and close. Haydn himself conducted, and the work was a great success although it was not repeated until nine years later, when the composer made considerable revisions to the score, shortening some numbers and adding choruses.

There is little, if any, difference between this kind of work and the old *opera seria,* and so the oratorio appears like something from an earlier age. The arias are immensely long, rich in orchestration and vocal coloratura, conventionally used, and the introductory ritornellos are in proportion. Haydn had no stage considerations in mind so he expanded the music freely. The result is yet another work which, despite its obvious beauty and the excellence of its craft, remains a museum piece.

The changed conditions and the increased salary provided for in the contract of 1779 were rewards that Haydn might have expected in the course of time. But we must assume that the new contract might never have been issued had not Prince Nikolaus felt the need to tighten the ties that bound Haydn to him. The more indispensable Haydn became at Esterháza, the more allowance the prince was prepared to make. The engagement of Luigia Polzelli as singer in the opera theater, and of her sickly husband as violinist in the court orchestra, and their continued presence, despite her mediocre voice and his unreliable health, may well be further evidence of the prince's enlightened self-interest. Indeed, as the decade of the 1770s closed, it may have seemed to Haydn that Luigia's coming to Esterháza was the only bright spot on his horizon.

PART IV

Mozart, Genius Apparent

CHAPTER XIV

The Wunderkind Years: 1756–73

The case of Mozart, like that of the Bachs, almost forces one to speculate about the relationship between genes and genius. Wolfgang's father, Leopold Mozart, was the eldest of six sons of an Augsburg bookbinder. His superior intellect seemed to promise a career in the Church or the law, and it is surprising that he abandoned his studies in 1738 to take up the violin, while earning a living as a *valet de chambre*. In 1747 he married Anna Maria Pertl, who bore him seven children, of whom only two lived for more than a few days. The survivors were Maria Anna (1751–1829), always called Nannerl in the family, and Wolfgang Amadeus, born on 27 January 1756, and christened the following day under the resonant names of Joannes Chrysostomus Wolfgangus Theophilus. He was his parents' seventh and last child.

By 1756 Leopold's reputation had spread beyond Salzburg, where he held the post of court-composer and Vice-Kapellmeister. His compositions were enjoyed throughout the German-speaking world, and his famous book, *A Treatise on the Fundamental Principles of Violin Playing*, together with the theoretical works of Quantz and Emanuel Bach, constituted the great teaching works from the middle of the eighteenth century (see pages 28–31).

Wolfgang's talent was discovered at the age of three, when he started to attend his older sister's keyboard lessons. For teaching purposes, Leopold compiled a collection of pieces by various masters of the time, just as J. S. Bach had earlier assembled the *Notebook for Anna Magdalena*, his second wife. Although the book was intended for Nannerl, it is clear that Wolfgang used it as well, for their father inscribed on it the day and year when the boy learned certain pieces and the time he took to learn them. Accounts of the child's astonishing progress have come down to us through these annotations and from the anecdotal recollections of friends and family, recorded many years after the event. His progress in all aspects of music was evidently exceptionally rapid. An example of this is the oft-told story that he played the violin part in a trio sonata without any training, after having simply observed his father.

This famous engraving by Delafosse from a painting by Carmontelle, shows the Mozart family as they must often have appeared in public performances around 1763–64.

Wolfgang's first attempts at composition also appear in Nannerl's piano book, thriftily written on the empty pages. They date from shortly after his fifth birthday, a fact carefully noted by Leopold when he made the fair copy of these works that survive today Their interest lies not so much in their musical quality as in the evidence of the child's incredible development from one piece to the next. The very first piece (*ACM* 34), K.1a, consists of ten bars in which a random sequence of tonic-bound figures are given some sense of structure through repetition. One can imagine the child happily stringing together pleasing clichés. Approximately eight months later, in December 1761, the randomness is gone, and the *Menuetto* K.1d (*ACM* 35) is informed by a strong, clear harmonic structure and a repeated cadential figure. Also of note is the interrupted cadence in m.18. This is a device that the composer adopts from now on, which in this case serves to strengthen and delay the final cadence.

THE FIRST TOURS

As soon as possible, Leopold Mozart decided to begin the series of tours across Europe that would spread the name of Mozart far and wide.

These trips started Wolfgang the boy on the road to becoming the cosmopolitan traveling man, at ease everywhere. The first tour in early 1762 took both parents and their children to Munich and lasted for three weeks; beyond the fact that it was a success no details are known. Much of our knowledge of Wolfgang's early life and travels comes from letters written by his father to their landlord, banker, and friend Lorenz Hagenauer, and because the Munich tour was so short, Leopold evidently felt no need to correspond.

In the fall of the same year the family left Salzburg for Vienna, giving concerts on the way, and meeting with such acclaim that their fame preceded them. They were already the talk of the town when they arrived on 6 October, and within a week they were commanded to appear before the empress at Schönbrunn, where Wolfgang charmed and astonished everyone by his self-assurance and his skill. Here he met Wagenseil, whom he invited to turn pages for him in a performance of one of that composer's concertos, behavior tolerable only in a precocious six-year-old. From Vienna a trip into Hungary for two weeks brought such financial success that Leopold felt able to decline the offer of a further Viennese concert on the way back to Salzburg, where they arrived just twenty-two days before Wolfgang's seventh birthday.

These tours, important though they were, were only a prelude to Leopold's grander plan. In June 1763, the Mozarts (by now being driven in their own carriage) set off with servants from Salzburg, not to return for over three years. Traveling via Munich, Augsburg, Stuttgart, Schwetzingen, and Brussels, they reached Paris on 18 November, where they spent the next five months.

The nineteenth century never tired of recreating the eighteenth through romantic eyes. Here, the painter depicts the child Wolfgang in 1762 when he first played for the Empress Maria Thesea at Schönbrunn. (Mozart Museum, Salzburg)

Mozart's capacity to absorb and retain impressions has often been noted. The journey must have offered great promise, some of which was fully realized. The first disappointment, however, occurred in Stuttgart, where Jommelli was Kapellmeister to the Duke of Württemberg. The duke would not receive the Mozarts, and Leopold placed the blame for this on Jommelli's antagonism toward Germans. On the other hand, in Schwetzingen, Wolfgang had his first experience with the Mannheim orchestra; both he and his father were impressed.

PARIS The Paris stay was important. A month went by before the French court acknowledged the prodigy's arrival. Then, however, the reception was extremely flattering, for the queen spoke to them in German and fed them delicacies from her table, while the princesses kissed the children and were kissed back. The only sour note was sounded by the Marquise de Pompadour, the king's mistress. She, we are told, refused Wolfgang's kisses, whereupon he is reported to have said, "Who does she think she is? I have even kissed the empress."

Once royal favor was shown, the nobility were quick to follow suit, and the Mozart children were invited to perform all over Paris. There is a famous picture which shows Wolfgang playing the *clavecin* during a tea party at the palace of the Prince de Conti—a common enough occasion for the little boy. Of interest to us is the fact that the Prince de Conti's resident harpsichordist was Johann Schobert, whom many consider one of the most important influences upon Mozart's compositional style. Also on the Prince's staff were Gossec and the composer of *opéras comiques,* Josef Kohaut (1738–93).

This is a detail from a larger painting, *Le Thé à l'Anglaise* by Michel Ollivier, in which the tiny Wolfgang is seen at the harpsichord, as described in the text above. (Musée du Louvre, Paris)

It is difficult to estimate the effect that the Paris visit had on Mozart. He cannot have been unaffected by the atmosphere where not only Schobert but also Eckhard and Honauer reigned as harpsichord virtuosos and exemplified the modern German keyboard style in a French setting, and where Gaviniès and Le Duc preserved the French tradition of violin playing while blending it with the Italianate. Yet, neither at this time nor later did any of the Mozart family express any praise for French musicians or any liking for French music—rather the opposite.

LONDON Early in April 1764, the family left Paris for London, where they lived for fifteen months in the society of two of the most polished musicians of the age, Abel and Christian Bach. Of course, the children were well received by members of the gentry, the nobility, and royalty. But for us there are two important events that mark the London visit: first, young Mozart's abilities were tested "scientifically" and the results were noted and have come down to us; and second, the pace of his compositional activity increased markedly and he composed his first symphonies.

The eighteenth century, as we have observed, was an age of scientific discovery, blending naiveté, skepticism, and inquiry. Daines Barrington, who reported to the Royal Society on Mozart, was a typical man of his age, a lawyer and scholar with a variety of interests. He had observed the child and determined to test him as carefully and objectively as possible. Here is an extract from his longer report:

> I carried to him a manuscript duet, which was composed by an English gentleman to some favourite words in Metastasio's opera of Demofoonte. The whole score was in five parts, viz. accompaniments for a first and second violin, the two vocal parts, and a base *[sic]*. I shall here likewise mention, that the parts for the first and second voice were written in what the Italians stile the *Contralto* cleff; the reason for taking notice of which particular will appear hereafter. My intention in carrying with me this manuscript composition, was to have an irrefragable proof of his abilities, as a player at sight, it being absolutely impossible that he could ever have seen the music before. The score was no sooner put upon his desk, than he began to play the symphony in a most masterly manner, as well as in the time and stile which corresponded with the intention of the composer. . . Happening to know that little Mozart was much taken notice of by Manzoli *[sic]*, the famous singer, who came over to England in 1764, I said to the boy, that I should be glad to hear an extemporary *Love Song* , such as his friend Manzoli might choose in an opera. The boy on this (who continued to sit at his harpsichord) looked back with much archness, and immediately began five or six lines of a jargon recitative proper to introduce a love song. He then played a symphony which might correspond with an air composed to the single word, *Perfido*. It had a first and second part, which together with the symphonies, was of the length that opera songs generally last: if this extemporary composition was not amazingly capital, yet it was really above mediocrity, and shewed most extraordinary readi-

> ness of invention. Finding that he was in humour, and as it were inspired, I then desired him to compose a *Song of Rage,* such as might be proper for the opera stage. The boy again looked back with much archness, and began five or six lines of a jargon recitative proper to introduce a *Song of Anger*. This lasted also about the same time with the *Song of Love;* and in the middle of it, he had worked himself up to such a pitch, that he beat his harpsichord like a person possessed, rising sometimes in his chair. The word he pitched upon for this second extemporary composition was *Affetto*. After this he played a difficult lesson, which he had finished a day or two before: his execution was amazing, considering that his little fingers could scarcely reach a fifth on the harpsichord. His astonishing readiness, however, did not arise merely from great practice; he had a thorough knowledge of the fundamental principles of composition, as, upon producing a treble, he immediately wrote a base under it, which, when tried, had very good effect. He was also a great master of modulation, and his transitions from one key to another were excessively natural and judicious; he practised in this manner for a considerable time with an handkerchief over the keys of the harpsichord.[1]

EARLIEST WORKS The compositions from the London visit offer an interesting spectrum. In Wolfgang's earliest works one suspects that Leopold, while transcribing, may also have done a little touching-up. The paternal pen may well be visible in the first symphony in E♭, K.16. How else can one explain the innumerable felicities of this work by an eight-year-old except by assuming that the precocity of nascent genius was guided by the hand of experience? In its structure the work resembles the majority of sonata-binary movements composed at this time, in which Wolfgang seems to prefer equality of proportion between the two halves. The balance is beautifully preserved. The repeated material at the opening of the first movement is reiterated at the start of the second half, but now it is in the dominant key and subjected to the tonal flux that is desired. The difference in length between the two halves (58 bars as opposed to 62) is brought about by the lengthening of the texturally contrasting passage (mm. 23–30) which becomes 12 bars long in the second half (mm. 81–92) in order to accommodate the modulation. Otherwise everything else is symmetrical, and the balanced binary structure presents the repeated material in its customary, yet ever-fresh inverse relationship to the exposition. The part-writing is squarely in the Viennese tradition of chamber-music textures in symphonic music. The passage which best illustrates this tendency is in mm. 31–36, where the downward scale in thirds enlivens all the string parts. Finally, the conclusion to each half creates a strong link with the modulating material (mm. 23–30).

Others have pointed out how the second movement in the relative

1. Otto Erich Deutsch, *Mozart: A Documentary Biography* (London, 1965), pp. 96–98.

minor, with its texture of repeated triplet notes against melodic duplets, is an early example of a distinguished family of slow movements. The child's ingenuity can be seen in his creation of a variegated and vital texture in mm. 29–32. The last movement, quite different in mood, also demonstrates this same inventiveness which no one has ever attributed to Leopold's compositions, and which we must take as native to Wolfgang's genius.

During August and September 1764, Leopold became seriously ill, and all the concert-giving, travel, and lessons were abandoned. During the illness the Mozart family moved to the village of Chelsea, in the hope that the country air and pleasant surroundings would hasten Leopold's recovery. Wolfgang was obliged to be very quiet, and, as a consequence, devoted himself more than ever to composition. Of the greatest interest is a collection of small pieces on two staves, generally called the "London Notebook," in which he freely worked out and wrote down whatever interested him. This collection most clearly shows how clumsy Wolfgang could be, and how he or his father must have polished those works that were intended for publication. Some of these compositions are indistinguishable from Mozart's normal keyboard style of the time, whereas others appear to be sketches for orchestral works, and one looks as if it were intended for organ. The strong echoes of Baroque atmosphere and cliché, side by side with modernisms sometimes of the most blatant kind, are perhaps not so surprising.

Contrapuntal experiments, harmonic and rhythmic crudities abound, and all reflect the incredible strength of inquiry in the mind of this extraordinary child. At times he seems not to be restricted by his instrument or by the small stretch of his child-size hand. If these compositions were indeed intended for keyboard, they show that the eight-year-old Mozart possessed a technique sufficient to perform anything being written by his contemporaries at that time.

Example XIV–1: W. A. MOZART

a. "London Notebook" No. 2 (K.15b)

b. "London Notebook" No. 21 (K.15v)

One of the pieces from the "London Notebook," (*ACM* 36; K.15p) is in the key of G minor, later to play an individual and important role in Mozart's scheme of keys and their *Affekt*. Its structure is a balanced binary of a kind that might serve as the last movement of a sonata or a symphony—the prevalence of repeated notes or tremolo figures leads one to think that this may have been intended to be orchestrated and used as part of a symphony. Underneath that structure, however, young Mozart still seems to strive for the greatest asymmetry. The opening five-bar unit is elided into its repetition, but in the second half of the movement, a five-bar group balances a four-bar group. Even in the close (mm. 26–33 and mm. 65–72) an eight-bar grouping is divisible into 3+3+2 measure units. Such unexpected irregularity and the feeling of tension brought about by elision of phrases are heightened by other factors. The opening chain of diminished sevenths is most unusual at any time before 1790; the prevalence of the rhythmic motive 𝄾 ♫♩ | ♩ and its further extensions 𝄾 ♫♩ | ♫ ♩ and 𝄾 ♫♩ | ♫ ♫♫ | ♩ work toward strong unity and tautness; and finally, the tonal excursion to the key of the major sixth degree of the scale (E minor, mm. 47–56) makes for the greatest tonal contrast imaginable within a small piece. Perhaps even more than the symphony K.16, this piece reveals Mozart's early genius, and although the mature composer created works of astounding originality, his schooled imagination never again created a work of such primitive, naive force.

Quite as important as the opportunity to experiment was Mozart's exposure to the opera and to the art of singing. He was on the friendliest terms with two of the most celebrated *castrati* of the age, Giovanni Manzuoli (1720–82), referred to above by Barrington, and Ferdinando Tenducci (1735–90), who were as famous for their acting ability as for their vocal technique. (He may even have taken some lessons from Manzuoli.) Indeed, a host of Italian singers and instrumentalists were in London for the season, and Wolfgang's mastery of vocal writing increased noticeably with their acquaintance. It was here that he finished his first operatic composition, the aria "Va, del furor portata" from Metastasio's *Ezio*. It is tempting to connect this aria with Barrington's account, already cited, and to see in it the "song of rage" to which he refers. But this is hard to verify since Leopold asserted that Wolfgang wrote fifteen arias in London and Holland, of which only two survive.

The last months in London were not as successful, either financially or socially, as the first, and at the end of July 1765, the Mozart family departed, intending to stop again in Paris on their way home. They were persuaded to visit Holland, however, a decision which Leopold later came to regret. For in The Hague, in September, Nannerl fell so ill that, despite the best medical help, her life was despaired of and she was given extreme unction. In mid-November, as she recovered, Wolfgang came down with the same undiagnosed disease, finally recovering enough to start work again in mid-January 1766. Nevertheless, the stay in Holland, which lasted until April 1766, produced an amazingly rich crop of compositions, including a symphony, an aria, and six sonatas for violin and keyboard. Then it was back to Paris for two months and slowly to Salzburg—a five-month journey during which the family concertized extensively and enjoyed great success.

BACK HOME: SALZBURG AND VIENNA

On 30 November 1766, the Mozarts arrived home after what was to prove the grandest and longest tour of Wolfgang's lifetime of travel. The immediate rewards were obvious: the family's financial circumstances were greatly improved; the name of Mozart was now known in all the courts of Europe; the fame of the child prodigy was growing as the flow of original compositions increased. But the price of such success was high: Wolfgang had had a series of sicknesses which left him undersized for his age; but even more significant, he had grown accustomed to praise from the great, and was fully aware of his extraordinary gifts. From this knowledge arose an attitude all too easily interpreted as arrogance, which made enemies for him and surrounded him with resentment throughout his life. As has often been said, the miracle is that Mozart grew up to be as normal as he was, for what modern authority on child rearing could approve of the way Nannerl and Wolfgang lived, and what modern parent would seriously write, as Leopold did:

> God . . . has bestowed such talents on my children that, apart from my duty as a father, they alone would spur me on to sacrifice everything to their successful development. Every moment I lose is lost forever. . . . You know that my children are accustomed to work. But if, with the excuse that one thing prevents another, they were to accustom themselves to hours of idleness, my whole plan would crumble to pieces. Habit is an iron shirt. And you yourself know how much my children, and especially Wolfgang, have to learn.
>
> (*Letters,* 10 Nov. 1766)

In Salzburg there was pause of ten months while Wolfgang worked and Leopold developed his plans. For having seen his son triumph in the west and the north, he now looked again toward the east and Vienna, and for the first time south toward Italy.

The Mozarts arrived in Vienna in September 1767, but had to flee shortly thereafter because of a widespread outbreak of smallpox. Despite this precaution, Wolfgang contracted the disease toward the end of October, and Nannerl a little later, so that it was the end of the year before the children were out and about. In the New Year they were received at Court, where the widowed Maria Theresa and her son, the new Emperor Joseph II, were extremely affable. Leopold writes that the emperor asked Wolfgang if he would like to compose and conduct an opera, and from this chance remark there resulted, in July 1768, *La finta semplice* (The Pretend Simpleton), K. 51, to a libretto by Marco Coltellini after Goldoni. This comic work gave rise to a series of events more suitable to tragedy: quite suddenly the singers, who had been happy with their arias, complained that they could not sing them; the orchestra complained about having a child conduct them; nasty rumors were spread indicating, on one hand, that the music was worthless and the child not sufficiently conversant with Italian, and, on the other, that the father had written the work. Leopold, with all the zeal of the self-righteous, appealed to Metastasio and Hasse for help. But it was all in vain. The opera was not staged, and Leopold went to the extreme of petitioning the Court to rectify his grievances. Whatever happened during the proceedings is not known, but Leopold did not ingratiate himself or his family with either the emperor or his mother. From that time on, the empress, although courteous to their faces, spoke and wrote derogatorily about the Mozarts, and her negative opinion probably affected Wolfgang's career adversely for the rest of his life.

The Vienna sojourn was not an entirely negative experience, for Wolfgang had his little opera *Bastien und Bastienne,* K.50, performed at the house of their rich friend Dr. Mesmer. This work, the earliest of Mozart's theater works to maintain its complete effectiveness in performance, is modeled after Rousseau's successful *Le Devin du village* (1752). It is a typical *Singspiel* with its spoken dialogue and its short, compellingly melodic vocal pieces, which are called "arias" but which are really strophic songs. The subject matter and music, entirely consonant with the abilities and the mentality of a twelve-year-old genius, are irresistible, as the young composer shows his mastery of the Arcadian idiom of refined rusticity, as well as of the truly rustic in his imitation of bagpipes.

THE ITALIAN TOURS

Almost the whole of 1769 was spent in Salzburg, but in mid-December Wolfgang and Leopold set out to conquer Italy. However disappoint-

Leopold describes Wolfgang sitting for the artist, Saverio dalla Rosa of Verona, in a letter of 7 January 1770. (Private collection)

ing Vienna had proven, they were amply rewarded by the successes of this tour, the first of three visits to Italy, which lasted fifteen months, and which took them to all the major cities as far south as Naples. In Italy, Wolfgang came to know Sammartini, the famous symphonist and opera composer, described by Leopold as a "true friend." Perhaps even more important was the historian and contrapuntist Padre Martini, who succeeded in convincing young Mozart of the value of counterpoint to an extent that studying Fux with his father had never achieved. Wolfgang was honored by the Pope, who received father and son in audience and who conferred upon the boy the Order of the Golden Spur—of a grade previously awarded only to one other composer, Orlando di Lasso, and higher than that given to Gluck and Dittersdorf. It is sad that his knighthood never made life any easier for him, nor did it salve the burning need he always felt for open acknowledgment of his worth by his social superiors. In Rome, Wolfgang performed the famous feat of writing from memory the parts of the *Miserere* by Gregorio Allegri (1582–1652), after only one hearing. And in Bologna the *Accademia filarmonica,* after a severe test, admitted the fourteen-year-old to membership, waiving the regulation that members should be at least twenty years old. More important than these honors, however, was the *scrittura* (commission) to write the first opera for the next season in Milan. As was customary, the contract called for the recitatives to be sent to Milan in October, while the composer himself was due there by

1 November so that the arias could be written with full knowledge of the singers and their capabilities. Mozart did not start work on the opera at once but enjoyed a relatively carefree Italian summer of study and travel. When he returned to Milan on 18 October the recitatives had already been written, and there remained the overture and twenty-four vocal numbers to be composed and adjusted to the singers' voices and demands. The boy worked frantically, and the first rehearsal in the theater took place on 19 December. There followed separate recitative rehearsals, another stage rehearsal, and then, on the 22nd, the dress rehearsal. On 26 December 1770, Mozart's first commercial *opera seria,* entitled *Mitridate, rè di Ponto,* was brought before a public that expressed its satisfaction with tumultuous applause and great praise. In that season the opera was given more than twenty times, and each time the house was packed. Scarcely three weeks later, in January 1771, the journey back to Salzburg was begun, and after stops at various places to visit or give concerts, the travelers arrived home on 28 March 1771.

During the brief period from 1770 to 1772, Mozart's future seemed assured. Honors were thrust on him from all sides, he moved easily and constantly in aristocratic society, on a footing of seeming equality with his hosts, and important commissions continued to pour in. Following the success of *Mitridate,* he was asked to write the Lenten oratorio *La Betulia liberata,* K.118, to a text of Metastasio for Padua; he received another contract for an opera for Milan (*Lucio Silla,* K.135) for the 1772 season, at a higher fee; and he was chosen to write a *serenata teatrale,* a ceremonial opera, called *Ascanio in Alba,* K.111, to celebrate the wedding of Maria Theresa's son to an Italian princess. The *serenata* was yet another great success, and the bridegroom, Archduke Ferdinand, considered taking Mozart into his service, until he received a letter from his mother, in which she wrote: "What I say is intended only to prevent your burdening yourself with useless people and giving titles to people of that sort[.] if they are in your service it degrades that service when these people go about the world like beggars[.] besides, he has a large family."[2]

Wolfgang and Leopold arrived back in Salzburg after their second trip to Italy on 15 December 1771. Their employer, Archbishop Schrattenbach, who had always been so tolerant of their absences from his court, was about to celebrate two anniversaries—the fiftieth year of his priesthood and his birthday—and Wolfgang had prepared an *azione teatrale* entitled *Il sogno di Scipione* (Scipio's Dream), K. 126, as a gesture of thanks. The archbishop, however, died on the very day after their return and the opera, with the smallest of alterations, was offered as a celebration of the new archbishop, Count Hieronymus Colloredo, who has earned immortality as the villain of the Mozart legend (see p. 295ff).

2. Deutsch, *op. cit.,* p. 138.

Despite the fact that all Mozart's works for Italy were successful, they led to nothing. Neither the Archduke Ferdinand nor anyone else offered him a permanent position there. *Lucio Silla* was his last opera commissioned in Italy, and after its production and with no further prospects, father and son returned to Salzburg on 13 March 1773. They had been so happy and free under Archbishop Schrattenbach, and his successor, the Prince Archbishop Colloredo, had already shown himself to be both effective at cutting expenses and an unsympathetic personality. Leopold, dealing with the repeated disappointments they had recently endured, philosophically surmised that "God has probably some other plan for us." (*Letters,* 27 Feb. 1773) But after the excitement of Italy, to return to the drudgery and boredom of Salzburg must have been very hard.

CHAPTER XV

Early Style

We remember Leopold telling Lorenz Hagenauer that his children were accustomed to hard work, and in Wolfgang's case the volume of his compositions proves that. In his fifth and sixth years, he wrote several small pieces for keyboard. In his seventh year the pace picked up with three sonatas and more short pieces. When he was eight, he completed the first symphony, seven sonatas, and miscellaneous other pieces, and so it went until his twelfth year, during which he produced five symphonies, two operas, several Masses, and a volume of other works. Not only did the rate of composition increase but the style matured, and in this first period we can easily trace the abandonment of all vestiges of Baroque practice as his compositional language became more and more refined.

Many of Mozart's works from this period are unfortunately and irretrievably lost. Some are mentioned in correspondence; others are listed in the catalogue of his son's work that Leopold compiled in September of 1768 when rumors were rife that the child could not have written what was attributed to him. How we would like to hear the Trumpet Concerto that Leopold described to Hagenauer:

> On the feast of the Immaculate Conception the new church of Father Parhamer's orphanage will be consecrated. Wolfgangerl has written for this feast a Solemn Mass, an Offertorium and a Trumpet Concerto for one of the boys.
>
> (*Letters,* 12 Nov. 1768)

Even more tantalizing are those works of which we have the incipits, such as the keyboard sonatas included in the Breitkopf catalogue but otherwise unknown.

THE FIRST KEYBOARD WORKS

Since Wolfgang's fame was initially based on his harpsichord playing, it is doubly regrettable that no keyboard sonatas survived from this first period. However, the "London Notebook" does give us a good idea of the skill with which Wolfgang was addressing the keyboard, and it is all the more surprising that none of the complete compositions or the sketched ones from this book seem to have been utilized subsequently.

The two sets of variations on Dutch tunes for solo keyboard, K. 24 and 25, composed some time before 7 March 1766 in Holland, demand less from the player than the accompanied sonatas composed at the same time. They are of some interest, however, in that, on the one hand, Mozart included an *Adagio* variation near to the end of each set, as he did so frequently in later variations, but on the other hand, both sets preserve the same meter throughout—a practice Mozart avoided in later years.

Two sonatas for piano duet, K.19d (1765) and K.123a (1772),are more interesting. We know that Christian Bach improvised duets with Wolfgang, the child sitting on the man's knee. We also know that Leopold boasted that Wolfgang had written his first work for piano four-hands in London, and, he added, "no one had ever written a four-hand work before." K.19d starts off exactly as we would expect from a man and a child, with one playing and the other imitating, but this quickly changes into a melody and accompaniment. The later sonata surprisingly shows little advance, given the fact that Mozart was later to make this chamber music medium so definitively his own.

His first published work, the two sonatas for harpsichord with optional violin (K.6 and 7), dedicated to Princess Victoire of France, was compiled in 1764 from works written earlier. Originally composed for keyboard alone, the optional violin parts were added to meet the Parisian taste of the time. In the "throwing together" of the sonatas, K.6 comes out with four movements, F/S/Minuet and Trio/F, while K.7 follows the popular Viennese pattern of F/S/Minuet and Trio. The slow movement of K.7 is the first example of what has already been referred to as the "dream" *Andante.* It consists of a constant stream of triplet sixteenths in the middle of the texture against a singing melody in duplets, accompanied by a bass. In its layered appearance it resembles one of Schobert's compositional techniques and it may bespeak his influence. It should be noted as well that Schobert had made it acceptable in Paris to publish works in pairs, as opposed to three or six, more usual elsewhere.

Two more sonatas (K.8 and 9) quickly followed, dedicated to a Comtesse de Tessé. It is tempting to see in the second of these a stylistic advance over the earlier sonatas, not simply in the structure of the first movement with its effective use of something very like a false recapitulation, nor yet in its coherent and mobile bass line, but especially in the variety of its textures.

These two publications, issued in Paris as Opp. 1 and 2, were quickly followed by Op. 3, a set of six sonatas with the accompaniment of violin and cello, published in London and dedicated to Queen Charlotte. Perhaps Christian Bach's influence is to be glimpsed in the fact that three of these works are in two movements. The accompanying violin parts typically fill in the gaps at the ends of phrases, effecting a bridge between different melodic materials in the keyboard part, while the cello is restricted to its *continuo* function of doubling the bass or playing a simplified version of it. There are some striking felicities, and even some good imitative effects:

Example XV–1: W. A. MOZART, Sonata K.13, I

During the Mozarts' visit to Holland, Wolfgang wrote a further set of accompanied sonatas (K.26–31), K.26 alone in three movements and the rest in two. They show a more developed sense of melody than the earlier works, as well as a better balance between the violin and the keyboard.

Example XV–2: W. A. MOZART, Sonata K.26, III

STRING QUARTETS

The first seven of Mozart's string quartets were all conceived and executed in Italy before the family returned to Salzburg in 1773. The first and least typical is K.80, which was composed at Lodi in 1770, and is said to show the influence of Giovanni Battista Sammartini. Originally written in three movements (the fourth was added later), the writing is quite unlike Wolfgang's later ideas of what a string quartet should be. The first two movements have the cello and viola performing a *continuo*-like bass line while the violins share most of the material in trio-sonata style, giving the score the appearance of many contemporary symphonies.

The next six quartets, K. 155–160, were composed in Italy, probably late in 1772 and early 1773. None of the autographs bears a date, but it is likely that they were conceived as a set around a descending circle of fifths and that they were composed in the order D, G, C, F, B♭, and E♭.

By 1772, Mozart had left the stolidity of the earlier works behind. Melodies are built according to principles of coherence and containment; short phrases balance each other in antecedent/consequent relationships, and these relationships are not created simply by meter and rhythm, but also by upward and downward melodic direction—very like inversion—and by cadence, as in Example XV-3. Textures are var-

Example XV–3: W. A. MOZART, Quartet K.156, I

ied and are constantly interesting. At times the part-writing achieves the ideal quartet style, the essence of which lies in the integrity of each part's contribution to the whole. This can be demonstrated in passages like:

Example XV–4: W. A. MOZART, Quartet K.156, I

Here, the relationship between each part is clear, yet it is dependent neither upon imitative counterpoint nor upon a distinctive texture or figuration for each instrument. Instead, each of the upper three parts uses two kinds of material, the rhythmic figure of two sixteenths and an eighth note, and the melodic arch of eighth notes. The two violins are in the closest relationship, alternating material every two measures, while the viola mediates between them in its own way. The cello alone is quite different, providing discreet yet strong harmonic support.

Example XV–5: W. A. MOZART, Quartet K.157, I

By the time this set of quartets was composed, Mozart had fully developed the art of creating musical vitality from a single note, an art in which none of his contemporaries could approach him for skill or inventiveness. The above example is a Mozartian elaboration of the most common cliché of invertible counterpoint at the octave, occurring between the first violin and the cello, using the notes E, D, C, B. The cello plays the unornamented notes, whereas the first violin turns them into an elaborate melody. The viola doubles the cello on the beginning of every second beat, but actually carries the same melody as the first violin, hence it is in canon at the octave with the first violin. All that is left for the second violin, in this oscillating tonic and dominant harmony, is a pedal note, G, held for sixteen beats. The composer could have written a long, tied G, or reiterated eighth notes on G. This passage is fine testimony to the total concentration which Mozart bestows on his composition, and to the constant interplay of his intellect and his imagination, for he creates the illusion of a third contrapuntal voice from the pedal G. He gives it the dotted rhythm and the trill, essential to the character of the upper parts, but he inserts rests in the pedal where the first violin and the viola have none, in order to clarify the effect of the two moving parts. Such attention to detail is not confined to this work and the single-tone pedal can be activated and ornamented in a variety of ways. It is no wonder that such music is so popular with players to this day, and Mozart's second-violin parts are uniformly interesting. Even at this early date, we can recognize in Mozart the quintessential composer of chamber music. His later masterpieces will only confirm this through their greater refinement and through the intensification of part-writing and expressivity. Moreover, this same quality suffuses not only the works written for the chamber but also those for the theater, the church, and the concert.

SYMPHONIES

Mozart wrote at least twenty-three symphonies between 1770 and 1773, a greater number than at any other time in his life. The first four works in this genre, composed in 1764–66 in London and The Hague, have several structural features in common. They are all three-movement works, F/S/F, with rounded binary first movements in common time. Slow movements are all in 2/4 time, and final movements are all in 3/8 time. Two slow movements are set in subdominant relationship, while the other two are in the relative-minor mode.

A useful comparison may be made between Mozart's orchestral works and those that Haydn (then a man of thirty-two or so) was writing at the same time. Such a comparison shows that Mozart's ideas on how to use the string section were more modern than Haydn's. Where Haydn ties his violas to the bass and writes trio-sonata textures, Mozart has four real parts more often than not. It can also be noted that right from the beginning Mozart tends to introduce imitative counterpoint in two, three and four parts, and even though the effect may at times be simple, his intention to create greater independence and integrity among the four strings is clear. (See Example XV–6.)

Even when he was not relying on imitative counterpoint, the child Mozart demonstrated an innate genius for creating something out of nothing in his distribution of rhythmic interest among the strings, and

Example XV–6: W. A. MOZART, Symphony K.19a, I

in his ability to give each instrument a distinctive profile. Mozart's delight in creating a detailed and elaborate score was a lifelong characteristic.

Example XV–7: W. A. MOZART, Symphony K.22

The next group of symphonies comprises approximately seven works composed in Vienna and Salzburg. These, too, appear to fall into a group defined by overall structural irregularities. First, all the symphonies are in four movements with a Minuet and Trio inserted in third place. There is one exception: K.45a is a three-movement work which, interestingly, is a revision of an earlier work composed in The Hague in 1766; structurally it belongs to the first group. All set their slow movements in the sub-dominant key. The relationship between Minuet and Trio is more variable. Of course, the first Minuet is in the tonic key, but the Trio is found in the relative minor and the dominant, as well as the subdominant. In the last two works of this group (K.48 and K.73) Mozart writes his first complete symphonic recapitulations, and

In 1777 Mozart was painted in his sober, professional black garb, wearing the insignia of a knight of the Golden Spur, which Pope Clement XIV had given him in 1770. (Bologna: Civico Museo Bibliographico Musicale)

in K.48 for the first time he writes a symphonic first movement in triple time.

At the end of 1769, Leopold and Wolfgang set out on the first Italian tour, which lasted, as mentioned above, almost fifteen months. During this time Mozart composed at least five symphonies (K.81, 97, 95, 84, and 74) three of which are in three movements and two in four. All of these works share the peculiarity of the Italian opera overture by not repeating the exposition. Only one of them has the incomplete recapitulation of the rounded binary structure.

All the delights of Italy and the rich lessons that Wolfgang learned in so many areas of music seemed to come to full flower when he returned to Salzburg. Between the end of March 1771 and August 1772 he wrote a dozen symphonies. It is hard to believe that Archbishop Colloredo was not impressed by such industry. Moreover, in these symphonies there is evidence of the complete maturation of the artist, who, at sixteen, had already accomplished more than most do in a lifetime. In this group of works each movement of each symphony demonstrates an increase in expressive potential, and each shows the composer more in control of his craft, more able to produce the effect he wants.

The first movements of symphonies are now almost invariably in sonata form with complete recapitulations. They are almost equally divided between duple and triple meter. From the earliest works in this form, Mozart demonstrated his use of textural and dynamic contrast at the opening of the first movement. In the Symphony in A, K.114, he develops a *cantabile* opening into the modulatory material used to escape from the tonic and move forward:

Example XV–8: W. A. MOZART, Symphony K.114, I

This same ability to expand an idea is shown with more traditional material in Example XV–9 on p. 284.

Mozart's freedom with form and structure, and his sense that such freedom can be used to express humor or high spirits, is seen in the Symphony in D, K.133, where the opening of the movement reappears, not at the beginning of the recapitulation but as a final utterance.

The first movement of the Symphony in C, K.128, is remarkable in that it creates a sense of large-scale instability. The attention-getting tutti chords of m.1 put a strange stress on the second beat, the effect of which is further heightened by the empty third beat. The three measures of triplets that follow are elided into a repeat of the opening. Thus eight measures are cast in an awkward asymmetry. The harmonic movement of the whole exposition needs to be seen to be believed, since the impression of tonal instability is so much more pronounced here than in the middle section. This music is Mozart's response to that current of emotionalism called *Sturm und Drang* usually associated with

Example XV–9: W. A. MOZART, Symphony K. 133, I

the minor mode. In the context of C major, the emotional effect is magnified still further.

One of the most polished and perfect attestations to Mozart's newly attained maturity is to be found in the first movement of the Symphony in A, K.134 (*ACM* 37). In the opening of this work, the composer displays a method of spinning out a melody akin to Haydn's intellectually governed compositional process. The resulting music is utterly removed from Baroque *Fortspinnung,* the effect of which can often be likened to the flight of a paper dart: at the launching, who can say how long the flight will be? Here the structure at all levels is governed by antecedent/consequent relationships created from tiny, schematic particles of music that symbolize the great forces of music—the rhythmic and the melodic—and through them to exemplify the usual Mozartian and eighteenth-century pairing of rhythm with the masculine and melody with the feminine.

The opening eight measures warrant examination. In mm. 1–2, there is the typical, simple opposition of an upward leaping arpeggio (rhythm) followed by a long, non-harmonic tone resolving downward by semitone (melody). But much more complicated interpretations are possible. The first figure, the arpeggio, begins on a downbeat while the second figure properly begins on an upbeat so that the dissonance is prepared in an orthodox manner. The first figure also has a tendency to extend itself to the second and third beat, since such an outburst of energy as that of the upward arpeggio, like a ball thrown into the air, has to bounce a little before reaching stability and repose. Mm. 3 and 4 illustrate what has been called "extension by complementary opposites" (not inversion). Mm. 5 and 6 telescope the first four measures, compressing into three beats the process that originally took five beats, and at the same time the shape of these two measures becomes a complementary opposite to mm. 1–4. And mms. 7 and 8 offer the orthodox conclusion, which we all might be able to write, given the first six bars. A repetition of the opening eight measures, without winds and an octave lower, leads to the start of the modulation and a ten-measure period based on the sequential use of mm. 5 and 6, but now starting once again with an upward arpeggio. The impression of a three-part exposition is more forcibly conveyed in this work than in any other, since the first 26 measures and the last 19 out of a total of 68 measures are concerned with the opening material. Interesting also is the coda, which, in a completely different way, separates the melodic material (mm. 156–161) from the arpeggio material (mm. 162–168). Each element is expanded in its own manner.

CONCERTOS

The reports of Mozart's first effort at concerto composition come down to us in a letter of 24 April 1792 from Andreas Schachtner (1731–95) to

Mozart's sister. Schachtner had been court trumpeter at Salzburg and a family friend. His account in shortened paraphrase runs as follows:

> Once I went to your home where four-year-old Wolfgang was busy with pen. His father asked him what he was doing; he replied that he was writing a piano concerto and that the first part was already finished. The pages were covered in ink blots because the child dipped the pen too deeply into the ink. After some laughter the father saw that beneath the blots the work was written correctly, but that it was so difficult as to be almost unplayable. Wolfgangerl said: "That's why it's a concerto—you have to practise it hard to be able to play it."[1]

No traces of such a work nor of any other concerto from this period have survived. There are, however, seven concertos for keyboard and orchestra which the boy compiled in pastiche fashion from sonata movements and whole sonatas by other composers. The first four (K.37, 39, 40, and 41) date from the first half of 1767 and are orchestrated for strings with oboes and horns. Each movement of each concerto in this group is an arrangement and orchestration of a separate sonata movement: four are by Raupach, four by Honauer, and one each by Eckard, Schobert, and Emanuel Bach. There is also one movement whose authorship is not yet traced. More interesting are the three concertos, K.107, arranged for keyboard and strings from whole sonatas of J. C. Bach, which survive in a manuscript written by Wolfgang and Leopold together around 1770. A comparison of movements shows how the Mozarts conceived concerto structure at this time and how the double exposition and the ritornellos could change a sonata into a concerto.

It is a fine coincidence that the child who was destined to become the supreme master of the piano concerto and of the opera produced his first examples of both genres at the same time; the pasticcio concertos date from April to July 1767, and *Apollo et Hyacinthus,* K.38 was given its first performance on 13 May 1767.

OPERATIC WORKS

For some years Mozart had been writing operatic arias for a variety of voices. He was accustomed to put on the mask of theatrical gesture at will and produced songs of love or rage at the drop of a hat. After the great European tour it was only a matter of time before he would produce a full-fledged opera. *Apollo et Hyacinthus* is called an intermezzo and is written to a comic Latin text (comic not in the sense that it is funny, but in that its ending is not tragic) for performance at Salzburg University. It consists of a small overture in one movement, followed

1. Deutsch, *op. cit.,* p. 451.

This design for stage machinery that simulates a storm-tossed ship is one of the illustrations of scientific and technological processes found in Diderot and D'Alembert's *Encyclopédie*.

by recitatives and arias, some of which possess a definite lyric charm. The seventh number is an aria for a desperate father whose son has just been killed, in which the text speaks of his being tossed like a ship on a stormy sea. Both the vocal line and the orchestral accompaniment show young Mozart's delight in rendering emotional content through the creation of a musical picture: the dynamics that change from measure to measure; the melodic line that moves constantly from high to low and back again. All elements work together to delineate the anguished soul and the storm-tossed ship.

Example XV–10: W. A. MOZART, *Apollo et Hyacinthus*, No.7.

8

16

25
a 2

The handling of the orchestra is exemplary and Mozart's power to devise appropriate textures which reach beyond the ordinary is astonishing. The long, *cantabile* melody of the Duet (No.8), played by the first violins, is accompanied by pizzicato notes on the beat in the bass and offbeat chords in the second violins, while the *divisi* violas in sixteenth notes playing with the bow anticipate the orchestration of *Così fan tutte*. Indeed, it is not going too far to see in *Apollo* evidence of a greater sophistication and more vivid musical imagination than we find in the later works of this period composed for Italy and Vienna.

Four months after the production of *Apollo et Hyacinthus* the Mozarts went to Vienna for their second visit, which was to last for well over a year. In late January 1768 Wolfgang was asked to write his next opera, *La finta semplice,* for Vienna. The history of this opera has already been described. All that remains to add is that despite all Leopold's efforts, it was not produced in Vienna but was probably staged in Salzburg the following year, 1769. The libretto is like so much eighteenth-century comedy in that it builds its story around the old characters of the *commedia dell'arte*. As we expect, each character conforms to a stereotype and neither the librettist nor the composer thought to create any of the distinctively human characterization that was to be Mozart's greatest contribution to the genre.

Mozart next glanced in the direction of German popular comic opera of the time. Legend, founded on a report by Mozart's early biographer, Nissen (who became Constanze's second husband), has it that *Bastien und Bastienne* K.50, was commissioned by Dr. Mesmer, the friend of the Mozarts who invented the medical use of magnetism, called mesmerism. There are, however, a number of questions about the accuracy of the story and it must remain unconfirmed and suspect. Whatever the case, this work shows Mozart as much a master of the short, melodic type of ariette, dependent upon a simple, songlike structure, as he was of the Italian aria, with its complex and necessary coloratura. A sad and surprising fact: Rousseau's *Le Devin du village* was performed at least 544 times between 1753 and 1829; Mozart's did not receive its official premiere until 1890.

Mozart's first, full-blown *opera seria* resulted from the commission from Milan in 1770 (see p. 272). The libretto for *Mitridate,rè di Ponto* (Mithridates, King of Pontus) K.87, was taken from Racine by Vittorio Cigna-Santi (1725–85), and has been described as "the best libretto for an *opera seria* that [Mozart would] ever have."[2] It is possible that Mozart was too young to do the libretto justice, since he still accepted certain conventions of the time (such as the application of aria types) in a way that a more experienced composer might have rejected. But the boy's concern was to please his singers first and his audience next, and he succeeded in both his aims. The opera was rapturously received, with numbers being encored (a rare occurrence), and repeated performances. The cost to the young Mozart in effort and anxiety must be gauged by the large body of sketches and revisions for this work, almost one-third the size of the score, that have come down to us. It is no wonder that he complained to his mother, in a letter written while he was working on the opera, that "I cannot write much, for my fingers are aching from composing so many recitatives." (*Letters,* 20 Oct. 1770)

From our perspective, the opera suffers from the fact that differentiation of characters or character types is difficult: of the seven singers required, four are sopranos, one is alto, and the other two are tenors, despite the fact that only two characters are female. Most of the arias fall into the pattern of *da capo* structures with truncated recapitulation and most have a concerto-like, long opening ritornello. The vocal writing includes much coloratura, and places are reserved for cadenzas for the soloists. Since almost all the arias are followed by the exit of the

2. Alfred Einstein, *Mozart* (London, 1969), p. 397.

soloist and his or her train of followers (soldiers, priests, guards, friends, etc.), it is perhaps surprising that the closing ritornello is often quite brief, leaving little time for clearing the stage. The role of the orchestra is reduced and the subtleties noted in the orchestration of *Apollo* are not to be found—presumably in order to take nothing away from the singers.

The success of *Mitridate* prompted Count Firmian, the governor of Milan, to suggest to the court in Vienna that Mozart might be allowed to compose one of the two theatrical works planned to celebrate the wedding of the Archduke Ferdinand to the Princess Beatrice d'Este. The wedding was to take place in October of 1771, and the works commissioned were *Il Ruggiero,* to be composed by Hasse, the grand old man of opera, and *Ascanio in Alba* (K.111), a *serenata teatrale,* by young Mozart. In performance, Mozart's work was much more successful than Hasse's, and Leopold, writing home, could not help gloating: "It really distresses me greatly, but Wolfgang's serenata has killed Hasse's opera, more than I can say." (*Letters,* 19 Oct. 1771) But Wolfgang, it seems, thought highly of *Il Ruggiero* and wrote to his sister that he knew "nearly all the arias by heart and so I can see and hear it at home in my head." (*Letters,* 2 Nov. 1771)

The score of *Ascanio* adds little that is new to what we already know of Mozart's work at this time, but it is interesting to note that the libretto calls for the extensive use of the chorus in song and movement, and of ballet. Hasse remarked that the Milan audience of that day was more concerned with spectacle than with recitative and that in *Ruggiero* there was little spectacle and a great deal of recitative.

It is worth taking a moment to reflect on the amazing fertility and the even more amazing industry Mozart displayed at this time. In the space of approximately one calendar year, from 29 September 1770 to 25 September 1771, he had composed four major works in the operatic genre: *Mitridate,* an *opera seria; La Betulia liberata*, an *azione sacra* or an unstaged play; *Il sogno di Scipione,* an *azione teatrale* or a staged play; and *Ascanio in Alba,* a *serenata* or *azione teatrale,* as well as pieces in other genres. In addition, he was conducting, playing harpsichord, and directing the performance of his theater works.

The last opera Mozart wrote for Italy was *Lucio Silla,* an *opera seria* to a libretto by Giovanni de Gamerra (1743–1803). In the elevated and moralistic tone of Metastasio, Gamerra devised a plot in which the fidelity of love leads to disloyalty and treachery. Instead of punishing the treachery by executing the perpetrator, the dictator Silla makes an all-encompassing gesture of forgiveness. Two voice types are required for the six characters: four sopranos and two tenors.

Despite the conventional plot and stock types of this work, Mozart gives early indications of his rapidly developing personal style. The orchestra is given much more to do and its effect is considerably richer

The first page of the 15-year old's oratorio *Betulia Liberata,* K.118, written for Padua to a text by Metastasio. The overture in three movements is Mozart's first *sinfonia* in a minor mode. (Staatsbibliothek zu Berlin-Preussischer Kulturbesitz, Musikabteilung)

than in *Mitridate* or *Ascanio*. The pervasive texture is reminiscent of chamber music in that all parts contribute vitally to the whole, rather than function simply as accompaniment. The *da capo* aria with its heavy load of coloratura is still prevalent but the sequence of aria types is varied. It is in the melodic and harmonic usage, however, that the most telling signs of the future are to be seen. Toward the end of the opera the hero sings an aria in a *Tempo di Menuetto;* the smooth, ingratiating quality of the main melody together with the strong supporting instrumental lines make memorable and affecting music that could have been written during Mozart's most mature years. Even more significant is the harmonic vocabulary with which he accomplishes the expression of mixed emotions. It is a commonplace of Mozartian criticism that the composer has the power to mingle the tragic with the comical, pathos with humor, to an unparalleled degree. The later operas *Don Giovanni* and *Così fan tutte* are perhaps the crowning examples of this. In *Lucio Silla* Mozart dealt with two similar dramatic situations in two different ways. In the first case the heroine, Giunia, rejects the tyrant, Silla, since she believes he killed her husband. Giunia's aria has a slow, reflective section, in which she speaks of her love for her husband, followed by a fast section in which she rejects her present suitor. The alternation of memory and reality creates an **A B A B** structure with coda. There is ample precedent for this kind of aria with its wild emotional swings. In the second situation, the supposedly dead husband, Cecilio, who is planning to kill Silla, sings an aria (not *da capo*) in which he describes his mixed feelings of hope and anger. The aria is in D major, but the subdominant area oscillates between G major and G minor, which, allied with powerful rhythmic substance and an orchestra with trumpets and drums, gives a foretaste of that moment in *Don Giovanni* when the gates of Hell are opened. Here are some of the first signs of the greatness to come.

Lucio Silla had an inauspicious first performance, which began three hours late and did not conclude until two in the morning. There were a number of other mishaps as well. The work itself was successful, but it failed to generate other commissions from Milan and it was never performed beyond that city. Moreover, it did not secure for Wolfgang the court appointment he hoped for.

CHURCH MUSIC

The last years of the eighteenth and the early years of the nineteenth centuries witnessed a broad strengthening of nonconforming sects of Christianity, with their emphasis on hymn singing as the main musical component of the church service. At the same time, the growth of reactionary political views and religious orthodoxy in Catholic countries led to a revival of a capella singing, both in practice and as an ideal. In this atmosphere, Mozart's church music, like all church music during the entire second half of the eighteenth century, fell into increasing disrepute even when his stock in opera and instrumental music was rising. Yet music for the church was an important part of the rounded education that Leopold sought for his son. As in the more important areas of Mozart's compositional development, the works of older, more established composers furnished models for the young boy, and in church music, as in the other genres, his "imitations" are remarkable for their mastery of material and thoughtful charm.

Mozart composed two extended solemn Masses before 1773: K.139 in C minor/major, probably written for the consecration of the chapel of Father Parhammer's orphanage, and K.44, the *Dominicus* , written to accompany the first Mass celebrated by Wolfgang's childhood friend Cajetan Hagenauer, ordained as Father Dominicus. It is obvious that Mozart wanted to give of his best in both these works, and the results are so striking that the "Orphanage" Mass was long believed to be a later composition. Both are extended *missae longae* or "number" masses, as opposed to *missae breves,* and therefore a larger orchestra as well as extensive use of solo voices was customary, all of which allowed the boy a certain exuberance of effect.

The *Waisenhausmesse,* or "Orphanage" Mass opens with a solemn call to attention (much as Bach's B-minor Mass) in which three trombones double divided violas with remarkable results. The *Kyrie* that follows is a traditional **A B A** structure, in which the third invocation is a *da capo* of the first. Those sections for solo voices, whether alone or in concert, are set simply and melodically, avoiding the coloratura of the opera and of much of his later church music.

Both these Masses share certain attributes. They both retain a certain naiveté from the past; for example, Mozart does not hesitate to set the text of the Creed "descendit de coelis" (he descended from Heaven) and later "ascendit in coelum" (he ascended into Heaven) with falling and rising lines, and at the words "judicare vivos et mortuos' (to judge the living and the dead) and "expecto resurrectionem mortuorum" (I believe in the resurrection of the dead) the tempo suddenly slows at the word "dead." The traditional fugues at the "Cum Sancto Spiritu" (with the Holy Ghost) and "et vitam venturi saeculi" (and the life to come) are effective in every way. But what distinguishes these works is the deeply felt and carefully worked setting of texts such as "Qui tollis" (Thou, who bearest) or "passus et sepultus est" (he died and was buried), in which words and music, religious feeling and emotional response, are balanced in novel and imaginative ways. In some of the smaller works for the church the same qualities are to be found, and one can only see this as evidence not only of the technical prowess but also of Mozart's emotional precocity.

The most popular religious work of this period, however, is one which falls outside the canon of the Mass. The motet *Exsultate, jubilate,* K.165, was written in 1773 for the *castrato* Venanzio Rauzzini (1746–1810), and was first performed on 17 January of that year. It is, in effect, a concerto for soprano, with two *Allegro* movements surrounding an *Andante,* and with its flashy coloratura, the final movement, *Alleluia,* makes a marvelous display piece.

While Mozart's contemporaries invariably referred to his youth, his success was never accounted for on those grounds; throughout his life, Mozart the composer competed with the best adult composers of the time, and was judged against them. As a performer, on the other hand, much was made of his quality as a *Wunderkind,* and for as long as possible. But his superabundant natural gifts might have counted for very little without the particular education that Leopold Mozart gave him. Along with the languages and the manners and the musical techniques and all the other things, perhaps the most important thing that he learned was the habit of hard work. Leopold fitted his son with an iron shirt and Wolfgang wore it freely and without constraint. Disciplined work became his second nature.

CHAPTER XVI

The "Colloredo" Years: 1773–81

THE PATRON

Mozart returned from his last Italian tour in March 1773 an accomplished master, acclaimed the equal or superior to many established composers in writing for the theater, and with a large number of instrumental and church compositions to his name. But like the prophet honored everywhere but in his own country, at home Mozart was treated like any other household servant, subjected to all the demands that court routine necessarily imposed, and not at all in the manner to which he had grown accustomed. But given the buoyant spirit of a seventeen-year-old, Wolfgang's enjoyment of both his work and his nonmusical pastimes was not unduly upset by the petty irritations of court life and an unsympathetic employer. That was soon to change.

Hieronymus Colloredo, the man elected in March 1772 to the Archbishopric of Salzburg, has earned a place in history as an example of the potential evils inherent in the patronage system. Whether he fully deserves his reputation must remain in the balance. To us it appears that he treated Mozart abominably, and we can only wonder how he can have failed to recognize that he had under his wing a supreme genius.

Yet if he had been dealing with a Haydn rather than with this Mozart, he might have been remembered quite differently. He was not a conservative or reactionary man—indeed, in some ways he was a reformer after the pattern of the Emperor Joseph II. Unfortunately, he did not have the ability to ingratiate himself to his subjects. He inherited a court which had been overlavish in expenditure, yet he kept on his large musical establishment, for he was fond of music. In his dealings with the Mozart family, he frequently lost his temper and acted hastily; he was always grudging in his praise, appearing to hinder rather than help his young charge's career. Nevertheless, he seemed prepared to be forgiving, and he never made Leopold pay for any of Wolfgang's transgressions.

Much of the reponsibility for the situation that evolved must rest on Mozart's shoulders, for there is no doubt that his conception of the

Hieronymus, Count Colloredo, painted by F. X. König in 1772. Had he not employed Mozart, he would now be quite forgotten. *Sic transit gloria mundi.* (Convent of St. Peter, Salzburg. Photo by A. Hahnl)

artists' place in society and of his own talent would have set him on a collision course with almost any patron. More than seven of his seventeen years had been spent touring throughout Europe, enjoying the status of a free-lance artist, consorting as house or dinner guest with members of the aristocracy. In addition, he was aware of the ideas circulating among intellectuals at the time which esteemed the brotherhood of man above considerations of rank or wealth. Long before he became a Freemason, he had been exposed to their ideas and was receptive to them, as well; by 1772, he had set a Masonic song, *Lobgesang auf die feierliche Johannisloge,* K.148 (Song of Praise for the celebrated Johannis Lodge).

We must remember that Mozart's estimation of his own talents was not shared by many of his contemporaries, and Burney reports in his *Travels* the following information about Salzburg, which he had received from a correspondent, and which casts a somewhat different light on what was going on there:

> The archbishop and sovereign of Saltzburg is very magnificent in his support of music, having usually near a hundred performers, vocal and instrumental, in his service. This prince is himself a *dilettante,* and good performer on the violin; he has lately been at great pains to reform his band, which has been accused of being more remarkable for coarseness and noise, than delicacy and high-finishing. Signor Fischietti [*c.*1725–after 1810] author of several comic operas, is at present the director of this band.

> The Mozart family were all at Saltzburg last summer [1772]; the father has been long in the service of that court and the son is one of the band; he composed an opera at Milan, for the marriage of the archduke, with the princess of Modena, and was to compose another at the same place for the carnival of this year, though he is now but sixteen years of age. By a letter from Saltzburg, dated last November I am informed that this young man, who so much astonished all Europe by his infant knowledge and performance, is still a great master of his instrument; my correspondent went to his father's house to hear him and his sister play duets on the same harpsichord; but she is now at her summit, which is not marvellous; "and," says the writer of the letter, "if I may judge of the music which I have heard of his composition, in the orchestra, he is one further instance of early fruit being more extraordinary than excellent."[1]

In summary, there can be no doubt that there were faults on both sides in the quarrels between Mozart and Colloredo. Posterity has tended to justify the Mozarts, who have left such an indictment of the archbishop on the pages of history and such a weight of evidence in their correspondence. At the same time, the situation was not as clear-cut as they made it out to be.

THE PRODUCTS OF PATRONAGE

Wolfgang settled back into life at Salzburg and threw himself into composition. Whatever was wanted from him he was prepared to provide, whether the work was for church or concert hall, chamber or outdoors, whether instrumental or vocal, and whether the request came from the archbishop or one of his friends. The productivity of these years is amazing: during the last nine months of 1773 Mozart wrote six symphonies, three divertimentos or serenades, one piano concerto, six string quartets, one string quintet, two Masses, as well as smaller works. The month of August alone, when the Mozarts were in Vienna, accounted for the six quartets, a serenade, and a set of piano variations.

QUARTETS, K.168–173 Most of the works from this period were designed for public performance, since it was by this means that both father and son saw the best possibility for advancement in the world. But the set of six quartets (K.168–173) cannot be passed over without comment, for they are the first Mozart conceived and arranged as a group, probably after he had become familiar with Haydn's Opp. 9, 17, and 20. As in Haydn's Op. 20, Mozart sometimes uses the *Menuetto* as a second movement, sometimes in third place, but whereas Haydn divided this position equally among the six, Mozart places the dance movements third in four quartets. The most significant likeness, per-

1. Burney, *Music in Germany,* II, pp. 322–23.

haps, is in the use of fugal finales. Haydn used formal fugue to end three quartets. For Mozart, the first and last quartet are sufficient for such a display, but it is remarkable that the remainder of them contain many more contrapuntal devices, such as imitation and inversion of subjects in movements not otherwise contrapuntal, than heretofore. Yet other movements, for example, the *Rondeaux* of K.170 and 171, display the most Frenchified, *galant* taste imaginable. It is clear that when he was writing these quartets Mozart was determined to impress the Viennese audience with the extent and breadth of his abilities, for they display an unusual variety of tonal relationships between movements and of tempo indications, both in the quartets written in Italy (K.155–160) and those composed in Vienna (K.168–173).

In the slow movement of the Quartet K.168 (*ACM* 38) the formal structure is clear, and perhaps its close at the repeat sign in the key of C minor rather than in A♭ major is a conscious archaism—at least it is unusual. What is chiefly interesting, however, is the way the piece progresses in a succession of what might be called "points of imitation." Thus mm. 1–7 expose the opening melody and the first violin introduces new material in mm. 5–11. At m. 10 the opening melody is heard as a cadential figure in the relative major. A cadence is reached in mm. 12–13, and in the cadential chord another figure is begun, which is treated imitatively, and so on. The whole makes an unusual slow movement, affecting through the shape of its melodic lines, and quite consonant with the tone of the rest of the quartet.

SYMPHONIES, K.183 and K.201 The effects of imitative counterpoint are henceforth felt throughout Mozart's lifetime, and it is a hallmark of his style in whatever medium that all parts of a composition are vitalized by their significance to the whole texture. In two important symphonies of the period, the G minor K.183 of October 1773, and the A major K.201 of April 1774, contrapuntal devices invigorate the orchestral parts and serve to increase the intellectual and emotional intensity of each work. Both are powerful works in four movements, in which it is difficult to imagine a single note being changed without damage. It is characteristic of Mozart's sonata structures that much greater weight is placed upon the exposition and recapitulation, and that the developmental process occupies only a small part of the whole. It is also characteristic that Mozart's developments are less of a "working out" than a period of tonal flux, often with little more than the slightest connection with what has gone before, rather serving, it would seem, to separate the exposition and recapitulation. Yet in both these symphonies the tension of the whole is maintained, and although the development sections are short, they achieve a heightened effect through the use of imitative counterpoint.

When Wolfgang and his father learned that the archbishop was going to Vienna, they obtained permission to precede him there, so that they could maintain and strengthen their professional contacts. As we have seen, however, the visit produced nothing in the way of an appointment, but resulted in a fine crop of compositions.

LA FINTA GIARDINIERA Most of 1774 was spent in Salzburg with the daily round of playing and composing. Wolfgang had been asked to write an opera for the Munich Carnival, and so, in customary manner, he began work in October, leaving the composition of the arias until he was on the spot with the singers at hand. The opera, *La finta giardiniera* (The Pretended Garden-Girl) K.196, was an enormous success, and the Mozarts had the distinct pleasure of seeing Archbishop Colloredo congratulated by all the Munich court on his having such a treasure as young Mozart. Leopold reported to his wife that "he [Colloredo] was so embarrassed that he could only reply with a bow of the head and a shrug of the shoulders." (*Letters,* 18 Jan. 1775) Their triumph was only temporary, for despite his success, no further contracts came Wolfgang's way, and father and son were soon back in Salzburg, Leopold resuming his long-held position as Vice-Kapellmeister with Wolfgang as one of the concertmasters (the other was Michael Haydn). This was destined to be Wolfgang's longest stay at home since he first started traveling, and it was also to be remarkably productive, particularly in the concerto genre—he wrote five for violin, probably for his own use, in the last eight months of 1775 alone[2]—and in serenade, divertimento, and Mass. Conspicuously absent is any completed symphony.

BROADENING EXPRESSIVITY

In this period Mozart experimented with any device that would serve to broaden expressivity. Tempo changes within movements are quite common: in the Violin Concertos K.216, 218, and 219, in the Piano Concerto K.271 (1777), and in the Sonatas for Violin and Piano K.306 (1778) and K.378 (1779), the last movements, cast in the rondo form, each have an episode in different tempo and/or meter. In some works, such as K.218 and K.306, the rondo subject itself consists of material different in both meter and tempo. A somewhat different case, perhaps Mozart's only use of this device, is to be found in his Violin Sonata, K.302 (1778), in which the formal structure of the first movement is so adapted that the first group is *Adagio* and the second group *Allegro*. Mozart, like Haydn, amused himself with the obvious transfer of vocal idioms or aria and recitative into instrumental terms. It is significant

2. There is a question concerning the dating of the violin concertos, and the first of them, traditionally assigned to 1775, may have been composed in 1773.

that Haydn's most successful examples should have been written for string quartet, while Mozart's finest example, arguably, occurs in the slow movement of his Concerto for Piano in E♭ K.271, written not for himself but for a French pianist, Mlle. Jeunehomme.

The correspondence reveals in numerous ways the increasingly strained relationship between the Mozarts and the archbishop. A year had barely passed since Colloredo's accession when in mid-1773, he informed Wolfgang that he "had nothing to hope for in Salzburg and would do better to seek [his] fortune elsewhere." (*Letters,* 1 Aug. 1777) Leopold reported to Padre Martini that the archbishop had said that Wolfgang "knew nothing and that he ought to betake himself to some conservatorio of music at Naples and study music" (*Letters,* 22 Dec. 1777)—a remark that demonstrates the way the archbishop could lose his judgment when he lost his temper. He was probably present when the Pope conferred a knighthood on Wolfgang; he undoubtedly knew about the boy's extraordinary admission to the Bologna Academy and was evidently simply trying to wound. The family developed a code by which they could talk about the archbishop in their letters without being discovered by the censors. And so it continued, as each side drew ever nearer to the breaking point. That point was reached in a letter dated 1 August 1777, when Wolfgang, after describing a history of requests by Leopold to be allowed to travel and a commensurate list of refusals by the archbishop, proceeded to lecture that man of the church on the teaching of the Gospel, and, finally, to request his release from the archbishop's service. Colloredo responded on 28 August with a furious broadside in which he dismissed not only Wolfgang but also his father, although when his temper cooled he rescinded his decision with regard to Leopold.

THE SECOND JOURNEY TO PARIS

Thus it was that Wolfgang, traveling this time with his mother since Leopold could not leave, set out in 1778 on the next step along the road to his personal and artistic maturation. The first stop was Munich, where *La finta giardiniera* had been such a success as the Carnival opera of 1775. But despite the reputation he enjoyed there, Mozart could get nowhere with the Elector, who reiterated that there was no vacancy in his establishment. It is clear from the conversation recorded by Mozart that the Elector's chief concern was not to offend Archbishop Colloredo by taking into his service the man whom he had just dismissed. Mother and son quickly moved on to Augsburg, where Wolfgang gave a concert and got to know his cousin, Maria Anna Thekla, with whom he carried on a correspondence notorious for its scatalogical vulgarity, a side of his nature which manifested itself in his letter writing and some of his canons. There was no post to be hoped for at Augsburg and they pushed on to Mannheim, where the Mozarts were to spend the next four months. Things appeared to go well and Wolfgang was befriended by Christian Cannabich as well as other members of the musical establishment there. Through their assistance he was able to play for the Elector, and thereafter to request permission to write an opera for the court. He received a degree of encouragement that filled him with the highest hopes, but he was not able to pin down anything definite. His compositions did not bring in enough to sustain the two travelers, and Leopold had to help them out with cash and advice. Leopold's frustration at being at home, knowing the ways of the world and fearing that his son did not, brought a degree of rancor into their correspondence which hurt them both. Perhaps it was Wolfgang's "unwillingness to crawl," as he says in a letter, which did more to injure his prospects at Mannheim than anything else. The Abbé Georg Joseph Vogler (1749–1814) was in charge of church music there, with the title of Second Kapellmeister. Mozart made it no secret that he thought him "a dreary musical jester, an exceedingly conceited and rather incompetent fellow" (*Letters,* 4 Nov. 1777) despite the fact that Vogler was high in the Elector's favor. So the only work he obtained was as a free-lance composer and teacher.

Apart from a group of sonatas for piano and violin, which critics spoke of as "an entirely new type," and a couple of piano sonatas, the most important compositions of this period were the result of a commission from an amateur flute player. Mozart was not fond of the flute and did not take the commission seriously; yet even in these works he demonstrated one of his chief stylistic traits of the time—his complete prodigality of material, which many of his contemporaries commented upon: one idea develops into another with the greatest ease and yet the whole remains coherent.

In Mannheim, while planning to move on to Paris where Leopold saw the only remaining possibility of success, Mozart met a family called Weber, and fell in love with one of the daughters, Aloysia, a most gifted singer, to whom he gave lessons. This was probably the grand passion of Mozart's life—all his plans now centered on furthering her career as a singer, forgetting about his own, or rather, seeing their two careers bound up together. Leopold brought him back to earth in a strongly worded letter, and after a long and uncomfortable journey, mother and son arrived in Paris from Mannheim on 23 March 1778.

Mozart's first commission was for eight choruses and recitatives for a *Miserere* by Ignaz Holzbauer, which are unfortunately lost, as is also the autograph of his second work written in Paris, the *Sinfonia concertante* for flute, oboe, horn, and bassoon, K.297b.[3] Among the compo-

3. It is possible that the *Sinfonia concertante* in E♭ for oboe, clarinet, bassoon, and horn may be an arrangement of this original work by Mozart—at least in part.

sitions Mozart produced in Paris there are works of real significance: he returned to the symphony with the so-called *Paris* Symphony, K.297 in D, a three-movement work scored for large orchestra including flutes, oboes, clarinets, bassoons, horns, trumpets, and tympani (see p. 274 below); the concerto is represented by K.299 for flute and harp; and there are two sonatas for violin and piano, four for piano alone, and four sets of variations for piano, among others.

Mozart had reasonable success in Paris, despite the fact that the Gluck-Piccinni quarrel was at its height (see p. 193). His symphony was performed at the *Concert Spirituel,* his ballet *Les petits riens,* K.299b, was given six times at the Opéra, and he had pupils among the aristocracy. He was offered the post of organist at Versailles but refused it on the grounds that it did not pay enough. But an old family friend, Baron von Grimm, who had helped the Mozarts on their first stay in Paris, wrote to Leopold that:

> Wolfgang is too kind-hearted, not active enough, all too easily deceived, too little concerned with the means that can lead him to his fortune. In order to make one's way here it is necessary to be crafty, enterprising and daring. I wish he had, for the sake of his success, half as much talent and twice as much address . . .[4] (*Letters,* 13 Aug. 1778)

On July 3rd, after a few weeks of various ailments, Anna Maria Mozart died. In addition to bearing his sorrow, Wolfgang had to make all necessary arrangements and in the most tactful way possible break the news to his father and sister in Salzburg. Late at night, directly after his mother's death (she died at 10:00 p.m.) he wrote a long letter to his father. In the first paragraph he said that his mother was very ill, and that while the doctors do not despair he has given up hope. Then he continued to talk about business, music, etc., in a tone of normalcy which is hard to believe. At two in the morning he began another letter to a Salzburg friend in which he told the truth and asked that the sad news be broken gently and carefully. This episode demonstrates clearly the extent of Mozart's self-discipline and strength. When he could have collapsed in paroxysms of self-pity, he controlled himself and acted a part with total conviction.

The expressive sincerity of some of the Paris compositions cannot be doubted. The Sonata for Violin and Piano in E minor, K.304 (discussed on pp. 310–12) and the Sonata for Piano in A minor, K.310, cannot be dated with complete accuracy, but they were written around the time of his mother's illness and death. Each is a controlled, mature masterpiece that displays a more complete command of all aspects of technique as well as a wider range of musical experience than any previous

4. The original of Grimm's letter has not survived, but this part of it was copied by Leopold into a letter to Wolfgang.

The interior of the Cathedral at Salzburg in an engraving by Melchior Küssell. From 1779 until he left the Archbishop's service, Mozart was organist here. (Museo Carolino Augusteum, Salzburg)

work. One has the feeling here that there is now no height or depth that Mozart was not able to reach, and that whatever he wished to accomplish in music he could achieve.

In late September, Wolfgang left Paris on the homeward journey, dragging his feet and hoping once again that a job might materialize in Mannheim. He sustained another hard blow *en route* when Aloysia Weber, now an accomplished artist, rejected his suit. He wrote to his father "today I can only weep, I have far too sensitive a heart," (Letters, 29 Dec. 1778) without telling Leopold the reason for his misery. Three weeks later, on 17 January 1779, he was back in much-hated Salzburg, soon to be on the payroll of the archbishop again, this time as organist in the place of the recently deceased Anton Adlgasser (1729–77). It says something for Colloredo that he not only took Mozart back into his household, but he gave him Adlgasser's salary of 450 gulden a year, which was three times what he had been earning before.

THE SALZBURG "EMPLOYEE" ONCE AGAIN

Once again, despite his surroundings, a string of masterpieces flowed from his pen during this year. Both the Concerto in E♭ for two pianos, K.365, and the *Sinfonia concertante* in E♭ for Violin and Viola, K.364, belong to this period. Alike in key and in setting two soloists against an orchestra, these two works embody the widest contrast between exuberance and introspection. Just how much Mozart is in control of his material can be seen in the passage from the slow movement of K. 364, in which imitative counterpoint—through its dissonance—becomes the most powerful means to the expression of agony. When set against this movement, in the same key, the slow movement of the E♭ Piano Concerto, K.271, appears "operatic" and too theatrical to be quite sincere.

Beside the concertos mentioned above, the Serenade K.320 for orchestra, and the Divertimento in D, K.334, for two violins, viola, bass, and two horns must be mentioned since each constitutes the most perfect example of its genre.

Since 1775 Mozart had no opportunity to write for the stage. In 1779 he renewed his interest in two endeavors: the incidental music, consisting of choruses and entr'actes, for the heroic drama *Thamos, König von*

The whole Mozart family painted by Nepomuk della Croce in 1780-81. Frau Mozart, who died in 1778, appears to dominate the family from her lofty perch on the wall. (Mozart Museum, Salzburg)

Aegypten, K.345, and the unfinished *Singspiel, Zaide,* or *Das Serail* (The Seraglio), K.344.

The year 1780 was not very productive, probably because of Mozart's unhappiness in Salzburg, but in the fall of the year he received a commission to write the 1781 Carnival opera for the court of Carl Theodor at Munich. He began work on it in October of 1780, becoming totally absorbed in the task, and went to Munich in November in order to be near the singers while he was writing their arias.

IDOMENEO Although *Idomeneo* is an *opera seria* seemingly in the Metastasian style, only the language used to express the emotions can be called Metastasian, for the stage situations and the active use of the chorus betray the French origins of the work. Mozart approached writing it as an experienced composer of opera of all kinds, yet this is the first of his works in which he shows himself to be a true creative genius of the theater, capable of innovating, abandoning convention, and doing whatever may be necessary to ensure that the finished work shall be as convincing theatrically, yet as full of verisimilitude, as possible. Since Varesco, the librettist, was in Salzburg and Mozart was in Munich from the beginning of November, Leopold acted as intermediary between the two, and thanks to this arrangement we have a record of one of the most illuminating exchanges on the subject of the composer's aesthetic and his dramatic ideals that has ever survived. In the very first letter to his father, written almost before he had had the time to unpack, the keynote of Mozart's relationship to Varesco (and to all his subsequent librettists) is struck. He says: "Some slight changes will have to be made here and there, and the recitatives will have to be shortened a bit."(*Letters,* 8 Nov. 1780) He goes on to ask for the modification of an aria, otherwise good, because it contains an aside, the effect of which is spoiled when it has to be repeated with the *da capo.* Subsequently he asks for more changes.

Shortly before the opera was to be produced, a rumor began circulating that Mozart had set some Italian badly because of his ignorance of the language. (The same accusation had been leveled against Gluck, with as little basis in fact.) Mozart's reply shows how strongly he believes that a large part of music's function is to enhance or represent the words. He says:

> I should like to tell that whoever said such a thing knows very little Italian. The aria (Raaff's aria "Mare funesta") is very well adapted to the words. You hear the *mare* and the *mare funesta* and the musical passages suit *minacciar,* for they entirely express *minacciar* (threatening). (*Letters,* 27 Dec. 1780)

That he took real pride in this aspect of his operatic composition is shown in the way he cites examples of the same kind of thing in later correspondence, without the need to rebuff criticism.

Mozart wanted his operas to be true to life. Yet the tenor Anton Raaf, who was 67 years old when he sang the title role in *Idomeneo,* appeared on stage immaculately clad after a terrible storm at sea. (Deutsches Theatermuseum, Munich)

The opera was a success. The Mozart family and several Salzburg friends traveled to Munich to take part in the Carnival celebrations, and to celebrate Mozart's birthday, the opera's dress rehearsal (on the same day, 27 January), and the first performance (on 29 January 1781). The archbishop, in Vienna because of the illness of his aged father, undoubtedly was kept informed of the opera's fate, for three Salzbourgeois were noted in the libretto as being in his service: the composer, Mozart; the poet, Varesco; and the translator, Schachtner. And although Wolfgang enjoyed his operatic success and the Carnival to the full, he still found time for composition, turning out two arias, an isolated and important *Kyrie* in D minor, K.341, and his famous Quartet for Oboe and Strings, K.370. The most impressive composition of this period is undoubtedly the Serenade in B♭, K.361, for 13 wind instruments, which was begun in Munich and completed in Vienna. It unites rich and refined orchestration with an exuberance of spirit and a heartfelt emotional quality so that one can hardly conceive of any serenade ever covering a wider expressive range and yet remaining a serenade in spirit. He gave an unusual name to this unusual work, calling it a *Gran Partita*. Why he wrote it is unknown, but speculation will not be far wrong if we believe it was written to attract the attention of a potential patron. It did not succeed in this, however, and during its composition he received a summons to join the archbishop in Vienna. March of 1781 saw Mozart settled in the city that was to be his home henceforth, and which, a mere ten years later, provided him with a pauper's grave. That was still in the future, however, and the greatest work was still to come.

CHAPTER XVII

The High Salzburg Style

The Mozartian style comes to full maturity early in the early seventies and the works he composed during this time have found favor with connoisseurs ever since. The composer's progress from youth to manhood is reflected in the development of his musical style, as his craft becomes more complex and his melodic inventiveness richer. Above all, he becomes increasingly capable of creating music imbued with a uniquely deep and passionate expressivity.

KEYBOARD WORKS

A group of piano sonatas, which are the first examples of this genre to survive, dates from the second half of 1774 and the beginning of 1775. Mozart composed the first five of a set of six one after the other, having decided at the outset to use only the "easy" major keys (those with the simplest key signatures). The arrangement is made by following a descending circle of fifths from C to E♭, the most extreme of the easy keys on the flat side, then upward by fifths from the starting point, C, to G and D; thus the set is composed in the order C, F, B♭, E♭, G, and D (K.279–284). A couple of months intervened between the composition of the fifth and sixth sonatas. It appears likely that these works were written for Mozart's own use in Munich at the time of the first performance of *La finta gardiniera,* and in family correspondence, he refers to them as the "difficult" sonatas. Each is in three movements, but beyond that basic similarity, Mozart tried to make them as different as possible: three use the subdominant as the variant key for the middle movement, one uses the tonic minor, and two use the dominant; and the music ranges from the carefree *galanterie* of the first movement of the C major or the B♭ to the gnomic, aphoristic, and deeply felt opening of the E♭ (Example XVII–1) or the coda of the slow movement of the Sonata in G. The last sonata of the set, in D, is the longest and has as its final movement one of the most imposing sets of variations Mozart ever wrote.

Example XVII–1: W.A. MOZART, Sonata K.282, I

Almost three years elapsed before the last three sonatas of this period were composed. Mozart's travels to Mannheim and Paris engendered a number of important works, among them the Piano Sonatas in C, K.309, and in D, K.311, both written in Mannheim in late 1777, and the Sonata in A minor, K.310, written in Paris in the summer of 1778.

These three works are more ambitious and more mature than the earlier set. They are the product of the years in which Mozart experienced the miseries of unrequited love, thwarted aspirations, the duplicity of his fellow composers, and personal bereavement. Few artists have had to endure such prolonged anguish. No composer is less likely to be autobiographical in music than Mozart, but as the range of his personal experience broadened, his expressive powers became more and more profound. In these sonatas we see the ever increasing evidence of Mozart's control of asymmetrical phrase structures and of idiosyncratic harmonic usage within the *Affekt* of *galanterie* that must have placed his music beyond the grasp of his contemporaries.

The first 20 bars of K.309 contain phrases of different lengths being elided and yet the whole appears balanced and controlled. In the last movement of K.310 the composer concentrates on the harsher and unusual sonority of the open fourth:

Example XVII–2: W. A. MOZART, Sonata in A minor, K.310, III

This sonority is further expanded in mm. 37–40. That this harshness is deliberate is beyond doubt, since Mozart softens the effect by leading the voices differently when the passage is repeated in the minor of the relative major. On the other hand, the slow movement of this sonata contains some of the lushest textures in all of Mozart's compositions for piano.

Example XVII–3: W.A. MOZART, Sonata in A minor, K.310, III

In addition to the Capriccio, K.395, during this period Mozart wrote at least six sets of variations for piano alone, including his most celebrated set on the French tune "Ah vous dirai-je, Maman," better known in the English-speaking world as "Twinkle, twinkle, little star." Some of these works involved a high degree of virtuosity and afford a better example of Mozart's technical prowess than do the sonatas.

The only four-hand Sonata he wrote at this time, K.358 in B♭ (1774), is an empty, unattractive work which shows almost no advance in technique over the Sonata K.19d. It is a piece of social music that, for some reason, did not catch the composer's imagination, a fact all the more remarkable in the light of his supreme command of the medium in the next work he wrote for it, the Duet Sonata, K.497, in F (1786).

ACCOMPANIED SONATAS

Most significant are the accompanied sonatas of this period. A set of six sonatas "Pour Clavecin Ou Forte Piano Avec Accompagnement D'un Violon" was assembled to be dedicated to the wife of the Elector of the Palatinate. Most of them were composed while Mozart was trying to land a job in Mannheim, because, as he said, that type of thing was popular there. They also reflect Mozart's admiration for similar works by Joseph Schuster (1748–1812). The last two works of the group were written in Paris and the whole set was first published there so Mozart at least had a printed score to give to the Electress on his way back to Salzburg.

The majority of these sonatas are in two movements (the reader will recall that the sonatas of Christian Bach for the same instruments are also in two movements), and they are varied and complex. Later in 1778, shortly after these sonatas were composed, Leopold commended the instrumental works of Bach to his son as models worthy of emulation in the following terms:

> If you have not got any pupils, well then compose something more . . . But let it be something short, easy and popular . . . or you imagine that

> you would be doing work unworthy of you? If so, you are very much mistaken. Did Bach, when he was in London, ever publish anything but similar trifles? *What is slight can still be great,* if it is written in a natural, flowing, and easy style—and at the same time bears the mark of sound composition. Such works are more difficult to compose than all those harmonic progressions, *which the majority of people cannot fathom,* or pieces which have pleasing melodies, but which are *difficult to perform*. Did Bach lower himself by such work? Not at all. Good composition, sound construction, il filo—these distinguish the master from the bungler—even in trifles. (*Letters,*13 Aug. 1778)

The proportions of the ensemble sonatas are ampler than those of the solo sonatas: the shortest exposition of the accompanied sonatas (K.296) is almost twice as long as that of the solo sonatas (K.279). These larger proportions result from the repetition or sharing of melodic materials between the instruments, and from Mozart's use of a long, *cantabile* melody, more appropriate to the flute or violin, perhaps, than to the piano. There is no *cantabile* melody in the piano sonatas of the period comparable to the opening of K.301:

Example XVII–4: W. A. MOZART, Sonata K.301, I

Such melodies are far removed from the clipped, contrasting figures of the language of *galanterie*.

One work from this Mannheim set of accompanied sonatas particularly deserves comment. The Sonata in E minor, K.304 (*ACM* 39), is written in a key that Mozart rarely uses, and it has long been acknowledged as one of the composer's outstanding works in the minor mode.

This is not one of those pieces in minor that cannot wait to move to the major. After twenty-eight insistent measures in minor, the move to establish G major for the second group is colored by G minor in mm. 41–44. When G is firmly in place, the music begins to slide back toward E minor, as in mm. 53–55, or right into the key, as in mm. 67–71 and mm. 82–84. Indeed, few eighteenth-century works have used the affective minor mode so thoroughly that there is almost no trace of major except in the second half of the exposition. The effect is particularly poignant in the recapitulation where, in those spots when the music slides into the minor mode in the exposition, the harmony serves to establish the major mode, emerging for a moment from the surrounding sea of minor, only to be dragged under again (see mm. 167–171).

Example XVII–5: W. A. MOZART, Sonata K.304, I, four opening phrases

The melody of the first movement is tightly knit. In those minor-mode works by Mozart traditionally called "emotional," melodies are generally controlled and shaped rigorously into balancing periods. Thus, in this sonata the eight-measure opening tune is divided into four sections, each with a closely related rhythmic profile. The first phrase is different from the other three in that it rises straight up and its melody is completely disjunct. The remaining three have similar shapes and move conjunctly, apart from the last interval of a falling fifth. Transposed to begin and end on the same note the three phrases are virtually identical (see Example XVII–6, p.312). This opening melody with its upward direction and unique emotional *Affekt*—the outcome of its unique contour—occurs five times in the movement, suffering no modification except in the accompaniment that surrounds it. It is the beginning and the end. No sonata-form movement in the whole of Mozart's oeuvre remotely parallels this achievement, since no other work has a similar inexorable aim to express. The first statement, mm. 1–8, is a *piano* unison; the second, mm. 13–20, sets the violin with piano accompaniment at a dynamic of *piano;* the third on the dominant, mm. 85–92, introduces a countersubject, the first gesture of which is the minor ninth; the fourth, mm. 113–120, is the recapitulation, in which the final note of each melodic unit is harmonized dissonantly and with a *sforzando;* the fifth and last, mm. 193–200, like the second, sets the violin melody against a static, brooding accompaniment in the piano.

Example XVII–6: W. A. MOZART, Sonata K.304, I, phrases 2, 3, and 4 transposed

The second and final movement of this sonata is a Rondo in *Tempo di Menuetto* with a modified refrain. The 16–bar melody is a four-line strophe **A B A' B'** in which the bass movement has such a strong downward movement in **A** and **A'**, repeated with each refrain, as to seem almost like a ground bass. Unlike its predecessor, this movement, despite the depressed nature of the main melody, offers, in its first episode (mm. 33–62) an escape into G major. The second episode (mm. 94–127) reveals the consolatory possibility of E major. The last return of the refrain must be seen in the light of what Mozart does in its second appearance. The reader will note that in the final appearance of the material, much of the chromatic movement in the bass has been replaced by a pedal E and the descending motion has been replaced by ascending motion. Whereas the melody of the refrain was characterized by a bass falling from E, the coda (mm. 148–170) features a rising bass moving repeatedly through G A B C to G A B E. The grim, determined final bars emphasize the minor mode moving toward the archaic final chord, the thirdless E and B—not an ambiguous major / minor, but a definite minor chord without the third.

In this glorious testimony to the human need to communicate, Mozart achieves what is commonly attributed to Beethoven, i.e., a consistent use of musical materials to convey a sequence of affective states. The sequence is arranged in such a manner that the thoughtful and reflective listener is urged to look for more particular significance that might reasonably account for the arrangement. The accompanied sonatas of this period represent a dimension of instrumental music that Mozart had not achieved before—a dimension which few ever achieve.

In August of 1776, Mozart had written a three-movement work for violin, cello, and keyboard, entitled *Divertimento a 3* , K.254. In relation

Example XVII–7: W.A. MOZART, *Divertimento a 3,* K.254, III

to the piano-trio genre, this work falls squarely between Haydn and late Mozart since it is largely a piano sonata with occasional passages for violin and in which the cello largely doubles the bass line. It would not deserve singling out for special mention were it not an early example of metrical alteration, which became an important feature of Mozart's style. In the first movement, mm. 116–121, there is a passage of 2 / 4 meter within 3 / 4, in other words, hemiola. The phrasing indications together with dynamic markings of *forte* and *piano* create an impression of cross-meters and produce unusual and striking effects. The last movement contains a passage in which a variety of meters are forced into triple time twice and at one point (mm. 67–68) the hands of the keyboard player are required to articulate different meters.

CHAMBER MUSIC WITHOUT KEYBOARD

The abundant chamber music without keyboard that Mozart wrote during this period was scored for a wide variety of instrumental combinations. For strings alone there is the set of six quartets K.168–173 (see p.258) written in August 1773, after Mozart's Italian trip, when he was trying to cultivate a relationship with the Viennese publisher Artaria.

Just as the sets of quartets are preceded by a solitary quartet, K.80, so the great string quintets are preceded by a solitary quintet, K.174. This work was written in Salzburg in 1773 after Mozart's return from Vienna, and its instrumentation tempts the composer into experimenting with texture; the richness offered by the combination of two violins, two violas, and cello brings out new effects, the first of which is that of a string trio with violin and viola soloists. Later the higher strings are paired against the violas and all four upper strings participate. Perhaps the most striking difference between this work and the later quintets is the role of the cello. Here its function is that of a bass instrument in a supporting role. Indeed, Mozart labeled the lowest staff *Basso,* and whether the part should be played by cello or double bass or both is not clear.

For about four years, between the end of 1773 and 1777, Mozart wrote almost no concerted chamber music. The one noteworthy exception is the Sonata for Bassoon and Cello, K.292, possibly from 1775, which one can imagine being, for Mozart, the work of only a few hours, and which is not so much a duet as a sonata for bassoon with bass to be realized in any number of ways.

The mixed works for winds and strings, beginning with the Flute Quartets of 1777 and 1778 were certainly produced on commission, but they also reflect a vogue at this time for unusual ensembles in all kinds of instrumental music. We know that Mozart reminded his father that he could not stand the flute and that his dislike made composing for it all the harder. Yet, particularly in the first of these quartets, the composer pours out his melodic gifts with a prodigal hand. The Quartet for Oboe and Strings in F, K.370 of 1781, has likewise set an unbeatable standard for that performing combination.

Glorious though many of the sonatas and chamber works of the period 1773–81 are, it is not in the realm of private but in public music that Mozart made his most substantial contributions. Almost none of the chamber works of this period, however charming, can realistically be compared in technique or expressive power with works for the same combinations written during his last ten years. But in the concerto, the symphony, the serenade, the divertimento, and in the opera, standards were established which the composer himself only occasionally surpassed.

SYMPHONIES

Mozart wrote a dozen symphonies that cluster in 1773–4 and in 1778–80 (the years between belong to the concerto and the divertimento). The earliest symphonies, dated in March and April of 1773, undoubtedly reflect some of the lessons Mozart learned in Italy. It is noteworthy that K.184 in E♭ Is the first symphony in which two bassoons are scored throughout, and not merely taken for granted. For the most part, the bassoons simply doubled the cellos and basses. In the slow movement, however, they remain independent and, in the final bars, become part of a solo wind choir. The last movement sees an almost total independence, not only of bassoons from bass line but of winds and strings—an innovation which is not repeated for some time.

Between 5 October 1773 and 6 April 1774, Mozart wrote three symphonies—in G minor, K.183, in C, K.200, and in A, K.201—often regarded as a junior trilogy, comparable to the last three symphonies "within narrower limits."[1] K.183, in which the mood ranges from the noisily defiant to the quietly pathetic, has long been famous as an early example of Mozart's typically affective use of the key. It is the only example of a *Sturm und Drang* concert symphony by Mozart,[2] and, as is so often the case with this composer, the listener may interpret the work as an expression of a serious emotional state, or as an imitation of the gestures of an emotional state (just as the child Mozart had put on the masks of love and anger for Daines Barrington, see pp. 265–66). Nevertheless, the intensity of the expression and its unremitting force (letting up for only a moment in the G-major trio of the minuet) make this one of the most single-minded of compositions. It is hard to imagine how Mozart envisaged using it in the normal surroundings of either a public or private concert.

The Symphony in A, K.201, is quite different in every respect. Here,

1. Einstein, *op. cit.*, p. 222.
2. The three-movement overture to *Betulia liberata*, K.118, is in the key of D minor and, moreover, shows a unification in thematic material between the first and last movements.

in a work whose expressive ambit ranges from the graceful to the stately, from the serious to the frivolous, the composer creates textures in which the integrity of the orchestral voices is enriched by counterpoint, and a loving elaboration of detail seems to inform every measure. The character of each movement is fundamentally different, yet they belong together. If K.183 was single-minded in its expression and in the unity of its material, the A-major Symphony encompasses a world of different ideas.

While in Paris in 1778, Mozart received a commission to compose a symphony for the *Concert Spirituel* and the resulting work in D, K.297, bears the sobriquet, the *Paris*. Johann Stamitz had greatly influenced French taste for instrumental music as a result of his visit and the training he gave Parisian orchestras in 1754. Despite the passage of time and rapidly changing fashions, Parisian symphonic taste was still more closely aligned to the work of the Mannheim School than to any other current of musical thought. The commission for the *Concert Spirituel* rather put Mozart in a quandary for he and his father did not particularly like the music of Stamitz (usually they meant Carl, the son) and they rarely had anything good to say about French music, either. Since they believed the Parisians were fond of noisy music, the symphony Mozart composed for them uses the largest orchestra to this point: flutes, oboes, clarinets (appearing for the first time), bassoons, horns, trumpets, drums, and strings, in fact, all the instruments available and customarily used in the orchestra of the *Concert Spirituel*. *Cantabile* melodic substance is abandoned in favor of arpeggio-based melodies of rhythmic character. Cadences and cadential formulas are extended at great length with dazzling and noisy orchestration. The sonata-form structure of the first movement is clear, although no repeats are called for and the middle section is exceptionally short. Most striking is the effect which Mozart introduces into his recapitulation at the point of transition (mm. 174–185). This is the point in the structure where Mozart devised some of his most astonishing developments, either theoretic or tonal, and the *Paris* Symphony represents an early example of a mature trademark. Its slow movement was judged to be too long by Joseph Legros (1739–93), the impresario, and Mozart wrote a substitute which was published with the first edition. The substitute movement lacks all the charm of melody and richness of orchestration which characterized the first version, and its reliance on cliché reflects the composer's opinion of Parisian taste. How surprised Mozart must have been to find the third (and last) movement of this symphony the most appreciated. Difficult to play and involving fugato, it was as much a challenge to players as to listeners.

The Symphony in G, K.318, is an Italian overture. But what an overture! Various reasons have been suggested for the composition of this work: that it was to be the overture to the *Singspiel, Zaide;* that it was

Example XVII–8: W. A. MOZART, Symphony in G, K.318, I

to be part of several other dramatic works; that it was to be a substitute overture for an opera by another composer. Whatever the case, not even in the G-minor Symphony, K.183, has Mozart written music of a more strongly defined character. The first subject is made up of strongly profiled, rhythmic material at the unison that sums up all that is imperious. The second tonal area brings a melody of an equally strong but different cast, and the closing theme unites the rhythmic opening in counterpoint with a development of the secondary, melodic material in a texture of extreme brilliance. In the middle section the opening musical substance is developed: over a long pedal on B, a sequence of extremely dissonant harmony seems to be leading to E minor, a move frustrated by a sudden turn to C and then to D. The recapitulation would normally be expected at this point, but in its place there follows a gentle, *cantabile* slow movement in the tonic, G. The recapitulation that finally follows the slow movement is incomplete, i.e., it begins with the lead-in to the second group, now in the tonic. A uniquely Mozartian stroke occurs in the coda of this symphony, mm. 256–262, where, in the midst of radiant tonic G and its dominant, the opening of the work is heard again, but altered to increase its expressive power. Much of the force of the opening resides in the tiny C♯ in m. 2 and m. 257—a tritone away from the tonic. The third repetition of the rhythmic gesture (mm. 258–259) involves C♯ and D♯, and clearly opens the door to the key of E minor—a rare key for Mozart, which takes us into the troubled domain of the Sonata K.304, discussed above. This awful door to E minor opens, giving a glimpse of the world within, emphasized by the dotted-rhythm chord of E minor, set for 2 bassoons, 4 horns, 2 trumpets, and tympani. Just as quickly as it opened, the door closes again, and strings, flutes, and oboes modulate gently to the subdominant and quickly back to the tonic. The marvel of this structure is that what strikes the listener as a new idea has been carefully prepared: the effect of mm. 258–259 was already foreshadowed in mm. 3 and 4; and the long pedal on B (mm. 85–94) leads us to expect E minor—expectations that are gratified finally in m. 259. In these few measures, in this revelation of elemental power in the smallest musical gesture, we see another quality of Mozart's genius, part of the essence of which lies in his ability to put a world of disparities into a nutshell. Difficult to grasp because it seems to us understated, Mozart's message is not, like Beethoven's, a call to action, but a contemplative observation. As clearly as any artist he can see and portray Heaven and Hell, but he prefers Heaven. This small and marvelous overture/symphony has both realities within its small dimensions.

The final two symphonies of this period, in B♭, K.319, and in C, K.338, do not retreat from the deep waters in which Mozart henceforth swims, although, of course, their nature is quite different. In orchestration, Mozart has now completely forsaken the old-fashioned, and he has no more lessons to learn about handling winds in the orchestral context. The writing in these two symphonies is quite up to the standard of the most mature symphonies. The luminous quality of the single bassoon in mm. 42–44 of the first movement of K.338 shows an appreciation of this instrument quite foreign to the symphonies of 1774 and earlier.

SERENADES AND DIVERTIMENTOS

In the *General History of Music* by Thomas Busby, printed in 1819, Mozart's superior abilities in writing for winds are characterized as "so well known" that they need no further description. He says:

> . . . with Mozart, it was a *natural* resource. The breathing sweetness of the flute, pouring reediness of the hautboy, and mellow murmuring of the bassoon, accorded with the passive delicacy of his nerves, and lively tenderness of his sensations.[3]

3. Thomas Busby, *A General History of Music* (London, 1819; facsimile reprint, New York, 1968) II, p. 413.

Where had this perception of the nature of wind instruments been developed and perfected? Perhaps the answer may be found in that area of music which is neither symphony nor concerto nor chamber music, but that amalgam of all things, the Serenade / Divertimento.

Mozart's more than forty serenades, divertimentos, or cassations, as some earlier works of this type are called, fall into three categories: those for small groups of wind instruments alone; those for mixed chamber combinations; and those for orchestra. There are, of course, important works that do not fit neatly into any of these categories. It is well to recall first of all that the term "divertimento" is a general rather than a specific term, and denotes more a function than a structure—the divertimento is social music often designed for specific celebratory occasions.

The Divertimentos for Winds have been described as "open-air music," and, since they are orchestrated for varying numbers of paired instruments (most often oboes, clarinets, bassoons, horns) they combine the greater penetration and carrying power with the bucolic connotations of the instruments themselves. From this period there are two divertimentos for ten instruments (the instruments mentioned above plus two *cors anglais*), each similarly laid out in five movements with only one Minuet. The unique work, K.188, has six movements and is orchestrated for two flutes, five trumpets, and tympani, a curious combination of Mozart's least favorite instruments. The five divertimentos for six instruments (oboes, bassoons, and horns) are in four movements (K.253 is in three), and they all contain writing as sophisticated and musical material as refined as that to be found anywhere. The gavotte-like *Andantino* from K.270 (written in January 1777), like much of the best eighteenth-century art, purges the pastoral of any reality and realizes an ideal.

The group of divertimentos for strings and winds (most usually string quartet and two horns: K.205, 248, 251, 287, and 334) inhabit a world between chamber music and music for a public audience. The first violin holds a special place in these works and employs a degree of virtuosity unrivaled by the other players. Unlike the wind divertimentos, these works, as well as the serenades for orchestra, begin and end with a march designed to bring the players into position and to take them away after the music is over. It has been said of K. 247, K.287, and K.334 that they are "among the purest, gayest, most satisfying and most perfect [works of their kind] that ever assumed musical form. [They are] a lost paradise of music."[4]

The Serenades for orchestra (K.185, K.203, K.204, K.239, K.250, and K.320) have a *concertante* character that differentiates them substantially from the symphonies. A prime example is the *Serenata notturna*

4. Einstein, *op. cit.*, p. 198.

K.239, orchestrated for strings and tympani but with a concertino body consisting of two violins, viola, and double bass. The Serenades for larger orchestra, then, tend to use the instruments in a soloistic fashion. These works are in seven or eight movements, not counting the introductory and concluding marches, and they all include a two- or three-movement violin concerto, set in a different key from the rest of the work. In the course of the last big serenade, K.320, the concerto element is fulfilled by two movements, which Mozart himself entitles *Concertante*, for two flutes, two oboes, two bassoons, and two horns, with *ripieno* strings.

These Salzburg years, though increasingly uncomfortable for the Mozarts because of the archbishop's hostility, must have had their compensations in the jovial relationships they had away from the court—we know from their letters how the Mozarts enjoyed "target-shooting" parties. The significance of these family friendships is to be seen in the divertimentos and serenades which were produced for them—more at this period than at any other—and one can only marvel at a period of history in which the lighter, more robust pleasures are immortalized through music of such elegance. It is because of such artworks that our own times have come to see so much of the eighteenth century as a vision of Eden before the Fall of Man.

CONCERTOS

The Salzburg years are also the richest in the production of concertos for a variety of instruments. In addition to half a dozen piano concertos, all the violin concertos belong to this time together with the concertos for flute, oboe, bassoon, and those for flute and harp, for two violins, and for violin and viola. There are some of the most tantalizing fragments of concertos remaining: one for piano and violin, and one for violin, viola and cello. Lost are concertos for cello, for oboe, and a *sinfonia concertante* for flute, oboe, horn, and bassoon.

All the violin concertos, except the first, date from 1775. In their avoidance of the deeply serious and their devotion to music of high polish and high spirits or gentle melancholy, they resemble the serenades of the same period. But it is remarkable what a leap forward in dimension and virtuosity the 1775 concertos take. K.219 in A major uses an interesting formal device never taken up again by the composer. After the orchestral tutti the solo violin enters in an *Adagio* "introduction" which is, however, connected thematically with the *Allegro* through melodic and rhythmic extension of the tonic triad. The finale of the same concerto mingles exotic, minor-mode elements of Turkish and Hungarian Gypsy music with the courtly Minuet, and this use of *Sturm und Drang* techniques in a comic context casts a curious light on the movement.

This 1777 engraving of a concerto performance in Zurich by Johann Rudolf Holzhalb once again shows a woman instrumentalist taking a leading role at the keyboard while pairs of flutes, violins, and horns, plus a solitary cello make up the accompanying forces.

The *Sinfonia concertante* in E♭, K.364, for solo violin and viola, is a complete departure from the serenade atmosphere. Indeed, this is one of the concertos that is truly unique, for while its instrumentation and structure have forebears and descendants, what it has to say is without parallel. And in such cases historical considerations become less important than critical ones. E♭ major has been described as the "Masonic" key, the three flats of the signature being accorded a mystical significance. Perhaps more to the point is the realization that for Mozart E♭ is one of the richest keys, allowing for a wide range of expression, from the queenly-regal, dignified, and commanding without being imperious, to the exuberant and the energetic. Something of the emotional content of this work is revealed by Mozart's use of C minor as the tonic for the slow movement. The minor mode used in binary or sonata-form movements allowed him to intensify his second tonal area in recapitulation, and Example XVII–9 (see p. 322) shows first how the expression is heightened, and second, how counterpoint, in Mozart's music, is associated with expressive intensity.

The first group of completely original piano concertos belongs to this period and includes K.175, K.238, K.246, and K.271 for one piano and orchestra, K.365 for two pianos and orchestra, and K.242 for three pianos and orchestra. Of these six works, K.271 and K.365 are among the greatest of their genre, but for different reasons.

K.271 in E♭, as mentioned earlier, was written for a Mlle. Jeunehomme, about whom nothing is known, and it dates from January

Example XVII–9: W. A. MOZART, *Sinfonia concertante,* K.364, II

1777. The characteristic features of the work are outstanding. The outer movements begin and end with the piano asserting itself with unusual vigor and with no regard for decorum. It is unique in that it brings in the soloist before the first orchestral tutti, a procedure taken up by Beethoven over twenty-five years later. Few works of Mozart are more strongly rooted in the initial motives of the orchestra, a well-defined unison arpeggio with rhythmic force, which is immediately taken up by the piano and turned into a fluent melody. If Mozart perceived rhythm as the masculine element in music and melody the feminine (and there are undeniable cases where he made this association), then it is hard to avoid the conclusion that the soloist is cast in a feminine role and that the orchestra is the piano's masculine complement. The orchestral tutti is richly textured and full of substance. As is customary in the Mozart keyboard concertos, the soloist plays two parts: that of the *continuo* player, supporting the orchestra from a background position, and that of soloist, supported by the orchestra. Here, at the beginning of the solo exposition, is a classic example of how Mozart induces the coy soloist to emerge from the background: over the last material of the tutti, the soloist enters on a long dominant trill, which, when the orchestra falls silent, turns into new melodic material, based upon the opening. The close of the first movement is unusual, for after the cadenza, the soloist again embarks on a long dominant trill over the same orchestral material as in the first solo entry. Now, however, instead of repeating the "new" material, the soloist uses assertive downward arpeggios to confirm the tonic key after the orchestra's cadential chords. The movement is superb in every detail.

The slow movement in C minor, the first of Mozart's concerto movements in the minor mode, seems to exist on a high plane of pathos, yet there is something theatrical about it which makes it a little unbelievable—perhaps it is too "operatic." Mlle. Jeunehomme might have been able to affect the listener through her portrayal of pathos, as her instrument sobbed and broke down (mm. 12–16, 49–53, and at the close) in that kind of musical asymmetry which Mozart was later to develop into one of his most powerful means for expressing frenzied distress. But despite the broken, incoherent phrases of recitative that speak of despair, here is a case where Mozart's sentiment is sentimental and not sincere, mask and not reality. Too much of the movement is in the relative major, and the cadential conclusion to the recitative tells us that our heroine is of such strong will that she is not to be pitied. Each time, the *forte* chords that follow emphasize the artist's willpower and bring the listener back to metrical reality with a jolt. The assertion is one of reason or intellect over feeling and emotion, as is most common with Mozart. Emanuel Bach said that in order to move his audience the musician must be moved. Mozart demonstrates the opposite proposition: even when moved, he is still in control.

The final movement is brilliant and taxing. Its effect of strength and impetuosity is heightened by the interpolated Minuet, each strain of which is repeated with ornamentation. As a whole work this concerto can stand beside any of Mozart's finest.

The Concerto for Two Pianos in E♭, K.365, is one of a kind. The world it inhabits is one of youthful exuberance, high spirits, and gentle melancholy, and as such it resembles much of the idealized social music of Salzburg. For the players its chief virtue lies in the interplay between the pianos, consisting of close imitation, transposed repetition, and the almost arbitrary division of the figures between the performers. This composition is such a perfect example of its kind that one wonders whether Mozart himself could have equaled it had he composed another.

OPERATIC WORKS

Mozart did not write as many operas during these years as he had in the preceding ones, but he did complete three works, an *opera buffa, La finta giardiniera;* a *serenata, Il rè pastore;* and an *opera seria, Idomeneo,* the first of his "great" operas.

On 13 January 1775, Mozart's comic opera *La finta giardiniera,* K.196, was given its first performance in Munich. The play is described as a farce, and the libretto (author unknown; thought formerly to be by Coltellini but more likely by the less well-known Petrosellini) is the kind of thing that, five years later, he would probably have rejected. It is, however, an effective vehicle, full of misunderstandings that create stage situations of broad comedy. The music reflects the plot magnificently; for example, in the opening, the main characters sing together about the happy day on which everything breathes contentment. Then in the middle of a ternary structure, the characters each tell their own story, and of course, each person is miserable for one reason or another. With the return of the **A** section, all repeat the blissful opening. Later in the opera the main characters are in pursuit of each other in a forest in the middle of the night, with nobody able to see anybody else—the audience, of course, seeing all.

Despite the occasional duet, this is an opera of arias and the exit aria dominates, a sure sign that Mozart was not yet fully emancipated from the *seria* tradition. We have here the first of the real Mozartian finales, in which the crowd on stage becomes larger and larger and the dramatic situation more and more tense; but the essential feature of the later finale, the interplay of characters, is absent. Despite its great charm, *La finta giardiniera* falls far short of the greatness still to come. Like *Lucio Silla,* it was not taken up elsewhere, despite the enthusiasm it aroused initially.

Mozart's work on *Il rè pastore* (The Shepherd King), K.208, must have started as soon as he returned to Salzburg from Munich. Commissioned to celebrate a visit to Salzburg by the Archduke Maximilian, this is a *serenata* composed to a libretto by Metastasio which had been set by many composers since its first appearance around 1750. The *serenata* required little staging, and the libretto called for only a succession of varied recitatives and arias. Although Mozart lavished invention and craftsmanship on the score, it remains merely a fine example of a genre already outmoded.

Mozart's next theatrical venture, though incomplete, shows him striking out in new areas as the maturation process continues. In 1778 the Emperor Joseph II founded a national theater in Vienna to encourage German opera. Undoubtedly with the aim of establishing a strong Viennese contact, Mozart began the composition, in 1780 or earlier, of a *Singspiel* called *Zaide* to a libretto by the old family friend Johann Andreas Schachtner. The work remains an interesting torso embodying the only fruits of Mozart's short-lived enthusiasm for the style of word-setting called "melodrama" (music interspersed with the spoken word). Why it was never finished is not known: perhaps because the death of the old Empress, Maria Theresa, closed the Viennese theaters for a period of mourning, or perhaps because he became fully occupied with a commission to compose the Carnival opera for Munich—and Munich had been for years a goal quite as attractive as Vienna. Indeed, it must have seemed to Mozart that finally the chance he had been waiting for had arrived. He wrote to his father from Mannheim:

> Do not forget how much I desire to write operas. I envy anyone who is composing one. I could really weep for vexation when I hear or see an aria. But Italian not German; seriosa, not buffa. (*Letters,* 4 Feb. 1778)

In the fall of 1780, three years after offering his services to the Elector, he was asked to write for the orchestra he most respected—the Mannheimers—and for voices he knew, an opera in Italian, not German, and *seria,* not *buffa.* That Mozart put his heart and soul into this commission is evident from the score, as well as from the letters exchanged between him and his father. The score, when viewed in relation to the conventions of the background from which it emerges, is quite simply the richest, most imaginative and innovative of any operatic score of Mozart's. The aria structures breathe new life into oft-repeated formulas; the ensembles and chorus parts are both challenging and deeply rewarding, the orchestration is sumptuous. On every page there is evidence that the dramatist in Mozart has finally emerged in full maturity, and the miraculous balance between the eternal enemies, Action and Music, is struck for the first time.

The play chosen by the Munich court was the French tragedy *Idomenée,* which had been set by André Campra (1660–1744) in 1712, and in 1756 as an Italian *opera seria* by Baldassare Galuppi. It is possible that Mozart sent a copy of this libretto to his old Salzburg acquaintance, the court chaplain, Abate Giambattista Varesco (died 1825), whom he asked to adapt the libretto for his purposes, and strengthen its connections with the French original. The story deals with an old myth. Idomeneo, king of Crete, returning home from Troy is beset by storms at sea, and promises to sacrifice to Neptune the first living thing he meets if he can but come safely to land. Neptune accepts the bargain, and Fate sets Idomeneo's son, Idamante, in the king's path. Idomeneo tries to avoid fulfillment of his vow but all his maneuvering cannot deliver him from his contract. Neptune sends a sea monster to ravage Idomeneo's lands. Although Idamante slays the monster, there appears to be no way out of the dilemma, and Idamante is about to be sacrificed when Neptune is appeased by the offer of Ilia, Idamante's betrothed, to die in his place. The *lieto fine,* or happy ending, is brought about when Neptune punishes Idomeneo by forcing him to abdicate the throne in favor of his son.

Mozart left Salzburg for Munich in early November 1780. It is clear from the correspondence that while in Salzburg he had planned the course of the opera thoroughly with Varesco and his father, and that both father and son perceived the commission to be of the highest importance. It is also clear that Act I must have been almost entirely composed in Salzburg. In his first letter from Munich, Wolfgang gives us the first written evidence of his scrupulous approach to opera, and at the same time gives us some sympathy with poor Varesco, whose job was never done. Having just said that the libretto will be printed in Munich and that the Abate should not copy it out again, he says:

> I have just one request to make of the Abbate *[sic]*. Ilia's aria in Act II, Sc. 2 should be altered slightly to suit what I require. "Se il padre perdei, in te lo ritrovo"; this verse could not be better. But now comes what has always seemed unnatural to me—I mean, in an aria—and that is, *a spoken aside* . In a dialogue all these things are quite natural, for a few words can be spoken aside quite hurriedly; but in an aria where the words have to be repeated, it has a bad effect, and even if this were not the case, I should prefer an uninterrupted aria . . . (*Letters,* 8 Nov. 1780)

In his next letter, he refers to what seems to have been an argument between Varesco and his father and him about the reasonableness of Varesco's having the king alone on the ship in a terrible storm, and asks for alterations. He also says that:

> The second duet is to be omitted altogether—and indeed with more profit than loss to the opera. For when you read through the scene, you will see that it obviously becomes limp and cold by the addition of an aria or duet, and very *genant* for the other actors who must stand by doing nothing; and besides, the noble struggle between Ilia and Idamante would be too long and lose its whole force. (*Letters,* 13 Nov. 1780)

He reverts to the same point of length in another letter, when he is speaking of the supernatural intervention that creates the happy ending.

> Tell me, don't you think that the speech of the subterranean voice is too long? Consider it carefully. Picture to yourself the theatre, and remember that the voice must be terrifying—must penetrate—that the audience must really believe it exists. Well how can this effect be produced if the speech is too long, for in this case the listeners will become more and more convinced that it means nothing. If the speech of the Ghost in Hamlet were not so long, it would be far more effective. It is quite easy to shorten the speech of the subterranean voice and it will gain thereby more than it will lose. (*Letters,* 29 Nov. 1780)

Mozart is not concerned with abstract or theoretical ideals. His aim is trueness to life, and his yardstick is what will make the desired effect upon a demanding audience. To this end, cuts and alterations were made whenever improvements came to mind, right up to the first performance.

Mozart had trouble with two of his singers. Raaff (Idomeneo), Mozart's old and dear friend, at the age of sixty-six was too old, and the *castrato,* Dal Prato (Idamante; "mio molto amato castrato dal Prato;" *Letters,* 15 Nov. 1780) was too young and too stupid; a poor actor and a mediocre voice. The others were fine voices and old friends. Mozart's enthusiasm translated into lavish, richly colored chamber music textures, as the following extract from Ilia's aria "Se il padre perdei" (No.11) shows.

Example XVII–10: W. A. MOZART, *Idomeneo,* No.11

Here, the voice, with solo flute, oboe, bassoon, and horn, becomes part of a concertino in which all soloists share the material of the aria, a device that Mozart was to use again with even more dazzling though less dramatic effect the following year. The formality of the two-part aria is kept in some instances, but Mozart invests many of the numbers with novel devices which serve to move the *opera seria* away from its conventionalized stock-in-trade, toward the realms of real human feeling and urgent drama. Mozart knew Gluck, his music, and his ideas, and asserts his allegiance to them, not only throughout the opera, but literally in the last bars of the overture, where the echoes of Gluck's overture to *Iphigénie en Aulide* are unmistakable.

The overture and Scene I of *Idomeneo* (*ACM* 40) illustrate the composer's inventiveness. The overture is set in the key of the opera, D major. But at the close of the overture, D has become the dominant of G major/minor, and the music flows almost imperceptibly through the rising curtain and into Ilia's accompanied recitative, which is the overture's tonal resolution. Progressive tonality and the shaping of the music to expressive ends has an early exposure here. The *recitativo,* whatever its internal tonalities and emotions, begins and ends on G, leading to an aria in G minor. There are two ideas in its verse: first, that in the cause of fighting the Greeks, Ilia has lost father and brothers. Then the transition: she says "And shall I now love a Greek?" The second idea is that she knows she is betraying her own blood, but she cannot hate the face of her loved one, Idamante. The verse lends itself perfectly to a *da capo* setting, but Mozart chooses to make it a balanced binary form, flowing out of and back into recitative, thus allowing no applause to interrupt the forward movement of the action. The voice enunciates the first musical idea in G minor, which sets the first idea from the text. The second idea is set in B♭. Typical of Mozart's pursuit of forward motion in the drama, the recapitulation of the first verbal idea contains the modulation by which it returns to G minor. Mozart's unusual, thoughtful way of setting the text allows him to accomplish several things at the same time: the G-minor tonality is expressive of loss of family and hatred; the second verbal idea—that she has betrayed her family through her love for the son of their murderer—is set first in the relative major, then in the tonic, allowing for the richest possible exposure of Ilia's tormented position in the drama while remaining within her character; and finally, it sets the tone of urgency that must color the whole opera.

The magnificent quartet (No.21) of the third act is another example of Mozart's sovereign control of structure and his insistence on turning the power of structure to expressive ends. Here the four main characters speak of their separate, and conflicting, emotions. Idamante, commanded by his father into exile and not knowing the reason, says he will leave and in wandering find death. Ilia says that she will accompany him in life and death. Idomeneo inveighs against Neptune's cruelty. And Electra, promised to Idamante and thwarted by Ilia, seeks revenge. The structure is clear from the text repetition and from the key structure. Once again a binary structure is chosen, in which the second half recomposes the material to such a degree that it almost appears to be new. This recomposition enables Mozart to do two things: first to make the four voices reach a climax of chromatic and contrapuntal movement of extremely strong impact; and second, to have Idamante close the quartet as he opened it, with Mozart's elemental setting of musical grief. The quartet, its stasis underlined by the end and the beginning being one and the same, is nevertheless one of the strongest dramatic touches in the whole opera, and it is no wonder that the Munich court thought the third act of *Idomeneo, rè di Creta* even better than the first.

RELIGIOUS MUSIC

Mozart's years in the service of Archbishop Colloredo resulted in the composition of more music for the church than at any other time in his life. Six *missae longae,* five *missae breves,* plus about a dozen other religious works, many of which are long, multi-movement compositions, make up the sum of this eight-year period. However, the strictures that the archbishop imposed on music for the divine service were surprising. In a letter to Padre Martini of 1776, Mozart describes these limitations as follows:

> Our church music is very different from that of Italy, since a mass with the whole Kyrie, the Gloria, the Credo, the Epistle sonata, the Offertory or Motet, the Sanctus and the Agnus Dei must not last longer than three quarters of an hour. This applies even to the most solemn Mass said by the Archbishop himself. . . . At the same time the Mass must have all the instruments—trumpets, drums and so forth. (*Letters,* 4 Sept. 1776)

The expansion of musical ideas, so dear to the composer's heart, has to be abandoned, and yet brilliance of effect must be retained.

The music itself is full of internal contradictions, undoubtedly brought about by the Mozart family's animosity toward the archbishop, and Wolfgang's growing ambivalence toward the Church's dogma combined with his constant need for support and assistance from the Almighty in his endless search for a suitable post. He was like the rational skeptic who nonetheless crosses his fingers for luck. As a result, much of his music for the church service appears to juxtapose the serious and the deeply felt with the flippant and the superficial. He quite often allows the effect of a work to be marred in one way or another, almost as though he cannot resist the impulse to mock his employer, even though it may mean spoiling his own creation. Of course, Leopold's comments in letters about the archbishop (and how many more savage comments must there have been in conversation) did not help his son make the best of things, but merely served to exacerbate the situation.

Perversely, the archbishop's requirements caused Mozart to reduce his use of counterpoint; to avoid basing vocal arias on liturgical phrases or words; to exploit those formal devices usually associated with instrumental music; and to expand on the use of "modern" melody in a religious context where it would seem hardly to belong.

The Mass in C, K.317, will serve to demonstrate what was both good and banal in Mozart's church music during the 1770s. Usually called the *Coronation* Mass, this work was written to commemorate the crowning of a miraculous statue of the Virgin in the Church of Maria Plan. The orchestration, typical of the Salzburg Mass, consists of strings with no separate viola part (it is assumed that the violas merely doubled the bass line) but on this occasion enriched by oboes, horns, trumpets, trombones, and tympani. The short *Kyrie* has an impressive slow introductory passage that leads to a faster tempo and a "modern," songlike extension of the *Kyrie* prayer, set for solo soprano and tenor. The *Christe eleison* is totally submerged within the melodic structure and is barely heard. A return to the opening material indicates that the "Introduction" was not really an introduction, but rather the first section of an **A B A** form, one in which text and music do not coincide. The *Gloria* appears as an instrumental form and is often described as a sonata structure. The text "Quoniam . . ." recapitulates the music first associated with "Gloria . . . ," and "Amen" appears at that point associated with the second tonal area and the words "Domine Deus." The text from "Qui tollis" through "Miserere nobis . . . Suscipe . . . Qui sedes" forms the "development." Similar devices are heard in the *Credo,* where a remarkable *Adagio* central section begins with the text "Et incarnatus" through to "sepultus est." Here, apart from the completely chordal writing of expressive harmonies, the most striking element is the thirty-second note passagework in the first violins, which bears a strong resemblance to the figures accompanying "Et incarnatus" in J. S. Bach's Mass in B minor. The recapitulatory effects of this movement set "Et resurrexit" at the point of return, but most remarkable is the contrapuntal picture-painting of "descendit de coelis" in the first part, which becomes the neutral but conclusive "Amen" of the second part.

Once the *Sanctus* and the jubilation of the *Osanna* are through, a childlike *Benedictus* follows, perhaps exemplifying the saying of Christ that the kingdom of Heaven shall be barred except to those who become as children.

The triple invocation of the *Agnus Dei* is set in modern fashion, with a melody whose opening phrase Mozart was later to use to beatify the suffering of the Countess in *Figaro.* At the last appearance of the tune the text changes to "Dona nobis pacem" and Mozart reverts to the solo material of the opening *Kyrie*—an effect which might have been perfectly fitting musically had it not been followed by a coda, *Allegro con spirito,* in which the choir takes this same songlike material and turns it into a ludicrous parody of itself by increasing its speed. It is quite traditional for the *Dona nobis* section of the Mass to leave the congregation feeling at peace in a prayer already granted, and in most instances Mozart accomplishes this by adopting a different meter from that of the *Agnus* (often a 3 / 8) and a faster tempo. But here he sets the dismissive text to the supplicatory music of the *Kyrie.*

Among the compositions for the Mass, the short instrumental interludes between the *Gloria* and the *Credo,* which Mozart refers to as *Epistle* sonatas, should here be mentioned. In these seventeen short sonata movements set mostly for two violins and *continuo* (although a few are for large orchestra and use the organ as a solo instrument), the composer strikes precisely the right tone for the occasion. If beauty combined with brevity was the archbishop's wish for the Mass, his orders could not have been better fulfilled.

Apart from entire Masses, Mozart completed a significant number of Psalm settings, and it is perhaps in these that his finest efforts may be found. The full range of his abilities as a church musician and a master of both the old and the new styles can be discerned in the two sets of Vesper Psalms, K.321 and K.339.

The *Laudate Dominum* (Psalm 117) from the Solemn Vespers *de Confessore,* K.339, composed in Salzburg in 1780 (*ACM* 41), requires little explanation. The orchestra is small, consisting of two violins, cello, basso, and organ. The three trombones usually present are omitted and a solitary bassoon may be added, *ad libitum.* Like a song, this Psalm has a constant accompaniment, with basses throughout sounding the first and fourth beats of 6 / 8 meter, while second violins arpeggiate the harmony in sixteenth notes. The entire text is set to a continuously unfolding melody, first announced by ten measures of violin ritornello. The ritornello melody is then taken up in the voice and expanded to thirty-one measures. This *bel canto* vocal melody, which has in it nothing of the virtuosic or the secular / operatic, is one of Mozart's miracles, for its shape is not dictated by text or by musical repetition. All that can be said about it is that it cadences on V (m. 24) and subsequently moves back to I. There is no direct repetition of material, but certain measures (mm. 20–22, 27–29, 37–39) and certain cadences show some indirect relationship. The doxology ("Glory be to the Father," etc.) is set for choir, and the "Amen " sets the soloist and choir together in the most expressive molding of the line first seen around m. 20.

Many authorities have described this composition as exceptional but having nothing of the churchly or religious about it. It certainly bears no relationship to anything typically operatic either. Perhaps on this account we ought to see it as among Mozart's sincerest tributes to the power that created and controlled his destiny. Like Anatole France's juggler, who had only his skill and tricks to offer to the Virgin, perhaps Mozart is offering the only thing he has—his unique musical gift, embodied in unparalleled melody.

PART V

The Classical Style at its Apogee: 1780–1800

CHAPTER XVIII

Years of Revolution and Change

SCIENCE AND INDUSTRY

Important scientific advances were made during the last twenty years of the eighteenth century, and although they were not as immediately significant as other factors molding society, their importance for subsequent years cannot be overestimated. From all the countries of western Europe came contributions to the world's central core of knowledge, but perhaps the greatest number of discoveries were made by the Frenchman Antoine Laurent Lavoisier (1743–94), generally regarded as the father of modern chemistry. He was a scientist of many interests, active in the reform and modernization of weights and measures and the creation of the decimal system. He established the basis of the modern theory of elements, named oxygen, and first accurately described the process of oxidation. As a result of his experiments with combustion, he was able to refute the old idea that burning was made possible by the presence of a hypothetical gas, called Phlogiston, and to show that in the process of burning, matter was not lost but changed; he formulated the Law of the Conservation of Matter, which states that matter can neither be created nor destroyed. This optimistic view did not prevent Lavoisier's life from being taken on the guillotine—but then, human life is not matter.

In Britain, the only European nation actively engaged in developing industrial power, innovations were increasing productivity at an astounding rate. In fact, the progress of that industrialization may be measured by the invention of a series of machines to spin and weave raw cotton, essential to a burgeoning textile industry: James Hargreave's spinning jenny (1767) allowed one man to work up to eighty spindles; Edmund Cartwright's power loom (1785) made it possible for the cloth to be woven automatically; Eli Whitney's cotton gin (1793), which separated the cotton fiber from the seed, was an early American contribution to the budding age of the machine. With the entire textile market available, and with no real competition, Britain was able to

The fellow Prentices at their Looms
Representing Industry and Idleness

Hogarth shows two weavers' apprentices in a rare state of cleanliness and order. His satire is all the more telling when we learn their names: Industry and Holiness.

amass unprecedented wealth, nor was its preeminent position challenged until the United States and Germany did so in the closing years of the nineteenth century.

The most obvious social change brought about by the Industrial Revolution was the replacement of individual crafting of goods for sale by the factory system. In the early eighteenth century the proto-capitalist would buy the raw material and place it with suitable artisans, who would work it into finished articles, for which he would pay a predetermined piece rate. The artisan contributed his skill at making, and the "capitalist" contributed his skill at buying and selling; of course, the latter undertook the greater risk. As the machinery that produced goods faster and cheaper was developed, home production became less practical and the worker had to go to the factory where the bulky and costly machinery was kept. The location of the factory was determined by a number of considerations, chiefly the availability of transport to move the finished goods and the availability of fuel for power. Where these conditions were optimal, not only one but many factories were built; hence, existing towns grew into cities and new communities were created. The labor force was mobile, moving where work was available.

Today, we look back with horror upon the conditions created by the factory system: the fifteen-hour workdays, six days a week, the use of child labor in contact with primitive, unguarded machinery, and the unsanitary conditions in which the working people lived before effective sewage-disposal systems were devised. Squalor, misery, disease, and short life expectancy were their lot in those early days of capitalism, and it is hard to accept the fact that people flocked to the new industrial towns because, bad as the conditions were in those new towns, they were better than certain starvation in the rural areas.

Because people were living so much closer together, there was more frequent exchange of political and religious ideas. And because people moved around, accepting work wherever they could find it, the nature of society began to shift away from the hierarchical order based on status (the possession of property) to one based upon contracts between employer and worker; the paternalistic relationship that often existed between landowner and tenant was giving way to an opportunistic relationship in which each side felt less responsibility to the other. The resulting social changes were profound, inevitably affecting the industrializing societies of western European countries during the following century.

Set in a pleasant, wooded valley, the architecture of this cotton mill is severely functional. In this painting, Joseph Wright of Derby makes the mill a source of light and a thing of beauty.

THE FRENCH REVOLUTION

Although France did not experience the effects of industrialization at this time, there were powerful forces within the state working to bring about social change, forces which, by the 1780s, had become irresistible. The inevitable social cataclysm called the French Revolution began in 1789 with the fall of the Bastille and lasted until the end of the Reign of Terror in 1794. The causes of the Revolution were complex, but can be summarized as follows: first, there was an urgent need for a written constitution to assure all citizens of equality before the law; second, the inequities of a system of taxation under which most of the wealthiest members of society—the nobility and the princes of the church—paid no taxes at all demanded redress; and third, an end to a variety of feudal privileges was called for. Furthermore, the country was in desperate financial straits. The French had supported the American War of Independence and the French army and navy had fought with great valor, but the cost of the war had been covered by borrowing; by the early 1780s, the national debt had grown to a monstrous level. Add to this financial situation a population divided by the self-interest of the various large groups within it and an utterly discredited monarchy and you have a country ripe for revolution.

The course of the Revolution was marked by its progress from limited, rational beginnings through a series of crises, after each of which a more radical group took power. Initially there was little thought of doing away with the monarchy, since so many aims had been accomplished relatively peacefully: feudalism was abolished, a declaration of the rights of man was adopted, taxation was equalized, Church lands were seized, and the Constitution of 1791 was drawn up. With the passage of these measures, the middle class and the peasants were largely satisfied, but the city dwellers, in particular the people of Paris, saw little cause for settling down. Thus, the "Third Estate" (peasants and middle class) who had brought about the Revolution and who had largely achieved their goals, now saw themselves opposed by a more radical faction who wanted to push things still further. This factionalism was to continue and become exacerbated. The king, Louis XVI, lost whatever public support he had in 1792 when he was accused of being allied with foreign governments and convicted of treason. His execution, in January of 1793, shook all the thrones of Europe, and many of the countries around France joined forces against her. Thus, with the country threatened by foreign enemies from without and the fear of enemies from within, the Reign of Terror was introduced and defended on the grounds that those who opposed the Revolution had to be destroyed before they could destroy it. The return of more rational government in 1794 was to be a short prelude before the dictatorship of Napoleon, whose career must be accounted a most extraordinary phenomenon, only possible in the aftermath of the Revolution.

A riot in Paris in 1789. The engraving shows the impetus of the mob pressing forward but does not remotely anticipate the destructive power of that mob three years later.

The events in France typify the violent contrasts that coexisted during the last part of the eighteenth century: on the one hand the excesses of the Terror, and on the other the rational achievements that pointed the way to the future. The scientific metric system was instituted and replaced old, idiosyncratic systems of weights and measures; a plan for public education was inaugurated; the French state was separated from the Church (for a while, Christianity was banned and the worship of Reason was instituted, but this attitude later gave way to one of tolerance toward religion); and a new calendar was introduced with a week of ten days—this idea also was of mercifully short duration.

While the Revolution made monarchs and governments tremble, the effect upon the younger intellectuals and artists was exhilarating. The poet William Wordsworth (1770–1850) wrote:

> Bliss was it in that dawn to be alive,
> But to be young was very heaven![1]

The young artist envisaged a new era: the institutionalized *ancien régime* would be swept away and replaced by a new order that would, in the words of William Blake (1757–1827), "build Jerusalem" among the "dark, Satanic mills" of the modern industrial world. These were the artists who called themselves Romantics and saw themselves as fundamentally

1. Wordsworth, *The Prelude,* Bk. xi, lines 108–109.

different from their forefathers in both ideals and actions. They therefore considered revolution as the most readily available solution to all social problems. As Wordsworth saw it, the last years of the eighteenth century were a time for optimism and for striding into the future, confident that one's greatest expectations for society and humanity might not be unreasonable.

CHANGING PHILOSOPHIES

During the last two decades of the eighteenth century, we see the beginnings of a schism between the practice of art and its aesthetics, which, perhaps more than any other single factor, lies at the heart of the inevitable alienation of the artist from society. During the whole of the eighteenth century, the single criterion of artistic acceptability was the notion that art must give pleasure: in theory, *mimesis* conforms to this principle in that the closer the work of art is to the object it is imitating, the greater the pleasure involved in the experience of it. In practice, "good taste" was the seal of approval given to that art which pleased more than that art from which "taste" was absent. The distinction between the beautiful and the sublime can also be seen in the light of this general principle, since the beautiful is pleasurable while the sublime is ecstatically, painfully pleasurable. That which gives no pleasure is not art!

While earlier philosophers had tended to make personal experience the basis of general, even universal statements, Immanuel Kant (1724–1804) attempted to establish principles of art and beauty completely independent of our experience of them. In defining "taste" he contrasted interested pleasure (that which arises in us from the appeal of the work, the object it represents, etc.) with disinterested pleasure (that which arises from the contemplation of the work itself, its shape, structure, etc., with no admixture of personal response). He said that "everyone must admit that any judgement on beauty remotely tinged with interest is very partisan and no genuine judgement of taste."[2] The work of art must not have a purpose outside itself, or the appreciation of it ceases to be disinterested. The disparity between Kant's views and those of earlier philosophers can perhaps best be measured in the following statement:

> Beauty has nothing to do with being moved, a sensation, that is, in which pleasure is aroused only by a momentary damming of vital force followed by a more powerful surge. But the judgement of sublimity (with which the sense of being moved is connected) requires a different yardstick from that required by the judgement of taste. A pure judgement of taste is thus

2. Immanuel Kant, *The Critique of Judgement.* Cited in le Huray and Day, *op. cit.*, p. 216.

> conditioned neither by charm nor emotion. No sensation is, in short, the substance of aesthetic judgement. [3]

Kant argued that the beautiful in music (that is to say, its universal quality, as opposed to the pleasurable in music, or that quality which can be defined as its appeal to an individual) is the result of the contemplation of its form, and that the mathematical / acoustical basis of music affords the means whereby the individual perceives that form.

He defined genius as "the inborn human aptitude through which nature provides art with rules."[4] He further maintained that every art presupposes rules if it is to be called artistic, yet no concept can be formed of how the artwork is created; thus, the fine art itself cannot formulate rules governing its product, and hence, fine art must be produced by a genius. Thus, genius must be defined as the aptitude to create something for which no rule can be postulated, and therefore, its prime quality must be originality. However, since there is such a thing as original nonsense, what a genius produces must be exemplary, although not the product of imitation. The genius, he said,

> does not himself know how the ideas for it came to him, nor does it lie within his power to calculate them methodically or, should he so wish, to communicate them to others by means of principles that would enable others to create works of equal quality.[5]

Kant's ideas on aesthetics were generally rejected by the young artists of the time, who were experiencing the first ardors of Romantic passion. The most influential spokesman for the opposing viewpoint was Johann Gottfried Herder (1744–1803), one of Kant's pupils. More than any other, Herder's influence affected the interest shown by German artists and intellectuals in the art of folk poetry, in Shakespeare, and even in music.

Herder tried to refute Kant's idea of the subjectivity of emotion, and the centrality of disinterestedness, i.e., emotional uninvolvement, in judging either poetry or music. He believed in the universality of the experience of sound; thus, he says that "every person is none the less endowed with a basic pattern of varying emotional and tonal responses."[6] And he rejected the Kantian idea that the tonal and aesthetic basis of music is to be found in the mathematical properties of acoustics. He said:

> If it were true that music is nothing more than a mathematical sleight of hand in which musical pleasure derives from numerical relationships and intervallic calculations—an idea that I find quite meaningless—I should be

3. *Ibid.*, p. 220.
4. *Ibid.*, p. 227.
5. *Ibid.*, p. 338.
6. Johann Gottfried Herder, *Kalligone*. Cited in le Huray and Day, *op. cit.*, p. 254.

> frightened off it for ever. Whoever counts or calculates when he experiences music's deepest and life-giving joys?[7]

Herder spoke of the slow emancipation of music from mime and word and its establishment as a completely independent art. He asked what it was that freed music from external control, answering the question in these terms: "It was religious awe. Religious awe raises the individual above words and gestures so that nothing remains to express the emotions but sounds."[8]

Here, clearly, is much of the theoretical substance behind musical Romanticism, and other writers during the last years of the eighteenth century reflected similar attitudes. No one better exemplified the passive surrender to music, the avid grasping at the emotional experience that was such a strong part of the Romantic movement, than Wilhelm Heinrich Wackenroder (1773–98). For him,

> Music is the breath of the spiritual in its highest form, its finest manifestation, the invisible stream as it were from which the soul draws sustenance for its deepest dreams. Music engulfs the human spirit. It means both everything and nothing. It is a finer and perhaps subtler medium than language. The spirit can no longer use it as a vehicle, as a means to an end, for it is substance itself and this is why it lives and moves in its own enchanted realm.[9]

Through such panegyrics, instrumental music is seen to have come of age, and need no longer be attached to words or ideas. It is not surprising that music's capacity for dealing with musical ideas should be rationalized into something comparable to the power of language to manipulate concepts. Friedrich von Schlegel (1772–1829), writing about the philosophical nature of music, said:

> Many people tend to find it curious and absurd that musicians should talk about the "ideas" in their compositions; and yet it may frequently occur that one is apparently more conscious of their thoughts "in" their music than of their thoughts "about" it . . . The person who goes more deeply into the question will discern that a certain element of philosophical speculation is not at all foreign to the spirit of pure instrumental music. Must not purely instrumental music create its own text? And is not its theme developed, confirmed, varied and contrasted, just as is the object of a sequence of philosophical speculations?[10]

This perception of Schlegel's points squarely at the most important achievement in musical thought during the last twenty years of the

7. *Ibid.*, p. 256.
8. *Ibid.*, p. 257.
9. Wilhelm Heinrich Wackenroder, *Phantasien über die Kinst.* Cited in le Huray and Day, *op. cit.*, p. 250.
10. Friedrich von Schlegel, *Das Athenäum.* Cited in le Huray and Day., *op. cit.*, p. 247.

eighteenth century. For through the manipulation of tonality, melody, rhythm, and harmony, the musician had succeeded in creating a pseudo-language, a means to develop, confirm, vary, and contrast. And if we remember the famous remark of Fontenelle of many years earlier, "Sonate, que me veux-tu?" (Sonata, what do you want from me?) we shall see that, by the end of the century, a cogent reply to the question had been formulated. The answer is—understanding.

By the end of the century there were two opposing camps: on the one side the Kantian philosophy of Beauty required "disinterested" judgment, and on the other side "emotion" and "expression" needed a response conditioned in some way. The opposition between head and heart, with which the artist had dealt throughout the century in his compositions, had now become the subject of abstract philosophical inquiry, and differences in point of view became visible where earlier there seemed to be none.[11] These ideas affected much nineteenth-century thinking, and the Wagner-Brahms battles of the later 1800s are inconceivable without them. Eduard Hanslick's influential writings are fundamentally Kantian, and such ideas flow through to the twentieth century in a composer like Stravinsky. Most of the creative poets and composers of the earlier nineteenth century, and the mass of the public, whose respective aim is to move and to be moved, stand at the opposite pole. As the century advances, however, the relationship changes, and the rift between the artist and the public, about which so much has been written, becomes more apparent. The situation at the beginning of the twentieth century, therefore, may be seen as a direct result of the last twenty years of the eighteenth century.

11. It is possible to view this difference in aesthetic as simply a sophisticated extension of the eternal oscillation between intellect and feeling. The earlier *Querelle des Bouffons* and the fight over the merits of French and Italian music may be seen as another aspect of it.

CHAPTER XIX

The Changing Status of the Musician

CONCERT SOCIETIES

The growth in the popularity of concerts in the last decades of the century continued unabated. Moreover, the organization and subsequent proliferation of concert series greatly affected musicians' lives, not only by making it easier for the free-lance player to make a living by joining an orchestra, and by providing more opportunities for solo performers, but also through the commissioning of new works to keep the series supplied with novelties.

PARIS In Paris, the old-established *Concert Spirituel,* which operated under license of the *Académie royale de musique,* suffered a decline in popularity. It lost its location in the Salle des Cent Suisses of the Tuileries palace where its concerts had been held since 1725, when the royal

The Palace of the Tuileries and its gardens. A focus of Parisian and court life since it was built in the 16th century, the palace was burnt to the ground in 1871. (A contemporary engraving by Martin Engelbrecht)

family began to use the palace as a residence in 1784. They moved to a larger hall in the palace, but many thought the sound was not as good as in the old room. Haydn's *Farewell* Symphony, No. 45, described in the records as "la symphonie où l'on s'en va" (the symphony in which they go away), was the final work performed before the move. The concert series ended in 1790, but it is interesting to note that in its last season each program contained at least one Haydn symphony.

In December 1780 a rumor began to circulate that the *Concert des Amateurs* was running into financial difficulties and in January of the following year, the society's dissolution was announced. A new organization took its place, the *Concert de la Loge Olympique,* whose greatest fame lies in its having commissioned Haydn to write the six *Paris* symphonies in 1784. The name was taken because the series was held initially in quarters of the *Palais royal* used by the Freemasons, whose lodge bore that name. In 1786 the series moved to the room in the Tuileries formerly used by the *Concert Spirituel,* now once more available. Since members of the royal family appeared at whim at the concerts, both audience and orchestra got into the habit of wearing dress clothes, making the performances as attractive to the eye as they were gratifying to the ear. The prosperity of this series enabled their organizers to engage the best soloists and to commission compositions.

As the Parisian mob took over the revolution anything that was associated with aristocratic patronage.was curtailed. Only when order was restored, under the Directorate, did concert life regain something of its old vigor. Meanwhile, the composer became involved in the propaganda machine of the revolutionary state. He was expected to organize massed choirs and to compose songs and hymns that taught the people all the correct revolutionary attitudes, and for a while many composers, including Jean-François Le Sueur (1760–1837), Luigi Cherubini (1760–1842), Charles-Simon Catel (1773–1830), Adrien Boieldieu (1775–1834), and Etienne-Nicolas Méhul (1763–1817), threw themselves into this activity. Perhaps the most important composer to lend his services to the Revolution was François-Joseph Gossec. He wrote more, performed more, was visibly in the vanguard more than any of the others, and he was clearly the most naive; when the Bourbons were restored to the throne of France in 1814, they never forgave Gossec for his cooperation with the regime during the Republic.

The status of the musician was particularly enhanced by the *Concert des Amateurs,* in which many aristocratic melomanes sat side by side with professionals to make music. When Gossec dedicated his Requiem (1760) to the administrators of that society upon its publication in 1780, he wrote that they had done more than most to elevate the status of the arts in France, for "élever l'âme des artistes, c'est travailler à l'agrandissement des arts" (to elevate the soul of the artist is to work for the betterment of the arts). It was Gossec who worked tirelessly for the formation of the *Ecole royale de chant* which was established in January of 1784. Thus, when the *Conservatoire national de musique* was created in 1795 it depended for much of its curriculum on innovations Gossec had already put in place. The *Conservatoire* was the first really modern institution established without charitable motives or church affiliations. Its curriculum, its student body (boys and girls from all *départements* of the country), and its teachers enhanced the reputation of the musical art and hence the dignity of the professional musician. In 1816 Gossec was forbidden to teach there, and spent the last eleven years of his allotted ninety-five shunned by society and largely forgotten.

LONDON In London the Bach-Abel concerts were replaced in 1783 by the series of Professional Concerts, founded by a group of musicians that included Muzio Clementi, Johann Cramer (1771–1858), and Johann Salomon (1745–1815), without the assistance of aristocratic patronage. This series was successful for ten years, introducing new works and presenting the best soloists to an eager public.

Haydn had received several invitations to visit England from the Professional Concerts, but he had always refused. Salomon happened to be in Germany when Prince Nikolaus died and Haydn became a free man. The contract that resulted in Haydn's two visits to London—in 1791–92 and 1794–95—was signed between them in 1790. While Salomon was setting all this up, the organizers of the Professional Concerts tried to create a profitable rivalry by engaging Haydn's pupil Ignace Joseph Pleyel (1757–1831) as their star attraction. But Haydn's enormous success led to the demise of the Professional Concerts in 1793, despite Pleyel's popularity. After Haydn's final departure for Vienna in 1795, the Salomon Concerts also ceased to exist. Thus, despite the great variety of concert activity in London, only one major series reached across from the eighteenth to the nineteenth century: The Concert of Antient *[sic]* Music, founded and organized by members of the aristocracy in 1776. It will be recalled that they operated under a blanket regulation that no music less than twenty years old was to be performed, and the series lasted until the 1840s. By that time, the nucleus of modern concert repertoire based on the work of Haydn, Mozart, and Beethoven had been formed, and there was no further need to urge concertgoers and music lovers to preserve the past, for the past increasingly was dominating the present.

In 1784, then thought to be the centennial of Handel's birth, London musical life caught fire as great celebrations were planned for a Handel Festival. A variety of works, but chiefly oratorios, were to be presented in Westminster Abbey and other halls. The performances were remarkable for the large forces used, and critics commented about the "sublime" effect of the music in such surroundings. The celebration was immensely successful and served to place the oratorio, and vocal music in general, at the heart of the tradition of public music in England. The

The arrangement of choirs and audience in Westminster Abbey for the Handel Commemoration of 1784 can be clearly seen in this contemporary engraving.

effect was felt across the Continent as well, and the Handel Festival of 1784 must be seen as one of the earliest occasions to focus attention on the past, and set standards by which the present can be judged.

BERLIN The founding of the *Singakademie* in Berlin in 1791 was another significant event, since that institution rapidly developed into a center of the Bach cult. Here Bach's cantatas were collected, treasured, and performed as nowhere else in the world.

LEIPZIG In Leipzig, on the other hand, where eighteenth-century concert activity had never been dependent upon aristocratic funding, but grew out of the widespread love of music among the bourgeoisie and the university population, the construction of a substantial concert hall brought about a concert series that has survived from that time to the present. The new Gewandhaus (Cloth Hall, so named because it was the meeting place of the Guild of Clothiers) erected in 1781, not only gave its name to the orchestra that played there every Thursday during the season (conducted by J. A. Hiller) but also was rented to distinguished visitors (Mozart gave a concert here in 1789). The Gewandhaus name has become almost synonymous with music in Leipzig, and even when the location of the concerts was moved, the name was preserved. Above the stage in the old Cloth Hall was the

A watercolor painting by Felix Mendelssohn of the old Gewandhaus in Leipzig. (Courtesy of the Gertrude Clarke Whittall Collection, Music Division, The Library of Congress)

inscription *res severa verum gaudium*—"Real Joy Is a Serious Thing." These words reveal a great deal about the bourgeois attitude to music and to the arts in the late eighteenth century, not only in Leipzig but everywhere.

VIENNA The situation in Vienna remained as it had been. Public concerts in halls and theaters, such as the Burgtheater, or those in the Mehlgrube or the Augarten, were organized by the artist for his own benefit. Mozart's subscription concerts, for which he composed so many of his piano concertos, were held in those halls. The earliest concerts that may be described as a series were those of the *Tonkünstlersocietät* (Society of Musicians) which took place each year after 1772 at Christmas and Lent, to raise funds for this benevolent institution for musicians.

MUSIC PUBLISHING: THE BEGINNING OF AN INDUSTRY

But although concert life in Vienna did not change very much, the practice of making music among a rapidly growing European population resulted in an explosion of music engraving and printing there, intense enough to compensate for earlier inactivity. The establishment of Artaria and Co. has been noted (see p. 127), and their success bred many rivals. First among these is the publishing house of Christoph

Toricella, who, like Artaria, was a dealer in art and copper engravings, and not a native of Vienna. In 1781 Toricella issued his first publication, which made use of the engraving talent of an expatriate Parisian publisher, Huberty. In succeeding years he published works by Haydn, Mozart, Christian Bach, and others. In the end, however, he could not compete with Artaria and in 1786 he went under, most of his plates having been bought by his rival.

During this period, two composers of considerable reputation, Leopold Kozeluch (1747–1818) and Franz Anton Hoffmeister (1754–1812), both originally trained in the law, began publishing their own work in order to increase their earnings. Kozeluch's venture, while successful, was to be of secondary importance, since he quickly achieved great renown as a pianist and composer, but Hoffmeister was both more prolific as a composer and had much more influence as a publisher. In 1783 he was simply printing his own works, but by 1785 he was running a full-fledged business from his home. A friend of Mozart's, Hoffmeister is perhaps best remembered for having commissioned the piano quartets, but he also published first editions of Beethoven and Haydn, as well as many other reputable composers. In 1800 he set up a business relationship with Ambrosius Kühnel (1770–1813) in Leipzig, and although Hoffmeister continued to publish in Vienna until 1806, more and more of the business was transacted in Leipzig. The firm of Hoffmeister und Kühnel lasted until 1806, when Hoffmeister withdrew. Upon Kühnel's death in 1813, it was bought by C. F. Peters (1779–1827), and eventually became one of the most important publishing houses of the nineteenth century.

Publishing was not confined to the largest centers. The historic company of Schott was founded at Mainz, probably in the year 1780, and its catalogue grew to enormous proportions in the nineteenth century. Nicolaus Simrock, old friend of the Beethoven family, founded the house of Simrock at Bonn in 1793. Like Schott, it came to be of the greatest importance in the second half of the nineteenth century as Brahms's favorite publisher.

The steady development of the publishing industry in centers like Leipzig, Vienna, Mainz, and Bonn cut into the markets traditionally held by the old publishers of London, Paris, and Amsterdam. This fact, together with the increased popularity of Viennese music, led to the gradual decline of publishing in these older centers. Despite important activity elsewhere, Germany and Austria dominated the field increasingly during the nineteenth century.

To conclude this brief survey of music publishing as the eighteenth century drew to a close, mention must be made of Alois Senefelder (1771–1834), who developed the process of lithography, a method of etching onto a stone surface, rather than onto a metal plate. The potential importance of this process was recognized soon after its discovery, and in 1797 the first major compositions to be printed by the process—some keyboard sonatas of Haydn—were issued. Shortly afterward, Senefelder discovered true lithography, a method of printing based upon the principle that water repels grease, while grease absorbs grease. This process, called "chemical printing," was much less expensive than printing from engraved plates, but it must also be said that many of its early products were not as clean as those produced by more traditional methods.

THE VIRTUOSO

The period 1780–1800 witnessed the gradual abandonment of the "amateur" ideal of instrumental playing, and its replacement with the ideal of the "virtuoso." The instrumental soloist began to assume an importance comparable to that of the star singer, and to be rewarded accordingly. Musicians have always traveled, but in this period there was a great deal more touring, not in search of a patron, as heretofore, but to take advantage of opportunities as they might present themselves throughout Europe.

Typical of such an enterprising life is that of Muzio Clementi, who, having perfected an uncommon keyboard technique, embarked on his first Continental tour in 1780, leaving London for Paris, where he stayed for a little over a year. Report has it that he gained the favor of Marie-Antoinette, who recommended that he go to Vienna, where her brother, the Emperor Joseph II, would be interested in receiving him. It would seem that his original plan had been to go to Berlin, but he took the queen's advice and by December of 1781 was in Vienna, where Joseph II arranged the famous competition in pianism between Clementi and Mozart. In May 1782 he left Vienna, and did not arrive back in London until over a year had passed. Typical of the modern virtuoso, Clementi was, from the age of twenty-one and for the remainder of his life, on his own, a completely free man.

Among the virtuosos of the time it is remarkable that a proportionately larger number than before or since were young women. Women keyboard players abounded in London and in Paris, and as we recall, two of Mozart's greatest works were written for women: the E♭ Piano Concerto, K.271, for Mlle. Jeunehomme, and his Sonata for Violin and Piano in B♭, K.454, for the violinist Regina Strinasacchi (1761–1839).

For many musicians, life in the last decades of the eighteenth century and the early years of the nineteenth became increasingly difficult. We know how young Mozart resented the great difference in treatment which he received from various members of the aristocracy, treated as an equal by some and as a servant by others. There were two contradictory social trends destined to intensify over the next fifty years: egalitarianism, fostered by the Revolution and all the ideals that had led up to it; and class distinction, brought about by old aristocracy defending itself against new, industrial wealth, and by new industrial wealth asserting its superiority over the rest of society. The virtuoso moved among all kinds of people, the equal to his hosts at times, and at other times segregated from polite society by a physical barrier. Later, in the nineteenth century, Spohr would insist on the respect accorded by silence during his playing, and Liszt would stride over the silken rope meant to preserve and emphasize class differences. In the late eighteenth century, many composers and performers sought a more secure and profitable position in society by going into music publishing or instrument manufacture, replacing the plaudits of the multitudes with the comforts of respectability.

THE MUSICIAN AS AUTHOR

The histories of Burney and Hawkins in English prompted Johann Nikolaus Forkel (1749–1818) to write his *Allgemeine Geschichte der Musik* (General History of Music), of which the first volume appeared in 1788 and the second in 1801. At the same time, his *Allgemeine Literatur der Musik* (General Writings on Music; 1792) breaks new ground in providing a comprehensive bibliographical survey of the literature about music. Important treatises on the art and craft of composition were produced by Beethoven's counterpoint teacher, Johann Albrechtsberger, whose *Gründliche Anweisung der Composition* (Basic Instruction in Composition) appeared in 1790, and Heinrich Christoph Koch (1749–1816) whose *Versuch einer Anleitung zur Composition* (A Guide to Composition) was brought out between 1782 and 1793. The *Clavierschule* (1789) of Daniel Gottlob Türk (1750–1813) is the last major work in the lineage of Emanuel Bach's *Essay* and is worthy of comparison with it. Türk not only gives instruction on fingering, ornamentation, etc., but also attempts to inculcate a sense of style in the student; hence the *Clavierschule* forms an invaluable testimony to the performance practice of the 1780s.

The earlier eighteenth century had witnessed the development of a critical literature about music, as well as a network of publications designed to report on performances and carry discussions of intellectual interest in this or that city. The Leipzig publishing house of Breitkopf, which had become Breitkopf und Härtel in 1796 and had a long record of technical and practical innovation, was determined to enter the field of periodical publishing. In 1798 the first issue of the *Allgemeine Musikalische Zeitung* (General Musical Newspaper) appeared. The function of this newspaper was to print essays on various composers, provide criticism of new compositions, and announce recent publications. Although Johann Friedrich Rochlitz (1769–1842), who was editor of the journal from 1798 to 1818, was fundamentally conservative, the *A.M.Z.* achieved a dominant position among music periodicals of the day, and it remains for us the most informative about critical attitudes. It was published until 1848.

The success of such an enterprise hints at the growing number of people who were prepared not only to play music and to listen to it but also to read about it and discuss it. The critical viewpoint, particularly that of the editor, established Bach, Handel, Mozart, and Haydn as the standards by which more modern composers should be judged. The earlier yardstick of "good taste" is, in Rochlitz's writing, replaced by the idea of "correctness." The *A.M.Z.* and its first editor, like the Handel Festival of 1784 in London, became a powerful force at the turn of the century, compelling music lovers to look back toward earlier models and inculcating the idea of an exemplary "Classical" period of composition.

CHAPTER XX

Solo and Chamber Music

It has long been acknowledged that the music written during the last twenty years of the eighteenth century included some of the greatest achievements of Western civilization, in any art at any time. These achievements are attributable to the two giants, Haydn and Mozart. Their most important works during this period included symphonies, concertos, and operas, as well as solo and chamber music. During the last decade of the century they were joined by Beethoven, considered by nineteenth-century music lovers as the truly supreme genius of the age. Haydn and Mozart were looked upon with affectionate condescension, and their music was valued only insofar as it provided a foundation for Beethoven's surpassing accomplishments.

In our day we have carried a similar evaluative process several steps further, and deem it necessary to examine the music of those numerous *Kleinmeister,* who were industriously composing in the late eighteenth century. Their work enables us to perceive that while the music of Haydn and Mozart remains supreme in fertility of invention, formal imagination, and intuitive perception—in other words, the highest union of discipline and fantasy, of craft and art—it is not and cannot be the whole story.

THE DECLINE OF THE *CONTINUO*

During this period, the almost two-hundred-year-old tradition of *basso continuo* effectively ceased to influence the texture of musical composition, although the technique was still taught as part of practical musicianship and harmony. Some string composers, such as Kreutzer and Giovanni Battista Viotti (1755–1824), wrote sonatas for violin and *continuo* until the very last years of the century, but these are exceptions and can be considered works for solo violin with cello or double bass accompaniment. Even the the way composers wrote for the cello was changing, the harmonic conditioning of the bass line becoming less obvious as the melodic function became stronger, resulting in a much closer relationship between the bass line and the total musical texture. It is as if the principles of Liberty, Equality, and Fraternity, so much in the air at the time, were emancipating the bass from its role of service to the upper instruments.

FROM THE HARPSICHORD TO THE FORTEPIANO

The closer we draw to the time when the "Romantic" artist begins to emerge, the further away we get from the eighteenth-century composer's ideal of catering to the tastes and the abilities of the amateur as well as the connoisseur. The Romantic sees himself set apart from the rest of society, and virtuosic mastery of an instrument is a means of demonstrating that apartness. The keyboard sonata of this period therefore demands a more professional level of technique—indeed, a pronounced virtuosity—which was only occasionally glimpsed in the preceding period.

EMANUEL BACH The last representative of an earlier aesthetic who was still active at the beginning of this period is Emanuel Bach, whose work and style have been discussed in several chapters of this book. Like his father, who had been charged with an inability to change with the times but who nevertheless demonstrated a thorough awareness of the music of his stylish young contemporaries, so, in the last years of a long and productive life, Emanuel revealed new facets of his innovative imagination, looking quizzically around him at the music that is so different from his.

For there is little doubt that Emanuel's old age, while secure in material possessions and honorifics, must have been somewhat embittered by the realization that his music was no longer in the mainstream, and that none of his pupils was interested in carrying on his artistic ideals. He must also have seen the way the wind was blowing when, after having a subscription list of 519 for the first volume (1779) of his *Sonaten für Kenner und Liebhaber,* the list dwindled with each of the succeeding five volumes until only 288 expressed any interest in the last one (1787).

It is well known that Emanuel, like so many of his contemporaries, composed far more than he ever sent for publication, and it has previously been noted that the sonatas comprising the first volume *Für Kenner und Liebhaber* were on average about eleven years old by the time they reached the public. In the five succeeding volumes, for whatever reason, Emanuel mixes sonatas with rondos and fantasias, so that in each of the last three volumes there are only two sonatas. A certain tendency can be seen, not only to decrease the number of sonatas for publication but also to make them more and more up-to-date in some ways—probably many of the late ones were composed especially for the publication—and to make them shorter. Just at the time when the sonatas of other composers were expanding, in some cases to heroic lengths and sometimes to long-windedness, Emanuel's sonata becomes smaller and more succinct. Where other composers created sectionalized works in which harmonic movement is often slow, and melodies often lyric in their expression and self-containedness, Emanuel created first movements in which nothing seems stable and in which motion is so flexible and rapid as sometimes to defy the listener's full comprehension. A thread of influence may be postulated here between the ideals and procedures of Emanuel Bach and the late Beethoven of the Bagatelles, the Sonata Op. 109, and the String Quartet Op.135.

With both repeats, the first movement of the Sonata in D, H.286, from the 1787 set (*ACM* 42), composed in 1785, requires perhaps two minutes of playing time. It is a quiet, wispy piece of music that sounds like a fantasy since it seems to have so little stability. Closer scrutiny reveals, however, that all components of first-movement sonata form are not only present, but are constructed with astonishing strictness. The exposition, middle section, and recapitulation are each 24 measures in length. The materials in the exposition and recapitulation correspond perfectly, *mutatis mutandis:* the first 8 mm. of each (which can be split into 4 + 4) end with a half close; four measures of transitional material look into E minor and D major; and twelve measures in the key of A (V) can be divided into 2–bar groupings according to texture. In the same way the development is strictly bound to the textural process of the exposition: its first 16 bars correspond exactly to mm. 9–24 of the exposition, as it intensifies metrical and harmonic irregularities. It touches on a number of tonalities: G, A, B minor, F♯, etc. The rate of harmonic change is immensely variable; thus five measures which repeatedly emphasize the tonality of G are followed by three measures of rapid secondary dominants, which lead, in m. 33, to a sequence of slower and stable harmonic progression, taking eight measures to establish B minor in m. 40. From this position the composer easily moves back to the tonic.

The question arises how a sonata movement whose shape is so regular can appear to be so fantastic. The answer lies only partly in dynamics and tonal fluidity, but largely in rhythm and meter, where the *irregularities* go beyond anything being written in 1785, even by Mozart. From the outset there is an uncertainty whether the accent in the 3 / 8 meter is to be perceived in the usual place, 1–3, 1–3, or differently: 1 2 –, 1 2 –. The first two bars expose this dilemma with their 1–3, 1 2 –. But the question of meter becomes still more vexing when these problems arise in the secondary tonal area, at m. 13. From this point, Emanuel uses the power of the repetition of musical figures to make a mockery of the barlines. Indeed, the music is completely free in meter and cannot be definitively barred except in the arbitrary way Bach has done. In Emanuel's score, the notes fight against their imprisoning barlines, and the result is an *Affekt* in which notes seem to tumble over one another in jostling haste.

Example XX–1: C. P. E. BACH, Sonata in D, H.286. Inverse relationships between exposition and mid-section of first movement

A comparison of mm. 13–22, just discussed, with mm. 29–38 emphasizes the strict nature of Emanuel's compositional process, since the metrical irregularities from the exposition are mirrored completely in the development (as they are also in the recapitulation mm. 61–72) but with one intensification: the metrical groupings of 4 / 16 and 2 / 16 in m. 14 become 3 / 16 and 3 / 16 in m. 30. N.B. the inverse relationship of melodic direction in the first five measures of each example.

Another aspect of Emanuel's late sonata style is perhaps surprising in view of his ideal of smaller proportions. As early as 1750, he had published a set of sonatas with varied repeats. These works, because of their written-out and ornamented repeats, were much too long, both for the player and for the publisher, and while Emanuel did not immediately abandon this idea he seems to have written only a few more works in this full-blown style. Starting around 1780, he returned to this method of structuring a movement in several works. Moreover, he experimented further with the idea, and tried truncating the varied repeats in order to make the sonata still more epigrammatic. One of his last sonatas, composed in Hamburg in 1786, perhaps after his final volume was in press, was written in this way. It is a fine example of the way in which the strictest parallelism of sections can produce a completely different effect when ornamented (see *ACM* 43).

There is a kind of perverse obstinacy in Emanuel Bach, which his father and older brother also had in large measure and which caused all of them great trouble. In Emanuel this trait shows itself in his determination to go his own compositional way. When everyone else is writing sonatas that are bigger, he writes miniatures; when other composers contrast melody and virtuoso passagework, he makes his textures more homogeneous; when other composers look upon the rondo as a light, short, loose composition suitable for ending larger works, he writes rondos that are bigger than many of his entire sonatas; and finally, when the rondo seems the most appropriate form for the amateur, he makes it demanding to play and the most complete example of the composer's craft.

The Rondo in G, H.271 (1780) printed in the third set (see *ACM* 44), is one of the shortest rondos that Emanuel wrote and yet it demonstrates most of the devices that he uses. The first eight measures constitute the rondo theme, the "Classical" construction of which is to be noted. Nothing could be more regular and balanced, and in that quality it is unlike any of the sonatas we have met. The only incongruous note is found in mm. 7 and 8 where the move to the cadence suddenly changes to *forte,* reinforced by a chain of trills. The reprise of the theme (mm. 9–16) is ornamented with a jump in register every two bars: thus the first two bars are lowered an octave and the second two bars are raised an octave, and so on. The player might begin to conceive of this as a humorous procedure were it not for the balanced progress of the melody, which maintains a straight face, as it were, during its stately dance. Mm. 17 and 18, the beginning of the episode, turn what was a complex melodic line into a straight downward line, which has a slightly more expressive effect than the opening. This effect is echoed in mm. 25–26 at a *forte* level, followed by a measure in striking opposition to what has immediately preceded it. M. 27 can only be construed as an attempt to change something emphatic (mm. 25–26) into something expressively tentative. The answer in mm. 28 and 29 has undeniable power and surely it is here that the humor of the work and its parodistic effect are apparent. In the musical language of Emanuel Bach it is clear that a sledgehammer is being used to crush a butterfly.

Now we are halfway through the first episode (plus the one odd bar that was interpolated) and Emanuel changes the direction of the melody; as in m. 31, what had fallen begins now to rise. Mm. 38 and 39 carry the process further with all proper decorum, but then, just as the downward motion exploded into its most emphatic gesture in mm. 28 and 29, so now in mm. 40 and 41 the upward motion bursts out in a figuration often used by Emanuel, and by Haydn as well, as an expressive musical counterpart to laughter, and the first episode ends with a fermata that leaves the listener and player wondering what can happen next. The rondo theme, which at the outset was so stately, now is heard as incongruous at its recurrence in m. 42. The next episode (mm. 50–84), while strictly bound to the melodic material of the rondo theme and drawing all its substance from it, modulates constantly and leads to a recurrence of the rondo theme in C♯ major at m. 85, and the last episode gathers together elements of both the first and second episodes. After a final recurrence of the theme, a tiny four-bar extension peters out in a couple of hiccups and the final surprise is given by the last chords.

This rondo shows Emanuel Bach building a composition strictly and taking his material beyond the bounds of what seemed to be the preordained set of the first musical substance. In other rondos he achieves similar ends by using other means. The theme of a Rondo in F (H.266), composed in 1779 and published in 1781, runs as follows:

Example XX–2: C. P. E. BACH, Rondo in F, H.266, theme

Here the progress of downward thirds is an obvious element of the basic material, which Emanuel later seizes upon to turn into:

Example XX–3: C. P. E. BACH, Rondo in F, H.266

Nor does the first motive of the theme escape being turned into a mocking parody of itself:

Example XX–4: C. P. E. BACH, Rondo in F, H.266

Since Emanuel intends his rondos to be fantastic, not surprisingly he incorporates much of the effect of fantasy into them. The theme of the third Rondo (H. 267) from the 1783 set is:

Example XX–5: C. P. E. BACH, Rondo in B♭, H.267

Later in the work the theme is irregularly augmented and appears like this:

Example XX–6: C. P. E. BACH, Rondo in B♭, H.267, treatment of rondo theme in *fantasia*.

This same rondo concludes with a fantasy passage of unbarred, expressive writing over a dominant pedal, and this is particularly significant, since in his old age Emanuel seems to have found the fantasy more and more to his liking. In his *Essay* written twenty years earlier he had described the fantasy as requiring "only a thorough understanding of harmony and acquaintance with a few rules of construction."[1] In his last years, however, he notated more of his improvisations than ever before. It may well be that the late keyboard music of Emanuel Bach is

1. C.P.E.Bach, *Essay*, p. 430.

the last music to enshrine the soul of the clavichord, for whether the form of composition is the sonata, the rondo, or the fantasy, the composer's aim appears to have been the expression of an intimate and personal emotional state, and we know that he considered the clavichord more suitable than the harpsichord or the fortepiano for this kind of music. But at the time of Emanuel's death, intimacy and private utterance had ceased to be the chosen language of the solo keyboard sonata, and increasingly its function was to speak to a larger audience in tones much more striking and virtuosic, produced by a larger and stronger instrument. Emanuel's hope of addressing "connoisseurs and amateurs" was doomed to failure, for in the 1780s there were few connoisseurs—let alone amateurs—who were not swept along with the new currents. Like his father before him, Emanuel died still attached to a style that had fallen from favor.

COMPOSER / PIANISTS As the popularity of the clavichord and the harpsichord declined, the piano gained favor and the number of virtuoso keyboard composers writing for it during the period is astounding. Some of the more significant names may be mentioned, such as Johann Franz Xaver Sterkel (1750–1817), active and respected in southern Germany; Leopold Kozeluch, a Bohemian who spent most of his active life in Vienna, where he enjoyed royal favor as well as popular esteem, and who was Mozart's successor as court composer; Joseph Wölfl (1773–1812), born in Salzburg and chiefly remembered for his competitive playing with Beethoven; Joseph Gelinek (1758–1825), whose playing was praised by Mozart, and who made a substantial fortune from writing many sets of variations, which met with enormous success, despite their sameness and lack of originality; Daniel Steibelt (1765–1823), born in Berlin, whose virtuoso career began in Paris in the last years of the eighties; and Johann Baptist Cramer (1771–1858), born in Mannheim, son of Wilhelm Cramer, a respected violinist and composer, who moved to England in 1772; and a host of others. The period also saw the first successes of the younger generation of composers, like John Field (1782–1837) and Johann Nepomuk Hummel (1778–1837), who look forward to the new age of the nineteenth century in their pianism but who remain strongly attached to the eighteenth century in their compositional ideals and techniques. The two outstanding composer / pianists of this period, however, were Jan Ladislav Dussek and Muzio Clementi.

Recognizing that the younger generation generally wrote two kinds of sonatas—those for their own use and those for teaching or publishing purposes—it may be said that they all show certain common characteristics, whether written for the Viennese or the English piano. The dimensions of all movements tended to expand, just as the number of movements increased, with four movements becoming almost the rule in virtuosic sonatas. As the size grew bigger the relatively homogeneous textures of Haydn and Mozart gave way to a kind of layered structure, defined by melody and its alternation with passagework (rapid scalic or arpeggio passages). The complex interplay of textural change of earlier days became simplified and a typical sonata exposition came to consist of an extended melodic section in the tonic, leading to a modulating section of short note values exploiting some pianistic figure and often built around a small rhythmic motive derived from the opening melody. With the new key established, the composer once again would go to his well of lyric inspiration and draw up a melody comparable to the opening, which in turn was followed by passagework lasting until the closing theme, which might be either *cantabile,* like the first two melodies—indeed, most probably derived from the first—or a combination of melody and virtuosity. This scheme is fundamentally the same for the concerto and string quartet at the close of the century, and while it produced some extremely beautiful music, it inevitably revealed the basic error of separating form and content, and seeing structure simply as a container for certain elements in a fixed order. The lesser composers had to rely on models, and in this music we begin to see coming into existence the kind of formulas that left such a mark on composers like Berlioz and Schumann, who believed this was the essence of "Classical" music. In other words, much Romanticism is based upon a misconception of the Classical.

DUSSEK Jan Ladislav Dussek was born in Bohemia in 1760 and demonstrated his musical talent early. By the time he was nineteen, he had traveled to northern Europe, where his career was to be based. In 1782, while performing in Hamburg, he met Emanuel Bach and may have had lessons from him—at the least it is possible that he received advice from him. In 1783 he went to Russia, and in the following year he undertook an extensive tour throughout Germany. Toward the end of 1785 he went to Paris where he won favor with the queen, Marie-Antoinette. With the first rumblings of the Revolution, Dussek fled to London, where he had phenomenal success as a virtuoso pianist. He appeared with Haydn in concert, and the great man wrote a testimonial letter to Dussek's father in which he describes the son as "a most honorable and polished man who is a distinguished musician," and says, "I love him just as you dearly as I do you . . ."[2] In England, Dussek married and went into the music-publishing business with his father-in-law. They could not survive in the cut-throat, competitive world of commerce, and in 1799 they went bankrupt. Dussek fled abroad to escape prison, leaving everything behind: wife, daughter, and debts. For two years he was in the service of Prince Louis Ferdinand of Prussia (1772–

2. *Haydn Correspondence,* p. 131.

1806), a soldier, a first-rate pianist, and the talented composer of a small handful of chamber works. Louis Spohr (1784–1859), the brilliant violinist and celebrated composer, describes in his *Autobiography* how Dussek, at the prince's request, invited him to join them on maneuvers. Spohr writes:

> I therefore proceeded to Magdeburg, and found in the house which the Prince had taken for himself and his suite, a room also, for me. I now led an extraordinary, wild and active life, which nevertheless suited my youthful taste right well for a short time. Frequently at six o'clock in the morning, were Dussek and I roused from our beds and conducted in dressing gown and slippers to the Reception-saloon, where the Prince was already seated at the pianoforte in yet lighter costume, the heat being then very great, and indeed, generally in his shirt and drawers only. Now began the practice and rehearsal of the music that was intended to be played in the evening circles, and from the Prince's zeal, this lasted frequently so long, that in the meantime the saloon was filled with Officers decorated, and bestarred. The costume of the Musicians contrasted then somewhat strangely with the brilliant uniforms of those who had come to pay their court to the Prince. But this did not trouble his Royal Highness in the least, neither would he leave off until everything had been practised to his satisfaction. Then we finished our toilet in all haste, snatched as hasty a breakfast, and rode off to the review. I had a horse appropriated to me from the Prince's stud, and was permitted to ride with his suite. In this manner for a time to my great amusement, I took part in all the warlike evolutions.[3]

Unfortunately the prince was killed in battle, and Dussek joined the household of the Comte de Talleyrand in Paris, in whose service he remained until his death early in 1812, fat and dissipated, but still playing like an angel.

As a pianist, Dussek was famous for the *cantabile* sounds he coaxed from the keyboard. To us he is probably most remarkable for his uncanny foreshadowings of later styles. For example, in a sonata composed in 1807, twenty-three years before Brahms's birth, we find the following:

Example XX–7: J. L. DUSSEK, Sonata Op. 70, I

3. Spohr, *Autobiography*, pp. 86–87.

While it is easy to be swept away by such stylistic anticipations, it must be remembered that they are all aspects of Dussek's own style, and that in his day they were not looked upon as clairvoyant glimpses at the music of the future.

The Sonata in G, Op. 35, No. 2. (*ACM* 45) was composed between 1790 and 1799, during Dussek's stay in London. It is possible that Haydn's influence may be seen in several of Dussek's works of this time (as indeed it can in some of Clementi's as well) through the strong unification of the melodic materials of the first and second tonal areas—the principle of monothematicism. This sonata, however, is not one of those, creating instead a sense of independent melodic areas. The placement of the opening chord suggests the sonorous English piano.

The opening phrase, with its antecedent / consequent relationship, does not conclude on a final note, but moves forward into dissimilar rhythmic material (mm. 5–11) and the whole forms an **A B** structure cadencing in m. 12, where an elision leads into a varied repetition of the opening material. It is clear from a glance at the printed page that the passagework begins in m. 16, yet the prevalence of the opening material until m. 23 must be noted. The rhythmic / compositional thread which runs through the whole passage is clear, and the sense of harmonic flux, springing as it does from the quasi-improvisatory movement of the fingers on the keyboard, speaks of fantasy.

The subsequent material (mm. 41–60) consists of the most imposing, self-contained melodic development of the movement. Although not split up by emphasized cadences, this twenty-bar period can be divided into five groups of four bars, in which the first and fourth groups are identical, the second is unique, and the third and fifth are closely related rhythmically and opposed melodically. It should also be observed that the fifth group of four bars has a direct rhythmic link with mm. 5–6, and a melodic link with mm. 9–10. The subsequent passage is more orthodox than the earlier work, and less venturesome—its purpose is to stabilize the key before the closing theme (m. 81). The final bars of the exposition (mm. 91–96) hark back to the opening, but where the music was open-ended there, here it is closed.

The middle section or development is one of Dussek's larger ones. It moves twice through a cycle of fifths, first from B to F, and then from E to E♭. The first part of this section (mm. 97–115) consists of two layers of material; two measures of the rhythm that was present in both parts of the exposition, followed by seven measures of effectively new material. The second layer leads to a false recapitulation in the subdominant, immediately after which a strange juxtaposition of the opening and the closing materials takes place. If a purpose is to be sought for this curious placing of material, it may be found in the way the closeness clarifies the compositional derivation of the closing material from the opening. The remainder of the middle section continues to develop tonal flux out of the opening material of the movement, until a dominant pedal (mm. 147–153) brings the return.

The recapitulation of the opening four measures is followed by a fermata which leads to another shocking juxtaposition—that of the large, secondary area melody, but set here in E♭ with no more aural justification than the melody note, D, preceding it. (During the fermata, D changes from being the fifth degree of G to become the seventh of E♭). Again the action is so provocative as to prompt the question of purpose, and the plausible compositional answer is to be found in the transposition of the melodic third, which had earlier united the opening and closing material, into a harmonic process. The composer establishes E♭ and then causes the bass movement to rise through F to G, after which an orthodox although shortened repetition of the material in the tonic key is heard. Having used two original surprises in this movement, Dussek, in traditional fashion, concludes with a reiteration of all the secondary key area material, in the tonic and in the original order. Only small changes are to be found, but it is important to observe that the extension of the trill (mm. 198–294) and the closing theme (mm. 213–214) give effects of color which are also powerful allusions to the tonal scope of the movement.

Although Dussek's Op. 35 sonatas are not his most celebrated, this movement demonstrates that he deserves serious consideration as a composer. Much of his compositional style depends upon improvisatory effects and yet, as with all good composers, his work has backbone achieved by thorough craftsmanship allied with innovative imagination. His influence upon his contemporaries was considerable, perhaps the greatest of any pianist/composer. But after his death his popularity faded quickly in the face of the growing reputation of Beethoven on the one hand, and the rise of the younger generation of Weber, Hummel, and Spohr on the other. In the mid-nineteenth century, however, interest in his works revived and modern editions were issued by Litolff and others.

CLEMENTI In this twenty-year period Clementi composed most of his sonatas for piano, and while there is no doubt that the virtuoso element is often powerful, it is rarely manifested in the étude-like sequences of thirds and sixths seen earlier. Like Dussek, Clementi cultivated a wide audience for his works by writing in a variety of styles, which ranged from the simple and accessible to the complex, both technically and musically. Perhaps because he was more concerned about the amateur audience his published music would find, Clementi appears generally more conservative than Dussek, and devices such as the Alberti bass are still part of his stock-in-trade. On the other hand, his compositional profile is quite as personal and strongly developed as Dussek's. His early training in Rome and his mastery of Bach's "48" left him with an abiding taste for fugue and polyphony. The sonatas from this period abound in points of imitation and he even writes whole movements in canon. Passages of free polyphony, such as the following example from the Sonata in E♭, Op. 12, No. 4, dating from 1784 or earlier, are as typical of Clementi as they became typical of Hummel:

Example XX–8: M. CLEMENTI, Sonata Op. 12, No. 4, I

Throughout his long life Clementi was fond of creating highly pungent textures, largely from two devices: unprepared dissonances arising from the movement of voices over a changing harmony, and the dissonance that results from voices moving over a pedal harmony. In his sense of structure, he was conservative, often resorting to a textbook kind of regularity in sonata-form rondo movements. On the other hand, some works reveal originality of thought equal to the best of his time. The Sonata in G, Op. 37, No. 2 (*ACM* 46), illustrates the best of Clementi's ideas on structure, melody, and texture. Everything here is determined by musical content rather than by virtuosic potential, and the effect is one of great variety and of an emotional range from the flippant to the deeply serious.

Example XX–9: M. CLEMENTI, Sonata Op. 7, No. 3, I

VARIATIONS The popularity of the folksong reached a peak at this time. Not only were actual folksongs dressed up in modern arrangements by celebrated composers such as Haydn, Beethoven, Pleyel, and Kozeluch, but they also influenced the nature of original melodies by composers who wanted to give their work a popular touch. Perhaps most important, familiar, well-loved folksongs were used in movements in larger works, such as string quartets or piano concertos. That it was the fashion of the time to use Scottish folksongs exclusively, even in those countries with a wealth of indigenous folk materials, is a tribute not only to the lasting effect of *Ossian* but also to the fact that almost everything Scottish—countryside, history, Mary Queen of Scots, climate—seemed to strike a responsive chord in the hearts of the proto-Romantics. Similarly, it is the melody of the Scottish folksong that shaped the short, lyric poems of Robert Burns (1757–92), for the majority of these were written as parodies, i.e., to fit preexistent tunes.

The variation form also became enormously popular at the same time, and for the same reason: it, too, relied on a preexistent melody that was familiar to the audience. While they could be complex at their most sophisticated, variations were, essentially, simple things. All the composer had to do was to add figurations to the given melodic / harmonic basis. The development of the new piano and the virtuosic technique that arose from its exploitation provided an almost inexhaustible array of colors with which to embroider the chosen melody. It is no wonder that this form of music became so popular with the growing audience; not only did it provide a vehicle for the amateur composer and the amateur virtuoso, but it allowed the amateur listener to recognize and bask in a familiar tune, albeit tricked out in a variety of disguises.

A typical example of variation is the Abbé Gelinek's highly successful *Variations on the Queen of Prussia's Favourite Waltz*. (*ACM* 47 consists of the theme and the third variation.). It is particularly hard for us to surmise what the attraction of this kind of music could have been. An insipid waltz with trio is subjected to variations in which the object is clearly not to uncover or develop aspects of the theme in a coherent manner, but to maintain the harmonies, the introductory left-hand chords, and the opening anacrusic, dotted figure. Beyond that the harmony is overlaid with figuration of a certain brilliance. This kind of composition is a testimony to the naive taste of a large portion of the public, who were more interested in demonstrating some accomplishment at the keyboard than connoisseurship; it is also a tribute to the pernicious influence of the virtuoso ideal.

THE "BATTLE PIECE" The naive taste was widespread, and in those times of war and revolution, composers attempted to capitalize on the situation by writing pieces that described historic events, often in order

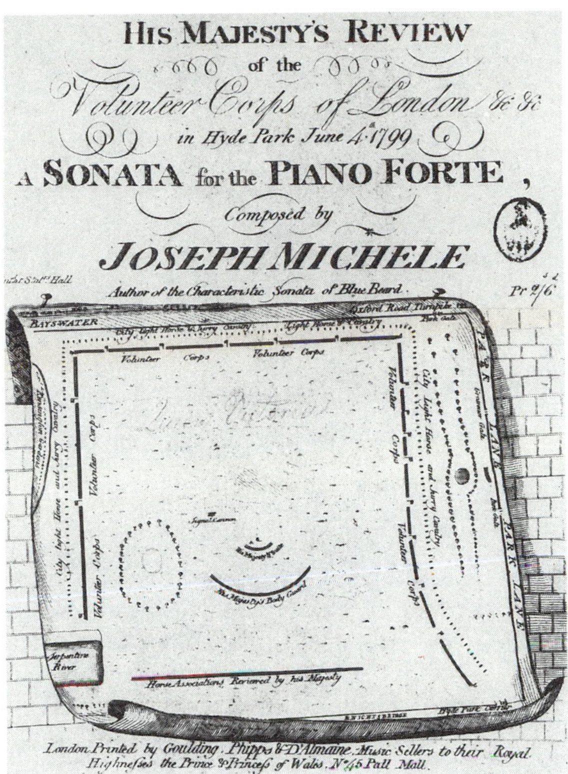

Cheaply produced with no artistic pretentions, this title page from 1799 imitates a wall poster commemorating an event of passing interest.

to stimulate nationalistic sentiment.[4] The genre of the "battle piece" has a long history, but in the last years of the century, amidst the prevailing political strife, these battle pieces became the musical counterpart to the old broadsheet ballads that had been peddled around the countryside, giving lurid details of some gruesome murder or some famous criminal's last moments. As fine a composer as Dussek wrote music to describe the pitiful fate of Marie-Antoinette, and, in another work, to follow the events of a naval battle fought by Admiral Duncan.

Above, you will find the title page of a so-called Sonata for the Piano-Forte, Op. 2, by one Joseph Michele written to portray His Majesty's Review of the Volunteer Corps of London in Hyde Park, 4 June 1799. The page shows a rough map of Hyde Park and the deployment of the troops, in an amateurish engraving hardly beyond the power of an apprentice engraver and far removed from the artistic title pages that are to be found at this time. The composer is described as being "Author of the Characteristic Sonata of Blue Beard." The work has nothing to do with either the structure or the principle of the sonata but consists

4. This is the age of national anthems: the British, the French, and the Austrian anthems were all widely exploited at this time to arouse patriotic feelings.

of a number of sections in different tempos, each of which has an informative sentence at the beginning, such as:

a. The Volunteers March to their respective Stations.
b. Cannon Announce the Approach of His Majesty.
c. Troop of Horses precedes His Majesty. etc.

It is remarkable, in this music designed for amateurs of the most mediocre taste and ability, that the idiom, harmonic and melodic, is that of simplified Haydn, Pleyel, and Mozart, and the pianism is that of elementary piano tutors. The interest of such works is primarily sociological, for they testify to a level of taste that is easy to overlook, but which sheds light on some critical reactions to far greater works at this time.

PIANO DUETS Music for piano four-hands or for two pianos became very popular during this period, attesting to the growth of interest in music for the home. The advantages in composing for four hands were quickly realized, and pianist/composers like Clementi, Dussek, Kozeluch, and Sterkel exploited the idea of constant exchange of material to the hilt. While original works for this combination prevail, we also find many arrangements of compositions originally for other instruments. This use of the four-hand medium was to become more and more important throughout the nineteenth century, since it allowed pianists to become familiar with compositions otherwise inaccessible except

The medium of piano four-hands fosters a sense of musical ensemble and allows for the furthering of close personal relations. Such social uses of music played a large part in the literature and drama of the time. A 1781 engraving by Johann August Rosmaesler.

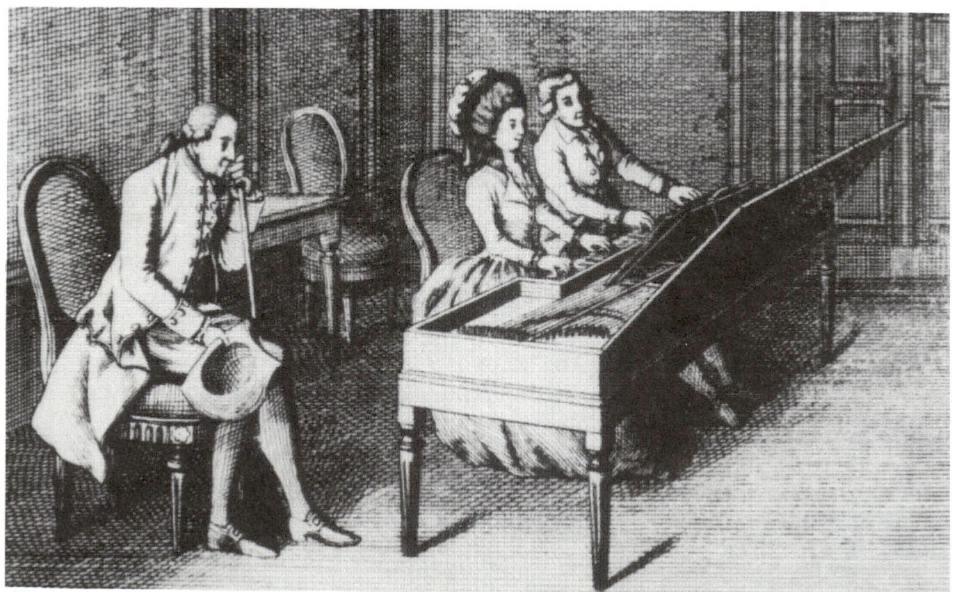

through rare live performances. A real industry developed around arranging orchestra and chamber works for piano four-hands, and many composers, such as Brahms, increased their income by arranging their own works. Thus Pleyel produced a number of compositions for piano duet, all of which turn out to be arrangements of other works, ranging, in their original form, from duets for two violins through string quartets to symphonies.

THE ACCOMPANIED KEYBOARD SONATA

The accompanied keyboard sonata continued to be popular, and a range of examples attests to the variety of composers' approach to the genre. The style of sonata previously discussed, in which the keyboard is accompanied by a subordinate "melody" instrument (violin or flute) that never gets the melody, continues to be produced; there is also the "dialogued" sonata in which each instrument has an approximately equal share of the material, but which is still called—by publishers and composers alike—a "keyboard sonata with accompaniment of . . ." Quite as common is the keyboard sonata with two accompanying instruments, in which the range of possibilities is still greater: for example, the sonata for piano in which the other instruments (generally violin or flute and cello) are given no initiative at all; the sonata for piano in which the dialogue exists only between the piano and the upper melody instrument and the cello has no initiative; and the sonata in which the dialogue involves all the instruments in varying degrees.

The accompanied keyboard sonata was astonishingly popular, and when we see that the great pianist / composers of the time wrote just as much for these combinations as for piano solo, we realize how salable such works were. For example, during this period, Clementi wrote approximately 46 solo sonatas and 43 accompanied sonatas. He treats the accompanying instruments as utterly subordinate and nothing is lost, apart from color, if they are not used. Dussek, on the other hand, whose total output of 27 solo sonatas is outweighed by approximately 75 accompanied sonatas, exhibits a clear move from the subordinate style to the dialogued style. Kozeluch produced a total of 36 solo sonatas as against 47 accompanied sonatas. Pleyel wrote over 40 accompanied sonatas for piano trio, and, as might be anticipated in such a famous pupil of Haydn, his style of instrumentation is close to that of his master—i.e., with dialogued violin and keyboard and optional, subordinate cello. Particularly interesting, in view of what has been said about the popularity of the variation, is the fact that many of Pleyel's trios use Scottish folksongs and popular tunes as raw thematic material.

In the piano trio of this time, we find a manner of scoring that has become obsolete but is of some significance. Instead of placing the string

A case of publisher's piracy or a business arrangement? This fine title page was used by both French and English publishers with only a change of language.

parts on staves above the piano score, as they are printed today, composers of the time, including Mozart, wrote a four-stave score in which the violin part was on top, the next two staves were for the piano, and the bottom line was the cello part. This arrangement helped to preserve the cello's *continuo* function and to link it as a coloring agent to the piano's left hand. It was more difficult for the average composer to envisage the kind of antiphonal setting that would pit both the strings against the keyboard.

The photograph of an early edition of No. 5 in Pleyel's *Six Sonatas for the Pianoforte or Harpsichord, with an Accompaniment for a Flute or a Violin and Violoncello: Composed and Dedicated by Permission to Her Majesty The Queen of Great Britain* (*ACM* 48; first movement) is of interest not only because of the music but because of its layout. The flute/violin part was printed, as normal, above the keyboard, but the cello part was considered so unimportant that it was only printed as a separate part. The first movement is a fine example of a monothematic sonata structure in which all parts of the work are built upon one two-beat fragment of material. In this respect Pleyel shows himself a worthy pupil of Haydn, but it is interesting to note how much less important the development section is; while thorough and interesting, it is nevertheless only one-third as long as the exposition. The rest of the sonata consists of a short, melodic slow movement in C, the subdominant of the relative major, and a rondo in which the minor-mode theme alternates with episodes in the relative and tonic major. To Pleyel's credit it must be said that the obvious conclusion in the major is avoided, and counterpoint intensifies the final appearance of the theme, making the whole an extremely successful work.

CHAMBER MUSIC FOR STRINGS

In music written for the home, developments in combined string instruments without piano are of the highest importance at this time on two counts: first, because the number of published works ranging from duets to quintets increased markedly; and second, because the great composers, Haydn and Mozart, produced their greatest works in this field, and Beethoven composed his first set of quartets, Op.18, as well as his finest string trios.

While the preeminence of Paris and London as centers of publishing did not significantly lessen, the influence of publishing in German-speaking lands grew, particularly in Vienna. The effect of this growth was, of course, to make it much easier for German or Austrian composers to be printed in their own languages, and to diminish the importance of making a success in Paris.

DUETS The duet for two violins, violin and viola, violin and cello, or two cellos was popular in its own right, both for playing and for teaching. Along with the minor players and composers who contributed to it are a number of important composers, such as Mozart, whose two duets for violin and viola (K.423 and K.424) were composed to help Michael Haydn, Joseph's younger brother, out of a difficult situation. Bréval wrote many sets of duos which were published in Paris, for either two violins or two cellos. Pleyel contributed charming works to this repertoire, some of which were arranged for every combination of instruments. Viotti's production of duets extends over a period of nearly thirty-five years. They are all for two violins, and, together with those of Franz Krommer (1759–1831), may be looked upon as the finest duet compositions of the late eighteenth and early nineteenth centuries. Generally these works are composed on the *concertante* principle with both instruments sharing melodic and virtuosic material, but there is inevitably an overbalancing in favor of the first, or upper, instrument.

STRING TRIOS The string trio, as noted in a previous chapter, remained a kind of stepchild of music, with the combination of two violins and cello predominant and the combination of violin, viola, and cello less popular. It is difficult to see why the string trio was so overlooked, since there are such good examples, mostly for two violins and cello, by Boccherini, Haydn, Pleyel, Viotti, and a host of others. The Divertimento K.563, by Mozart, and the Trios, Op. 3, 8, and 9 by Beethoven are all large, imposing works for violin, viola, and cello, completely worthy of standing beside the contemporary string quartets of these masters. Few other composers of the time thought to use the string trio in this way.

STRING QUARTETS The string quartet covers the whole spectrum of musical needs of the time. Indeed, it is arguable that no other medium was able to fill the gamut of social demands as well. The great works of the masters, with their immense expressive range from the humorous to the serious, from the naive and rustic to the sophisticated and refined, satisfy the eternal human longing for the highest attainable in art. The lesser masters entertain magnificently without offering quite the same scope, nor do they make the same demands on the players and listeners. In addition, there are original string quartets that embody the then-modern trend of emphasizing the primacy of melody by using folk tunes, either quoted directly or used for reworking, like any other musical substance. There are even numbers of multi-movement string quartets built upon the most popular operatic airs of the day. All this is, of course, in addition to arrangements of entire symphonies, operas, and oratorios. No other medium could do as much as the quartet and none lent itself more readily to handling by carefree amateurs or by the most learned and imaginative minds of the time.

In 1784, Wolfgang Mozart wrote to his father:

> I must tell you that some quartets have just appeared, composed by a certain Pleyel, a pupil of Joseph Haydn. If you do not know them, do try and get hold of them; you will find them worth the trouble. They are very well written and most pleasing to listen to. You will also see at once who was his master. Well, it will be a lucky day for music if later on Pleyel should be able to replace Haydn. (*Letters,* 24 Apr. 1784)

PLEYEL Ignace Joseph Pleyel was only a year and a half younger than his fellow countryman, Mozart. He is said to have taken lessons with Vanhal and with Haydn at Eisenstadt. He remained with Haydn for five years. After some travel and service as Kapellmeister to Count Erdödy, he became assistant to Richter, the Mannheim musician who was made Kapellmeister of Strasbourg Cathedral in 1769, and whom he eventually succeeded. Given the currents of atheism which the French Revolution fostered, religious services in the cathedral were interrupted, and in 1795 Pleyel went to Paris, where he opened a music store and undertook the publishing of other composers' works as well as his own. In 1807 he began to manufacture pianos, and it is this commmercial enterprise that has carried his name down to our age. After 1800 he composed very little new music and in 1834, three years after his death, the company he had founded ceased the publication of music altogether.

The greater part of Pleyel's output falls between 1780 and 1800, and during this period the popularity and circulation of his works was enormous, possibly exceeded only by that of his master. Mozart's judgment about Pleyel's replacing Haydn is, in the light of 1784, most perceptive and accurate.

His more than sixty string quartets are mostly in three or four movements (although there are several in two). First movements, generally *Allegro* in 4 / 4, are usually written in the French *concertante* style, which demands a fairly high degree of virtuosity from all the instruments in turn. The form is usually complete sonata structure, in which occasional interesting modifications somewhat offset the impression that Pleyel is a composer with only a modest melodic gift. Slow movements tend to be shorter than is usual in Haydn and Mozart, but of a length and style comparable with the likes of C. F. Abel: very *cantabile,* with rarely any excursions or developments away from the first melodic statements. Such slow movements often seem to be merely interludes between the outer movements. In the quartets with four movements, the third is usually a Minuet and Trio, while in the three-movement works, the third is often either a Minuet and Trio or a *Tempo di Minuetto*. The fourth movement tends to be a rondo either in 6 / 8 or 2 / 4 meter. The *concertante* influence can be expected to remain strong, but Pleyel's rondo themes, in common with those of many of the lesser masters of this period, often display a naiveté in their melodic/harmonic structure which makes them sometimes appear trite and trivial to modern ears. The search for simplicity and naturalness which can be observed in contemporary fashions of dress and in some political philosophies have their egalitarian counterparts in melodic structures such as the following:

Example XX–10: Typical populist themes

a. G. B. VIOTTI, Concerto No. 23 in G, III

b. I. J. PLEYEL, Quartet (Benton 356), III

C. I. J. PLEYEL, Quartet (Benton 305), III

This style of quartet writing accurately took the measure of the public's pulse and was immensely popular. Whether the reasons for this are the simple, direct melodies, the uncomplicated and oft-repeated formal structures, the easy yet fluent virtuosity which generally falls smoothly under the fingers and which flatters the player, or whether they are to be sought elsewhere, the *concertante* recipe for success was followed by numbers of composers in all the major centers. Some of its noted exponents are Franz Anton Hoffmeister, Giuseppe Cambini, and Adalbert Gyrowetz (1763–1850). And while no composer remains entirely free of the style, the great composers tend to depend on it to a lesser degree, as do some minor composers, notably Emanuel Aloys Förster (1748–1823), Leopold Kozeluch, and Carl von Dittersdorf, all of whose quartets are written with wit and inventiveness.

MUSIC FOR VOICE AND PIANO

During the last quarter of the eighteenth century the song for voice and keyboard imperceptibly increased in popularity. The charming and innocent little songs discussed previously continue to be produced by many composers, but among more and more composers there is clearly an urge to deepen the effect of the strophic song and to increase the theatrical effect of ballad settings or songs which tell a story.

Johann Rudolf Zumsteeg (1760–1802) has long been recognized as one of the most influential of Schubert's forerunners. The text of his song *Nachtgesang,* (Night Song) in three stanzas, is a typical, pre-Romantic effusion in which the poet muses on the darkness and his tears, and then, casting his eyes upward, asks whether there is peace up there, far from this world of vanity (*ACM* 49). Zumsteeg preserves the strophic structure of the verse in the vocal melody, which, with minor variations, repeats itself for each verse. However, the harmonization is different in each stanza. To be sure, there are places where the composer cannot avoid repetition, but the aim is to set each verse with a fresh impact. The harmonic language of the song is unusually chromatic.

The function of the keyboard in songs of the 1790s was much more advanced than in earlier times, although *Nachtgesang* does not demon-

This watercolor, entitled *Aria,* commemorates a New Year's morning in 1792 and the gift of a portrait and a song, the latter performed by the daughter of Pehr Hilleström, the artist. (Statens konstmuseer, Stockholm)

strate this. Strophic songs were usually written on three staves, and frequently the accompanying figures in the keyboard part were designed to heighten or reflect the verbal imagery of the poem, while yet remaining within the capabilities of the amateur player.

Particularly important at this time and for the first fifty years of the following century was the musical setting of the poetic ballad (see p. 116 for general discussion). There were essentially two ways of constructing such a setting. The poet usually wanted his poem to be left intact so that his artistry might be fully appreciated. After all, a long ballad of twenty or thirty stanzas preserves its rhythm and meter and rhyme scheme throughout. On the other hand, the musician wished to use his art to heighten the emotional impact of the story by creating music that enhanced it.

Johann Friedrich Reichardt (1752–1814) set Goethe's famous ballad *Erlkönig* (*ACM* 50) in a manner that matched the first ideal to perfection. Indeed, Goethe himself praised Reichardt's settings of his poems, saying, "His settings of my songs are quite unparalleled by anything I know of their kind."[5] We, who are used to Schubert's setting of the same words, find Reichardt's quite limited, and, conscious as we are that this kind of song writing has become merely a curiosity, it is with effort that we remember how closely this setting conformed to the poet's ideal.

One of the most famous German ballads of the day is *Lenore* by the

5. Cited by Walter Salmen in his preface to "Reichardt, Goethes Lieder." Vol. 58 of *Das Erbe Deutscher Musik* (Munich, 1964) I, p. v.

poet Gottfried August Bürger (1747–94). It is a poem in thirty-two stanzas telling the story of a maiden, waiting for the return of her lover from the wars. When he does not come back, in despair she refuses to accept what God has decreed. Then William, the lover, appears on a black horse and gallops off, Lenore contentedly behind him. At the graveyard he turns into a skeleton and Lenore's hoped-for marriage bed is the grave, thus pointing up the moral that we should accept whatever God sends without complaint. This ballad had a very strong appeal when it was written and was set many times. In one setting (1788) by Friedrich Ludwig Aemilius Kunzen (1761–1817)(*ACM* 51) the text is used as a springboard for the composer's imagination; he calls his setting "ein musikalisches Gemälde" (a musical painting), and he envisages not merely one singer but a narrator and three singers: Lenore, her mother, and the ghostly William. After the first line of text is spoken by the narrator, the music starts, depicting Lenore in her troubled sleep. A fully developed march for the piano paints the picture of the soldiers returning from the wars and their happiness, and so on, to the end.

This is the kind of composition that belongs to the byways of musical history. In its own time, it might take the place of opera in the home, affording to the performers an opportunity to act and to sing, and to make their listeners' flesh creep. When such a ballad setting is able to match the piano figuration so aptly with the text and to create such a vivid heightening of it, it is unthinkable that the strophic song should remain aloof. In the bulk of Schubert's production for voice and piano a very large proportion is taken up with the composition of through-composed ballads. Kunzen's experimental work from 1788 shows vividly the way in which music in the home was groping its way toward new ways to effect a marriage between word and music.

CHAPTER XXI

The Preeminence of the Symphony and the Concerto

As the eighteenth century drew to a close, the means of bringing music to the public increasingly came to depend on groups of people (e.g., committees, boards of directors, etc.) concerned with ensuring the financial stability of an organization rather than on individuals (the Bachs, the Abels, the Legros, etc.) whose prime motive was personal profit. With such a change in concert organization, an interesting phenomenon was observable: what has been called the Great Repertoire—those works that form the nucleus of concerts, whether in Vienna, Paris, London, or New York—came into being. At the heart of the Great Repertoire is the symphony, and the first of the truly international symphonists was Haydn. Most of the other works programmed with the Haydn symphonies at that time—the concertos, the *symphonies concertantes,* the arias—are today either entirely forgotten or confined to historic recordings.

Earlier it was possible to point to a number of composers of roughly equal stature, whose works had local currency, but whose names were less likely to appear on public concert programs in other cities; for example, not one Abel symphony was programmed by the *Concert Spirituel* in Paris between 1770 and 1784, although the majority of symphonies performed were by Mannheimers like Toeschi and other Germans like Sterkel and Eichner. But beginning around 1779/80 the works of Haydn came to dominate the symphonic portion of concerts. The programs of the *Concert Spirituel,* for example, generate the following approximate but interesting statistics: in 1777, Haydn's symphonies occupied 3.5% of the time allotted to symphonies; in 1780 that percentage had risen to 21%; in 1782 it was 39%; in 1784, 66%; and in 1790, the year the *Concert Spirituel* closed, 78%. Although these percentages do not necessarily pertain elsewhere, they do reflect a general trend. Even in Vienna, Haydn-resistant as it was, the late 1790s reveal a similar pattern. Nothing comparable had ever happened, for Haydn's work made the symphonies of all his contemporaries seem routine and mediocre by comparison.

THE SYMPHONY IN VIENNA

MICHAEL HAYDN Vienna was a focal point for the production of symphonies at this time, and its position as the most important center for instrumental music in the world was assured. Of all the lesser symphonists of the period perhaps the most interesting was Johann Michael Haydn, Joseph's younger brother, whose early training took place in Vienna. The greater part of his life was spent in Salzburg, where he was an honored colleague of the Mozarts. He wrote 41 symphonies, of which approximately half were created between 1780 and 1800. Most are in three movements, F/S/F, whereas the earlier symphonies are usually in four. First movements are often simple sonata structures, with more than half in triple time; one symphony of this period, in two movements only, has the surprising opening signature of 3/8. Slow movements tend to be rondo, song form, or variation structures, and they are set most frequently in the dominant (subdominant and the tonic minor are also used, but less often). Last movements are frequently rondo structures, and four finales are headed *Fugato*.

Unlike his brother, Michael Haydn worked within the accepted symphonic forms. His individuality lies in his melodic inventiveness, at times drawn out to lengths quite beyond the power of most of his contemporaries, and in his use of solo instruments in the orchestra for novel coloristic effects. The opening sectional melody from the two-movement Symphony in D (1786) extends over an unusual length without having to rely on the usual phrase repetition.

Example XXI–1: M. HAYDN, Symphony in D (P.23), I

The slow movements of Michael Haydn's symphonies often present extended melodies with a solo orchestration. Instruments favored for these solos are violin, flute, oboe, and bassoon, and in one slow movement the violin and *cor anglais* perform a duet throughout. Many of his richest effects are in these movements, and the kind of sparse, two-part writing associated with his brother's earlier symphonies is not favored. The first page of a D-major symphony from 1781 (Example XXI–2) reveals how arresting and unusual Michael Haydn's orchestrations could be.

Example XXI–2: M. HAYDN, Symphony in D (P.43), I

DITTERSDORF Two years younger than Michael Haydn, Carl Ditters, later and more commonly called von Dittersdorf, was one of the most prolific symphonic writers at this time, but unfortunately, he continued writing instrumental music after the demand for it had disappeared. Only his comic operas, phenomenally successful in their own day, kept his name alive. In his symphonies, Dittersdorf, like Leopold Mozart, often attempted to catch audience interest by associating extra-musical ideas with the music. Thus, a symphony of *c.* 1770 is entitled "The Battle of the Human Passions," another of *c.* 1773 is called "The Carnival," another "National Symphony in the Style of Five Nations."

In the early 1780s, he wrote a series of twelve symphonies based upon stories taken from the Latin poet Ovid's *Metamorphoses,* of which only six survive in their full, orchestral version. The attraction of the subject matter was twofold: it allowed for programmatic effects, which Dittersdorf develops with taste and discretion; and since the subjects were taken from familiar Latin literature, the composer could count on his classically educated audience to associate the ongoing musical events with the well-known narrative. The *Ovid* symphonies are in four movements: three are arranged as church-sonata symphonies, S/F/Minuet/F. and three are arranged in the modern style, F/S/Minuet/F. There is one outstanding tonal anomaly among them: in the first of the six, a church-sonata symphony, the Minuet is set outside the tonic in the key of the relative minor. Normal practice is to set the first Minuet in the tonic, and occasionally the second Minuet, the Trio or, as Dittersdorf calls it, the *Alternativo,* in the relative minor. In the second movement of this same symphony, at the point of return to the tonic key area in the recapitulation, the preparation concludes on a pedal E and ends with a chord of E major. There follows a hiatus, a complete break lasting one and a half measures with a fermata; then the opening material is taken up in the tonic key, C. This process, already rather old-fashioned in the 1770s, is something of an anachronism in the mid-1780s.

Even more interesting from the point of view of formal structure is the fact that in four of the six symphonies, the Finales end with a change of tempo and material. All six Finales are marked *Vivace* or *Presto;* one, the fifth, alternates *Adagio* and *Vivace*. The G-major Symphony (No. 3), based on the story of Actaeon changed into a stag by Diana and killed by his own hounds, concludes its *Vivace* hunt music with Actaeon's death, and the music dies away with no change of tempo. The other four symphonies conclude with extended, slower movements to the fast Finale joined without a break: the *Presto* of the first ends *Allegretto;* the *Vivace* of the second concludes *Andantino;* and the fourth and sixth close with a *Tempo di Minuetto*. Each of these conclusions is a coda, by definition, but not a coda that serves to tie up loose ends in the music. Here, Dittersdorf, like Haydn in the Symphony No. 45, steps out of his role as storyteller and provides a formulaic resolution—as fairy tales end with "and they all lived happily ever after." The *Allegretto* ending of the first of the *Ovid* symphonies even includes a folksong-like tune to reinforce the effect of stepping outside the narrative context of the symphony.

Example XXI–3: C. DITTERS V. DITTERSDORF, *Ovid* Symphony No. 1, conclusion.

KOZELUCH Leopold Kozeluch's eleven fully authenticated symphonies were all written within this period and they are mostly four-movement works. His melodic style—and the symphonies depend for their effect upon the consistent grace of the melody—is easy, fluent, and as close to a *galant* style as it is possible to imagine in 1790. There is a certain predictability in the frequent repetition of a phrase a third higher than at its first appearance:

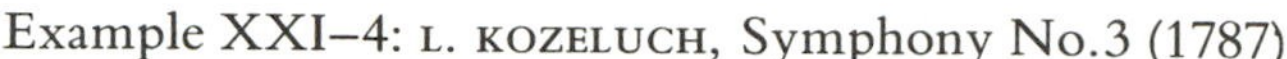

Example XXI–4: L. KOZELUCH, Symphony No.3 (1787)

The symphonies rely greatly upon repeated eighth notes in the lower strings—a characteristic of early Haydn's symphonies—but the resulting texture is clear and vital.

Other prominent symphonists of this period in Vienna include Antonio Salieri, F.A.Hoffmeister, Adalbert Gyrowetz, and Joseph Leopold Eybler (1765–1846).

Ignace Pleyel's symphonic production largely dates from the mid-1780s to the early years of the nineteenth century, when his compositions in other fields had already won him widespread celebrity. But his symphonies do not reflect his talent as well as his chamber works. In the latter, there is a tautness of structure, which, despite an obvious over-willingness to gratify expectation in the nature of the melody and the alternation of melody and passagework, keeps the composition coherent and interesting. The symphonies, however, tend to become long-winded and lose both momentum and proportion in the relationship of movements.

Minor composers faced knotty problems in the last two decades of the eighteenth century. By definition the lesser symphonists were lesser composers, and therefore were imitators of models. This application of the Kantian dictum in no way belittles the quality of the music that can be written under such circumstances. These lesser composers may not have known the symphonies of Mozart that might have served as models for them, and those of Haydn that they had heard were too recent to have been thoroughly assimilated. Therefore their models were found in the works of their predecessors and their peers. Thus, through the closing years of the century, *Kleinmeister* like Kozeluch, Salieri, and Gaetano Brunetti (1744–98) perpetuated the symphony of the previous generation, confining their search for immortality to enlarging the orchestra, exploiting its effects, and composing in a more modern melodic style. Other lesser masters, like Pleyel, sought to impose their stamp on the symphony by enlarging the proportions of the first movement, and by creating an unprecedented degree of difference between first and second group material. A comparison between Pleyel's Symphony No. 20 in D[1] dating from 1791 and Beethoven's Fifth Symphony, composed approximately fifteen years later, shows that Pleyel's first tonal area is almost as long as Beethoven's entire exposition. Moreover, the main substance of the second tonal area has absolutely nothing in common with the movement as a whole, and at each of its three appearances that lack of connection is emphasized. Pleyel was not alone in his use of non-integrated material, and it may be argued that Hummel's Sonata Op. 13, and Beethoven's Sonata Op. 2, No. 1, contain examples of the same aesthetic practice. The use of material only remotely connected with the rest of the sonata-form movement clearly fulfilled an expressive need for composers in the 1790s that we, today, feel less strongly.

Why did Pleyel's audience fail to see the problems that are so obvious to us? It would seem that the audience of the day did not fully appreciate the originality of Haydn and Mozart, and Pleyel's work was not compared to theirs. They saw in Pleyel's work an attempt to climb the heights of the grandiose and to create enjoyable music; they could only applaud his achievements, particularly since he did not require them to strain their understanding. To use Burke's definitions, Pleyel won over his audience by offering them beautiful music cloaked in the proportions of sublimity.

THE CONCERTO

In London and Paris, the two great and wealthy centers of music in western Europe, it was not the symphony that formed the nucleus of the public concert during these years of the eighteenth century, but the concerto. The English terminology used at the time is typical and informative: a concert was divided into two "acts" and each "act" was opened by an "overture." The overture might be a big symphony by Haydn or a little symphony by a lesser composer, but in a verbal sense, at least, it might be perceived as the introduction to the arias and concertos that followed. In other words, the interest of the concert might be seen to lie primarily in the activities of the solo artists who either sang arias or played concertos. In both London and Paris a concert might well consist of two symphonies, several vocal pieces, and two or three concertos or *symphonies concertantes*.

1. Pleyel, Symphony No. 20 in D (New York: Garland, 1981)

The variety of instruments for which concertos were written is of interest, for it illustrates the difference between audiences then and now. In fifty concerts given by the *Concert Spirituel* during the years 1780 and 1781 the following numbers of concertos for the following instruments were performed (the figures do not take into account the repetition of works):

1780/1781	Flute - 15	Oboe - 9	Clarinet - 12	Bassoon - 7
	Horn - 12	2 Horns - 6	Harp - 3	Piano - 3
	Violin - 43	Cello - 13	*Symphonies concertantes* - 4	

During the years 1788 and 1789, the number of concertos performed declined slightly, but the distribution among solo instruments shows more significant differences:

1788/1789	Flute - 0	Oboe - 6	Clarinet - 10	Bassoon - 8
	Horn - 3	2 Horns - 0	Harp - 3	Piano - 11
	Violin - 42	Cello - 5	*Symphonies concertantes* - 18	

Notice how persistent was the popularity of the concerto for solo violin, and the growth in importance of the *symphonie concertante* and the piano concerto.

PARIS The French capital enjoyed a long tradition of excellent violin playing by the likes of Jean-Marie Leclair, Pierre Gaviniès, and many others. The so-called French Violin School, however, was founded by the Italian-born Giovanni Battista Viotti, whose influences could be traced back to Corelli. In 1782 Viotti went to Paris and appeared as soloist in one of his own concertos. His style of playing, with its broad tone and wide variety of bowing techniques, strongly affected the playing of Rodolphe Kreutzer, Pierre Baillot (1771–1842), and Pierre Rode (1774–1830; the only one of the three who was actually a pupil of Viotti's). Viotti's twenty-nine violin concertos followed a structural principle which made an impression all over Europe, since with minor variations it is also the scheme of Kreutzer's nineteen concertos, Baillot's nine, and Rode's thirteen.

The structure of these concertos is not dependent upon the idea of recapitulation, nor upon the development of thematic material, nor upon the manipulation of tonalities, although, of course, these are all present to some degree. Their coherence seems to be based rather upon the violin and its capabilities, emphasizing as they do the broad *cantabile* tone of the instrument as well as its formidable agility.

VIOTTI A Viotti concerto typically opens with a long orchestral tutti, which may occupy as much as a quarter of the total length of the movement, *Allegro* or *Moderato* in tempo, and in 4/4 time. Usually between

70 and 100 measures long, it is, on average, somewhat longer than Mozart's. Two of the concertos have slow introductions, comparable to those in symphonic first movements, and they are both linked thematically to the ensuing *Allegro*. Viotti prefers to open his first tutti quietly, and several that open *forte* move quickly to *piano*. The extended *cantabile* melodic opening usually stands in marked contrast to the more rapid, *forte* passage-work which separates the first and second melodic elements. From this point it becomes less easy to generalize, because Viotti tends to do different things. Most frequently, a *cantabile* second melody and sometimes a third will follow, sometimes with mode change from minor to major, and sometimes with modulation, but there is also the possibility (e.g., Concerto No. 23) that the opening material in the tonic key will be repeated at this point. Following further rapid passagework there may be a further *cantabile* conclusion or not, but inevitably the orchestral *tutti* will conclude on a strong reiterated cadence whose purpose is clearly to create the right theatrical atmosphere for the entry of the soloist. Whether *forte* or *piano,* whether on the beat or with anacrusis, the soloist's entry is on long notes, not designed to be ornamented as in the earlier style but to be left as single notes which exploit the instrument's capacity for sustained sound and expose the quality of the soloist's tone. The period of Viotti's concertos also saw the ideal of the modern violin bow perfected in Paris by the three generations of the Tourte family—indeed, tradition has it that Viotti's advice is embodied in the mature Tourte bow. The shape and structure allowed for more hair under greater pressure to be brought into contact with the string, thus producing a fuller, rounder, more penetrating sound, which became the ideal violin sound of the nineteenth century. At the same time legato bowing was cultivated to a far higher degree than earlier, hence it is possible to assert that Viotti's style (and that of his pupils) is dependent upon the new bow, and that the style of violinists from Viotti to Spohr is the basis for the modern ideal of violin sound.

Example XXI–5: G. B. VIOTTI, Concerto No. 28 in A minor, I

a. Opening orchestral melody

b. Soloist's embellished version of (a).

The *cantabile* melody of the soloist is itself a forward-looking thing, extending from sixteen to twenty measures, but its relationship to the opening melody of the orchestral tutti is sometimes obscure. It may well involve some repetition of motives, but it is not typically built upon dynamic contrast, nor upon antecedent/consequent relationships, nor upon the contrast of rhythmic phrase with conjunct melodic phrase. In other words, it is not a Mozartian statement; its origins lie rather in the song. The next example shows the soloist's opening melody from the Concerto No. 20, an **A A'** structure, and the stanzaic form of melody, **A A B A,** of the Concerto No. 28 can be seen in the previous one.

Example XXI–6: G. B. VIOTTI, Concerto No. 20 in D, I, soloist's opening

These melodies remain in the same register. Perhaps more typical, not only of Viotti but also of Kreutzer and Rode, is the melody that is repeated once in high register and once in low register, in order to show that the violin possesses two distinct registral sounds, the G-string sound and the E-string sound. The opening solo melody of Viotti's Concerto No. 29 and of Rode's Concerto No. 8, both exemplify the way in which the violin itself dictated the structure of concertos written for it around 1800.

Example XXI–7

a. G. B. VIOTTI, Concerto No. 29 in E minor, I

b. P. RODE, Concerto No. 8 in E minor, I.

After the opening *cantabile,* as might be expected, there follows strongly contrasted passagework which serves to introduce the second *cantabile* melody.[2] Further technical brilliance reaches a conclusion in a long trill, which is followed by a short orchestral tutti. The middle section of the form is occasionally separated from the rest of the movement by being couched in triplets instead of duplet eighths and sixteenths, but it is the start of what is, in essence, the third big block—the first is the orches-

2. In the 23rd Concerto there is no real second melody.

tral tutti, the second is the soloist's entry up to the concluding trill, and the third block runs from the soloist's second entry to the end of the movement. Viotti barely emphasizes the point of recapitulation, and occasionally he proceeds in a very unusual manner. Thus, in the Concerto No. 22 the material had been presented as follows:

(read down columns)

Exposition			Recapitulation	
Ia	in tonic (A min)	recapitulates	Va	in tonic major, flowing into
Ib	in tonic major	in reverse	Ib	in tonic major
Va	in dominant major	order, as . . .	Ia	in tonic minor

In the 23rd Concerto in G, after a false recapitulation in E, the real recapitulation, in a movement 348 bars long, occurs 62 bars from the end. It is clear that Viotti's principles in structuring the first movement of a concerto are based upon considerations different from those of the symphony and string quartet.

Slow movements tend to be short and simple in structure and substance. The orchestral introduction to the slow movement of the Concerto No. 22 in A minor (*ACM* 52) has been compared to Beethoven, and even more reminiscent of the Beethoven of the Romances for Violin and Orchestra are the violin melody and its accompaniment; the movement to subdominant harmony in m. 15 is particularly striking. All this is hardly surprising, knowing, as we do, of Beethoven's attraction at this time to things French, and the influence of the French Violin School on his writing.

Viotti stands beside Haydn and Beethoven as one of the greatest humorists in music around 1800. The last movements of his concertos tend toward drollery (particularly Nos. 22 and 23) in their extended rondo structures. He was also among the first composers to use the polonaise as a last movement, an innovation which resounded throughout the nineteenth century.

PIANO CONCERTOS No piano concertos written during these years made a lasting impression apart from those by Mozart and the young Beethoven. Indeed, it has been pointed out that no concertos written between Mozart's last Concerto (K.595) of 1791 and Chopin's first Concerto (the F minor was composed in 1829, before the E minor) survive in current repertoire except for those of Beethoven. There were no keyboard developments comparable to those of the French Violin School. This is particularly surprising when you consider that the great virtuosos Clementi and Dussek together with a host of other players, were very active at this time. It has been suggested that the late eighteenth-century piano could not compete in volume of tone with the orchestra, but this argument falls before the success of Mozart's and Beethoven's concertos.

In the hands of virtuosos such as the Abbé Sterkel and Leopold Kozeluch, the piano concerto really does not change in form or manner. Like the earlier concerto of Christian Bach, their works demand no more than an average amateur technique from the pianist. The keyboard textures depend heavily upon Alberti bass patterns in closed position in the left hand; arpeggios written in such a way that they can be divided between both hands so that the thumb does not have to move under the fingers; and passagework consisting largely of scalar patterns. The relationship between keyboard and orchestra is largely limited since either the orchestra plays alone or the piano plays alone or with the most rudimentary accompaniment. There is no rich interaction between orchestra and soloist. Even in the Dussek concertos the situation is not very much better. He is more apt than either Kozeluch or Sterkel to use the hands in open position, spanning either an octave or a tenth with wrist movement, and his right-hand *fioriture* are much more elaborate than theirs, but in his concertos written before 1800 he does not use the resources of the instrument as fully as in his sonatas on the same period.

STEIBELT Around 1800, however, a change took place in the nature of pianism in the concerto, as a stronger emphasis is placed upon virtuosity. Daniel Steibelt, the Prussian-born and Paris-based virtuoso, best exemplifies this trend. As the early Clementi Rondo (*ACM* 17) clearly puts more importance upon the quality of the pianism than upon the quality of the music, an idea which Clementi quickly abandoned, so Steibelt's sonatas and concertos, more than any others, rely primarily upon the impression that the pianist makes on the listeners. Steibelt's Third Piano Concerto, Op. 33, often referred to as *The Storm,* was published in 1799. It foreshadows many of the structural and pianistic trends in the virtuoso piano concerto of the next thirty years. In its day this concerto was enormously popular for it was deliberately aimed at a naive audience with pretensions to culture (see Example XXI–8). Steibelt's foreword to the printed edition (Example XXI–8a) is addressed to those for whom the use of the pedals is not second nature. In attempting to remedy this situation, Steibelt makes one of the very first references to the exact use of the sustaining pedal "that raises the Dampers" and the "Piano Pedal." The slow movement (*ACM* 53) is built on a Scottish folksong; and the last movement carries the heading: "a Rondo Pastoral. in which he introduces an Imitation of a Storm." [*sic*]

The large-scale form is that of a typical piano concerto of this period: ritornello, solo, rit., solo, rit., solo, rit., rather than that of Viotti's late concertos, outlined above. An open hand position is required most of the time. Steibelt uses the entire range of the instrument in scales, double-octave scales, and arpeggios. Example XXI–8b, the conclusion of the first solo, in which an original figuration of a diminished seventh down the keyboard is followed by an upward scale, leads to the climactic trill, which builds through five bars to the cadence. In Examples XXI-8c and 8d, taken from the storm movement, Steibelt is reviving the Schobert's *tremolando* technique from thirty years earlier.

Example XXI–8: D. STEIBELT, Concerto No.3, Op.33, figurations from movements I and III

a. Foreword to the printed edition

The Author wishing to make more Variety on the Piano Forte, finds it neceſsary to make use of the Pedals, by which alone the tones can be united; but it requires to use them with Care; without which, in going from one Chord to another Discord & Confusion would result. Hereafter the Author in all his Compositions will make use of the following signs to denote the Pedals.

⊕ *The Pedal that raises the Dampers.*

△ *The Piano Pedal.*

✱ *To take the Foot off the Pedal that was us'd before.*

b. Figurations and lengthened approach to cadence, I

c. Left- and right-hand octave figures, III

d. Tremolando, III

With such displays of pianistic technique Steibelt enjoyed great success, and while very little of his technique is original in the sense that Chopin's is—i.e., he did not develop new figurations—it is clear that he struck a responsive chord with the public. The young generation of pianists needed the formality of the Classical concerto structure to make their greatest effect. The grandiose introduction by the orchestra, the climactic and everlasting suspended trill at the conclusion of the solo section, the brilliant domination of the keyboard from top to bottom, and even the expanded range of the keyboard (Steibelt's tonic key is here dictated by his top note, B, on the keyboard), all these things are part of the trappings of the virtuoso as superman.[3] And one senses that formalism now is coming to take precedence over form; we are on the verge of seeing that the way things are said is becoming more important than what is said.

3. It is interesting to remember that Spohr, whose musicianship took precedence over his virtuosity, was most apt to experiment with the structure of his violin concertos, making them shorter and shorter, while Paganini (1782–1840), the archetypal virtuoso, used the "Classical" concerto form, like Steibelt's *Storm* Concerto.

CHAPTER XXII

The Various Faces of Musical Theater

THE *OPERA SERIA*

Rational thinkers, like the Italians Durazzo and Algarotti, worked for opera reform along French lines, but their ideas had little impact in their homeland. The only aspects of French opera that made any lasting impression were certain plot elements of the *comédie larmoyante* and the true-to-life situations of the *opéra comique;* these Italian *opera buffa* incorporated and adapted wholeheartedly, creating from them a new genre of opera that lay between the tragic and the comic: the semi-serious. A paradoxical situation arose, which persisted into the nineteenth century: while Italy was still universally acknowledged as the natural home of opera, it was progressively falling out of step with the way France and Germany were marching. In those countries, the impact of instrumental music and the idea that "real joy is a serious thing" were making music a means of uplifting mankind. However, in Italy at this time instrumental music counted for less and less, and the use of opera for social criticism was virtually unheard of. It is as if Italy had become so conditioned to the exportation of its composers and their music that all developments and advances from outside were considered irrelevant. Somewhat later, in 1817, when Spohr was traveling in Italy he remarked on the poor quality of playing there. In Naples he met Niccolò Zingarelli (1752–1837), the composer and director of the conservatory, and reported him as saying, concerning Mozart:

> "Yes, he . . . was not deficient in talent, but he lived too short a time to cultivate it in a proper manner; if he could only have continued to study ten years longer then he would have been able to write something good."[1]

The best Italian operas in this period are not *opere serie* The simplification of harmonic language necessary to earn the approval of a popular

1. Spohr, *Autobiography*, II, p. 17

Italian audience effectively deprived composers of the means to explore the darker sides of operatic emotion. Thus, the plot of Cimarosa's most celebrated *opera seria,* entitled *Gli Orazi ed i Curiazi,* 1796, concerns the age-old conflict between love and duty: in a battle between two rival families, the heroine's brother kills her husband. At the beginning of the following *recitativo accompagnato,* Sabina discovers her husband's body:

Example XXII–1: D. CIMAROSA, *Gli Orazi,* No. 19

The brother and sister then sing a duet, during which she ultimately provokes him to kill her as well.

Example XXII–2: D. CIMAROSA, *Gli Orazi,* No. 19

When the brother, overcome by anger at her taunts, kills Sabina, the crowd celebrates his victory over the enemy. However, overcome with remorse, he rushes off, to the following music:

Example XXII–3: D. CIMAROSA, *Gli Orazi,* No. 20

This is a typical *opera seria* plot, affording opportunities for nobility, despair, and tragedy in music; but Cimarosa, arguably the greatest composer of Italian opera alive in the 1790s, can do no more than create pretty, major-mode clichés, where there should have been devastating dramatic impact. The popular musical language of the time in Italy, the language that Cimarosa spoke so well, is not the language of tragedy but of sentimental comedy, and because this was the only language the Italian audiences understood, the statuesque nobility of Gluck's latest style, however successful in Paris and Vienna, could make no headway there.

THE FLOURISHING *OPERA BUFFA*

It was quite otherwise in comic opera, with its admixture of gentle melancholy, sympathetic tears, and laughter. The two outstanding masters of the last twenty years of the century were Giovanni Paisiello and Domenico Cimarosa, both of whom excelled in either *seria* or *buffa*. For us their immortality rests in the latter. Paisiello's most famous work is the sentimental comedy entitled *Nina, ossia La pazza per amore* (Nina, or Mad for Love) of 1787, but he had already made his reputation with *Il barbiere di Siviglia* (The Barber of Seville) in 1782. This setting of Petrosellini's adaptation of Beaumarchais's play was first heard in St. Petersburg, a city which, during the reign of Catherine the Great (1729–96), supported a thriving Italian opera, usually placed an Italian in charge of the opera theater, and commissioned many new works. It held the stage so strongly for thirty years that when Rossini wanted to compose his own *Barber* he wrote to old Paisiello saying that he intended no slight. The two operas stand up well to comparison. Petrosellini's adaptation is closer to Beaumarchais than Rossini's libretto. Thus the opening of the Paisiello does not need the rather silly comedy of Rossini's band of musicians, and Paisiello's Rosina is a lady, as is Mozart's immortal Countess. Rossini's Rosina, who announces herself as a self-possessed and scheming baggage, is hardly Countess material and seems far more likely to lead the Count a merry dance, rather than ever allow him to deceive her.

Paisiello's score abounds with the verve of the early symphony's first movement—there is never a dull moment—and although much of the action takes place in recitative, the pace is such that there is no sense of *longueur*. The story concerns Count Almaviva,[2] who loves Rosina, the ward of an old curmudgeon, Dr. Bartolo. Since the Count wishes to be sure of being loved for himself alone, rather than for his wealth, title, and position, he has disguised himself as a poor student, Lindoro. Figaro, a former servant of the Count, helps to plan the elopement in the nick of time, for Bartolo intends to marry Rosina himself for her money, aided by Don Basilio, her music teacher. The plot involves

2. His name means "lively spirit" and thus Rossini's opening scene, which makes him look a fool, is misjudged.

disguises and deceptions and is one of the most ingenious comedies in Western literature. Over half the numbers in this score are ensembles, Paisiello saving the largest of them for the conclusion so that there is a real climax toward the end. He uses the voices in blocks but is also adept at the comic effect resulting from four or five voices in rapid interchange. Just before the final dénouement, there is a quintet. The Notary, whom Don Basilio had brought along to conclude the marriage between Rosina and Bartolo, has just married the Count and Rosina, with Don Basilio, who can always be bribed, as witness. Commenting on the fact that money can always work miracles, the five voices split into two groups, the high voices—Rosina, soprano, and the Count, tenor—against the low voices—Figaro, the Notary, and Don Basilio, all baritones. Bringing the five voices together again, Paisiello then creates an antiphonal effect between the groups (Example XXII–4), alternating two eighth notes. After two such exchanges, the time interval becomes reduced to a single eighth-note alternation, and finally sixteenth notes are introduced. The delicious effect (also used by Mozart) is over in a flash, but fortunately, it is, like everything in this style, repeated at least once more.

Example XXII–4: G. PAISIELLO, *Il barbiere di Siviglia,* Finale, Act II

In another quintet, one of the highlights of Beaumarchais's brilliant stagecraft, Don Basilio unexpectedly appears and is sent home to bed by Rosina, the Count, Figaro, and Bartolo, who has been temporarily deceived. In Example XXII–5 on p. 401 we see the comic effect of Paisiello's writing reinforcing the comic effect in the plot, as the audience has just been transported from a moment of tense uncertainty to the relaxation of knowing that all is well—for the time being.

Two excerpts from this opera deserve mention. The first (*ACM* 54) is a comic trio between Dr. Bartolo and two of his servants, named Wideawake and Young'un (*Lo Svegliato* and *Giovanetto*) because Wideawake is always half asleep and Young'un is an old, old man. To help the Count defeat Bartolo, Figaro the surgeon/barber, has surreptitiously given Wideawake a sleeping potion and Young'un a sneezing powder. Low comedy perhaps, but effective. In his setting Rossini did not use this scene, possibly because he could see no way in which he might improve on Paisiello's work.

The second excerpt (*ACM* 55) is a short *Cavatina* for Rosina with which the first act of the opera concludes. The influence of Paisiello's Rosina upon Mozart's Rosina, who has now been married to the Count for a few years, has been mentioned, but the similarity between this *Cavatina,* composed in 1782, and the Countess's opening *Cavatina* from *The Marriage of Figaro* (*ACM* 66) is really quite striking. The key is identical; the pairing of wind instruments and the way they are used is

Example XXII–5: G. PAISIELLO, *Il barbiere di Siviglia,* Quintet, Act II

the same; and the initial shape of the melody is similar, not simply in the opening phrase but in the whole first sentence. Paisiello's and Mozart's conception of Rosina's character is not shared by Rossini, who sees Rosina in a more vulgar light.

Domenico Cimarosa's *Il matrimonio segreto* (The Secret Marriage) was first presented in Vienna in February 1792, just two months after Mozart's death. It pleased the Emperor Leopold so much that he first ordered

Example XXII–6: D. CIMAROSA, *Il matrimonio segreto,* Act I, Scene 3, Aria

dinner for the whole cast, then demanded a complete repeat of the opera—the longest encore in history, it is said—and gave the composer a gift of money almost equal to two years of Mozart's salary, plus a diamond-studded snuffbox.

Unlike Paisiello's *Barbiere,* the pace of Cimarosa's *Secret Marriage* is leisurely. The harmony tends toward excessive simplicity with tonic and dominant harmony and perfect cadential figures in the bass reiterated again and again; the harmonic rhythm is slow. In those places where there would appear to be a quickening of harmonic rhythm, i.e., in scalar passages, the voices and instruments are almost invariably set in unison, thus avoiding making explicit in the harmony what was merely implied. Much of the work proceeds in ensembles, and Cimarosa gives variety to both arias and ensembles by making them sectional and changing tempo frequently. Yet the attraction of the work is undeniable, and *The Secret Marriage* is one of the few eighteenth-century comic operas, apart from Mozart's, to be staged in modern times. In Cimarosa's grateful melodic style, in his rhythmic verve, and in his manner of setting the voice in monotone against a melodic orchestra (Example XXII–6) he shows himself to be Rossini's progenitor, and Rossini himself, when asked which was his favorite among his own operas, jestingly replied, "*Il matrimonio segreto.*"

THE TRAGÉDIE LYRIQUE

Christoph Willibald Gluck dominated serious Parisian opera through the Revolution and well into the nineteenth century, even though he himself had left Paris late in 1779, following the failure of his last opera, *Echo et Narcisse*. So completely had Gluck effected a unique amalgam of styles in his great French operas of the 1770s that neither the Italians nor the Germans could see how much they had contributed to them. They made no impression whatsoever in Italy and only received a *succès d'estime* in Germany. Niccolò Piccinni, the man summoned to Paris to do battle with Gluck (see p. 193), remained there after the latter's departure and produced a succession of operas in which he too donned the French dress of accompanied recitative, active chorus, and reduced arias with fair but short-lived success. It will be recalled that Gluck had abandoned his setting of *Roland* as soon as he heard that Piccinni was working with the same libretto. Piccinni's *Roland* had been produced in 1778, and the sister opera, *Atys,* in 1780. Both these works were composed to revisions by Marmontel of the Quinault librettos, originally set a hundred years earlier by Lully. The most successful of Piccinni's French operas was *Didon* (1783), also to words by Marmontel. The libretto of this opera is skillfully worked to invest the simple old story with a sense of inexorable tragedy leading to an unavoidable climax. The character of Dido herself is marvelously drawn and her words are of such poetic strength that they can be read without the music. Unlike Gluck's, however, Piccinni's music lacks the power to equal the subject or the words, and although the composer was so deeply moved during his working on the score by Dido's plight that he wept over it, he nevertheless did not possess the talent or the language to transfer his noble simplicity into noble tragedy. The success he achieved with *Didon* was as dependent on the acting and singing of the woman who played the title role as on his compositional skills.

Antonio Salieri had the great good fortune to enjoy Gluck's favor, and his opera *Les Danaïdes* (1784) shows that he deserved it. Here, the conflict between love for a father and love for a husband is turned into a blood-and-thunder opera of such extreme violence that one marvels that Salieri attempted the subject. (At the same time one shudders to think what a movie producer would do with it today.) In order to exorcise his hatred for his brother, Danaus gathers together all fifty of his nephews, and under the pretense of ending the quarrel between their father and him, gives each nephew one of his fifty daughters in marriage. Then he commands his daughters to kill their husbands on the wedding night. They agree, but one daughter, Hypermnestre, helps her husband, Lyncée, to escape, and he returns, kills Danaus and his daughters, the Danaïds. Hell opens up and swallows them, and in the last scene we see their torments.

Of course, to modern ears Salieri's language is not equal to the task the libretto imposes, but one wonders whether Gluck's would have been, or even Mozart's. The eighteenth-century audience had none of the problems that we have with the setting, since they recognized that Salieri was taking them to the limits of the musically acceptable.[3] They were content to peek into Hell's open door, whereas we might want to go right in and look around. But Salieri's language is a great deal more complex than Piccinni's and his technique more sophisticated. His orchestra is large and his use of color selective. The strings form both the foreground and the background of the orchestra, and they depend on rapid scales, arpeggios, and tremolos for unusual effects. The diminished seventh is the chord that is most frequently used to express extremes of emotion, and other seventh chords are staple fare. Salieri's harmonic language can deal with modulation in more extreme keys than Piccinni's. Example XXII–7 shows a few measures of recitative in which Hypermnestre pleads with her father for the life of her husband.

In the last scene of the opera, set in the palace, the chorus describes what is about to happen. They say: "The earth trembles; the heavens thunder; do you hear the thunder resound? Hell is opening to engulf in its deep vaults this place of blood. Let us flee . . ." Then the stage directions read:

> The palace, shattered by thunder and devoured by flames, crumbles and disappears. The scene changes into a representation of Hell. The Tartarus [treated here as a river] flowing with waves of blood on its banks, and in the middle of the stage is Danaus, chained to a rock; his bloody entrails are

3. Eighteenth-century aesthetic dictates that whatever the dramatic circumstances and the expressive need, the music accompanying the drama must always be beautiful. As Mozart succinctly said: "The music must never cease to be music."

Example XXII–7: A. SALIERI, *Les Danaïdes,* Act IV, Scene 1

> being eaten by a vulture, and his head is repeatedly struck by thunderbolts. Some of the daughters of Danaus are chained together in groups and tormented by Demons and eaten up by serpents; others, pursued by Furies, fill the stage with their movements and with their screams. A rain of fire falls forever.

The modern reader, used to all the resources of the cinema of fantasy, must wonder how such directions could be realized on the eighteenth-century stage. The answer must be sought in the power of suggestion of the choreographed movement, and in the extent of imagination which the audience brings to the performance.

Beaumarchais intended his libretto of *Tarare* (1787) for Gluck because he knew of Gluck's interest in reforming opera, an interest he shared. But with Gluck's refusal he offered it to Salieri, who went to Paris and lived with the author and his family while working on the opera. Beaumarchais had definite views why he, a music lover, found opera boring. He said: "Notre Opéra pue de musique" (Our opera stinks of music). "The fault of our grand operas is too much music in the music. . . . Whenever the actor sings, the action stops and whenever the action stops the interest drops."[4] Tarare, a virtuous, humbly born soldier, has a good wife, Astasie, who is desired by a tyrannical king, Atar. After many vicissitudes, Atar kills himself, and the reluctant Tarare is named king. Astasie's aria in Act IV shows Salieri's mastery of Gluckian techniques and Beaumarchais's approval of them in the way the recitative and air intermingle, simply and naturally. Perhaps the most striking thing about this opera, however, is Beaumarchais's idea of writing a prologue in which Nature and the Genius of Fire discuss human existence, and ask the impassive, unborn souls of the main characters of the opera what they wish to be. It is hard to imagine a greater blow to the very roots of French classical tragedy than the prelude to this drama. Beaumarchais, ever the gadfly and proto-revolutionary, has Nature say to the unborn soldier, Tarare, and the unborn despot, Atar, "Children, embrace. Equal by nature, how removed from that state will you be in society!"

On the eve of the Revolution, in June 1787, *Tarare* was produced in Paris. Its egalitarian sentiments were in the air; its subject matter—the overthrow of a tyrant—was apposite; its moral—the triumph of virtue and the virtue of loyalty—was popular. All these, together with the excellence of the musical setting, made it a great success. It has been said that every political regime could find support for its ideals in this opera, whether democratic, royalist, or republican.[5] Six months later, early in 1788, the opera was presented in Vienna under the title *Axur,*

4. Beaumarchais, *Préface de Tarare*. Cited by Arthur Pugin, ed. "Tarare" in *Chefs d'Oeuvres Classiques de l'Opéra français* (Reprint, New York, 1971), pp. 3–4.
5. Rudolph Angermüller. Preface to Salieri's, *Tarare* (Munich, 1978), I, p. vi.

ré d'Ormus. Lorenzo da Ponte had made some adaptations and translated the words into Italian, and Salieri had revised the music. The process of changing a modern French opera into an Italian *opera seria* involved considerable rethinking, and resulted in the removal of the Prologue with the unborn souls and the excision of Beaumarchais's political pin-pricks, as well as much musical remodeling.

The Revolution affected the whole of musical life in Paris and throughout France. The massive musical occasions organized for political celebrations, in which hundreds, even thousands, of performers took part, must have been impressive.[6] Their effect was not slow to penetrate the theater. Operas built around revolutionary themes received government support, and many items in the repertoire were weeded out if they were thought to have a corrupting influence on the public. The prominence of the Opéra, which was renamed the Théâtre des Arts, declined as the *tragédie lyrique,* with all its time-honored traditions, gave way to the *opéra comique*. During the Reign of Terror (1793–94) many artists were frightened by the threat of the guillotine into abandoning their artistic standards in order to prove their political orthodoxy to the revolutionary demagogues who held the power of life and death.[7] Under such conditions many strange things were produced, one of the most curious being an *opéra comique* entitled *The Congress of Kings* (1794), which concludes with the Kings symbolically embracing the Revolution and the cause of the populace, and which was worked on by no less than twelve composers, including some of the greatest names of the time: Cherubini, Grétry, and Méhul.

THE EFFECT OF THE REVOLUTION ON THE *OPÉRA COMIQUE*

During the years immediately before the Revolution, Grétry's *opéras comiques* were most popular. This kind of opera had hardly changed since Rousseau's *Le Devin du village,* with its emphasis on short num-

6. It was not only the Councils of the Revolution that sought massive numbers of participants in their celebrations. The First Handel Commemoration had taken place in London in 1784, only five years before the Fall of the Bastille. This was a time in which vast dimensions, huge performing bodies, and stupefying volume of sound were equated with sublimity.

7. Antoine Lavoisier and twenty-three others were tried before a revolutionary tribunal in the morning, declared guilty of aristocratic connections, and guillotined in the afternoon. He asked for time to write down the results of his scientific experiments, which was denied. His defense described him as one of the most brilliant men of France. The chairman of the tribunal replied, "La Révolution n'a pas besoin de savants" (the Revolution does not need learned men). It was observed at the time that it took but a second to cut off his head, but the whole of France would not produce such another in a hundred years. How vulnerable to such charges were musicians who, until five years before, had been dependent upon aristocratic patronage!

bers, charming and naive melodic structures, the most basic harmony, and the simplest textures. Grétry's *Richard Coeur-de-lion* was first produced in 1784. Like all this composer's work, it is musically slight, but it is important on several counts nevertheless. It deals with the rescue of King Richard I of England from captivity in Germany by his friend, the minstrel, Blondel. The period is that of the Crusades. Recognized as one of the first examples of the historical opera, it was also one of the earliest examples of the rescue opera, in which a hero or heroine in the greatest peril is saved. The peril may be at the hands of a villain or from the forces of nature, and as such it is a universal aspect of dramatic motivation. What makes the genre special at this time was the fact that musicians, playwrights, and audiences recognized the possibility of relating the subject matter on stage directly to contemporary events. Thus the drama became an obvious allegory and the dramatic events could touch the audience more deeply.

Richard Coeur-de-lion falls between two stools. Its libretto contains allusions to the kind of problems that brought about the Revolution: one character tells that his father was killed by a nobleman for shooting a rabbit on his property; and there is talk of the equality of people whose condition in life is very different. Yet the overall moral of the opera serves to glorify loyalty to the monarch. Hence, after *Richard* enjoyed success for a few years, it was soon out of favor, and Grétry had to defend himself against attack on the grounds of his aristocratic associations.

With the Revolution a number of changes in the *opéra comique* that had been evolving for some time became apparent. Monsigny's *Le Déserteur* (1769) with its sentimental plot and serious overtones illustrates a tendency to deepen the subject matter of the *opéra comique* as well as to complicate its musical techniques. Given the inclusion of spoken dialogue and simpler musical material, it was obvious to revolutionary government and to musicians alike that the *opéra comique* was the best possible means to reach the public. During the 1790s there were two theaters in Paris that staged such operas, one called the Opéra Comique National and the other the Théâtre Feydeau, and almost all important operatic activity was carried on at one or the other of them. In 1801 the two merged.

One aspect of the literature of the period is the cultivation of horror to an extent not experienced in European history for close to two hundred years. The most obvious manifestations of this are the ballad and the "Gothic" novel. In opera its effects are to be seen in the use of subject matter dealing with dungeons and darkness, the oppression of women (including the imprisonment in castle towers of those who resist sexual advances), and the evil lust for power or money, or both. Librettists and composers used such subjects with delight for the opportunity of developing new and ever more forceful effects. There can be no doubt that Salieri's *Les Danaïdes* was chosen, at least in part, because its forty-

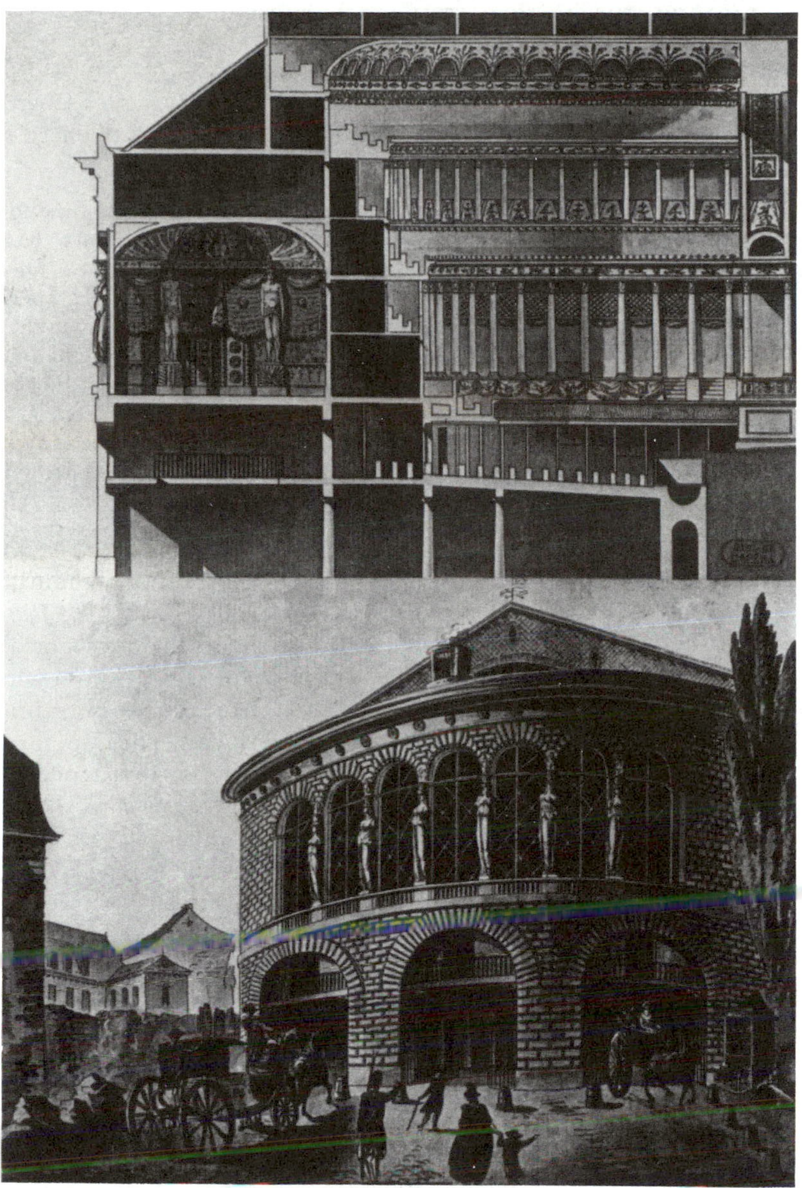

The Théâtre Feydeau in Paris, 1791; engravings of the exterior and a cross section of the theater; the latter clearly shows the relationship of seats and stage, and also the magnificent decor of the interior. (Paris: Bibliothèque de l'Opéra)

nine murders and fifty killings (49 nephews, 49 daughters, and Danaus) would raise a potent *frisson d'horreur*. The other powerful way of exciting strong emotion was to use stage effects and scenery in grandiose ways—in this period the grandiose was almost always mistaken for the sublime.

The Parisian operas of the early 1790s had to vie with the events of the streets, with the guillotine hard at work; composers and librettists mounted impressive competition. Thus, in the last act of Cherubini's *Lodoïska* (1791) the villain's castle is under attack with the hero inside, and at this point the stage directions read as follows:

> The back wall of the gallery crumbles and opens the rest of the fortifications to the view; various towers connected by bridges all seem to be aflame. The fire is wreaking enormous damage. All at once the stage is filled with warriors, Tartars against Poles, and on the ramparts other fighting soldiers are to be seen . . . At the height of this tumult the flames reach the tower where Lodoiska is imprisoned; part of the tower crashes down. Lodoiska, surrounded by flames, is about to be burned when Floreski [the hero] at the top of the fortress, crosses a bridge which leads to his loved one. He flies across to her, grabs her, and tries to return the way he came, but at that moment the fire destroys the bridge and the two lovers fall into the arms of the Tartar soldiers . . .

The moral of the opera is a common one for the period. The villain's punishment is hateful captivity for having extinguished all humanity in his soul. Cherubini's opera *Eliza* (1794) has as a subtitle *The Journey to the Glaciers of Mount St. Bernard*, and at its climax there is a storm scene in which an avalanche sweeps the hero into a precipice—from which he is safely dug out. Le Sueur's opera *La Caverne* is a story of brigands whose lair is a cave which collapses for the climax. The taste for scenic effects in French *grande opéra* of the 1840s and in Wagnerian opera of the 1850s and later has its origins in the French *opéra comique* of the 1790s.

The *opéra comique* has little of the comical about it at this time. Its subject matter has become as serious as that of the *tragédie lyrique,* and there is now little to distinguish the humbler medium, except for the spoken dialogue and an occasional comic character. Composers recognized that this genre afforded them the most varied means of dealing with the alliance of word and music and drama. The *tragédie lyrique* joined word and music in two ways—recitative and air—and the differences between these two were minimized as much as possible. The *opéra comique* had the extreme contrast of the melodic air with the spoken word, and in addition composers used the accompanied recitative as well as melodrama, i.e., the spoken word interspersed with affective, descriptive music for the full orchestra.

The two most important composers of opera in the 1790s were Etienne Méhul and Luigi Cherubini, but in fact they were only the brightest stars of a galaxy of active and popular composers that included Rodolphe Kreutzer, the violinist and composer, whose setting of *Lodoïska* (1791) was more popular in Paris than Cherubini's; Jean-François Le Sueur, the teacher of Berlioz and a man stronger in imagination and influence than in the technical command of music; André-Erneste-Modeste Grétry; Pierre Gaveaux (1761–1825), the singer and composer; Henri-Montan Berton (1767–1844); Nicolas-Marie Dalayrac (1753–1809); Charles-Simon Catel; and many others.

To Cherubini falls the honor of having written the only opera of the 1790s (apart from Mozart's) to survive on the modern stage. His *Médée* (1797) is, like so many great works, a culmination, a gathering together of a number of historical strands. It is an *opéra comique*—that is to say, it has, properly, spoken dialogue.[8] Yet it seems to gather together the myth-based *tragédie lyrique,* and the Gluckian opera of the 1770s, as well as the allegorical opera of the Revolution.

The story concerns the sorceress Medea, who helped Jason capture the Golden Fleece, and had two children by him. Now she is being abandoned so that Jason can marry again, and her two little sons are to be taken from her. In her fury she exacts a terrible revenge, killing Jason's bride-to-be by sending her poisoned wedding presents, and finally killing her own children. The plot can be interpreted as a protest against such treatment of a mother, and certainly, despite the horror of the situation, both the libretto and the music create sympathy for Medea. In 1797, the plot could also be taken as an allegory of the mad Revolution/mother killing her own children: it should be remembered that Danton, Robespierre, St. Just, Marat, and a host of other revolutionary leaders had ended their lives on the guillotine. At the end of the opera Jason is left with neither bride nor children. By 1800, anyone thinking of *Médée* as an allegory might see Robespierre's protégé, Napoleon, as Jason. Allegory works like that.

Many of Cherubini's contemporaries thought of him as the greatest living composer. Born in Florence, he was a pupil of Giuseppe Sarti (1729–1802) and after spending two years in London, he arrived in Paris in 1786, where he was to make his home for the rest of his life. If aspects of the French Violin School penetrated into Beethoven's writing for that instrument, then with at least as much justification it can be said that Beethoven's style of the early 1800s is prefigured by Cherubini's in the 1790s. His melodic gift may not be as strong as that of some of his contemporaries, but in all other ways his skill as a composer is far superior to any of them. Cherubini was a master of counterpoint, of harmony, and of the orchestra, and he and Mozart stand alone as the two opera composers of the time with sufficient technical ability and artistic *savoir faire* to be able to accomplish what they set out to do. His *Médée* deserves to hold the stage as the best representative of a style of opera otherwise hardly remembered. The score of the opera is rich in variety and texture, and is particularly distinguished by Cherubini's fertile invention of rhythmic figures which serve to identify and unify sections of the music. (Example XXII-8 on p. 412 shows the upper string parts of mm. 21–32 of the overture.) The contrapuntal anticipations in the viola and second violin of the opening melody in the first violins give

8. That it has been heard latterly as an Italian opera, with sung recitatives instead of spoken dialogue, is a modern example of the tyranny of thinking of opera as an exclusively Italian art form.

Example XXII–8: L. CHERUBINI, *Médée,* Overture

an unusual richness to the whole. In the next example, we see an interlocking figure from mm. 44–46, which began as an accompanying figure to the first violin's melody (see above) and has become the principal

Example XXII–9: L. CHERUBINI, *Médée,* Overture

melody in close imitation.[9] Cherubini's use of figures allows him to intensify textures. In Example XXII–10 the first and second violin parts of an aria interlock in an extremely satisfying way, but a few measures later the flute is added (see 10b).

Example XXII–10: L. CHERUBINI, *Medée,* Act I, Scene 1, Dirce's Aria

9. Example IX-4 on p.159 shows the embryonic beginnings of this imitative technique used symphonically by Cannabich.

Cherubini's handling of the orchestra combines great textural richness with clarity, yet he can also use economy to enable individual tone colors to emerge. (See Example XXII–11, the first few measures from the Introduction to Acts II and III of *Médée*.)

The melody of Medea's first-act aria in which she excites the audience's sympathy has many Mozartian turns, and the accompaniment exemplifies many of the points already mentioned. As a whole, it is an

Example XXII–11: L. CHERUBINI, *Medée,*

a. Act II, Introduction

b. Act III, Introduction

(D'un côté, et dans une partie du fond, le théâtre représente une montagne garnie de rochers et d'arbres touffus. Une grotte paroît au pied; il en sort une source qui tombe avec rapidité. Sur la croupe de la montagne, dans le fond, s'élève un temple dont la porte est ouverte, et où l'on voit brûler une lampe. Un escalier conduit à ce temple, et à la droite un chemin tortueux et escarpé, conduit du temple au sommet de la montagne. De l'autre côté, s'élève une aile du palais de Créon, des jardins et des édifices.)

example of the manner in which Cherubini's dramatic aims are completely matched by his compositional skill; the result is high artistic achievement.

From the turmoil of the Revolution, French opera during the last two decades of the century emerges as the most imaginatively experimental opera in all of Europe. It reaches beyond the confines of the theater in its striving for grandiose effects; it puts aside much of the pretty simplicity of the older *opéra comique* and becomes satisfyingly complex, both in its librettos and in its music; and perhaps most important, it ceases to be mere entertainment and strives to better mankind.

THE *SINGSPIEL*

Not until well into the nineteenth century did German-speaking countries give up their love affair with Italian opera. The big courts maintained Italian opera companies, and even those theaters presenting opera in German for the most part took their repertoire from Italy or from France with translated librettos. The power of the well-established Italian composers in the major cities of Europe to hinder or totally block any operatic activity that might be seen as against their interest is well documented. The biographies of Mozart and Haydn present enough cases to prove that point.

Although serious German opera hardly existed, the *Singspiel* flourished, springing from two distinct traditions. In North and Central Germany, the eighteenth-century *Singspiel* developed, as has been said, first from an infusion of elements from the English Ballad Opera, and secondly from the importation of subjects from the French *opéra comique*. It is a measure of the increased stature of this tradition that Goethe wrote a number of plays for composition as *Singspiele* in order to explore the relationship between word and music.

Among the prominent composers of *Singspiele* in the 1780s is Johann André, whose works were staged mostly in Berlin, where he had been appointed Kapellmeister in 1776. Goethe thought highly of his work and asked him to set his play *Erwin und Elmire* in 1775. Most curious is the fact that he set the Bretzner libretto entitled *Belmont und Constanze, oder Die Entführung aus dem Serail* (May 1781) at about the very same time Mozart was beginning to work on the adaptation of the same libretto for his *Entführung*.[10]

A similar coincidence in 1798 has Reichardt in Berlin and Zumsteeg in Stuttgart setting the same libretto, an adaptation by Friedrich Wilhelm Gotter (1746–97) of Shakespeare's *The Tempest,* entitled *Die Geisterinsel* (The Isle of Spirits) within four months of each other. Gotter's preferred composer would have been Mozart. This libretto exemplifies the fashion for setting "magic" subjects, a fashion as strong in Vienna as in Berlin. In Vienna the *Singspiel* had the advantage of being a native tradition that was treated by some significant composers, and enjoyed the support of the emperor. In 1778, as a part of his plans to foster a strong nationalistic spirit within his disparate realms, Joseph II had ordered the founding of a National *Singspiel* Theater. The first work presented in the Burgtheater, the new home for popular musical plays, was entitled *Die Bergknappen* (The Miners) by Ignaz Umlauf (1746–96). Because of a dearth of native Austrian works to stage, the new *Singspiel* Theater turned quickly to translations of French and Italian works, but the

10. The author, Bretzner, published a protest against Mozart's unauthorized use of his work which is famous because of its opening: "A certain individual, Mozart by name, in Vienna has had the audacity to misuse my drama *Belmont und Constanze,* for an opera text . . ." Had he but known!

The elegant facade of the Kärntnertor Theater in Vienna, beside the city walls and the gate from which it takes it name. (Historisches Museum der Stadt Wien)

emperor valiantly tried to persevere with his original idea. In 1781 he asked Salieri, the Kapellmeister of his Italian opera, to write a German opera, and the result was *Der Rauchfangkehrer* (The Chimney Sweep) of 1781, a successful work which Mozart surely knew. The company and the voices for which Salieri wrote were those for whom Mozart tailored *Die Entführung,* and so Salieri also uses Cavalieri and her "glib gullet" and Ludwig Fischer with his deep bass voice and phenomenal range.

In 1783 the National *Singspiel* Theater company was disbanded, and although performances of German opera were started again in 1785 in the Kärntnertor Theater, they only continued until 1788, when the company was disbanded for good. During these years Carl von Dittersdorf produced a number of scintillating works with great success, beginning with his most famous *Doktor und Apotheker* (Doctor and Apothecary) of 1786, and followed by a number of others. He commanded a variety of styles, and with equal ease could write into his score a street song or an Italian aria. Overall he displayed the Viennese fluency of melodic style, which Mozart shared, and which is so inimitable. Coming as they do after 1786, Dittersdorf's *Singspiele* are dependent upon the construction of complex scenes in which the music carries the action forward; they are much less dependent upon spoken dialogue. Whether the example of his friend Mozart was an influence upon

Dittersdorf is impossible to say, but his capacity for building an ensemble Finale like the one at the conclusion of the first act of *Hieronymus Knicker* (1789) is exceptional. He concludes the entire work, however, not with such a Finale but with a Vaudeville.

With the closing of the *Singspiel* Theater, that type of entertainment moved into theaters outside the city walls, such as the Theater auf der Wieden, where Emanuel Schikaneder (1751–1812) became manager in 1789, and where he produced *The Magic Flute* in 1791. Theaters like this catered to a lower class of audience, much given to elaborate stage effects and farcical comedies.

A number of composers tried to capitalize on the success of *The Magic Flute,* including Peter von Winter (1754–1825) whose opera *Das Labyrint* (1798) attempted to provide a sequel to *The Magic Flute*. Paul Wranitsky (1756–1808) wrote an *Oberon* (1789) which deserves mention as part of this fashion.

The other strain of Viennese *Singspiel* is much more homely and comfortable and full of light comedy. Its most famous exemplars are *Die Schwestern von Prag* (The Sisters of Prague; 1794) of Wenzel Müller (1767–1835), and *Der Dorfbarbier* (The Village Barber; 1796) of Johann Schenk (1753–1836), which was perhaps the most popular of all.

OPERATIC ENTERTAINMENT IN LONDON

Italian opera preserved its role at the center of musical entertainment in London. The Italian colony was thriving, sustaining composers and librettists. Luigi Cherubini lived happily among them during the years 1784–86, producing two successful operas there, and Haydn's last opera, *L'anima del filosofo,* was written on a commission from London. Apart from Italian opera, however, musical theater steadily drifted toward the cruder kind of entertainment typified by the pantomime, comic songs and character pieces. Indeed, there is a curious parallel to be seen between the situation in London and that of the Viennese *Singspiel,* except that London's theaters never produced a *Magic Flute*.

William Shield (1748–1829), a violin and viola player and a pupil of Avison, did not produce his first opera, *The Flitch of Bacon,* until 1778, but it was an immediate success. From 1772 he composed primarily for Covent Garden. He wrote a number of full-length works with spoken dialogue, as well as afterpieces, those one-act operas that served to conclude an evening's dramatic entertainment. Many of his operas mix original pieces with borrowed material, and much of his borrowed material was taken from the folk repertoire. Shield had a gift for writing short, melodic songs, but he had little sense of the theater, nor could he perceive the need for modern opera to create drama through the music.

As the development of English opera in the seventeenth century had

This elaborate title page was printed in 1798 for Michael Kelly's opera *Blue Beard or Female Curiosity*. The music for this work was partly composed by Kelly and partly selected by him from the works of Paisiello. The pastiche was very successful and was performed 64 times in one season.

suffered a crushing setback with the early death of Henry Purcell in 1695 at the age of thirty-six, so English musical theater lost two of its greatest talents prematurely almost a hundred years later. Thomas Linley, Jr. (1756–78) was a precocious composer, who, at the time of his death at the age of twenty-two, had many compositions to his credit. He had studied in England with William Boyce (1711–79) and violin with Nardini in Italy, where he met and became friends with Mozart. Stephen Storace (1762–96) realized much more of his talent than Linley had time to do. He was of Italian extraction, and studied in Italy and probably also had lessons from Mozart.[11] Stephen had two Italian operas produced in Vienna, but in 1787 the Storace family returned home to London,[12] where his first successful stage work was produced in 1789. *The Haunted Tower* is an opera more "Gothic" in name than in substance. It is a pastiche that mixes original numbers by Storace with songs by other popular composers of the day—Pleyel, Paisiello, Sarti,

11. His sister, Nancy, was Mozart's first Susanna, and there is much to suggest that Mozart was more than a little in love with her.

12. The departure of the Storaces undoubtedly led Mozart to think of following them to London, and perhaps here is the origin of the last three symphonies.

Linley, and Martini—as well as Welsh, English, and French folksongs. Of considerably greater substance is *The Pirates* (1792), which is perhaps Storace's masterpiece. Here the music ranges from the tuneful, short, strophic song to the aria with extensive coloratura, and to ensembles employing the devices of imitative counterpoint. The writing is always professional and competent, sounding like pale Mozart. It is clear, however, that in writing in this manner Storace is aiming at the London audience, and although he did much to raise that audience's standards, he was capable of so much more than they demanded.

As the eighteenth century closed there can be no doubt that London's position as one of the world's greatest centers of opera was lost. With the benefit of hindsight it is also clear that London in 1800 had already turned into the theatrical desert which persisted throughout so much of the nineteenth century. In the constant oscillation of the balance of power, Paris had become the place where innovation and imagination were to be found, and the influence of Parisian opera of the 1790s was dominant everywhere in Europe throughout the nineteenth century.

PART VI

Haydn, the Acknowledged Master

CHAPTER XXIII

The Last Years at Esterháza: 1780–90

DAILY LIFE AND RESPONSIBILITIES

By the beginning of this decade, Haydn had worked for nearly twenty years for the Esterházy family, and while the financial and artistic rewards were sufficient to elicit his lasting loyalty to Prince Nikolaus and to the princely house, his job was exhausting in its reponsibilities, and restrictive by its very nature. Thus it was that during this time Haydn began to feel more and more that his duties as a servant were chafing, and expressed his increasing need to be his own master. All through the 1780s he tried to change the circumstances of his life, little suspecting how suddenly and completely the following decade would see the realization of his dreams.

Late in 1779, it will be remembered, the opera theater and the ballroom at Esterháza had burned down with the loss of musical instruments, several unique Haydn manuscripts, theatrical costumes, and much more. This disaster obviously shortened Haydn's winter stay in Vienna and took him back into Hungary. His relationship with his wife has already been described, and his marriage had never been happy. But life at Esterháza afforded some consolations since he did not hesitate to look elsewhere for the comfort his wife had never provided, and it is possible that he had, by now, formed an attachment to Luigia Polzelli, the wife of an elderly violinist, who had joined the musical staff as a singer the previous March. At the age of forty-nine, Haydn was obviously deeply in love and over ten years later he wrote to her from London on 4 August 1791, after the death of her husband:

> . . . The poor man had suffered enough. Dear Polzelli, perhaps, perhaps the time will come, which we both so often dreamt of, when four eyes shall be closed. Two are closed, but the other two—enough of all this, it shall be as God wills . . .[1]

1. *Haydn Correspondence,* p. 117.

and on 13 December 1791:

> . . . . for I esteem and love you as I did on the very first day . . .[2]

Good Catholic that he was, divorce never entered his mind.

The other two eyes—those of Haydn's wife—closed forever in March of 1800 and in May of the same year Haydn signed this statement:

> I, the undersigned, promise to *Signora* Loisa Polzelli (in case I should consider marrying again) to take no other wife than said Loisa Polzelli . . .[3]

He left her money in his will and looked after her two sons, the second of whom may have been his. He even managed to keep her on salary for a year at Esterháza after she had been dismissed. While he would have married her in 1780 had he been able, by 1792 his tone had changed and he speaks encouragingly (and hopefully) of the possibility of her marrying again, saying "I hope. . . you will write me if you get married again, for I would like to know the name of him who is fortunate enough to have you."[4] By 1800, when he was sixty-eight, marriage had obviously lost its attractions.

Life at Esterháza continued as it had been when the opera theater was established in 1775—with the prince offering his constant guests an endless round of entertainment, which, in turn, created endless work for Haydn. The number of opera performances now averaged close to one hundred per season. Each season, an average of six new and six previously performed operas was presented. As the decade wore on, while the number of operas that were performed increased, there were fewer new operas among that number.

As was the custom of the time, every new opera had to be carefully revised by the music director. Instrumentation had to be added or deleted, depending upon the availability of instruments, and often substitute or additional parts were required as the orchestration was changed. Some arias would be cut and new arias composed to suit the voices of the available singers in Haydn's troupe. Ornamentation and cadenzas might have to be supplied.

At the same time, the demand for Haydn's compositions increased as his fame spread across Europe. In 1780 he became a member of the Philharmonic Society of Modena, Italy. In 1781, he received a commission from Spain to write music for a special Lenten service in the Cathedral of Cadiz. In the same year he entered into prolonged and very fruitful negotiations with the publisher and instrument maker William Forster of London. In 1783 he was invited to England to conduct the Professional Concerts in London. In 1784 he received a commission for

2. *Ibid.*, p. 122.
3. *Ibid.*, p. 169.
4. *Ibid.*, p. 126.

six symphonies from the *Concert de la Loge Olympique* in Paris, and a commission came from the king of Naples for some concertos for *lira organizzata,* or hurdy-gurdy. The *European Magazine* in October 1784 printed "an Account of Joseph Haydn . . ." which contains, along with a number of biographical inaccuracies, the following accurate evaluation:

> The universality of Haydn's genius cannot be more strongly proved than by the vast demand for his works all over Europe. There is not only a fashion, but also a rage for his musick; and he has continual commissions from France, England, Russsia, Holland &c . . .

and it goes on to characterize him thus:

> As a man, he is friendly, artless, and undesigning;
> As a husband, affectionate, tender, and exemplary;
> As a performer, neat, elegant, and expressive;
> As a composer, chaste, masterly, and original.[5]

Incidentally, the myth of the feud between Haydn and Emanuel Bach (see p.225) is to be found in the same article.

Haydn was becoming increasingly aware of the amenities which the civilized life of Vienna afforded. He began to taste the sweetness of life during the wintertime when he could forget that he was a servant and see himself as the equal of his prosperous middle-class and aristocratic friends. It is possible that he may have become acquainted with Mozart as early as 1781—indeed, it would be strange if he had not—although the earliest documentary evidence of their friendship is dated 1784. In that year we know that they played string quartets together, and Leopold Mozart related Haydn's famous observation that his son "is the greatest composer I know, either personally or by reputation."(*Letters,* 16 Feb. 1785) Mozart also dedicated six string quartets to him, ever after called the *Haydn* Quartets. At Mozart's urging, Haydn applied for admission to the Society of Freemasons and was admitted early in 1785.

Between 1789 and 1792 Haydn wrote a series of letters to Marianne von Genzinger, who, with her husband, the Esterházy physician, was resident in Vienna. Theirs was a comfortable relationship, based upon a musical affinity which led to something very like love in Haydn, and the concern which both he and she express when one of Haydn's letters goes astray in 1790 arouses the modern reader's curiosity. When Haydn says:

> Your Grace need have no fear, therefore, either about the past or about the future, for my friendship and the esteem in which I hold Your Grace (tender as they are) will never be reprehensible.[6]

5. Pages reproduced in facsimile in Landon *Hadyn,* II, p. 497.
6. *Haydn Correspondence,* p. 101.

he is clearly close to the borderline separating the tender from the reprehensible. And we remember the terms in which he writes to Luigia Polzelli such a short time later!

Perhaps what Haydn most needed from Frau von Genzinger is best expressed in a letter of 9 February 1790.

> Nobly born
> Most highly respected and kindest Frau von Genzinger
>
> Well, here I sit in my wilderness—forsaken—like a poor waif—almost without any human society—melancholy—full of the memories of past glorious days—yes! past alas!—and who knows when these days shall return again? Those wonderful parties? Where the whole circle is one heart, one soul—all these beautiful musical evenings—which can only be remembered, and not described—where are all these enthusiastic moments?—all gone—and gone for a long time. Your Grace mustn't be surprised that I haven't written up to now to thank you. I found everything at home in confusion, and for 3 days I didn't know if I was *Capell*-master or *Capell*-servant. Nothing could console me, my whole house was in confusion, my pianoforte which I usually love so much was perverse and disobedient, it irritated rather than calmed me, I could only sleep very little, even my dreams persecuted me; and then, just when I was happily dreaming that I was listening to the opera, *Le nozze di Figaro*, that horrible North wind woke me and almost blew my nightcap off my head; I lost 20 lbs. in weight in three days, for the good Viennese food that I had in me disappeared on the journey; alas! alas! I thought to myself as I was eating in the mess here, instead of that delicious slice of beef, a chunk of a cow 50 years old; instead of that ragout with little dumplings, an old sheep with carrots; instead of a Bohemian pheasant, a leathery joint; instead of those fine and delicate oranges, a *Dschabl* or so-called *gros Sallat* ; instead of pastry, dry apple-fritters and hazelnuts—and that's what I have to eat. Alas! alas! I thought to myself, if I could only have a little bit of what I couldn't eat up in Vienna.—Here in Estoras no one asks me: Would you like some chocolate, with milk or without? Will you take some coffee, black, or with cream? What may I offer you, my dear Haydn? Would you like a vanilla or a pineapple ice? If I only had a good piece of Parmesan cheese, especially in Lent, so that I could more easily swallow those black puddings and noodles . . .[7]

It is obvious that Haydn had had enough of the rigors of Esterháza and was becoming accustomed to the good life of Vienna. The world was beckoning to him in every conceivable way, and the temptation to leave his good Prince Nikolaus was great. During the whole decade that temptation would grow ever greater, yet Haydn consistently found the gratitude and loyalty to resist.

Whatever his feelings, Haydn was able to set them aside and find consolation or distraction in composition; his productivity continued unabated. His interest in the sonata for solo piano declined after 1780,

7. *Ibid.*, pp. 96–97.

and in the last twenty-nine years of his life he composed only eight, five during this decade. At the same time his focus was shifting from the harpsichord to the piano, and by the end of the decade his style of writing for keyboard had changed completely, becoming entirely pianistic.

THE SOLO KEYBOARD SONATAS

In 1784, Artaria published a set of three sonatas in G, B♭, and D (Hob. XVI: 40, 41, 42) dedicated to the Princess Marie Esterházy, the style of which has little precedent. They are each two-movement works of unequaled simplicity, not to say naiveté, including only one sonata form among their six movements. Of the remainder, four are variation or ternary forms involving variation, and one movement is free. It would appear that Haydn, around 1780, was experimenting with using the same theme in different ways. He is on record as saying that the most difficult thing about composition is finding the melody. In this set the first sonata's first theme is quite clearly the subject of the sonata's second movement as well.[8] Also noteworthy is the consistent and emphatic

8. When Haydn dedicated a set of six sonatas to the Misses Auenbrugger in 1780, he wrote to the publisher as follows:

> Incidentally, I consider it necessary, in order to forestall the criticism of any witlings, to print on the reverse side of the title page the following sentence, here underlined:
>
> *Avertissement*
>
> Among these 6 Sonatas there are two single movements in which the same subject occurs through several bars: the author has done this intentionally, to show different methods of treatment.

For of course I could have chosen a hundred other ideas instead of this one . . .

Haydn Correspondence, 25.

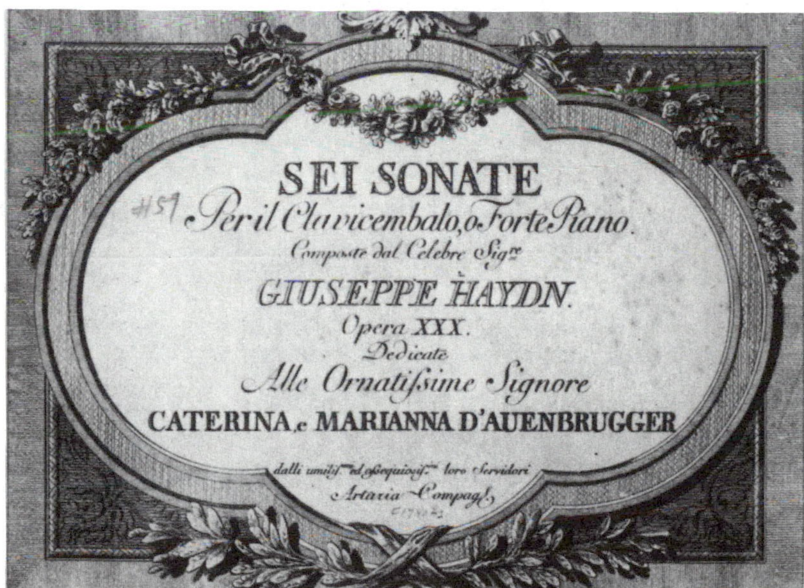

use of the submediant area, to which Haydn had turned frequently in the past but which here seems to have something of the systematic about it.

The remaining two sonatas of this decade both date from 1789/90. The first (Hob. XVI:48; *ACM* 56) was written for Christoph Gottlieb Breitkopf (1750–1800) and it has been suggested that Haydn may have wanted to make a striking entrance onto the German scene.[9] Whatever the reason, he composed a first movement consisting of one of the most complex amalgamations of double variation and free fantasia ever written. This movement, which reveals a complete understanding of the piano's potential as opposed to the harpsichord, must be counted as one of Haydn's most successful and significant works for keyboard.

The last sonata of this decade (Hob. XVI:49) was written for his Viennese hostess, Marianne von Genzinger, and is filled with delightful touches. The slow movement in particular excites our interest, for it was this movement to which Haydn referred in a letter of 20 June 1790, saying:

> . . . only the Adagio is quite new . . . it contains many things which I shall analyse for Your Grace when the time comes; it is rather difficult but full of feeling. Oh! how I do wish that I could only play this Sonata to you a few times; I could then reconcile my staying for a while in this wilderness . . .[10]

THE ACCOMPANIED KEYBOARD SONATA

As his interest in works for solo piano waned, the sonata for piano accompanied by violin and cello became an ideal medium for him. In the six years between 1784 and 1790 he composed thirteen, Hob. XV: 5–17, published in five sets, all of the highest quality, displaying great invention in harmony, modulation, and structure.

At this time Haydn was establishing contacts with publishers in Paris and London, and it was the contract with Forster of London that initiated the spate of piano trios that was to follow. In this contract Haydn carefully agrees that:

> Forster is the sole proprietor of the said works, that I sold them to him as such, and that I cede and transfer to him all my rights and covenants thereto.[11]

The works included symphonies, divertimentos, and two sets of "Sonatas for Harpsichord, with accompaniment of a Violin" *[sic]*; the first

9. Landon, *Haydn,* II, p. 643.
10. *Haydn Correspondence,* p. 105.
11. *Ibid.,* p. 55.

two works of the first set are, however, sonatas by Pleyel for harpsichord and violin with a cello part added.[12]

Among the trios of the period there is one movement exceptional in its scoring. As is well known, Haydn's Trios were rooted in the *basso continuo* tradition and with few exceptions the cello part always duplicates the left hand of the piano. But Haydn's scoring of these works is resourceful and in no way mechanical. The first movement of Hob. XV:9 in A is unique in that Haydn treats the violin and cello as a single body and as a counterpoise to the keyboard (Example XXIII-1); hence, the cello is frequently quite independent of the left hand of the keyboard player, playing in higher than normal register and using the tenor clef. So unusual is this style among the trios that one wonders whether this movement was written for a specific player. At the least, it shows Haydn's awareness of the possibilities of the cello sonority in a trio, and it would also indicate that the sonority Haydn habitually uses in his trios was adopted deliberately. For the rest, the cello is sensitively scored in the majority of the works, occasionally taking a middle, melodic voice when the left hand of the keyboard has some kind of Alberti bass, occasionally dropping out of the texture altogether. Indeed, these trios demon-

Example XXIII–1: J. HAYDN, Trio (Hob. XV:9, I)

12. It is something of a mystery why Haydn should have included works by Pleyel as his own. It is less of a mystery why Haydn should have sold works to Forster when he had already sold them to another publisher; many have accused Haydn of being overly fond of money. At a later date a legal dispute arose between Forster and another London publisher, Longman and Broderip. When Forster reproached Haydn over his double dealing, the latter attempted to shift the blame onto Artaria and Longman. He writes to Forster on 28 February 1788: "This much I promise you: that as long as I live neither Artaria nor Langmann [*sic*] shall have anything from me, directly or indirectly." In no way did this promise to Forster affect his relationship with his main publisher, Artaria. Undoubtedly, Haydn thought he would never be called to account for this sharp practice, which shows him in a very bad light, but there is some evidence that the case of Forster v. Longman came to court when Haydn was in London and that he was called as a witness.

strate the distance that Haydn had already traveled from *basso continuo* to a more modern sonority.

Sensitive as Haydn is to the extended color of the accompanied sonata, he is equally aware of the extension of harmony that the increased use of chromatic passing chords over pedals can create. Particularly successful are passages such as the following:

Example XXIII–2: Haydn's chromatic harmony

a. Trio (Hob. XV:5, I)

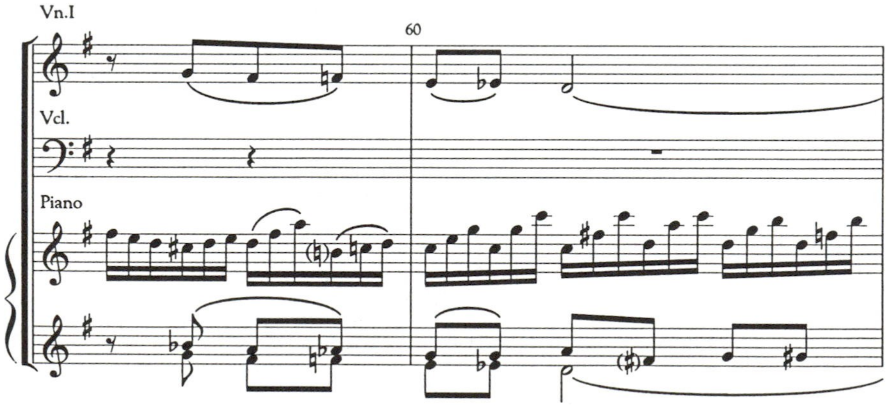

b. Trio (Hob. XV:8, I)

The second, and final, movement of the Trio in C (Hob. XV:13; *ACM* 57) is monothematic, with typical instrumental distribution, but of serious and innovative structure. The exposition is, as might be expected, well crafted and almost unremarkable, except for the strong establishment of A minor at m. 34 *en route* to G at m. 44. Then, once G has been established, there is a rapid modal exchange to G minor, and at m. 52 the bass descends chromatically from G to D. The player/listener may pass over these events without noticing them, but they have their effect in the middle section, in the recapitulation, and in the coda. The middle section opens with a surprise, for immediately following a cadence in G, a quick modulation takes the music to A minor and for about 20 bars there is a variety of modulations. At m. 120 A minor is established over a dominant pedal on E. Obviously, the passage in mm. 120–26 has an exact parallel in mm. 138–44, but the second occurrence is on a pedal B and the tonality is E. But both these passages result in a chord of F (m.128 & m.144). The first F is reached as the bass moves slowly upward through the chromatic scale E to B, and it is heard as the flattened sixth; the second F is sensed as a shock, as the chord slips semitonally from E to the flattened second degree, the Neapolitan, the most affecting chord in the vocabulary of the late eighteenth century. (N.B. the way in which the *Affekt* is heightened by the dotted rhythm in unison at the second occurrence.)

Recapitulation is effected quickly, back to C from E minor, but Haydn's sense of tonal balance is not yet satisfied. As the middle section was largely centered on A and E, three and four steps on the sharp side of the circle of fifths, now the flat side must be brought in as a counterpoise, and mm. 176–196 modulate to E♭ (3 steps on the flat side). Starting in m. 187, an upward chromatic movement in the bass rises from E♭ to A♭, the same kind of movement as in mm. 127–38, but a semitone lower. An augmented sixth on A♭ brings the tonic key back. Lest the listener feel that the balance around the circle of fifths is not yet properly adjusted, Haydn adds a passage in the coda (mm. 231–42) which establishes A♭ (four steps below the tonic as E was 4 steps above it) before reconciling that key to C major as the flattened sixth. This kind of structural and tonal thinking is to be seen more and more in the 1780s, and that Haydn should treat the medium of the accompanied sonata with such seriousness shows how highly he regarded it. Nothing comparable is to be found in his solo keyboard sonatas.

THE STRING QUARTET

The 1780s also mark Haydn's return to the string quartet. Between Op. 20, published in 1772, and the six Quartets, Op. 33 (Hob. III:37–42; 1781), he had not approached the medium, but then a single Quartet,

Op. 42, (Hob. III:43) appeared in 1785; six Quartets Op. 50 (Hob. III:44–49) in 1787; two sets of three Quartets, Opp. 54 and 55 (Hob. III:57–62), in 1788; and a further six, Op. 64 (Hob. III: 63–68) in 1790. In addition to these full-length works, Haydn made a quartet arrangement of *The Seven Last Words on the Cross,* consisting of seven successive slow movements with an introduction and a fast conclusion representing the earthquake signaling Christ's death.

Much has been made of a statement that survives in two letters Haydn wrote—one to a prince and the other to a Swiss writer, neither of whom was personally known to him—trying to interest them in the purchase of a manuscript set of Op. 33 at the high, pre-publication price of six ducats a set.[13] He offers them this work, "written in a new and special way, for I have not composed any for 10 years." In both letters the wording is virtually identical. Throughout the eighteenth century, novelty was highly prized, and to advertise something as "new and special" was not unique to Haydn. But many writers have tried to discern what is new and special about Op. 33: some have said that there is nothing new, and others have drawn up lists of innovative devices. Had Haydn's two letters not survived there would probably have been no controversy, for there is no denying that these quartets are less grand than those of Op. 20, smaller in structural scale and often in gesture, as well as lighter in texture; but there might well have been agreement that this set of quartets embodies a kind of humor that is quite new in his music.[14]

Haydn's ability to perceive the incongruous—an aspect of the *empfindsamer Stil*—was keen, but his humor had been, to this point, somewhat intellectual, consisting of jokes for those in the know. In the Op. 33 quartets, there is a quality of silliness, of tomfoolery, and of directness that is quite unusual, except in the works of Emanuel Bach. The silliness is well exemplified in the distortion of the tune in the last movement of the B♭ Quartet, Op. 33, No. 4 (Hob. III:40).

Example XXIII–3: J. HAYDN, Quartet, Op. 33, No.4, IV, Haydn's humor

13. This method was also used by Beethoven in the selling of his *Missa solemnis*.
14. Only Emanuel Bach, at precisely this time too, was developing a similar kind of humor in his Rondos.

In the entire history of music, there is no more laughable composition than the first movement of Op. 33, No. 4 (Hob.III:40; *ACM* 58), in which the humor ranges from the witty to the slapstick. Short and crisp (89 measures), the movement appears at first sight to be correctly proportioned. As is quite obvious, the first phrase consists of a long note harmonized with a dissonance resolving to a consonance, which is then strongly reinforced. The wit of the movement is to be found in the constant repetition of this process on different degrees of the scale and in different ways, leaving the listener totally confused. This confusion is reinforced at m. 51 when the recapitulation takes place earlier than expected. In a movement only 89 bars long, direct relationships with the opening (which starts on the third beat of a bar of anacrusis, hence described as m. 0:3) occur in mm. 2:3, 31:3, 33:3, 48:3, 50:3, 51:3, 53:3, 76:3, 78:3, and 85:3; less direct but unmistakable relationships also occur in mm. 13:3, 17:3, 18:3, 19:3, 20:3, 64:1, 65:1, 66:3, 67:3, and 68:3; this makes a total of 20 times or once in every four bars. The only element of the movement which is not connected to the opening phrase is the closing theme (mm. 26–30 and 80–84). Another witty aspect of the movement is the structural modification in the recapitulation in which a development of the turn followed by two eighth notes (m. 4:4) is interpolated and expanded over a pedal through mm. 71–75.

The cello is the butt of the slapstick humor of this movement. The listener clearly hears the balanced repetition of phrases at the opening, and all is clear and easily comprehensible. Thus the first phrase antecedent (8 beats in length) is balanced by a similar consequent. In m. 4 all the instruments play another small antecedent (six beats in length) which is balanced by a similar consequent. The second half of m. 7 reveals a third antecedent/consequent relationship beginning, as the antecedent moves to a sensible conclusion, with a unison D in m. 9 on all instruments. The consequent phrase ought to move to a perfect cadence at the beginning of m. 11 with the first violin playing notes such as C C A A | B♭, complemented by the bass line E♭ E♭ F F | B♭, but this does not happen. Instead, all instruments repeat the antecedent's close. What follows, emphasized by the dynamics, is an urgent move to a *forte* perfect cadence followed by another unison F and D, and a still more emphatic final close in m. 12—a normal extension. The cello, however, playing the buffoon, cannot count and adds yet another F and D, which ruins the cadential effect entirely. At the recapitulation in the analogous place (m. 63) the transposition that had occurred in the exposition is omitted and the bridge here is made by changing the *forte* chords that had finalized B♭ before the cello's blunder, into *piano* chords that move the tonality toward E♭. This time the cello, with sublime self-confidence, inverts the first violin's notes and plays A♭ and F, caring nothing that it is creating a naked and shocking augmented fourth with the second violin, and even dragging the viola into the same "error," which they continue for two more measures. The way in which their rhythm has to change from weak/strong to strong/weak, and the way in which the cello and the viola reconcile themselves completely to the texture five and a half bars later, is remarkable. At the conclusion of the movement, this piece of slapstick has been worked out. The cello has finally learned its lesson and does not add another pair of F♯ and a D.

The isolated Quartet in D minor, Op. 42, may well be part of a commission from Spain for a group of little quartets, which Haydn wrote about in 1784. It will be remembered that Boccherini, active in Spain at this time, divided his quartets and quintets into two kinds: *quartetti* and *quartettini,* and *quintetti* and *quintettini*. Why Haydn never completed the set is not known, and why this quartet is in four movements when Haydn referred to a commission for three-movement works is also not known, although one can easily postulate that a fourth movement was added in order to sell the work when he decided not to finish the set.

At the beginning of 1787, Haydn was occupied with the quartet arrangement of the *Seven Last Words,* and starting a new set of six quartets as well. Possibly during the composition of the fourth quartet, Haydn, who had received a valuable ring from King Frederick William II of Prussia shortly before, asked his publisher to dedicate the new set of quartets to the cello-playing monarch, who had succeeded his uncle, Frederick the Great, in August of 1786. What is surprising is that none of these quartets shows any particular intention to flatter the king by the inclusion of grateful cello melodies. If anything, they are just as sparse in texture and as terse in structure as Op. 33. In Op. 50, No. 1, Haydn uses the simple marking of *Allegro* with the crossed-C time signature for the first time. It is easy to forget that Haydn was twenty-seven years old when Handel died, and this new style is a signal departure from his old-fashioned notational habits. Also one senses that the sonorities of Mozart's great quartets are resounding in Haydn's ears in certain parts of No. 2, which contains, in its slow movement, one of the most magical reharmonizations (see Example XXIII–4 on p. 436). It is through such devices as this reworking that the language of eighteenth-century music reveals its depth and extraordinary capacity for "speaking great truths."

No. 4 in F♯ minor concludes with a 6/8 *Allegro* fugue reminiscent of Op. 20, which, after 60 measures of counterpoint, retreats to a sternly homophonic conclusion.

The last twelve quartets of the decade, Opp. 54, 55, and 64 (Hob. III:57–68), are all dedicated to Johann Tost, a man about whom little is known, but who seems to have had at least two careers: that of a very good violinist in the orchestra at Esterháza, and that of a wholesale merchant. In the former capacity he developed an enormous appetite for chamber music, while in the latter he developed the ability to pay

Example XXIII–4: J. HAYDN, Quartet Op. 50, No. 2, slow movement reharmonization

for the numerous chamber works he commissioned—at least for a while. The first six quartets, Opp. 54 and 55, demonstrate a fondness for taking the cello from low to high register through arpeggios, which seems to be a novel device, and which effectively uses the cello's two personalities. Also noteworthy is the quasi-improvisatory style of writing for the first violin in the slow movements of the second and third quartets. Op. 54, No. 2 has been noted as one of the most unusual quartets in overall structure that Haydn ever wrote, for after an orthodox first movement there is an *Adagio* (*ACM* 59), which one critic has described as free-form, but which is, in reality, an eight-measure ground, above which the first violin wails and sobs, giving the impression of improvising in the wildest Hungarian Gypsy manner. This ground is played four times, and followed by a three-bar coda. The Minuet and Trio is characterized by strong emphasis on the augmented triad, which creates a sonorous effect unique in its time, and the last movement is rich and slow, enclosing an incongruous *Presto*.

The Quartets Op. 64 are all works of the highest quality and, like the earlier works discussed, they have highly individualized profiles. One notices immediately that there are two quartets in this set in which the Minuet is placed before the slow movement. There is no doubt that Haydn feels himself less bound to the conventional movement order of F / S / Minuet / F in a quartet than in a symphony, and can, instead, observe the principle of contrast between movements; for example, in the approximately thirty-five symphonies composed between 1780 and the end of Haydn's life, there is not a single example of the Minuet in second place,[15] while in eight quartets out of forty-five written in the same period a Minuet serves as second movement.

15. The last time Haydn wrote a symphonic Minuet as second movement was for Symphony No. 44 (Hob. I:44), composed some time before 1772.

Example XXIII–5: J. HAYDN, Quartet Op. 64, No. 3, Menuet

The relationship of the four parts and their contribution to the texture of the whole, as well as the subtle matter of each player's role within the group seem to undergo further refinement in this set. The finale of Op. 64, No. 5 (Hob. III:63), is written soloistically for the first violin in *moto perpetuo* style, yet the movement breaks into an episode in double fugue, an apparent reconciliation of a soloistic texture with an egalitarian texture, and a contrast that sets the popular beside the learned. The example above reveals, within the context of a minuet, Haydn's subtle distribution of instrumental initiative, for clearly at the outset the cello has the lead, which on the eighth beat is taken over by the violins for four beats, etc. Also to be noted is the reliance upon variation techniques in the slow movements of this set.

SONGS

Haydn also published twenty-four songs, the first set of twelve in 1781 and the second in 1784. Like most of Mozart's songs, these are unpretentious pieces, written on two staves, and they bear little relationship to the nineteenth-century Lied. Haydn was pleased with them and wrote to Artaria on 23 June 1781 saying that "they surpass all my previous ones in variety, naturalness, and ease of expression." It is sad that we have none of his previous ones for comparison. He dedicated the first set to a Mademoiselle Clair, whom he described as "the darling of my Prince"; they are utterly charming in their simple, folklike melodies, many of which would fit perfectly as themes for slow-movement variations or as subjects for last movements in his later symphonies. A month later, on 20 July 1781, he wrote again to Artaria:

> You will find the words of the 4th, 8th and 9th *Lieder* in Friebert's *Lieder,* as published by Herr von Kurzböck, but in case you cannot get them, I

> shall send them to you. These 3 *Lieder* have been set to music by *Capellmeister* Hofmann, but between ourselves, miserably; and just because this braggart thinks that he alone has ascended the heights of Mount Parnassus, and tries to disgrace me every time with a certain high society, I have composed these very three *Lieder* just to show this would-be high society the difference: *Sed hoc inter nos*.
>
> . . . I pray you especially, good Sir, not to let anyone copy, sing, or in any way alter these *Lieder* before publication, because when they are ready, I shall sing them myself in the critical houses. By his presence and through the proper execution, the master must maintain his rights: these are only songs, but they are not the street songs of Hofmann, wherein neither ideas, expression nor, much less, melody appear.[16]

The second set, equally beautiful but perhaps less naive, concludes with a deeply felt song with the title *Auf meines Vaters Grab* (On my Father's Grave). Haydn's father had rejoiced at seeing him in Esterházy uniform in 1761 and had died in 1765. What would he have thought to see him, twenty years later, with his advantageous Esterházy contract and international fame?

SYMPHONIES

Haydn composed approximately twenty symphonies during this decade, by the end of which his most mature style was established. All of them are four-movement works with a fast first movement, a slow movement, a Minuet and Trio, and a fast Finale. The church-sonata symphony has now disappeared, and as a replacement for it, the symphony with slow introduction has become more common. Increasingly, Haydn's symphonies result from foreign commissions and commitments, and are composed with a specific audience in mind. As a result, the local conditions of Esterháza play an ever-diminishing role. The list on the facing page is helpful.

From the earlier part of the decade, the 77th Symphony is remarkable in that its fourth movement is a rigorously monothematic sonata form, exemplifying Haydn's tendency to use folksong-like themes in extremely contrasting ways—with the barest accompaniment, or as a subject for complex imitative or Fuxian counterpoint.[17]

We know that Haydn's contacts with Paris and London were through publishers who approached him or whom he approached for business reasons. In 1784, however, Haydn received a commission to write six symphonies from the directors of the *Concert de la Loge Olympique,* a group with Masonic connections, which was at that time the largest

16, *Haydn Correspondence,* p. 31.

17. The score is available in the *Norton Anthology of Western Music.*

No.	Key	Name	Date	First published	Composed for
73	D	*La Chasse*	1780–2	Vienna, 1782	
74	E♭		1780–1	London, 1781	
(75)			1779		
76	E♭		1782	Paris, 1783	
77	B♭		1782	London, 1784	
78	C minor		1782		
79	F		1783–4		
80	D minor		1783–4	Vienna, 1785	
81	G		1783–4		
82	C	*L'Ours*	1786		
83	G minor	*La Poule*	1785		The *Concert*
84	E♭		1786	Vienna, Dec. 1787	*de la*
85	B♭	*La Reine*	1785	Paris, Jan. 1788	*Loge Olympique*
86	D		1786		
87	A		1785		
88	G		1787	Paris, 1788	Johann Tost
89	F		1787		Johann Tost
90	C		1788		
91	E♭		1788	Paris, 1790	Comte d'Ogny
92	G	*Oxford*	1789		

concert-giving organization in Paris (see p. 345). Haydn's symphonies had been increasingly popular in Paris for twenty years, and German instrumental music had held a special position in that city for still longer. The orchestra of the *Concert de la Loge Olympique* was one of the finest and largest in Europe and superior to anything Haydn had ever worked with. In the Symphonies nos. 82–87, known ever since as the *Paris* Symphonies, one senses a greater depth and breadth of musical substance. First movements have all the crash and bustle of earlier symphonies, but in addition to the usual chords and arpeggios there is stronger melodic material. The number of *Adagio* movements of serious, quasi-religious quality gradually increases, replacing variation movements built on folksongs in *Andante* tempo or faster. Minuets show less change, while more Finales are based on popular tunes, rather than those tags and scraps of melody that lend themselves to contrapuntal treatment.

After the *Paris* Symphonies, there were five more completed by the end of the decade. Nos. 88 and 89 were written for Johann Tost, who took them to Paris and sold them to a publisher there. The Symphony No. 88 has always been recognized as one of Haydn's finest, and it is certainly one of his most popular. Perhaps more than any other, it demonstrates the fact that the modern symphony could no longer rely upon stock gestures of unison chords, or rapid scales, or tremolos, or any of the other standard devices from which the symphony had, until now, been constructed. In the mid-1780s, in fact, the symphonic style of Johann Stamitz's generation disappeared, and henceforth composers who continued to use the old clichés were considered old-fashioned.

The three Symphonies Nos. 90–92 were probably commissioned by the Comte d'Ogny, one of the aristocratic Parisian melomanes, who may also have been influential in the commissioning of the *Paris* Symphonies. They demonstrate Haydn's most advanced orchestration, particularly in his use of woodwind. One of these Parisian symphonies, No. 92, is commonly nicknamed *The Oxford* because Haydn chose this work to be played on the occasion of his being awarded an honorary doctorate by the university in that city.

CONCERTOS

Haydn played many instruments although he claimed to be a virtuoso on none; his main calling was to be a music director and composer, and his main instrument was the orchestra. In his time, no one excelled him as a virtuoso on that instrument. Perhaps as a direct result of this practical situation, wildly humorous and deeply serious symphonies poured from his pen in profusion. But his concertos, although attractive and full of charm, are both far fewer in number and less enterprising than the symphonies in every way.

The date of composition of the D-major Piano Concerto (Hob. XVIII:11) cannot be fixed more precisely than the early 1780s. It is a work more closely related to the concertos of J. C. Bach than to the great concertos of Mozart of the 1780s. Nevertheless, it has an individuality, and, particularly in its Rondo, a direct appeal to audiences. The Cello Concerto in D (Hob. VIIb:2), which dates from 1783, is of all Haydn's concertos perhaps the most virtuosic and demanding. It was written for Anton Kraft, one of the cellists in the Esterháza orchestra, and remains the only Haydn concerto in the regular repertoire of the major solo instruments (piano, violin, and cello).

One of the most curious commissions that Haydn ever received was from the king of Naples in 1785 or 1786 to write "three concertos for two organized lyres for his Majesty . . . one in the key of C, the second in F, and the third in G. Please take care that the ritornelli are shorter than those of your first concerto . . ." The *lira organizzata* is basically a hurdy-gurdy, an instrument of the common people but with technical improvements, and the king of Naples had learned to play this strange instrument very well. There are five extant concertos for two *lire organizzate,* Hob. VIIh:1–5, and Haydn took his instructions seriously for he built the works not like concertos but like chamber works for nine players, mostly grouped in pairs: 2 violins, 2 violas, 2 horns, 2 *lire*

The *lira organizzata* in operation. The instrument's appeal lay in the ease with which it could be played. Watteau's *Gentleman Playing a Hurdy-Gurdy* (Barber Institute of Fine Arts)

organizzate, and cello. He uses all kinds of combinations of these players, of course, but chiefly he has one group converse with another in pure chamber style, and as chamber works these are among Haydn's most delightful, in sound and structure.

If the concertos for *lira organizzata* resulted from a curious commission, a commission from 1785 resulted in a curious payment. In that year Haydn was asked to write music for the Lenten service for the Cathedral of Cadiz. In this service the officiating bishop would speak the first of the seven last phrases of Christ on the Cross, and would deliver a sermon on that phrase: "Father, forgive them for they know not what they do," then he would prostrate himself before the altar. Haydn's commission was to compose seven slow movements, each about ten minutes in length, to be played during the moments of prostration. This he did, with great difficulty, providing also an introduction and a final movement called *Terremoto* (Earthquake) to follow the seventh and last phrase: "Into Thy hands, O Lord, I commend my spirit." Haydn was deeply moved, man of faith as he was, in the composition of these "sonatas" for orchestra, as he called them, and they proved to be immensely popular; he himself arranged them for string quartet, for choir and orchestra, and possibly for piano. It has been observed that there was an increased depth and spirituality in his instrumental music following the fulfillment of this commission. His reward took another form as well: Haydn received a little box from Cadiz and upon opening it, he saw to his surprise a chocolate cake. Angrily he cut into it, only to find it filled with gold pieces.[18]

THE OPERAS

Far from relaxing his operatic efforts, Haydn composed three works for the Esterháza theater during this decade. The first, *La fedeltà premiata* (Fidelity Rewarded), a *dramma giocoso,* was designed for the celebration of the opening of the new opera house, built despite many difficulties to replace the one that had burned to the ground in 1779. The opera was completed in 1780, and first performed in 1781, to a libretto whose plot is so complex that it is hardly comprehensible. Its characters are four men and four women; one pair are the serious lovers whose faithfulness through the hardest trials is ultimately rewarded. It makes the greatest use of dramatic irony—that situation where the audience knows what is going on and someone on stage does not—and the comic characters range from the ridiculous poltroon, the Count Peruchetto (Littlewig), the self-seeking shrew, Amaranta, to the Priest of Diana, goddess of virginity, who lusts after Amaranta.

Haydn's score is, in some ways, a great advance on his earlier operas. No longer are the arias composed as massive set pieces, undramatic in their structure and impossibly slow in movement. Instead, opening *ritornellos* are short and focused, recapitulating forms are used for the comic characters, whereas serious characters at moments of intensity use arias of varying tempos, and coloratura passages are reduced in length and number. In other words, theatrical considerations begin to assert their importance in the face of purely musical considerations. There are moments of great imaginative originality in the instrumentation and melodic writing. The pure beauty of the accompaniment in passages of Fileno's aria No.30, "Se dei begli occhi tuoi," and the strength of the affective melody in the same character's *recitativo stromentato,* No. 38a, are noteworthy. A comic effect of orchestration is also noteworthy; in the aria where the lovesick priest is talking about the conduct of rival bulls in a pasture with cows, the constant bellowing of the two horns is irresistibly funny.

Against these positive features must be set some critical problems which this opera will always pose to modern audiences. Haydn seems quite incapable of arriving at a style that will allow him to distinguish between his serious and his comic lovers in similar situations. Thus,

18. Geiringer, *Haydn,* p. 78.

serious Celia has a beautiful aria at a dramatic moment, which is followed by comic Amaranta singing an aria provoked by a similarly intense situation. Haydn not only fails to distinguish between these arias, but makes Amaranta's more beautiful and more affecting. Furthermore, the serious Fileno opens a passionate aria with a dotted rhythm that forces us, in that context, to see him as a comic character. These are errors of judgment that Mozart would never make.

Haydn's tonal structures in this opera do not arise from the dramatic but from abstract ideas of instrumental music. The first Finale is a perfect case in point. We have earlier noted Haydn's fondness for keys a third apart (see pp. 427–28). This Finale opens in B♭, then proceeds to set the different parts of the text in a variety of tempos and keys as follows:

mm	1 –101	B♭	*Vivace assai*	C
	102–133	G	*Adagio*	3/4
	134–169	G min.	*Presto*	2/4
	170–304	E♭	*Presto*	6/8
	305–385	C	*Vivace assai*	C
	386–433	A♭	*Adagio*	[Alla breve] crossed C
	434–512	G min.	*Presto*	2/4
	513–583	B♭	*Presto*	C
	584–653	G min.	*Vivace*	3/4
	654–822	B♭	*Presto*	[Alla breve] crossed C

It is clear that these keys are arbitrarily chosen, even though the move from one to the next is often made with considerable forcefulness, and each area is set off from those that follow. But there is no affective consistency of tonalities, and equally there is no sense of a greater or lesser movement away from a central tonic around a circle of fifths. Compare this method of choosing keys with Mozart's when he wants to show Osmin losing his temper (see p. 484).

Next came *Orlando Paladino,* a *dramma eroicomico* mixing the serious with the comic and the heroic, which was first performed at Esterháza in 1782. The plot concerns the love of Orlando, nephew of Charlemagne, for Angelica, who is in love with Medoro. Orlando's frustrations drive him mad and the complications caused by his madness are sorted out by Alcina, the all-powerful sorceress. By the power of her magic, she turns him to stone and procures forgetfulness for him from the River Lethe.

This is Haydn's comic masterpiece, and while the characters of the knights, Rodomonte and Orlando, and the sorceress Alcina are familiar subjects of the *opera seria,* here it is impossible to take them seriously or to believe for a moment that Haydn wanted that. Rodomonte, king of Barbary, is a braggart who is, fortunately, never put to the test, but

A pen and pencil drawing by Pietro Travaglia of a stage set for the first scene of *Orlando Paladino* showing desolate, mountainous wilderness. (Széchenyi National-bibliothek, Theatersammlung, Budapest)

Haydn's first aria makes him sound like Mozart's self-important Dr. Bartolo, and nothing happens later to change that impression. Orlando is given big arias which parody the old style, and lack all credibility. The two lovers, Angelica, queen of Cathay, and Medoro are practically identical with the sentimental lovers of *La fedeltà premiata*. Their music is extremely beautiful and finely wrought. The obvious *buffo* parts of Eurilla and Pasquale, shepherdess and squire to Orlando respectively, are well drawn, and the aria in which Pasquale pretends to play the violin, trilling, drawing out long notes imitating the *castrato* voice, etc., is the best and funniest of its kind that Haydn ever wrote.

Haydn adapted himself very quickly to the world of opera outside Esterháza, and here he is completely flexible in his aria introductions; sometimes they are of substantial length, sometimes they are non-existent. The opera is rich in accompanied recitative carrying long soliloquies. The Finales of Acts I and II are also fine, that of Act I being remarkable for its tonal shifts by half-step. Again, throughout *Orlando* Haydn uses harmonic sleight of hand to move about extensively, and his favorite modulations are to keys a third apart. *Orlando Paladino* was successful in its own day, but eventually slipped into oblivion. It remains, however, the Haydn opera most distinguished by its portrayal of the comedic and the ridiculous and most modern in its structural devices.

Haydn's last opera for Esterháza was *Armida*. Composed during 1783 and first performed in February of 1784, this, it is said, was Prince Nikolaus's favorite. In that it reverts to an older style of *opera seria,* it fits modern critical standards less well than his comic operas, but there are fine moments throughout the score. Since this is an *opera seria,* Haydn writes largely for the solo voice, which is shown off in arias, and for visual effect, with the princely soldiers in full uniform playing a significant part as stage extras. Since the arias are more concerned with musical than dramatic suitability, the larger introductory ritornello is used, and there are usually concluding cadenzas before the final ritornello. Coloratura is called upon for its peculiar kind of vocal splendor, which was highly appreciated everywhere, as well as to deepen the emotional affect that the talented singer could produce from its judicious use. After finishing this work, Haydn restricted his writing for the Esterháza opera theater to a few substitute arias for insertion into other composers' operas.

CHURCH MUSIC

Similarly, despite his eagerness to praise God, his *Missa Cellensis* (Hob. XXII:8; 1782) is his only large-scale composition for the church during this decade, and in fact, he did not write another Mass until 1796. The reforms of Emperor Joseph II were, in part, designed to simplify the music for the church service, just as he hoped that all activities of the church might be simplified and rationalized, and it may well be that Haydn found the restrictions on the use of the orchestra in the service too irksome and too remote from his wishes. The *Missa Cellensis* was written as a short, serviceable Mass with a reasonable amount of orchestral brilliance. There are few signs that Haydn was vastly enthusiastic about the work, but there are signs of haste in composition. The three parts of the *Kyrie* use the same material, the fugues at the customary places are perfunctory, and the composer borrows material from his own opera *Il mondo della luna*. In short, this work gives no indication of the heights to which Haydn's Mass composition will rise in later years.

CHAPTER XXIV

Freedom at Last

In his letter of 9 February 1790 to Frau von Genzinger, quoted earlier, Haydn bemoans the fate that forces him to return to Esterháza from the comforts of Vienna. Hardly more than two weeks after writing those words, an event occurred of the greatest importance to the whole establishment of Prince Nikolaus Esterházy: on 25 February his Princess, Maria Elizabeth, died. Haydn describes the efforts he made to cheer the prince. He writes:

> The death of his wife so crushed the Prince that we had to use every means in our power to pull His Highness out of this depression, and thus the first 3 days I arranged enlarged chamber music every evening with no singing; but the poor Prince, during the concert of the first evening, became so depressed when he heard my Favorite Adagio in D that we had quite a time to brighten his mood with other pieces.
>
> On the 4th day we had an opera, on the 5th a comedy, and then our theatre daily as usual . . .[1]

But the prince was 76, and after what must have been for Haydn a cheerless summer, his old friend and patron, Nikolaus "the Magnificent" died in late September, following a brief illness. His heir was his son, Paul Anton, who did not care for music. He must have been preparing for his succession for some time, for two days after his father's death he dismissed almost all the musical and theatrical establishment with no notice. Haydn was left a pension of 1000 gulden a year for life in his old friend's will, and he was kept on by the new prince at a nominal salary of 400 gulden with no duties and permission to accept other engagements. He lost no time in leaving Esterháza behind him for now, to all intents and purposes, he was no longer a servant but finally his own man.

1. *Haydn Correspondence,* pp. 98–99.

HAYDN IN LONDON

When the news of Prince Esterházy's death spread abroad, various people began to think about Haydn and his possible availability. Pleading loyalty to his new prince, he refused an offer to become Kapellmeister to Prince Grassalkovics, whose court was at Pressburg (now Bratislava), since that would merely be exchanging one servitude for another. Johann Peter Salomon (1745–1815) was another who acted quickly on hearing the news. He was a German violinist and impresario, resident in London, who had been in correspondence with Haydn trying to arrange a visit there for him. He was traveling in Europe and immediately turned toward Vienna. According to Griesinger the story then runs as follows:

> Towards evening someone knocked at Haydn's room: Salomon walked in and his first words were, "Get ready to travel. In a fortnight we go together to London." Haydn began by resisting the proposal. He pointed to his ignorance of the English language and to his inexperience in travel. These objections, however, were soon put aside. It was agreed that Haydn should receive three thousand gulden for an opera and a hundred gulden for each new composition he conducted in twenty concerts. Haydn was thus already covered up to five thousand gulden and this sum was to be deposited . . . in Vienna as soon as Haydn should tread upon English ground.[2]

Dies tells much the same story in different words:

> . . . a strange man one day walked unexpectedly into his room and said bluntly, "I am Salomon from London and I have come to fetch you. Tomorrow we shall conclude an agreement."[3]

Prince Anton was perfectly agreeable that Haydn should go to London, and the remaining days in Vienna were filled with preparations. Much time was spent with Mozart, the world traveler, who on one occasion said, "You have had no training for the world, and you speak so few languages," to which Haydn replied, "My language is understood all over the world."[4] Dies adds:

> When Haydn had settled . . . his household affairs, he fixed his departure and left on December 15, 1791 [1790], in company with Salomon. Mozart on this day never left his friend Haydn. He dined with him and said at the moment of parting, "We are probably saying our last farewell in this life." Tears welled from the eyes of both. Haydn was deeply moved, for he applied Mozart's words to himself, and the possibility never occurred to him that the thread of Mozart's life could be cut off by the inexorable Parcae [Fates] within the following year.[5]

2. Griesinger, *op. cit.*, p. 22.
3. Dies, *op. cit.*, p. 119.
4. *Ibid.*, pp. 119–20.
5. *Ibid*, p. 121.

The port of Calais in northern France as it looked some time before 1760. The Age of Steam had not reached the sea, and Haydn's crossings were dependent upon favorable wind. (A reversed print published by Daumont of Paris)

Haydn and Salomon set off, traveling via Munich, Bonn (Salomon's birthplace and where Haydn had his first contact with Beethoven), and then to Calais for the Channel crossing. They avoided Paris because of the uncertain state of things there, and they arrived in England on New Year's Day, 1791. Haydn was not yet fifty-nine and threw himself with gusto into the life that London offered.

At that time, London was the biggest, most flourishing city in the world, with a large and vital mercantile and professional middle class, as well as a cultivated aristocracy. Its musical life was richer and perhaps more varied than anywhere else, as artists flocked there to make their fortunes. At the time of Haydn's arrival, London boasted two rival opera houses and several subscription series of concerts, including, of course, the Salomon Concerts and their chief rival, the Professional Concerts. Obviously no arrangements could be made to prepare for Haydn's concerts before he got to London, and the speed with which Salomon acted is remarkable. On 15 January 1791, the following announcement appeared:

> HANOVER SQUARE. MR.SALAMON *[sic]* respectfully acquaints the Nobility and Gentry, that he intends having TWELVE SUBSCRIPTION CONCERTS in the course of the present Season. The first of which will be on Friday the Eleventh of February next, and so continue on the succeeding Fridays. Mr.HAYDN will compose for every Night a New Piece of Music, and direct the execution of it at the Harpsichord.
>
> The Vocal as well as Instrumental Performers will be of the first Rate, and a List of them will appear in a few Days.
>
> Subscriptions, at Five Guineas, for the Twelve Nights, to be held at Messrs.Lockhard's, No.36, Pall-Mall.
>
> Tickets transferable Ladies to Ladies, and Gentlemen to Gentlemen.[6]

From the beginning Haydn was overwhelmed with visitors so that on the very first evening, he reports, he had to move to larger quarters.

6. The programs given are as cited in Landon, *Haydn,* III, pp. 43 and 49.

On 18 January, he was present at a court ball for the queen's birthday and was greeted with a bow from the Prince of Wales, even though he had not yet been presented. His future in London was made! The prince, who played the cello, was a patron of the Professional Concerts, the rival organization, but he proceeded to make music with Haydn on numerous occasions. The Professional Concerts also impressed Haydn by sending him a small ivory plaque with his name on it, granting him admittance to all their concerts. He told Griesinger that no one in Vienna had ever thought to extend such a courtesy to him.

After several postponements, the first of the Haydn-Salomon Concerts took place on 11 March 1791, as the following announcement attests:

> HANOVER-SQUARE. MR. SALOMON respectfully acquaints the Nobility and Gentry, that his Concerts will open without further delay on Friday next, the 11th of March, and continue every succeeding Friday.
>
> PART I.
> Overture – Rosetti.
> Song – Sig[nor] Tajana.
> Concerto Oboe – Mr. Harrington.
> Concerto Violin – Madame Gautherot [Composed by Viotti].
> Recitativo and Aria – Signor David [Composed by Rusi].
> PART II.
> New Grand Overture – Haydn
> Recitative and Aria – Signora Storace
> Concertante, Pedal Harp and Pianoforte – Madame Krumpholz and Mr. Dusseck,
> Composed by Mr. Dusseck.
> Rondo – Signor David [Composed by Andreozzi].
> Full Piece – Kozeluck *[sic]*.
> Mr. HAYDN will be at the Harpsichord.
> Leader of the Band, Mr. SALOMON,
> Tickets transferable, as usual, Ladies to Ladies and Gentlemen to Gentlemen only.
> The Ladies' tickets are Green, the Gentlemen's Black.
>
> The Subscribers are intreated to give particular orders to their Coachmen to set down and take up at the Side Door in the Street, with the Horses' Heads towards the Square.
>
> The Door in the Square is for Chairs only.

For the next three months with only one week off, Haydn rehearsed the orchestra and conducted from the harpsichord at one concert per week. The concerts, as the announcement above indicates, did not feature many works by Haydn but aimed at appealing to a variety of tastes; hence, each concert consisted of a mixture of operatic favorites, new symphonies and concertos, new chamber music, and popular songs.

The opera which Haydn had written for London was never performed because of difficulties with the theater, but Haydn was not unduly disappointed. He had received payment already and so lost no money; nor did he lose the time necessary to prepare the work.

One of the most important events for Haydn was his attendance at the Handel Festival in May of 1791. It will be recalled that the celebration of Handel's hundredth birthday had been organized in 1784 and had been an enormous success, with repetitions, produced by ever-growing forces, in 1785, 1786, 1787, and the fifth in 1791. It was a gorgeous and impressive occasion in Westminster Abbey with the king and queen in court dress. It is said that there were 1,068 performers on this occasion. Haydn was enormously impressed, as he was to be again, when, a year later, he saw a ceremony in St. Paul's Cathedral, which he recorded in his notebook as follows:

> 8 days before Pentecost I heard 4,000 charity children in St. Paul's Church sing the song noted below. One performer indicated the tempo. No music ever moved me so deeply in my whole life as this devotional and innocent . . . [7] [there follows Haydn's notation of the melody.]

Haydn was honored by Oxford University. In July of 1791, at the urging of Dr. Burney, the university awarded the composer an honorary Doctorate of Music, and although Haydn told his biographers that he felt silly in his gown, he attributed much of his success in England and the reception he received in great houses to his possession of the degree. Somewhat later, he told his fourth prince, the overbearing Nikolaus, that a Doctor of Music of Oxford University ought not to be addressed as if he were a lackey. Thereafter he was addressed as Herr von Haydn.

Haydn's success with the Salomon Concerts prompted the rival Professional Concerts to try to induce him to break his contract. Although they offered substantial financial advantage, Haydn refused; therefore they embarked upon a campaign to weaken his position in the eyes of the public. In particular, they alleged that this old man was now "written out" (indeed, friends of Haydn had openly wondered how much longer his inspiration and productivity could last) and that in the next season they would have Ignace Pleyel, Haydn's former pupil, under contract, offering a new composition at each concert. As it turned out, Pleyel's coming to London with a substantial number of new compositions put Haydn under a great deal of pressure, but he was able to meet the challenge; subsequently he and Pleyel went to the theater together and were as good friends as ever. The younger man did not succeed in putting Haydn and the Salomon concerts out of the picture; it was the Professional Concerts that collapsed in 1793.

The concert of 23 March 1792 saw the first production of the Symphony No. 94 in G *(The Surprise)*, which was, from the beginning, one of Haydn's most popular symphonies. The nickname comes from the

7. *Haydn Correspondence*, p. 261.

A pencil drawing of Haydn in 1794 by George Dance, whose portraits are famous for their accuracy. (Historisches Museum der Stadt Wien)

sudden *fortissimo* chord in the slow movement. Griesinger records the anecdote as follows:

> I asked him once in jest whether it was true that he had composed the Andante with the Drum Stroke to waken the English who fell asleep at his concert. "No," came the answer, "but I was interested in making a brilliant debut, so that my student Pleyel, who was at that time engaged by an orchestra in London (in 1792) and whose concerts had opened a week before mine, should not outdo me. The first Allegro of my symphony had already met with countless Bravos, but the enthusiasm reached its highest peak at the Andante with the Drum Stroke. Encore! Encore! sounded in every throat, and Pleyel himself complimented me on my idea."[8]

Later that same year, Haydn met the Astronomer Royal, William Herschel, who had begun life as an oboe player before turning to astronomy. Haydn was most impressed by his telescopes and one wonders whether his conversations with Herschel may have left him with ideas for the "Representation of Chaos" in *The Creation*.

Among the many famous people whom Haydn met was the anatomist, surgeon, and teacher, John Hunter, whose wife, Anne, was a

8. Griesinger, *op. cit.*, p. 33.

great admirer of the composer and wrote several verses which Haydn set as songs. For many years, Haydn had suffered from the effects of a nasal polyp. Just before leaving England in late June 1792, he had an experience in London which Dies recounts as follows:

> Haydn had several times already submitted to surgical operations [for his nasal polyp] and, even under the hands of the celebrated Brambilla, had been so unfortunate as to forfeit a piece of the nasal bone without being wholly freed of the polyp.
>
> In London Haydn chanced on the acquaintance of the celebrated surgeon H[unter]; "a man," said Haydn, "who undertook surgical operations almost daily and always successfully. He had inspected my polyp and offered to free me of this complaint. I had half agreed, but the operation was put off, and I finally thought nothing more about it. Shortly before my departure Mr. H[unter] sent to ask me with pressing reasons to come to him. I went. After the first greetings several big strong fellows entered the room, seized me, and tried to seat me in a chair. I shouted, beat them black and blue, kicked till I freed myself, and made it clear to Mr. H, who was standing all ready with his instruments for the operation, that I would not be operated on. He wondered at my obstinacy, and it seemed to me that he pitied me for not wanting the fortunate experience of his skill. I excused myself for lack of time, due to my impending departure, and took my leave of him."[9]

Despite this encounter, Haydn remained friends with the Hunters and spent time with them on his second visit to England.

RETURN TO VIENNA

Haydn arrived back in Vienna about four weeks after leaving London, in late July. His journey had taken him through Bonn, where arrangements were probably made for Beethoven to follow him to Vienna as pupil, and possibly to return with him to England the following year—for Haydn was contracted to return. No notice was taken of his arrival in Vienna and he quickly settled back into the comparative anonymity of the city where he was taken for granted, undoubtedly enjoying the rest.

He was due to return to London early in January 1793, but for unknown reasons he did not. Perhaps he needed time to gather a portfolio of compositions. A contributing factor may well have been the death at the age of thirty-nine of Marianne von Genzinger, his dear friend and correspondent, who had provided him with a second home in Vienna. Of the many women in Haydn's life she was one of those he loved most, although she was happily married. Another possible factor

9. Dies, *op. cit.*, pp. 151–52.

was the presence in the Haydn household of Pietro Polzelli, Haydn's pupil, and Luigia's (and Haydn's?) son. It was not until the following January, in 1794, that Haydn found himself once more on the road to London. His third prince, Paul Anton, did not wish him to leave, although he had no particular occupation to offer him. Dies says that it was because he believed Haydn had acquired enough fame and enough money. But in the end he gave in, and on 19 January 1794, the long journey was once again undertaken. Only three days after Haydn's departure Prince Paul Anton suddenly died.

BACK TO LONDON

Incredible as it seems, the first concert of Haydn's London season took place on 10 February 1794, only six days after his arrival, and others followed a week apart. These were times of national crisis and an enormous surge of patriotism swept across England. The wars with revolutionary France that were to last until Waterloo in 1814 were just beginning. There is no doubt where Haydn's sympathies lay. A staunch supporter of the established order, Haydn could feel nothing but horror at the execution of Louis XVI of France in 1793. That the former Austrian princess, Marie-Antoinette, queen of France, should follow her husband to the guillotine later in the same year must have seemed like the collapse of all that was good and solid in the world. He was certainly infected by the sense of patriotic pride around him, and the frequent singing of the national anthem "God Save Great George, our King" made him resolve to compose something similar for his own emperor, which he did when he finally returned to Austria.

In 1795, when the next Salomon Concert Series was to be announced, the entrepreneur published a letter to his patrons saying that he could no longer carry on, thanking them for their support and Haydn and Viotti, and all the other "Professors" (professional musicians) for their assistance. These concerts were replaced by the "Opera Concert," so called because it met in the King's Theatre, Handel's old opera house. The orchestra united the talents of the defunct Professional Concerts with those of the Haydn-Salomon Concerts.

After having been formally introduced to the king and queen, Haydn had become more intimate with the royal family, and Griesinger describes their relationship:

> One evening when Haydn had been playing the pianoforte before the Queen for a long time, the King, who always spoke German, said he knew that Haydn had formerly been a good singer, and he would like to hear him do a few German songs. Haydn pointed to one joint of his little finger and said, "Your Majesty, my voice is now not even that big." The King laughed, and then Haydn sang his song *Ich bin der verliebteste*.

> The King and Queen wished to keep him in England. "You shall have a place in Windsor in the summers," said the Queen, "and then," she added with an arch look toward the King, "we shall sometimes make music tête à tête." "Oh!" replied the King, "I am not worked up over Haydn, he is a good honest German gentleman." "To keep that reputation," answered Haydn, "is my greatest pride." On repeated urging to remain in England, Haydn claimed that he was bound by gratitude to his Prince's house, and that he could not separate himself forever from his fatherland or from his wife. The King offered to send for the latter. "She will not cross the Danube, much less the sea," Haydn replied. He remained unmoved, and he believed that on that account the King never gave him anything. Of the royal family, only the Duchess of York came to his benefit concert, and she sent him fifty guineas.[10]

Why Haydn chose not to stay in England is hard to guess. He had little to keep him in Vienna, and he must have known that in refusing the pressing offer of the king and queen he was likely to offend them. Both Haydn and Mozart had experienced the effect of a monarch who was not enamored of their music, and there is certainly a question whether the initial poor reception of *The Seasons* in England may not have been a direct result of Haydn's refusal to settle there. The thought of all those poor people in Austro-Hungary, two brothers, a large number of nephews and nieces, and friends, who occupied such a place in his heart that he remembered them in his will, may perhaps have called him back. It may be that he could not refuse the request of his fourth prince, Nikolaus II, to return and set up the Esterházy musical establishment once again. Whatever the reasons, in August of 1795 he left England, rich in memories as in compositions, and with a libretto for an oratorio, *The Creation*. Griesinger says:

> Haydn counted the days he spent in England among the happiest of his life. He was universally respected there, a new world was opened up to him, and he was enabled by generous profits at last to pull out of the limited circumstances in which he had grown old and gray; for in 1790 he had hardly two thousand gulden capital of his own.
>
> He earned in a three-year stay in England something like twenty-four thousand gulden, of which about nine thousand went for the journey, his support, and other expenses.[11]

The Vienna he returned to was the Vienna of Beethoven's early Trios, Op. 1, and the Piano Sonatas, Op. 2.

THE FINAL RETURN

The prince whom Haydn returned home to serve was a difficult and

10. Griesinger, *op. cit.*, p. 35.
11. *Ibid.*, pp. 23 and 35.

proud man. Thirty years old in 1795, his interests lay primarily in the visual arts and the theater. In music his tastes were for old-fashioned church music and for little else. He reached such eminence that Napoleon suggested he be made king of Hungary, and it speaks well for him that he was not to be bought by such a bribe but remained loyal to the imperial crown. His activities as a soldier and philanderer did much to dissipate the enormous wealth of the Esterházy family.

For Haydn he was an unsympathetic and arrogant patron. Haydn's duties, however, remained light, consisting initially of rebuilding his musical establishment, concentrated less in Esterháza and more in Vienna and Eisenstadt. During these last years of the eighteenth century, Haydn cemented relationships with many of the aristocratic families of Germany and Austria, and the great advantage of his position lay in the fact that it allowed him time to concentrate on what he wanted to compose. One of his first wishes was to rearrange his celebrated *Seven Last Words on the Cross* for choir and orchestra, and he asked Gottfried, Baron van Swieten (1733–1803) to write words to the series of slow movements which make up the work; later, he wrote the words for *The Creation* and *The Seasons*.

Baron van Swieten figured prominently in the musical life of Vienna from the 1780s into the nineteenth century, and in the lives of Haydn, Mozart and Beethoven. He was trained as a diplomat and in that capacity had been sent to Berlin and to London. In Berlin he came into contact with the Bach cult; while in London he experienced the early stages and the growing tradition of Handel performance; and when he returned to Vienna in 1777 he established his Sunday musicales to propagate the new faith of Bach and Handel, in which Mozart played such a prominent part as instrumentalist and arranger. (Not only did Mozart provide him with modern orchestrations of *Messiah, Acis and Galatea,* and *Alexander's Feast,* but he also arranged a number of Bach fugues for string quartet and trio.) It was van Swieten who advised Mozart's widow not to spend much-needed money on a more elaborate funeral for her husband. He was an amateur composer of symphonies, and Beethoven dedicated his First Symphony to him.

He has been described as a "stiff" man, but an invitation he made to Beethoven, who had ingratiated himself with him by his playing of Bach fugues, has an endearing quality to it. In the early 1790s the sixty-year-old van Swieten wrote to the twenty-year-old Beethoven thus:

> To Hr. Beethoven in Alstergasse No.45 with the Prince Lichnowsky. If there is nothing to hinder you next Wednesday I should be glad to see you at my house at half past 8 with your nightcap in your bag. Give me an immediate answer. Swieten.[12]

This was the man with whom Haydn worked closely on the two

12. Alexander Wheelock Thayer, *Life of Beethoven* (Princeton, 1964) I, p. 161.

Baron Gottfried van Swieten: the portrait shows him as he must have looked when Haydn was working with him—an obstinate, opiniated man.

projects that occupied so much of his creative energies during the next five years. In Mozart we have a composer who bullied his librettists; in van Swieten we have a librettist who tried to bully his composer. He believed that his conception of the words and music was the correct and the best one, and that Haydn's job was to realize his ideas. Haydn was experienced in dealing with difficult people, but he found the fight exhausting, particularly during their collaboration on *The Seasons* . Perhaps even more galling to Haydn was van Swieten's proprietary attitude to *The Creation,* speaking of it as though he were the sole author.

During 1796, while working on the sketches for *The Creation,* Haydn busied himself with other compositions. That year he produced the famous Trumpet Concerto, four Piano Trios, and the first two Masses composed for performance on the nameday of Princess Marie Hermenegild, wife of Nikolaus II, and Haydn's devoted admirer.

The following year, 1797, Haydn's work on *The Creation* demanded much more of his concentrated attention and kept him from other work. Indeed, he rented accommodation in Vienna near van Swieten's house to facilitate their meetings. Despite the trouble he experienced with this oratorio, it is probably his most popular work, and one that is recognized by millions to whom the name Haydn is quite unknown.

It may very well be that Haydn conceived the idea of composing an Austrian national anthem, for we know how impressed he had been by that piece and the patriotic purpose it had served. However, there are other versions of the story of its origins: one has Haydn talking it over with van Swieten, who then approached the President of Lower Austria, a Count Saurau, who then had verses written for that purpose.

Count Saurau's version of the story is slightly shorter, omitting both Haydn's and van Swieten's contributions and claiming the idea was his. Whatever the true story might have been, the Hymn was sung at all theaters on the emperor's birthday, 12 February 1797 by order of the Austrian government. The plan worked to perfection, and *Gott erhälte Franz den Kaiser* (God save Franz, the Kaiser) stands as one of the most solidly built musical edifices of all time. Completed by the middle of this year, also, were the six String Quartets Op. 76, dedicated to Count Joseph Erdödy. Several of these works were probably already finished in 1796, but they were not published until 1799, since Count Erdödy would have had the exclusive use of them for a period. For the remainder of 1797, Haydn worked on *The Creation*.

Late in the year, Haydn was made an honorary member of the *Tonkünstlersocietät,* that organization to which he had applied in 1778 for insurance for his wife and himself and which had demanded large compositions from him whenever required as a condition for his admittance. It will be remembered that when Haydn refused this condition his application was rejected. Now, all rancor was forgotten, and the Society received very great benefits from Haydn's goodwill and the performances of his oratorios.

Haydn was a man of fixed work habits, and his day is described, possibly by his trusted amanuensis, copyist, and valet Johann Elssler (1769–1843), and set down by Dies, as follows:

> Haydn rose in the warmer season at half-past six, and shaved at once; up to his seventy-third year, he allowed no strange hand to do this for him. Then he dressed completely. Were a student present while he dressed, he had to play the lesson assigned him on the clavier. Mistakes were noted, a grammar lesson based on them was delivered, and then a new problem set for the next lesson.
>
> At eight Haydn had his breakfast. Immediately afterwards Haydn sat down at the clavier and improvised until he found some idea to suit his purpose, which he immediately set down on paper. Thus originated the first sketches of his compositions.
>
> At half-past eleven he received visits, or he went for a walk and paid visits himself.
>
> The hour from two to three was devoted to the midday meal.
>
> After dinner he always took up some small domestic business or went into his library and took a book to read.
>
> About four o'clock he returned to musical tasks. He then took the morning's sketches and scored them, spending three to four hours thus.
>
> At eight in the evening he usually went out, but came back to the house around nine and either set himself to score-writing, or else took a book and read till ten o'clock. The hour of ten in the evening was set for supper. Haydn had made it a rule to have nothing in the evening but wine and

> bread. This rule he only now and then violated if he were invited somewhere to supper.
>
> He liked jocularity at table and cheerful conversation in general.
>
> At half-past eleven he went to bed, in old age even later.
>
> Winter time made no difference in his daily schedule on the whole, except that Haydn rose a half hour later in the morning . . .[13]

Who would have known Haydn's schedule and work habits better than Elssler, his constant companion?

In April of 1798 *The Creation* went into rehearsal in preparation for its first performance, which took place before an invited audience on the last day of that month, at the Schwarzenberg Palace. It was greeted with an enthusiasm that has made it, ever since that day, the preeminent oratorio for the Viennese. Prince Schwarzenberg gave Haydn a roll of a hundred ducats, which was in addition to the honorarium guaranteed under the business arrangement that van Swieten had made with a number of backers to cover all the expenses of the performance. Haydn told Griesinger that during the performance "now I would be ice cold in my whole body, now a burning fever would come over me, and I was afraid more than once that I should suddenly suffer a stroke." In the exhaustion that followed the frenzied activity, Haydn, it seems, became ill and was confined to his room. Probably this period of confinement was the time in which he composed one of his three finest Masses, the *Missa in angustiis* (Mass for Troubled Times), or *Nelson* Mass, the third of the six for Princess Marie, first performed on 23 September 1798.

Early in 1800 Haydn's wife died in Baden, where she had spent years having treatments for her arthritis. Her death in itself meant little if anything to her husband, for they had lived apart for years, but to his old *amour,* Luigia Polzelli, who had had letters extending the proposal of marriage "when two pairs of eyes shall be closed," it meant renewed hope that now she might have her sixty-eight-year-old. But Haydn was not about to exchange an old wife who had always meant expense and trouble, for a young one who might prove equally costly and difficult for an old man.

Later that year Haydn had the pleasure of meeting Lord Nelson, the hero of the anti-Napoleonic world, who, with his mistress, Lady Hamilton, stayed at Eisenstadt for a few days. Haydn and Lady Hamilton made music together and Haydn gave her a copy of a song of his. Still later, Haydn gave his last concert at Esterháza.

But Haydn's main occupation was now his second great oratorio, *The Seasons.* Once again working with van Swieten, Haydn had to cope with his collaborator's vanity and constant instructions on how the music

13. Dies, *op. cit.,* p. 204.

Vienna's imposing Burgtheater. The first public performance of Haydn's *Creation* took place here in March, 1799.

should be written. From the start the oratorio aroused criticism for the amount of word painting in the score, an aspect of music of which van Swieten was very fond. Perhaps as a result of this criticism, Haydn, talking to Griesinger, put the burden of this fault upon van Swieten's shoulders.

> *The Creation* and *The Seasons* have been criticized for depicting objects foreign to the nature of music, which is inherently subjective and not objective, and this imitation is indeed not unconditionally commendable. In the midst of so many excellences, however, such passages are only minor blemishes, and Haydn himself set small store by them. When correcting the clavier edition of *The Seasons* he found the croaking of frogs too strongly expressed, he observed that this place really belonged to Grétry, and Baron van Swieten wanted it that way. In the full orchestra this vulgar notion would disappear soon enough but it would not do in the clavier edition.[14]

They quarreled about the music and for a while would not speak to one another, but the surprising thing is that the score is so completely successful. To us, who are less self-conscious than the intellectuals of the early nineteenth century and who benefit from a much broader histor-

14. Griesinger, *op. cit.*, pp. 40–41.

ical perspective, the incidents of tone painting do not stand out even as much as Beethoven's in his Sixth Symphony. The modern critic, indeed, would find it hard to choose between *The Creation* and *The Seasons,* accounting for the greater popularity of the earlier work because of its its biblical reference.

The Seasons was first performed on 24 April 1801, and it created a profound impression, confirmed in the ensuing years. Doubting notes were heard from some who adversely criticized the text, but Haydn's setting was universally admired. Shortly after the first performance, Haydn made his will, and it speaks for his physical fatigue and mental exhaustion that the two events followed one another so closely. The will is confirmation of Haydn's assertion that his simple life would enable him to leave more to his poor relations, and he seems to have remembered all of them generously.

He may not have expected, however, that later that same year he would finish the fifth of his great Masses, usually called the *Creation* Mass, a work of very high quality which takes its name from a small quotation of music from the oratorio. Moreover, he was also working on a lucrative contract that he had drawn up some years earlier with a Scottish publisher, to make arrangements of Scottish folksongs, a job that required little effort and paid well. And there was still one great work to come in 1802, the *Harmoniemesse* (Wind-band Mass).

The year 1803 saw the composition of two movements of an unfinished string quartet, called Op. 103, in D minor. The work was still unfinished in 1806 and was published in its incomplete state, for by this time it was clear that Haydn's state of health and advanced years would never allow him to finish it. It consists of a slow movement and a Minuet, both quite fine. It is significant that Haydn completed the composition of the easier movements, since his failing powers were not adequate for the first and last movements, which would have required much greater concentration. After the Minuet, there is printed in a small rectangle the size of a visiting card, a quotation from Haydn's song *Der Greis* (The Old Man), "Hin ist alle meine Kraft, alt und schwach bin ich." (All my strength is gone, old and weak am I).

Haydn's last years were rich in honors and memories. The mounting fame of *The Creation* brought him a gold medal from Paris. Another French medal accompanied his election to the Institut de France. He was given honorary membership in the Felix Meritis Society of Amsterdam. The inhabitants of a small town on an island in the North Sea off the German coast wrote to thank the composer of *The Creation* and received from him the following beautiful letter:

> Gentlemen,
>
> It was indeed a most pleasant surprise to receive such a flattering letter from a part of the world where I could never have imagined that the products of my poor talents were known. But when I see that not only is my

name familiar to you, but my compositions are performed by you with approval and satisfaction, the warmest wishes of my heart are fulfilled: to be considered a not wholly unworthy priest of this sacred art by every nation where my works are known. You reassure me on this point as regards your fatherland, but even more, you happily persuade me—and this cannot fail to be a real source of consolation to me in my declining years—that I am often the enviable means by which you, and so many other families sensible of heartfelt emotion, derive, in their homely circle, their pleasure—their enjoyment. How reassuring this thought is to me!—Often, when struggling against obstacles of every sort which oppose my labors; often, when the powers of mind and body weakened, and it was difficult for me to continue in the course I had entered on;—a secret voice whispered to me: "There are so few happy and contented people here below; grief and sorrow are always their lot; perhaps your labors will once be a source from which the care-worn, or the man burdened with affairs, can derive a few moments' rest and refreshment." This was indeed a powerful motive to press onwards, and this is why I now look back with cheerful satisfaction on the labors expended on this art, to which I have devoted so many long years of uninterrupted effort and exertion. And now I thank you in the fullness of my heart for your kindly thoughts of me, and beg you to forgive me for delaying my answer so long: enfeebled health, the inseparable companion of the grey-haired septuagenarian and pressing business deprived me till now of this pleasure. Perhaps nature may yet grant me the joy of composing a little memorial for you, from which you may gather the feelings of a gradually dying veteran, who would fain even after his death survive in the charming circle of which you draw so wonderful a picture. I have the honor to be, with profound respect,

Your wholly obedient servant,
Joseph Haydn

Vienna, 22 September, 1802[15]

Honors continued to pour in from France, from Russia, from Sweden, from Vienna, and became the stuff of his daily life as he found physical activity more and more difficult.

Haydn's last public appearance is perhaps his most famous. On 27 March 1808 a performance of *The Creation* was mounted in the Old University in Vienna. It was to be a celebration of Haydn's seventy-sixth birthday. Prince Esterházy sent his carriage to drive Haydn to the place, through crowds so large they had to be controlled by the military. He was greeted at the door and carried in to a fanfare. His "good angel," Princess Esterházy, wrapped her shawl around his shoulders to keep him warm, and many other ladies followed suit. He was so overwhelmed by the music and the reception accorded him that it was thought he was too fragile to stay after the first part of the oratorio. Everyone there knew that they were seeing Haydn in public for the last time, and as he was carried out, Beethoven, thirty-eight years old and now a

15. *Haydn Correspondence,* pp. 208–209.

Haydn's last public appearance, on March 27, 1808 in the hall of the Old University in Vienna, for a performance of *The Creation*. From a watercolor by Balthasar Wigand. (Historisches Museum der Stadt Wien)

celebrated composer, knelt before him and kissed his hands and forehead. By this act he acknowledged to the world that he was indeed Haydn's pupil, paying tribute to the master he had refused to recognize twelve years earlier. Thereafter, he who had so often spoken slightingly of Haydn would permit no word of adverse criticism.

In May of 1809 the French were bombarding Vienna, and when they had occupied the city, Napoleon placed a guard of honor in front of Haydn's door. On 26 May he went to the piano and played the Austrian Hymn, and five days later, on 31 May, he died. Because of the difficult times his funeral went almost unnoticed. Two weeks later a memorial service did him all the honor that was due to him.

THE LAST COMPOSITIONS

Haydn's compositions for keyboard during the last nineteen years of his life comprise three sonatas for solo piano, Hob. XVI:50–52, and fourteen sonatas for piano with accompaniment of violin and cello, Hob. XV:18–31. It is not possible to date these works exactly since autographs survive for only three of the seventeen works, and Haydn's notebook, in which he had listed all the works he composed in England, has been lost, but the probability is that they all date from sometime in 1794 to early 1797.

PIANO SONATAS It is likely that all the sonatas for piano solo were written for the virtuoso pianist, Clementi's pupil Therese Jansen, at whose wedding to Gaetano Bartolozzi in London Haydn acted as witness. The C-major Sonata, Hob. XVI:50, bears all the signs of not having been conceived as a whole. The first movement is one of the most impressive monothematic sonata-form movements in the whole of Haydn's oeuvre, but the second movement does not compare with it in any way. The short last movement is a tense and surprising kind of Scherzo, and it balances the opening of the work, as it compensates in power for what it lacks in length. The Sonata in D, Hob. XVI:51, like the previous work, appears to be thrown together, yet its two movements are individually fine. The Sonata in E♭, Hob. XVI:52 (*ACM* 60), is acknowledged as Haydn's greatest, and probably most famous, solo work for piano. It is a well-balanced, three-movement work in which the large, sonata-form outer movements surround a ternary-form middle movement set in the key of E major, a semitone above the tonic, E♭.

This is a work conceived for the piano and, it would seem, for public performance, although it is not known whether it was played in concert at the time of its composition. The first movement is remarkable for its monothematicism, and it is an excellent example of the structural modification Haydn often makes to prevent prolixity. A richly promising thematic group is exposed in mm. 1–8 and the repetition begun in m. 9, becomes a bridge to the dominant in mm. 13–16. M. 17 opens the second group, which continues to m. 43. In the recapitulation these crucial measures (exposition mm. 9–26) are drastically reorganized to cut out a further repetition of the opening measures (recapitulation mm. 86:3–97). A further example of the way in which Haydn modifies repeated material to create the unexpected may be found by comparing m. 38 with mm. 109–110. The effect of the twice-flattened B instead of the expected B♭ is shocking for it is clearly a "wrong note" which Haydn then reconciles. It startles both the listener and the player alike.[16]

It is unthinkable that the slow movement of this sonata could have been conceived for any other sonata since the themes of the first two movements are so closely allied, one being developed from the other (taking into account the change of meter which Haydn always thought desirable). One can almost see it emerging under the composer's hands in improvisation upon the opening of the first movement. It shares with the first movement a richness and variety of texture that make them perfectly complementary. The last movement establishes its relationship with the first through the chromatic direction of its melody, upward at all times except in the conclusion of the middle section. The impression of resolution as the chromatic scale changes its direction is again an example of Haydn's understanding and control of the small elements of music.

16. The relationship of these notes to the key of F♭/enharmonic E major, which some critics cite as a preparation for the key of the following movement, and justification of the development passage in m. 88 is incontrovertible yet far-fetched, since the effect on the ear is not that of a tonality but of a single wrong note.

PIANO SONATAS WITH ACCOMPANIMENT The accompanied sonatas appeared, as follows:

Nov. 1794 announced . . .	Hob. XV:18–20
May 1795	Hob. XV:21–23
Oct. 1795	Hob. XV:24–26
Apr.1797 announced	Hob. XV:27–29
Composed in 1796	Hob. XV:30
Composed in 1794–5	Hob. XV:31

All four sets are dedicated to women: the first to the widow of his third Prince Esterházy; the second to the wife of his fourth prince, Marie Hermenegild, to whom he had already dedicated the group of piano sonatas in 1784 and for whom he would write his last six Masses; the third to the widow of the well-known pianist and composer Samuel Schroeter, Rebecca, whom he would probably have married had he been free, and with whom he almost certainly had an affair; and the fourth set to the virtuoso Therese Jansen-Bartolozzi.

The accompanied sonatas show little change over those of the preceding decade. The writing for cello is surprisingly retrogressive, for in these works the cello is even less independent than in the accompanied sonatas of 1787. On the other hand, the music gains constantly in depth and richness, revealing a quality of introspection at times as exalted as any string quartet Haydn ever wrote, and at other times as exuberant as expected. There is, in these works, a kind of improvised ornamentation that goes beyond anything in the solo keyboard sonatas, often juxtaposed with rigorous and sinewy two-part writing, e.g., Nos. 23 and 24. Sensuous harmonic effects, as shown in Example XXIV-1 are unlike anything to be found in the works of Haydn's contemporaries, and clearly result from his habit of improvising and then composing at

Example XXIV–1: J. HAYDN, Trio (Hob. XV:23), II

the keyboard. Although Haydn had no reputation as a pianist, it is interesting to note that the pianistic figuration he generates from his fingers is more original than in the solo sonatas (Example XXIV–2). So fertile in inspiration, so inspired in workmanship, Haydn's late trios constitute a body of instrumental music on an artistic level with the late

Example XXIV–2: J. HAYDN, Trio (Hob. XV:27), I

symphonies and late quartets. Our comparative ignorance of them can only be attributed to the fact that the performing combination for which they were written is no longer fashionable, since cellists generally wish to participate more fully than Haydn allows. The trios may come into their own once more as the practice of early music revives our sensitivity to the rewards of *continuo* playing.

STRING QUARTETS There are fifteen string quartets from these last years:

Opus No.	Number	Dedicated to	Composed	Published
71	3	Count Apponyi	1793	London, 1795
74	3	Count Apponyi	1793	London, 1796
76	6	Count Erdödy	1796–97	Vienna, 1799
77	2	Prince Lobkowitz	1799	Vienna, 1802
103	1		1803	Leipzig, 1806

The Quartets Opp.71 and 74 are really one set of six which was split by the publisher into two sets of three. This was a common practice of the time, enabling the publisher to come onto the market with the first three of a set, while the other three were still in preparation. It is not usual for the two parts to have different opus numbers. More often the publisher will distinguish the parts of an opus as *1er. Livraison, 2me. Livraison,* etc. (literally, 1st delivery, 2nd delivery).

These late quartets were written with public as well as private performance in mind. They were presented to an eager public in Salomon's concerts by the quartet led by Salomon himself, and hence they are often referred to as the *Salomon* Quartets. An important difference between these and earlier quartets is immediately apparent: in five of the six quartets an introductory passage opens the first movement. In one case the introduction is slow; in the other four, they are in tempo but strongly contrasting in texture or dynamics. It is clear that the introduction serves many purposes, among which must be reckoned the practical (quieting the audience) as well as the musical (thematic).

In the Quartet Op. 74, No. 1 (Hob. III:72), the two introductory chords provide the seed from which the whole movement germinates. This is perhaps the best example of Haydn's growing predilection for much closer and more obvious thematic/motivic work. Indeed, the first movements of these quartets demonstrate this kind of technique consistently, juxtaposing it with passages of sixteenth notes to create an effect of brilliance and virtuosity. Various writers have noted the deepening quality of seriousness and gravity of Haydn's slow movements in this last period, particularly in the quartets but also in the symphonies, to the point where they become the emotional, expressive heart of the work.

Haydn obviously reached the apogee of his style and technique in the six quartets of Op. 76, producing one masterpiece after another. The first of the set (Hob. III:75) displays an almost Mozartian use of counterpoint, so easy, natural, and unconstrained as to appear instinctive. For example, at m. 144 of the first movement, where a canon at the octave between first and second violins produces a string of intervals of a fourth. The addition of the viola part cleverly makes all well.

Example XXIV–3: J. HAYDN, Quartet, Op.76, No.1, I

The slow movement *Adagio sostenuto,* with its echoes of the Priests' March from *Die Zauberflöte,* attains a sublimity that Haydn exceeded only once. The *Menuetto* with a *Presto* marking is Haydn's first real Scherzo in that its meter is felt as one beat to the measure.

The second quartet, in the key of D minor, inevitably recalls Mozart's K. 421, also the second of the set, in its texture and in the initial downward octave, but the prevalence of the opening intervals identifies it most clearly as Haydn. The *Menuetto* is famous for its sustained canon with the upper strings set against the lower strings, a unique kind of sound.

The third quartet is perhaps the most famous, since it includes the variations which Haydn wrote on his own Austrian national hymn. The tune itself is a multi-faceted inspiration, and Haydn's harmonic and textural treatment is rightly judged one of the sublime things in music.

The fourth quartet is nicknamed *The Sunrise* because of the beautiful opening in which the long-spanned melody of the first violin emerges from the quiet, sustained chords of the lower strings and takes shape. The secondary material in the dominant begins with a modified inversion of the opening, a procedure followed by Beethoven in his first piano sonata, and which obviously did not disturb the inventor of the nickname.

The fifth quartet in D opens with a curious movement that is certainly a set of variations, but these variations are not bound by the harmonic structure of the theme. There is given a strong tendency to the tonality of B minor, and since Haydn sets his slow movement in F♯ major, this quartet can be looked upon as a *locus classicus* of his use of mediant and sub-mediant key areas.

The sixth quartet opens with a set of variations which concludes with a fugue, followed by a second movement entitled *Fantasia.* This movement, one of Haydn's wildest experiments in modulation and structure, is followed by another Scherzo, again entitled *Menuetto,* but the real joke is to be found in the *Alternativo* or Trio, in which Haydn plays with a scale and its inversion.

The two Quartets Op. 77 (Hob. III:81 and 82), were to have been part of a set of six, of which Haydn wrote two and a half. Why he did not complete the set is not known, but one plausible suggestion concerns the appearance of young Beethoven's Op.18 quartets (also dedicated to Lobkowitz) at about the time Haydn was working on Op. 77. It is possible that the old man felt his quartets suffered by comparison and so he withdrew from the field. It is certainly possible that his contemporaries might have found Haydn's work old-fashioned in 1800, but today we can only regret the loss of masterpieces that might have been. Both works adopt the Scherzo type of Minuet, and although Haydn still calls these movements *Menuetto* there is not a shred of the minuet's periodicity left. Indeed, perhaps the only characteristic of the dance that remains is to be found in the opposition of duple with triple meter. Rich as the outer movements of both works are, it is in the poignant and valedictory slow movements that we find the center of gravity that claims our attention.

Based upon a four-bar theme, the figure of mm. 1 and 2 in the slow movement of Op.77, No.1 (*ACM* 61) recurs thirteen times in the course of the monothematic and loosely structured sonata form. It is the expressive curve of this figure that imbues the entire movement with a feeling of acceptance, of finality with no regret, and of the permanence of the beautiful.

SONGS While he was in England Haydn published two sets of songs each entitled *Six Original Canzonettas.* The first set (1794) was composed to verses by Anne Hunter, wife of the famous (and over-eager) surgeon John Hunter, and one of the many women who seem to have been strongly attracted to the famous sexagenarian; the second set is composed to various poets, including Shakespeare, Metastasio, and also Anne Hunter. These songs differ from the earlier sets in that they are written on three staves, and the accompaniment is more dense; nevertheless, the vocal part is still almost always doubled in the right hand of the piano part. They show a definite attempt to make music heighten the effect of the word, although none of them goes beyond the normal techniques of opera. Generally, the songs are strophic, but there are also examples of through-composed and modified strophic structures. Despite the fact that most of them are clearly the jottings of an idle half hour or so, some attain heights of beauty that make one regret the loss of so many other Haydn songs.

SYMPHONIES With the twelve symphonies composed for his two London visits, Haydn reaches a personal pinnacle, setting a standard of excellence by which every symphony of the late eighteenth century is measured. Each visit was the occasion for six new symphonies:

No.	Key	Composed	First performed
93	D	London, 1791	17 February 1792
94	G (*Surprise*)	London, 1791	23 March 1792
95	C minor	London, 1791	1791
96	D (*Miracle*)	London, 1791	1791
97	C	London, 1792	3 or 4 May, 1792
98	B♭	London, 1792	2 March, 1792
99	E♭	Austria, 1793	10 February 1794
100	G (*Military*)	London, 1794	31 March, 1794
101	D (*Clock*)	London, 1794	3 March, 1794
102	B♭	London, 1794	2 February, 1795
103	E♭ (*Drum Roll*)	London, 1795	2 March, 1795
104	D (*London*)	London, 1795	4 May, 1795

No composer ever produced twelve major symphonies in such a short time, and when we consider that at the same time, Haydn also composed six string quartets, fourteen piano trios, three piano sonatas, an opera, and many smaller works, we realize that Bach's achievement from 1723 to 1730, Mozart's from 1780 to 1787, and Beethoven's from 1803 to 1808, is equaled by Haydn, a man in his sixties. The symphonies are all marvels of freshness of inspiration, as rich in details of orchestration and in elaborate contrapuntal devices as they are inventive in structure.

The Symphony No. 102 in B♭, considered one of the very best, shows some of the qualities shared by all of them. It resembles the first six in the omission of clarinets in its orchestration. Of the second group, only Nos. 101 and 102 do not use clarinets. Eleven of the twelve *London* Symphonies begin with a slow introduction, each of which serves a different purpose within the compositional process. There are those like Nos. 94 and 104 where a relationship between Introduction and *Allegro* is so abstruse as to cause the listener to doubt whether any connection is intended by the composer, and in consequence, whether there need be any connection at all. There are those, like No. 97, where a phrase at the opening and closing of the Introduction is almost literally repeated toward the conclusion of the *Allegro*. There is the case of No. 103, where the long Introduction recurs towards the close of the first movement and makes its relationship to the material of the whole movement obvious. And there is the case of Symphony No. 102, where, following an arresting unison B♭ with *crescendo-decrescendo,* a melody follows with two clearly differentiated parts: mm. 2–5 constitute the melody in which a legato beginning (mm. 2–3) is concluded by a series of staccato notes (mm. 4–5). A repetition of this opening leads to a modulating development in which the figure stated by the first violins in m. 2 is relayed throughout the orchestral texture. It is this figure that might be called

Example XXIV–4: J. HAYDN, Symphony No. 102, I

the musical germ from which the symphony springs. Clearly, the opening of the *Vivace,* mm. 23–26, is a quickened and elaborated version of

Example XXIV–5: J. HAYDN, Symphony No. 102, I

mm. 2–5. In m. 57 the beginning of the second group consists of the first figure together with its inversion. The working-out of the figure

Example XXIV–6: J. HAYDN, Symphony No. 102, I

can be followed easily throughout the movement. The material, mm. 81–92, is not easy to see as springing from the germinal material, however, yet even this, so affectively different, proves its identity with the opening. (See Example XXIV–7.)

The melodies of both the Minuet and Trio bear a recognizable relationship to the opening of the symphony. The slow movement seems to have no particular connection with the first movement, and indeed, it may be that it was composed before the rest of the work. The same slow movement, but in the key of F♯ major, is also used in the last trio

Example XXIV–7: J. HAYDN, Symphony No. 102, I

dedicated to Mrs. Schroeter, Haydn's last love, and it may be included in both works because it perhaps had a particular significance for them both.

The last movement, however, contains another instance of Haydn's amazing humor which is both funny and structurally significant for the whole of the work. This sonata-rondo appears to be based more upon the interval of a third than on the fourth, which was the basis of the first movement. The material between mm. 78–99 shows the first signs of an obvious connection. When this material is repeated in mm. 234 and beyond, the process of decomposition and recomposition is started in mm. 261–285. The *piano* chords in mm. 284 and 285 are a prelude to one of the strangest events in the Haydn oeuvre, the *fortissimo* passage, mm. 286–310, which is then repeated at *piano*. The passage is so anomalous in the context of the last movement, where nothing except the

Example XXIV–8: J. HAYDN, Symphony No. 102, IV

long flute passage (mm. 222–232) has foreshadowed it, that the listener is forced to think back to the opening of the symphony to find its justification.

In none of Haydn's other symphonies is there anything like this musical dig in the ribs, which, at the same time, conveys a feeling of the composer's satisfaction at his display of masterful technique. He has built one of his greatest works, full of the most varied affective content, from a small, insignifcant sequence of notes. Yet with all the variety the symphony contains, as in so many of Haydn's great works, it is remarkable that one senses no element of pathos.

CONCERTOS There are two concertos that survive from this period, and possibly two others (one for two horns and one for bassoon) that are lost. The Concertante in B♭ was written for Haydn's second concert season in London in 1792, in direct response to the Professional Concerts' importation of Haydn's pupil Ignace Pleyel as a rival attraction. Pleyel was Kapellmeister at Strasbourg at this time—not until 1795 did he move to Paris—and in France the *symphonie concertante* was one of the most popular genres. Haydn's manuscript, normally neat and tidy, betrays the haste in which this charming, three-movement work was written. The solo instruments are violin, cello, oboe, and bassoon, and fulfill their roles in the orchestral body, emerging at times as a group and as individuals. A surprising feature of the last movement is the introduction of instrumental recitative for the solo violin, which intervenes before the composer introduces the main melodic material. It is as if Haydn were anticipating the structure of the last movement of Beethoven's Ninth Symphony, but with none of its significance.

The Concerto for Trumpet in E♭ dates from the time of Haydn's final return to Vienna,and it was written for a friend who had invented a trumpet with keys. Probably the most celebrated of all trumpet concertos, it is also Haydn's most famous virtuoso work. In the customary three movements, the work is scored with complete mastery. The very existence of this concerto is something of a miracle: written in 1796, it was first performed in 1800 and then it was unheard of for 129 years, surviving in a single copy.

OPERA Salomon's original contract with Haydn specified that the composer should write an opera for London. The result of this stipulation was the *dramma per musica* entitled *L'anima del filosofo* (The Philosopher's Soul) or *Orfeo ed Euridice*. The libretto was by Carlo Badini, an Italian resident in London for many years. Unlike the Gluck version of the story, Haydn and his librettist return to the ancient myth of Orpheus, who, after the second death of Euridice, forswears love and pleasure offered to him by the Bacchantes and dies at their hands. The work is in the style of an *opera seria,* depending very largely on a sequence of aria and recitative, but Haydn had a chorus in London, which made the aural effect of this opera different from any of his others. From Euridice's first scene, where we would have expected a solo aria following an accompanied recitative, Haydn surprises us with an aria for solo voice with unison chorus, and what would have been static becomes dramatic through the interaction of the characters on stage. The orchestra—bigger by far than heretofore—is used throughout. Particularly noteworthy is the dramatic pace of the deaths of Euridice and Orfeo, for in an opera that contains one of Haydn's most extravagant coloratura arias, the restraint, the brevity, and the dramatic impact of both these passages is striking. The opera concludes with an effect something like an eighteenth-century *Götterdämmerung,* for after the Bacchantes have killed Orfeo a marvelous storm arises, and the river overflows and washes away the mob of wild women. Orfeo's river-god father carries his son's body away too, and a sad calm returns.

ORATORIOS When Haydn left England for the last time he carried with him a libretto on the subject of the biblical Creation, destined to become the greatest oratorio of the second half of the eighteenth century and in many ways Haydn's single most significant work. The origins of the libretto have been a matter of discussion, since the putative English original by an unknown "Mr. Lidley" cannot be found. The balance of evidence, however, points in the direction of there having been an English libretto, based upon the Bible and Milton's *Paradise Lost,* which was adapted and translated into German by van Swieten, the English version of the libretto retaining much from the original English. During the composition of this work Haydn, the man of faith, was inspired by his devotion, and every day fell on his knees to pray for help and guidance in its composition. Yet much has been made of the Masonic influence on the libretto and the fact that it deals with a God far removed from the notion of the Trinity. Whatever its theology, for Haydn the work was an expression of his simple belief in the story from Genesis, and the finer points of doctrine paled into insignificance beside his certainty of God in the scheme of things.

The music cost Haydn immense effort, and the almost careless ease with which he had tossed off earlier symphonies gave way to painstaking planning of effect. There can be no doubt that the opening of this oratorio constitutes some of the most original and powerful pages in the history of Western music.[17] What Haydn has done in these pages is to extend the reach of eighteenth-century harmony to the point where the dissolving of tonality becomes conceivable through the further extension of what he has developed here. Extension of nonharmonic tones, constant semitonal movement in voices, interruption of movement to cadence, and diminished harmony are the most obvious means which Haydn uses to create an effect of Chaos, a state where nothing is

17. The score in available in the *Norton Anthology of Western Music.*

solid, a state of restlessness, melancholy because it lacks the word of God to create order, stability, and significance. It is hard to think of anything comparable, except possibly Wagner's Prelude to *Das Rheingold.* Both Haydn and Wagner use their Preludes to induce a particular state of mind in the listener: Haydn by enlarging his means and Wagner, paradoxically, by restricting himself to almost minimalist principles.

All aspects of the composition of *The Creation,* whether accompanied recitative, unaccompanied recitative, aria, or chorus, all receive the blessing of Haydn's inspired and imaginative intellect, and in the all-embracing miracle of the oratorio, that goes beyond any one religion in speaking to all mankind, childlike naiveté and mature intellect are united, much as in Mozart's *Die Zauberflöte.* And as with *Die Zauberflöte,* Haydn's *Creation* met with popular and widespread success, again demonstrating that the ideals of eighteenth-century music were not exclusive but inclusive, and they reached over boundaries of class, nationality, and religion to embrace all thinking and feeling people. Haydn's achievement places him beside Mozart and Beethoven as one of the great humanists of music.

His next oratorio, *Die Jahreszeiten* (The Seasons), matches *The Creation* in every respect. To a libretto by van Swieten taken from an epic poem of the same name by James Thomson, an early eighteenth-century Scottish poet, Haydn wrote the richest score of his entire life. While not possessing anything as innovative as "The Representation of Chaos" this subject offered Haydn a broader canvas to work on; it is one thing to contemplate the divine and to marvel at revelation, but another to think of the ordinary man in his year-round activities. Griesinger reports Haydn in old age as saying:

> I had a hard time in my youth, and I strove even then to earn enough to be free of care in my old days. In this I succeeded, thank God. I have my own comfortable house, three or four courses at dinner, a good glass of wine, I can dress well, and when I want to drive out, a hired coach is good enough for me. I have associated with emperors, kings, and many great gentlemen and have heard many flattering things from them, but I do not wish to live on an intimate footing with such persons, and I prefer people of my own status.[18]

Haydn's last will and testament is dated hardly more than a week after the first performance of *The Seasons;* in it he divides his worldly goods almost entirely among the descendants of his family and upon peasants and humble folk whom he has known and worked with. It was his pride to remember everyone, for *The Seasons* is about the life of these people, affected by the weather, the ploughing, the harvest, the drinking and the dancing, the hunt, and the kill, all the activities that measure

18. Griesinger, *op. cit.,* p. 55.

the span of man's life in full touch with nature. And one senses that Haydn, in writing *The Seasons* , was making a sentimental journey back to his roots and remembering how he too used to hunt with delight. Haydn might well have written a superscription at the head of *The Seasons* identical to that which Beethoven wrote at the opening of his *Pastoral* Symphony, "Joyous feelings upon arriving in the Country," for *The Seasons* is Haydn's *Pastoral*. In it he has come full circle, returning to the home of his childhood with all his memories bright as only an old man's can be, having traveled the world and met with success, and now knowing where truth, beauty, and essential life are to be found. The sounds of nature which he incorporates so often in this work are all evoked by musical means and are as natural to Haydn and as significant musically as any trick of counterpoint, any shade of harmony, or any device of structure. Now, perhaps, for the first time since this work's premiere, we can listen to it with ears and aesthetic conceptions that approximate Haydn's, without any of the pretentious snobbery that has characterized criticism of this work from Beethoven's time almost to the present.

MASSES In Haydn's old age his active reemployment by his fourth prince required him to write a Mass for the nameday of the Princess Marie Hermenegild. With her many kindnesses and with her open admiration for Haydn, the princess compensated in large measure for her husband's haughtiness and authoritarian manners, and Haydn wrote Masses for her with love. Six works resulted from this duty, the first two of which cannot be accurately dated:

1. *Missa in tempore belli* (Mass in Time of War) 1796. Also known as *Paukenmesse* because of the prominent part for tympani.
2. *Missa St. Bernardi von Offida* 1796. Often called *Heiligmesse*.
3. *Missa in angustiis* (Mass for Troubled Times) 1798. Also known as the *Nelson* Mass.
4. *Theresienmesse* 1799. The Empress of Austria, Maria Theresa, may have sung this work in performance.
5. *Schöpfungsmesse,* (Creation Mass) 1801. So called because of a quotation from *The Creation*.
6. *Harmoniemesse* (Wind-band Mass) 1802. So called because of the importance of the wind writing in it.

Unlike the *London* or the *Paris* Symphonies, which are of uniform excellence, the last six Masses seem to betray a varying enthusiasm, and Haydn's ability to become rapt in the process of composition seems to have forsaken him at times. Thus there are many pages in these works which seem to go through the routine and cliché procedures of reiterating expected cadential phrase and orchestral textures. The kind of richness of melodic thought and texture which distinguishes *Die Schöpfung* and *Die Jahreszeiten* is much rarer here, but it is noteworthy that the Masses become more thoughtful and richer with the passage of time. Whether he felt in 1796 that he had said farewell to life when he left London, or whether he loathed the thought of once again actively working for the Esterházys, away from Vienna in Eisenstadt, or whether it was simply that in 1796 he was burdened with other work cannot be known. But the first two Masses may impress the listener as perfunctory, despite some remarkable movements. The cello *obbligato* in the *Credo* and the tympani effects in the *Agnus Dei* from the *Mass in Time of War* are outstanding, however.

In the *Missa in angustiis* it is quite evident from the outset that the composer is completely involved with striking and original results. The setting of the solo soprano against the choir in the *Kyrie* is shockingly brilliant. The orchestration of strings and brass, without woodwinds, contributes to its effectiveness. It is believed that an unexpected fanfare of trumpets in the *Benedictus* was inserted when Haydn heard of Nelson's victory over Napoleon in the Battle of the Nile.

While the *Theresienmesse* steps back from the brilliance of the previous Mass to be quiet and introspective, the two final Masses set the crown on Haydn's achievement in church music, and there can be no question of his total absorption in the task at hand. The *Schöpfungsmesse* and the *Harmoniemesse* both contain melodic material that is original and strikingly beautiful, and the textures are carefully worked out to the last detail.

These works show no sign that Haydn the composer was almost exhausted. Indeed, the astonishing thing is that to the end he showed such energy and vitality, allied with the sensibility that he had always possessed but which grew deeper with advancing years. His legacy to mankind is perishable only if one can conceive of humanity without music. In a world of ever-changing aesthetic values, we can once again see the value of the Haydn of the operas and the Masses, in a way denied to the generations of the nineteenth and earlier twentieth centuries, and we can acknowledge Haydn's greatness now as it was in his own day.

Griesinger quotes Haydn in old age as saying that

> . . . instead of the many quartets, sonatas and symphonies, he should have written more vocal music. Not only might he have become one of the foremost opera composers, but also it is far easier to compose along the lines of a text than without one.[19]

We can see, as Griesinger perhaps could not, that these are the dreams of an old man on what might have been. And although we can recognize once again the inherent beauty in Haydn's vocal works, yet there are few who would not change them for more "quartets, sonatas and symphonies" for we recognize in them one of the rarest alliances of intellect and imagination ever to have existed.

19. *Ibid.*, p. 63.

PART VII

Mozart, Genius Achieved

CHAPTER XXV

The Last Ten Years: 1781–91

Because all the Mozarts traveled to Munich to enjoy Wolfgang's triumph with *Idomeneo,* there are no family letters describing the first performance, on 29 January 1781, or the stir that the opera made. There is little doubt that the celebrations following the realization of this grandest of all operas, occurring only two days after the composer's 25th birthday, must have been both festive and gratifying.

Several friends of the Mozarts also travelled to Munich for the occasion but not the archbishop, despite the fact that the Italian librettist, Varesco, the German translator, Schachtner, and the composer, Mozart, were all in his service. He went in the opposite direction, to Vienna, whence he summoned Mozart to join him on 12 March. Wolfgang arrived there from Munich on 16 March 1781.

BREAKING WITH COLLOREDO

During the next two months matters between employer and servant reached crisis point. Blame cannot be accurately apportioned, but it is clear that both Wolfgang and the archbishop were guilty—from the other's point of view—of gross provocation, and the final rupture between them, which had been building for so long, was inevitable. For Colloredo, Mozart was a troublesome, conceited servant, whose undeniable talent required constant indulgence. He always wanted permission to be away from Salzburg, obviously looking for a better position, which he never got. The world might think the archbishop lucky to have someone of Mozart's talent in his service, but the world could never know the cost. ("I shall certainly fool the archbishop, and how I shall enjoy doing it" [*Letters,* 4 Apr. 1781]).

To see Mozart's point of view one must remember that to him and to his family the world appeared to be inhabited by few friends and many enemies. It may be that they were right. Colloredo was always seen as an obstacle to success, and in the last months of their connection he seems to have tried to bring Mozart to heel by making his life a misery, requiring him to be in constant attendance like any ordinary servant. Mozart's letters detail a whole catalogue of annoyances: he was compelled to eat at the servants' table in the archbishop's house, yet outside he was constantly invited to dine with members of the aristocracy as an equal; he was asked to give his services at a charity concert, which would have been good for his reputation, but the archbishop refused permission, until members of the nobility persuaded him to reverse his decision (how galling for Colloredo!); and, for a final concert at the archbishop's, Mozart had composed three new works and received as a reward four ducats, whereas had he not been obliged to play for Colloredo he would have been able to accept an invitation to play at Countess Thun's house, for which he would have received 50 ducats. Moreover—bitterest of all—the emperor had been present at Countess Thun's, and to make himself known to the emperor was Mozart's dearest wish. The litany of frustrations and lost opportunities was endless. The most revealing statement about all this is in a letter to his father in which, writing about the payment of musicians, Mozart says: "For, as we have always been different in every way from the other court musicians, I trust we shall be different in this respect too." (*Letters,* 24 Mar. 1781) This quotation sums up the quarrel, for while this was Mozart's view, it was most emphatically not Colloredo's. Mozart did see the archbishop's point too, for it was put to him. He says that the chief accusation made against him in respect of his service was:

> I did not know that I was a valet . . . I ought to have idled away a couple of hours every morning in the antechamber. True, I was often told that I ought to present myself, but I could never remember that this was part of my duty, and I only turned up punctually whenever the Archbishop sent for me. (*Letters,* 12 May 1781)

The affair dragged on until the middle of June 1781, with Leopold using all the power of persuasion that a lifetime of governing his son had given him. But Wolfgang's mind was made up. He believed that luck was beginning to run in his favor ("Now please be cheerful, for my good luck is just beginning, and I trust that my good luck will be yours also." [*Letters,* 9 May 1781]) and that concerts, pupils, fame, and fortune awaited him from a public enamored of his talent. He was convinced that only the archbishop stood in his way. He also had another reason to believe that his future lay in Vienna rather than in Salzburg because he was once again in love, and with a woman of whom his father could not possibly approve, Constanze Weber.

He was literally kicked out of the archbishop's service. The infamous boot in the backside was administered some time before 13 June, and was reported in a letter of that date. The court official who executed Colloredo's orders was Count Arco, a friend to the Mozarts and hitherto quite helpful, who finally lost patience with Wolfgang. We can guess the extent of Leopold's anxiety at the news. We can also see Wolfgang boiling over with rage at the insult, and threatening to exact a dreadful vengeance for it in public In another supreme act of self-control, in order to calm his father and distract himself with thoughts of the glorious future rather than the hateful past, Mozart, within three days, was discussing the possibility of a libretto from Johann Gottlieb Stephanie (1741–1800), an actor and successful author of a number of stage pieces. Hot blood cools, and within three weeks Mozart promised his fearful father that he would not exact his revenge upon Count Arco in public, and urged his father not to be afraid of the archbishop, an oft-repeated cry which demonstrates his independence from Colloredo and from his father.[1]

MOZART'S MARRIAGE

The second half of 1781 was not much better than the first. In early May, when he was being pushed from pillar to post by the archbishop, he moved into the Weber household. It will be remembered that when Mozart and his mother were *en route* to Paris in 1778, Wolfgang had fallen in love with a young singer, Aloysia Weber, and that she had at first encouraged him. But a few months later, when her prospects seemed brighter, she threw him over. She was making a good salary singing in Munich, enjoying the favor of the Elector, and looking forward to a brilliant future as a royal favorite.

At that time, Leopold Mozart had been concerned that his son's infatuation with Aloysia would wreck his career. How dismayed he must have been to find the Weber family resurfacing in Vienna! Father Weber had died, and the mother and her remaining daughters had moved from Mannheim to Vienna, where Madame Weber now took in male lodgers and drank. Aloysia's royal "protector" had tired of her, and her career in Munich had lasted hardly more than a year. So she had married the widower Josef Lange, an actor and painter, who agreed to contribute to his mother-in-law's maintenance. It was into this household that Wolfgang moved. Barely three months later, father Leopold heard rumors

1. Among the many myths about Mozart, one of the hardest to quash is that his psychological growth was stunted through his dependence upon his father. That he was always a loving son cannot be doubted. That he was a self-disciplined, mature, and independent adult, fit to be husband and father, is shown in a letter in which he writes: "I implore you, dearest, most beloved father, for the future to spare me such letters [of criticism] . . . for they only irritate my mind and disturb my heart and spirit; and I, who must now keep on composing, need a cheerful mind and a calm disposition."(*Letters,* 9 June 1781) Mozart at twenty-five is a different person from Mozart at twenty-one.

Constanze Mozart: a portrait painted in 1783.

that his son was about to marry one of the two Weber girls still at home; but Wolfgang took pains to deny that he was in love:

> I will not say . . . that I do not speak to her [Constanze]; but I am not in love with her. I fool about and have fun with her when time permits (which is only in the evening . . .) and that is all. If I had to marry all those with whom I have jested, I should have two hundred wives at least. (*Letters,* 25 July 1781)

A month later, on 22 August, he tells his father of a pupil (Josephine von Auernhammer) making unreciprocated advances to him. After almost no mention of the Weber name, Wolfgang bursts out with "Oh how gladly would I have opened my heart to you long ago, but I was deterred by the reproaches you might have made to me . . ." (*Letters,* 15 Dec. 1781) On 7 August 1782, three days after his marriage to the middle daughter, Constanze Weber, Mozart wrote to his father. Leopold's reluctant consent to the marriage arrived after the wedding. All Wolfgang's pleading on Constanze's behalf, his repeated assurances of her goodness, modesty, thriftiness, etc., had done little to persuade Leopold that the match was a good one, but he was hardly in a position to deter his son. Wolfgang and Constanze were now united; while one could imagine a better wife for Mozart, she was the one he had chosen, and she undoubtedly brought him happiness as well as tribulation—just as he did to her.

AN IDEAL REALIZED: *DIE ENTFÜHRUNG*

While all this was going on, Wolfgang was frantically composing *Die Entführung aus dem Serail,* and he distracted his father from thoughts of the Weber household and its scheming women with endless details about the opera. He received the libretto on 30 July, 1781, and when writing to Leopold two days later, told him of his plans and of the sections he had already composed. Leopold's reaction, when he learned that the heroine of the new opera, like Fräulein Weber, was named Constanze, can be imagined.

Die Entführung was to have been performed in the middle of September, 1781 to celebrate the visit to Vienna of a Russian grand duke, and Mozart set to work with the greatest enthusiasm and haste. He was totally absorbed in the composition and he was pleased with the results.

> All my enthusiasm is for my opera, and what would at other times require fourteen days to write I could now do in four. I composed in one day Adamberger's aria in A, Cavalieri's in B♭ and the trio, and copied them out in a day and a half. (*Letters,* 6 Oct. 1781)

Two other letters contain the most succinct expression of Mozart's ideas on what an opera should be, and how the remodeling of librettos is carried out, as well as on the relationship of music and word, of music and expression. The first is worth quoting in its entirety. N.B. the irony of the second line.

> MON TRES CHER PERE! VIENNA, 26 September 1781
>
> Forgive me for having made you pay an extra heavy postage fee the other day. But I happened to have nothing important to tell you and thought that it would afford you pleasure if I gave you some idea of my opera. As the original text began with a monologue, I asked Herr Stephanie to make a little arietta out of it—and then to put in a duet instead of making the two chatter together after Osmin's short song. As we have given the part of Osmin to Herr Fischer, who certainly has an excellent bass voice (in spite of the fact that the Archbishop told me that he sang too low for a bass and that I assured him that he would sing higher next time), we must take advantage of it, particularly as he has the whole Viennese public on his side. But in the original libretto Osmin has only this short song and nothing else to sing, except in the trio and the finale; so he has been given an aria in Act I, and he is to have another in Act II. I have explained to Stephanie the words I require for the aria—indeed I had finished composing most of the music for it before Stephanie knew anything whatever about it. I am enclosing only the beginning and the end, which is bound to have a good effect. Osmin's rage is rendered comical by the use of the Turkish music. In working out the aria I have (in spite of our Salzburg Midas) allowed Fischer's beautiful deep notes to glow. The passage "Drum beim Barte des Propheten" is indeed in the same tempo, but with quick notes; and as Osmin's rage gradually increases, there comes (just when the aria seems to be at an end) the allegro assai, which is in a totally different meter and in a different key; this is bound to be very effective. For just as a man

in such a towering rage oversteps all the bounds of order, moderation and propriety and completely forgets himself, so must the music too forget itself. But since passions, whether violent or not, must never be expressed to the point of exciting disgust, and as music, even in the most terrible situations, must never offend the ear, but must please the listener, or in other words must never cease to be music, so I have chosen a key foreign to F (in which the aria is written) but one related to it—not the nearest, D minor, but the more remote A minor. Let me now turn to Belmonte's aria in A major, 'O wie ängstlich, o wie feurig'. Would you like to know how I have expressed it—and even indicated his throbbing heart? By the two violins playing octaves. This is the favorite aria of all those who have heard it, and it is mine also. I wrote it expressly to suit Adamberger's voice. You see the trembling—the faltering—you see how his throbbing breast begins to swell; this I have expressed by a crescendo. You hear the whispering and the sighing—which I have indicated by the first violins with mutes and a flute playing in unison.

The Janissary chorus is, as such, all that can be desired, that is, short, lively and written to please the Viennese. I have sacrificed Constanze's aria a little to the flexible throat of Mlle. Cavalieri, 'Trennung war mein banges Los und nun schwimmt mein Aug' in Tränen'. I have tried to express her feelings, as far as an Italian bravura aria will allow it. I have changed the 'Hui' to 'schnell', so it now runs thus—'Doch wie schnell schwand meine Freude'. I really don't know what our German poets are thinking of. Even if they do not understand the theatre, or at all events operas, yet they should not make their characters talk as if they were addressing a herd of swine. Hui, sow!

Now for the trio at the close of Act I. Pedrillo has passed off his master as an architect—to give him an opportunity of meeting his Constanze in the garden. Bassa Selim has taken him into his service. Osmin, the steward, knows nothing of this, and being a rude churl and a sworn foe to all strangers, is impertinent and refuses to let them into the garden. It opens quite abruptly—and because the words lend themselves to it, I have made it a fairly respectable piece of real three-part writing. Then the major key begins at once pianissimo—it must go very quickly—and wind up with a great deal of noise, which is always appropriate at the end of an act. The more noise the better, and the shorter the better, so that the audience may not have time to cool down with their applause.

I have sent you only fourteen bars of the overture, which is very short with alternate fortes and pianos, the Turkish music always coming in at the fortes. The overture modulates through different keys; and I doubt whether anyone, even if his previous night has been a sleepless one, could go to sleep over it. Now comes the rub! The first act was finished more than three weeks ago, as was also one aria in Act II and the drunken duet (per i signori viennesi) which consists entirely of my Turkish tattoo. But I cannot compose any more, because the whole story is being altered—and, to tell the truth, at my own request. At the beginning of Act III there is a charming quintet or rather finale, but I should prefer to have it at the end of Act II. In order to make this practicable, great changes must be made, in fact an entirely new plot must be introduced—and Stephanie [the libret-

> tist] is up to the eyes in other work. So we must have a little patience. Everyone abuses Stephanie. It may be that in my case he is only friendly to my face. But after all he is arranging the libretto for me—and, what is more, as I want it—exactly—and, by Heaven, I do not ask for anything more of him. Well, how I have been chattering to you about my opera! But I cannot help it. Please send me the march which I mentioned the other day. Gilowsky says that Daubrawaick will soon be here. Fräulein von Auernhammer and I are longing to have the two double concertos. I hope we shall not wait as vainly as the Jews for their Messiah. Well, adieu. Farewell. I kiss your hands a thousand times and embrace with all my heart my dear sister, whose health, I hope, is improving, and am ever your most obedient son
>
> W. A. MOZART (*Letters,* 26 Sept. 1781)

And from the second:

> Now as to the libretto of the opera . . . I am well aware that the verse is not of the best, but it fitted in and it agreed so well with the musical ideas which already were buzzing in my head, that it could not fail to please and I would like to wager that when it is performed, no deficiencies will be found. . . . Besides, I should say that in an opera the poetry must be altogether the obedient daughter of the music. Why do Italian comic operas please everywhere—in spite of their miserable libretti . . . ? Just because there the music reigns supreme and when one listens to it all else is forgotten. Why, an opera is sure of success when the plot is well worked out, the words written solely for the music and not shoved in here and there to suit some miserable rhyme. . . . The best thing of all is when a good composer, who understands the stage and is talented enough to make sound suggestions, meets an able poet, that true phoenix; in that case no fears need be entertained as to the applause even of the ignorant. (*Letters,* 13 Oct. 1781)

It is clear that Mozart includes himself among the "good" composers.

The Russian grand duke came to Vienna and departed, but *Die Entführung* was not performed until 16 July 1782. The staging of two of Gluck's operas caused the delay, and Wolfgang was greatly annoyed, for on receiving the commission he had set to work at once and completed the first act very quickly. Leopold, always on the alert for plots against his son, believed that Gluck was responsible for the opposition to the work, but this is most unlikely, since it was probably Gluck who put Mozart's name forward for the commission. There certainly was some organized antagonism, however, for a claque operated during the first two nights and tried to spoil the opera's reception. They were not successful, and once staged, it proved to be one of Mozart's most popular works, both in Vienna and abroad. Within three weeks after the first performance, Mozart brought his own "elopement" to a successful conclusion and married Constanze.

This unfinished portrait by Mozart's brother-in-law, Joseph Lange, captures the totally focussed concentration of which he was so capable. (Mozart Museum, Salzburg)

LIFE IN VIENNA

On 24 December a competition in piano playing between Mozart and Clementi was set up by the emperor, who, by this time, had had numerous opportunities to hear Mozart, and who may even have had a bet riding on his shoulders. We hear about the affair in two of Mozart's letters; the first tells of the event and the second describes it as follows:

> Now a word about Clementi. He is an excellent cembalo player but that is all. He has great facility with his right hand. His star passages are thirds. Apart from this, he has not a farthing's worth of taste or feeling; he is a mere mechanicus. (*Letters,* 16 Jan. 1782)

In his autobiography Carl Ditters von Dittersdorf gives an account of a conversation with the emperor, in which the latter asks Dittersdorf how he would compare Mozart and Clementi. Dittersdorf replies: "Clementi's playing is art simply and solely; Mozart's combines art and taste."[2]

By August 1782, despite the fact that Mozart had been in Vienna for well over a year, despite the Clementi competition, and despite the emperor's admiration for Mozart's piano playing, no official appointment was yet forthcoming. Mozart himself was well aware of his failure in this direction and speaks to his father of offering himself to Paris or London, but these were words of bravado and nothing was to come of them.

Instead, Mozart had a growing list of pupils and his concerts were well attended—he was in demand by the private citizenry, and so the

2. Karl von Dittersdorf, *Autobiography* (reprint, New York, 1970), p. 251.

security of an appointment was not of overwhelming concern. He describes his life as it was before his marriage in a letter to his father at the end of 1781.

> Every morning at six o'clock my friseur [hairdresser] arrives and wakens me, and by seven I have finished dressing. I compose until ten, when I give a lesson to Frau von Trattner and at eleven to the Countess Rumbeck, each of whom pays me six ducats for twelve lessons and to whom I go every day . . . I have arranged with the Countess that . . . if I do not find her at home, I am at least to get my fee. (*Letters,* 22 Dec. 1781)

Nor was his social life any less busy. He and Constanze both enjoyed themselves as much as any people of their age. Mozart may well have been flirtatious before his marriage (see letter 25 July 1780, above); afterward he became even more so, and he seems to have allowed no opportunity to pass him by, secure in the knowledge that he was a married man. Carnival time in Vienna, as elsewhere, was a time for dancing. Indeed, we learn from the memoirs of Michael Kelly, an Irish tenor who sang the parts of Don Basilio and Don Curzio in the first performance of *The Marriage of Figaro,* that Mozart often said that his talent lay in the direction of dancing rather than music. After asking his father to send his fancy dress he says:

> Last week I gave a ball in my own rooms, but of course the chapeaux [the men] each paid two gulden. We began at six o'clock in the evening and kept on until seven. What! Only an hour? Of course not. I meant, until seven o'clock next morning. (*Letters,* 22 Jan. 1783)

Despite all these distractions, the flow of composition continued. 1782 saw the production of one opera, one symphony, one large serenade, three piano concertos, one horn concerto, one horn quintet, and the first of the six great string quartets to be dedicated to Haydn. But the fact that reveals more than anything else about the frantic pace of Mozart's life is that, for one reason or another, he left more compositions in a fragmentary or unfinished state during this year than at any other time in his life.

Wolfgang and Constanze had six children during their nine-year marriage, only two of whom survived their father, the elder living to the age of 74. It is surprising that any survived at all when one reads in Mozart's letter to his father after the birth of their first son, who was destined to live only a couple of months:

> I was quite detemined that whether she should be able to do so or not, my wife was never to feed the child. Yet I was equally determined that my child was never to take the milk of a stranger! I wanted the child to be brought up on water, like my sister and myself. However, the midwife, my mother-in-law and most people here have begged and implored me not to allow it, if only for the reason that most children here who are brought up on water do not survive, as the people here don't know how to do it properly. (*Letters,* 18 June 1783)

In 1783 Mozart met Lorenzo da Ponte (1749–1838), the man who would achieve immortality as the librettist of three of his greatest operas. Da Ponte had recently fled from Italy to escape a jail sentence for adultery. He arrived in Vienna shortly after the death of Maria Theresa and attached himself to Salieri, hence Mozart, longing to write another opera, did not expect that his request to da Ponte for a libretto would be fulfilled. He wrote to his father:

> The Italian opera buffa has started up again here; it is successful—the buffo is especially good. He is called Benucci.—I have read through easily 100 or more librettos but I have hardly found one with which I could be happy;—at the very least much would have to be changed here and there . . . We have here as poet a certain Abate da Ponte . . . he has to write a completely new libretto for Salieri. It won't be finished for two months—he has promised to do one for me then; who knows whether he can keep his word—or will!—These Italian gentlemen are very nice to one's face!—enough! we know them!—if he has an understanding with Salieri, I will never get one from him as long as I live. (*Letters,* 7 May 1783)

It seems he was right—for the moment.

Mozart was in great demand as a concert pianist. The program of a concert given in the Burgtheater on 23 March 1783 runs as follows:

1. The *Haffner* Symphony. K.385
2. Aria "Se il padre perdei " from *Idomeneo*. K.366
3. Piano Concerto in C. K.415
4. Scena "Misera dove son?" K.369
5. Concertante from Serenade in D. K.320
6. Piano Concerto in D. K.175
7. Aria "Parto, m'affretto" from *Lucio Silla*. K.135
8. Fugue for piano
   Variations for piano. K.455
9. Rondo "Mia speranza adorata ." K.416
10. Last movement, *Haffner* Symphony. K.385

Every work is by Mozart in this concert, which was attended by the emperor, and the inclusion in the program of an improvised fugue was designed to impress him.

1784 was a particularly busy and productive year. Mozart's concert career demanded the composition of concertos, and his genius enabled him to produce six (K.449, 450, 451, 453, 456, and 459), each of which seems to eclipse its predecessor in wealth of ideas and interest. With the first of these concertos, Mozart began a catalogue of his works. Into a little notebook he entered on a blank page a date, a number, a title, and the instrumentation; on the facing page, ruled with staves, he notated the incipit, reducing everything to short score of two staves. On the front page of the notebook he wrote: *Verzeichnüss alle meine Werke* (Catalogue of all my works) from the month of February 1784 to the month—Wolfgang Amade Mozart. This invaluable catalogue is not without errors, since the composer did not always enter works upon completion. But it affords strong evidence that Mozart's method of composing allowed him to work on more than one piece at a time. The year 1786, for example, shows the following sequence of dates and works:

3 Feb.	[K.486]	*Der Schauspieldirektor.* "A comedy with music."
2 Mar.	[K.488]	"A Piano Concerto" in A.
10 Mar.	[K.489]	"A Duetto" Soprano, Tenor & Orch. "for my opera *Idomeneo*"
10 Mar.	[K.490]	"Scena con Rondò with solo violin" Soprano & Orch.
24 Mar.	[K.491]	"A Piano Concerto" in C minor.
29 Apr.	[K.492]	*Le Nozze di Figaro.* "opera buffa in 4 acts."
3 Jun.	[K.493]	"A Quartet for piano, violin, viola and violoncello."
10 Jun.	[K.494]	"A short Rondò for piano solo."
26 Jun.	[K.495]	"A Waldhorn Concerto for Leutgeb."
8 Jul.	[K.496]	"A Trio for piano, violin and violoncello."
1 Aug.	[K.497]	"A piano sonata for 4 hands."
5 Aug.	[K.498]	"A trio for piano, clarinet and viola."
19 Aug.	[K.499]	"A quartet for 2 violins, viola and violoncello.
12 Sep.	[K.500]	"12 Variations for piano solo."
4 Nov.	[K.501]	"Variations for piano, 4 hands."
18 Nov.	[K.502]	"A Trio for piano, violin and violoncello."
4 Dec.	[K.503]	"A Piano Concerto" in C.
6 Dec.	[K.504]	"A Symphony" (the "Prague").
27 Dec.	[K.505]	"Scena con Rondò with piano solo for Mlle. Storace."

—an amazing succession of masterworks testifying to immense industry and inspiration.

Two events of the greatest importance for Mozart must be noted in connection with 1784, and both arise from his concert giving. During the first part of the year, he played often at the house of Count Johann Esterházy, an active Freemason. Mozart was admitted to the order in December, and it was to become for him a source of the greatest spiritual comfort and inspiration. And he became personally acquainted with Haydn.

In that same year Wolfgang's sister, Nannerl, married well and left home. The relationship between her and her brother had been of the closest up to the time of their marriages, but thereafter, as is to be expected, they drifted apart as their marital responsibilities increased.

The years 1784/85 seem to be the most successful period in Mozart's adult life. He was living in comfortable lodgings, his concerts were well attended, his second son, Karl (1784–1858), was healthy and happy, and the loss of their first-born was largely forgotten. Even father Leopold had much to be proud of. A letter of his to Nannerl well conveys his sense of satisfaction with his son, with his son's family, his life, and his success.

In this painting of a reception at a Freemason's Lodge in Vienna, the figure on the extreme right may be Mozart, while the man in the center might possibly be Prince Nikolaus Esterházy. (Historisches Museum der Stadt Wien)

> That your brother has very fine quarters with all the necessary furniture you may gather from the fact that his rent is 460 gulden . . . we drove to his first subscription concert, at which a great many members of the aristocracy were present. The concert was magnificent and the orchestra played splendidly . . . we had a new and very fine concerto by Wolfgang, which the copyist was still copying when we arrived, and the rondo of which your brother did not even have time to play through . . . I met many acquaintances there who all came up to speak to me. I was also introduced to several other people.
>
> On Saturday evening Herr Joseph Haydn . . . came to see us and the new quartets were performed, or rather, the three new ones which Wolfgang has added to the other three which we have already. The new ones are somewhat easier, but at the same time excellent compositions. Haydn said to me: "Before God and as an honest man I tell you that your son is the greatest composer known to me either in person or by name. He has taste and, what is more, the most profound knowledge of composition."
>
> On Sunday evening your brother played a glorious concerto which he composed for Mlle. Paradis for Paris. I was sitting only two boxes away from the very beautiful Princess of Württemberg and had the great pleasure of hearing so clearly all the interplay of the instruments that for sheer delight tears came into my eyes. When your brother left the platform the Emperor waved his hat and called out "Bravo, Mozart!" And when he came on to play there was a great deal of clapping. (*Letters,* 16 Feb. 1785)

Mozart and his family lived in the house with the bay window from Sept. 1784 to April 1787. This was where Mozart received Haydn and Beethoven. (Historisches Museum der Stadt Wien)

The incessant activity around the Mozart household ("We ourselves do not go to bed until midnight and we get up at half past five or even five. . ."(*Letters,* 26 May 1784]), the concerts, the rehearsals, the lessons, concealed from Leopold the fact that money was going out faster than it was coming in, and by the end of the year the first signs of the financial embarrassment that was to dog the composer's footsteps for the rest of his life began to appear. Writing to the composer and publisher F. A. Hoffmeister he said: "I turn to you in my distress and beg you to help me out with some money, which I need very badly at the moment." (*Letters,* 20 Nov. 1785).

MOZART AND DA PONTE

At this time Mozart and da Ponte were finally working together—on an adaptation of Beaumarchais's *Le Mariage de Figaro*. This play had been first produced in Paris the year before, and as early as 31 January 1785, the Emperor Joseph II had expressed his concern that if it were to be translated into German and performed in Vienna, it would need considerable alteration. Mozart's choice of this work may have been influenced by his own feelings on the subject, or by his belief that the subject was fashionable, and hence that the opera was likely to be a commercial success; but it is more than possible that this choice worked against his best interests with the emperor. We already know the kinds of demands that Mozart imposed on his librettist during the adaptation of the play. Da Ponte was clearly a clever wordsmith of malleable nature, and although we have no records of their working relationship, we must assume that things went well.

The opera, *Le nozze di Figaro,* was first performed on 1 May 1786 at the Burgtheater in Vienna. Opposition to its production delayed but could not cancel its appearance. In 1786, there were nine performances of the work in Vienna. It was not staged there again until 1789, and more performances followed in 1790 and 1791. After that, neither of the court theaters in Vienna staged any Mozart opera until 1798, clear testimony to the lack of favor he enjoyed with the court, and to the enmity he aroused among his confrères.

For some time Mozart had felt that although his activities in Vienna had popular support, they lacked the official seal of approval they ought to have had from the emperor. It was one thing to carry on all the activities of the artist under the contractual protection of some great patron, but it was quite another matter to exist as a free-lance artist with all the financial uncertainty that involved. In numerous letters, he made his dissatisfaction over his failure to achieve an official post known to his father. For some time he had contemplated going to England for an extended period in order to recoup his finances. As late as 1786 Mozart had advanced plans for a journey, had practiced his English, and was ready to go. However, essential to his plan was that father Leopold would look after the children, since he was not prepared to leave Constanze behind with them. Unfortunately, Leopold was at that time fully occupied looking after his other grandchild, Nannerl's son, Leopold, and was not prepared to undertake the charge.

Whatever disappointment the Mozarts may have felt over this refusal was compounded by the death of their third son at the age of one month. It was therefore very heartening to hear, at the end of 1786, the news from Prague, where *Figaro* had been produced early in December. A newspaper report of 12 December says that "no piece . . . has ever caused such a sensation as has . . . Figaro" and passes along a rumor that Mozart himself was thinking of coming to Prague to see how much better his opera was produced there than in Vienna. (A later issue of the same paper reported that Mozart was preparing to travel to London in the spring.) Mozart did go to Prague, and told his father that there, "nothing is played, sung or whistled but 'Figaro' " (*Letters,* 15 Jan. 1787), giving a much-needed boost to his self-confidence. Moreover, *Figaro's* wild success in Prague led to the commissioning of another opera, *Don Giovanni,* on which Mozart worked during 1787.

At the end of January 1787, Count August von Hatzfeld, Wolfgang's "dearest, best friend," died at the age of 31—Mozart's own age. A few months later, Wolfgang wrote to his father (it was to be the last letter he would ever write to him) expressing his concern over the state of Leopold's health and his thoughts about death, in words that are both memorable and revealing:

> I need hardly tell you how greatly I am longing to receive some reassuring news from yourself. And I still expect it; although I have now made a habit of being prepared in all affairs of life for the worst. As death, when we come to consider it closely, is the true goal of our existence, I have formed during the last few years such close relations with this best and truest friend of mankind, that his image is no longer terrifying to me, but is indeed very soothing and consoling! And I thank my God for graciously granting me the opportunity (you know what I mean) of learning that death is the key which unlocks the door to our true happiness. I never lie down at night without reflecting that—young as I am—I may not live to see another day. Yet no one of all my acquaintances could say that in company I am morose or disgruntled. (*Letters,* 4 April 1787)

Leopold died on 28 May 1787. A year earlier he would have been able to die with a more optimistic view of his son's future prospects. But by May of 1787, the Mozarts had had to move into smaller lodgings in order to reduce expenses, and Leopold knew very well that the tide was turning against Wolfgang.

Don Giovanni was brought to the stage on 29 October 1787, and the Prague audience received it with a rapture that Vienna would never accord to one of its own citizens. Mozart had taken Constanze with him to Prague and the two of them fully enjoyed their celebrity there.

FINANCIAL PROBLEMS

When Gluck died on 1 November 1787, his death created a vacancy to which Joseph II appointed Mozart on 7 December. The position of *H. M. Kammermusicus* (chamber composer for the court) was largely honorary, entailing almost no duties except for filling occasional requests to provide dance music. Gluck had received 2000 gulden a year with the sinecure. Mozart was offered—and accepted—800; "too much for what I do, too little for what I could do," he is reported to have said.

In 1788, one of the most humiliating episodes in Mozart's life began: he wrote a series of begging letters to anyone who might help. Indeed, for the next three years, and until a few months before Wolfgang's death, the Mozarts lived from hand to mouth, borrowing from a brother Mason, Michael Puchberg, and repaying, only to borrow again. Indeed, a variety of documents exist that show that Mozart got money from a number of people at this time. Why this should have been necessary cannot be ascertained. A plausible case has been made that he was given to gambling, and it is certain that some of his friends were. It has also been suggested that he may have fallen into the hands of usurers, or that he may have been too concerned about keeping up appearances of prosperity, but whatever the cause, Mozart had many friends who cannot have suspected the financial difficulties he was in or they would have offered assistance. During the last years, Constanze was frequently ill and went to Baden, a small spa near Vienna, to rest and recover. We also learn, from Mozart's letters, that, despite his pleas for financial aid, he kept his valet to look after him.

A welcome break from the never-ending problems of survival came when Prince Lichnowsky invited him to go to Prussia, for Mozart was always happy traveling, insulated from the day-to-day cares and savoring the chance experiences of the road. The journey began on 8 April 1789, and took the travelers through Prague, Dresden, and Leipzig to Berlin, bringing him into contact with old friends: In Prague he saw the Duseks[3] and met the impresario Domenico Guardasoni (1731–1806), with whom he talked about a future opera. In Dresden he heard Johann Wilhelm Hässler (1747–1822) play the organ and judged him harshly; in Leipzig he himself played the organ in the Thomaskirche before a rapt congregation, and met Johann Friedrich Doles (1715–97), J. S. Bach's successor. Doles showed Mozart the parts of Bach's motets; Mozart, it is said, spreading them out on the floor, read them avidly, and said that here, at last, was something from which one could learn. He was eagerly awaited in Potsdam by King Frederick William II, the cello-playing monarch of Prussia, who patronized music lavishly. The king asked him for six string quartets, of which he completed three, and six easy piano sonatas for the princess, of which he completed one. Mozart was very well rewarded by the monarch, but by the time he arrived home two months later, he had virtually no money left. On 12 July 1789, he wrote the following letter to his reliable friend, Puchberg:

> DEAREST, MOST BELOVED FRIEND AND MOST HONOURABLE B.O.
> Great God! I would not wish my worst enemy to be in my present position. And if you, most beloved friend and brother, forsake me, we are altogether lost, both my unfortunate and blameless self and my poor sick wife and child. Only the other day when I was with you I was longing to open my heart to you, but I had not the courage to do so—and indeed I should still not have the courage—for, as it is, I only dare to write and I tremble as I do so—and I should not dare to write, were I not certain that you know me, that you are aware of my circumstances, and that you are wholly convinced of my innocence so far as my unfortunate and most

3. František Xaver Dušek (1731–99) and his wife Josefa (1754–1824) were close friends of Mozart in Prague. She had a fine voice for which Wolfgang wrote three arias.

distressing situation is concerned. Good God! I am coming to you not with thanks but with fresh entreaties! Instead of paying my debts I am asking for more money! If you really know me, you must sympathize with my anguish at having to do so. I need not tell you once more that owing to my unfortunate illness I have been prevented from earning anything. But I must mention that in spite of my wretched condition I decided to give subscription concerts at home in order to be able to meet at least my present great and frequent expenses, for I was absolutely convinced of your friendly assistance. But even this has failed. Unfortunately Fate is so much against me, though only in Vienna, that even when I want to, I cannot make any money. A fortnight ago I sent round a list for subscribers and so far the only name on it is that of the Baron van Swieten! Now that (on the 13th) my dear little wife seems to be improving every day, I should be able to set to work again, if this blow, this heavy blow had not come. At any rate, people are consoling me by telling me that she is better—although the night before last she was suffering so much—and I on her account—that I was stunned and despairing. But last night (the 14th) she slept so well and has felt so much easier all the morning that I am very hopeful; and at last I am beginning to feel inclined for work. I am now faced, however, with misfortunes of another kind, though it is true, only for the moment. Dearest, most beloved friend and brother—you know my present circumstances, but you also know my prospects. So let things remain as we arranged; that is, thus or thus, you understand what I mean. Meanwhile I am composing six easy clavier sonatas for Princess Friederike and six quartets for the King, all of which Kozeluch is engraving at my expense. At the same time the two dedications will bring me in something. In a month or two my fate must be decided in every detail. Therefore, most beloved friend, you will not be risking anything so far as I am concerned. So it all depends, my only friend, upon whether you will or can lend me another 500 gulden. Until my affairs are settled, I undertake to pay back ten gulden a month; and then, as is bound to happen in a few months, I shall pay back the whole sum with whatever interest you may demand, and at the same time acknowledge myself to be your debtor for life. That, also, I shall have to remain, for I shall never be able to thank you sufficiently for your friendship and affection. Thank God, that is over. Now you know all. Do not be offended by my confiding in you and remember that unless you help me, the honor, the peace of mind, and perhaps the very life of your friend and brother Mason will be ruined.

Ever your most grateful servant, true friend and brother
W. A. MOZART

at home, 14 July 1789.
O God!—I can hardly bring myself to dispatch this letter!—and yet I must! If this illness had not befallen me, I should not have been obliged to beg so shamelessly from my only friend. Yet I hope for your forgiveness, for you know both the good and the bad prospects of my situation. The bad is temporary; the good will certainly persist, once the monetary evil has been alleviated. Adieu. For God's sake forgive me, only forgive me!—and—Adieu!

Things could hardly have been worse: Constanze was pregnant again, and taking the "cure" at Baden, and the gossip about his wife's conduct in public was causing Mozart some concern. He must have been cheered by the revival of *Figaro,* and the arrival of a commission to write *Così fan tutte.* The new opera absorbed Mozart's attention during the remainder of 1789, and it was successfully staged in January 1790. Shortly after, on 20 February 1790, the emperor, who had suggested the subject of *Così fan tutte* to Mozart and da Ponte and had given them the commission for it, died. In the administration of the new emperor Leopold II, Mozart kept his job and salary, although Salieri, sensing that he did not enjoy the favor of the new emperor as he had that of Joseph II, decided to resign his direction of the opera theater. It was Joseph Weigl (1766–1846), however, and not Mozart who succeeded to Salieri's post. The perpetual round of begging letters continued.

At the end of 1790, the possibility of Mozart's going to London was reopened. In fact, we believe that he had two offers, one by word of mouth from Salomon, who wanted to take Mozart as well as Haydn with him, and one in a letter from a man named O'Reilly. Why he took up neither of these offers remains something of a mystery, and it is possible that Emanuel Schikaneder and he were already planning to write a *Singspiel* together. The year 1790 had seen some of Mozart's darkest hours, and there can be little doubt, both from his own complaints and from the observations of other people, that in addition to all his money and family problems, his health was beginning to deteriorate. But by the end of the year there were unmistakable signs that dawn was about to break after the long financial night. He had added few compositions to his catalogue in 1790, but the Quintet in D, K.593, shows that once again he was writing life-enhancing music of incomparable beauty.

During the spring of 1791, Mozart was working on *The Magic Flute* and the opera was virtually completed by July. In that month, two things happened to interrupt Mozart's work on the *Singspiel,* as reported some seven years later.

> He set *The Magic Flute* to music for the theater of the well-known Schikaneder, who was an old friend of his. The music for the opera *La Clemenza di Tito* had been commissioned by the Bohemian Estates for the coronation of the Emperor Leopold. He began this latter work in the coach on the road from Vienna, and finished it in Prague in the short space of eighteen days.
>
> The story of his last work, the Requiem already mentioned, is as remarkable as it is mysterious. Shortly before the time of the coronation of Emperor Leopold, even before Mozart had received the order to journey to Prague, an unsigned letter was delivered to him by an unknown messenger, which, after many flattering remarks, asked whether Mozart would undertake to write a Requiem, how much he would ask to do it, a and when would he be able to deliver it?

> Mozart, who never took the smallest step without his wife's full knowledge, told her of this remarkable commission, and straightaway told her of his wish to try his hand at this genre of composition, all the more since the noble and moving style of church music had always appealed to him. She advised him to accept the commission. And so he wrote back to the unknown patron that he would write the Requiem for a certain sum; he could not precisely state how much time would be needed to complete it; and he wished to know where he should deliver the work when it was ready. After a short time, the selfsame messenger appeared again, bringing with him not only the sum that had been agreed upon but also the promise that, since Mozart had been so modest in his demands, there would be a considerable additional payment upon receipt of the work. Above all, he should write according to his own mood and feeling; however, he should not trouble himself to discover the identity of the patron, for such efforts would assuredly be in vain.
>
> In the meantime Mozart received the flattering and advantageous commission to write an *opera seria* for the Coronation in Prague of the Emperor Leopold. To go to Prague! to write for his beloved Bohemians! the offer was far too attractive to refuse.
>
> Just as Mozart was climbing into the coach with his wife, the messenger appeared like a ghost. He tugged at her coat and asked:. "What about the Requiem?" Mozart excused himself, citing the necesssity for the journey, and the impossibility of communicating with his unknown patron; in any case, it would be his first task upon returning, and it was up to the unknown person to decide whether he wished to wait so long. The messenger was completely satisfied with the reply.
>
> While in Prague Mozart became ill and ceaselessly tried remedies; he was pale and looked sad, although in the company of his friends his happy good humor still manifested itself in joking.
>
> On his return to Vienna he at once took up his Requiem and worked on it with great energy and lively interest; but his illness visibily became worse and made him gloomy and melancholy. His wife was disturbed to notice it. One day, when she was driving with him in the Prater to give him a little distraction and raise his spirits, and they were sitting alone, Mozart began to speak about death, and asserted that he was making this setting of the Requiem for himself. The eyes of this sensitive man filled with tears: "I feel so very much," he continued, "that I shall not go on much longer; I am sure that someone has given me poison! I cannot put this thought out of my mind."[4]

Modern scholarship has refuted the idea that *La clemenza di Tito* was written in the very short time between mid-July, when the impresario Guardasoni left Prague for Vienna, presumably to give the libretto to Mozart, and 6 September 1791, when the opera was first performed. The commission for the opera originated with the Bohemian Estates (i.e., the Parliament). Such things do not simply happen but are moved forward by individuals. Guardasoni was above all a mover, and by

4. Franz Xaver Niemetschek, *Ich kannte Mozart* (I knew Mozart) (Facsimile reprint of 1798 edition, Munich, 1984), pp. 32–34. Author's translation.

whatever means, he persuaded the Estates to authorize him to appoint "a celebrated composer" to write the score. The most celebrated composer in Prague was, of course, Mozart. It must be presumed that Mozart and Guardasoni had prepared for the possibility of this state-occasion opera, and that much of the revision of the Metastasian libretto and even some of the composition actually preceded the commission. At least one aria, "Non più di fiori," was sung in concert in late April by Mme. Dušek. There is no doubt, however, that Mozart worked very hard to get the work ready on time, and had his pupil Franz Xaver Süssmayr (1766–1803) write the recitatives. The opera was not a success with the monarchs it was designed to entertain. The Italian-born empress pronounced it "una porcheria tedesca" (a piece of German piggery) and that phrase has conferred on her an immortality that she would not otherwise possess. Yet *Tito* was to be the opera that would carry Mozart's name to the London stage and hold it there. Recently, it has received more critical attention and productions have been mounted with increasing frequency.

Mozart had never lowered his standards in order to speak to a wider public; nevertheless *The Magic Flute* had interested him from the moment he and Schikaneder began discussing it, even though it must have seemed to necessitate some degree of "writing down." Whether it was the universal truths underlying the fable; or whether it was the chance to practice, on stage, some of the tomfoolery that he always enjoyed in private life; or whether it was the enticing opportunity to join together all styles of music, juxtaposing the most serious and the most lighthearted;[5] or whether Mozart finally saw that he had a chance of winning a Viennese audience, no matter what class, we cannot know. The psychological spark that enabled the composer to identify himself fully with the subject matter and that moved him to see all its possibilities was there. It was certainly the last of his operas into which he poured all aspects of his craft and creative imagination.

The Magic Flute was his first vindication; it showed him that success was possible, even for him. The opera's reception was such that in the days before his death, he would take out his watch and estimate where the singers would be in the opera on that night's performance, hearing and seeing everything in his imagination. More than any other of his works it exemplifies the man himself with all his personality quirks, as it joins together sophistication and naiveté, idealism and realism, complexity and simplicity, experience and innocence.

The Requiem occupied him to the end but was left in an unfinished state. For many years people believed, with Mozart, that the messenger was sent to him from the other world, but the simple truth, finally revealed in 1964, was far more down to earth. The messenger, a man

5. The author has in mind, for example, the music for the three Genii, those ageless boys in *Die Zauberflöte* who unite wisdom, knowledge, and experience of old age with the appearance and the voices of childhood, the characteristics we see in Mozart himself.

named Leitgeb, who was an official in the estate administration of a Count Walsegg, was simply doing his employer's bidding. The count was a melomane who made it a practice to pass off other people's quartets and chamber music as his own. Upon the death of his young wife he wanted to make it appear as though he had written a Requiem for her himself—hence the anonymity. For Mozart, the truth of the matter was unimportant. His incipient disease made him feel dreadfully ill, and having endured so much illness in his lifetime, he could tell that what he was experiencing was of an unusual nature.

Mozart died on 5 December 1791, just short of his thirty-sixth birthday. Had he lived, the history of music would have been very different, since he had just been chosen as the next Kapellmeister of St. Stephen's Cathedral in Vienna, and commissions from various parts of Europe were pouring in. In the last months of his life he had broadened his style to include a simpler and more popular vein, making his music accessible to an audience previously put off by its complexity. The amalgamation of this popular style with his skill, imagination, and intellect produced an ethereal music of such elemental simplicity that it is hard to believe it was not produced by the gestures of divinity.

Lest fanciful phrases convey a wrong impression, the last words shall be left to Niemetschek, whose description of Mozart's appearance gives a stronger impression than any surviving portrait. He wrote:

> There was nothing exceptional about the physical presence of this extraordinary man; he was small and his appearance gave no sign of his genius, apart from his large intense eyes. His look was unsteady and absent-minded, except when he was seated at the keyboard; then his whole countenance changed! Then his eyes would become serious and filled with concentration; every movement conveyed the feeling that he was expressing through his playing and that he could awaken so powerfully in the listener.
>
> He had small, beautiful hands; in playing he moved them so quietly and naturally over the keyboard that the eyes no less than the ears had to be equally enchanted. It is a marvel that he could stretch so far with them, particularly in the bass. By his own admission this phenomenon was due to his assiduous study of Bach's works.
>
> His ungainliness, his small size, arose from the early overtaxing of his brain and from his lack of exercise in childhood. Yet he was born of handsome parents and was himself a beautiful child; but from the age of six he was compelled to lead a sedentary life, and in addition, he started to compose from that age. During his lifetime, how much this man wrote, particularly in his last years! As Mozart was well-known to prefer playing and composing at night, and as his work was often very pressing, it can easily be imagined how much his physique suffered from such habits. His early death (if indeed it was not brought about unnaturally) must be attributed mainly to these causes.
>
> But in this ungainly body there dwelt an artistic genius such as Nature rarely bestows even upon her most treasured darlings.[6]

6. Niemetschek, *op. cit.*, pp. 44–45. Author's translation.

CHAPTER XXVI

The Great Works of the Final Decade

There are a few well-known occasions where a striking alliance of inspiration and industry has produced a great masterpiece. Handel's composition of *Messiah* in three weeks and Wagner's conception of *The Ring* carried to completion over twenty years are both examples of this phenomenon. But for sustained productivity and inspiration nothing in the whole history of music can surpass Bach's first years in Leipzig (1723–*c.*30) and Mozart's last ten years in Vienna. The similarities between the two composers and their situations are striking: both set out for their final destinations, Leipzig and Vienna respectively, with the highest hopes—hopes that were to be quickly dashed; both worked in an idiom that was essentially that of their contemporaries, but their contemporaries accused them of being lost in pursuit of the "science" of music at the cost of their art; both received nominal appointments from their sovereigns that acknowledged their worth and at the same time openly undervalued it; and both, at the end, saw their mastery of the art of music as the justification for their existence. Both Bach and Mozart knew the extent of their talents and both suffered frequent attack. "Too many notes, my dear Mozart," said the emperor, after a performance of *Die Entführung*. "Not one note too many, Your Majesty," replied Mozart.

The compositions of the last ten years show Mozart unfailingly improving upon every genre he touched. From the shortest, most trivial song to the larger forms of chamber music, the symphony, the concerto, and the opera, he found the means to give each work a unique personality and to convey the impression that his creative imagination had, for a lesser or greater time, been totally absorbed in the composition of the work in hand. A convincing case has been made that Mozart's method of composition involved notating short ideas as they occurred to him, then taking them up at a later date to work out and complete. Even the fragments of unfinished compositions often bear the stamp of total absorption that the completed works carry, and convince us that many of them were simply awaiting further elaboration.

THE LATE PIANO WORKS

There are various theories concerning the composition dates of the first four of Mozart's last nine sonatas for solo piano, and no help is forthcoming from Mozart's own catalogue since they antedate it.

Sonata in C	K.330	1783	Vienna?
Sonata in A	K.331	1783	Vienna?
Sonata in F	K.332	1783	Vienna?
Sonata in B♭	K.333	1783	Linz?
Sonata in C minor	K.457	14 Oct. 1784	Vienna
Sonata in F	K.533	3 Jan. 1788	Vienna
Sonata in C	K.545	26 Jun. 1788	Vienna
Sonata in B♭	K.570	Feb. 1789	Vienna
Sonata in D	K.576	Jul. 1789	Vienna

Based upon handwriting and watermarks, most recent scholarship substantiates the dates shown above, despite their misleading Köchel numbers. At least three of the sonatas of 1783 form a group, and they were published as such in 1784. The fourth was published in another group of works (including K.284 and K.454) also in 1784. There is a quality of expansiveness about these works attributable not to increased length but to their technical demands. K.330 is perhaps the most orthodox and unremarkable, despite the charm of its slow movement. K.331 is one of the most famous since its first movement, a set of variations, is built on a theme that has been used by at least one other composer, and its *Rondo alla Turca* has been arranged in many ways outside its sonata setting. Most interesting, technically, is the use Mozart makes of the cross-hand technique to impart a peculiarly rich resonance to the piano.

Example XXVI–1: W. A. MOZART, Sonata K.331, I, variation No. 4

K.332 provides a perfect illustration of Dittersdorf's criticism of Mozart:

> He is unquestionably one of the greatest original geniuses, and I have never yet met with any composer who had such an amazing wealth of ideas; I could almost wish he were not so lavish in using them. He leaves his hearer out of breath; for hardly has he grasped one beautiful thought, when another of greater fascination dispels the first, and this goes on throughout, so that in the end it is impossible to retain any one of these beautiful melodies.[1]

In the first movement of this sonata the prevalent Alberti basses of K.330 are replaced by constantly changing textures and a grand display of melodic invention. It is surprising to find the slow movement dominated almost throughout by old-fashioned, broken-chord patterns in the left hand. Also surprising are passages reminiscent of a typical Schobert texture, such as those noted in the earlier sonata K.310 and in some variations composed in Paris.

The Sonata in B♭, K.333, with all its charm and melodic extravagance, seems to be a throwback. Its opening theme recalls Christian

Example XXVI–2: W. A. MOZART, Sonata K.333, II

1. Dittersdorf, *op. cit.*, pp. 251–52.

Bach's Op.17, No.4, and its long, written-out cadenza in the third movement also points to an earlier time. The slow movement, however, contains such harmonic excess, created by extended appoggiaturas, that it hardly seems to belong to this sonata.

K.457 in C minor (*ACM* 62)carries the special aura that surrounds so many of Mozart's minor-mode works. Nineteenth-century criticism held that his minor-mode works escaped the superficiality that characterized many of his major-mode works by speaking in the language of true feeling rather than conventionalized utterance. They thought, in effect, that Mozart was a closet revolutionary. It is hard to believe that as late as the beginning of the twentieth century, Edward MacDowell, great pianist, admired composer, and newly appointed professor of music at Columbia University, could describe these sonatas as "entirely unworthy of . . . any composer with pretensions to anything beyond mediocrity. They are written in a style of flashy harpsichord virtuosity such as Liszt never descended to."[2]

Mozart dedicated K.457, together with the Fantasia in C minor, K.475, to his pupil Frau von Trattner, and it is clearly a work that carries a great deal of emotional weight in its dynamic and melodic content. Yet its structure allows for only a slight middle section in the first movement, the smallest in any of these works relative to the exposition. It is not to any developmental process that this work owes its power; it very rarely is with this composer. If its secret resides anyplace accessible to verbal logic it is in the variety of directions the music takes: thus, the upward thrust of the opening has, at first, a conventional response. But observe that the dominant pedal of m. 9 really resolves 11 bars later. Notice that mm. 51–56 hold one harmony, after which the bass rises to cadence, and that rising bass direction gives power to the material which closes the exposition. At the analogous place in the recapitulation the strength of the bass is increased by its chromatic quality. It is the function of the unusually extended coda to resolve all this energy to stillness, stability, and composure. That Mozart accomplishes this demonstrates his complete control of every dimension of the movement, from the largest to the smallest. The slow movement anticipates Beethovenian sound (m. 32) and intricacy, while the last movement, with its abruptly broken flow, hiatuses, and unexpected modulations, is a disturbing composition.

The Sonatas in F, K. 533, and D, K. 576, both demonstrate Mozart's increasing tendency to treat the solo sonata as chamber music, in which left and right hands exchange material, collaborating to make an ensemble. The following example shows an entire fragment consisting of the first 19 measures of a Piano Sonata in B♭, K.569a, that Mozart never completed:

2. Edward MacDowell, *Critical and Historical Essays* (Facsimile reprint, New York, 1969), p. 194.

Example XXVI–3: W. A. MOZART, Fragment of a keyboard sonata, K.469a, I

This, together with another fragment (K.590b) and the two completed sonatas referred to above, supports the conception of the piano sonata as chamber music. The natural language of all these works is contrapuntal. Even when the material appears to be of conventional mold, it is susceptible to contrapuntal treatment. K.533 is unique in that its technical devices seem to point to something beyond themselves. The opening (mm. 1–2) and the conclusion of the exposition (mm. 99–102) are widely separated. The first action of the middle section is to bring them together (mm. 103–107). That in itself is unusual enough, but the device is applied again when the secondary material of the second tonal area (mm. 66–69) returns in the recapitulation (mm. 193–196). It then undergoes a further partial recapitulation (mm. 201–205) with the opening subject in contrapuntal combination.

The uncommonly rich slow movement contains one of the most astonishing passages of harmony and voice-leading in all of Mozart's compositions (mm. 60–72). This is the kind of music that oversteps the bounds of Mozart's own aesthetic "that the music must never cease to be music" and passes into a realm where, for a moment, the inexorable repeating pattern of notes creates dissonance of an almost expressionistic quality.

Omitting consideration of a number of other works for piano left in fragmentary state, mention must be made of the *Rondo* K.511, the *Adagio* K.540, the *Gigue* K.574, and the *Menuet* K.355 (revised K.576b). In these works, particularly K.511, the composer transcends anything he had written for the piano. In particular, the effect of the right hand carrying two voices in three-part polyphony, and indeed the constant assimilation of contrapuntal techniques, is remarkable. During this period Mozart also composed several sets of variations, with those on a tune of Gluck, K.451, generally accounted as the finest.

PIECES FOR PIANO FOUR-HANDS Within the ten-month period from 1 August 1786 to 29 May 1787, Mozart completed three works for piano four-hands that have no precedent and, it may be argued, no successors. The Sonata in F, K.497, anticipates the rich sonority and intricate part-writing of the great string quintets, and its character is quite different from the later Sonata in C, K.521, in which Mozart's writing is less polyphonic and more dependent upon pianistic figuration. In the latter work the tendency, already noted, of treating the two hands of the solo piano sonatas as separate contributors to an ensemble has increased, and the two players become left and right hands—with ten fingers instead of five. The set of variations in G, K.501, is closer in style to the later sonata and, while *concertante,* in the sense that both players must possess a measure of virtuosity, it is nevertheless the realization of a chamber music ideal. These three works deserve to be considered among the greatest of Mozart's pianistic accomplishments in technique, in content, and in essential musicality.

The Sonata in D, K.448, for two pianos, four-hands is as good an example as one can find of Mozart's capacity to adapt his style to any instrumental combination. The work was written in late 1781 for performance by Mozart and, as he tells us, the fat pupil who made advances to her piano teacher and was rejected, Josephine von Auernhammer.[3] In this work almost all material is repeated by each player, and the result is a perfect piece of social music making. Mozart also left some extensive fragments of compositions for two pianos, four-hands which show that, had the opportunity arisen, he would have left us with more than one masterpiece for this combination.

MECHANICAL ORGAN WORKS The delight which the eighteenth century took in mechanically produced music (something comparable to our own day) was not shared by Mozart; at least, when he was asked to write some pieces for mechanical organ, at the end of 1790, he confessed to being bored with writing for a machine in which "the works consist solely of little pipes, which sound too high-pitched and childish

3. Josephine von Auernhammer, as well as being a fine pianist, was a published composer.

for my taste." (*Letters,* 3 Oct. 1790). The resulting three compositions, K.594, K.608, and K.618, hardly reflect Mozart's boredom, except possibly the first. Written on four staves (594 and 608) and three staves (618), the first two are usually played by four hands on the piano, or on the organ. All three are serious, contrapuntal works, but the last is a prime example of Mozart's latest manner, mixing the simple with the complex, the happy with the sad, the sweet with the bitter.

SONATAS FOR VIOLIN AND PIANO

The sonatas for piano "with violin accompaniment" fall into three groups. The first, comprising K.379, K.376, K.377, and K.380, date from 1781, the time of the rupture with the archbishop and shortly thereafter. The second group consists of a substantial number of unfinished works dating from the year of his marriage. And the last group contains the large sonatas K.454 in B♭ (1784), a concert work written for the violinist, Regina Strinasacchi, at the first performance of which it was noticed that Mozart was playing from blank pages: he had only had time to write out the violin part; K.481 in E♭ (1785), K.526 in A (1787), and a small sonata in F, K.547. Each of the large works is, in its own particular way, excellent and all three redefine the standards of writing for the two instruments. From K.481 one feature must be singled out for comment, for this work takes up in a coda material which had been first exposed in development, a device that historians usually attribute to Beethoven. In the first movement of K.526, carefully differentiated articulation in different voices brings about a sense of metrical fluidity,

Example XXVI–4: W. A. MOZART, Sonata for Violin and Piano, K.526, I

which is a facet of Mozart's mature style easily overlooked. Indeed, the texture of the entire sonata is one in which voices intertwine in a freely contrapuntal style. The slow movement is a unique mixture of the austere and the emotional. The moving octaves of the opening, which predominate throughout the movement, provide a backdrop for moving, vocal-style interjections. This texture surely influenced Beethoven's Violin Sonata Op. 24. In the same slow movement, Mozart displays

Example XXVI–5:

a: W. A. MOZART, Sonata for Violin and Piano K.526, II

b: L. VAN BEETHOVEN, Violin Sonata Op. 24, II

a marvelous ability to focus the iridescence of a whole tonal spectrum upon the everyday key of D major, lifting it out of itself by sheer magic (see Example XXVI–6 on p. 508).

THE PIANO TRIOS

Mozart devoted so much thought and inspiration to the sonatas for piano with violin, and for piano with violin and cello, that they retain an importance and beauty beyond what was considered the norm in his day. Having written nothing for piano trio since 1776, Mozart suddenly produced three masterworks, K.496 in G, K.498 in E♭, and K.502 in B♭, between July and November, 1786. Then, after a pause of almost exactly two years he wrote three more, K.542 in E, K.548 in C, and

Example XXVI–6: W. A. MOZART, Sonata for Violin and Piano K.526, II

K.564 in G, composed between June and October, 1788. That these works are, from the outset, real trios as opposed to accompanied piano sonatas is shown by the following excerpt from K.496:

Example XXVI–7: W. A. MOZART, Trio K.496, II

The cello, while supporting and coloring the bass for the most part, is now midway between the role of the *continuo* and Beethoven's *obbligato* cello—fully at home participating as solo voice, as conversationalist with the other parts, or as accompaniment to the other parts. In scoring these works Mozart placed the cello in the lowest position, with the piano in the middle and the violin on top. With the cello placed there, what is more natural than having it sound the bass line. The surprise is that it so often functions as an independent voice.

The trios are occasional pieces, written for private performance by friends, like so much of Mozart's music, and this is the reason he composed a number of works for unusual combinations of instruments: for example, the oboe quartet, K.370; the duets for violin and viola, K.423 and 424; the works for glass harmonica; those for mechanical organ. Also among this list there is the trio K.498, mentioned above, for piano, clarinet, and viola. It is perhaps surprising that 498 contains a strong *concertante* or virtuosic element, not encountered in the other trios.

THE PIANO QUARTETS

Two quartets for piano, violin, viola, and cello, K.478 in G minor and K.493 in E♭, were to have been a set of three to be printed by Mozart's friend, composer and publisher F. A. Hoffmeister. After the poor reception given to the first, Hoffmeister begged to be released from the contract, and the second work, already written—indeed, already partly engraved—was later published by Artaria. The third, unfortunately, was never written. Of the very first piano quartets, these two are among the best, and it is hard to see why they should have been rejected. To be sure, there is something of the piano concerto in the keyboard parts, but nothing more taxing than in the accompanied keyboard sonatas.

Where Mozart went beyond public expectations, however, was in the string parts; here the contrapuntal web woven by the strings exceeded normal accompaniment patterns. Unlike the string quartets of the time, both the piano quartets are in three movements, F/S/F, which places them in the "divertimento" category of the sonatas and trios; yet the musical material is of the highest order, covering the widest range from gravity to humor and incorporating all that is most significant from the vocabulary of instrumental music and comic opera.

THE PIANO QUINTET

The Quintet K.452, for piano, oboe, clarinet, horn, and bassoon, dates from 1784, and Mozart confessed to his father that he thought it one of the best works he had ever written. Leopold wrote that he "had the great pleasure of hearing so clearly all the interplay of the instruments that for sheer delight tears came into my eyes." (*Letters,* 16 Feb. 1785) He might well have been speaking of such music as the following excerpt, in which the interplay of instruments is one of the most important aspects of the music:

Example XXVI–8: W. A. MOZART, Quintet K.452, II

During the last ten years of his life the public knew Mozart as a pianist, but in his private life, when making music with his friends, he often played the viola. In his days at Salzburg he had been known as a violinist of some brilliance. In Vienna by choice he slipped out of the limelight and into the middle of the texture where the dark sound of the viola and the interplay of the instruments could best be savored.

CHAMBER MUSIC FOR STRINGS ALONE

In the field of chamber music for strings alone, duet, trio, quartet, and quintet, Mozart set a standard that could not be surpassed. The criteria by which such works are judged cannot be simply stated, but they must be taken to include instrumental interplay, satisfying melodies encompassing a broad range of emotional expression, harmony ranging from simplest to most complex in modulation and in dissonance treatment, a perfect perception of the vital life of rhythmic figures, and a complete command of textural variety.

THE STRING DUETS At the time of Mozart's visit to Salzburg with his wife in 1783 he had occasion to write two duets for violin and viola to help out his friend Michael Haydn, who could not complete a commission. These works, K.423 in G and K.424 in B♭, completely fulfill the musical and textural possibilities of their instrumentation, in a way quite beyond Michael Haydn's albeit wonderful capacities.

THE STRING TRIO A solitary trio, K.563 in E♭, for violin, viola, and cello was written in 1788 for Michael Puchberg, the friend and fellow Mason to whom Mozart turned on so many occasions for financial help during his last years. In six movements, the work is properly entitled "Divertimento."

THE STRING QUARTETS The last ten string quartets comprise three groups: the *Haydn* Quartets, K.387 in G, K.421 in D minor, K.428 in E♭, K.458 in B♭, K.464 in A, and K.465 in C; the solitary *Hoffmeister* Quartet K.499 in D; and the *Prussian* Quartets, K.575 in D, K.589 in B♭, and K.590 in F.

The *Haydn* Quartets, so called because they were dedicated to that composer, were published in 1785. In the dedication, Mozart describes these quartets, "his children," as "the result of long, hard labor," and his manuscript shows the extensive revisions that the works underwent. The six quartets fall into two groups of three, the first written in seven months between December of 1782 and June/July 1783, and the second group written in three months between November 1784 and January 1785. Leopold describes the second group as lighter than the

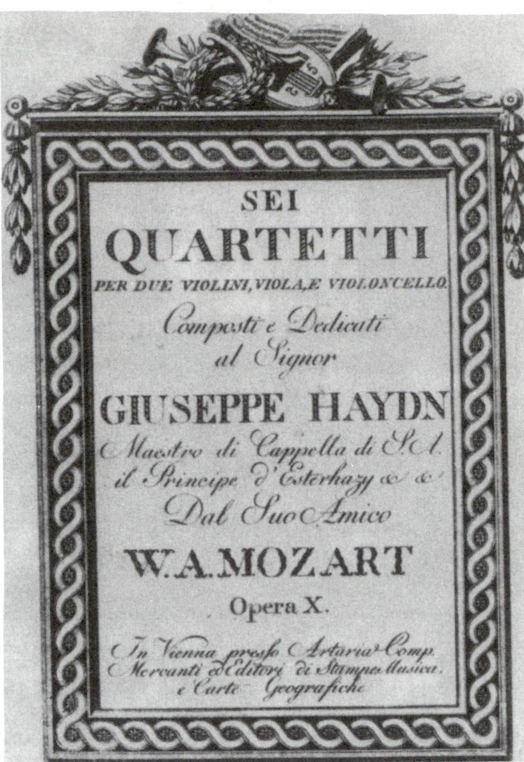

SEI
QUARTETTI
PER DUE VIOLINI, VIOLA, E VIOLONCELLO.
Composti e Dedicati
al Signor
GIUSEPPE HAYDN
Maestro di Cappella di S. A.
il Principe d'Esterhazy &c &c
Dal Suo Amico
W. A. MOZART
Opera X.
In Vienna presso Artaria Comp.
Mercanti ed Editori di Stampe Musica,
e Carte Geografiche

The elegant title page of the first edition of Mozart's six quartets dedicated to Haydn and published by Artaria.

first. If any one set of six string quartets can be thought to epitomize "Classical" string quartet style this set must be the one. Craft and art in perfect balance, direct and enticing in melody, straightforward yet sophisticated in harmony, each instrumental part is laid out so that no note is wasted, and each player is rewarded not only in the beauty of the whole but in the knowledge that his part is essential to the whole. From moment to moment the technique and texture change and the instruments almost cease to exist as instruments and become voices. All virtuosic efforts are abandoned in the realization of the score, and there can hardly be a player in these quartets who has not been moved to marvel at them. They constitute a summit of artistry in which everything happens so smoothly that any sign of striving is hidden from view. This is music that justifies what Joseph Haydn said to Leopold (see p.357). Indeed, these quartets reveal Haydn's superlatives to be inadequate.

It has been said that Haydn showed Mozart how to write string quartets and then Mozart showed Haydn how string quartets should be written. The question of Haydn's influence on Mozart's string quartets remains open. One can observe that Haydn's Op. 20 appeared in 1772 and that when the next set (Op. 33) was published in 1781, they were advertised as being in quite a new style. Mozart seems to have followed the same pattern by writing no quartets between K.173 (1773) and K.387 (1782). To deduce therefore that Mozart wrote the *Haydn* Quartets under the older composer's influence is to err on the side of the simplistic. Mozart heard and assimilated most of the music of his time. His artistic development—like Haydn's—was continuous. Of course they influenced each other and of course they gave each other the sincerest form of flattery in their mutual admiration and imitation. Each was *sui generis*.

The remaining four quartets are quite different. The *Hoffmeister* and the *Prussian* Quartets show equal mastery of all techniques, but the manner has changed. Whether the exuberance of the early Vienna years has waned, to be replaced with something else, is hard to say. But henceforth, although energy, resolve, and impetus are present at times, there is also an introversion that casts a grave shadow over the works.

In the *Haydn* set the composer steadfastly avoids the use of any element that comes from the world of the public concert. The opening fanfare to warn the audience that the music has already begun is a commonplace in the symphony and the concerto. Mozart's sense of the essential difference between various types of composition makes him avoid anything that smacks of the soloistic, the *concertante,* or the virtuosic. (Haydn, incidentally, is more apt to mix elements of public music and private music.) In the last three quartets Mozart moves away from this ideal. These works were written for King Frederick William II of Prussia, the ardent amateur cellist and patron of Boccherini, who had works dedicated to him by most of the famous composers of the day, including Haydn and Beethoven. Mozart intended to write six quartets for the king, although only three were finished. The prominence given to the cello part is balanced by a tendency toward *concertante* writing for all the instruments—in other words, there are stretches written in either soloistic or purely accompanimental style, in marked contrast to the ever-changing relationships in the *Haydn* set. It is curious to observe that the effect of brilliance created by the *concertante* writing is to some extent mitigated by the restricted use of tempo contrast. For example, the first *Prussian* Quartet, K.575, has an *Andante* slow movement and three others all marked *Allegretto*.

THE STRING QUINTETS While it might be argued that Haydn and Beethoven had at least equaled Mozart's excellence in the string quartet, no one else enriched the string quintet genre as he did. With the exception of K.174, Mozart's quintets date from the last four years of his life: K.515 in C from 19 April 1787; K.516 in G minor, 16 May 1787; K.593 in D, December 1790; and K.614 in E♭ from 12 April 1791. To this list must be added a Quintet in C minor arranged from the Serenade for Winds, K.406, dating from 1787 or 1788. We do not know why Mozart composed them at this particular time. Apparently they were not designed for a friend or for a publisher; perhaps there was a plan to offer them to a patron, but that, too, is speculative. It is certain, however, that combining a larger number of instruments in the context of chamber music brought out the best in the composer who clearly delighted in creating new sonorities by setting one group of instruments against another.

Each of these works is as different as possible while remaining within the limits of a single style, and each is a flawless masterpiece. The Quintets in C and G minor form one of those famous pairs of works (compare the Piano Concertos K.466 and K.467; K.488 and K.491; and the Symphonies K.550 and K.551) in which Mozart appears to be creating complementary opposites—works for the same medium which are worlds apart in spirit.

The quintets repeatedly demonstrate not only Mozart's technical mastery of all compositional devices, but also a degree of structural innovativeness more usually associated with Haydn, and a use of dissonance not seen again until Schubert. The slow movement of K.614 exemplifies both formal and harmonic innovation (*ACM* 63). A hybrid structure, crossing the ideas of rondo and variation (a favorite Haydn device), the theme is one of the last of the slow Gavotte tunes that have appeared periodically in his music. This theme, like so many by Mozart, unites simplicity with symmetry, grace with melancholy, and joins the subtlest artistry with universal appeal. By m. 53 an episode variation carries the musical idea away into new areas. The way Mozart returns (mm. 78–88), using unprepared dissonance of an unusually pungent nature, is a technique he favored in his late works, i.e., the use of scale passages repeated with intervallic modifications that obscure both the tonality he is in and that to which he is going.

All things are brought together in the quintets: strict canon, assimilated fugue, imitation, textural and harmonic play, the opera house, the concert hall, all united to produce works of unsurpassable richness. The *Haydn* Quartets with their teeming invention are here equaled, but on a bigger scale, and there is nothing of the depressed introversion of the *Prussian* Quartets about them. Mozart has no rivals in this medium.

THE SONG

There is one more area of private music that Mozart enriched: the song. It is not unusual for writers to say that a couple of Mozart's songs anticipate the glories of nineteenth-century Lieder, but in fact the few he wrote epitomize several important currents in eighteenth-century song. He acknowledges the taste for sentimental melancholy, with its emphasis on tears, sadness, comfort, graves, wounds, loneliness, and suffering several times, e.g., K.391, K.390, and reaches an apotheosis in K.523, *Abendempfindung an Laura* (Evening Feelings to Laura). This song not only approaches the nineteenth century in emotion, but also in its arpeggiated accompaniment figure acting as a continuum against which the through-composed melody wends its eloquent way. The satirical song, which depicts and mocks customs and characters—e.g., K.524 and K.518—is represented by a masterpiece in K.517, *Die Alte* (The Old Woman). Here the text bemoans modern times and the music mocks the text in its archaisms. The eighteenth-century ballad is also brought to mind in Mozart's only Goethe setting, *Das Veilchen* (The Violet), K.476, a through-composed song with discontinuous textures that is held together at the end by the repetition of a phrase from the beginning .

In Mozart's day the Viennese Lied was a slight thing, the creation of a few minutes, designed to amuse amateur musicians. Hence the genre was not one into which Mozart would invest great effort. The wonder is that such slight poetic prompting could, from time to time, evoke such a response from him.

THE SYMPHONY

The Vienna years produced no symphonies specifically written for that city. Indeed, in the last ten years of his life, Mozart wrote only six works in this genre:

K.385 in D	1782 (the *Haffner*)
K.425 in C	1783 (the *Linz*)
K.504 in D	1786 (the *Prague*)
K.539 in E♭	1788
K.550 in G minor	1788
K.551 in C	1788 (the *Jupiter*)

We must not make too much of this paucity, however, for the fact is that Mozart wrote symphonies only for special occasions. He used works of this type, as we have seen (p.488), to open and to close his concerts or academies. For this purpose a symphony could be cut up so that movements 1, 2, and 3 might serve as an overture, while movement 4 would work well as finale. The main emphasis in the concert lay in the varied nature of the solo contributions: concertos, arias, etc.

THE *HAFFNER* Originally written as a Serenade, this was the second he had written for his Salzburg friends of that name. When he needed a new symphony to dismember at one of his concerts, Mozart asked his father to send the score back to Vienna, where, by dropping the extra movements and adding flutes and clarinets to the orchestration, he created a symphony that surprised him by its excellence. The Serenade had been written in such haste that he had really forgotten everything about it. For us, the symphony is unforgettable, particularly the first movement, its festive D-major flourishes united with the contrapuntal working of a rhythmically piquant theme, that in itself lacked any charm. Mozart's treatment of it and his superabundant invention make grandeur and humor, pathos and exuberance coexist.

THE *LINZ* Returning to Vienna from Salzburg at the end of October 1783, Wolfgang and Constanze were the guests of Count Thun in Linz for three weeks. Mozart wrote to his father

> I am going to give a concert in the theater here—and since I have not a single symphony with me, I am head over heels into the composition of a new one, which has to be finished on time. (*Letters,* 31 Oct., 1783)

They had arrived in Linz on 30 October , and the symphony, which received its first performance on 4 November, was an immediate success.

This is the first of three symphonies in which Mozart placed a slow introduction before the first movement—a fact which some scholars attribute to Haydn's influence at this time. Perhaps of greater significance is the fact that in this nineteen-measure introduction a process is taking place that is quite different from anything Haydn does (*cf.* his Symphonies Nos. 84, 85, 86, 88). Thematically more independent, Mozart's introductions are more usually lengthy harmonic or melodic excursions, conveying a greater feeling of obscurity or complexity. In the *Linz,* the entire introduction is composed, fantasia-like, on a descending scale, and the opening fanfare and the ensuing polyphonic play are brought to an end only by the underlying bass progression.

THE *PRAGUE* The next symphony, K.504 in D, the *Prague,* was composed late in 1786, and received its first performance early in 1787 at a concert directed by the composer, who was in Prague to conduct *The Marriage of Figaro.* We know that Mozart was thinking at that time of going to London to seek his fortune, and it may be that this unique symphony was written for the audiences of that city. It is a three-movement work, distinguished by the longest of Mozart's slow introductions leading to an *Allegro* movement that relies heavily upon the use of contrapuntal textures. The movement also contains a striking example of unusual string orchestration in its climactic final measures. Here the enormous space between first and second violins is filled by the density of wind sound, yet the texture conveys an almost Beethovenian sense of strain. The slow movement is like an island of sensuous languor between the energetic first and third movements. The fullness of the woodwind orchestration and the chromatic writing create an effect of unequaled richness, and there are passages in which the winds prevail over the strings to an extent that presages what is to happen to the orchestra at the hands of Beethoven and Schubert between 1800 and

Example XXVI–9: W. A. MOZART, Symphony K.504 , the *Prague,* I

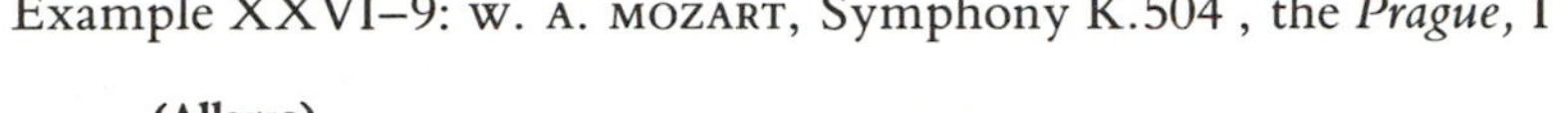

1830. No orchestration in the last twenty years of the eighteenth century was as forward-looking as Mozart's.

THE LAST THREE SYMPHONIES It is possible that Mozart intended them to be his "London" symphonies, but, in the absence of clear evidence, we cannot be sure exactly why he wrote the last three, which he entered into the catalogue of his own works, under the year 1788, as follows:

[K.542]	22 June	A Trio for Piano, Violin and Cello.
[K.543]	26 June	A **Symphony** - 2 Vlns, Fl., 2 Cl., 2 Bsn., 2 Hn., 2 Trp., Tym., Vle., & Bassi.
[K.544]	26 June	A little March - Vlns., Fl., Vla., Hn., & Cello.
[K.545]	26 June	A little Piano Sonata for beginners.

[K.546]	26 June	A short Adagio for 2 Vlns., Vla., & Basso for a fugue which I wrote a long time ago for two pianos.
[K.547]	10 July	A little Piano Sonata for beginners with Violin.
[K.548]	14 July	A Trio for Piano, Violin and Cello.
[K.549]	16 July	A little Canzonetta for 2 Sopranos and Basso.
[K.550]	25 July	A **Symphony** - 2 Vln., Fl., 2 Ob., 2 Bsn., 2 Hn., Vle., & Bassi.
[K.551]	10 August	A **Symphony** - 2 Vln., Fl., 2 Ob., 2 Bsn., 2 Hn., 2 Trp., Tym., Vle., & Bassi.
[K.552]	11 August	A Song - *Beym Aufzug in das Feld*

It is unbelievable that all these works were composed within the approximately eight-week period indicated; yet the list stands as proof of the impossible, for these symphonies have no equals in the eighteenth century. In technique and perfect control of all means, they stand alone. As a group they make an interesting trilogy, and there are a number of ways in which in which the differences between them can be seen as mutually complementary.

The E♭ Symphony has been called the *Masonic* (E♭ and C minor, the keys with three flats, are those Mozart most frequently uses for his ceremonial Masonic music and the ties in the theme of the first movement have been held to symbolize the bonds of brotherhood in Freemasonry). Symbolism aside, this is the third and last symphony with a slow introduction, the grandeur of which, with its rich counterpoint of textures, with the violence and the inevitability of its dissonance, and with its mysterious closing canon, all serve to heighten the rhythmically hesitant, motivically organized melody that opens the *Allegro*. It is also the only symphony to use that device most commonly associated with Haydn, but which Mozart increasingly makes his own—monothematicism. The last movement of the E♭ Symphony is a sonata structure in which the main thematic areas share the head motive and bear the strongest resemblance to each other (see Example XXVI–10). The energetic first motive of seven notes permeates the entire movement, and when it is used to end the symphony abruptly, the listener can only conclude that Mozart's intention, in using such bathos, is not to communicate weighty ideas but to express humor and high spirits.

The G-minor Symphony[4] has long been regarded as Mozart's highest achievement in expressivity, but it was not always so perceived. For the nineteenth century it was, in Schumann's words, "a model of Grecian lightness and grace." Schumann saw the work through the eyes of

4. The score of the G-minor Symphony is available in the *Norton Anthology of Western Music*.

Example XXVI–10: W. A. MOZART, Symphony K.543, IV. Interrelationship of themes:

the young Romantic composer and pictured Mozart as a formalist, concerned only with balance and shape; for him the symphony was an epitome of Classical art. The late nineteenth and twentieth centuries felt that an apology was needed for Mozart, who was clearly so much less "powerful" than Beethoven, and they found the excuse in the idea that Mozart was really a social critic who was compelled by circumstances to produce courtly art. This thinking led to the widely held belief, still current in some circles, that Mozart's minor-mode works are the really "great" works, into which the composer invested his true personality. But today we can accept the fact that a great actor can play tragedy one night and comedy the next and be equally great in both; the Shakespeare of the tragedies and the Shakespeare of the comedies is still Shakespeare. We must acknowledge that Mozart, likewise, is a composer who writes with unsurpassed excellence in major or minor mode, and both modes come equally close to fulfilling the composer's expressive needs.

The quintessence of the G-minor Symphony, then, is to be found partly in the response that great works must necessarily evoke, and partly in its structure. In significant ways it is different from the E♭ Symphony, as it also differs from the symphony which follows it. In K.543 Mozart deliberately establishes a strong first movement, rich in variety of material, and concludes with a humorous, monothematic structure. In K.550 he strives to create a sense of balance and equality between first and last movements, with resemblances set up in a variety of ways, not the least of which is imitation.

The opening measures demonstrate the subtle ways in which the composer makes his musical elements work against one another to create a feeling of tension and instability. At first sight nothing could be more stable than the initial melody with its stolid, although *piano*, accompaniment. The violas *divisi* play a background figure that emphasizes the strong beat of the measure, both by starting on the beat and by sounding a lower note on that first beat. The well-known melody in the first violins is a finely calculated tune in which each phrase balances the next, and antecedent/consequent relationships are immediately apparent. It, too, seems to accentuate the strong beats of the measure, but it begins with an anacrusis, unlike the accompanying figure, and the first note of this upbeat is strongly dissonant with the harmony. Being dissonant it attracts to itself an agogic accent that makes it stronger than its resolution; the sense of downbeat is weakened, and thus the metrical alignment of melody and accompaniment is dislocated. What at first had seemed to work together is now seen to pull apart. The resulting *Affekt* is one of unease, where one feels that something is wrong but cannot tell precisely what it is.

A similar but much stronger pulling apart is found in the last movement where, after the double barline, the strongly metrical main theme of the movement is subjected to the most painful dislocation of melody, harmony, rhythm, and tonality. Where the first movement communicated a sense of unease, here the violence of the expression is unmistakable.

Example XXVI–11: W. A. MOZART, Symphony in G minor, K.550, IV

The third symphony of the trilogy, K.551, has been aptly nicknamed *Jupiter*. For as Jupiter was the father of the gods whose weapon was the lightning bolt and thunder, so the symphony wields superhuman power and moves with sovereign ease through the biggest symphonic architecture of the century. The first movement contains a wealth of material, completely disparate and ranging from the majestic (mm. 9–23) to the trivial (mm. 101–10); from the terrifying (mm. 81*ff*) to the tender (mm. 56*ff*). Its effects range from the humorous to the intellectual in the creation of an exacting first movement, and yet it is in the fourth movement (*ACM* 64), justly famous as one of the greatest technical *tours de force* in all of music, that the listener is overwhelmed. Here, several short motives are fashioned into a web of counterpoint, without parallel in its vigor and strength. It is Jupiter-like, or Jovian, in that its dazzle and power can hardly be comprehended, any more than its technique can be apprehended; it can only be wondered at.

THE CONCERTOS

Mozart composed twenty-two concertos during his last decade, of which seventeen are for piano, four for French horn, and one for clarinet. To say that each is a masterpiece and capable of defining the ideal of the medium is a wearisome repetition, but no less than the truth. Most of the piano concertos were written for the composer's own use in his Viennese concerts and hence were composed between 1782 and 1786, when his concert-giving was at its height:

1782 - K.413 in F	K.414 in A	K.415 in C
1784 - K.449 in E♭	K.450 in B♭	K.451 in D
K.453 in G	K.456 in B♭	K.459 in F
1785 - K.466 in D minor	K.467 in C	K.482 in E♭
1786 - K.488 in A	K.491 in C minor	K.503 in C

All these works consist of three movements, F/S/F, with a slow movement in a different but related key, most commonly in the subdominant. Mozart, however, shows an amazing capacity for varying the detail of the concerto shape, more so in the piano concertos than in the others. The point of return to the tonic key and the first material is usually where one finds the most interesting variations since here the opening orchestral exposition and the following solo exposition are combined into one recapitulating section. In general, Mozart personifies the piano soloist in a variety of roles, as we have already seen in K.271, where the soloist, particularly in the slow movement, appears in the character of the tragic operatic heroine. For example, in K.467 and K.503 the shy soloist has to be coaxed and enticed from the role of *continuo* player and to participate in the action as a principal player.

Example XXVI–12: W. A. MOZART, Hesitant solo entries

a. K.467, I

b. K.503, I

What a surprise to find these two works among the most taxing and virtuosic! On the other hand, K.466 and K.491 both present the soloist in a kind of Hamlet soliloquy, opening the solo part with a melancholy piece of new material. Even those works that appear orthodox, such as

Example XXVI–13: W. A. MOZART, Solo entries in soliloquy

a. K.466, I

b. K.491, I

K.488, in which the first orchestral tutti appears to be duplicated, note for note, in the first solo, the element of surprise is retained by having the soloist revise the third solo to include new material which had been introduced only after the first tutti and first solo had reached their conclusion.

To single out any one of these works for study is difficult since each has unique and distinctive qualities of imagination. But perhaps the most unusual structural modification—indeed it is used once only—occurs in the last piano concerto, K.595 in B♭. This work, unlike all others, not excluding K.466 in D minor and K.491 in C minor, breathes an atmosphere oppressive with resignation, weariness, and defeat in its first movement. In order to achieve this, Mozart uses a number of expressive devices, none of which is unique, but which cumulatively create an effect that can hardly be mistaken.

Example XXVI–14: W. A. MOZART, Piano Concerto K. 595, I

a. Melody conveying an impression of a downward progression or of falling:

b. Repetition of a melody with different coloring:

c. Extensive use of the Neapolitan area:

d. Various kinds of hiatus or effects of disorientation:
1. Interruption of climax

2. Rhythmic

3. Tonal

The distinctive profile given to the soloist is one that emphasizes the depressing *Affekt* of the work. The soloist enters with an ornamented repeat of the orchestra's opening material (mm. 81–96) and then moves into seven measures of very orthodox passagework, terminated by a strong cadence of dotted rhythms in the orchestra (mm. 97–105). From mm. 106–19 the soloist introduces material that has not been part of the orchestral exposition, and is strongly Neapolitan. This new material remains the soloist's exclusive property in the recapitulation as well. In fact, the recapitulation seems to proceed in the most routine manner, with all the events of the exposition recalled as expected. But after the final trill (m. 334), which ought to herald the final ritornello and the cadenza/conclusion, Mozart inserts an anomaly: material that had been the property of the orchestra and had not been alluded to since the first ritornello is now brought back by the soloist. Here, although the material is exactly as at its first appearance, the fact that it is now given to the soloist places it in a new light. The close juxtaposition of rhythmic hiatus, Neapolitan area, chromaticism, and subdominant area, all confirm the elegiac nature of what stands as one of the most poignant musical experiences Mozart has left us.

Example XXVI–15: W. A. MOZART, Piano Concerto K. 595, I

There is no great composer who took advantage of the opportunity to write for his friends more than Mozart. The four concertos for French horn, K.412, K.417, K.447, and K.495, and the single one for clarinet or basset horn, K.622, were all written for friends, and they form the backbone of the concert repertoire for those instruments. We do not know whether Mozart gained financially from writing these works, however in variation of detail and constant freshness of material, as well as the indefinable matter of personal identification, they do not approach the great piano concertos of the same decade.

SERENADES, DIVERTIMENTOS, AND DANCES

Mozart's activities in Vienna gave him less opportunity to write serenades and divertimentos, forms associated with the earlier period in Salzburg. There are only two additional works for winds alone: the Serenade K.375 (1781) in E♭, and the Serenade K.388 (1782) in C minor, both for 2 oboes, 2 clarinets, 2 horns, and 2 bassoons (K.375 also exists in a version for 2 clarinets, 2 horns and 2 bassoons). These great works conclude Mozart's writing for *Harmoniemusik* (wind band) yet their echoes resound through the rest of his music in the "serenade-like" episodes within several piano concertos, and in the wind writing of the symphonies and operas. A set of five tiny Divertimentos for 2 clarinets (basset horns) and bassoon, K.439b (1783), also creates marvelous effects in a small space.

Mozart wrote a solitary serenade for strings which has become one of the most popular pieces of music in existence: the Serenade in G, K.525, *Eine kleine Nachtmusik*. The German description is taken from Mozart's own catalogue and means "A Little Night Music (i.e., Serenade)." Mozart's own title is generic, but for the English-speaking world it has become specific.

Two engravings by Daniel Chodowiecki, entitled *La Dance,* which contrast proper posture and elegance, manliness and femininity, with ridiculous, mincing affectation and exaggeration.

Least known and in some ways most important among Mozart's works written for specific social occasions in public are the many dances which he composed as *H. M. Kammermusiker* to Joseph II. Mozart, like Beethoven and Haydn, had written dances throughout his career. Dancing played a large part in eighteenth-century life, and Mozart, as we know, liked it and was very good at it. In his position as chamber composer for the court, he produced nineteen works, according to his own catalogue, consisting of sets of Minuets, German Dances, *Contretänze,* and *Ländler.* The range of invention is immense and the variety, particularly of the Minuets, astonishing. The second Minuet from K.601 (1791; *ACM* 65) is singled out because it illustrates the extremes of range in this form, from the most *galant* to the music of country bumpkins. (Note in particular the bassoon part in the *galant* Minuet and the bagpipe effect of the hurdy-gurdy in the rustic Minuet.) Since the majority of these dances date from Mozart's last year, 1791, we cannot help but regret that such a wealth of idea, imagination, humor, and feeling should have been spent on ephemera instead of string quintets, concertos, or symphonies.

OPERAS

It was during the last decade of his life that Mozart wrote his greatest operas, but these works were not uniformly spaced throughout the period. He went to Vienna in 1781, immediately after the production of *Idomeneo* in Munich. 1782 saw the staging there of *Die Entführung aus dem Serail* (The Abduction from the Seraglio), K.384, the *Singspiel* with which Mozart hoped to reap profits from the emperor's establishment of a German opera. In 1783, Mozart began the composition of two operas which were left incomplete, and wrote a number of substitute arias for other people's operas, working very hard and achieving very little. Total operatic silence reigned in 1784, while in 1785 he composed only three substitute ensembles. In 1786, a short, one-act piece, *Der Schauspieldirektor* (The Impresario), K.486, appeared, as well as *Le nozze di Figaro* (The Marriage of Figaro), K.492, followed shortly after by *Don Giovanni* , K.527, in 1787. Then there was a three-year gap until *Così fan tutte* (All Women Behave in This Way), K.588, in 1790, and *Die Zauberflöte* (The Magic Flute), K.620, as well as *La clemenza di Tito* (Titus's Mercy), K.621, in 1791.

Mozart lavished the utmost care on the two operas of 1781–82: on *Idomeneo* because he hoped it would lead to employment in Munich; and on *Die Entführung* because he hoped it would bring him favor with the emperor and employment in Vienna. Each demonstrates his complete mastery of two utterly different styles of opera. Underlying the stylistic differences, however, there is Mozartian unity in attention to detail; in both operas he devotes great thought to the drama and its progress, and to the nature and motivation of the characters. Evidence for this is to be found in the correspondence, which, although not as extensive for *Die Entführung* as for *Idomeneo,* nevertheless tells us a great deal. (See the letter from Mozart to his father of 26 September 1781, pp.483–85.)

As a comic opera *Die Entführung* uses patter throughout for comic effect and much of the panoply of Italian opera is put aside in favor of short, simple effects. For example, the emphasis on the ritornello is lessened and many of the numbers open with only a preliminary chord before the vocal entry; in two cases, the verses of strophic songs are separated by the insertion of spoken dialogue; the melodic material, even of arias, is strongly influenced by the German popular style. It has another quality that helps to make it great: Mozart's psychological identification with the characters. He was quite aware of the similarity between the situation of the hero, Belmonte, and the heroine, Constanze, and his own, and spoke about it in these terms. Like Belmonte, he too was bound by love to rescue his Constanze, and like Belmonte he had to battle many adverse forces. His victory is assured through the success of his hero, and his psychological identification enables him to speak movingly and sincerely through the mouths of each character. Even the villain, Osmin, becomes a means of revenging himself upon his old enemy Colloredo.

Der Schauspieldirektor, or *The Impresario,* was a small occasional piece based on an idea of the emperor and first performed at a gathering at

Schönbrunn on 7 February, 1786.[5] It consists of an overture, two arias, a trio and a quartet with a large amount of spoken dialogue and the plot concerns the rivalry of singers. It is a slight piece that did not cost the composer much effort but brought him both the emperor's notice, and some money. The score contains, nevertheless, moments of surpassing beauty.

The commission for *The Impresario* interrupted work on *The Marriage of Figaro,* which Mozart had begun late in 1785. While *Figaro* was the first of Mozart's well-known collaborations with his most famous librettist, Lorenzo da Ponte, it will be remembered that they first met in 1783 when da Ponte was writing for Salieri. The original play, *Le Mariage de Figaro,* by Pierre-Augustin de Beaumarchais, had been written in 1779, but because of the controversial nature of its subject matter, it was not staged until April 1784. Less than a year later it was being prepared for performance in Vienna in February 1785. The court in Vienna was quite as sensitive to subversive material on the stage as the court in Paris, and this performance was forbidden by Joseph II. Strangely, however, the printing of the play in translation was not banned, and a copy of it was found among Mozart's books after his death. In casting around for a subject, Mozart and da Ponte may have hit upon the idea of setting a play that had been in trouble with the censors, in order to attract an audience. The excellence of the play itself and the fact that it formed a sequel to *The Barber of Seville* (1775), Paisiello's setting of which was in the repertoire of the court opera, must have provided an additional attraction. In his memoirs, da Ponte relates that it took Mozart only six weeks to compose the opera. Considering the number of works that Mozart was committing to paper between October 1785 and 1 May 1786, when the first performance took place, this astounding statement becomes more credible, since he could not have spent more time on it. Modern scholarship has made a strong case for its having been composed between mid-October and the end of November, 1785.

Various intrigues are reported by da Ponte and by Michael Kelly (1762–1826), who sang Don Basilio in the first performances, in his *Reminiscences* (1826). It certainly appears strange that an interval of five months could elapse between the completion of the work and its first performance, and doubly strange that it should have received only eight performances before disappearing from the Viennese stage for three years. *Una cosa rara* by Martín y Soler (1754–1806) displaced *Figaro* and became the rage with Viennese audiences. It was only when *Figaro* became a wild success in Prague that Viennese curiosity was aroused and Mozart was asked to revise it for a new production in 1789.

5. For that same occasion Salieri produced his tiny Italian opera *Prima la musica e poi le parole* (First the Music and then the Words).

By setting *Una cosa rara* beside *Le nozze di Figaro* we can see something of Viennese taste in the 1780s and discover why Mozart's music was found difficult to accept. Martín's work has all the charm of melody that is to be found in Mozart, but where Mozart connects the music to the drama by some unexpected and delicious modulation or by some textural change, Martín cannot be shaken from his simple path of primary triads and consistent textures. In ensembles, Martín's voices move together in thirds and sixths, and any counterpoint of different emotions and different dramatic motivations in one and the same composition is quite beyond his power. Martín's appeal lies in his simplicity and in the immediate attractiveness of his melody; Mozart's has the same appeal, in far greater measure, but the immediacy of his impact is mitigated by his harmonic, contrapuntal, and dramatic complexity. The Viennese audience could appreciate Martín's work at first hearing because it did not challenge them. Mozart's work is infinitely more profound and hence more demanding. The Prague audience was prepared to give Mozart what the Viennese audience would not: a sympathetic and attentive hearing.

The plot of *The Marriage of Figaro* centers on the infidelities of Count Almaviva, the idealistic and handsome young nobleman hero of *The Barber of Seville,* who, several years after his marriage and a sequence of *amours,* wishes to seduce Suzanne[6] before her forthcoming marriage to Figaro. Upon his marriage to Rosine (the Countess), the Count had voluntarily given up his *"droit de seigneur"*—the right to spend the first night with any bride on his estates.[7] Now he begins to wish he had not been so hasty. Some time in the past Figaro had borrowed money from an elderly woman, Marceline, promising her marriage as security. Unknown to anyone, Figaro is actually the long-lost fruit of an illicit liaison between Marceline and old Dr. Bartholo, the Countess's former guardian and would-be husband. The Count schemes to use Figaro's debt and contract with Marceline to prevent his marriage to Suzanne, but with the discovery of Figaro's true relationship to the older woman the plans for their marriage come to naught and the old enmity is converted into love. After many intrigues and complications, the Count and Countess are reconciled and everything ends happily.

If any librettist could ever lay claim to genius, then it must be da Ponte, for the adaptation of Beaumarchais's play into a concise opera is hard to fault. Perhaps cutting all reference to the liaison and promise of marriage between Marceline and Dr. Bartholo and the birth and loss

6. French spelling of the characters' names refers to the Beaumarchais play; Italian spelling refers to the characters in the opera libretto.

7. A French critic has wittily described the character of Beaumarchais's Count as one "who perceives the end of his privileges drawing closer and wishes to abuse them before having to renounce them. Afflicted with a cold heart, if he lights so many fires [his affairs] it is only to warm himself up at them for a moment."

Taken from the first edition of Beaumarchais's play, *Le Mariage de Figaro,* the illustration of this famous *coup de théâtre* dates from 1785.

of their child, all of which Beaumarchais carefully prepares, was a mistake, since it makes the discovery that Figaro is their long-lost child resemble a comic-opera device. It is possible that the exclusion of this part of Beaumarchais's dramatic exposition was part of the clean-up that the play had to undergo in order to be allowed on stage in Vienna. The campaign against loose sexual morals begun by Maria Theresa may have persisted, and one notes that da Ponte and Mozart, in addition to rendering the love affair between Bartholo and Marceline innocuous, have made Chérubin's sexuality that of an adolescent, not only by writing the role for soprano voice but also by cutting out some of the more suggestive dialogue and making him into a sometime-in-the-future lover. In the play, the Countess, pleading for Chérubin in Act I, says, "Alas, he is so young!" to which the Count, who knows how many compromising situations the young man has been in, replies, "He is not so young as you think." Most obvious is da Ponte's removal of all direct reference to the "first-night right," despite the fact that this is the core of the play. Only by making such cuts could the composer and librettist get the emperor's support for staging their opera. And even after these and larger cuts were made, the opera was considered longer than normal.

Perhaps Mozart's most important contribution was his ability to communicate, through musical gestures, subtleties of characterization beyond that which words could achieve alone, never resorting to the stock, cardboard figures with which operas had always been populated.

The Countess's dejection is established before she says a word, (*ACM* 66) by the short melodic phrases that all resolve downward, and yet her dignity and strength of character are also clearly shown by the richness of the orchestration and the quiet emphasis upon the strong beat of the measure. Compare this *Cavatina* of Mozart with the one by Paisiello (*ACM* 55). Mozart's Rosina is not one-sided but is, like a real human being, a complex person full of contradictions. Bartolo's fatuous self-importance is demonstrated by pompous orchestration, by his use of patter, and by the juxtaposition of musical incongruities. Cherubino's romantic fixation is established in two ways: his breathlessness by tempo and rhythm, and his obsessiveness by the *ostinato* quality of the rhythm. These are only a few obvious examples.

Mozart's clear perception of character and of each character's relationship to the drama is greatly abetted by the incomparable ease with which he differentiates personalities within an ensemble. For example: late in Act I, the Count discovers Cherubino hidden in a deep chair covered by a sheet. He is furious! Don Basilio, who is enjoying the situation, is hypocritically stirring up trouble while seeming to pour oil on the already troubled waters. Susanna is terrified. In the excerpt from the trio (see below), Mozart combines these contradictory emotions, each character attaining emotional credibility. This same ability is demonstrated in the Sextet where Figaro discovers that he is the son of Marcellina and Bartolo; it is a masterpiece of comedy, a set piece which nevertheless moves the action forward and one of Mozart's own favorites. It also allows for the development of the great finales to Acts II and IV.

Example XXVI–16: W. A. MOZART, *The Marriage of Figaro,* Act I, No. 7

The following outline shows the way the finale of an act of an *opera buffa* should be constructed, according to the Mozartian ideal. The action before the finale of Act II of *Figaro* is as follows: the Count has been led, by an anonymous letter from Figaro, to believe that the Countess has a lover. The Countess and Susanna have been dressing Cherubino, an adolescent godson of the Countess, in women's clothes when the Count arrives unexpectedly. Cherubino hides in a closet and is locked in by Susanna. The Count demands that the door be opened, suspecting that the lover is inside. The Countess refuses, and the Count takes her with him as he goes to look for tools to force the door. Meanwhile, Susanna unlocks the door, lets Cherubino out through a window, and then locks herself in the closet. The audience knows what has happened; neither the Count nor the Countess has the least inkling that anything has changed when they return, and the Finale, which is almost one thousand bars in length, begins.

Section & length	Key	Meter	Tempo	Action
a. 121mm.	E♭	C	*Allegro*	Count and Countess. He threatens to force the door and to kill whoever is inside. He reproaches his wife with infidelity. She names Cherubino as the person inside the closet but says he and she are both guiltless.
4mm. of transition which changes the tempo and raises expectation.				
b. 41mm.	B♭	3/8	*Molto andante*	Susanna emerges from the closet. When the Count goes in to see whether anyone is left inside, Susanna tells the Countess how Cherubino escaped.
c. 161mm.	B♭	C	*Allegro*	Count sues for pardon for his suspicions and the ladies make the most of their advantage.
d. 70mm.	G	3/8	*Allegro con spirito*	Figaro enters, saying that everything is ready for the celebration of the wedding, and tries to force the Count to agree to let it go ahead. The Count, recognizing a crucial point in the game, holds back and pulls out . . .
e. 69mm.	C	2/4	*Andante*	the anonymous letter from Figaro, telling him of the Countess's rendezvous for that evening. Figaro denies any knowledge of it despite the Countess and Susanna's broad hints that all is in the open. The three plead that the wedding be allowed to proceed, when . . .

f. 138mm.	F	C	*Allegro molto*	in comes the gardener, complaining that too many people throw things out of the castle windows, that they have just thrown a man out, and that the rascal ran away. The Count's suspicions are re-awakened.
g. 92mm.	B♭	6/8	*Andante*	Figaro says it was he who jumped out of the window when the Count came. Of course, we know it was Cherubino. But in jumping he has dropped a paper which the gardener hands to the Count, who now asks Figaro to identify it, since it must have dropped from his pocket. Figaro has no idea, but bit by bit the ladies convey to him that it is Cherubino's commission in the army which he had to bring back because it had not been officially sealed.
h. 243mm.	E♭	C	*Allegro assai*	Marcellina, Bartolo, and Basilio enter asking for the Count to judge the justice of their case against Figaro and his debt. The whole ends with all the solo characters, divided clearly into the good ones and the bad ones, singing against each other. At this point in the opera, when the curtain falls, it looks as though the characters whom we do not like are going to be triumphant.

Vienna may not have taken instantly to *Figaro* but Prague did. The opera was produced there early in December 1786, and Wolfgang and Constanze went at the beginning of 1787 to enjoy its success. In February 1787, Mozart returned to Vienna with a contract for a new opera for Prague. *Don Giovanni,* first produced on 27 October 1787, which many have regarded as the greatest of all operas, was the result, and once more it came about from uniting the talents of Mozart and da Ponte.

The idea for the story had been popular for a number of years, although regarded as vulgar by many with pretensions to taste; indeed, that same year Giuseppe Gazzaniga set the same subject to words by Bertati. What Mozart and da Ponte created was immeasurably greater than anything that had been done before, and they raised the fable from the level of the tawdry and popular to that of supreme art. The plot is relatively simple, compared to that of *Figaro:* a rich nobleman, whose pleasure is the pursuit of women, attempts, in disguise, to rape the daughter of a

The National Theater in Prague was the scene of Mozart's most gratifying triumphs when *The Marriage of Figaro* and *Don Giovanni* were first performed there.

neighbor. He fails, but is forced to duel with her father and kills him. The daughter vows that she will find the guilty man. When she realizes that their friend and neighbor was the would-be rapist she tries to unmask him, but revenge is taken out of her hands by her father's ghost. Some time later, Don Giovanni and his servant, Leporello, are hiding in a cemetery. The statue erected in memory of the dead father warns the Don of his approaching fate, saying that he will not be laughing by morning. Don Giovanni, in foolish bravado, invites the statue to dine with him; the statue accepts, and when it arrives at the Don's house, calls upon him to repent. He refuses, and the statue drags him to Hell.

The score of *Don Giovanni* is even richer in orchestral color than that of *Figaro,* and the effects that Mozart obtains through harmony, instrumentation, and dynamics in the statue scene remain hair-raising to this day. Like *Figaro, Don Giovanni* contains at least one show-stopper of a tune. In the former it was "Non piu andrai," Figaro's march-like aria teasing Cherubino about the life awaiting him in the army. In *Don Giovanni* it is "La ci darem la mano," a duet of seduction between the hero and Zerlina, the peasant girl whom the Don unsuccessfully pursues throughout the opera. Both these tunes were immediately popular, and have remained so ever since.

The incredible pace of *Don Giovanni*'s opening scene is unlike anything that has preceded it. One of Mozart's dramatic constants is verisimilitude. The stop-and-go style of eighteenth-century opera, in which recitative carries action forward and aria conveys reflection or emotional response, is, in itself, far removed from life, yet in the first scenes of *Don Giovanni* the action is carried forward at a speed usually associated with spoken drama, despite its musical repetitions and symmetries. No other opera plunges the audience into the middle of the action so quickly. When the curtain rises, Leporello is alone on stage, keeping watch for his master, who is attempting a rape. Leporello tells us where his master is, and that he is a gentleman. We assume that an orthodox dramatic exposition is to take place, when Donna Anna and Don Giovanni enter, and the present action begins. Indeed, the need for a dramatic exposition is negligible since the whole drama is created before the audience's eyes. The scene proceeds from Leporello as watch, through the entrance of Donna Anna and Don Giovanni, and the struggle between them, to Anna's exit and her father's entry, his forcing Don Giovanni to fight, and Giovanni running him through, to the pensive trio of the three men, with similar voices and strongly differentiated lines, as the Commendatore dies. All this takes place in 190 bars of music and about four minutes of time. The pace of action in these four minutes is varied; action and reflection are both present, and the musical symmetries are readily perceptible. The audience is even encouraged to associate musical motive with action, as the prominent bass line from the opening of the overture (mm. 5–11) becomes the upper line during the duel (Scene 1, mm. 167–72) which then becomes the music of the Commendatore's death (Scene 1, mm. 190–93). This is also the music for Don Giovanni's own death and damnation (Act II, Scene 15, mm. 594–97). Mozart has crammed all this into the first scene, during which he has not given up control of the timing for one second. Everything happens just as he intends: making allowance for minutely faster or slower tempos—the duel, for example, cannot be lengthened or shortened; moreover, the stage director who will ignore what Mozart saw as a duel with swords, does so at his peril.

A novel bit of characterization takes place when Donna Elvira, a woman who believes herself to be Don Giovanni's wife, enters. Mozart gives her an imperious, queenly, virtuosic aria in which she vows to tear out Don Giovanni's heart. Unknown to her, however, the Don and Leporello observe her, and twice during her aria Don Giovanni speaks. His speech cuts across her music and the effect of all her virtuosity, the strength of her cadence, and all her resolve is lost, for her vows count as nothing in the face of his commanding character. (See Example XXVI–17.)

The finale to the first act of *Don Giovanni* takes place in the Don's palace. A big ballroom has two other rooms leading off it. In each of the rooms is an orchestra, strings and winds in the main room and strings alone in the other two. In each room a different kind of dance is played, and while the action builds up to the proposed seduction of Zerlina, the other characters dance, according to their wishes, either an aristocratic Minuet, a livelier *Contretanz,* or a wild German dance, ancestor of the waltz. In conceiving and realizing this whole scene, Mozart, as in the finale to the *Jupiter* Symphony, creates a complex of such richness allied with such multiplicity of event that, even after repeated hearings, the ordinary human brain can hardly comprehend it

Example XXVI–17: W. A. MOZART, *Don Giovanni*, Act I, Scene 5

The first edition of *Don Giovanni* published by Breitkopf und Härtel in 1801 had a boyish Don in the clutches of a large Commendatore on its title page.

all. For the music alone is enticing enough, but above that are the dialogue and the several actions taking place simultaneously. The little orchestras enter successively and Mozart even notates their tuning up. In Example XXVI–18 on p. 540, the complete Minuet appears in the bottom two staves and the melodies of the other two orchestras on the two upper staves.

Don Giovanni has given posterity a great deal of trouble. Puritans like Beethoven found the entire subject and the main character immoral; many serious-minded dramatists and poets saw the death of the protagonist, Don Giovanni, as the proper tragic conclusion to the story. Some modern critics have seen Mozart's final scene as one of the composer's rare dramatic mistakes. However, we must acknowledge that only with Mozart's moralizing conclusion can the true flavor of the human comedy be brought out, and we accept it as one of his finest commentaries on mankind. The question we are forced to face is whether Don Giovanni is a heroic character, worthy of tragic status, or is he not? Mozart allows us to draw our own conclusions.

The Vienna performance of *Don Giovanni* took place, after some revisions by the composer, on 7 May 1788. The opera was greeted coolly and was judged "too difficult" and "hard on the voices." Hence, no more commissions came until after the successful revival of *Figaro*

Example XXVI–18: W. A. MOZART, *Don Giovanni,* Act I, Ballroom Scene

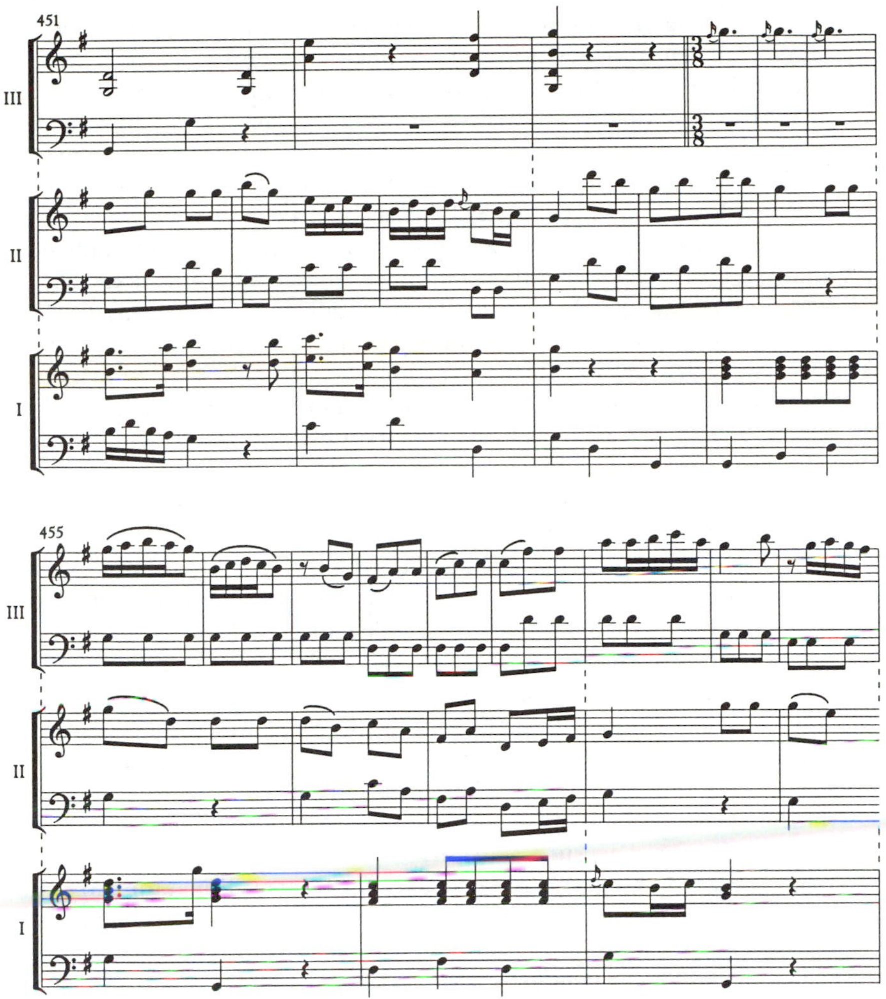

in 1789, which may have prompted the Emperor to remember Mozart. In any event, he commissioned the same composer and librettist to write another comic opera, even giving them the subject, which appears to have an historical basis. *Così fan tutte, ossia La scuola degli amanti* (All Women Behave in this Way, or, The School for Lovers), tells of two young officers, engaged to be married, who bet with an old cynic that their fiancées will remain faithful under all circumstances. The cynic has them go away, return in disguise, and woo each other's fiancée. The cynic wins the bet. The whole topic has been seen as repulsive by many since Mozart's time, and despite its promising reception it became the least-often staged of his great comic operas. There have always been those, however, who have been able to perceive that Mozart's position is not critical of feminine weakness (the moralists' position is that no one in this opera is without fault) but rather is one of deep sympathy with the human condition, with human weakness and particularly with human suffering. If the characters in this story, and we who watch it unfold, have learned anything when the original couples are reunited, it must be that one's expectations of other human beings must not be set too high.

None of Mozart's comic operas lives in a more idyllic atmosphere. A nineteenth-century critic wrote of it that "the air is so soft that one has only to breathe it in order to be happy." And yet in none is the audience so often close to tears, both at the dramatic situation and at the sheer beauty of the music. *Così fan tutte* has been called an opera of ensembles, and Mozart must have experienced considerable pleasure in putting together a first act in which everything works perfectly, with not a moment wasted, and where 12 out of 17 numbers are ensembles. The Quintet No.9 and the Terzet No.10 exemplify the peculiar bittersweet quality of *Così fan tutte.* The men are pretending they have to leave for the army, and the women, sobbing, ask them to write every day. Pretense for the men is reality for the women. Mozart composes the quintet with the most banal introduction he has ever written—a simple vamp that could go on for a longer or a shorter time, above which the sobs are set exactly as one might expect. The sustained line in the violas provides the sole element of the unexpected. Then Mozart's broader vision changes the whole focus. The pretended parting, with all its deceit and petty pride, with its sentimental women and self-centered men, becomes a symbol for all parting—not the parting that is such sweet sorrow, but the loss of present happiness and the uncertainty of its ever returning. The sobs at the outset are realistic, and yet were the whole quintet composed in such a manner it would become laughable and would descend to the level of ordinary comic opera. But at the moment when the sobs become legato melody, realistic sorrow is transfigured into musical sorrow and the particular becomes the universal; the characters are no longer people of flesh and blood but disembodied voices whose nature is sounding spirit. This opera stands alone among Italian operas, an Everest of art whose foundation lies in the unfathomable depths of the human psyche. Mozart is not a tragedian whose characters perish nobly for great causes. All his important characters are fallible, but they achieve rewards despite their folly, their greed, their lust, and all the other human frailties they embody. Like Shakespeare's last plays, the so-called Romances, his great operas glow with the virtues of sympathy, trust, generosity, and tolerance.

Die Zauberflöte or *The Magic Flute,* is a *Singspiel* which Mozart conceived with an old friend and fellow Mason, Emanuel Schikaneder, for presentation in Schikaneder's Theater auf der Wieden. In the late 1780s it was fashionable to use fairy tales and exotic stories with magic as the subjects of operas in Vienna, and possibly as early as 1789 Mozart and Schikaneder may have discussed the story, which combines real people and real love with the world of magic and the supernatural. Composition of the opera, begun early in 1791, was interrupted by the commission to prepare an *opera seria* for the Prague celebration of Leopold II's coronation as king of Bohemia. This opera, *La clemenza di Tito* (Titus's Mercy), was given its first performance on 6 September 1791 with Mozart directing, and just over three weeks later, *The Magic Flute* was first performed on 30 September 1791 in Vienna, also with Mozart directing.

Many hold that *The Magic Flute* is among the greatest human documents, worthy to stand beside Bach's *St. Matthew's Passion*. The plot alone would hardly seem to justify that claim. Pamina, the daughter of the Queen of the Night (evil), has been taken away from her mother by Sarastro, the head of a brotherhood devoted to Truth (good). The Queen of the Night persuades Tamino, an idealistic prince, to rescue her daughter by showing him Pamina's portrait. She gives him, in his quest, a magic flute to help him in time of need. Tamino goes to Sarastro's realm, discovers the goodness of the brotherhood and the Queen of the Night's deceit, and decides to join the brotherhood. After undergoing various trials and rites of purification, Tamino and Pamina are united. Such is the main plot, in which the Queen and Sarastro have supernatural powers, she through the exercise of magic and he through wisdom. Tamino and Pamina are quite human, experiencing love and working toward the realization of their ideals. A vital part of the whole opera is Papageno, who becomes Tamino's servant and companion. Papageno is a bird-catcher for the Queen of the Night and is dressed in a costume of feathers in order to show that while he is human yet he is closer to the animal world than is, for example, Tamino. Papageno has ideals, or rather goals, but they are purely physical: food, drink, and a wife like himself. Mozart and Schikaneder make this trite and far-fetched plot with its ordinary, one-dimensional characters into an allegory of the brotherhood of all humanity, and the musical means adopted by Mozart reflect this broad approach.[8] No other opera by Mozart unites such stylistic disparities, and yet in no opera do separate and disparate parts fit together so well. Wagner's *Tristan und Isolde* is often looked upon as the opera in which the musical means are most strongly intertwined with the emotional substance of the drama. Sixty-eight years

8. Like many great works of art, *The Magic Flute* can be interpreted on a number of levels. In addition to the broad, humanistic thrust of the text, many believe that the opera was written as an allegory of Freemasonry and it cannot be denied that there are many elements of Masonic ideals embodied in the work. (Some have even gone so far as to suggest that Mozart was poisoned by the Freemasons because he betrayed their secrets.) It was also widely believed that the Queen of the Night symbolized the Empress Maria Theresa, who had been opposed to Freemasonry, while her son, Joseph II, was represented by the hopeful hero, Tamino, whose attitudes to religion were more tolerant. In these ways, the artwork can be seen as a mirror, reflecting those attitudes and ideas that we bring to it.

before *Tristan, The Magic Flute* made its musical means a fundamental part of the all-embracing allegory of the drama.

The Queen of the Night uses all the devices and the vocal technique required in the arias of the Italian *opera seria*. Sarastro's musical language is couched in strophic songs which have a distinctly hymnlike quality. Tamino and Pamina speak the human language of the *Singspiel,* comparable to that of Belmonte in *The Abduction,* but raised to a still higher level of expressiveness (e.g., in Pamina's G-minor aria). Papageno speaks with the irrepressible verve of the popular song. But perhaps most surprising of all, after the Overture, which is a fine piece of Mozartian counterpoint, is the duet of the two armed men, those figures of horror at the gateway to the trials by fire and water, who stand and sing, an octave apart, a contrapuntally figured, Bach-like chorale—a real measure of the solemnity with which this part of the work must be approached.[9] In addition to these disparate styles, the work contains a substantial passage of accompanied recitative which revitalizes the eighteenth-century medium and makes it meaningful to modern ears. And throughout, the connecting tissue of ensembles is carried on in an angelic euphony which is as simple in texture and structure as Papageno's music but which is purged of all earthiness. This music belongs to the "supernaturals"—the three ladies of the Queen of the Night and the three Genii.

In an opera filled with great moments one would think the greatest would be hard to find, but there is a place in *The Magic Flute* that, better than any other, exemplifies Mozart's art of understatement as well as his love of simplicity, qualities which overlap but are not always the same. Tamino and Pamina have been separated as part of his trials. He has not been allowed to speak to her, and she, in despair, has been about to kill herself. The two are finally allowed to meet again, to speak to each other and to undergo the trials of fire and water together. The excerpt on the facing page shows the moment of meeting, after which Pamina leads Tamino through safely. A brief moment of perfect statement, of deep seriousness, exemplifying the uniqueness of *Die Zauberflöte*.

In the finale of Act I of *The Magic Flute (ACM* 67) an ethereal atmosphere is conjured up by the music of the three boys (Genii), stately yet bright and almost motionless. Tamino's long accompanied recitative illustrates how the listener can be carried forward, both musically and dramatically at the same time. The remainder of the finale shows how a trite, moralizing text and hymnlike music can be set side by side with no loss of effect.

Much of *La clemenza di Tito,* Mozart's last *opera seria,* was put together in the eighteen days of legend, but it is now absolutely certain that some

9. *The Magic Flute* in places pulls the theatrical and the religious experience close together in a process that Wagner was later to complete in *Parsifal*.

Example XXVI–19: W. A. MOZART, *The Magic Flute,* Act II, Finale

of it was written in the first part of the year. This is an *opera seria* far removed in style from *Idomeneo* of ten years earlier. Where the earlier opera had been luxuriant in its orchestration and innovative in devising new relationships of structure with the drama, *La Clemenza* seems to have engaged the composer to a lesser degree. In line with Mozart's practice in his Italian comic operas and in his last *Singspiel,* brevity is of the utmost importance. His librettist, Caterino Mazzolà (1745–1806), shortened the Metastasio text by about a third as well as making other alterations; he himself shortened individual numbers by cutting down the opening ritornellos of arias and ensembles and reduced the complexity of the forms. Nevertheless, *La clemenza* still has some formidable set pieces. The basset horn is used as an *obbligato* instrument in two of the arias—something that Mozart has not done elsewhere—but unique to this opera is the handling of the chorus. Unlike those in *opere buffe,* the chorus in *La Clemenza* is not merely a device that affords a measure of aural relief for the audience but it is rather a character in the opera: the Roman people, who comment on the action. But unlike *Idomeneo,* the chorus here functions with ensembles of soloists and with Tito himself in three large numbers, a usage that anticipates the nineteenth century. The whole "soundscape" of the opera takes on a new dimension through this device, and it makes grandiose antiphonal writing between soloists and chorus possible. It also allows the chorus to comment on the unfolding drama in a manner never before attempted by the composer.

Although it was not a success at its first performance, *La clemenza* gradually built an audience, and Mozart had the pleasure of knowing before he died that his last two operas were successful.

CHURCH MUSIC

After his precipitous departure from Salzburg, Mozart had no reason to write more music for the Church service, and the two large-scale Mass compositions which he undertook remain unfinished, mighty though they are. The religious aspects of Freemasonry seemed to absorb the composer, who wrote a number of works for his brother Masons.

The first incomplete Mass composition, K.427 in C minor, was vowed as offering in thanksgiving for his marriage with Constanze (mentioned by Mozart in his letter of 4 January 1783). Why it was never completed we do not know. What music Mozart added to give it the appearance of being complete at its first performance we do not know. Tradition has it that it was first performed on 25 August 1783 in Salzburg with Constanze as soprano soloist, but again, we cannot be certain. What we have in complete form are a *Kyrie, Gloria, Sanctus,* and *Benedictus* with parts of a *Credo,* and this is enough to show that Mozart's conception of music for the Mass had developed and deepened immeasurably. Incomplete as it stands, the C-minor Mass cries out for comparison with the Bach in B minor or Beethoven in D. There is a seriousness in its whole conception that had heretofore been present only in part. That seriousness undoubtedly results from a level of involvement with the musical substance that generated greater richness and variety than in any other ecclesiastical work by Mozart. The "Christe eleison," the "Laudamus te", and the "Et incarnatus est" are for soprano solo—for Constanze—and the flavor of operatic aria is pronounced in all of them. But in no way does that detract from the conviction that they carry. The "Et incarnatus" has a trio of flute, oboe, and bassoon soloists who have an extended cadenza with the soprano. But there is nothing frivolous or worldly in the sound. Rather one must admit that the words of the liturgy have never been set in a more heavenly way. Even the *Benedictus* for four solo voices, so often a way station for a pleasant bit of relaxation, is a demanding movement: in A minor, the secondary material in C first appears in mm. 21–26, but on its return in the original key, it is modified (mm. 73–82). Clearly this huge and impressive fragment represents one of the greatest losses to posterity. Completed it would have been, without doubt, Mozart's greatest composition for the Church.

Example XXVI–20: W. A. MOZART, Mass K.427, *Benedictus*

The tiny composition, *Ave verum corpus* (Hail, true body) K.618 (*ACM* 68), only 46 measures in length, epitomizes the neoliturgical style of Mozart's last period, and hence is quite the opposite of the style of K.427 or the Requiem, K.626. Here, the slightest hint of counterpoint is merged into a kind of transfigured simplicity in which every note is inevitable yet never trite. Deservedly one of the best known of Mozart's small pieces, it was written, like so many others, to please a friend.

Mozart's final work, the Requiem K.626, embodies a great deal of his art and most of his craft in liturgical music. In particular, the Requiem shows at all points in its structure his command of counterpoint so completely assimilated as to be a natural language. He plumbs the depths of the science of harmony, which his contemporaries found so disturbing in his work in general. (The example below shows the way Mozart modulates from A minor to F in mm. 24–40 of the *Confutatis*.)

Example XXVI–21: W. A. MOZART, Requiem, *Confutatis,* Enharmonic progression

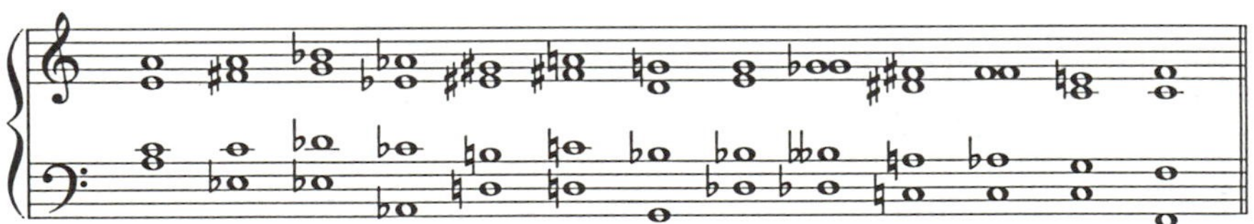

Although Mozart had probably begun composing the Requiem in early summer of 1791, the pressure of other obligations forced him to postpone working on it, so that at the time of his death relatively little was complete. The Introit *Requiem aeternam* and the *Kyrie* fugue were actually the only sections with completed voice parts and orchestration.

For the rest, in those movements which Mozart had sketched, there were instrumental introductions completely or partially scored and voice parts fairly fully indicated. The *Sanctus,* the *Benedictus,* and the *Agnus Dei* were not written down at all, and we can only assume that what we hear today embodies, in some measure, the ideas that Mozart was able to communicate verbally.

Constanze wanted to have the work finished so that she could receive payment for it in full. Even more important, she must have dreaded being called upon to repay the advance of fifty ducats that her husband had accepted at the time of the commission. She first asked Joseph Eybler to complete it. Although we do not know the exact dates at which various parts of the Requiem were composed between the master's death and its performance, Eybler cannot have spent long with the manuscript, which we know he received on 21 December 1791. He handed it back to Constanze, having added some missing orchestration and virtually nothing else. Constanze then asked Süssmayr, Mozart's pupil and helper and the last person with whom Mozart had discussed the work, to try his hand with it. Süssmayr completed it sometime in the first half of 1792, and the Requiem as we know it is by Mozart with additions by Süssmayr.

Looked at dispassionately, we can only regret that Mozart was not able to cast his eye over the completed work. It is difficult to believe that he would have left the *Tuba mirum* with the long trombone solo that sounds so anticlimactic to modern ears and, as one critic has put it, goes on sounding long after it has called all the resurrected before God's throne. It is equally difficult to believe that Mozart could have improved on the *Requiem aeternam,* with its contrapuntal craft in the winds accompanied by the strings and its atmosphere of gravity purged of all passion. Perhaps the Requiem, in its very incompleteness, conveys to us a stronger message of mourning than might have been possible had the work been neatly concluded.

ENVOI

More romantic legend has accumulated around Mozart than about any other composer of his time. His prodigious abilities as a child, his relationship with the archbishop, his rejection of patronage to become the trail-blazer for all subsequent free artists, his life in Vienna and his friends and cronies there, the circumstances of his death and his burial—all these have created a popular picture of the man and his work that bears little relationship to the truth in many instances. Modern research paints quite a different picture. Now, the emphasis is much less upon the spontaneous genius who tossed off compositions with one hand while managing a billiard cue with the other, than it is upon his incredible self-discipline in meeting commitments, for which there is a great deal of evidence. We can see that compositions frequently were begun and put aside only to be taken up later. Mozart's own catalogue and its dates must be used carefully since completion dates do not necessarily tell the whole story. Seeing him more as a human being than as a manifestation of divine genius, we now tend to place greater emphasis upon the difficulties that Mozart experienced during composition in certain genres, such as the string quartet, and we understand the truth behind his words that the *Prussian* Quartets were still more so.

Perhaps the greatest puzzle about this composer and the least susceptible to a plausible answer is why the quality of his music was not more appreciated by his contemporaries, when to us it is so superior to anything being written at the time. As a child, his incredible abilities had brought him to everyone's attention. As a grown man he had been given the highest praise by Haydn, universally recognized as the greatest composer of the age. Yet for the broad public of music lovers he failed to hit the mark that composers like Cimarosa and Martín y Soler in opera and Haydn in instrumental music reached with every composition.

The answer was perhaps most effectively given by Joseph II when he said to Mozart that there were too many notes in the score of *The Abduction*. The complexity of Mozart's compositions for the Viennese audience of the 1780s is not easy for us to understand, since to our ears it is divinely simple. But the audience of 1780 was used to music much less filled with event than Mozart's, whether in the theater, the concert hall, or the chamber. He himself was aware of this fact, and from time to time he wrote in a deliberately simplified style.

What also worked against Mozart in Vienna was the fact that no one in the court was ever wholeheartedly in favor of him: Maria Theresa had written that letter in which she faulted the Mozarts for traveling around like beggars; Joseph II always preferred the music of the Italians and had reservations about Mozart's music; even though he recognized his musical greatness he gave Mozart neither the public recognition of a post early enough to preserve his buoyancy of spirit nor a salary commensurate with his worth. Mozart cherished some hope for recognition from the Emperor Leopold, but this, too, was to be denied, and there is documentary evidence to show that his profligate ways, his poverty, and his debts worked against his reputation, very much as he had feared they would.

Does the modern view of the hard-working Mozart change or lessen the miracle of Mozart? Only partially: now we can recognize that the miracle of his genius was not based on the supernatural, but on the superhuman.

PART VIII

Beethoven: 1770–1827

CHAPTER XXVII

The Giant Astride the Centuries

THE BEGINNINGS IN BONN

Arguably, no composer in history has exercised a greater influence upon the world of music during and after his own time than Ludwig van Beethoven. At a moment in history when music was widely recognized as the highest art, when instrumental music was considered the most satisfactory manifestation of that art, and when the symphony was acknowledged as the vehicle for the most profound utterances in music, mediating between God and man, Beethoven reigned as the undisputed master of the symphony, the sonata, and the string quartet. Like the other contemporary superman Lord Byron, Beethoven came to be universally accepted as the standard-bearer of the new age, a man typical of the new ideal of genius, for whom art was everything.

Nothing in his origins could have aroused expectations beyond the routine and the normal. To be sure, his grandfather had been court Kapellmeister and a man of substance, but Beethoven's father never rose above the rank of singer in the chapel, and by all accounts was a weak man and a bully. His mother was the daughter of a chef and the young widow of a valet, hence of a lower class than his father, but Beethoven was fiercely attached to her. Ludwig was the second child of the marriage and the second christened Ludwig, the first having died shortly after birth. His baptism took place on 17 December 1770, but the date of the actual birth is uncertain with all likelihood pointing to the 16th. Until his fortieth year, the composer believed that he had been born in 1772. The reason for this was simple: when young Beethoven first demonstrated musical ability, his father, determined to capitalize on his son's talent and to make him seem an infant prodigy, lopped two years off his age and advertised 1772 as his year of birth. Ludwig was small and the deception worked.

He must have started keyboard lessons very early for there survives a concert notice from 26 March 1778, in which Ludwig is said to be six years of age and his father's pupil. The announcement says that he will play various concertos and trios and that he "will give complete enjoyment to all ladies and gentlemen, the more since . . . [he has] had the honor of playing to the greatest delight of the entire Court."[1] His education was rounded out by lessons on the violin. For the rest, his formal instruction outside music was not pursued with any enthusiasm by his father, and Beethoven remained to the end of his days largely self-taught in literature, languages, politics, and philosophy (although there is record from a later date of his having attended some lectures at Bonn University in philosophy). Moreover, it would appear that the basis for his anti-social behavior and his solitary and difficult social life was established by his father's insistence that any time not spent in school should be spent in practice.

Sometime in his eighth year his father realized that his son needed teachers of greater ability than his, and the records show a succession of instructors, the most outstanding and influential being Christian Gottlob Neefe (1748–98). Neefe came to Bonn in 1779 and in 1782 he succeeded to the post of court organist. It was Neefe who introduced Beethoven to the *Well-Tempered Clavier,* and who taught him thoroughbass and composition; it was Neefe who first instilled in Beethoven those ethical and moral attitudes which became such a fundamental part of his thinking; and it was Neefe who, in 1783, set down the first printed word that compared Mozart and Beethoven.

FIRST COMPOSITION By this time Beethoven's first composition had been published.[2] The *Variations pour le clavecin sur une Marche de M. Dressler, composées . . . par un jeune amateur Louis van Beethoven agé de dix ans* were in fact composed in 1782 or even 1783, and the indication on the title page, quoted above, that Beethoven was ten years old at the time demonstrates the way documentary evidence supported the notion that he was two years younger than his actual age.

1. Alexander W. Thayer, *Life of Beethoven,* rev. & ed. Elliott Forbes (Princeton, 1964). pp. 57–58.

2. Beethoven was among the earliest composers to depend upn his publishers for much of his living. Moreover, the period of his greatest compositional activity coincided with the enormously rapid expansion of the circulation of music in printed copies, rather than in manuscript; he was probably the first of the great composers to see most of his work in print during his own lifetime. At the beginning of his career, he appears to have had an exalted view of the term opus, reserving it for large, multi-movement works or groups of works. Often he sent smaller works, e. g., songs or sets of variations, to be published without requiring that they be assigned an opus number. Hence Beethoven's output can be divided into two categories: those works that were printed with opus numbers and those that were printed without opus numbers or remained in manuscript. The opus numbers generally convey an idea of chronology but must be treated with care since some early works were only published years after they were written. The less significant works and those unpublished at the time of the composer's death are identified by the letters WoO., an abbreviation for the German words **We**rke **o**hne **O**puszahl (works without opus number). These works are arranged according to genre, and therefore the number following the letters does not indicate a chronological ordering.

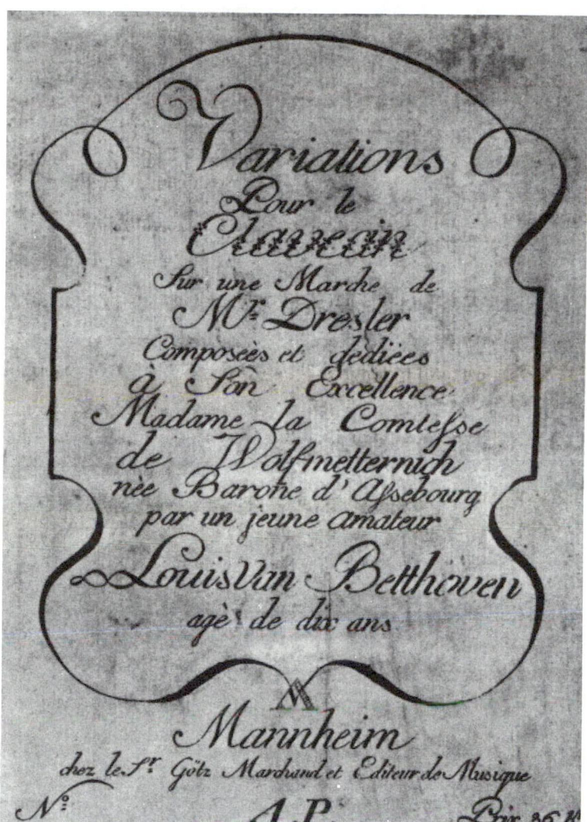

Variations
Pour le
Clavecin
Sur une Marche de
Mr. Dresler
Composées et dediées
a Son Excellence
Madame la Comtesse
de Wolfmetternich
née Barone d'Assebourg
par un jeune amateur
Louis Van Betthoven
agé de dix ans

Mannheim
chez le Sr. Götz Marchand et Editeur de Musique
N°. A.P. Prix 36 K

The title page of Beethoven's first printed composition, the *Variations on a March of Mr. Dressler.*

EARLY PROFESSIONAL LIFE The following year, in mid-1783, Neefe named Beethoven harpsichordist in the opera orchestra, a position of enormous responsibility for a young boy, and one from which he drew a substantial knowledge of the operatic repertoire of the day, as well as a rare ability to read full scores at sight.

In the reminiscences of his friends we read that Beethoven was poorly dressed and even dirty as a child. We now learn that, as court organist, his full dress consisted of:

> Sea-green frock coat, green knee breeches with buckles, stockings of white or black silk, shoes with black bow-knots, embroidered vest with pocket flaps, the vest bound with real gold cord, hair curled and with queue [pigtail], crush hat under the left arm, sword on the left side with silver belt.[3]

In mid 1784 the old Elector died and the uniform changed to one of scarlet and gold when the Archduke Maximilian Franz, the youngest brother of the Emperor of Austria and of Marie-Antoinette, queen of France, became the new Elector and Archbishop of Cologne. For a number of years he had been most interested in Mozart and is said to

3. Gottfried Fischer, *Reminiscences.* Cited in O. Sonneck, *Beethoven, Impressions of his Contemporaries,* (New York, 1967), p. 8.

have wanted him to be his Kapellmeister. It is not known why this did not come about, and one may well wonder how different the history of music might have been had Mozart gone to Bonn in 1784. Max Franz did, however, succeed in attracting a large number of fine minds to Bonn, both as a result of his funding of institutions to foster scientific and artistic knowledge, and because of the progressive and free-thinking atmosphere he encouraged. As soon as he took office, Max Franz required reports on all branches of his court, and we learn the following from the documents:

> Ludwig van Beethoven, age 13, born at Bonn, has served two years, no salary . . . but during the absence of Kapellmeister Luchesy he played the organ, is of good capability, still young, of good and quiet deportment and poor.[4]

Beethoven certainly benefited from the intellectual society of Bonn, and his association with many of the prominent families at court helped add polish to his manners. He also benefited from the new Elector's passion for Mozart, and, in 1787, went to Vienna, perhaps to take lessons from the older composer. There is an oft-told anecdote that Mozart showed no interest in Beethoven's playing until the young man began to improvise. Whether he was sufficiently impressed to give him any lessons is not known, but it is unlikely since Mozart was very busy and Beethoven only stayed in Vienna for two weeks at the most. His hasty departure was caused by the news that his mother was very sick, and some weeks after his return Maria Magdalena Beethoven died at the age of forty. Before she died, she had undoubtedly charged her eldest surviving son to look after the household and to ensure the well-being of his father and brothers. Thus, at the age of seventeen Beethoven became the *de facto* head of the household, and for the next five years, until his father's death in 1792, he made sure that his father did not drink away all the family's subsistence. And he did it well and with all proper consideration.

Beethoven, the young orchestral player, seems to have fitted well into a congenial company. The new Elector was a good administrator and around 1788 he set about gathering together an orchestral body of young, enthusiastic virtuosos, for the performance of concerts and opera. In this group Beethoven played viola for four years and was not considered the brightest talent among them. Their number included Anton Reicha (1770–1836), the nephew of the orchestra's director, a flutist destined to become a fine composer of wind music, and teacher of Berlioz, Liszt, and Franck; Bernhard Romberg (1767–1841), the virtuoso cellist and composer in all fields although remembered today for his music for his own instrument; his cousin, Andreas Romberg (1767–

4. Thayer-Forbes, *op.cit.*, p. 79.

A silhouette of young Beethoven in his mid-teens, dressed in the uniform described on p. 555. (With permission of the Beethoven-Haus, Bonn)

1821), a fine violinist and composer of memorable string chamber music and choral work; Nicolaus Simrock (1751–1832), a hornist and lifelong neighbor of the Beethovens, who founded, in 1793, the great publishing house that bore his name. Beethoven's teacher, Neefe, was also a member of this group. There were also other fine executants, and the orchestra achieved an extraordinary level of accuracy and musicianship in performance, creating a reputation comparable to that of the Mannheim orchestra forty years earlier. The French Revolution and its repercussions led to the dissolution of the orchestra in 1792, and perhaps hastened Beethoven's departure for Vienna in November of that year.

The benefits of these years upon Beethoven's musical and social development are impossible to overestimate. His orchestral and theatrical experience acquainted him with a repertoire of works that he otherwise might never have known, for he never spent much time studying the compositions of other people. And mixing with cultivated, educated people on equal and familiar terms, sharing literary, philosophical, and political interests, and discussing problems of the moment convinced him that genius ranked far above social status (as he asserted on a number of occasions).

EARLY SUPPORTERS The von Breunings became Beethoven's spiritual family. It was in their midst, we are told, that Beethoven "received his first acquaintance with German literature, especially poetry, as well as his first training in social behavior"[5] Madame von Breuning,

5. Franz Wegeler, *Notizen,* cited in A. Thayer, *op. cit.,* p. 84.

widow of Court Councillor von Breuning, had four children, the eldest of whom, Eleonore, was just over a year younger than Beethoven. The family was wealthy and cultivated, and after his introduction to them (probably in 1784) he rapidly became an intimate friend "spending in the house the greater part of his days . . . [and] also many nights."

The arrival in Bonn of Count Ferdinand von Waldstein in 1788 brought the second most important formative influence into Beethoven's life. Devoted to music making and to intellectual pursuits, the count became a kind of protector for the young pianist and composer, willing to help Beethoven's financial situation by gifts so discreetly given as to make it seem that they came from the Elector. Had Waldstein or the von Breunings thought of Beethoven as no more than an artist, they would have had little compunction in offering him money.[6] In normal eighteenth-century manners among the well-bred it was more acceptable to go hungry than to accept charity; while it was perfectly in order for Beethoven to receive gifts and money from the Elector, it would have been demeaning for his friends to help him directly. In maneuvering thus with Beethoven, Waldstein was exercising the tact that good manners required between equals. Today we remember Waldstein best as the person to whom the Piano Sonata Op. 53 is dedicated. But he is also remembered for his words in the album that Beethoven's friends prepared as a memento on his second and final departure for Vienna in 1792:

> Dear Beethoven! You are going to Vienna in fulfillment of your long frustrated wishes. The Genius of Mozart is mourning and weeping over the death of her pupil. She found a refuge but no occupation with the inexhaustible Haydn; through him she wishes to form a union with another. With the help of assiduous labor you shall receive Mozart's spirit from Haydn's hands.
>
> Your true friend
> Waldstein Bonn, October 29, 1792.[7]

This inscription may be dismissed quickly as a flowery, fanciful piece of verbiage, but it does give us an idea of the esteem in which Beethoven was held in Bonn. It is clear that in these circles Mozart was looked upon as a genius and Haydn was not. In all probability Haydn's popularity would be reason enough for these intellectuals to deny him genius; the genius, after all, is an original and always something of an outsider. How much quiet contempt in the term "the inexhaustible Haydn"! Beethoven was to inherit the mantle of genius, and hence was already superior to Haydn. Small wonder that Beethoven's relations with Haydn

6. In the first years of the nineteenth century, Louis Spohr, a doctor's son, was financed by the Duke of Brunswick, who, acting as an old-style, enlightened patron, made sure he had the best possible teachers and experience to encourage his talent. Spohr was grateful to his patron.

7. Quoted in Thayer-Forbes, *op. cit.*, p. 115.

were often strained until the latter's death in 1809, after which Beethoven could hardly find terms glowing enough to praise the man whom, in life, he had so often attacked.

THE EARLY YEARS IN VIENNA

Some time on or before 10 November 1792, Beethoven arrived in Vienna, supported by his patron, the archbishop of Cologne, and armed with letters of introduction to the music-loving nobility, as well as an invitation to study with Haydn. He appears to have settled down quickly and to have begun his studies promptly, remaining in the pupil/teacher relationship until around the end of 1793 (Haydn left for England early in 1794). This was the time when Haydn, at the height of his powers, was in constant demand throughout Europe. Perhaps for this reason he could not devote the kind of time or the energy to Beethoven's instruction that the younger man felt entitled to, or perhaps it was that Haydn, who was self-taught, believed that his was the proper path to follow. Whatever the reason, the lessons were not a success. Beethoven had to resort to the elaborate subterfuge of taking lessons from Johann Schenk (1753–1836), who, out of pure altruism, agreed to teach him strict counterpoint without charge and to correct his exercises, on condition that Haydn never know of their relationship and that Beethoven recopy his work after Schenk had corrected it. The arrangement worked well. Nevertheless, Beethoven must have absorbed a great deal from Haydn in the area of free composition, as his later works demonstrate.

Late in 1793, Haydn wrote to the Elector/Archbishop in support of a request for renewed financial subsidy for Beethoven, enclosing a number of Beethoven's compositions as evidence of his industriousness. Once again Beethoven seems to have embraced deception as a reasonable method of conduct; the Elector wrote a scathing letter back to Haydn in which he said that, with the exception of one fugue, all the music Haydn sent had been written and performed at Bonn before Beethoven's departure, and that given the amount of money Beethoven was getting, he ought not to be in financial need. One must assume that Beethoven is the guilty party in this case. The very worst that can be charged against Haydn is that he did not take the trouble to ascertain that the compositions he forwarded were really new.

Why would Beethoven act in this way? Perhaps the answer lies in his absolute conviction that he was above the rules and conventions that bind ordinary people. There is certainly plenty of anecdotal evidence to support this idea, e.g. Ferdinand Ries[8] reports the following story:

8. Ferdinand Ries (1784–1838) a student of Beethoven's and personal friend. He moved to London and there acted as Beethoven's agent.

> Once, while out walking with him, I mentioned two perfect fifths, which stand out by their beauty of sound in one of his earlier violin quartets, in C minor. Beethoven did not know of them and insisted it was wrong to call them fifths. Since he was in the habit of always carrying music-paper about him, I asked for some and set down the passage in all four parts. Then when he saw I was right he said: "Well, and who has forbidden them?" Since I did not know how I was to take his question, he repeated it several times until, much astonished, I replied: "It is one of the fundamental rules." Again he repeated his question, whereupon I said: "Marpurg, Kirnberger, Fuchs, etc., etc., all the theoreticians!" "And *so I allow them!*" was his answer.[9]

It is clear that Beethoven was conscious of his lack of formal training in music and missed the sense of historical context that he believed such training would have given him. He had studied Bach counterpoint but his only experience with Fuxian or species counterpoint had been during those sessions with Schenk. Therefore, after Haydn's departure for London in 1794, Beethoven began his studies with the greatest contrapuntist of the day, J. G. Albrechtsberger. These lessons continued for over a year.[10] He also valued Antonio Salieri's advice on free composition, particularly in regard to the setting of Italian words. A further report from Ries tells of the reaction of Beethoven's teachers to their pupil:

> All three [Haydn, Albrechtsberger, and Salieri] valued Beethoven highly, but were also of one mind touching his habits of study. All of them said Beethoven was so headstrong and obstinate that he had much to learn through harsh experience which he had refused to accept when it was presented to him as a subject of study.[11]

These early years in Vienna saw Beethoven's first publications, the Three Trios for piano, violin and cello Op. 1, which, although probably completed by the end of 1793, were not issued by Artaria until July or August 1795. Of course, Beethoven had written many works before these, but it is significant that the composer had not considered any of them of sufficient importance to receive an opus number. The trios received their first performance[12] at a private gathering in the home of one of Beethoven's noble patrons. They were well received by the audience, which included Haydn, who, while complimenting Beethoven, advised him against publishing the third trio (in C minor). Beethoven attributed Haydn's remark to jealousy. In the event, he did wait a while

9. Ferdinand Ries, *Biographisches Notizen über Ludwig van Beethoven.* cited in O. Sonneck, *op. cit.,* pp. 49–50.

10. One is reminded of Franz Schubert's decision, in his last year, to take counterpoint lessons from the greatest teacher of the day, Simon Sechter.

11. Ferdinand Ries *Notizen.* cited in Thayer-Forbes, *op. cit.,* p. 149.

12. This concert must have taken place at the end of 1793 and before 16 January 1794, for on that date Haydn left Vienna for his second visit to London.

before publishing them, using the time to gather an impressive list of subscribers and to make some revisions.

Beethoven could not, at first, depend upon composition: he earned his living playing the viola—and keyboard where required—in orchestras. It was, however, his extraordinary ability as a keyboardist that established his fame. During his early years in Vienna, Beethoven had occasion to compete with some of the finest pianists on the local scene, one of whom was the Abbé Gelinek, composer of brilliant, routine music much admired in its day. Beethoven's pupil of later years, Carl Czerny (1791–1857), recounts the following anecdote:

> I can still remember Gelinek's telling my father, one day, that he had been asked to spend the evening at a gathering where he was to break a lance with an unknown pianist. "We will give him a first-class drubbing," Gelinek added. The following day my father asked Gelinek how the battle of the preceding night had turned out.
>
> "Oh," said Gelinek, quite downcast, "I shall think back on last night many a time! That young fellow was full of the very devil! Never have I heard such playing! He improvised on a theme I had given him as I have never heard Mozart himself improvise. Then he played compositions of his own which are in the highest degree astonishing and grandiose and he displayed difficulties and effects on the piano beyond anything of which we might have dreamed."[13]

On another occasion the pianist, Daniel Steibelt was the victim in an incident fully recounted by Ferdinand Ries:

> When Steibelt, the famous piano virtuoso, came from Paris to Vienna, in all the glory of his fame, several of Beethoven's friends were afraid the latter's reputation would be injured by the newcomer.
>
> Steibelt did not visit Beethoven; they met for the first time in the home of Count Fries, where Beethoven gave his new Trio in B-flat major, Op.11, for piano, clarinet and violoncello, its initial performance. It does not give the pianist much of an opportunity. Steibelt listened to it with a certain condescension, paid Beethoven a few compliments, and felt assured of his own victory. He played a quintet he had composed, and improvised; and his *tremolandos,* at the time an absolute novelty, made a great impression. Beethoven could not be induced to play again. Eight days later there was another concert in Count Fries' home. Steibelt again played a quintet with much success and besides (as was quite evident), had practiced a brilliant fantasy for which he had chosen the identical theme developed in the variations of Beethoven's trio. This roused the indignation of Beethoven and his admirers; he had to seat himself at the piano to improvise, which he did in his usual, I might say unmannerly fashion, flinging himself down at the instrument as though half-pushed. As he moved toward it he took the violoncello part of Steibelt's quintet, purposely put it on the piano-rack

13. Carl Czerny cited in O. Sonneck, *op. cit.,* p. 23.

> upside-down, and drummed out a theme from its first measures with his fingers. Then, now that he been definitely insulted and enraged, Beethoven improvised in such a way that Steibelt left the room before he concluded, refused ever to meet him again, and even made it a condition that Beethoven was not to be invited where his own company was desired.[14]

The way to fame and fortune in Vienna seemed assured, and Beethoven even appears to have attempted to acquire some social graces—certainly necessary considering the number of times he thought he was passionately in love. But no part of this future was to be fulfilled. In his late twenties Beethoven had become aware that his hearing was deteriorating (it is believed that he had some serious illness, possibly typhus, around 1796–97, although there is no record of it) and by 1800 it was clear to him that he was going to have to rethink his career as a musician. Beethoven had been taught to think of himself as a genius, destined to walk down roads which few could follow. The rest of his life was, in fact, an almost steady decline to stone deafness some time late in the second decade of the century. Had he not been so afflicted, who can tell how his career might have played out, for the peculiar greatness of the man did finally lie in the vigorous and desperate struggle through which he converted personal disaster into creative energy.

RECOGNITION AND SUCCESS

The year 1800 marks a watershed in Beethoven's life for two reasons, both of which served to establish his reputation as a composer. First, on 2 April 1800, a remarkable concert was given in which Beethoven appears on an equal footing with the most revered composers of the time. To begin with a symphony by Mozart and to end with the first performance of Beethoven's First Symphony in C, Op. 21, in the first year of the new century seems like a conscious acknowledgment that a new age was beginning. The program was as follows:

1. A Grand Symphony by the late Kapellmeister Mozart.
2. An Aria from *The Creation* by the Princely Kapellmeister Herr Haydn, sung by Mlle. Saal.
3. A Grand Concerto for the Pianoforte, played and composed by Herr *Ludwig van Beethoven*.
4. A Septet, most humbly and obediently dedicated to Her Majesty the Empress, and composed by Herr *Ludwig van Beethoven* for four stringed and three wind instruments, played by Messrs. Schuppanzigh, Schreiber, Schindlecker, Bär, Nickel, Matauschek and Dietzel.
5. A Duet from Haydn's *Creation*, sung by Herr and Mlle. Saal.
6. Herr *Ludwig van Beethoven* will improvise on the pianoforte.
7. A new Grand Symphony with complete orchestra, composed by Herr *Ludwig van Beethoven*.

14 Fe nand Ries, *Notizen* cited in O. Sonneck, *op. cit.*, p. 51

Second, after nearly two years of hard work, Beethoven finished his first set of six string quartets. Until this time, almost all his published work was written for his instrument (fourteen of the first nineteen opus numbers involved the piano principally). He had already demonstrated his mastery of the piano sonata, and now, in 1800, he entered the two remaining arenas he was to dominate for the whole of the nineteenth century and arguably to this day: the symphony and the string quartet. In this same year, Prince Lichnowsky settled a small annuity on him, which gave him enough financial independence so he could compose according to his inclination (see Diderot's dictum about commissioning works from artists, p. 18), and did not feel a pressing need to accept any and all publishers' offers.

THE HEILIGENSTADT TESTAMENT The reordering of his life was not something that Beethoven could accomplish overnight. In a fit of depression over the decline of his hearing, Beethoven penned the following document, always called the "Heiligenstadt Testament," after the village where he was staying when he wrote it. Although addressed to his brothers (Johann is not named, for some reason), it was never sent, nor was it seen until after Beethoven's death. It tells much about his inner thoughts at this time, including his brief contemplation of suicide. The fact that he copied out the whole so carefully and preserved it makes it into a kind of *apologia pro vita sua,* destined not for his brothers alone but, like his musical utterances, for mankind. Here it is in its entirety:

> Heiligenstadt, October 6, 1802
>
> For my brothers Carl and [Johann] Beethoven
>
> Oh my fellow men, who consider me, or describe me as, unfriendly, peevish or even misanthropic, how greatly do you wrong me. For you do not know the secret reason why I appear to you to be so. Ever since my childhood my heart and soul have been imbued with the tender feeling of goodwill; and I have always been ready to perform even great actions. But just think, for the last six years I have been afflicted with an incurable complaint which has been made worse by incompetent doctors. From year to year my hopes of being cured have gradually been shattered and finally I have been forced to accept the prospect of a *permanent infirmity* (the curing of which may perhaps take years or may even prove to be impossible). Though endowed with a passionate and lively temperament and even fond of the distractions offered by society I was soon obliged to seclude myself and live in solitude. If at times I decided just to ignore my infirmity, alas! how cruelly was I then driven back by the intensified sad experience of my poor hearing. Yet I could not bring myself to say to people; 'Speak up, shout, for I am deaf'. Alas! how could I possibly refer to the impairing *of a sense* which in me should be more perfectly developed than in other people, a sense which at one time I possessed in the greatest perfection, even to a degree of perfection such as assuredly few in my profession possess or have ever possessed—Oh, I cannot do it; so forgive me, if you ever see me

withdrawing from your company which I used to enjoy. Moreover my misfortune pains me doubly, inasmuch as it leads to my being misjudged. For me there can be no relaxation in human society, no refined conversations, no mutual confidences. I must live quite alone and creep into society only as often as sheer necessity demands; I must live like an outcast. If I appear in company I am overcome by a burning anxiety, a fear that I am running the risk of letting people notice my condition—And that has been my experience during the last six months which I have spent in the country. My sensible doctor by suggesting that I should spare my hearing as much as possible has more or less encouraged my present natural inclination, though indeed when carried away now and then by my instinctive desire for human society, I have let myself be tempted to seek it. But how humiliated I have felt if somebody standing beside me heard the sound of a flute in the distance and *I heard nothing,* or if somebody heard *a shepherd sing* and again I heard nothing—Such experiences almost made me despair, and I was on the point of putting an end to my life—The only thing that held me back was *my art.* For indeed it seemed to me impossible to leave this world before I had produced all the works that I felt the urge to compose; and thus I have dragged on this miserable existence—a truly miserable existence, seeing that I have such a sensitive body and that any fairly sudden change can plunge me from the best of spirits into the worst of humors—*Patience* —that is the virtue, I am told, which I must now choose for my guide; and I now possess it—I hope that I shall persist in my resolve to endure to the end, until it pleases the inexorable Parcae to cut the thread; perhaps my condition will improve, perhaps not; at any rate I am now resigned—At the early age of 28 I was obliged to become a philosopher, though this was not easy; for indeed this is more difficult for an artist than for anyone else—Almighty God, who look down into my innermost soul, you see into my heart and you know that it is filled with love for humanity and a desire to do good. Oh my fellow men, when someday you read this statement, remember that you have done me wrong; and let some unfortunate man derive comfort from the thought that he has found another equally unfortunate who, notwithstanding all the obstacles imposed by nature, yet did everything in his power to be raised to the rank of noble artists and human beings.—And you, my brothers Carl and [Johann], when I am dead, request on my behalf Professor Schmidt, if he is still living, to describe my disease, and attach this written document to his record, so that after my death at any rate the world and I may be reconciled as far as possible—At the same time I herewith nominate you both heirs to my small property (if I may so describe it)—Divide it honestly, live in harmony and help one another. You know that you have long ago been forgiven for the harm you did me. I again thank you, my brother Carl, in particular, for the affection you have shown me of late years. My wish is that you should have a better and more carefree existence than I have had. Urge your children to be *virtuous,* for virtue alone can make a man happy. Money cannot do this. I speak from experience. It was virtue that sustained me in my misery. It was thanks to virtue and also to my art that I did not put an end to my life by suicide—Farewell and love one another—I thank all my friends, and especially *Prince Lichnowsky* and *Professor Schmidt.* I would

> like Prince L[ichnowsky]'s instruments to be preserved by one of you, provided this does not lead to a quarrel between you. But as soon as they can serve a more useful purpose, just sell them; how glad I shall be if in my grave I can still be of some use to you both—Well, that is all—Joyfully I go to meet death—should it come before I have had an opportunity of developing all my artistic gifts, then in spite of my hard fate it would still come too soon, and no doubt I would like it to postpone its coming—Yet even so I should be content, for would it not free me from a condition of continual suffering? Come then, Death, *whenever* you like, and with courage I will go to meet you—Farewell; and when I am dead, do not wholly forget me. I deserve to be remembered by you, since during my lifetime I have often thought of you and tried to make you happy—Be happy—
>
> Ludwig van Beethoven
>
> For my brothers Carl and [Johann]
> To be read and executed after my death—
> Heiligenstadt, October 10, 1802—Thus I take leave of you—and, what is more, rather sadly—yes, the hope I cherished—the hope I brought with me here of being cured to a certain extent at any rate—that hope I must now abandon completely. As the autumn leaves fall and wither, likewise—that hope has faded for me. I am leaving here—almost in the same condition as I arrived—Even that high courage—which has often inspired me on fine summer days—has vanished—Oh Providence—do but grant me one day *of pure joy* —for so long now the inner echo of real joy has been unknown to me—Oh when—oh when, Almighty God—shall I be able to hear and feel this echo again in the temple of Nature and in contact with humanity—Never?—No!—Oh, that would be too hard.[15]

It must be remembered, however, that although the moods of the Heiligenstadt Testament are central to Beethoven's life, at other times he was capable of exuberant delight in music, especially composition. "I live entirely in my music," "I feel equal to anything," are two of his typical statements to friends, which tell us much about the man, for at the same time as he is talking about his death, he is writing to publishers, offering works which he describes as completely new in conception. The musical evidence of this side of his nature is to be found in the richly textured and emotionally vital Second Symphony in D, Op. 36, finished around the time of the Testament.

THE BEGINNINGS OF THE "NEW STYLE" During 1803, together with many other projects, Beethoven was working on his Third Symphony, which, we are told by Ries, initially bore the title "Buonaparte," for Beethoven had long admired Napoleon, comparing him to the consuls of ancient Rome. Actual work on the symphony started in 1803, at which time Beethoven was seriously contemplating forsaking Vienna for Paris. He always had a strong love/hate relationship with

15. Emily Anderson, *The Letters of Beethoven* (London, 1961), III, pp. 1351–54. This edition will be referred to hereafter as *Beethoven Letters*.

France and things French, perhaps because he was a Rhinelander, and perhaps because he had had direct experience of having the Bonn Court and all his connections with his homeland destroyed by French expansion in 1792 and 1794. Yet he admired and was influenced by much of the work of the French violin school. He had met the French violinist Rodolphe Kreutzer and dedicated to him the great Sonata, Op. 47, for violin and piano. His contemplated move to Paris had been discussed with his friends. But before he could fulfill his intention, Napoleon, who had been more a military dictator than a republican Roman consul, crowned himself emperor. According to the well-supported anecdote, Beethoven ripped the title page of the symphony in two, saying: "Is he, then, nothing more than an ordinary human being? Now he, too, will trample on the rights of man and indulge only his ambition. He will exalt himself above all others, become a tyrant!" Beethoven's ambivalence towards Napoleon has been interpreted in terms of admiration and betrayal.[16] The betrayal did not totally eradicate the admiration, however, and several years later, in 1809, Beethoven very seriously considered accepting the offer to become Kapellmeister to Napoleon's brother, King Jerome of Westphalia, but that was still far in the future.

It was to be expected that out of his experience playing in the theater orchestra Beethoven would want to write an opera. An operatic project begun in 1803 with Emanuel Schikaneder, the author of the libretto of *Die Zauberflöte,* had fallen through, and in 1804 he started work on what was to become, ten years later, his only work in this genre, *Fidelio.* Strongly influenced by the idealistic atmosphere of much late eighteenth-century thought, Beethoven found a subject which glorified married love and exemplified the genre of "rescue opera." The main plot concerns the rescue of a political prisoner from imminent death by his wife and is based, it is said, upon a real incident.

Initially scheduled for production in October, bad luck dogged the opera. It was finally brought to the stage with the title *Leonore* for three performances, the first taking place on 20 November 1805, just a week after Napoleon's victorious armies entered a conquered Vienna. In the circumstances—playing in an occupied city from which the royal family, the aristocracy, and the wealthy had fled—it was no wonder that *Leonore* was not a success. We are told that for the second and third performances the theater was completely empty. The score was put aside until 1806, when it was revised and the action speeded up. It was staged again on 29 March with the title *Fidelio* to a slightly better reception. But Beethoven withdrew the opera because he suspected that he was being cheated out of receipts, and it lay dormant until 1814, when it was performed once again on 23 May after more extensive revision.

Despite the upheavals occurring at the time and his hatred of the

16. Maynard Solomon, *Beethoven* (New York, 1977), pp. 132*ff.*

French occupying Vienna, despite the opera's lack of success and the depression that followed, Beethoven was intensely productive during these middle years of the first decade of the century. Between 1804 and 1808 he composed the Fourth, Fifth and Sixth Symphonies, the Fourth Piano Concerto, the Violin Concerto, the Concerto for Piano, Violin, and Cello, three String Quartets Op. 59, two Piano Trios, Op. 70, one Sonata for Cello and Piano, Op. 69, and three large Sonatas for Piano Solo, Opp. 53, 54, and 57. Such an array of masterpieces is hard to match.

ENLIGHTENED PATRONAGE AND OTHER SOURCES OF INCOME

At this time Beethoven was trying to assure himself a steady income, but with the fluctuation of currencies caused by the Napoleonic Wars, with the changing fortunes of his patrons in those uncertain times, and without an official position, such security was not possible. The annuity from Prince Lichnowsky continued until 1806, when it may well have ceased after Beethoven refused to play for a number of French officers who were Lichnowsky's guests. In the years immediately after, Beethoven seriously contemplated leaving Vienna. It will never be known whether he really intended to accept the offer from Napoleon's brother, King Jerome, or whether he used the invitation as a ploy to force his wealthy supporters, friends, and admirers to make a counteroffer. In fact, after a few weeks of discussion, a contract was drawn up as follows:

AGREEMENT:

The daily proofs which Herr Ludwig van Beethoven is giving of his extraordinary talents and genius as musician and composer, awaken the desire that he surpass the great expectations which are justified by his past achievements.

But as it has been demonstrated that only one who is as free from care as possible can devote himself to a single department of activity and create works of magnitude which are exalted and which ennoble art, the undersigned have decided to place Herr Ludwig van Beethoven in a position where the necessaries of life shall not cause him embarrassment or clog his powerful genius.

To this end they bind themselves to pay him the fixed sum of 4000 (four thousand) florins a year, as follows:

His Imperial Highness, Archduke Rudolph	FL.	1500
The Highborn Prince Lobkowitz	FL.	700
The Highborn Prince Ferdinand Kinsky	FL.	1800
Total	FL.	4000

> which Herr van Beethoven is to collect in semi-annual installments, *pro rata,* against voucher, from each of these contributors.
>
> The undersigned are pledged to pay this annual salary until Herr van Beethoven receives an appointment which shall yield him the equivalent of the above sum.
>
> Should such an appointment not be received and Herr Ludwig van Beethoven be prevented from practicing his art by an unfortunate accident or old age, the participants grant him the salary for life.
>
> In consideration of this Herr Ludwig van Beethoven pledges himself to make his domicile in Vienna, where the makers of this document live, or in a city in one of the other hereditary countries of His Austrian Imperial Majesty, and to depart from this domicile only for such set times as may be called for by his business or the interests of art, touching which, however, the high contributors must be consulted and to which they must give their consent.
>
> Given in Vienna, March 1, 1809.[17]

A comparison between this contract and the one offered to Haydn in 1761 (see p.184) is instructive, for it shows that the ideal proposed by Diderot in 1763 had been realized by the Archduke Rudolph and the Princes Lobkowitz and Kinsky. The age of these noblemen at the time of signing (twenty-one, thirty-five, and twenty-seven respectively) demonstrates how strongly Beethoven's music appealed to the young.

It would seem that, from this point, Beethoven's life should have proceeded in an orderly fashion, but this was not the case. The devaluation of Austrian currency in March 1811 reduced the buying power of Beethoven's income drastically, and he complained that the intention of the contract was not being fulfilled. Archduke Rudolph immediately agreed to increase the stipend; Prince Lobkowitz was financially embarrassed and after September 1811 could pay nothing for four years; and Prince Kinsky, having agreed to pay full value plus back payments, was killed in a fall from his horse. To add to the confusion, Lobkowitz resumed his payments in 1815 but died in 1816. After negotiations with the Kinsky and Lobkowitz estates, Beethoven's pension, reduced to 3400 florins, was reestablished and back payments made.

Like all great composers of the time, Beethoven took a certain number of pupils in both piano and composition, but his irascible personality almost guaranteed that most did not stay with him long. We are told that wrong notes hardly excited comment from him but any failure to observe marks of expression would make him angry. Ferdinand Ries studied with Beethoven between 1801 and 1805 and remained one of his staunchest supporters throughout his life. He tells the following story:

17. Thayer-Forbes, *op cit.,* p. 458.

> Beethoven had given me his beautiful Concerto in C minor in manuscript so that I might make my first public appearance *as his pupil* with it. . . . I had asked Beethoven to write a cadenza for me, but he refused and told me to write one myself and he would correct it. Beethoven was satisfied with my composition . . . but there was an extremely brilliant and very difficult passage in it, which, though he liked it, seemed to him too venturesome, wherefore he told me to write another in its place. . . . I did so. . . . When the cadenza was reached in the public concert Beethoven quietly sat down . . . When I boldly began the more difficult one, Beethoven violently jerked his chair; but the cadenza went through all right and Beethoven was so delighted that he shouted 'Bravo!' loudly. . . . Afterward, while expressing his satisfaction he added: 'But all the same you are willful! If you had made a slip in the passage I would never have given you another lesson.'[18]

Certainly, his most faithful student in both piano and composition was the Archduke Rudolph. Despite occasional unkind words in letters to friends, Beethoven was genuinely fond of this young man, who studied with him from around 1803 to 1820. There is also no doubt that Beethoven benefited in innumerable ways from the influence that Rudolph could and did use on his teacher's behalf.

With the onset of serious deafness, Beethoven's career as a performing pianist fell away rapidly, but concertizing remained a source of income for him since the "music academy" was still fashionable. In 1803, a concert was staged which consisted of the first two symphonies, the third piano concerto, and the oratorio *Christus am Oelberge* (Christ on the Mount of Olives), as well as a number of vocal compositions. There followed a long period in which no similar activity took place until December 1808 when the following advertisement appeared in the *Wiener Zeitung:*

> MUSICAL AKADEMIE
>
> On Thursday, December 22, Ludwig van Beethoven will have the honor to give a musical *Akademie* in the R.I. Priv. *Theater-an-der-Wien*. All the pieces are of his composition, entirely new, and not yet heard in public. . . . First Part: 1, A Symphony, entitled: "A Recollection of Country Life," in F major (No.5). 2, Aria. 3, Hymn with Latin text, composed in the church style with chorus and solos. 4, Pianoforte Concerto played by himself.
>
> Second Part. 1, Grand Symphony in C minor (No.6). 2, Holy, with Latin text composed in the church style with chorus and solos. 3, Fantasia for Pianoforte alone. 4, Fantasia for the Pianoforte which ends with the gradual entrance of the entire orchestra and the introduction of choruses as a finale.
>
> Boxes and reserved seats are to be had in the Krugerstrasse No.1074, first story. Beginning at half past six o'clock.

18. Ries, cited in Thayer-Forbes, *op. cit.*, p. 355.

The Theater an der Wien was the scene of the first performance of *Fidelio,* as well as of the Third and Sixth Symphonies and the Violin Concerto. (Historisches Museum der Stadt Wien)

During the last years of Napoleon's adventures in Europe, when it was clear that his star was waning, Beethoven had considerable success with the *Battle* Symphony, composed to celebrate the victory of the Duke of Wellington over Napoleon's armies at Vittoria on 21 June 1813. It was first performed in December of that year at a concert given in aid of wounded soldiers, at which Beethoven conducted an orchestra which included many of the best musicians in Vienna. The concert included the first performance of Beethoven's Symphony No. 7 and the entire event was extremely successful. During the Congress of Vienna—that coming together of all the statesmen of Europe in the winter of 1814–15 to decide the Continent's post-Napoleonic geography—a series of three concerts was given which also paired the Seventh and the *Battle* Symphonies, and these too were generally successful. It is of interest to note that in the concerts around this time and later, Beethoven was, in effect, an honorary conductor. Even when his hearing was adequate he had never been very effective in front of an orchestra; Spohr described how he would crouch down behind the music stand so that he could hardly be seen, for a *pianissimo,* and then leap up into the air to elicit a *fortissimo.* Now, by the second decade of the century there seems to have been general agreement that whether on the concert platform or in the orchestra pit—for Beethoven conducted the first performance of the revised *Fidelio* on 23 May 1814—the players and the singers would follow the leader of the orchestra rather than the conductor. At that performance of *Fidelio*

> . . . his ardor often rushed him out of time, but Kapellmeister Umlauf,

> behind his back, guided everything to success with eye and hand. The applause was great and increased with every representation.[19]

For the first performance of the Ninth Symphony in 1824, this position of honorary conductor is noted in the advertisements for the concert, which, after indicating the time and the place, the works to be performed, and the soloists, advises that:

> Herr Kapellmeister Umlauf [has undertaken] the direction of the work . . . as a favor. Herr Ludwig van Beethoven will himself participate in the general direction.[20]

It was at this concert that a well-known and touching incident occurred: at the conclusion (of the whole symphony or of the Scherzo is not accurately known) one of the soloists, Fräulein Unger, had to tug at Beethoven's sleeve, so engrossed was he in the score and oblivious of the applause, to get him to turn around and acknowledge the wildly enthusiastic audience. Despite the success of the first performance the receipts were so disappointingly small that Beethoven accused his friends and the management of swindling him. Two weeks later the concert was repeated and this time created a deficit.

PUBLICATION PRACTICES. Beethoven also earned a living from the publication and sale of his compositions. As has already been described, the growth of the publishing industry in the early years of the nineteenth century was astonishing, but it was not yet governed by any international copyright laws. In his dealings with publishers, Beethoven had to strike agreements with individual publishers in different places; in addition to the time and energy he expended personally, negotiations on his behalf were carried on by his brothers and friends. The result was a tangle of correspondence, riddled with accusations and misunderstandings, often hard to unravel.

One persistent complication arose from the prevailing custom that commissioned works often were the exclusive property of the person who commissioned them for a specified period of time. A letter from Caspar Carl Beethoven to Breitkopf in Leipzig, written in December 1802 describes the arrangement, as follows:

> . . . he who wants a piece pays a fixed sum for its exclusive possession for half or a whole year, or longer, and binds himself not to give the manuscript to *anybody*; at the conclusion of the period it is the privilege of the composer to do what he pleases with the work.[21]

Beethoven frequently created situations that were both an embarrassment and a nuisance to his friends. While he lived in London, Ferdinand

19. Cited in Thayer-Forbes, *op. cit.*, p. 583.

20. *Ibid.*, p. 908.

21. *Ibid.*, p. 311.

Ries was always willing to help his old teacher with his English contacts, and Beethoven, careless of the trouble to which he was putting Ries, did not hesitate to ask him. Beethoven promised the Philharmonic Society exclusive use of his new symphony (the Ninth) for eighteen months, and promised Ries the dedication; he also said that he would dedicate the *Diabelli* Variations to Mme. Ries. Neither dedication materialized. Ries actually concluded a contract for the English publication of the variations, and the English edition was to have been dedicated to Mme. Ries, but by the time the publisher received Beethoven's manuscript, he already had a copy of the Viennese edition in hand, dedicated to Antonie Brentano. Ries had a similar experience when he made arrangements with Clementi to publish the last two Sonatas for Piano, Opp. 110 and 111. Beethoven had given Ries these assurances on 25 April 1823:

> . . . In a few weeks too you will receive a new set of 33 variations on a theme, a work which I have dedicated to your wife. . . do see that the C minor sonata is engraved immediately. I promise the publisher that it will not appear anywhere else first. . . But it must be engraved at once—As the other one in A flat, even though it may already have arrived in London, has been engraved inaccurately, well then, the English publisher if he engraves it too, can announce his edition as the correct one. [22]

By the time the manuscript of Op. 111 arrived in London, it had already appeared in print in Paris. In summary, it can be said that Beethoven's dealings involving the publication of his music all too often had the distinct aroma of double-dealing, no doubt justified in the composer's mind by his oft- repeated belief that publishers were nothing but villains.

THE LAST YEARS

After 1814, which had seen the successful revival of *Fidelio* and during which Beethoven had been presented to kings and emperors, his popularity seems to have waned and the number of performances of his works diminished. There are fundamentally two reasons for this. First, there is evidence that points to a change in the kind of music the Viennese wanted to hear in concert. Spohr, who directed music at the Theater an der Wien from 1813 to 1815, and whose departure from Vienna was commemorated by Beethoven with the gift of a specially composed canon, wrote in 1815 in praise of concerts in Munich, that

> At every concert, a *whole* symphony is performed; (which is the more praiseworthy, from its becoming unfortunately daily more rare, and that the public for that reason are losing more and more the taste for that noble kind of instrumental music . . .[23]

22. *Ibid.*, pp. 1026–27.
23. Spohr, *op. cit.*, p. 213.

All Beethoven's symphonies, except the last, had been written by this time, and it would appear that the composer, sensing popular taste, tried to recapture his audience by composing more works for voices and orchestra. The other reason for his declining popularity is the fact that increasing numbers of Viennese thought that Beethoven had been at his best in his early work, and fewer and fewer could follow his more recent compositions with pleasure. In other words his reputation as Vienna's greatest composer was based upon works remote in time. A contemporary report says:

> In opposition to his admirers, the first rank of which is represented by Razumovsky, Apponyi, Kraft, etc., . . . who adore Beethoven, is found an overwhelming majority of connoisseurs who refuse absolutely to listen to his works hereafter.[24]

Beethoven had long thought of going to England to make money. He had friends there and publishers waiting for his works. Late in the year 1817, the English piano manufacturer John Broadwood and Sons shipped one of their pianos, "a six-octave Grand Pianoforte," to Beethoven in Vienna as a gift, and it came into his delighted hands early in 1818. But despite a contract with the Philharmonic Society of London to produce two symphonies and probably an opera in the winter of 1817/18, he did not go, pleading illness. Indeed, from this time on, the gradual decline in the state of his health became more and more obvious. Schindler wrote in 1820: "You were very well two years ago; now you are always ailing."

From around this same time there survives the earliest of the many "Conversation Books," notebooks which Beethoven, who by this time was completely deaf, would offer his visitors so that they could write their part of the conversation, and Beethoven would answer in normal speech. After his death, the Conversation Books came into the hands of his biographer, Anton Schindler, who destroyed a number of them; he subsequently used the information they contained selectively, to convey an idealized portrait of the composer.

Like Haydn in his old age, Beethoven enjoyed the honors he received from the great and the powerful, although he always pretended this was not the case. He took delight in dedicating works to the Archduke Rudolph, a clear demonstration to the world of his connection with His Imperial Highness. He underwent a period of great indecision over the dedication of the Ninth Symphony, hovering between Ferdinand Ries, the king of France, the king of Prussia or the emperor of Russia. The king of Prussia finally won (Ries did not stand much of a chance against the competition). He was infuriated when there was neither a gift nor a word of acknowledgment from the Prince Regent of England in response to his request that he be allowed to dedicate the *Battle* Symphony to

24. Cited in Solomon, *op. cit.*, p. 226.

him. But perhaps he was most gratified at the reaction to his plan to raise money from the composition of the *Missa Solemnis,* op.123, by selling manuscript copies of the score, for the large amount of 50 ducats each, to the crowned heads of Europe. His invitation was taken up by the czar of Russia, the kings of Prussia, Saxony, France, and Denmark, the Princes Radziwill and Galitzin, and a couple of grand dukes. He was overjoyed with the large gold medal sent to him by Louis XVIII of France, showing on one side the image of the monarch and on the other the inscription "Given by the King to M. Beethoven" surrounded by a wreath.

Beethoven's relationships with women have been the subject of much interest. He evidently had many romantic attachments, even in the early Vienna days, as his friend F. G. Wegeler writes:

> Beethoven never was out of love, and usually was much affected by the love he was in at the time. . . . In Vienna Beethoven, at least as long as I was living there, [1794–96] always had some love affair in hand, and on occasion made conquests, which many an Adonis would have found it difficult, if not impossible, to accomplish.[25]

Ferdinand Ries reports similarly, but adds the revealing statement: "He was very often in love, but as a rule only for a short time."[26]

There is no doubt that Beethoven thought of marriage and proposed it, at least twice. But gradually there emerged "the standard pattern of Beethoven's love affairs: his attraction to a woman who is firmly attached to another man,"[27] and this pattern continued to reproduce itself until a relationship which brought Beethoven's self-doubts to a decisive conclusion.

After Beethoven's death there was found among his effects a letter addressed to a woman whom he calls "my Immortal Beloved." The letter is dated July 6th and the 7th, but the year is lacking, as is the place where it was written and its destination. It is not known whether the letter was ever sent, or sent and returned, but Beethoven kept it until his death, just as he did the Heiligenstadt Testament. Both these documents represent milestones in Beethoven's life and both are testimony to his constant battle to find and accept the realities of his own character and of his own existence. The text runs as follows:

> July 6th, in the morning
>
> My angel, my all, my very self.—Only a few words today, and, what is more, written in pencil (and with your pencil)—I shan't be certain of my rooms here until tomorrow; what an unnecessary waste of time is all this—Why this profound sorrow, when necessity speaks—can our love endure

25. F. G. Wegeler, *Notizen,* cited in Sonneck, *op. cit.* p. 19.
26. F. Ries, *Notizen,* cited in Sonneck, *op. cit.,* p. 54.
27. The discussion that follows owes much to the work of Maynard Solomon, who has demonstrated the peculiar way in which Beethoven's relationships with women and with his nephew affected his compositional life.

without sacrifices, without our demanding everything from one another; can you alter the fact that you are not wholly mine, that I am not wholly yours?—Dear God, look at Nature in all her beauty and set your heart at rest about what must be—Love demands all, and rightly so, and thus it is *for me with you, for you with me*—But you forget so easily that I must live *for me and for you;* if we were completely united, you would feel this painful necessity just as little as I do—My journey was dreadful and I did not arrive here until yesterday at four o'clock in the morning. As there were few horses the mail coach chose another route, but what a dreadful road it was; at the last stage but one I was warned not to travel by night; attempts were made to frighten me about a forest, but all this only spurred me on to proceed—and it was wrong of me to do so. The coach broke down, of course, owing to the dreadful road which had not been made up and was nothing but a country track. If we hadn't had those two postillions I should have been left stranded on the way—On the other ordinary road Esterhazy with eight horses met with the same fate as I did with four—Yet I felt to a certain extent that pleasure I always feel when I have overcome some difficulty successfully—Well, let me turn quickly from outer to inner experiences. No doubt we shall meet soon; and today also time fails me to tell you of the thoughts which during these last few days I have been revolving about my life—If our hearts were always closely united, I would certainly entertain no such thoughts. My heart overflows with a longing to tell you so many things—Oh—there are moments when I find that speech is quite inadequate—Be cheerful—and be for ever my faithful, my only sweetheart, my all, as I am yours. The gods must send us everything else, whatever must and shall be our fate—

Your faithful Ludwig

Monday evening, July 6th

You are suffering, you, my most precious one—I have noticed this very moment that letters have to be handed in very early, on Monday—or on Thursday—the only days when the mail coach goes from here to K[arlsbad].—You are suffering—Oh, where I am, you are with me—I will see to it that you and I, that I can live with you. What a life!!!! as it is now !!!! without you—pursued by the kindness of people here and there, a kindness that I think—that I wish to deserve just as little as I deserve it—man's homage to man—that pains me—and when I consider myself in the setting of the universe, what I am and what is that man—whom one calls the greatest of men—and yet—on the other hand therein lies the divine element in man—I weep when I think that probably you will not receive the first news of me until Saturday—However much you love me—my love for you is even greater—but never conceal yourself from me—good night—Since I am taking the baths I must get off to sleep—Dear God—so near! so far! Is not our love truly founded in heaven—and, what is more, as strongly cemented as the firmament of Heaven?—

Good morning, on July 7th

Even when I am in bed my thoughts rush to you, my eternally beloved, now and then joyfully, then again sadly, waiting to know whether Fate will hear our prayer—To face life I must live altogether with you or never see you. Yes, I am resolved to be a wanderer abroad until I can fly to your

> arms and say that I have found my true home with you and enfolded in your arms can let my soul be wafted to the realm of blessed spirits—alas, unfortunately it must be so—You will become composed, the more so as you know that I am faithful to you; no other woman can ever possess my heart—never—never—Oh God, why must one be separated from her who is so dear. Yet my life in V[ienna] at present is a miserable life—Your love has made me both the happiest and the unhappiest of mortals—At my age I now need stability and regularity in my life—can this coexist with our relationship?—Angel, I have just heard that the post goes every day—and therefore I must close, so that you may receive the letter immediately—Be calm; for only by calmly considering our lives can we achieve our purpose to live together—Be calm—love me—Today—yesterday—what tearful longing for you—for you—you—my life—my all—all good wishes to you—Oh, do continue to love me—never misjudge your lover's most faithful heart.
>
> ever yours
> ever mine L.[28]
> ever ours

In the history of Beethoven biography nothing has caused more discussion and disagreement than this letter, which various writers have seriously conjectured to have been written shortly after 1800. There is now general agreement that the letter dates from 1812, and the recipient was probably Antonie Brentano, a married woman of noble birth who outlived Beethoven by forty-two years and preserved many mementos of him. The letter attests to Beethoven's refusal to allow her to leave her unfulfilling marriage in order to be with him; more clearly than anything else, it reveals his ambivalence.

For three years before the letter was written, Antonie had lived in Vienna, where her relationship with Beethoven had progressed so far that she was prepared not to return with her husband to their home in Germany. For Beethoven, the crisis lay in his realization that he could not embark upon a lasting relationship with a woman. After this crisis we know of not a single love relationship in Beethoven's life. There would never be "that woman who some day will perhaps share my fate . . ." [letter 5 March 1807] and Beethoven was destined to remain alone.

Perhaps the most consuming interest of his last decade, aside from music, was his nephew, Karl, and Karl's mother, his sister-in-law. Beethoven had opposed the marriages of both his brothers. When the elder, Caspar Carl, married in 1806 Beethoven was working on the *Razumovsky* Quartets, and on a sketch of the slow movement of Op. 59, No. 1, he added the note, "A weeping willow or acacia tree over my brother's grave," presumably in the belief that his brother was lost

28. *Beethoven Letters,* pp. 373–76.

to him, even though such was not the case. Nephew Karl was born three and a half months after the wedding, and nine years later, in 1815, Caspar Carl's early death brought to an end a marriage that seems to have been anything but happy. The day before he died, Caspar Carl realized that his brother, whom he had appointed co-guardian of Karl together with his wife, was going to try to take the young boy away from his mother completely. To prevent that situation he wrote a codicil to his will saying that he did not wish the son to be taken from the mother. Nevertheless, within two weeks of his brother's death, Beethoven was embarking on a legal process to take the nine-year-old boy out of the hands of a woman for whose vileness he could find no adequate description.

Over the years, the "mystery" surrounding Beethoven's birth reinforced his fantasy that he was of noble blood—indeed, the rumor circulated that he was an illegitimate son of the king of Prussia, and he did nothing to quash it. In opening the legal battle for custody of Karl, Beethoven addressed himself to the *Landrecht,* the court of law that dealt exclusively with cases involving the nobility, and, owing to his many friends among the aristocracy, initially he won. In 1818, however, Karl's mother petitioned for the removal of Beethoven's authority to direct his nephew's education. During the course of the proceedings, and in reference to his nephew, Beethoven let drop the phrase "if he were but of noble blood . . ." The Court pursued the question which Beethoven had raised, and since he could not bring forward the proof of his nobility, the case was referred to the Vienna Magistracy, the court that dealt with common folk. Beethoven was hurt by this judgment and feared that the decision would go against him. But he did not abandon thoughts of his nobility. The Conversation Books contain the following remarks by Beethoven on this subject: ". . . when it [*sic*] learned that my brother was not of the nobility . . . there is a hiatus here which ought to be filled, for my nature shows that I do not belong among this plebeian m[ass]."[29]

In this long, sorry tale, the subject of the wrangling, Karl, becomes lost in the tangle of his uncle's complex psyche, as Beethoven seems actually to want to be the father of the nephew, and, possibly, the husband of the sister-in-law. Certainly, in his last letters to his uncle, nephew Karl begins by writing "Dear Father" and concludes with "Your loving son, Karl." Eventually, the struggle between the two reached a point in 1826 where Karl shot himself in the head in a suicide attempt. After an extended and recuperative stay together in the country, Karl, who had decided to go into the army, left to join his regiment in January of 1827, less than three months before Beethoven's death. He did not return to Vienna for the funeral.

29. Thayer-Forbes, *op. cit.,* p. 712.

Beethoven's funeral, unlike Haydn's and Mozart's, did not pass unnoticed. Thousands of people from the artistic and literary world of Vienna followed him to the cemetery. A watercolor by Franz Stöber. (With permission of the Beethoven-Haus, Bonn)

Beethoven died after being confined to his bed for over three months and an autopsy revealed cirrhosis of the liver as the cause of death. The news of his mortal illness spread fast, and during the last months, those of his old friends who were still living, together with his admirers, Schubert among them, gathered round to pay their last respects. When he died on 26 March 1827, there were two people in the room: Anselm Hüttenbrenner, a wealthy young amateur musician and close friend of Schubert, and a woman whom Hüttenbrenner identified as Frau van Beethoven. We cannot be certain who this woman was, but it is possible that she was the sister-in-law he had hated so vociferously for so long, and whom he had perhaps finally come to realize that he loved. At his funeral, three days later, as many as 20,000 people participated in the elaborate ceremonial as Vienna laid its greatest son to rest.

CHAPTER XXVIII

The Entire Oeuvre

THE FIRST STYLE PERIOD TO 1802

For many in the nineteenth century, Beethoven was revered as the man who freed music from the tyranny of sonata form and formalistic thinking. This view of Beethoven as liberator has had a great deal of currency and accounts in large part for the attraction he exerted over the younger generation of Romantic composers (Mendelssohn, Schumann, etc.) as well as those who dominated the later part of the century (Wagner, Brahms, etc.). Yet Beethoven's life straddles the bench mark of 1800 almost equally, and while we must not make too much of that date as a dividing line, the inevitable question arises: does he belong, with Haydn and Mozart, in the triumvirate of the Viennese Classical School or was he the first of the Romantics. Is it possible to isolate certain aspects of Beethoven's music so that one can say "Here, he is a man of the eighteenth century, whereas here he is the harbinger of things to come?" Although we have resolutely avoided any attempt to define the term "Classical" in relation to music, the question might be thus rephrased: when is Beethoven Classical and when Romantic?

Many scholars have remarked on the continuity of styles from the Classical to the Romantic; it must therefore be expected that categorical distinctions, such as can more easily be made between Baroque music and Classical music, will neither be obvious nor easily defined.

Beethoven's compositions for string quartet, orchestra, and piano were considered both seminal and terminal by musicians of later times. For Wagner and Berlioz, deterministic as they were in their thinking, his work in the symphony constituted the end of an historical process, and they believed that no composer could expect to be able to write symphonies as Haydn, Mozart, and Beethoven had written them. For Wagner the music drama was the road to follow, and for Berlioz the dramatic symphony. For others, like Schumann, the close study of Beethoven scores was a necessary precursor to composition. However viewed, this body of work constitutes the single most important musical fact of nineteenth-century history.

SONATAS FOR PIANO SOLO

Between 1782, when, at the age of twelve, he wrote the *Variations on a March of Dressler,* WoO 63, and November 1825, when he wrote his last composition for piano, two little dances, WoO 85 and 86, Beethoven was rarely without some piano piece on his worktable. The resultant oeuvre is so rich and important that the sonatas for piano have been styled "The New Testament of Music." The list below shows how this sonata production was distributed throughout Beethoven's working life.

WoO 47	3 Sonatas (Sonatinas) (E♭, F minor, D)	1782/3
WoO 52	Sonatina	1791/2
Op.2	3 Sonatas (F minor, A, C)	Completed in 1795 using some older material.
Op.7	1 Sonata (E♭)	1796/7
Op.10	3 Sonatas (C minor, F, D)	1796/8
Op.13	1 Sonata (C minor) (*Pathétique)*	1798/9
Op.14	2 Sonatas (E, G)	1798/9
Op.22	1 Sonata (B♭)	1799/1800
Op.26	1 Sonata (A♭)	1800/01
Op.27	2 Sonatas (E♭, C♯ minor) *quasi una Fantasia*	1800/01
Op.28	1 Sonata (D) *(Pastorale)*	1801
Op.31	3 Sonatas (G, D minor, E♭)	1801/02
Op.49	2 Sonatas (G minor, G) *Sonates faciles*	1795/96
Op.53	1 Sonata (C) *(Waldstein)*	1803/04
Op.54	1 Sonata (F)	1804
Op.57	1 Sonata (F minor)*(Appassionata)*	1804/05
Op.78	1 Sonata (F♯)	1809
Op.79	1 Sonata (G)	1809
Op.81a	1 Sonata (E♭) *(Das Lebewohl)*	1809/10
Op.90	1 Sonata (E minor)	1814
Op.101	1 Sonata (A)	1813/16
Op.106	1 Sonata (B♭) *Grosse Sonate für das Hammerklavier*	1817/18
Op.109	1 Sonata (E)	1820
Op.110	1 Sonata (A♭)	1821
Op.111	1 Sonata (C minor)	1821/22

Leaving the so-called Sonatinas out of the discussion, in the years 1795–1802—i.e. the time when Beethoven was actively performing as a pianist—he wrote 19 sonatas, nearly three per year; in the seven years 1803–10 he wrote six; and in the eight years 1814–22 he also wrote six. These groupings roughly conform to the commonly accepted notion of Beethoven's three stylistic periods.

With the publication (1796) of the three Sonatas, Op. 2, Beethoven makes one of his strongest statements about his own personality in relation to his great predecessors. Haydn and Mozart certainly gathered works together in half-dozens or threes, and they ensured that each work in the collection contributed to the overall effect. At no time, however, did they group together three works more different from each other and so remote from what has preceded them.

Op. 2, No.1, in F minor (*ACM* 69), a model of terseness and compression, has a most conventional first statement (mm. 1–2), a "Mannheim rocket" topped by a turn. In the 8 measures that constitute the first period, the first 2 measures (the upward arpeggio and the downward/upward melodic turn) are immediately repeated in the dominant. Mm. 5–6 repeat mm. 2 and 4, and mm. 7 and 8 form both the melodic climax and the cadence. The first real sign of tension begins in m. 9. The transition could have started with the normal repetition of the opening, but Beethoven has no time for that. Instead, he repeats the opening on the minor dominant and in the next 11 bars has effected a transition to the secondary area of A♭, reached through E♭, which remains as a dominant pedal through mm. 20–25. The melodic material of these first bars of the second tonal area is a free inversion of the first two measures, in which the tonic arpeggio of m.1 becomes the downward spread of the dominant minor ninth. The turn of m. 2 becomes a similar but inverted turn (N.B. the emphasis given to this turn figure by the *sforzando).* In the first instance (m. 2) the E♮ placed in a rhythmically weak position, is the strongest harmonically and melodically. Now E♮ (m. 22) changes its name and function, becomes rhythmically strong, and, as F♭, falls to E♭.

As the movement proceeds the player realizes that Beethoven has chosen the turn as the center of his dialectic,[1] and in particular, the function of E♮ moving to F, and E♮(F♭) moving to E♭ and then to A♭ (one leads to minor mode and the other leads to relative major). Thus, mm. 33–41 use dynamic *sforzandi* to emphasize the skeleton of the E♭, F, A♭, and the concluding theme, mm. 41–48, is built on the minor third turn, C♭, B♭, A♭, G, A♭ within the major mode on A♭.

Example XXVIII–1: L. BEETHOVEN, Sonata, Op. 2, No. 1, I

1. Dialectic may be defined as that process in which seemingly irreconcilable opposing ideas merge into a higher truth.

The middle section, again, appears to open with a conventional gesture—the opening material in the relative major—but it continues to unfold surprisingly in its length and the manner in which the return is constantly postponed. The dramatic ebb and flow of this section can almost be compared to the way a dramatist like Shakespeare creates a climax of unbearable tension by alternating between tension and relaxation and back to tension again, thereby putting off an event that is inevitable.

The return is modified in a few ways, but most noteworthy is the fact that the second group is not modified in recapitulation except in pitch and modality. All events occur in due sequence.

The coda to the movement (mm. 147–52) is short and offers the clinching statement of the seminal motive. In the context of a dynamic *fortissimo,* Beethoven emphasizes rhythmically weak chords with *sforzandi*. It is no accident that the melodic component of these chords, A♭, G, F, followed by *fortissimo* F, E♮, F, is the same as the melodic material of m. 2. The dialectic has not resulted in any kind of synthesis here but in the uncompromising confirmation of the minor mode.

After such a closely argued first movement, the *Adagio* (whose main melody is taken from an early piano quartet) and the Menuetto and Trio offer a quiet interlude before the last movement takes over where the first left off. Indeed, the last movement might almost be described as a sonata-form fantasia based on the last chords of the first movement. If Beethoven's musical dialectic is based upon E♮ rising to F, as opposed to E♮ = F♭ falling to E♭/A♭, then both aspects are still to be found in this finale. Immediately after the opening measures of F, E♮, F, the E♭ to A♭ element becomes the focus of mm. 5–8. It does not remain so, however, and the secondary tonal area of this movement is around the minor dominant, C. This neglect of A♭ tells us something about the first movement, too. The middle section of this movement, a broad melody without precedent in all the preceding material (except tonally), appears as the eye of the hurricane. Its place in the scheme of things is undoubtedly as the ultimate conclusion of the argument that had E♮ as F♭, leading to A♭ major.

In this sonata, Beethoven reveals his spiritual affinity with the intellectual Haydn and with Emanuel Bach. Beethoven himself could hardly appreciate the directness of that lineage, dazzled as he was with the idea of Mozart's genius and with his own as well. Haydn's use of motives as a source of melodic substance and overall unity is part of his stock-in-trade, but rarely did Haydn thrust his musical substance into a situation where the musical atoms are being pulled in two directions, thus creating a sense of stress whose resolution becomes imperative. And this in the very first of the mighty corpus of Beethoven's piano sonatas!

Each work is unique in its shape and material. The subsequent sonatas of this opus operate on different principles that are equally convincing. In Op. 2, No. 2, Beethoven creates a sense of formal balance in the normal tripartite way, while in No. 3, a much misunderstood work of ripest humor, the tripartite sonata is taken back to something like its origins with an enlarged coda almost the size of the middle section; the resulting overall shape is **A B A B.** (Remember that although this is Beethoven's first use of this structure, he had Mozartian precedent.) In this group of sonatas, which range in size from large to enormous, there are a few shared features: each is in four movements rather than three; there is an even stronger emphasis on mediant relationships than in Haydn or Mozart (e.g., the Sonata in A centers its development on C, and the Sonata in C has a slow movement in E, etc.); and the style of pianism in all three is light years ahead of Haydn's or Mozart's.

Completely congruent with the pace of gentle experimentation set by the first sonatas are the subsequent works of this first period. Beethoven can do nothing more with dimension, for in Op. 2, No. 3, Op. 7, and Op. 10, No. 3, he has gone as far as possible, but within certain limits other possibilities open. Thus, Op. 13 allows an apparent introduction to reappear at crucial places in the structure as it disintegrates; Op. 14, No. 1 has a middle section in which the composer expands a long melody without clear relationship to the whole, except as a kind of fulcrum around which the rest of the movement balances; Op. 26 and Op. 27, seemingly more experimental than the earlier works, together constitute a return to the Mozart and Haydn sonatas in which a sequence of different movements scarcely hints at "sonata form." The title applied to both works in Op. 27, *Sonata quasi una fantasia,* shows Beethoven's acknowledgment of the opposition of emotion and reason, of heart and head, that many late-eighteenth-century artists were able to keep in balance so beautifully. A *fantasia* is a piece of spontaneous music generated on the slenderest structural basis that requires far less craft from its maker than the composition of a sonata.[2]

The three Sonatas, Op. 31 were the last published as a group, and like Op. 2, the differences between them in mood and structure are pronounced. To the G-major Sonata belongs the honor of being the first of Beethoven's oeuvre in which the second tonal area is set in the major/minor mode upon the mediant of the key. Although this tonal device became a commonplace in later works, in this case it is impossible to take it seriously. The whole sonata, indeed, must be an essay in satirical humor for the music is repetitious and melodically weak, the pianism is of the kind that emphasizes its futility by roaming all over the keyboard to get nowhere, and the mediant area shifts mode in the most slippery way imaginable. The same remarks can be applied to an excessively long slow movement which is too highly and nonsensically ornamented. The last movement is the most deceiving because the

2. C. P. E. Bach, *op. cit.,* p. 430.

melodic substance is so appealing, yet the overuse of sequence in development and the shifting of material from hand to hand becomes difficult to believe in. A sardonic coda puts the whole into perspective, and one can only imagine that in this work Beethoven was commenting savagely on the work of some of his contemporaries.

The second work in D minor, nicknamed *The Tempest,* is as serious as the first is flippant, and as rich in all its material as the first is impoverished. This work deals with the elemental opposition of notes moving by step and notes moving by skip. All three movements are strongly unified and the sonata's growth process as a work of introspection can be measured by looking at the first two notes of the first movement, C♯ and E, and juxtaposing the last two notes of the third movement, F and D (incidentally, the last two notes of the first movement as well). The intervening composition can be seen as a working out of these two intervals in all their expressive/emotional and structural ramifications—justly one of Beethoven's most celebrated compositions.

The third in E♭ is the last four-movement sonata Beethoven wrote for fourteeen years and it is a genial composition. With its gentler vein of sentiment, far removed from the acid humor of No. 1 and the heights and depths of No. 2, it provides a fitting balance to conclude the set.

From his first composition to the end of his life, Beethoven was busy writing variations, either as separate, self-contained works or as part of larger compositions. During the first period there are many examples but perhaps most significant are the two sets Op. 34 and Op. 35. Beethoven himself described them to the publisher, Breitkopf und Härtel, as follows:

> Both sets are worked out in quite a *new manner,* and each in a *separate and different way . . . Each theme is treated in its own way and in a different way from the other one.* Usually I have to wait for other people to tell me when I have new ideas, because I never know this myself. But this time—I myself can assure you that in both these works the *method is quite new so far as I am concerned—.*[3]

Op. 34 is particularly interesting since each variation is set in a key a third lower than the preceding. Thus, the theme in F is followed by a variation in D, then another in B♭, then G, E♭, C minor, then F to conclude. Moreover, unlike the typical Mozart variation in which motion and texture increase in complexity, here Beethoven writes completely discontinuous variations in which the key determines the character of the variation, and each variation resembles a character piece. The short character piece for piano was becoming popular at this time, and Beethoven himself contributed to this kind of music with his Bagatelles Op. 33.

3. *Beethoven Letters,* pp. 76–77.

THE SONATAS FOR PIANO WITH ONE INSTRUMENT

Beethoven composed sixteen sonatas, with opus number, for piano with a single instrument. The chronological list below shows that twelve of those may be considered as belonging to the first period:

2 Sonatas	Cello and Piano (F, G minor) Op.5	1796
3 Sonatas	Violin and Piano (D, A, E♭) Op.12	1797–8
1 Sonata	Horn and Piano (F) Op.17	1800
1 Sonata	Violin and Piano (A minor) Op.23	1800–1
1 Sonata	Violin and Piano (F) Op.24	1800–1
3 Sonatas	Violin and Piano (A, C minor, G) Op.30	1802
1 Sonata	Violin and Piano (A) Op.47	1802–3
1 Sonata	Cello and Piano (A) Op.69	1807–8
1 Sonata	Violin and Piano (G) Op.96	1812–13
2 Sonatas	Cello and Piano (C, D) Op.102	1815

CELLO SONATAS Of the early works the two Sonatas for Cello and Piano Op. 5, are perhaps the most remarkable since they, more than the others, were composed with the express purpose of creating a structure that could hold an enormous amount of material; in other words, rather like the first movement of the Piano Sonata Op. 2, No. 3, these cello sonatas rival those of Mozart in their prodigal display of wealth of idea. In scale, in richness and density of texture, and as a demonstration of Beethoven's facility in relating more distant keys to his central tonic, these works, particularly the first, are without parallel in their time. In Op. 5, No. 1, a 34–measure introduction presents a typically rhapsodic, preludial opening in which the extraordinary length is matched by the density of the piano writing. A long melody opens the *Allegro,* which, although repeated, is shortened in recapitulation and seems to attain its real shape only as the last utterance of the long coda. One of Beethoven's early experiments in broadening harmonic relationships occurs when the secondary tonal area of this Sonata in F major appears to be in A♭ major, but this is only a tentative first step in the direction of mediant tonalities, and A♭ here turns out to be the flattened sixth of C. A true pupil of Haydn, Beethoven does not allow the A♭ color to be an isolated event, and three times in the course of the long secondary area (mm. 73*ff,* mm. 98*ff,* and mm.127*ff*) the emphasis on A♭ within C major is reiterated. A coda of enormous length (59 bars) terminates this amazing work.

THE TRIOS AND LARGER WORKS WITH PIANO

It is perhaps in the area of composition for piano, violin, and cello that Beethoven demonstrates his uniqueness most impressively. There are six large works for this combination, together with two sets of variations, and a trio in which clarinet substitutes for violin, as well as some smaller works, as follows:

3 Trios	P.V.Vc.	(E♭ G, C minor)	Op.1	1793–4
1 Trio	P.Cl. Vc.	(B♭)	Op.11	1798
Variations	P.V.Vc.	(E♭)	Op.44	c.1800
2 Trios	P.V.Vc.	(D, E♭)	Op.70	1808
1 Trio	P.V.Vc.	(B♭) *Archduke*	Op.97	1811
Variations	P.V.Vc.	(G)	Op.121a	1815–16

The Trios Op. 1 were designed to impress Viennese society, and they represent an enormous advance over anything that Beethoven had composed to this time. Even so, their superiority rests almost entirely in the composer's conception of the piano trio rather than in any particular of musical style. For other composers of the time, the piano trio was still largely thought of as an accompanied sonata for piano, designed to provide mild entertainment. Beethoven gave it four movements instead of three, thus raising its status from that of social music to that of significant music, comparable to the symphony or the string quartet. And he created parity among the instruments, largely freeing the cello from its *continuo* role, although it still frequently doubles the left hand of the piano. Indeed, Beethoven's cello writing in the piano trio creates a sonority in which the cello sound becomes dominant for the very first time. It was this rich cello sound coupled with the harmonic potential of the piano that made the trio the favorite small combination of the nineteenth century, and, even more than the string quartet, the typical sonority of the period (e.g., Op. 1, No. 1, II, mm. 20–29).[4]

The early piano quartets, WoO 36 of 1785, are a curious mixture of piano sonata with accompaniment and *concertante* elements. Although written almost exactly at the same time that Mozart was writing his piano quartets, they bear no relationship to the Viennese works, seeming far closer in technique to those of Schobert, which date from about twenty years earlier. In the *Allegro* movements, the strings tend to double the more highly ornamented piano part, whereas in the variation movement of No. 2, each of the strings has a highly ornamented solo variation.

The Quintet Op.16 for piano, oboe, clarinet, bassoon, and horn also exists in a version as a quartet for piano and strings, and is said to be modeled on Mozart's Quintet K.452 for the same combination. Beyond the combination of instruments, the number and order of movements,

4. The piano trio was a favorite combination for arrangements of larger works throughout the nineteenth century. Beethoven set the example for such use with arrangements of his Second Symphony, Op. 36, and of his Septet, Op. 20.

and the key, it is difficult to find any "modeling," and the work unjustly suffers from this comparison. The piano figuration is most Beethovenian, yet it is undeniable that the melodies have a formal balance more reminiscent of Mozart.

Before Beethoven began writing string quartets he gained considerable skill in writing for strings alone by composing five string trios for violin, viola, and cello, to which is customarily added a Serenade for flute, violin and viola:

Trio	V.Vla.Vc.	E♭	Op.3	1792
Serenade	V.Vla.Vc.	D	Op.8	1796–7
3 Trios	V.Vla.Vc.	G, D, C minor	Op.9	1796–8
Serenade	Fl.V.Vla.	D	Op.25	1796–7?

This group of works, although originating early in the composer's career, forms the backbone of the literature for string trio; aside from these, there are few other masterpieces and the rest are by minor composers.

THE STRING QUARTET

The string quartet for two violins, viola, and cello lies at the center of Beethoven's musical legacy, and this inheritance comes to us from each period in his life.

Early	6 Quartets	F, G, D, C minor, A, B♭	Op. 18	1798–1800
Middle	3 Quartets	F, E minor, C	Op. 59	1805–06
	1 Quartet	E♭	Op. 74	1809
	1 Quartet	F minor	Op. 95	1810
Late	1 Quartet	E♭	Op.127	1822–5
	1 Quartet	B♭	Op.130	1825–6
	1 Quartet	C♯ minor	Op.131	1826
	1 Quartet	A minor	Op.132	1825
	1 Quartet	B♭ "Grosse Fuge"	Op.133	1825
	1 Quartet	F	Op.135	1826

The six string quartets of Op.18 were written over a two-year period, during which the composer had some second thoughts; as a result there are two versions of the Quartet No. 1 in F. He presented a copy of the first version to his friend Karl Amenda in 1799. Two years later, in July 1801, he wrote to Amenda, "Be sure not to hand on to anybody your quartet, in which I have made some drastic alterations." A comparison of the two versions shows that the changes are largely of detail, but when we remember that Beethoven wrote to George Thomson[5] (19 Feb., 1813): "I do not usually revise my compositions; I have never done so, convinced as I am that every alteration of detail changes the character of the composition," we must conclude that Beethoven approached this genre with uncharacteristic uncertainty. When writing string quartets, Beethoven could not rely upon his ability to improvise or to invent new textures with his ten fingers at the keyboard. Haydn's last and greatest quartets were being composed in the same small city at the same time as Beethoven was taking his first faltering steps with his; Mozart's last quartets were written earlier in the same decade. Beethoven's problem, one that he does not yet completely overcome, involves the integrity of voices, not depending upon formal counterpoint. In other words, the motivic technique which he displays in his keyboard sonatas (e.g. Op. 2, No. 2, mvt. 4, mm. 8–12) now has to be extended. In fact, in these early quartets, what Beethoven calls "voices in strict relationship," i.e., counterpoint, is used more extensively for this purpose than in other works of the time, and it is interesting to note that many of those passages are built upon that useful chord the diminished seventh (Example XVIII-2).

Example XXVIII–2: L. BEETHOVEN, Quartet Op. 18, No. 1, I

5. The event that caused this letter to be written is of interest. George Thomson (1757–1851) was a Scot who had entered into correspondence with Beethoven in 1803, when he asked him to compose some sonatas. Beethoven asked an exorbitant price which Thomson did not accept. Thomson was concerned with public education and later asked Beethoven to provide accompaniments to Scottish songs, which Haydn, Pleyel, and Kozeluch had already done. Now, in 1813, Beethoven has written accompaniments for 62 songs which Thomson has accepted, returning 9 because the ritornellos were difficult. Beethoven writes to him in French saying: "I am very sorry not to be able to do what you ask [change the accompaniments] [Here follows the excerpt above.] I am sorry that you will lose money because of this, but you cannot blame me for it, since you ought to have made me more aware of the taste of your countrymen and of their small powers of execution."

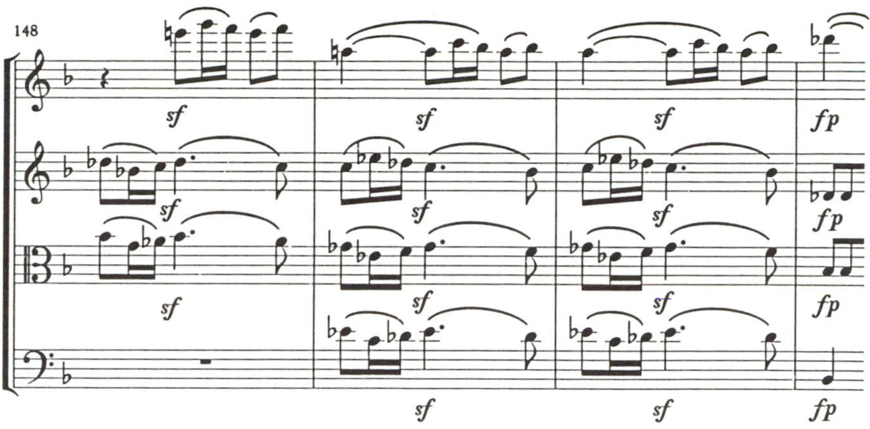

Each of the quartets in the set has great attractions, but critics have noted that they do not achieve the balance between technique and expressive aim found in other works of the time. Their textures are often richer than anything in Haydn or Mozart, and Beethoven from time to time finds it necessary to write *Adagio* movements in which the ornamentation is of a florid extravagance resembling that of J. S. Bach. It is remarkable that some of Beethoven's contemporaries, Krommer and Cherubini, for example, often seek a similar goal in *Adagio* writing for their quartets. Formal orthodoxy is offset in the sixth quartet by a harmonic experiment which is ahead of anything in its time. The last movement is entitled *La Malincolia* (Melancholy, Example XXVIII–3a), beneath which Beethoven has added "Questa pezzo si deve trattare colla più gran delicatezza" (This piece must be played with the greatest sensitivity). It consists of a slow introduction (melancholy) followed by an *Allegretto* (Example XXVIII–3b) that is interrupted twice by a weakening "melancholy." The *Allegretto,* which has presumably "conquered" melancholy, concludes this set of quartets.

There is no doubt that Beethoven often had images from life or literature in mind when he was composing, and that he pictured the relationship of music to things outside itself clearly. We know that he was thinking of the death scene in Shakespeare's *Romeo and Juliet* when composing the slow movement of Op. 18, No. 1. Whether or not he had a definite picture in mind during the composition of Op. 18, No. 6 there is no doubt that *La Malinconia* is intended to represent a musical parable of introspection being overcome by innocent joy. It is a remarkably fitting way to conclude a group of works intended for social recreation, which, although not the ripest of Beethoven's works for quartet, nevertheless point to the heights to be gained later.

Example XXVIII–3: L. BEETHOVEN, Quartet Op. 18, No. 6, IV

a. *La Malincolia*

b. *Allegretto*

MUSIC FOR LARGER CHAMBER ENSEMBLES

A solitary String Quintet, Op. 29, was composed at the same time Beethoven was completing the Op. 18 Quartets, and a Septet Op. 20, for violin, viola, cello, bass, clarinet, horn, and bassoon, was written during 1799. The Quintet is among Beethoven's least-known compositions (undeservedly so), while the Septet was so famous in the composer's lifetime that he became quite sick of hearing about it. It is clearly anomalous since it is both private and public music—for the chamber and for the concert; indeed, its first public performance has already been referred to.

From around 1800, making music in the home was no longer restricted to small groups of performers. It was the means through which the whole of music became available to amateur performers and everything, from operas and oratorios to symphonies, was arranged for a wide variety of combinations. By the late 1790s, almost all music for chamber combinations had settled into a four-movement form, related very closely to that of the symphony. After 1800, many chamber combinations, varying in size from two violins to eight or nine mixed instruments, adopted the multi-movement form of the Serenade. These works range from four to seven movements, and often include elements of virtuosity for all instruments. The resultant style stands midway between the ideals of public and private music, and is symptomatic of the increasingly important role played by a listening, non-playing audience in the composer's calculations. Beethoven's Septet exemplifies this ideal form of social music, mixing chamber dialogue style with *concertante* elements, with moods ranging from the exuberant to the delicately melancholy, but almost always avoiding the furrowed brow and the racked heart.

THE CONCERTOS

Beethoven's concertos were written during the course of a relatively few years in his early and middle periods:

Piano Concerto in B♭	Op.19	1794–1801
Piano Concerto in C	Op.15	1795–8
Piano Concerto in C minor	Op.37	1800–2
Triple Concerto (P. V. Vc.) in C	Op.56	1803–4
Piano Concerto in G	Op.58	1805–6
Violin Concerto in D	Op.61	1806
Piano Concerto in E♭	Op.73	1809

Each of the first three piano concertos underwent a long period of gestation before reaching its final form, as Beethoven added compositional and pianistic improvements. Each is closely modeled on the Mozart concerto. Indeed, in the third concerto it is possible to see Beethoven deliberately copying the first-movement coda feature from Mozart's K.491 in the same key. The urge to increase dimensions is felt, particularly in the orchestral exposition of the third concerto, which is expanded to an extent that Beethoven never attempted again. But by and large, apart from the nature of the pianism, the early concertos are perhaps the least innovative of all his larger forms.

THE SYMPHONIES AND ORCHESTRAL MUSIC

The first two symphonies, composed during Beethoven's first period, give a much stronger indication of the composer's originality than do the early piano concertos. Neither survives in the composer's autograph.

Symphony No.1 in C	Op.21	1799–1800
Symphony No.2 in D	Op.36	1801–2
Symphony No.3 in E♭	Op.55	1803
Symphony No.4 in B♭	Op.60	1806
Symphony No.5 in C minor	Op.67	1804–8
Symphony No.6 in F	Op.68	1807–8
Symphony No.7 in A	Op.92	1811–2
Symphony No.8 in F	Op.93	1812
Symphony No.9 in D minor	Op.125	1822–24

To many listeners today the First Symphony sounds so orthodox—so like the symphonies of Haydn and Mozart in structure—that it is all too easy to forget that the work's first critic[6] found it full of art and novelty, and rich in ideas. That first critic was perceptive when he wrote that "the wind instruments were used far too much, so that it sounded more like wind-band music than music for full orchestra." Before the turn of the century, Beethoven had grasped one of the ways of the future, and his first novelty lies in the strength of his writing for the winds, wood and brass, and in the consequent diminishing of the role of the strings. The symphony opens with a slow introduction, which not only begins with a series of secondary dominant harmonies (which critics have noted *ad nauseam*) but which also suspends the definition of the tonic until the first note of the *Allegro*. Beethoven here succeeded in writing an innovative slow introduction to the first movement of a symphony, even after Haydn had created a wealth of creative solutions to the problem. One of the functions of the slow introduction was always architectural: to provide an impressive entry into the work, comparable to the grandiose gateway to the park of an eighteenth-century mansion. But the impressiveness of the gateway bore no necessary relationship to the length of the driveway between the gate and the house. Here, the composer imposes a kind of determinism on the dimension of the entire first movement, i.e. the length of time taken to establish the tonic during the introduction gives the listener a sense that the structure to follow will be big and impressive. The rigor of the motivic technique and the mathematical placing of events within the structure all justify Bee-

6. *Allgemeine Musikalische Zeitung,* III, October 1800, p. 49.

thoven's approach to this first movement and are evidence of the new insights that he brought to the form. Tovey calls the symphony "a fitting farewell to the eighteenth century." For many of Beethoven's contemporaries who heard his later works, this remained his best symphony.

The Second Symphony is a formally orthodox work, and breaks little new ground. The tonal device of the slow introduction that Beethoven had used so successfully in the First Symphony could not be repeated without becoming stale. Here he writes an introduction that is longer, richer, and more self-contained than in any of his other symphonies, with the exception of the Seventh, and much closer in style to the ideal of Mozart than of Haydn. He continues to expand his resources, making the orchestral palette richer and more sumptuous than anything dreamed of earlier (except perhaps by Mozart in the slow movement of Symphony No. 38). Early critics praised the slow movement, but found the third and fourth movements very hard to accept although they recognized the humorous intent. The self-confidence expressed in this work is at the opposite pole from the mood of the Heiligenstadt Testament, and yet these two documents existed side by side in the mind of their creator.

THE SECOND STYLE PERIOD: 1803–14

Beethoven's dissatisfaction with the pieces he wrote before 1802 resulted in the emergence of a very different style of composition. In works from the "first period" it is still possible to hear sonorities and perceive structures in which there are overtones of Haydnesque or Mozartian influence. After the middle of 1802 such overtones are less and less discernible.

PIANO SONATAS

It is not its first-movement dimension that makes the Piano Sonata Op. 53 fundamentally different from anything Mozart ever wrote, nor is it the use of E major in the context of C that affects the listener, but rather a quality of melody, of sonority, and of process. Op. 53 is the only work Beethoven dedicated to his earliest patron and supporter, Count Waldstein. How far removed it is from those works in which Waldstein first perceived Beethoven's genius! The first movement (*ACM* 70) begins with thick sonority in low register, which is repeated a tone lower in m. 5. The bass, beginning two octaves below middle C, progresses downward by chromatic step to G. Meanwhile, the right hand moves further and further away from the descending bass to F, two octaves and a fourth above middle C. This texture, which sets the hands in opposition moving further and further apart, and the resultant sonority are constants in Beethoven's pianism. Contemporary composers like Clementi, Dussek, and Hummel, among others, also used the entire piano keyboard but for other ends. The sense of strain and stress that this sonority brings about is an important element in Beethoven's style and an inseparable part of his musical imagination. Compare the thick, low textures of m. 1 with the thick, high texture of m. 72 to see the way Beethoven uses the whole range of the instrument and all its tonal possibilities. Mm. 31–34 provide an example of Beethoven's deliberate crudity in transition and modulation, to which he resorts more and more. The effect of this at this point is to throw into higher relief the rich harmonization and thick textures of the melodic material of mm. 35–41.

The middle section, clearly divided into four parts, each fulfilling a certain purpose, is surprising in its avoidance of anything unusual. The first part is made up of four linking measures which lead to the second part, consisting of the opening material at its lowest in register, developed in two-bar groupings through a string of secondary dominants. The third part takes the triplet material from mm. 50 and 51 of the exposition through a wide-ranging harmonic fantasia with gradually quickening harmonic rhythm, leading to the last part: a prolonged dominant preparation. The return to the *pianissimo* opening is anticipated by a dynamic crescendo and by dissonance. The left-hand *ostinato* repetition of the tetrachord C B A G is a diminution of the bass progression of the opening measures of the movement, and the right-hand sixteenth notes are a new and unforeseen development of the sixteenth notes in m. 3.

Beethoven's treatment of the secondary tonal area in the recapitulation and coda is unusual in that he presents the *cantabile* theme, first heard in E, in the submediant, A; then, moving through A minor, he takes it to the expected area, the tonic. In the coda this material is heard again, entirely in the tonic.

Beethoven originally intended to give his Op. 53 a long ternary-form slow movement (*ACH* 71), but after composing it, he replaced it with a much shorter and quite different composition entitled *Introduzione* (*ACM* 70). The *Introtuzione* acts as a nebulous interlude between the large outer structures and effectively makes Op. 53 a two-movement sonata like Op. 54.

Op. 57 marks a terminus; for the first time in his mature life Beethoven had no piano sonata on his worktable, nor did he return to the genre until 1809. When he took it up again it was with two tiny works, Op. 78 in F♯ and Op. 79 in G, and one weightier one, Op. 81a in E♭, written to commemorate the departure from Vienna of the Archduke

Rudolph, Beethoven's only real student of piano and composition, before Napoleon's invading army. This sonata carries the title *Das Lebewohl* (The Farewell) since Beethoven wrote "Lebewohl" over the first three chords of the slow introduction to the first movement. In the first edition, the full title is *Lebewohl, Abwesenheit und Wiedersehn* (Farewell, Absence, Return). As in the *Pastoral* Symphony, Beethoven is not intent on pictorializing events, but on creating music which expresses feelings—in this case, the experience of having a friend depart and return. The proportions of the first movement are as unusual as Beethoven's blurring of tonic and dominant harmonies in the coda.

SONATAS FOR PIANO AND ONE OTHER INSTRUMENT

There are two sonatas for piano and violin and one for cello and piano that were written during this period. The Sonatas for Violin Op. 47 and Op. 96 are as different as possible—hardly astonishing since they were written ten years apart. Op. 47, dedicated to Rodolphe Kreutzer and usually identified by his name, was composed at a time when Beethoven was cultivating things French because he was thinking of going to Paris. It is described on a sketch as "Sonata written in a very concertante style, almost like a concerto." The first four measures of solo violin (Example XXVIII–4) demonstrate the distance that Beethoven has traveled since this combination was universally considered a sonata for piano with optional accompaniment for violin. Op. 96, on the other hand, dedicated to the Archduke Rudolph, has a first movement that is introspective, rarely rising to a *forte* dynamic, and of an overall style more conversational than *concertante*. The Cello Sonata Op. 69, like Op.

Example XXVIII–4: L. BEETHOVEN, Sonata Op. 47, (*Kreutzer*), I

47, begins with the string instrument alone, but here the resemblance ends. The texture, while traditional in many ways, reveals a strengthened linearity of the right and left hand of the piano, resulting in three-part polyphony with the cello.

PIANO TRIOS

There were three important piano trios written during this period: Op. 70, No. 1 in D and No. 2 in E♭, and Op. 97 in B♭. Nowhere does Beethoven comment on these works, as he does on so many other compositions, but with the first measures of Op. 70, No. 1 it is obvious that the world of Mozart and Haydn has been left behind, and the relationship of these three instruments is now established for the next hundred years: the sonority of the melodic cello, playing above middle C, leads the way for its equal partner, the violin, to follow, accompanied by a sympathetic and supportive piano. Indeed, in an exposition of 73 measures it is remarkable that the piano is in a clearly dominant position for only 20 bars. But it is not simply a rehash of the old question of who accompanies whom. There is greater reliance upon the grainy textures of imitative counterpoint as Beethoven's motivic development goes its way, but counterbalancing this texture is something that can only be called proto-impressionism. This style is found most obviously in the slow movement of Op. 70, No. 1—a movement which gave this trio the nickname of *The Ghost*—in which, from time to time, a sense of line disappears to be replaced by tremolandos making a blur of sound. A similar effect of blurring is to be found in the first movement at mm. 59–69 and mm. 235–245; as it is in the late piano sonatas. The inventiveness in the two Op. 70 Trios is not exceeded in the more famous Op. 97, in which Beethoven replaces the quality of exuberance, so obvious in the earlier work, with a quiet expansiveness.

STRING QUARTETS

A similar expansiveness pervades the first of the three Quartets Op. 59 which Beethoven dedicated to the Russian amateur Count Razumovsky, including Russian themes in at least two of the three. These quartets are strongly differentiated from each other, with the third immediately perceived by Beethoven's contemporaries as the one that ought to make its way most easily with the public. They demand more from players and listeners than other works of the time, and it is likely that their failure to receive the acclamation which he thought was their due led Beethoven to make his next two Quartets, Op. 74 and Op. 95, more accessible to amateur performers. Beethoven does not pamper the players as he realizes the quartet's sonorous potential in precisely the same way he had done with the piano sonatas: for that instrument he had separated the hands and set them at the extreme limits of the keyboard; with the opening measures of Op. 59, No. 1 he expands a three-note texture contained within an octave through a crescendo to an eight-note texture covering over four octaves. As with other of Beethoven's works, particularly in this decade, one senses the composer's need to make his music communicate a logical process. Here the process clearly leads from the first measure in the cello to the viola's repetition of it in m. 374, to the viola's repeat (m. 378) and to the first and second violins taking off on the phrase (m. 384) to the sustained high C (mm. 386–391) and the quiet, floating glide down to C with the flattened B (mm. 391–393). Comparing the "heroic" symphonies with these quartets, one writer has said:

> [in the symphonies]. . . the hero marches forth, indubitably heroic, but performing his feats before the whole of the applauding world. What is he like in his loneliness? We find the answer in the Rasoumovsky quartets.[7]

Beethoven must have felt the suitability of the quartet medium to his communicative need, for he says in a letter of 5 July 1806, that he is "thinking of devoting myself almost entirely to this type of composition." In the event, however, it is not the introspective possibilities of the world of private music that speak most strongly to Beethoven. His urge to preach to the world his newly discovered message of *per aspera ad astra*—conquering through suffering—led him to public music such as the symphony and the concerto, and ultimately to the theater.

THE SYMPHONIES

Nowhere is evidence of Beethoven's "new road" in composition more striking than in the difference between the Second Symphony, finished late in 1802, and the Third Symphony, *Eroica,* begun in May 1803.[8] This is the time of the Heiligenstadt Testament, a time of psychological crisis for Beethoven; that he was able to descend to the depths and emerge so changed is little short of miraculous. The Third Symphony is an enormous work, but its size is not without precedent (see Op. 28). Rather, what is completely new is the way Beethoven manages the dimensions and the way he makes disparate materials relate together to communicate a spiritual attitude. From the early days in Vienna, like so many of his contemporaries, Beethoven had been accustomed to paint-

7. J. W. N. Sullivan, *Beethoven, his spiritual Development,* (London, 1964), p. 81.
8. For a score of this work see either P. H. Lang, *The Symphony,* or *The Norton Anthology of Western Music.*

ing on large canvases, creating compositions on an additive principle, i.e., by the cumulative application of different melodic material to a widely used form. As has been pointed out, one way of doing this is to include entire "lyric" stanzaic forms of melody, rather than the customary pair of short, balanced phrases. Beethoven rarely includes verse-form melodies (the notable exception is in the last movement of Op. 2, No. 1), but he certainly follows the additive principle, and the second group of the first movement of the *Eroica* contains a sequence of varied melodies and textures that is paralleled only by the corresponding section in his Ninth Symphony.

In contrast, the first tonal area (mm. 1–44) is terse and, since its melodies are triadic, is essentially monothematic while conveying an impression of variety. If the attentive listener makes a comparison between the nature of this exposition and its recapitulation, it will be obvious that it is the terse first tonal area that is changed when it returns, while the complex second tonal area remains unchanged in its broad structure, albeit with minor modifications in scoring and register. Such a contrast between material and treatment forces the listener to look for the cause of the effect, and the answer to the search is found in the development. For Beethoven's great predecessors the middle section is an architectural element that serves to separate, and hence to emphasize, the symmetry of a structure; it is an area of difference, of instability. For Beethoven it becomes unmistakably the purgatorial fire that purifies, and he intends to preserve the architectural principles of his forebears while presenting a parable in music of how man makes himself better. Thus, in this symphony, after a short introductory transition (mm. 152–165), there is a development which is divided into four major sections. The first and second sections (mm. 166–219 and mm. 220–283) begin in similar fashion, but while the first ends on the type of cadence that introduces the second tonality (mm. 43–45) the second contains the affective climax of the whole piece, with rhythmic and tonal chaos emphasized by horrible dissonance. The third and fourth sections (mm. 284–337 and mm. 338–397, respectively) clearly back away from the climax with the introduction of the famous new material in the third, and with an enormous dominant preparation in the fourth. It is this development, quite without precedent, that gives the *Eroica* its unique position in the history of the symphony and of sonata form, and has caused subsequent historians, looking back at the eighteenth century through *Eroica*-colored lenses, to misinterpret the symphony of Haydn and Mozart. It is from this symphony as much as from the Ninth that the nineteenth century derives the notion that the essence of music lies in development. More than the late quartets, the *Eroica* Symphony shows us why Beethoven was the standard bearer of the "Romantic" era, but it also shows us that in Beethoven's ordered, thinking, the symmetry-giving impulse toward repetition must be preserved.

Beethoven started composing his Fifth Symphony[9] very shortly after the completion of the *Eroica*. He was filled with enthusiasm to recreate the conquering hero in still more vivid musical terms. The reasons why he set the idea aside for a couple of years, returning to it only intermittently, can only be surmised, but the fact is that before working on the Fifth Symphony in earnest he composed the Fourth in B♭, which, in all ways, seems like a throwback to the past. Tovey says that "the Fourth Symphony is perhaps the work in which Beethoven first fully reveals his mastery of movement."[10] Certainly, the Fifth Symphony might be seen to possess the spirit of the *Eroica* combined with the terseness, the sense of movement of the Fourth. To look back from the Fifth to the *Eroica* is to look at the expansive Beethoven of the early sonatas. There is a kind of luxury about the *Eroica* which is totally purged in the Fifth. Where the *Eroica* pours from a cornucopia with Mozartian extravagance, the first movement of the Fifth reduces all elements of exposition to a schematic indication of structure. With that said, however, the listener finds a melodic continuity that contributes greatly to the sense of inexorable drive in the movement, a drive that the many fermatas and hiatuses do nothing to stem. Where previously Beethoven has used many materials and colors, this first movement is, as it were, cut from a single piece of cloth.

This symphony is an even clearer communication of heroic achievement than the *Eroica,* and the return of the minor sound of the third movement in the middle of the major-mode last movement is a stroke of genius that allows the composer to recreate, at the point of recapitulation, the effect of his brilliant transition between the third and the fourth movements, an effect as of light emerging from darkness. Sketches show that Beethoven originally had brought the Scherzo to a complete halt before embarking on the Finale.

Hard on the heels of the Fifth Symphony comes the Sixth in F, on the sketches of which Beethoven wrote the following disconnected phrases:

> It is left to the listener to find out for himself the situations.
>
> A Characteristic Symphony—or remembrance of country life
>
> A remembrance of living in the country
>
> All tone-painting, if it is pushed too far in instrumental music, loses its value.
>
> Sinfonie pastorella. Whoever has any idea at all of country life can grasp what the author's intentions are without a bunch of descriptive titles.
>
> Also anyone will recognize, without description, that the whole work is more a matter of feeling than of tone-painting.

9. This score is available in *The Norton Scores.*
10. Donald Francis Tovey, *Essays in Musical Analysis* (Oxford, 1943) I, p. 35.

Above sketches for the last movement is written:

> Expression of thanks. Lord, we thank thee.

Beethoven wanted the copyist to write all the German titles that he had decided to attach to each of the five movements in the first-violin part. They ran as follows:

> I Pleasant, happy feelings which awaken in humankind on coming into the country. Allegro ma non troppo.
>
> II Scene by the brook. Andante molto moto quasi Allegretto.
>
> III Joyful gathering of country folk. Allegro.
>
> IV Thunder storm. Allegro.
>
> V Shepherd's Song. Grateful thanks and feelings of indebtedness to the Godhead following the storm. Allegretto.

With so many words from a man who, by his own admission, would sooner have written a thousand notes than one word, Beethoven provides yet more evidence of his need to communicate, and of his belief that his music would speak to the attentive listener. And no attentive listener can fail to discern the amazing differences of language between the Fifth and Sixth Symphonies. Where the Fifth is all tension and brevity, here the first movement's slow harmonic rhythm, and its motivic figures, repeated over and over again, convey a feeling of spaciousness that is almost visual, and music becomes an art of landscape painting, even without the use of realistic imitation.

After a period of three years with no symphonies on his desk, Beethoven produced a seventh, completed 13 May 1812, and an eighth in October 1812. The Seventh Symphony rapidly became one of Beethoven's most popular compositions in Vienna, and was arranged for a variety of instrumental combinations.

The Eighth Symphony, although a twin of the Seventh in many ways, did not receive as warm a reception, and although it is said to have been Beethoven's favorite, and although the critics have valued it highly, it is generally rated with the other "even-numbered" symphonies as a lightweight work. Certainly its brevity and good humor place it in a class by itself, and it gave Beethoven very little trouble in conception and birthing, far less than its older twin.

CONCERTOS

Within a short period Beethoven composed three large concertos, the Triple Concerto, Op. 56, the Fourth Piano Concerto, Op. 58 and the Violin Concerto, Op. 61, all of which refine and clarify the established structure without innovative change. As is his wont in the concerto,

Beethoven intensifies the recapitulation, and what was at first quiet or tentative becomes confident; yet this assertiveness is attained without stress, using melodic and harmonic materials that give the impression of calm, quiet optimism. The expanded dimensions—for these three works are all very big—are not so much achieved through the additive principle of the first sonatas, but by a developmental technique, in which a melodic fragment is enlarged in different ways. Perhaps most indicative of Beethoven's stylistic direction in these works is the enormous amplification of the key scheme and the way in which melodies themselves wander from key to key, which almost becomes a mannerism of his writing at this time.

Example XXVIII–5: L. BEETHOVEN, Modulating melody

a. Triple Concerto Op. 56, I

b. Triple Concerto Op. 56, III

c. Piano Concerto No. 4, Op. 58, I

d. Piano Concerto No. 4, Op. 58, I

Three years later, in 1811, the last and most innovative of all the concertos was published. Like Op. 58, the Piano Concerto in E♭, Op. 73 (*The Emperor*)[11] was dedicated to Archduke Rudolph, but it appears

11. The score of this work is available in Paul Henry Lang, *The Concerto*.

to have been first performed in Leipzig rather than Vienna. The correspondent of the *Allgemeine musikalische Zeitung,* Friedrich Rochlitz, wrote about this work that "it is without doubt one of the most original, most full of imagination, most effective, and also one of the most difficult of all existing concertos." He continued with a description of the ideal performance by both soloist and orchestra, to the enchantment of the audience.

The opening of this work with the soloist's entry in fantasia style is one of the most noteworthy features in the concerto literature, and even with repeated hearings, it remains arresting. It consists of three chords, I, IV, and V, richly figured by the soloist in preludial style, after which the orchestral ritornello begins. Tempting as it is to call these measures "introduction," that would be misleading, since a similar passage occurs at the beginning of the recapitulation (mm. 359–368). What is at issue here is the style and what it says about the soloist's function. The opening puts the relationship between the soloist and the orchestra into a certain context, one which forces the soloist to fantasize. An important difference between the opening of this concerto and its recapitulation lies in the fact that what was, at first, free, is measured, made less fantastic, and more orderly at the return. What is surprising is that the soloist, after such an entry, maintains so many of the attributes of fantasia at the beginning of the solo exposition—indeed, throughout the work—while demonstrating such clarity of form. Thus, the soloist's entry (m. 104) under the pungent complete dominant minor ninth cannot be construed as the timid gesture of the Mozartian soloist; it is, rather, the confident preparation for taking over the orchestra's material (m. 108) with as full chords and voicing as the piano can muster. And even then, after four controlled measures of quiet force, the soloist's need for independence results in a free and fantastic move to cadence at mm. 112–122. Orchestral mm. 123–26 are the precise equivalents of mm. 20–23, but where G♭ in m. 24 is a chromatic passing note between G and F, now the soloist makes a fantasia on G♭ and the orchestra is forced to follow (mm. 127*ff).* A comparison of these passages (mm. 108–132 and mm. 379–389) will show how differently Beethoven treats the soloist's exposition of this material and his recapitulation of it.

Perhaps the most original aspect of this first movement, however, lies in the treatment of the coda (mm. 481 to the end), for here Beethoven presents the opening of the work greatly modified but manifestly the same. Of the three outbursts by the soloist, the first two are reduced to preludial arpeggios across the entire keyboard, and the third (formerly a dominant seventh, now a six-four chord), always the longest and freest, becomes the cadenza. However, the soloist is not allowed to improvise, as is customary. Beethoven writes out every note and also makes it an accompanied cadenza involving orchestral instruments. In the context of this examination, the written-out cadenza makes a great deal of sense. We know where it begins, because of the six-four chord, but we do not know where it ends, for there are two, perhaps three, major points of arrival (m. 513, m. 526, and m. 539). The attentive listener will observe that at m. 539 we hear again, and for the second time only, those grand measures that told us that the orchestral exposition was about to close (mm. 87*ff* equals mm. 539*ff*). Interestingly, mm. 539–547 have the same harmonic profile as the first seven measures of the movement and similar proportions. For the last time, as at the beginning, the minor-ninth harmony surrounds the upward chromatic scale, now in octaves, which takes eight beats each of the three times it occurs. Accompanied by a low E♭ pedal in the horn, the soloist quietly and with complete assurance slowly intones the diatonic scale downward for eight measures, defusing all exuberance in the solemn assurance of the tonic. Such achievement has to be celebrated, and mm. 566 to the end provide a fitting, jubilant cadence.

With this work, more than with any other, Beethoven completely emancipates himself from the influence of the Mozartian concerto. In this structure, more than in any symphony except for the Ninth, Beethoven achieves a unique solution to the problem of how to create something quite new while retaining all the power of the traditional structure.

FIDELIO

If drama can be defined as the creation and resolution of tension from the interplay of contrasting and complementary characters, then Beethoven is one of the great musical dramatists. Yet his one completed venture into musical drama, *Fidelio,* cannot be rated an unqualified success, even by its staunchest admirers. The story belongs to the genre of the rescue opera and concerns a wife (Leonore), who disguises herself as a boy (Fidelio), and takes employment as a jailer's assistant in order to deliver her husband (Florestan), a political prisoner, from death at the hands of his tyrant enemy (Pizarro). This slender plot is fleshed out with a small sub-plot to which the listener is introduced as the curtain rises: the jailer's daughter (Marzelline) becomes infatuated with Leonore/Fidelio. Since this sub-plot depends entirely upon the dramatic irony of the situation, the main outcome is never in question: Marzelline cannot marry Fidelio. What is at issue for the audience is whether Marzelline might spoil the rescue somehow, and how much more tribulation Leonore can support. High ideals of marital fidelity, devotion, and freedom from tyranny blinded Beethoven to the weakness of plot, for above all he wanted the opera to make a moral case. The result is musical drama with great moments but lacking in character development, full of conventional, unbelievable "cardboard" types, and of uncertain pace.

The first numbers resemble comparable compositions from other operas that Beethoven had seen and adopted uncritically, and to which he had added personal touches. Thus Marzelline's suitor is interrupted while professing his love by a knock at the door, which it is his job to answer. This is an old, worn stage device, reasonably effective the first time, but stale and unfunny when repeated indiscriminately. Beethoven, unlike Mozart, has no conception of "what will make a good effect." Similarly, the jailer's song praising the value of money is a stock little number which a mature Mozart would have excised from his libretto or turned into a revelation of character. However, the jailer subsequently is shown to be a man of high morals and deep humanity, not easily corrupted; thus his opening song actually works against his character. Yet even in this first part of *Fidelio,* essentially no different from countless other *Singspiele,* Beethoven rises above the mundane to the celestial. Marzelline's song (No. 2) begins in a conventional, breathless style, broken by rests and with an offbeat accompaniment. By the second phrase it flowers into coherent melody as she is carried away by the thought "Oh, if only I were already married to you, and could call you husband . . ." C minor is the key of the opening, while the second thought begins a modulation to E♭ major. Another ravishing moment occurs in the celebrated canon (No. 3): four characters—jailer/father, lovelorn daughter, disguised wife, and rejected lover—all stand motionless and, to the same music, voice disparate thoughts.

The serious numbers of the opera, which have always been recognized as emotionally expressive triumphs, penetrate to the heart of Beethoven's feelings of compassion for humanity, expressed so movingly in the Heiligenstadt Testament. The scene in which the prisoners are allowed out of their cells to enjoy the sunlight is one of the strongest indictments of man's inhumanity to man, and Florestan's soliloquy in the dungeon attains a height of pathos rarely equaled.

The overtures to this opera, four in all, have won a life of their own in the concert hall. *Leonore* No. 1 was the first to be composed, but was judged "too light and not sufficiently expressive of the nature of the work." It was put aside, not to be published until the 1840s, when it bore the opus number 138 and was erroneously described by the publisher as one of the composer's last works. *Leonore* No. 2 was used in the ill-starred first performances in 1805, and is a fine piece of theatrical music. But for the revised and shortened version of the opera *Leonore,* produced in the spring of 1806, in which much repetition was excised from individual numbers and the opera made tighter, Beethoven composed the greatest of all his overtures, *Leonore* No. 3, which has been described as the perfect symphonic poem. When he made the final revision in 1814, he wrote yet another overture, which since then has shared the name of the opera, *Fidelio.* This overture, completely suitable in every way for the opera it introduces, is now always used in performances; in some productions, the *Leonore* No. 3 serves as an *entr'acte*.

Napoleon's occupation of Vienna had completely overshadowed the first performances of *Leonore*. The third and most successful version of the opera, *Fidelio,* was performed at a time when Europe felt itself restored to the joys of freedom after the tyranny of the Napoleonic era. There is a certain poetic justice in the fact that its allegorical symbolism (as well as its musical greatness) caused the opera to be received with great enthusiasm. Its success encouraged Beethoven at a time of considerable personal difficulty.

THE THIRD STYLE PERIOD: 1816–27

Beethoven's problems with his hearing and with the guardianship of his nephew, Karl, brought his composing to an almost complete halt. Indeed, in some years of the last decade of his life, he hardly finished anything except a small canon or the like—the work of a moment. In his spurts of creative activity, however, he continually succeeded in finding new compositional ways to define the term "masterpiece."

SOLO PIANO WORKS

During this period, Beethoven composed five sonatas for solo piano—Opp. 101, 106, 109, 110, and 111—and one great set of variations, the so-called *Diabelli* Variations, Op. 120. Each work is of the highest quality and utterly unique. Only two years after the Sonata Op. 90, Beethoven wrote the Op. 101 in A major, which he wished to be identified by the German word for pianoforte, *Hammerklavier*. Around this time, there were concerted attempts to exclude foreign words from the German language in the name of nationalism, and Beethoven wrote humorously, but seriously, to his publisher of Op. 101, Sigmund Steiner, the following short letter:

> After a personal examination of the case and after hearing the opinion of our council we are resolved and hereby resolve that from henceforth on all our works, on which the title is German, instead of pianoforte *Hammerklavier* shall be used. Hence our most excellent L[ieutenant] G[eneral] and his Adjutant and also all others whom it may concern, are to comply with these orders immediately and see that they are carried out.
>
> Instead of Pianoforte
> Hammerklavier -
> This is to be clearly understood once and for all -
> issued etc., etc.,
> by the G[eneralissim]o
> on January 23, 1817.[12]

12. *Beethoven Letters,* p. 654.

Beethoven believed that the piano was a German invention[13] and justified the use of *Hammerklavier* on that basis. However, the title page for Op. 101 had already been engraved, and so the term became associated *only* with the Sonata Op. 106.

The E-major sonata, Op. 109 (*ACM* 72) the first of the three sonatas that occupied Beethoven during 1820/21, is also perhaps the most easily perceived of this trio. Like Emanuel Bach in old age, Beethoven is the consummate master of his material who does not want to do the same thing twice. Like Bach, he enjoys making his sonatas into terse, aphoristic statements, seemingly in free form, but actually strict and traditional in fundamental ways. The first movement appears both fantasia-like and irregular; its tempo changes five times and structural features merge into each other. Yet all the elements of a sonata structure are present: the opening *Vivace* serves both as a definition of tonality and a transition to the dominant; the *Adagio* comprises the second tonal area of the form; and at the *Tempo primo* the middle section begins. The recapitulation, with material considerably changed, comes halfway through m. 48 and the coda at the end of m. 65. The broad proportions show surprising balance:

Exposition	Group I	8–1/2 m.	*Vivace*
	Group II	7 m.	*Adagio*
Middle Section	(Development)	33 m.	*Tempo primo*
Recapitulation	Group I	9–1/2 m.	*Tempo primo*
	Group II	8 m.	*Adagio*
Coda		34 m.	*Tempo primo*

The logic of Beethoven's thinking becomes clearer still when one recognizes that the initial *Vivace* contrasts with the *Adagio espressivo* in almost all possible ways:

Vivace	*Adagio*
Diatonic	Chromatic
Major mode	Much minor mode coloring
Single note texture	Thick texture
Uniform texture	Variable texture
Almost uniform dynamic	Constantly changing dynamic
Regular direction of figures	Contrary motion of figures
Orthodox modulatory procedure	Side-slipping modulation
Small range	Entire range of keyboard
Regularity of rhythm	Fantasia/cadenza-like fluctuations of rhythm
Simple	Complex

13. *Ibid.*, p. 657.

The list can be extended almost indefinitely—so much so that we are pushed to think that Beethoven must have intended to make the opening sixteen measures an exercise in compressed musical opposition, more concentrated than ever. Each part, the *Vivace* and the *Adagio,* forms an opposing epigram. The middle section seems to continue the figuration of the opening, but it soon becomes apparent that changes are going to take place as the texture thickens: sudden dynamics are introduced, and the diatonic gives way to the chromatic. At the point of return the *Vivace* element is enormously changed in dynamic, register, and direction, but an equally important and more puzzling change is inserted into the *Adagio* element: in m. 61 there occurs a pronounced modulation to C major, which, in the context of this tiny work, is strongly emphasized by the fact that it takes up almost two measures before sideslipping into E. In the coda, the interpenetration of the *Vivace* and *Adagio* materials, i.e., the synthesizing of the opposing elements, continues on a variety of levels, the most impressive being that passage mm. 75–85 when the regular rhythm recalls the opening *Vivace* and the thickness of texture, chromaticism, and well-defined contrary motion all recall the *Adagio.* Mm. 86–92, in their oscillation between C and C♯, clearly make sense of the large C-major episode (mm. 61, 62) for the C serves as a flattened sixth to E major and as the diatonic sixth in E minor. The pull to the minor mode is an aspect of the sonata that is worked out in the second movement.

The last eight measures of the first movement of Op. 109 are among the miracles of music in that they make explicit what was implicit in the opening two elements.[14] Here the musician and the philosopher seem to sense the same current of thought moving in the times, and they express similar things in their own terms. Implicit in the *Vivace,* which is unemotional, abstract, and spiritual, is its explicit, final, upward flight. One can imagine this upward flight moving at least to highest E on the quarter rest, perhaps, in spirit, off the keyboard and beyond human hearing, were it not held back by the low, thick, final chord. But Beethoven interrupts its progress with a disturbing hiatus, and the soaring material is left hanging in a most uncomfortable position—hardly an ideal resolution! The *Adagio* material, which has been filled with changing passion and feeling, is now made explicit in this final earthbound chord, consisting of the tonic triad in both hands with the fifth of the

14. The philosopher G. W. F. Hegel (1770–1831), an almost exact contemporary of Beethoven, gave his name to that process of argument (Hegelian dialectic) in which seemingly irreconcilable, opposing ideas merge. Hegel believed such a process of thought to be universal. It is usually verbalized as follows: an idea (thesis) within a human mind generates other, opposite ideas (antithesis) and from the interaction of the two a third idea (synthesis) is generated, which then becomes the thesis to generate another antithesis and a further synthesis. This process, Hegel believed, could continue in circular fashion until the original starting position was reached again, but at this point all that was implicit in the first idea would now be explicit.

chord on top. Note the dissonant quality of this chord, which, because of its register and thickness, generates strong contradictory overtones, and note, too, the way Beethoven weakens its metrical position, and hence its finality. This conclusion clarifies the process in mm. 8 and 9, where the cadence flow A♯ to B is forced into A♯ to A♮. The final chord, then, can hardly be seen as a final resolution, any more than the rest which precedes it can be seen to resolve the *Vivace* material. The movement certainly presents a synthesis of opposites, but its final statement, in Hegelian fashion, is another thesis rather than the resolution which the musician/philosopher Beethoven needs. This three-movement work is all of one piece, and the coming together of its ideas and ultimate stability is not to be expected until the last movement. Thus, the first and second movements are simply separated by a fermata—itself a powerful symbol—over the last chord.

The *Prestissimo* second movement, set in the minor mode, relies heavily upon devices of counterpoint, imitation, canon, invertibility, etc.; perhaps its strongest effect is caused by the downward scale, taken from the bass of the sonata's opening *Vivace,* now set in the minor mode, with contrary motion between the hands moving to opposite ends of the keyboard. In this way the movement seems to be related to the preceding *Adagio,* but in its rigorously controlled, intellectual quality it seems quite different from the fantastic and utterly unpredictable nature of that material. Is it possible that Beethoven could intend this *Prestissimo* as a totally different synthesis of first-movement materials, or is it its complete antithesis? The movement itself, which is entirely assertive and decisive, does not compel the listener to ask such questions. The last eight measures should be noted, with their strong cadence on a wide-spaced E-minor chord, which has the root at the top and bottom of the chord, and contains a minor third but no fifth. There is no hint of dissonant, strong overtones spoiling the finality of this chord, and it is followed by a complete break before the work continues.

The last movement, a theme with six variations, carries the heading *Gesangvoll, mit innigster Empfindung* (Songful, with intense sentiment). In the theme lies the final resolution of the sonata. This must be so since Beethoven both opens and closes the movement with essentially identical statements of it. The theme itself is more singable than anything else has been to this point. Its structure (Example XXVIII–6) bears melodic relationship to the opening of the sonata and Beethoven sets it contrapuntally against an inexorably rising, scalar bass which brings the hands closer together. The harmonization of the melody further affirms

Example XXVIII–6: L. BEETHOVEN, Sonata Op. 109, III

the connection with the first movement, as chromatic movement emphasizes the note C♮ in its relationship to B and E; Beethoven also places a strong cadence on G♯ minor.

Of the six variations, only the first is free of connection with earlier movements. Indeed, it is quite isolated from the other variations in technique as well as spirit; whereas the others flow, each from the preceding (there is a rest between Nos. IV and V), the final cadence of the first has a distinctly different tessitura from the beginning of the second. Variation I is concerned with "songful" melody which, through its setting, high above its simple accompaniment, and its particular style of ornamentation, bears a strong resemblance to similar melodies in the slow movement of the Ninth Symphony and in the *Benedictus* of the *Missa solemnis,* all of which Beethoven was working on at the same time. The left-hand accompaniment may look like a waltz or mazurka, but its function is primarily sonorous; it enables the composer to cover a wide range without disturbing the slow tempo and without taking anything away from the melody. It is in the context of the theme and this first ecstatic variation that the subsequent variations now start their magnificent and stately progress, surveying what has been and leading us to new heights, alternating a slow, singing, melodic variation with a fast, contrapuntal one.

Variation II is a double variation in that it modifies the repeats of each strain of the theme in a way that first evokes the *Vivace* material of the first movement and then the first movement's *Adagio* Variation III is a series of fast invertible counterpoints in exaggerated contrary motion, unmistakably creating links with the second movement. The next two variations are less closely tied to the first and second movements of the sonata and seem to develop from the preceding two. Variation IV, with a tempo somewhat slower than that of the theme, is polyphonic in the first half and thickly textured in its second, while V is another double variation in which the varied repeat of both halves adds a running counterpoint of eighth notes to the already strongly contrapuntal texture.

In the sixth and final variation, Beethoven achieves complete freedom within the strictest discipline, bringing to mind a small number of compositions from Emanuel Bach's last years that are clearly the result of extreme compositional rigor but sound like improvisations. Here, a double variation of the theme builds by continuous development to a climax in which the first treatment of the second strain (thirty-second notes over a low dominant trill) sounds like a cadenza arising solely from the artist's desire to fantasize. At the conclusion of this passage the tessitura is lifted four octaves for the second treatment of the strain, so totally different from the first that one can hardly believe that they are fundamentally the same thing. After this variation Beethoven inserts a three-measure transition to the theme, arriving at the only imaginable conclusion.

The theme of this closely integrated set of variations is only slightly modified by the addition of bass resonance in the first half, and by even slighter modifications in the second half. It is worth noting that Beethoven's final cadence is spaced in a way that has the strongest overtones generated by the lowest note coincide with the sound of the actual, struck notes, giving the chord its clean, restful, and stable sound. His melody falls from the fourth degree, A, to the major third, G♯, a modal and melodic interval. This observation becomes significant when we note that in Beethoven's original conception, this sonata was to be in E minor. We have seen that much of its richness and complexity arises from the retention of some of the minor characteristics, yet while Beethoven's cadential chord with the major third on top may be looked upon as the confirmation of the major mode, it is perhaps more important to realize that the effect of the final G♯ is to avoid the conclusiveness of the last cadence and to keep the sound of the music floating on, after the vibrations on the air have stopped.

In the last movement of his Sonata in A♭, Op. 110, Beethoven creates a structure with even less precedent than the first movement of Op. 109. Indeed, the shape of the whole sonata is of an unusual cast. It is in three movements, the first of which, despite unusual material and modulations effected by side-slipping chromatic movement, is relatively orthodox. The second movement, *Allegro molto,* seems like a Scherzo and Trio, but in duple instead of triple time. The third movement resembles Op. 109 in that it too seems to set in opposition the heart, represented by songful melody, and the head, represented by fugue. It can readily be seen that Beethoven requires a profusion of dynamic markings and verbal directions in the songful parts and relatively few dynamics and almost no instructions in the fugal parts.

At the outset there is a three-measure instrumental introduction before a recitative, which is, of course, a vocal idiom transferred into instrumental music when the composer wishes to evoke the human voice in a dramatic situation. After the recitative there follows a bar and a half of instrumental introduction to what Beethoven calls a *Klagender Gesang* (Song of Lamentation) in A♭ minor, which leads to the first *Allegro* fugue. Its subject is built upon the first notes of the first movement, that epigram of eternal musical truth here stripped of its rhythmic profile and now on notes of equal length emphasizing melody alone. At its triumphal final cadence, however, it is interrupted by a side-slip into G minor and the Song of Lamentation renews itself with the direction *Ermattet, klagend* (exhausted, lamenting). The melody now undergoes a certain kind of ornamentation in which rapid, interjected notes are placed off the beat.[15] The melody of the *Klagender Gesang* is the same length as

15. Beethoven may have said that the *Pastoral* Symphony was "more an expression of feeling than tone painting," but we must recognize in that formulation a certain play on words. The question may be asked whether, here, Beethoven is more concerned

at its first appearance but now it has a lengthened transition to the *Allegro* fugue, which starts with its subject inverted. Fugal devices of various kinds, however, give way to a concluding, ecstatically manic extension of the fugue subject (Example XXVIII–7) treated now homophonically as a stretch of endless melody with each cadence becoming the start of the next phrase.

Example XXVIII–7: L. BEETHOVEN, Sonata, Op.110, IV

a. Fugue subject

b. Final extension

From these brief discussions it can be seen how different and yet how complementary Op. 109 and Op. 110 are, and it cannot be emphasized too strongly that all three of the late sonatas are closely related to one another: they seem to share something of the same expressive goal, realized through the same formal procedures of variation, fugue, and sonata and utilizing the same medium, the piano.

Shortly after completing Op. 110, Beethoven finished the Sonata in C minor, Op. 111. The stature of this work as a human document has been noted times without number, and its reputation is well deserved. It must also be acknowledged that a great composer's last work in any medium carries a certain aura. What is immediately apparent in this sonata is its relatively orthodox first movement. After Opp. 109 and 110, Op. 111 appears straightforward, with a slow introduction leading

---

with expressing the feeling of lamentation or with making a musical impression of breath caught between sobs. If he were to attempt to pictorialize "sobbing," might he have been able to do it any more efficiently than he has done?

to a monothematic exposition, a short and even perfunctory development, a regular recapitulation, and a short, effective coda. The second and final movement is a theme and variations. Critics have commented upon Beethoven's use of trills in his final period, and here, as in the final movement of Op. 109, he exploits the expressivity of the device more than in any other works. But these variations are quite different from those of Op. 109. There one could say that the variations related to the theme as points on the circumference of a circle relate to the center, for each was different from the others and although they flowed together, they were separate. In other words, one could imagine Beethoven inserting a number of other variations into the set, provided that the last variation remained where it was. In Op. 111, however, the variation idea is turned into a linear exercise in which one thought leads ineluctably to another. The ongoing factor is that of reducing note length, and the process, starting from the beginning, increases motion—perceptible as tempo—to the point where motion becomes quiet stillness, as a spinning top "sleeps."

Beethoven's last great piano work is the set of *Variations on a Waltz of Diabelli,* Op.120. This composition occupied him over several years, as he took it up and put it down again. In its final state it illustrates perfectly one extreme aspect of variation. There are as many theories concerning the structure of this set as there are critics and analysts who have studied it. This indicates one of two things: either the listener's perception of the structure was not an essential part of Beethoven's artistic goal, or he failed to achieve that goal. The impression one has is that there is no inexorable push to a final climax as there is in Op. 111, although the climax undoubtedly comes toward the end.

The origins of this composition are the basis of a well-known anecdote: the proofreader/composer, lately turned publisher, Anton Diabelli (1781–1858), thought to make his name as a publisher better known by issuing a set of variations upon a little waltz of his, but he did not intend to write the variations himself. The title under which the work was eventually issued explains his idea and demonstrates what a flair for publicity Diabelli had in a time of great patriotism. The title in translation runs: "The Union of Artists of the Fatherland. Variations for the Piano-Forte on a given theme, composed by the most outstanding Composers and Virtuosos of Vienna and from the Royal Austrian States." The publication came in two parts; the first part was Beethoven's set and the second was the Artists' Union set of 50 variations (plus two that were not published with the set). The composers who participated in this project range from famous names, such as Hummel, Liszt, and Schubert, through the middle ranks, like Czerny, E. A. Förster, Gelinek, Moscheles, Sechter, to the quite forgotten, such as Czapek, Huglmann, Panny, and von Szàlay and many more. "W. A." Mozart, son of the great composer,[16] contributed two variations, one of which was included, and Beethoven's pupil the Archduke Rudolph, is represented by a fugue. The set contains the first composition of Franz Liszt and the last composition of Emanuel Förster. The fifty variations are introduced by the theme of Diabelli and concluded with a long coda by Czerny.

While Beethoven called Diabelli's little tune a "cobbler's patch," he was able to show that it was pregnant with possibilities. The idea of contributing to a joint venture, as described above, must obviously have been repugnant to Beethoven, who never saw himself as one of the mass of musicians, and it is not surprising that he refused to take part. His interest in the theme can only be explained by the nature of the discipline it imposed upon him, but it is entirely characteristic that he should undertake to demonstrate his ability to "out-variation" all the other composers of Vienna. That he conferred immortality upon Diabelli in the process was of no importance.

CELLO SONATAS AND SONGS

Apart from the string quartets, the only other examples of private music that deserve mention here are the two Sonatas for Cello and Piano, Op. 102, and the song cycle Op. 98. The cello sonatas date from 1815 and are among the earliest works in which Beethoven's predilection for contrapuntal writing, so typical of his late style, manifests itself in formal fugue. The song cycle, *An die ferne Geliebte,* Op. 98, dates from 1816. While Beethoven wrote songs throughout his life, and while some were very attractive, for the most part they hardly surpassed those of Haydn and Mozart. This cycle marks a great departure, however; we do not really know why he wrote it, but these songs are unique in their heartfelt poignancy and in their apparent personal significance for the composer. Composed to verses that may have been especially written for Beethoven, they constitute the first cycle of songs in the nineteenth-century conception of the Lied. Beethoven's example possibly influenced Schumann more than Schubert, and his return to the opening melodic material at the close of the cycle was twice adopted by Schumann. In Beethoven's cycle, each song is linked to the next by a modulating passage, but this device was not taken up again.

16. Franz Xaver Wolfgang, Mozart's last child, was born on 26 July, 1791, and lived until 1844. He was a professional musician, who made his living primarily from teaching and from playing the piano; he also composed some small pieces. He was known by his father's names of Wolfgang Amadeus.

THE STRING QUARTET

The composition of the five final string quartets occupied Beethoven between 1822 and 1826, but the actual time he spent on them is closer to two years than four:

Op. 127 in E♭	—	Talked about in 1822. Possibly worked on from May 1824 to February 1825
Op. 132 in A minor	—	Completed in late July 1825
Op. 130 in B♭	—	Completed in November 1825
Op. 131 in C♯ minor	—	Completed in July 1826
Op. 135 in F	—	Completed in early October 1826
Op. 130 in B♭	—	Substitute Finale—completed in November, 1826

In earlier years, Beethoven had habitually worked on several major compositions at the same time, apparently moving from one to the other with the greatest ease. During the time Beethoven was writing these quartets he composed only a few small canons and album pieces—nothing of great significance. Moreover, they are the final embodiment of his stupendous craft. The spiritual experience of the *Missa solemnis* and the composition of the Ninth Symphony were behind him, and when he had completed the alternate finale for Op. 130, there were only a few days left before the onset of his final illness.

After completing the Piano Sonata Op. 111, Beethoven said to his friend Karl Holz, "The piano is, all things considered, an unsatisfactory instrument." In the string quartet, Beethoven found his ideal: one that could sing like the human voice and sustain legato lines in any tempo or register; one that could provide a dense texture across the whole gamut (by contrast, when the hands are far apart on the piano the middle range seems empty); one that could achieve a homogeneous sound yet had certain exotic color effects; and one that, while lending itself to the most private utterance, allowed the deepest communication among the players and the listeners.

The three Quartets, Opp. 127, 132, and 130 arose from a commission from the Russian Prince Galitzin, who, in 1822, requested "one, two, or three new quartets" from Beethoven. All three were completed in 1825 and, as usual, while there are similarities between them, each is very different from the others. They differ most obviously in their overall organization. Op. 127 is in four movements; Op. 132 has five, interpolating between the slow movement and the last an *Alla marcia* which concludes with a recitative that effects a transition to the last movement; and Op. 130 in its huge original form has six movements, an extra slow movement and a German dance added to the traditional four. In each of the quartets the technique of tempo alteration is used in the first movement in order to create a contrast between slow, aphoristic, and even enigmatic musical utterance and the more simple, songlike, and straightforward fast material. In each quartet there is a place where the contrast between movements is shockingly exaggerated: Op. 127 between movements 2 and 3; Op. 132 between movements 3 and 4; and Op. 130 between movements 5 and 6. In each quartet a deeply felt slow movement is followed without transition by incongruous material, and one is reminded of the way the younger Beethoven would ridicule an audience that was deeply moved by his improvisation by suddenly dropping both forearms onto the keys, *fortissimo,* and stalking off. The quartets reveal another attribute which has been referred to as "a determination to touch common mankind as nakedly as possible."[17] This is manifested by frequent use of song elements—folk or operatic—or songlike melody, together with the written word in the form of titles, tempo indications, and general performance instructions, in order to communicate the essence of the musical experience.

Op. 127 in E♭ has always been regarded as the most accessible of the late quartets largely because its thematic material is so singable and serene in the first two movements and exuberant and forthright in the third and fourth. In particular, not only the theme and variations constitute a unique musical experience of enormous variety, but the actual quartet writing is of a richness unparalleled by any of Beethoven's contemporaries.

The Quartet in A minor, Op. 132, opens with a slow statement of the notes G♯, A, F♮, E. This sequence of notes seems to permeate much of Beethoven's thinking in these quartets, and analysts have gone so far as to see the compositional purpose of the last quartets as an exploration of these intervals. The effect of the opening is felt throughout the movement although the introduction itself never recurs, for elements of the "motto" are used as a counterpoint to the first subject, and it forms a part of a strong conclusion in the coda, which is remarkable for shedding a new light on old material.

There follows a kind of German-dancelike movement with *Ländler* trio, remarkable for a meter offset by one beat. It precedes one of the most curious and celebrated Beethovenian movements, which carries the title *Heiliger Dankgesang eines Genesenen an die Gottheit, in der lydischen Tonart* (Holy song of thanksgiving to the Godhead from a Convalescent, in the Lydian mode). In this movement a slow, chorale-like theme with imitative interludes is followed by a D-major section, slightly faster in tempo, and headed *Neue Kraft fühlend* (Feeling new strength). Then each section is varied and finally Beethoven concludes with a polyphonic treatment of the first phrase of the chorale. This is one of the rare examples of music's capacity to transport the sympathetic player/listener in a way that words cannot do.

The Quartet in B♭, Op. 130, is in some ways the most curious. On

17. Joseph Kerman, *The Beethoven Quartets* (New York, 1967), p. 194.

the surface it appears to be a serenade or divertimento in six movements, but its content is far removed from the notion of "entertainment" music. Perhaps the last two movements deserve the most comment. Beethoven said of the slow *Cavatina* that it was "composed in the very tears of misery, and that never had one of his own pieces moved him so deeply."[18] It was originally followed by a vast fugal movement which was, and is still, so troublesome to play and to listen to that Beethoven was finally persuaded to remove it and publish it separately as *Grosse Fuge* (Great Fugue). In its place he composed a new Finale, which proved to be his last composition.

The two remaining quartets, in C♯ minor, Op. 131, and in F, Op. 135, are so different that they seem to have sprung from different parents. Op. 131 is at the furthest remove from Classical models, having seven movements, each of which flows without pause into the next. The publisher, Schott, had asked for something new, and when Beethoven sent it he described it as a "patchwork," immediately saying that all the material in it was new and unused. It is indeed a patchwork compared with any other quartet, but the short third movement functions like a transition and the sixth movement like an introduction. Indeed, had Beethoven himself not dignified them with numbers it is unlikely that we would look upon these as two separate movements (*cf.* Op. 132). The tonal scheme has first and last movements in the tonic key whereas the internal movements form a harmonic progression to the conclusion. The "patchwork" also includes the textures and structures of fugue, sonata, and theme and variations, as well as over twenty indications of tempo change, not counting *ritard* and *a tempo*. Nevertheless, Beethoven has clearly intended a strong onward flow: each movement is connected to the following by a notated, time-limited break and there is a constant underlay of thematic connection between movements widely distinct in other ways. It seems clear that here, once more, Beethoven has been intent on exploring, in musical terms, the abiding paradox of the relationship between freedom and discipline. Even a cursory examination shows the strict control beneath the surface in what appears to be his most fantasic, imaginative, and most unconventional quartet.

On the other hand, Op. 135 would seem like a step back in time were the language not so clearly that of late Beethoven. The sonata-form first movement has an unexpected terseness and brings to mind the sonatas of Opp. 78 and 109. However, the instrumental interplay, consisting of short exchanged motives, is unlike anything Beethoven had done for years, and definitely resembles much earlier eighteenth-century work. The Scherzo, however, has only a little of the previous century in it. Rhythmically complex and at times harshly dissonant, this movement

18. Cited in Thayer-Forbes, *op. cit.*, p. 975.

succeeds in developing humor beyond the means available to Haydn (see p. 433). Example XXVIII–8 shows part of this movement, in which large intervals and string crossing in the first violin change Haydn's comic amiability into something bitter and sardonic. The unison figure in the three lower parts is repeated thirty-two times *fortissimo,* and then another fifteen times *decrescendo* in a foretaste of minimalism that is even more taxing for the players than for the listeners. This most savage of Scherzos is followed by a slow theme and variations in an utterly contrasting devotional manner, which Beethoven conceived, in his words, as a "song of rest or peace." The last movement is a strange mixture of humor and seriousness with a title, *Die schwer gefasste Entschluss* (The decision reached with difficulty), and a musical motto at the beginning: *Muss es sein? Es muss sein* (Must it be? It must be). What the difficult decision may have been we do not know. But we can see from Op. 135, his last completed, multi-movement composition, that Beethoven was showing signs of setting off down yet another new road.

Example XXVIII–8: L. BEETHOVEN, Quartet, Op. 135, II

THE NINTH SYMPHONY

The Ninth Symphony in D minor, Op. 125, is Beethoven's last symphony. Had he lived there would have been more, for we know that his final years were filled with embryonic plans for symphonies, operas, and a Requiem; how these works might have developed we cannot imagine, for the late quartets strike out on paths of intimate revelation and all-embracing melodiousness, as well as more intellectual directions, and each of Beethoven's works is willfully individual. The Ninth Symphony is a unique solution to a unique problem, with nothing in the least deterministic about it. In other words, its shape, its thematic material, its use of choir, etc., have nothing to do with the power of anything outside itself, and Beethoven could have written a Ninth Symphony different in all respects from the Ninth he actually wrote.

This artistic flight of fancy would be ridiculous—Beethoven standing amidst a motley crew of instruments behind a conductor who cannot see his players—were the subject not so emotionally charged.

And we can be quite sure that Beethoven's Tenth, had he written it, would have been something else again.

The problem of the Ninth lies in Beethoven's determination to reach out to embrace mankind in a bearhug of brotherhood, using an idealistic text to preach the unmistakable message, and a choir of human voices to realize it: here the medium, the choir and the orchestra on stage, literally is the message. Beethoven has undertaken to justify, at the bar of tradition, the introduction of text and voices into a genre which, historically, had been instrumental, and which Beethoven himself had raised from the theater to the cathedral, from the secular to the pseudo-sacred, from the physical to the spiritual.

The first movement (*ACM* 73) cast a long shadow over the nineteenth century, as it blazed a trail for Bruckner and even Mahler. To this point, all Beethoven's symphonies have begun their *Allegro* with a statement—a graspable musical entity of melody, rhythm, and harmonic progression. Here, the music begins with a question rather than a statement, as its opening sonority defines neither rhythm nor tonality nor melody. But from this sonority there emerges fragments of melody which ultimately coalesce, in mm. 17–20, into a statement to end all statements. We know from experience that Beethoven almost inevitably presented the opposing elements of his sonata dialectic in the first few measures, and miraculously he found yet another way to expose essential opposition: something in a state of change, which might be called a process of becoming (mm. 1–16), set against something which does not change but simply is, which might be called a statement of being (mm. 17–20). Not only is the opening of the symphony radically different from anything that has preceded it, but also its continuation proposes new methods of exposition, which the listener accepts as necessary and fulfilling. After m. 20, what seems like an extension of the strong cadence lengthens into a curious passage that stresses the Neapolitan sonority (mm. 24–25) before moving to a dominant. After an elided cadence (mm. 34–35) Beethoven returns to the opening material, now in the tonic and beginning in m. 35. The "process of becoming" now leads to the key of the submediant, and the "statement of being" is so changed that it concludes on D, the third of the chord, rather than on B♭. The strong melodic progression in the bass, D, E♮, F, F♯, G, G♯, leads to a prolonged rest on A with a strong melodic profile (mm. 63–67). When repeated (mm. 68–72), this leads back not to D minor but to B♭, for the long, complex, and enormously varied second group, mm. 74–159. The middle section (mm. 162–300) begins exactly as the opening of the movement, until m. 170, when F♯ modifies the tonality; in the key of G minor Beethoven presents a much changed image of the downward arpeggio statement, abruptly cut off by four measures of fan-fare (mm. 188–191) and followed by six measures of new, but obviously derived melody (mm. 192–197). At m. 198 the "statement of being" is further changed for eight measures, making it more melodic and subject to modulation, a process which is interrupted exactly as before and by the same two elements, the "cutting-off" fanfare and the derived melody. Both processes have similarly marked *ritard* and *a tempo* indications; hence it is reasonable to see here a musical process that may be described as two attempts to go in a certain direction that are both frustrated by consistent development of material from the first and second group, which goes on without hindrance to the recapitulation.

Changed recapitulations have been a hallmark of Beethoven's style. Haydn and Mozart tended to build up to a recapitulation and reach it with a sense of release or repose, repeating literally what has been before, and only making changes in its continuation. Beethoven, from the outset increased the power of recapitulation by immediately changing the re-statement to make it more emphatic (see the first Piano Sonata, Op. 2, No. 1, *ACM* 69). In this work, Beethoven carries his aesthetic of recapitulation to the furthest imaginable point, and creates from a first inversion of the tonic major chord, a veritable hell that makes the center of the development of the *Eroica* appear like child's play.[19] Moreover, it

19. Twice before, a major first-inversion chord has been placed with comparable power and orchestration. Both are in Mozart's *Don Giovanni,* the first being the second chord of the overture, and the second being the analogous music where the statue appears and the chord is reharmonized as a $6^{6}_{\substack{5\\3}}$.

Beethoven's recapitulation in its sonorous power recalls nothing so much as Milton's description of the fall of Satan in *Paradise Lost:*

is not a repeat of the opening that we hear at the point of recapitulation. Instead, Beethoven gives us what we have heard at the beginning of the development, at the point where F♯ is introduced (m. 170) What had been heard at the beginning in B♭ major is now crushed into mm. 313–14, and what might be called the double exposition of the first group is now telescoped under great pressure into one utterance. The "process" part of the first group is shortened by two bars, while the "statement," because of the counterpoint in contrary motion now added to it, is lengthened by being separated into component parts. Thus, mm. 317 and 318, 321 and 322 are interpolated measures. What had been mm. 24–27, and in the recapitulation is mm. 326–329, becomes the means of transition into the second group, as Beethoven makes a three-part descending sequence to release the tension of what must be the most strained and awe-inspiring recapitulation in the whole history of sonata structure.

The rest of the recapitulation, i.e., the second group, proceeds as usual with no great changes, and the coda begins at m. 427 with a much modified form of the "statement" set against the *tremolando* in the middle strings that had accompanied the "process of becoming". Here it is repeated four times before it is reduced to a fragment and disappears into a swirl of contrary motion and cross-rhythm. A fleeting glimpse of major mode and the contrapuntal texture woven from "statement" motives is followed by halting *ritardandi*. Then the second most famous feature of this movement after the opening: the "new" material. Over an *ostinato* bass built on the filled-in fourth, the first interval of the "statement," a slow, marchlike tune with dotted rhythms, an unmistakable evocation of a funeral march, appears. For Beethoven's public, as for Mahler's, the pomp of a military funeral procession was a common experience, much more so than for a twentieth-century audience. Here, not only the rhythm but the falling third to the tonic and the orchestration all contribute to the overwhelming finality of this conclusion. A powerful musical symbol of frustration is to be found in mm. 531*ff*,., where the leading-note, C♯, is forced down to C♮. The final statement of the movement is a clear indication that the sonata dialectic has not worked out the thesis and the antithesis. There is no synthesis, no resolution. As there is no resolution, there is no affirmation. All the struggle has been in vain, for the last notes are a reiteration of what was at the beginning; what was "becoming" has disappeared, and what "was" still "is."

The law of contrast dictates that the Scherzo should follow this grave

---

Him the Almighty Power
Hurled headlong flaming from th' Ethereal Skie
With hideous ruine and combustion down
To bottomless perdition, there to dwell
In Adamantine Chains and penal Fire,
Who durst defie th' Omnipotent to Arms.

and grim first movement. It is, fittingly, an enormous *fugato* composition combining deftness and lightness with power—an iron hand in a velvet glove.

The slow movement is a double theme and variations, which, like the first movement, alternates between B♭ and D. Here the tonic is B♭ and the second part of the theme is in D major. Perhaps most significant in Beethoven's symbology is the last variation, in which the first violins carry a melismatic melody closely related to the violin solo in the *Benedictus* of the *Missa solemnis,* and with the first variation of Op. 109. The expression is one of rapt ecstasy and of utter abstraction in the world of the spirit. More than any other, this music approaches that of the cherubim and angels, who, it is said, with serious faces and slow steps, celebrate the peace of God in joy and gravity.

We may wish this state of the slow movement to go on forever, but Beethoven shatters the peace with a violent chord, *fortissimo* D, F, A, B♭. This chord announces the introductory section to the choral Finale of this symphony, a section in which the audience is prepared for the use of the human voice. Beethoven accomplishes the task by using (a) dynamically stressed dissonance, (b) wordless instrumental recitative, and (c) quotations from all three preceding movements. After the quotations (m. 77) Beethoven introduces the beginning of the famous theme of the "Ode to Joy" and the recitative, hitherto quite stripped of accompaniment, is encouraged by orchestral participation. There follows a full instrumental exposition of the theme, starting in the cellos and basses (m. 92) and gradually taken up by the entire orchestra. This is an important symbol for acceptance which we have seen Beethoven use before, in the coda of the *Eroica* first movement, for example. All should be well, but the progress is interrupted (m. 208) by the loudest dissonance, and the baritone soloist explains why. He says, in Beethoven's own words freely translated: "O friends, let us not have this kind of sound, but rather let us strike up more pleasant, more joyful music." The soloists and choir, requiring no further invitation or justification, join in.

Events determined that the last pages of the Ninth Symphony should be the composer's final utterance in the realm of grandiloquent, public music, and that statement is one of affirmation. His last words are words of reasonable confidence in mankind—a mankind sufficiently rational to give thanks in a realization of communal interest.

THE *MISSA SOLEMNIS*

No such affirmation concludes the work which preceded the symphony. Beethoven undertook to compose the *Missa solemnis,* or Mass in D, Op. 123, to celebrate the elevation of his long-time and favorite pupil and patron, the Archduke Rudolph, to the Archbishopric of

Olmütz. The news of this honor was given in June 1819, although Schindler tells us that it was already public knowledge by mid-1818. In the month of the announcement, Beethoven wrote a long letter of congratulation to his pupil, in which he says:

> The day on which a High mass composed by me will be performed during the ceremonies solemnized for Your Imperial Highness will be the most glorious day of my life; and God will enlighten me so that my poor talents may contribute to the glorification of that solemn day.[20]

It is likely that Beethoven had been thinking about and sketching the Mass for some time before he wrote this letter, but since the date for the ceremonies was already set for March 1820, he had only nine months to finish it. With preliminary composition already under way this may have seemed sufficient, but in fact, he did not complete the Mass until 1823. In mid-1819 Beethoven was entirely consumed with the struggle to remove his nephew Karl from his mother's influence, and at the time he wanted to begin it, he was only starting to emerge from a barren period; by the time he finished it he was producing with a facility only equaled in the early years of the century. During the composition of the Mass he became totally immersed in concentration as never before. Schindler recounts an event which he dates in August of 1819:

> It was four o'clock in the afternoon. As soon as we entered we were told that both Beethoven's maids had left that morning and that there had occurred after midnight an uproar that had disturbed everyone in the house because, having waited so long, both maids had gone to sleep and the meal they had prepared was inedible. From behind the closed door of one of the parlors we could hear the master working on the fugue of the Credo, singing, yelling, stamping his feet. When we had heard enough of this almost frightening performance and were about to depart, the door opened and Beethoven stood before us, his features distorted to the point of inspiring terror. He looked as though he had just engaged in a life and death struggle with the whole army of contrapuntists, his everlasting enemies. His first words were confused, as if he felt embarrassed at having been overheard. Soon he began to speak of the day's events and said, with noticeable self-control, 'What a mess! Everyone has run away and I haven't had anything to eat since yesterday noon.' I tried to calm him and helped him to make his toilet. My companion hurried to the bathhouse restaurant to order something for the famished master. While he ate, he complained to us about the state of his household. But, because of the circumstances I have already described, there was no solution. Never has such a great work of art been created under such adverse circumstances as this *Missa Solemnis*.[21]

Beethoven's preparatory studies for this Mass were unusually extensive and absorbing, and there can be no doubt that among his complex reasons for proposing its composition was his desire to ensure his immor-

20. *Beethoven Letters,* p. 948.
21. Anton Schindler, *Beethoven as I knew him*. Ed. Donald McArdle (London, 1966), p. 229.

tality: in other words, like Bach's *Art of Fugue* or Mozart's Requiem, this work was to embody his art at its height. It was also to signify his renewal as a composer and to refute those who were saying that he was written-out and exhausted.

The *Missa solemnis* is clearly descended from a long tradition of Mass writing, yet it is most original and free from the traditional interpretation of his contemporaries. While it treats the text phrase by phrase, the traditional sequence of self-contained sections, so typical of the "number" Masses of Bach or Haydn, is replaced by a return to the earlier principles of highly unified Mass composition, e.g., the germinal function of mm. 4–7 of the *Kyrie,* which surface in a variety of transformations as the work proceeds. Beethoven's study of Palestrina's Masses may also have contributed to his metrical freedom, in evidence from the very first chord of the *Kyrie*. Frequently throughout this work (and through the late quartets) the reader senses that Beethoven's orthodox use of the barline is something which stands in the way of the music. It has been pointed out that the common rhythmic setting for the opening Kyrie is c 𝅗𝅥. 𝅘𝅥 | 𝅗𝅥 (Ky - ri - e). Beethoven's use of the same rhythm is softened and more fluid c 𝄼 𝅗𝅥 | 𝅗𝅥. 𝅘𝅥 | 𝅘𝅥 (Ky - ri - e).[22] Repeatedly, he sets stressed syllables on weaker parts of the measure, evidence of his wish to emphasize the intellectual and significant aspect of the word and lessen the physical impact of regular rhythmic pulse. Beethoven expresses the word, as his contemporaries have done, yet infuses each occasion with a seriousness of artistic purpose. Thus, in the *Credo,* after "et sepultus est" (and was buried), he avoids the expected effect of the "et resurrexit," by isolating the "et" (and) and then setting "resurrexit tertia die secundum scripturas" (he arose on the third day according to the Scriptures) for the voices a capella. He thereby postpones the joyful music we are expecting until "ascendit in coelis" (he ascended into heaven). This is one place where our expectation is ultimately fulfilled in a novel and perhaps more rewarding way.

Beethoven followed the tradition of his time by setting certain parts of the text as fugues. Both the "et in vitam venturi saeculi, amen," from the *Gloria* and the "in gloria Dei patris, amen," from the *Credo,* are fugues. Both of them demonstrate the composer's complete mastery of eighteenth-century techniques, for he is one of the very few capable of making the fugue an expression of man's most elevated sentiments.

The Mass and the Ninth Symphony belong together as surely as any two works for church and concert hall can. They appear to be counterparts of each other, yet many commentators have noted that this Mass is not really at home in church and the Ninth Symphony goes as far as a secular form can go in turning music of the concert hall into a religious experience. In each case it is impossible to imagine a more pow-

22. Warren Kirkendale, "New Roads to Old Ideas in Beethoven's *Missa Solemnis,*" *The Musical Quarterly,* LVI, No.4, Oct. 1970.

erful expression of belief: in the symphony we are given a humanistic document in which struggle and contemplation of heroic proportions lead to a conclusion of energy and exuberance—the outcome of the workings of enlightened reason; in the Mass the plea for mercy is remote from human experience and divinely beautiful. But Beethoven, unorthodox as he was, cannot speak so strongly, and herein, perhaps, is to be found the evidence that identifies him as a man of the eighteenth century rather than the nineteenth. Thousands of years of belief do not weigh on Beethoven's scales as heavily as does the power of reason to reveal truth. His conception of the difference between divine and earthly joy and his realization of it in music is beyond the reach of ordinary humans, and yet it is tinged with doubt; the end of his *Missa solemnis* is not an affirmation.

When the French were invading Vienna, Beethoven said to their generals: "If I, a composer, knew as much about strategy as I do about counterpoint I would soon send you packing."[23] As a composer, his profound knowledge of music enabled him to expand the nature and the limits of every genre of composition that he touched. And yet he refused to follow the trends of the times uncritically. Underlying all his work there is a sense of order in which individual parts are subordinated to the final effect that he wished to create, and that final effect is not simply one of comfort and ease, but is always of serious import and strength. His criticisms of Rossini, Weber, and Spohr all resided in his view of himself as a serious composer of symphonies and Masses. Thus, Rossini should stick to comic opera, Weber should compose nothing but operas without polishing them too much, and Spohr's vein of melody was too chromatic. These quick judgments show precisely where Beethoven's allegiance lay as he advised the "lesser" men to stay clear of his ground: for him the rules of counterpoint, the harmonious relationship of parts which we call structure or form, and the elemental force of strong central tonality are the means that he utilized throughout his life.

Beethoven lived through the time of the French Revolution as a young adult, and he saw the high ideals of the middle class overthrown by progressively more extreme demagogues, as ideals collapsed into the Reign of Terror. He witnessed the rise of the dictatorship that followed the chaos, and following that, the restoration of the Bourbon monarchy and the widespread attempts to put the clock back throughout Europe. Yet despite this experience, that would have made cynics out of many, Beethoven preserved his belief in the power of humankind to raise itself through the exercise of Reason, and he carried on a heroic fight to preach that doctrine.

23. Cited in Thayer-Forbes, *op. cit.*, p. 466.

PART IX

The 18th-Century Heritage at Work in the Early 19th Century

CHAPTER XXIX

Post-Revolutionary Changes in Society and the Arts

The first twenty years of the nineteenth century saw the end of England's restrictive grasp on technology, and the consequent spread of industrialization throughout the Western world. At first confined to Belgium and northeastern France, it gradually spread to Germany and the United States. The growth of cities and the necessity of moving manufactured goods to ports and markets sparked the creation of an expanding network of rail and canal communications which facilitated the movement not only of goods and people but of ideas.

NAPOLEONIC POWER AND ITS CONSEQUENCES

The wars of conquest conducted by Napoleon changed the face of Europe and the attitudes of the population drastically. These wars persisted for the entire period he was in power: from before 1799, when he was elected First Consul, through 1804, when he declared himself emperor, to 1815, when he was defeated at Waterloo and banished to the remote island of St. Helena, where he died. It had become clear that he intended to found a Napoleonic dynasty, for he set his family and friends upon several important thrones of Europe. No king felt himself secure as long as Napoleon was redrawing the map, and in the face of this threat many monarchs promised their subjects a constitutional government, to be implemented when the "emergency" passed. Only a few of these promises were fulfilled, however. Many of the revolutionary and republican ideals had been swept away by Napoleon himself when he declared himself emperor and instituted a hereditary nobility designed to perpetuate his name and his form of government. The restoration of the Bourbon monarchy in France, the abandonment of promises of constitutional government, the concerted drive to thwart nationalistic movements, and the revitalized power of the Roman Catholic Church

In this portrait by Jean-Dominique Ingres, painted in 1800, the Emperor Napolean is crowned with all due pomp and ceremony. (Copyright, Photo, Musée de l'Armée, Paris)

were all signs of the widespread and deep-seated need to return to values and systems that seemed in retrospect to have been so stable and secure.

It was in Germany, Austria, and Italy that the spirit of nationalism most threatened the status quo. The effect of independence movements in Belgium, Bohemia, Hungary, and Italy on Austria's farflung European empire and the popular movement for German unification endangered the continued existence of the patchwork of German-speaking countries. The short-lived liberalism of the immediate post-Napoleonic era was quickly stifled, and the Carlsbad Decrees of 1819 put a reactionary stamp on the age by reinstating censorship, and suppressing the politically liberal and nationalistic student societies, or *Burschenschaften*.

ECLECTICISM IN THE ARTS

The constant fluctuation between liberalism and reaction that characterizes the political life of France during the first twenty years of the nineteenth century was also typical of the rest of Europe. The inherent social contradictions extended far beyond the arena of politics, however, and evidence of an increasingly complex society is manifest in the variety of styles that flourished in the fine arts, as well as in the decorative, or applied arts. Perhaps it is in the last-mentioned that we find the best examples of such eclecticism of taste. For example, in addition to an abiding love of the classical style as exemplified in Roman artifacts and a taste for the Gothic that arose in the eighteenth century, there is now a revival of the Chinese influence—the third wave of *chinoiserie* to hit Europe in 150 years—which merges into a composite style redolent of the Far East. It was made up of a mixture of Chinese, Japanese, and Indian effects; there is an Egyptian style, which became popular coincidentally with Napoleon's Egyptian campaign, and which adopts motifs from ancient Egyptian art (the scholarly study of Egyptian archaeology dates from this time, affording an interesting comparison with the effect upon the arts of the archaeological excavations of Rome in the middle of the eighteenth century); and a new rococo style emerged, in which the enviable grace of grandfather's time is emulated, but which the nineteenth century finds almost impossible to recover.

It is important to see in this eclecticism an expansive freedom, a sense of exuberance in the very fact that everything—from the past and from the present, from remote places on the globe as well as of native growth—was available to be enjoyed. Purity of style and the cultivation of exquisite taste was less important than reveling in the power to command anything. The multiplicity of styles in European art was a vivid symbol of empire and of the way the rest of the world now had to pay tribute to the European conqueror. It reflected the range of tastes held by the new classes of wealth and power. As industrialization spread, the old landed gentry found itself in competition with an aristocracy of the newly rich. They were similar in many ways to the nobility created by the upstart Emperor Napoleon and were as anxious to assert their equality with the old aristocracy as they were to distance themselves from the class from which they had sprung. It is at this point in the changing structure of society, as the status conferred by the hereditary possession of land diminished, and the power of money became dominant, that rich and poor, master and servant, were polarized. The time-honored paternalism of the eighteenth century fell away, and a new class system, which set the worker against the bourgeois/capitalist, increasingly divided society during the nineteenth century.

Such dramatic changes affected the fine arts profoundly. In both France and England, where the literary tradition was both long and strong, there was an obvious split between the new trends in literature and the old. The rhyming iambic pentameter, the "heroic couplet" of the late seventeenth and early eighteenth centuries, typical of the work of Dryden and Pope, continued to thrive in England until the 1830s, while in

France, the classical meter of the Alexandrine, a twelve-syllable line rhyming in couplets, typical of the work of Racine, Corneille, and Molière, survived in all its detail to the same point.[1] The literary form *par excellence* for the new age was the novel. The newly rich reached their position through ambition; they had no history. Their delight in the novel was to see their favorite characters succeeding, for this was their history; the novel offered both escape and fulfillment, the substance of their dreams and the satire of their reality. While epic poetry and drama both instructed and amused in earlier periods, the nineteenth century preferred the novel.

PHILOSOPHIC COMMENTARY ON THE ARTS

Developments in the study of aesthetics as a branch of philosophy during the first twenty years of the nineteenth century were such that the young discipline quickly achieved maturity. The work of Immanuel Kant was central to the thought of this period and influenced the entire century. The two most important philosophers of the time were Georg Wilhelm Friedrich Hegel (1770–1831), a systematic thinker whose work ranged widely in many areas of philosophy and who taught at the University of Berlin (1818–31), and Arthur Schopenhauer (1788–1860), whose most famous work, *Die Welt als Wille und Vorstellung* (The World as Will and Idea), was first produced in 1819 and was to have a profound effect upon Wagner.

We are not concerned, however, with tracing the developments of Romanticism and its aesthetic or exploring the way in which it affected the future, but to point out how, in the early years of the nineteenth century, a persistent and conscious attachment for the classical survived. That the peculiar character of the age consists in looking backward and forward simultaneously was recognized by August Wilhelm von Schlegel, a man remembered not so much for his original writing as for his incomparable translations of Shakespeare. In his *Vorlesungen über dramatische Kunst und Literatur* (1808; Lectures on Dramatic Art and Literature) he writes:

> Religion lies at the root of human existence. If it were possible for man totally to abandon religion, including the innate religion of which he is unaware, everything would become mere surface without any inner substance. . . .The Greek religion of the senses aimed only at the enjoyment of outward and transitory blessings; and immortality seemed a remote, vague shadow, if it was believed in at all, a faded image of this bright and vivid life. The Christian attitude is diametrically opposed to this. Every-

1. Victor Hugo (1802–85) felt it something of an achievement when he could write "J'ai disloqué ce grand niais d'Alexandrin" (I have dislocated this damned idiocy of the Alexandrine) as evidence of the structure's diminishing power.

> thing finite and mortal is lost in contemplation of the eternal; life has become shadow and darkness, and the dawn of our real existence lies beyond the grave. Such a religion is bound to awaken the clearest realization that we seek in vain for happiness here on earth; this is a premonition that slumbers in any sensitive soul: that no external object can ever entirely satisfy the soul, and that every pleasure is but a fleeting illusion. Now suppose the soul . . . sighs with longing for its distant home, how can the character of its songs be other than prevalently melancholy? The poetry of the ancients was, therefore, the poetry of possession, while ours is the poetry of longing; the former is firmly rooted in its present, while the latter hovers between remembrance and anticipation.[2]

This is one of the early nineteenth-century references to Greece and Greek art as synonymous with classical as opposed to modern, a synonym which is carried still further in Schlegel's discussion of form and content.

> Greek art and poetry originate from an unconscious unity of form and subject; in any modern art that has remained true to its own spirit, a fusion is sought of these two natural opposites. The Greeks solved their problem to perfection; but the moderns can only partially realize their endeavors to reach the eternal . . .

Thus, in moving into the nineteenth century, so-called classical ideals of the eighteenth century were retained by the older generation, because such ideals were still capable of creating the "unconscious unity of form and subject" to which Schlegel refers. When members of a younger breed attempted to adapt them, however, the results invariably failed at some level: what should have been vital was cold; what should have been balanced was formalistic. As Schlegel says of the works of these artists, "Because they give the appearance of imperfection, their products are in greater danger of being imperfectly appreciated." This is a critical perception of the highest order.

2. August Wilhelm von Schlegel, cited in Le Huray and Day, *op. cit.*, pp. 269–70. The remaining quotations from Schlegel are to be found on these pages as well.

CHAPTER XXX

The Business and the Institutions of Music

By 1800, the idea that music without words and a voice to sing them was an idle and insignificant amusement—a notion that many would have defended fifty short years earlier—was dead. Whether in the form of chamber music for one or more music lovers in the home, or in the longer and more demanding symphonies and concertos of the concert hall, instrumental music was widely accepted as the ideal form of the ideal art.

While this thought had a novel ring to it in 1800, there was nothing new about the identification of the beautiful with the good, an idea frequently reiterated during the eighteenth century. When these two concepts are joined, instrumental music comes to be seen as a moral force for good. The proliferation of concert-giving institutions and the construction of new concert halls was a natural outgrowth of this notion. The building of the Leipzig Gewandhaus (see p. 347) anticipated later events, for as soon as the Napoleonic Wars were over, European society was able to direct its energies to the pleasures of peace. But whereas the purpose of the eighteenth-century concert had been social and musical—another means of fighting boredom—the concert during the nineteenth century was a much more serious thing, since its function was less to amuse than to elevate its audience. As the century progressed, the respect in which music was held was reflected in the number of concert halls being built—ever vaster and more lavish cathedrals, dedicated to the noble art.

CONCERT ORGANIZATIONS

In addition, there were many more permanent institutions established to organize musical life than had been the case in the eighteenth century, the age of the amateur. In the nineteenth century, an increasing number of professional musicians possessed of a certain standard of technical competence became the foundation of a rich concert life. Indeed,

Imagine this audience at an orchestral concert at The Hague in 1808 in a modern concert hall and the enormous difference between performing conditions then and now will be immediately apparent. (Collection Haags Gemeentemuseum—The Hague)

the ability to attract and keep an audience through artistry, together with financial probity and administrative skills, assured the permanence of many concert-giving societies that arose in the early years of the new century and survive to the present. When we remember that in most cases the musician himself developed the necessary managerial skills, at the same time maintaining professional performance standards, the distance that musician had traveled during the course of fifty or so years is astonishing: from teacher/player/composer to publisher, instrument maker (or both), and finally, concert organizer. This widening of the sphere of activities demonstrates the intelligence and ambition of individual musicians, of course, but it also shows how strong was the need to increase the social status of the musician commensurate to the heightened status of the musical art in relation to the other fine arts. For despite the weakening of private patronage and the development of the market place, despite the success of many free-lance musicians, what Quantz had written over half a century earlier was still true, that "music seldom procures the same advantages as the other arts."

The nineteenth-century concert is fundamentally based upon a conception of the "Classical" exemplified by the instrumental music programmed in the early nineteenth century. The opera theater in 1820 is almost totally committed to the performance of works composed in the previous twenty years, yet the concert society remains fixed on the symphonies of Haydn and Mozart long after the works were composed and their composers were dead. A nucleus of symphonic repertoire was established during the period 1800–20, and the format of the typical program was set.

One of the results of the development of what has been referred to as the Great Repertoire is that it became increasingly difficult for new works to find a place on concert programs and in the public consciousness. Early in the nineteenth century, this situation was only beginning to become apparent, and concert programs were both longer and more varied than they had been at the close of the century. In the early 1800s, the program format was much the same as in Haydn's London concerts, mixing the new symphonic nucleus of the Great Repertoire with ephemera, works from the opera theater, and from chamber music.

Two specific organizations deserve mention. In Vienna the *Gesellschaft der Musikfreunde* (Society of Friends of Music) was founded in 1812, not so much with the objective of sustaining an orchestra but dedicated to the broader service of music. Since it was initially formed under the influence of the Handelian oratorio, there was a strong leaning toward the vocal and the religious in their concerts. And in London the Philharmonic Society was formed in 1813 by a group of professional musicians, who organized themselves not for profit but for the encouragement of orchestral and instrumental music. Their plan called for a society of thirty members who would each contribute three guineas (approximately $5 in modern terms, but of course worth far more then). Seven directors were appointed to look after the management of the concerts. Another category of associate membership was available upon payment of two guineas ($3.50) and no limit was set upon the numbers in this category. Because of the interest of most of the important musicians of London and because of the importance of the project, the members of the orchestra gave their services without payment and the concert series was successful in all ways. In the first season (1813) three symphonies by Mozart and four by Haydn were performed, as well as two by Beethoven, illustrating the firm establishment of the "Classical" nucleus of the repertoire.

The violinist and composer Ludwig Spohr was engaged to perform and direct the season of 1820, during which he initiated the use of the baton, instead of conducting, as was usual, either from the leader's desk of the first violins or from the keyboard. In his *Autobiography* Spohr also reports that tickets to the concerts of the Philharmonic Society were much sought after, and as many as 700 people were turned away from each concert.

In Paris, concert life became active again during Napoleon's reign and the Bourbon restoration, and there was an attempt to revive some of the concert societies that had flourished before the Revolution. None of these was completely successful, however, and it was not until the establishment of the *Société des Concerts du Conservatoire* in 1828, under the direction of the influential violinist and conductor François-Antoine Habeneck (1781–1849), that Paris could boast an organized concert life comparable to that of Vienna or London. The orchestra of these concerts comprised approximately eighty players, and from the beginning, in line with Habeneck's tastes, the works of Beethoven were at the heart of their repertoire.

MUSIC PUBLISHING

In the world of music publishing, Franz Hoffmeister, who had started his business in Vienna in 1785, set up an establishment in Leipzig in 1800 in partnership with Ambrosius Kühnel. It was called the Bureau de Musique, and they printed and sold music as well as musical instruments. In 1805 Hoffmeister withdrew from the Leipzig business and returned to Vienna, leaving Kühnel in sole possession. Upon Kühnel's death in 1813 the business was sold to C. F. Peters, a Leipzig bookseller, under whose name the firm became one of the two or three most important of the nineteenth and twentieth centuries.

There were several remarkable developments in music publishing during this period. One consequence of the backward-looking, "classical" ideal was the interest in complete-works editions of important composers, alive or dead. Hoffmeister und Kühnel in Leipzig had great plans along these lines and brought out editions of J. S. Bach's keyboard works and Mozart's string quartets and quintets. Breitkopf und Härtel established a tradition with the publication, during these years, of so-called *oeuvres complettes* of Mozart, Haydn, Cramer, Dussek, and Clementi—a tradition which made them arguably the most important publishers of the second half of the nineteenth century. Pleyel, who had established an important publishing business in Paris in 1795, issued, with the composer's approval, a complete edition of Haydn's string quartets in 1801, which subsequently had to be enlarged to include those works produced after the edition went to print. Pleyel also produced the first miniature scores, beginning in 1802 with the scores of four Haydn symphonies and continuing with chamber works by Haydn, Beethoven, Hummel, and George Onslow (1784–1853). In 1807, Pleyel, like Clementi in London, began to manufacture pianos. Characteristic of the growing trend to look to a former age for artistic ideals, the relatively small publishing house of Janet et Cotelle (Paris) printed a fine edition of the complete string quintets by Luigi Boccherini in 1814, at a time when one would expect the demand for them to have fallen away entirely.

The rapid growth in the circulation of printed rather than handwritten music led to a broadening in the range of available quality. The standard of engraving declined somewhat from the exemplary publications of twenty years earlier, and pages are often cramped as works become larger. It must be noted, however, that publishers and engravers of this period were still prepared to leave whole pages blank in order to avoid presenting a string- quartet player with an awkward page turn—a practice abandoned later in the century when publishers began to lay out the music much more generously. The most noticeable decline is in the quality of the paper used. During the last years of the eighteenth century, Parisian publishers printed on ever thinner stock. In the first years of the nineteenth century this practice spread across Europe and the fine, strong, white papers of 1775 were all too often replaced by thin, greenish, and grainy papers, the quality of which is frequently matched by the engraving and the title pages.

MUSICAL WRITINGS

The early years of the nineteenth century produced two important biographies which illustrate the way Protestantism and Catholicism had remained issues simmering beneath the surface of the previous century. Johann Nikolaus Forkel's *Über J. S. Bachs Leben, Kunst und Kunstwerke* (On J. S. Bach's Life, Art, and Music) published in 1802 set Bach up as the champion of Protestant church music. Even more prominent is Forkel's notion of Bach as a German nationalist composer. The following, taken from the preface to this volume, illustrates the point, sounding more like Wagner's mouthpiece, Hans Sachs, in 1868 than a humble scholar in 1802:

> For Bach's works are a priceless national patrimony; no other nation possesses a treasure comparable to it. . . . All who hold Germany dear are bound in honor to promote the undertaking [the publication of the complete works] to the utmost of their power. . . . For, let me repeat, not merely the interest of music but our national honor are concerned to rescue from oblivion the memory of one of Germany's greatest sons.

Forkel's work played an important part in the movement to revive Bach's works that was gathering momentum around the turn of the century. It manifested itself in publications of his music, and culminated in Mendelssohn's performance in 1829 of the *St. Matthew Passion*.

The other important biography was the *Memorie storico-critiche della vita e dell'opere di Giovanni Pierluigi da Palestrina* of Giuseppe Baini, published in 1828. This work did much to make that composer the knight in shining armor defending the music of the Church of Rome.

Both these books were of the greatest significance, not simply because they focused public awareness on the composers but also because they helped to crystallize two ideal styles of church music, as well as ideal performance practices. On one side is the a cappella style of Palestrina, with its ethereal sonorities, and on the other the affective harmonizations of Bach's metrical chorale tunes—the ideal of the heavenly versus the ideal of the human.

THE PARIS CONSERVATORY

Despite its changing fortunes around the time of Napoleon's defeat and the Bourbon restoration (1814–15), the Conservatoire de Musique of Paris continued to be in the vanguard of educational institutions. From our point of view its importance is based upon two considerations: it gave many of the leading musicians of Paris a new respectability, transforming them from simple instrumentalists or composers to teachers of a noble art, with the authority of the state behind them. The staff list of that institution, both at this time and throughout the century, contains the name of virtually every musician of note in the whole country. The second point is that the curriculum of the institution was drawn up on the theory that the art itself implies certain ideals and standards which must be propagated, and that the student has to be initiated, as it were, into the grand tradition. That tradition was provided not by the immediate present nor by the remote past, but by the immediate past—the Golden Age of music, the "Classical" age.

CHAPTER XXXI

Chamber Music in the Concert Hall

Entirely characteristic of the nineteenth century is the paradox that while the subject matter of the arts becomes more personal, intimate, unique, and "private," its means and its function become more public. Thus increasingly music tends to be evaluated according to its usefulness in performance and the whole course of the art is modified, on the one hand, by the vogue for virtuosity, and on the other by the development of the concert, both of orchestral music and of music written for chamber combinations.

THE TRANSFORMATION OF THE SONATA

Obviously, much of what has been satisfactorily designated as "private" music up to now ceases to be that with the passage of time. The most important casualty of this fashion was the solo keyboard sonata, which, during most of the eighteenth century, had been an important medium for the greatest composers and the most accessible for hosts of lesser composers, professional and amateur. Just as J. S. Bach's fine, contrapuntal art was produced at a time when the world was no longer particularly interested in it, so Beethoven continued to produce piano sonatas until 1822 while the fashion gradually shifted its emphasis. For during the first quarter of the nineteenth century, most composers tended to neglect the sonata more and more in favor of shorter pieces using simpler forms, fantasias of various kinds, and variations.

Composer/pianists active during the eighteenth century, like J. B. Cramer and Kozeluch, tended to continue along their own well-trodden paths. But two of the most important, Clementi and Dussek, broke their patterns of production in interesting ways. Dussek composed seven sonatas during 1800 and 1801 (Op. 43 in A; Op. 44 in E♭; Op. 45 in B♭, G, and D; and Op. 47 in D and G). Then, for five or six years he did not publish any solo piano sonatas; finally, in 1806–7, he composed the *Elégie Harmonique,* a Sonata in F♯ minor, Op. 61, commemorating the death in battle of his patron, Prince Louis Ferdinand. The large Sonata in A♭, subtitled *Le Retour à Paris* (The return to Paris), Op. 70, was also composed in 1807, again partially as a result of an external stimulus: Joseph Wölfl had written a virtuosic sonata to which he had given the title *Non Plus Ultra,*loosely translated as "you cannot go any further," in effect boasting that this work embodied the height of piano technique, and so Dussek wrote at the top of his own work *Plus Ultra*—this is further! Only three more sonatas follow, all from 1811 and 1812 (Op. 69/3 in D; Op. 75 in E♭; and Op. 77 in F minor).

Clementi, who, like Dussek, had produced a steady stream of sonatas, solo and accompanied, until 1800, suddenly changed his course. In 1802 he published three important sonatas, in G, B minor, and D; then in 1804 another in E♭. Thereafter, although he lived until 1832, he composed only four more sonatas: Op. 44 in B♭ (1820) and Op. 50 in A, D minor, and G minor (1821). The slow movement of the first of the sonatas Op. 50 (*ACM* 74) is a simple, ternary structure, but its plangent dissonance, its insistent polyphony at its highest points of emotional intensity, and its extensive use of canon make it unique.

Johann Nepomuk Hummel, John Field, Friedrich Kalkbrenner (1785–1849), and Carl Maria von Weber (1786–1826) set the standard for all pianists of the generation after Clementi, Mozart, Dussek, and Beethoven. These men, who were starting their careers as composers around 1800, found a much wider market for their smaller compositions, such as variations and sets of dances, and did not find the sonata as congenial as their elders had, even though their early works were strongly conditioned by the style of the eighteenth century. This is demonstrated very simply by the numbers of such works that they wrote: Hummel, probably 6; Field, 4; Kalkbrenner, 13; and Weber, 4. These figures are a far cry from Clementi's 63, Dussek's 27, Kozeluch's 36, not to mention Haydn's 51, Mozart's 20, or Beethoven's 32. Of the younger generation only Franz Schubert (1797–1828), who made no claim to be a virtuoso pianist, wrote a relatively large number of solo sonatas and few shorter pieces, apart from many dances.

The lack of interest in composing sonatas can be attributed to changing fashion, and, at least in part, to the sense that while this form had provided a time-honored and traditional structure for the revered composers of the past, it had nevertheless become confining, and the temper of the times was against such things. It is conceivable that Schubert's exceptionally large production of sonatas, finished and unfinished, the majority of which date from 1815–19, spring from a consciousness of the second of these factors. For Schubert, the Beethovenian sonata was the challenge by which he could measure his ability to follow in his idol's footsteps; at the same time, he had to establish his own identity by experimenting with structure and tonality, as well as with thematic material.

It is interesting to observe the legacy of the eighteenth century that persists in the works of these younger masters. Nine times out of ten the eighteenth-century sonata will open with a characteristic gesture, most frequently consisting of fast, energetic movement, either exuberant or resolute:

Example XXXI–1: Characteristic gestures of the 18th-century sonata.

a. W. A. MOZART, Sonata, K. 576, I

b. L. BEETHOVEN, Sonata Op. 13 (*Pathétique*), I

Those that open with a strongly profiled, individualistic melody are in the minority:

Example XXXI–2: Melodic openings.

a. W. A. MOZART, Sonata, K. 332, I

b. L. BEETHOVEN, Sonata Op. 78, I

The sonatas of the younger generation initially preserved this classical gesture (Example XXXI–3), but it was quickly transformed into

Example XXXI–3: J. N. HUMMEL, Sonata Op. 13, I

something new. The opening of Weber's first sonata (1812; Example XXXI–4) contains all the rhythmic piquancy of the Classical opening, and the necessary arresting quality is heightened by the diminished har-

Example XXXI–4: C. M. WEBER, Sonata Op. 24, I

mony, by the harmonic deception (failure to establish the tonality), and by the unusual placing of the melodic action in the bass. While this appears novel in 1812, to us it looks like a complete reawakening of the spirit of *Empfindsamkeit* that we saw in the work of Jiri Benda and Emanuel Bach (see p. 58ff).

In Weber's next Sonata, Op.39 in A♭ of 1816, the idea of an arresting and characteristic fanfare opening is preserved but changed almost beyond recognition. Here the slow harmonic rhythm of Beethoven's *Pastoral* Symphony is extended as, over an arhythmic tremolo, a distant horn call evokes a quietude in which musical time and motion seem to stand still. This effect is achieved by the internal contradictions among the elements present. A fanfare as used in the hunt, in battle, or ceremonial is loud and exciting; Weber's is quiet, set against a continuum of sound, a tremolo with no beat to mark the passage of time. Using what appear to be the ordinary, "Classical" means of an opening fanfare, Weber makes music that is atmospheric rather than immediate, contemplative rather than energetic, and spatial rather than temporal. The eighteenth-century *topos,* the rhetorical commonplace, the traditional formulaic motive has become the nineteenth-century symbol, rich through its significance beyond the bounds of music.

Example XXXI–5: C. M. WEBER, Sonata Op. 39, I

The tendencies, already noted, to melodicize the main tonal areas of the sonata and to initiate a succession of textural changes oscillating quite violently between melody and passagework continue to develop. No composer who had heard a Beethoven composition could resist the notion of a prevalent rhythmic motive, but when this idea was combined with melody the effect was often predictable and tame. (See Example XXXI–6.)

Much of the handling of transitional passages during this period is completely orthodox and in accord with late eighteenth-century "Classical" practice: the opening material is repeated and developed through a modulation to the area of the second group. There is also much that is experimental and not of concern to us here except to note that the experiments themselves are evidence of a weighty tradition of formal procedure, which the committed artist must make his own, one way or

Example XXXI–6: C. M. WEBER, Sonata Op.24, I

another. The need to establish a tonal framework for the sonata is evident, and composers like Dussek, Clementi, and Hummel accepted the traditional naturally and unselfconsciously. Weber and Schubert, however, follow procedures which might be called transitional, and which create, more often than not, unique structures.

The opening of the second group is often treated as a major point of arrival and, as we have seen, earlier composers wrote self-contained melodies and set them off with strong cadences, rests, and every device of emphasis. Now this place in the structure becomes fraught with danger of a kind that has never before existed. If the inspiration fails and if the melody is extended too far, this moment in the exposition can sag disastrously. Hummel, who is particularly fond of this area in the sonata, provides a good example of a flaccid and uninteresting melody above an arpeggiated left hand in his otherwise fine Sonata Op.13.

The close of the exposition is still generally marked by a return to some material related to the opening of the sonata, by a strong cadence, and by a repeat sign—a nod in the direction of classical practice.

The middle section, or development, tends to be retained and it may occupy a sizable portion of the whole. Thus Weber's second sonata has an exposition of 69 bars, a development of 66, and a recapitulation of 46. But in a sonata where the exposition moves over a wide range of tonalities, the old distinction between the tonally stable exposition and the tonally fluctuating development tends to diminish, its place being taken by the reiteration of characteristic melodic material from the exposition repeated sequentially. The recapitulatory function of the sonata is preserved most carefully, but composers felt freer to modify the recapitulating material in ways which might be construed as "significant" to the listener.

Franz Schubert has for many years been recognized as the greatest of those composers who straddled the changing aesthetic from the eighteenth to the nineteenth centuries—the "Romantic-Classic" of Einstein's designation.

Schubert is well known for his experimentation within the sonata structure, although the period of his experimentation occurred between the time he was eighteen and twenty-three. It is obvious that for him nothing is sacred in the late eighteenth-century tonal structure. The B-major Sonata, D.575, of 1817 opens with a wildly modulating and asymmetrical subject in the tonic, B; the next obvious melodic area is in E, not the expected F♯, and it is left to the closing area to establish that orthodox goal. The development area again modulates with extremely unusual sequential sonorities from B minor, through D, F, A♭, E♭ back to B major. The recapitulation is in the subdominant, a not uncommon device in Schubert, and everything else follows symmetrically from this point (second melodic area in ♭VII [A major] and close in B). Schubert created a tonally devious exposition that is literally repeated in recapitulation so often that critics used to call him lazy. We are in a better position to see that the most natural and the most thoughtful of composers, looking back on the high noon of the eighteenth-century sonata from the gathering twilight, sees it as a tonal form in which a sequence of textures and tonalities repeat themselves after a digression. For Schubert it is not as important to reestablish the primacy of a simple tonality as it is to recapitulate an interesting pattern whose defining features are a rhythmical melody followed by two (often related) lyrical melodies, the establishment of a tonic, and a conclusion at the end of the exposition marked by the repeat sign and a cadence, most commonly in the orthodox key relationship (V with a major tonic and III with a minor tonic). From this point in the structure the only effective generalization has already been made, i.e., literal recapitulation and tonic conclusion. Schubert's idea of the sonata as a repeating form in three parts has an honorable Viennese ancestry in the works of Mozart as well as minor masters. The origins of his tonal expansions can be traced back through Beethoven to Haydn.

Because of its roots in a formalistic tradition, the sonata for solo piano rapidly became a form more honored than practiced. For Felix Mendelssohn (1809–47) who wrote three, all juvenile works published posthumously, the sonata was a part of the imitative stage of his learning, and one can clearly see him self-consciously using Haydn's monothematic structure, Mozart's device of false recapitulation followed by startling development, and Beethoven's exploration of mediant and submediant relationships. After his apprenticeship years, however, he does not visit the piano sonata again. Both Frédéric Chopin (1810–49) and Robert Schumann (1810–56), like Schubert, treat the sonata more personally: Chopin tends toward the Hummel/Dussek presentation of spreading melody interspersed with passagework, while Schumann explores the sonata as fantasia. All four composers frequently use *ostinato* rhythmic figures in a way that is quite foreign to earlier composers. As aptly as any single form, the medium of the solo piano sonata in the nineteenth century illustrates the decline and fall of an eighteenth-century ideal. The frequent use of *ostinato* rhythmic figures by all of these composers affords proof that the ideal of rapid change and constant variety was subverted and replaced by obsessive monotony and single-minded, mechanical unity.

THE CHANGING ROLE OF THE PIANO

The piano's role in partnership with other instruments changed more rapidly now than in any previous period. The *continuo* function is very largely lost from sight, and its place is taken by an accompanying role more subordinate than the *continuo* had been. For increasingly, extemporization and improvisation in the art of accompaniment became less important as the virtuoso and the would-be virtuoso required a halo of harmony, discreetly sanctifying their superiority. The oom-pah or oom-pah-pah rhythm of the subordinate accompanying parts dominated whole continents of nineteenth-century music and appeared surprisingly early—in the work of Schubert, for example.

When not completely subordinated, the piano became part of many instrumental combinations unheard of in eighteenth-century "private" music. At the same time, the technical demands now being made on the pianist removed much of the repertoire from the amateur's grasp, despite advances in the general level of technical accomplishment. When music seems to exist more to be listened to than to be performed, then the boundary between private and public music becomes blurred and insignificant. Four-hand piano music was very popular, and many new and original works were composed. Sonatas for four hands, however, suffered a decline similar to those for solo piano, and while Dussek produced several during the early 1800s, of the younger generation only Hummel and Kalkbrenner wrote sonatas. The greatest and most prolific of all composers for piano duet, Schubert, typifies in his produc-

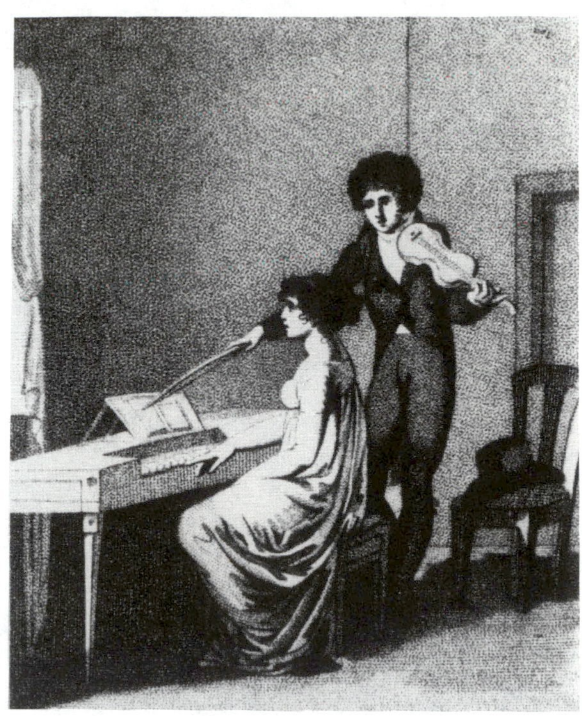

The Music Hour, 1801. In the early nineteenth century, music making is still an opportunity to demonstrate the equal participation of women and men.

tion the popular mixture of forms. In addition to two sonatas (in B♭, 1823, and in C, 1824) his extensive production of close to forty works includes dances, marches, variations, overtures, fantasies, and even arrangements of some of his own orchestral compositions. From this time and throughout the nineteenth century, the piano duet is more and more closely identified with arrangements of all kinds that are made for it. Not only were orchestral pieces, chamber works, and operas fair game for the arranger, but works for solo piano were arranged for four hands and thus brought within the reach of less accomplished players. The market was enormous and publishers took advantage of it.

The sonata for keyboard with optional accompaniment ceased to exist once the fashion for dialogued works grew strong. From force of habit, however, the nomenclature persisted long after the fact, and Beethoven's three Sonatas for Piano and Violin, Op. 30, for example, were still styled on the title page of the first edition of 1803, "TROIS SONATES / pour le Pianoforte / avec l'Accompagnement d'un Violon," etc., although the violin is clearly an equal partner to the piano. But perhaps a little of the solo keyboard attitude is retained in those chamber works—sonatas, trios, and quartets—where the keyboard demonstrably receives the lion's share of the attention.

The dialogued sonata for piano and another solo instrument continued to develop, and the number of instruments considered suitable partners for the piano increased. These sonatas, conforming to the common tendency of the time, bridged the worlds of private and public music. We have seen that Mozart wrote his B♭ Sonata, K. 454, for a famous violinist and first performed it in concert with only the violin part written out. A concert sonata, such as this, was distinguished from the chamber sonata not in number of movements, nor in the manner in which material was exchanged between the instruments, but in the degree of virtuosity required by the work. This distinction persisted well into the nineteenth century, the most famous example, perhaps, being Beethoven's *Kreutzer* Sonata in A, Op. 47 (see p. 595). Another curious example of this trend is found among the works of Schubert: three unassuming, four-movement compositions for violin and piano that he wrote in March and April of 1816 are each entitled by him *Sonate pour Pianoforte et Violon*. A year and a half later he wrote a virtuosic Sonata in A for Violin and Piano. The publishers distinguished between these two kinds of works by calling the first three *Sonatines,* despite Schubert's own title, and the last one *Sonate,* yet the only difference between them is in the technical demands of the latter work. Public performance is also at the heart of such unusual combinations as Beethoven's Sonata for Horn and Piano, Op. 17 and the Sonatas for Violin and Harp that Louis Spohr wrote for his wife and himself to use on their concert tours during the early years of the new century.

The development of the piano trio in the early nineteenth century perhaps reveals the greatest difference in the actual disposition of the instruments in the score, and in the resultant sonority of the combination. For whereas formerly the solo violin and the cello functioning as

Example XXXI–7: F. SCHUBERT, Trio Op. 99 (D.898), II– strings versus piano

bass could not easily counterbalance the fortepiano, now such a balance became possible, given the rapidly developing strength of the more modern piano, and the focus of attention is often directed away from the piano onto the paired strings (Example XXXI–7). The "emancipation" of the cello is, of course, the most important factor, making this the most enduring and effective, almost archetypical, combination of the age. From Schubert to Arensky, the piano trio's sonorities resounded through those homes in which music lovers were sufficiently schooled to tackle the technical problems posed by most of the works. At the same time the piano trio was a popular combination for arrangements of orchestral compositions.

THE PIANO IN LARGE CHAMBER ENSEMBLES

Early in the nineteenth century, composers began using the piano in larger combinations, a practice that increased with the passage of time. Fine piano quartets are contributed to the literature by Beethoven's pupil and imitator Ferdinand Ries and by Prince Louis Ferdinand, Frederick the Great's nephew. The quintet for piano and strings, a still more recent invention than the piano quartet, was scored for normal string quartet and piano, and for violin, viola, cello, double bass, and piano. Louis Ferdinand composed a good early example of the first type, while Hummel and Schubert produced the most famous examples of the sec-

Nicholas Aertmann: *A Late-18th-Century House Concert.* The widespread practice of making chamber music in the home led to the development of more varied and larger ensembles than had been common earlier. (Rijksmuseumn, Amsterdam)

ond. The quintet for piano and winds, created by Mozart (K.452) and imitated by Beethoven (Op. 16), was emulated by Franz Danzi (1763–1826) and Louis Spohr (Op. 52), while still larger combinations, for piano and strings or for piano and mixed instruments (septets and octets) were occasionally composed. The existence of this repertoire is a clear demonstration of how widespread the practice of making music in the home had become, and how many amateurs were capable of executing a difficult and demanding part in an ensemble. Clearly in some of this music the boundary line between chamber and orchestral music is obscured. However, the dialogued style, which derives its character from the reiteration and interchange of small motives, informed so much of the chamber music of the time that the distinction between the two remained clear. For example, the Nonet, Op. 31 and the Octet, Op. 32 of Spohr both depend upon such a dialogued texture, and a great part of the reward they give the players lies in the motivic interchange—a reward neither necessary nor expected in the professionally executed symphony.

STRING MUSIC AND VIRTUOSITY

Private music without piano tended to be more conservative in form although experimental in sonority. The increased emphasis on virtuosity in the concluding years of the eighteenth century manifested itself in the proliferation of works for solo violin, virtually abandoned since the days of Johann Stamitz. Students in mid-century had used sonatas (often called "Lessons" in England) as study material. Now, a stream of pedagogical compositions with some pretensions to musical value despite their technical orientation began appearing during the last twenty years of the century with the publication of *Etudes pour le Violin, formant 36 Caprices* Op. 3 (date unknown but possibly as early as *c.*1785) by Federigo Fiorillo (1752–1823?). This was followed in 1807 by the *42 Etudes* of Rodolphe Kreutzer and the *24 Caprices* of Pierre Rode in 1815. Each of these works represents an alliance of technique and expressivity of such potency that all three are basic to the modern violinist's development.

The string duet persists in unabated popularity. Many of the composers writing in this medium after 1800 were of the older generation and included Viotti, Kreutzer, Rode, and Baillot. In Germany Andreas Romberg, Franz Krommer, and Peter Haensel (1770–1831) all continued to use the familiar structures, while enlarging the *concertante* element of the duets. Indeed, the term *concertante* was clearly a strong selling point for the public and was widely used by publishers. Alessandro Rolla (1757–1841) was perhaps the most gifted of all Italian composers of instrumental chamber music in the first quarter of the nineteenth century, although we should mention that Gaetano Donizetti (1797–1848) and Gioachino Rossini (1792–1868) both wrote a fair quantity of instrumental music. Rolla left an impressive body of duet literature for two violins, violin and viola, two violas, and violin and cello that had great charm, yet posed considerable technical demands.

The most important compositions for string duo were those of Louis Spohr, whose published output represents all that was technically demanding and sonorously rewarding in his day. These multi-movement works generally display a clear-cut differentiation between the melodic and the virtuosic, and Spohr's use of sonata or rondo structure in the outer movements and ternary structure for the inner movements tends to be unadventurous and tradition-bound. But their sonority is completely novel because of Spohr's ingenious use of figuration, and particularly when he writes double-stops for both violins at once. It is as if the two violins were attempting to transcend their limitations and to emulate a string quartet. Spohr, largely self-taught, seemed to be anticipating the increased emphasis on polyphony, so characteristic of later nineteenth-century music. He acknowledged Mozart as his lifelong model and would probably have liked to trace the chromatic movement of his voice-leading to that master, but quite as potent an influence on his harmonic thought is the chromaticism of Haydn, whose turns of phrase often peep out from beneath Spohr's heavier draperies.

It is surprising that interest in the string trio, either for two violins and cello or for violin, viola, and cello, does not correspond to that shown in the string duet. Despite such works by Haensel, Viotti and Rolla, among others, nothing was produced that compared with the trios of Mozart and Beethoven.

During the whole of the nineteenth century the string quartet continued to flourish, and almost all composers, from the most talented to the least skillful, composed for that combination. Throughout the history of the quartet, the first violin had been treated as the first among equals and allotted the lion's share of musical material; the compositional principles of the dialogued quartet and the *concertante* quartet can both be seen as necessary measures to prevent undue dominance of the group by the first violin. During the last years of the eighteenth century and the first third of the nineteenth, however, the quartet's scope was broadened and it was found useful by traveling virtuosos in their concerts; called *quatuor brillant,* or "solo" quartet, this type of composition carried the domination by the first violin to its most extreme conclusion. In the *quatuor brillant* the business of the lower parts is solely for accompaniment without the expectation of any of the musical rewards of normal chamber music. From the point of view of sociological function this curious situation makes perfect sense, for it enabled the traveling virtuoso to pick up a scratch ensemble of violin, viola, and cello, professional or amateur, in almost any small town and perform concerto-like compositions with the harmonic and rhythmic backing of the group, and with almost no rehearsal. The quality of the players hardly mattered as long as they could count.

This kind of composition proved to be very popular at this time when audiences liked their music brilliant in effect and undemanding in texture. Indeed, there are documentary records showing that some audiences, even those with pretensions to musical culture, found the early quartets of Beethoven so difficult as to be incomprehensible. The best examples of the *quatuor brillant* are by Spohr; in his output of thirty quartets he carefully distinguishes between them, both in their title and by heightening the resemblance between the solo quartet and the concerto, the "brilliant" quartets, like concertos, consisting of three movements, while the chamber quartets have four. Spohr took the very popular works of Pierre Rode as his model for this type of quartet.

Many composers of the time sought to straddle the fence by writing quartets with brilliant first-violin passages as well as motivic dialogue among all the parts. Chief among the writers of this kind of quartet is Andreas Romberg (1767–1821), who produced twenty-eight. These mostly depend for their structure upon the succession of *cantabile* melody and virtuosity, so popular in the 1790s, although many display considerable originality and craftsmanship.

Perhaps the most popular composers of quartets published during this period, however, were Franz Krommer and Peter Haensel, whose works dominated Vienna's chamber music life. At a time when Spohr's works were criticized for the difficulty of their first-violin parts, when Pleyel's were becoming *passé,* and Beethoven's were not yet accepted, the quartets of Haydn and Mozart, together with those of Krommer and Haensel, represented the solid tradition of familiar, dependable music. Krommer was one of the great stream of Czech musicians who left their homeland to make a living in various musical centers of Europe. Self-taught in theory and having had formal instruction in violin and organ from an uncle, Krommer held a series of appointments before gravitating to Vienna and settling there, in 1795, to teach violin and composition. In 1810 he became director of ballet music to the court theater and upon the death of Kozeluch (1818) he was named chamber composer to the court. The many honors he received from different countries attest to his widespread popularity. His first quartets appeared in 1793, and during the next sixteen years he published a total of 73 quartets. Noticeable in the later quartets, written in the early nineteenth century, is the increased and perhaps self-conscious elaboration in the parts. Slow movements in particular appear to have been affected by the highly figured slow movements of Beethoven's Op. 18 quartets.

Peter Haensel was born in North Germany and was educated in Warsaw. He attained his first post as violinist at the age of seventeen and came to Vienna in 1791, at the age of twenty-one. In 1792 he began studying with Haydn. His first compositions, a set of three quartets, appeared in 1798 and his subsequent works were taken up by a number of publishers. A grateful vein of melody and effective part-writing were his strengths, but because of his reliance upon the *concertante* brilliance, and the quiet, unadventurous character of his music, his popularity did not survive him. In his work one can see the fruit of Haydn's teaching passed through the sieve of early nineteenth-century ideals.

LARGE CHAMBER ENSEMBLES

Because of the enormous popular demand for chamber music, the publication lists of the period are filled with the names of forgotten composers who wrote quartets, quintets, and works for larger combinations. Many of them were pupils of Haydn, and those who were not certainly admired Haydn's manner and imitated it. Perhaps most remarkable are the compositions for large chamber ensembles, often for mixed winds and strings, but also for strings alone. Thus Mendelssohn's Octet, Op. 20 (1825) for 4 violins, 2 violas, and 2 cellos, and Spohr's four Double Quartets Op. 65 (1823), Op. 77 (1827), Op. 87 (1828), and Op. 136 (1849) preserve the string chamber ideal, while Beethoven's Septet, Op. 20 (1799) for clarinet, horn, bassoon, violin, viola, cello, and double bass, Schubert's Octet, D.803 (1824) for clarinet, horn, bassoon, two violins, viola, cello, and double bass, and Spohr's Nonet, Op. 31 (1813) for flute, oboe, clarinet, horn, bassoon, violin, viola, cello, and double bass, mix strings and winds. The Octet of Spohr is worth noting because, like Mozart's Quintet K.407 for horn and strings, it has an unusual instrumentation, consisting of clarinet, two horns, violin, two violas, cello, and double bass.

Clearly, the period around 1800 is one in which the boundaries between serenade, symphony, and string quartet were crossed so often that lines of demarcation were effectively obliterated. Increasingly, the composer conceived music that would make an effect when performed before an ever more numerous audience seated in ever larger halls. Thus, although the term "chamber music" has persisted and has an undeniable usefulness, the notion of separating music according to public or private function, which has so frequently been used in this volume, becomes inappropriate and ceases to afford any illumination quite early in the nineteenth century.

CHAPTER XXXII

The Loss of Intimacy: Performance Triumphant

HAYDN'S LEGACY

The inhibiting effect of Haydn's immense popularity in the concert hall was felt and expressed in the very earliest years of the nineteenth century, as composers found themselves overwhelmed by the power of his symphonies and unable to escape from the weighty tradition they had established. Such an effect is not uncommon and is not restricted to music and musicians. Late in life, Goethe confessed to his amanuensis that he would never have been able to write as he had done, had he, as a young man, known the works of Shakespeare.

It was Haydn who perpetuated the Parisian preference for German symphonic music. As prominent a composer as Etienne Méhul admitted, when he set out to write symphonies, that he was fully aware of the risk he was running, but that he would write more of them "to accustom the public little by little to think that a Frenchman may follow Haydn and Mozart at a distance."[1] Those words, written in 1809, do not acknowledge the name of Beethoven, who was rapidly becoming the most powerful and inhibiting presence in the German symphonic tradition. In 1750, only an Italian could write opera; now, in 1810, only a German could write a symphony.

Indeed, the symphonists of the early years of the nineteenth century, like Pleyel and Kozeluch in the last years of the previous one, had the power to imitate but not to originate. In an effort to escape stagnation and in the fear of merely doing the same thing over and over again, a variety of devices were tried; these may appear either superficial or mechanical but they testify to the increasing regard for the overt unity of the symphonic form. Thus in Méhul's Symphony No. 4 (1809–10) the harmony and melody of the first four measures of the slow intro-

1. *The Symphony 1720–1840* (New York, 1986), Series D, Vol. VIII, David Charlton, ed., pp. xii-xiii.

duction to the first movement appear twice, embedded in the last movement. Something similar was used by Schubert in his First Symphony, written in 1813, in which he obliges his interpreter to set up a tempo relationship between the Introduction and the following *Allegro*—something that may have been desired before, but was rarely put into practice by the great composers of an earlier time.

If we consider Beethoven *sui generis,* there can be no doubt that Schubert was the most significant symphonist of the early nineteenth century. His first six symphonies, which follow more or less Classical models, may be outlined as follows:

No.	Key	Date	Cat. No.	Movements and their Keys			
				I	II	III	IV
1	D	1813	D. 82	D	G	D	D
2	B♭	1814/15	D. 125	B♭	E♭	C min	B♭
3	D	1815	D. 200	D	G	D	D
4	C min	1816	D. 417	C min	A♭	E♭	C min
5	B♭	1816	D. 485	B♭	E♭	G min	B♭
6	C	1817/18	D. 589	C	F	C	C

His later symphonies depart from traditional conventions to the point where one may observe, in the B-minor Symphony (*Unfinished*) D.759, a different structural principle underlying the first movement. It is incontrovertible that this composer was a genius as described by Kant, a creator of originals which may serve as models for others, and quite beyond the range of his contemporaries.

Schubert wrote his first symphony at the age of sixteen, by which time he may well have heard at least the first six of Beethoven's symphonies. Despite his ardent admiration of the older man, in none of his symphonies can he reasonably be accused of imitating him. Rather, the early works seem to look back to the Haydn of the *London* symphonies and to Mozart's of 1788, for Schubert would have had far more opportunity to hear and play their works than those of Beethoven. In particular, Haydn's influence seems to breathe through the slow movements of these early Schubert symphonies, as melodic structures of a folksong type follow similar modulatory procedures and lend themselves to similar treatment. Schubert's melodies, like those of both Haydn and Beethoven, frequently involve the use of short motives, but their *ostinato*-like repetition creates an effect outside the normal aesthetic goals of his predecessors.

More significant is the evidence that Schubert, while prepared to express his admiration for his masters in the time-honored way, i.e., by imitating them, was determined to give his originality free rein. The closest model for the procedure in the First Symphony is in the first movement of Mozart's Serenade K.320, which Schubert may have known since it was first printed in 1792. In this work, a short introduction of six measures *Adagio maestoso* reappears at the point of recapitulation as twelve measures of *Allegro con spirito,* but with a subtle and tricky difference between the two versions. Although a Serenade, this work circulated quite widely, with the number of its movements reduced to symphony proportions. An actual symphonic precedent may be found in Haydn's No. 103, where the Introduction is brought back at the end of the recapitulation. Even closer models exist in the formal procedures of some of Beethoven's piano sonatas. Schubert's practice of unifying a work by allowing introductory material to permeate the body of the work has ample precedent in Haydn, but the younger composer carries the process forward in a manner that looks to Liszt and Wagner, not only in his *Wanderer Fantasy* but in his last symphony. There is nothing in Beethoven or Haydn to compare with Schubert's obsessive use of a rhythmic motive throughout a movement, which appears in full bloom in the finale of his Second Symphony. Here, the rhythmic motive of a quarter note and two eighth notes persists for over 700 measures, and when it is not actually present, its obvious derivatives are. This characteristic practice is continued throughout Schubert's life and is an aspect of his musical personality that he does not inherit either from the eighteenth century or from Beethoven.

With a bow to tradition, Schubert allows one movement of a symphony (usually the slow one) to be set in a related key, and does so in his first, third, and sixth symphonies. As can be seen from the outline above, the slow movement of the Second Symphony is in the subdominant, E♭, and the third movement in the supertonic key of C minor. The Fifth Symphony likewise has a slow movement in the subdominant, but its third movement is in the submediant, G minor. In the Fourth Symphony too, Schubert attempts to broaden the traditional tonal limits—indeed, no composer did more to modify sonata form by enlarging its tonal sphere. The same inner expressive need that makes the Beethoven symphony a cogent and compelling experience forces Schubert to experiment with modulation, with tonality, and with dissonance, as well as form. The result is a series of symphonies that all contain the seeds of greatness.

Jan Václav Voříšek (1791–1825) was a Bohemian who, after working with Václav Tomášek (1774–1850), went to Vienna in 1813, at the age of twenty-two, to study the piano with Hummel. He wrote only one symphony, a fine work composed in 1823 in a completely traditional mold. It is interesting to observe that thirty-five years after Mozart wrote his last three symphonies, Voříšek's makes it appear as though time had stood still, so little difference is there between them. In contrast, there is a world of difference between Mozart's last three symphonies of 1788 and the the kind of symphony being written in 1753, thirty-five years earlier!

Example XXXII–1: J. P. VOŘÍŠEK, Symphony

a. I

b. IV

Voříšek was not a prolific composer like Schubert, and has left little besides this symphony. The distance between Schubert and Voříšek can be seen from a comparison of their symphonies, for Schubert's innate compositional strength enabled him to develop his own path, whereas Voříšek's admiration for Beethoven is seen in his imitation of that composer's procedures without the elemental force that lies behind them. In its motivic work and in its progression from the first motive of the first movement to the last melodic motives of the last movement, Voříšek's symphony communicates very much like a Beethoven work. Here is a progression of mental and musical states, leading to attainment not, however, in a Beethovenian *per aspera ad astra* style, but through the contemplation of a sequence of different kinds of musical beauty. The expressive strength of the first movement and its manipulation of its primary motives is as clear as its sonata-form structure is regular and orthodox. The two middle movements are beautifully developed examples of their kind, and it is impossible to conceive of any improvements to melody or to orchestration. Most of the last movement appears to bear little relationship to the first. But just as Haydn's Symphony No. 102 seems to drop all reference to its germ motive until the coda of the last movement, so Voříšek similarly concludes his symphony with the emphatic inverted form of his opening motive in all the woodwinds.

THE VIRTUOSO CONCERTO

While the early nineteenth-century symphony languished for want of a composer of sufficient stature to mold it according to present needs, such was not the case of the instrumental concerto. The violin concertos of the French Violin School have been discussed earlier, but it must be noted that Kreutzer and Rode were as actively performing and composing during the first decade of the nineteenth century as they had been in the last years of the eighteenth.

The concerto for solo piano and orchestra was equally vital and the reason is not far to seek. Whereas the Haydn symphony had been building in popularity since the 1770s, was internationally widespread in the 1780s, and was dominant in the 1790s, there was no comparable literature for the piano concerto. Yet it was increasingly popular, and many virtuosos wrote concertos for their own use. Unfortunately, as composers they were generally lightweight and their works ephemeral. The only great piano concertos—those by Mozart—were virtually unknown. Of Mozart's piano concertos, only the last appeared in print during his lifetime. The following list shows the curious relationship between dates of composition and dates of publication:

No.	Composed	Published	Difference between dates of composition and of publication
595 in B♭	1788/91	1791	no difference
537 in D	1788	1794	6 years
503 in C	1786	1798	12 years
491 in C minor	1786	1800	14 years
488 in A	1786	1800	14 years
482 in E♭	1785	1800	15 years
467 in C	1785	1800	15 years
466 in D minor	1785	1796	11 years

At the time when these works were beginning to appear in print, the ideal of the form had changed to one shaped by the evolving nature of the instrument. Works had appeared by a number of lesser composers who had an intuitive perception of the nature of the new instrument, allied with an intensive training and a finely polished technique. Had a similar situation obtained with the piano concerto as with the symphony, it may be postulated that Mozart's concertos would have been revered by 1820. In fact, they were all but swept away by those of John Field, Johann Nepomuk Hummel, Frédéric Kalkbrenner, Ignaz Moscheles (1794–1870), and others. The few that retained any place on the concert platform did so largely because of the composer's name and reputation.

Field's First Concerto had appeared in 1799 and has been noted because its slow movement was built upon a favorite Scottish air. The Second Concerto in A♭ (*ACM* 75) gives a contemporary arrangement for piano solo of the first movement) was first published in 1814. That it was composed as late as 1814 seems highly implausible, since Field was a popular concert pianist, and published several concertos in 1814. It is more likely that it dates from considerably closer to the beginning of the century, perhaps as early as 1804/1805, for virtuosos tended to be secretive about their compositions, avoiding print for fear of being imitated once their technical innovations were understood.

Like so many concertos of this period and later, this work serves to emphasize the heroic stature of the soloist by its large dimensions; the first movement is long, consisting of 504 bars of 4/4 meter in moderate tempo.[2] The lyrical essence of this concerto is conveyed at once in a long melody whose indivisible unity extends, with neither antecedent and consequent nor rhythmic/motivic/melodic repetition, over 8 bars to a pause on a half-close; it then returns to the opening, cleverly and subtly modified in melody, harmony, and orchestration, to reach a

2. It is notable that Mozart did not conceive the piano soloist (himself) as hero before 1785, but from that year on, his concertos grew in size, featuring more heroic gestures, and emphasizing climaxes to a greater degree.

conclusion at the beginning of the sixteenth measure. The next thirty or so measures provide the *forte* contrast, based on rhythms and melodic contours from the opening. A quiet link of two bars, mm. 46–47, introduces the next *cantabile* melody in the dominant, which is structured, like the first, on an eight-bar basis; but the second eight bars are elided into a new continuation, which eventually brings back the opening material. The orchestral exposition then is not built as in a Viotti concerto. It is clearly conceived as a three-part structure, beginning with a quiet melody on strings, moving to a *forte* development emphasizing rhythm, then returning by way of *cantabile* melody to the music that opened the composition.

The solo piano translates the opening lyricism into a heroic statement, combining strength (mm. 85–88) with tenderness (mm. 89–92). Its repetition (mm. 93–96), beautifully varied, contains a momentary and fleeting echo of Brahms in m. 95.[3] The *jeu perlé,* Field's pearl-like lyrical side, expands from four to twelve measures, and leads, suprisingly, to new material closely developed from the opening (mm. 110–118) and it is only subsequently that transition to the dominant takes place.

Mm. 134–141 demonstrate one of the most significant aspects of structural modification adopted into the sonata form, and now introduced into the concerto. The use of the dominant pedal, first observed in the symphony of the 1780s, where it was used to create a sense of tension before the recapitulation of the tonic key and the opening melodic/rhythmic material, is typically adopted at this point in the new concerto to create a climax and to herald the introduction of the second *cantabile* melodic area within the exposition! When the second *cantabile* melody is played by the soloist, there follows a quantity of passagework (mm. 165 and on) that brings about the climactic trill, thus concluding this part of the composition, which composers still want to make into a major point of arrival.

The second ritornello runs from m. 215 to m. 239 and centers on E♭, concluding with the opening material in that key, to announce the heroic soloist, this time in E♭ minor. Mm. 255–275 comprise an episode of unusual color, posing an interesting historical question: the similarity between these measures by Field (Example XXXII–2a) and mm. 159–166 from the first movement of Beethoven's Fifth Concerto, Op. 73 (1808/9; Example XXXII–2b) raises issues of priority and influence, which cannot be answered on any internal evidence, and for which external evidence is lacking. Structurally the passages play different roles in their respective works, but harmonically they are identical (although spelled differently) and their effect upon the ear is one of kinship. Pianistically, too, they are like blood brothers.

3. This reference to Brahms serves not to assert that Field foreshadows Brahms but to show the way in which Brahms, magpie-like, steals glistening bits of material from a wide range of his predecessors and stores them up for his own use.

Example XXXII–2: The Influence of Field's Style on Beethoven?

a. J. FIELD, Concerto No. 2 in A♭, I

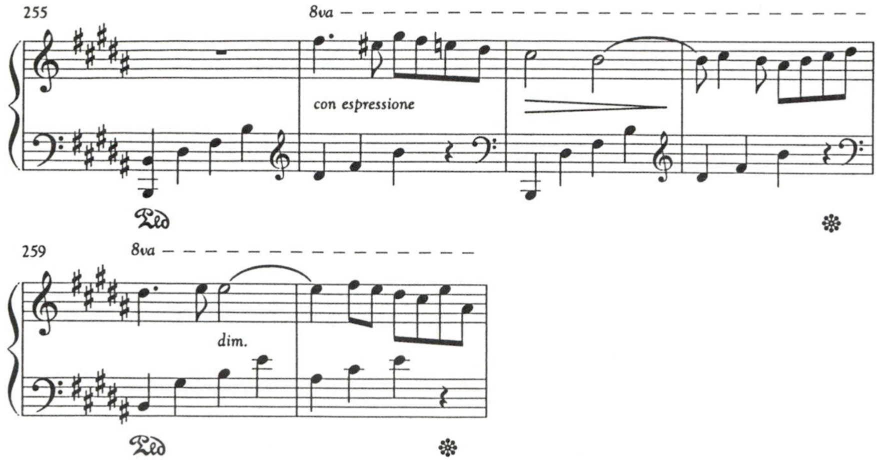

b. L. BEETHOVEN, Concerto Op. 73, *The Emperor*, I

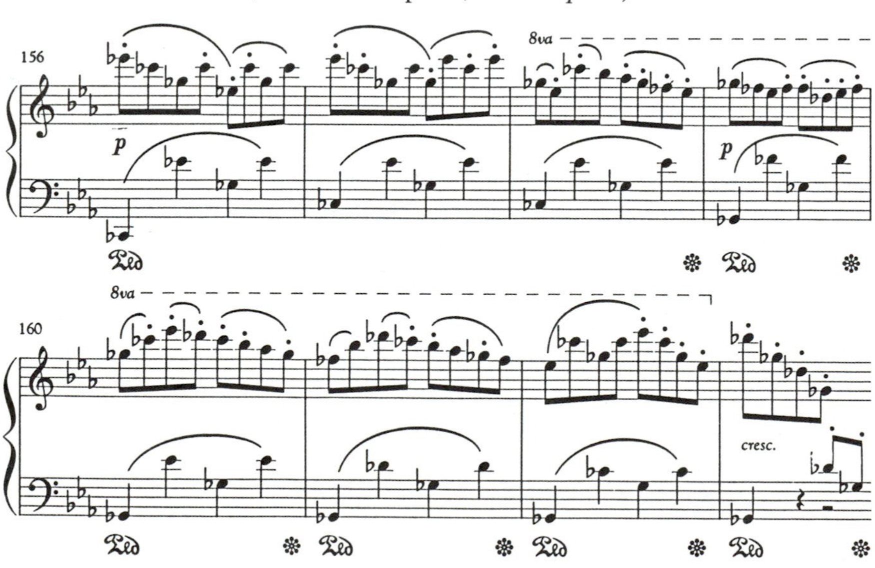

The remainder of Field's second solo section deals discursively with the material of the exposition and even reaches a climactic trill (mm. 372–373) but in the wrong key of F minor. In the next 35 bars there is a return from a false recapitulation in F minor to a real recapitulation in A♭ (m. 413). From here to the conclusion we have a drastically truncated review of the *cantabile* materials, juxtaposed and with almost all passagework removed, resulting in a final section less than half as long as the other two main divisions. There is no room for a cadenza.

This concerto is both exceptional and typical. It is exceptional in the way it captures the quality of the composer's aural imagination, both in piano sonority and orchestral color. Field's use of the orchestra is careful and skillful, and unlike many virtuoso composers from later in the nineteenth century, his sound education under Clementi and his own talent enabled him to devote as much attention to orchestration as to the solo part. His sense of voice-leading in the strings and his ability in modulation are also exceptional, perhaps not in comparison with Beethoven, but certainly when he is measured against his older contemporaries, such as Kozeluch, whose latest piano concertos date from around 1800.

Typical of the time is the desirability of conveying an impression of grand dimensions. Thus the orchestral exposition has to be long, and ideally it should lead to the introduction of the soloist with a climax of suspense which the soloist then releases. Hummel's A-minor Concerto, Op. 85 (1816), demonstrates these qualities when, after an orchestral exposition of 119 bars, the soloist enters quietly, and leads to a willful outburst of new material in a increasingly dissonant crescendo before settling into the first material of the exposition Also typical is the treatment of the second *cantabile* material. It might be argued that herein is a fundamental structural problem, created by the unsophisticated musical thinking of virtuoso pianists such as Field, Hummel, *et al.* Certainly the Mozartian concerto climaxes, set at the end of the exposition and before the last ritornello, retain their vitality through a combination of virtuosity and structural placement. In the early nineteenth-century concerto, the climax at this point is one of virtuosity alone, and can be

Example XXXII–3: J. N. HUMMEL, Concerto Op. 85, I

118
E
SOLO
I
p
cresc.
sf
118
E
calando
pp

compared with the little cadenzas or *roulades* which are inserted into operatic arias, slightly later in the century. Hummel writes 17 measures of piano figuration over a dominant pedal before settling onto his secondary material—a procedure which creates such expectation that whatever follows must be anticlimactic to some degree—and having created such a climax in this part of the structure, the need to extend and vary the climax at the end of the exposition and at the end of the recaptiulation becomes more acute. Example XXXII–4 shows the manner

Example XXXII–4: J. N. HUMMEL, Concerto Op. 85, I, conclusion of the exposition

in which the end-of-exposition trill of the Mozart concert has become bloated at the hands of his pupil.

The concerto and the *symphonie concertante* retained a creative vitality largely denied to the symphony at this time. Their sociological function as works designed to impress by direct musical impact is responsible for this, and the symphony, carrying its paraphernalia of tradition, of its charge to effect moral uplift, and of "real joy being a serious thing" cannot compete with it. The virtuoso concerto retained its eighteenth-century heritage of a large first movement and large dimensions within that movement throughout the century, and the Romantic concerto which sought to reject that inheritance (Mendelssohn, Spohr, Bruch, etc.) did not prevail. The concerto also retained its eighteenth-century heritage of having, whatever the specific gravity of its first movement, a final movement of much lighter substance, unconnected with the material of earlier movements; by contrast, symphony composers seemed more and more determined to unify the work, and eventually to place the greatest emphasis upon its conclusion. Thus, the great paradox in the relationship of these important mediums of the nineteenth-century concert hall: that the symphonic tradition, so firmly established by the large body of work from the eighteenth century and earlier, eventually underwent the greatest transformation of structure and purpose, while the concerto, far less firmly based in tradition, remained much closer to its origins.

THE PERSISTENCE OF THE OPERATIC TRADITION IN ITALY

In general it can be said that the music of the opera theater is more closely attached to the whims of fashion and is more apt to reflect the trends of the moment than other kinds of music. The roots of the nineteenth-century operatic fashions, particularly those dynamic and progressive forces of the French *grand opéra* and of German Romantic opera, go far back into the eighteenth century. Equally, the styles of eighteenth-century opera penetrate far into the nineteenth century before giving way to entirely new currents of thought. Romanticism has been geographically defined as a cast of thought native to North European countries, such as Britain, Scandinavia, Germany, etc., and alien to those countries, such as France and Italy, from which it derives its name. An element of justification for the notion may be found in the fact that opera in Italy simply refused to acknowledge that anything that was happening in the world of Gluck and Piccinni, or of Cherubini and Salieri, could have any impact upon Italian opera, which continued to adapt Metastasian librettos and to divide opera into the two polarities of *opera seria* and *opera buffa*. Indeed, at the opening of the century everything seemed to indicate that Italy was now in a backwater, overtaken by France and shortly to be overtaken by Germany as well.

Cimarosa had died in 1801, and Paisiello's best work was behind him. Expatriate Italians in France such as Cherubini and Gasparo Spontini (1774–1851) were active, but Cherubini's greatest opera, *Les deux journées,* had been produced in 1800 and his later operas were not particularly successful, while Spontini's first success, *La vestale,* was to come in 1807. In Italy itself, Niccolò Zingarelli (1752–1837), the Bavarian-born Simon Mayr (1763–1845), and Ferdinando Paer (1771–1839) were the most successful composers of opera, but none of these three was a talent of sufficient stature to make a strong impression on history. They were completely thrown into the shade by a younger generation of composers: Gioachino Rossini, Gaetano Donizetti, and Vincenzo Bellini (1801–35).

Rossini's operas fall largely into the two traditional categories of *seria* and *buffa*. So little had the *opera seria* changed over the years that when Rossini altered the ending of his early *seria* success, *Tancredi* (1813), from a happy to a tragic ending, public outcry made him change it back.[4] His greatest success, *Il barbiere di Siviglia* (1816), to a libretto by Sterbini, clearly shows the ways in which Rossini's style is an extension of that of his forebears.

ACM 76 contains a duet (No.7) between Figaro and Rosina from Act I of *The Barber*. The preceding *secco* recitative (not included) could have

4. Within a very few years, the opera-going public in Italy, as well as in the rest of Europe, would be expecting that an opera should end sadly.

been taken from any comic opera of the previous fifty years. The plot line has Figaro telling Rosina that the Count, masquerading as a poor student, is in love with her. This is fully explained in the words of the excerpt and runs parallel to Beaumarchais's original. However, where Beaumarchais keeps Rosina's behavior within the bounds of propriety and becoming modesty—a point that would not be lost on the sophisticated audience in Paris and at the French court—Rossini's libretto turns the situation into broader comedy, suitable for a wider and perhaps less polished audience, and transforms Rosina into an operatic coquette. The music uses the exchange of melodic lines between the characters to emphasize the comedy. Rossini makes a pretty point when he has Figaro repeat the coloratura that Rosina has just sung; not only is there a certain comic incongruity in his attempts, but while Rosina's words are an aside of self-congratulation, his words flatter Rosina as he maintains his dramatic superiority to her. The repetitive music conveys a sense of structure, and the rapid interchange of conversation moves the action forward, finally reaching the point where Figaro and Rosina sing together. At that point, Figaro becomes totally subservient to Rosina as his part provides the barest and most expected harmony. The elements that redeem his contribution from utter banality are the words themselves and their rhythmic setting. The instrumental agility of the vocal coloratura and the constant rhythmic vivacity are both part of the composer's personal style, one that swept Europe off its feet and made Rossini one of the most significant influences on the musical scene between 1810 and 1830. The extent to which he felt himself the product of an old tradition may be gauged from the fact that he wrote no more operas after his *William Tell* in 1829, in the belief that opera was taking a direction which he could not follow.

CHORAL MUSIC AT THE START OF A NEW TRADITION

The beginning of the nineteenth century saw something of a revival of composition for the Church, not only in Vienna where Joseph II's strictures against church music were relaxed after his death, but elsewhere as well. Eisenstadt and the Esterházy family brought into being Haydn's last half dozen Masses, discussed earlier, as well as three from Hummel, who was appointed to Haydn's post with the family in 1804, and one from Beethoven in 1807. Michael Haydn, one of the most important church composers in the late eighteenth century, composed two for Vienna, in 1801 and 1803, at the behest of the imperial family; Beethoven's *Missa solemnis* in D (1823) may also be thought to have originated with the imperial family since it was composed for the Archduke Rudolph. And in Paris, Cherubini, who had not enjoyed Napoleon's favor, was appointed one of the superintendents of the Royal Chapel at

An Oratorio Concert in the Theater at Covent Garden by Thomas Rowlandson, 1808. It was necessary to perform oratorios in theaters because the stages of most concert halls were too small to accommodate a choir, soloists, and an orchestra.

the time of the Bourbon Restoration, and he produced a number of Masses. However, the first of these was written before the Restoration and as a result of a visit to the Princess de Chimay. At this time, 1808, Cherubini, embittered by his failures, had almost given up composition, and was devoting himself to his hobbies of painting and botany. The local villagers asked him to compose something to be performed on St. Cecilia's Day in their church, and from this modest beginning there emerged a career in the composition of church music second to none at this time. His Mass of 1809 was followed in 1811 by a large Mass written apparently with no particular performance in mind. His first Requiem in C minor (1816) was written to commemorate the execution of Louis XVI, and it was this composition that caused Beethoven to say to his friend Holz that "he was better satisfied with Cherubini's setting of the Mass for the Dead than with Mozart's." "A requiem," he said, "should be a memorial to the dead and have nothing in it of the noises of the last trumpet and the day of judgement."[5]

Choral singing during this period was becoming the most popular way for amateurs to make music together, and while religious music

5. Cited in Thayer-Forbes, *op. cit.*, p. 985.

could satisfy the demand in part, the fact that in some places women were not yet allowed to sing in church choirs meant that it did not completely meet current needs. Part-songs for male voices, for female voices, and for mixed choirs, cantatas on a variety of poetic subjects, and oratorios, most frequently based upon religious subjects, all helped to make the choral movement one of the strongest influences upon the development of music through the nineteenth century and into the twentieth.

EPILOGUE

The musical life of a society is always of vital interest in that it illuminates the nature of humanity. The period covered in this book witnessed the creation of artworks of beauty, and philosophic explorations about the nature of music worth pondering. And there can be no doubt that the path we have followed has revealed the development of a Golden Age of music and its subsequent decline into a Silver Age.

The particular qualities of this period cannot be grasped through simplistic formulas: this Golden Age did not prize structure above significance, nor intellect above feeling, nor restraint above abandon, nor did the people of the time look back longingly to ancient Greece and Rome. Ultimately, the qualities that characterize so-called Classical music cannot be so defined, for they include everything within the limits of something essentially intangible: "good taste."

At the end of the eighteenth century, Immanuel Kant summed up the experience of his time when he wrote about original genius. Subsequently, his description was reduced to absurdity and taken for prescription (see pp. 340–41): to be a genius one merely had to be original.[6] But it is doubtful whether Mozart or Haydn ever sought originality as such. Indeed, the number and quality of the lesser masters of their times show that originality was not considered desirable; one sought, instead, conformity to accepted ideals of taste. Thus, the music of the late eighteenth century may sometimes be dull, but it is never pretentious or self-conscious.

Can an age become golden through effort and thought? Were the denizens of that Golden Age ever conscious that it was the best of all possible worlds? The answer is no! Shakespeare and his galaxy of brilliant contemporaries could not recognize what they had achieved, but only what more they might achieve; Haydn thought it sad to have learned how to use woodwinds so late in life; and Mozart was not able to finish the work that was to be his own Requiem. And Adam and Eve wanted more than the Garden of Eden could lawfully allow them. Only when

6. Kant was aware of the danger of his formulation and therefore spoke about the possibility of original nonsense.

the Age of Gold had passed could any understanding of what had been dawn on the contemplative.

The French painter, Nicolas Poussin (1593–1665) was one such person. In the painting below, called *The Arcadian Shepherds,* four figures, the woman dressed like a priestess, the men serious and intellectual in appearance, are pointing to the inscription on a tomb. It reads ET IN ARCADIA EGO—literally, "I, too, in Arcady." The words are ambiguous. They may mean that "I, the departed, like you, was once in Arcady," or that "I, Death, am here even in Arcady." What is not ambiguous is the sense of gravity, and beauty, and mortality. To contemplate the beautiful is to be reminded of its passing. The best music of the eighteenth century gives us an image of Arcadia. Like lost innocence, like all nostalgia, however, the perfection of Arcady cannot be regained but only recreated in the life of the mind.

(Musée du Louvre, Paris)

ET ⋆ IN ⋆ ARCADIA ⋆ EGO

Bibliography

The following bibliographical list is intended for the general reader, and must of necessity omit far more than it includes. The selection has been governed by practical considerations and does not include highly specialized studies or books in foreign languages, with the exception of the works catalogues. The existence of a paperback edition is indicated by an asterisk preceding the entry. Those requiring further information are advised to consult *The New Grove Dictionary of Music and Musicians,* ed. Stanley Sadie, 20 vols., London: Macmillan, 1980.

For information on works published since the *New Grove* the reader may also consult *RILM Abstracts of Music Literature.* (New York: CUNY, 1967 to the present), and *The Music Index.* (Warren MI: Harmonie Park Press, 1949 to the present).

Recommended one-volume reference works:

Baker's Biographical Dictionary of Musicians. (8th ed.). Ed. Nicholas Slonimsky. New York: Schirmer Books, 1992.

Cobbett's Cyclopedic Survey of Chamber Music. London: Oxford Univ. Press, 1963.

The New Harvard Dictionary of Music. Ed. Don Michael Randel. Cambridge: Belknap Press of Harvard Univ. Press, 1986.

The Norton/Grove Concise Encyclopedia of Music. Ed. Stanley Sadie. New York: Norton, 1988.

Complete editions of the works of many composers are to be found in numerous libraries. These editions are usually based upon the best available sources and compiled according to modern editorial practice. The reader is earnestly advised to consult these editions whenever possible, in particular with reference to the works of Haydn, Mozart, and Beethoven.

The bibliography is divided into six sections:

1. Works Catalogues. This is a very selective list.
2. General readings in political, diplomatic, or social history.
3. Aesthetics; the nature of music; thinking aobut music and the arts.

4. General works on music.
5. Works relating to Haydn, Mozart, and Beethoven.
6. Works relating to several other composers.

1. WORKS CATALOGUES

C. P. E. Bach. Helm, E. Eugene. *Thematic Catalogue of the Works of C. P. E. Bach.* New Haven: Yale Univ. Press, 1989.

J. C. Bach. Terry, Charles Sanford. *John Christian Bach.* (2nd ed.). London: Oxford Univ. Press, 1967, pp. 193–361.

L. van Beethoven. Kinsky, Georg, and Hans Halm. *Das Werk Beethovens: thematisch-bibliographisches Verzeichnis seiner sämtlichen vollendeten Kompositionen.* Munich and Duisburg: G. Henle, 1955.

L. Boccherini. Gérard, Yves. *Thematic, Bibliographical and Critical Catalogue of the Works of Luigi Boccherini.* Trans. Andreas Mayor. London: Oxford Univ. Press, 1969.

M. Clementi. Tyson, Alan. *Thematic Catalogue of the Works of Muzio Clementi.* Tutzing: Hans Schneider, 1967.

J. L. Dussek. Craw, Howard Alan. *A Biography and Thematic Catalogue of the Works of J. L. Dussek (1760–1812).* Ann Arbor: University Microfilms, 1964.

J. Haydn. Larsen, Jens Peter. *Three Haydn Catalogues* (facsimile ed.). Stuyvesant, N.Y.: Pendragon Press, 1979.

———. Hoboken, Anthony van. *Joseph Haydn: Thematisch-bibliographisches Werkverzeichnis.* Mainz: B. Schott's Söhne, 1957–1978.

W. A. Mozart. Deutsch, Otto Erich. *Mozart's Catalogue of his Works 1784–1791.* New York: Herbert Reichner, n.d.

———. Köchel, Ludwig von. *Chronologisch-thematisches Verzeichnis sämtlicher Tonwerke Wolfgang Amadé Mozarts.* (6th ed.). Wiesbaden: Breitkopf und Härtel, 1964.

F. Schubert. Deutsch, Otto Erich. *Franz Schubert Thematisches Verzeichnis seiner Werke.* Kassel: Bärenreiter, 1978.

L. Spohr. Göthel, Folker. *Thematisch-Bibliographisches Verzeichnis der Werke von Louis Spohr.* Tutzing: Hans Schneider, 1981.

G. B. Viotti. White, Chappell. *Giovanni Battista Viotti (1775–1824), a thematic catalogue of his works.* Stuyvesant, N.Y.: Pendragon Press, 1985.

2. GENERAL HISTORY

⋆Anderson, M. S. *Eighteeenth-Century Europe, 1713–1789.* London: Oxford Univ. Press, 1966.

⋆Briggs, Asa. *The Age of Improvement: 1783–1867.* London: Longmans, Green & Co., 1959.

⋆Brooke, John. *King George III.* London: Constable, 1972.

⋆Casanova, Jacques. *The Memoirs of Jacques Casanova de Seingalt.* Trans. Arthur Machen. New York: G. P. Putnam's Sons, n.d.

⋆Cobban, Alfred. *Aspects of the French Revolution.* London: Jonathan Cape, 1968.

⋆Guérard, Albert. *France in the Classical Age.* New York: Harper Torchbooks, 1965.

⋆Hervey, Baron John. *Lord Hervey's Memoirs.* Ed. Romney Sedgwick. New York: Macmillan, 1963.

Marshall, Dorothy. *Eighteenth-Century England.* London, Longmans, Green & Co., 1963.

Mitford, Nancy. *Madame de Pompadour.* London: Hamish Hamilton, 1968.

———. *Frederick the Great.* New York: Harper & Row, 1970.

⋆Ogg, David. *Europe of the Ancien Régime, 1715–1783.* New York: Harper Torchbooks, 1965.

⋆Sorel, Albert. *Europe and the French Revolution* (1885). Trans. and ed. Alfred Cobban and J. W. Hart. London: Collins, 1969.

Turberville, A. S., ed. *Johnson's England.* Oxford: Clarendon Press, 1952.

⋆Walpole, Horace. *Memoirs.* Ed. Matthew Hodgart. London: Batsford, 1963.

⋆Willey, Basil. *The Eighteenth-Century Background.* London: Chatto & Windus, 1940.

⋆Williams, Raymond. *Culture and Society, 1780–1950.* London: Chatto & Windus, 1958.

3. AESTHETICS: THINKING ABOUT THE ARTS

⋆Abrams, Meyer H. *The Mirror and the Lamp: Romantic Theory and the Critical Tradition.* London: Oxford Univ. Press, 1953.

⋆Brendel, Alfred. *Musical Thoughts and Afterthoughts.* London: Robson Books, 1976.

⋆Cone, Edward T. *The Composer's Voice.* Berkeley: Univ. of California Press, 1974.

⋆Dahlhaus, Karl. *Esthetics of Music.* Trans. William W. Austin. Cambridge: Cambridge Univ. Press, 1982.

Katz, Ruth and Karl Dahlhaus, eds. *Contemplating Music: Source Readings in the Aesthetics of Music.* Stuyvesant, N.Y.: Pendragon Press, 1987.

Kivy, Peter. *The Corded Shell*. Princeton: Princeton Univ. Press, 1980.

★———. *Music Alone*. Ithaca: Cornell Univ. Press, 1990.

Le Huray, Peter & James Day, eds. *Music and Aesthetics in the Eighteenth and Early-Nineteenth Centuries*. Cambridge: Cambridge Univ. Press, 1981.

Lippman, Edward A. *Musical Aesthetics: A Historical Reader*. Stuyvesant, N.Y.: Pendragon Press, 1986.

Oliver, Alfred Richard. *Encyclopedists as critics of music*. New York: AMS Press, 1966.

Reti, Rudolph. *The Thematic Process in Music*. London: Faber & Faber, 1961.

★Strunk, Oliver. *Source Readings in Music History*. New York: Norton, 1965.

Treitler, Leo. *Music and the Historical Imagination*. Cambridge: Harvard Univ. Press, 1989.

4. GENERAL WORKS ON MUSIC

Abraham, Gerald, ed. *The Age of Beethoven, 1790–1830*. London: Oxford Univ. Press, 1982.

Barford, Philip. "The Sonata Principle: A Study of Musical Thought in the Eighteenth Century." *Music Review*, XIII, 1952, pp. 255–263.

★Blume, Friedrich. *Classic and Romantic Music*. Trans. M. D. Herter Norton. New York: Norton, 1970.

Brook, Barry. "The Symphonie Concertante: An Interim Report." *The Musical Quarterly*, XLVII, 1961, pp. 493–516.

———, ed. *The Breitkopf Thematic Catalogue . . . 1762–1787*. New York: Dover, 1966.

Carse, Adam. *18th-Century Symphonies: a short history*. London: Augener, 1951.

———. *The Orchestra in the XVIIIth Century*. New York: Broude, 1969.

Demuth, Norman. *French opera: its development to the Revolution*. Sussex: Artemis Press, 1963. Reprint, New York: Da Capo, 1978.

Fiske, Roger. *English theatre music in the eighteenth century*. (2nd ed.). Oxford: Oxford Univ. Press, 1986.

Foster, Myles Birket. *History of the Philharmonic Society of London, 1813–1912*. London: John Lane, 1912.

Grout, Donald J. *A Short History of Opera*. (3rd ed.). New York: Columbia Univ. Press, 1988.

——— and Claude Palisca. *A History of Western Music*. (4th ed.). New York: Norton, 1988.

Helm, E. Eugene. *Music at the Court of Frederick the Great*. Norman: Univ. of Oklahoma Press, 1960.

Kerman, Joseph. *Opera as Drama*. New York: Alfred A. Knopf, 1956.

Kirkendale, Warren. *Fugue and Fugato in rococo and classical chamber music*. Trans. Margaret Bent and the author. Durham, NC: Duke Univ. Press, 1979.

Landon, H. C. Robbins. *Essays on the Viennese Classical Style*. London: Macmillan, 1970.

*Loesser, Arthur. *Men, Women, and Pianos: a Social History*. New York: Simon & Schuster, 1954.

Mackerness, Eric David. *A social history of English music*. London: Routledge, Kegan Paul, 1964.

Neumann, Frederick. *Essays in performance practice*. Ann Arbor: UMI Research Press, 1982.

Newman, William. *The Sonata in the Classic Era*. (3rd ed.) New York: Norton, 1983.

*Pauly, Reinhard. *Music in the Classic Period*. (3rd ed.). Englewood Cliffs: Prentice-Hall, 1988.

Ratner, Leonard. *Classic Music: Expression, Form and Style*. New York: Schirmer Books, 1980.

———. "Harmonic Aspects of Classic Form." *Journal of the American Musicological Society*, II, 1949, pp. 159–168.

Robinson, Michael. *Opera before Mozart*. London: Hutchinson, 1966.

*Rosen, Charles. *The Classical Style: Haydn, Mozart, Beethoven*. New York: Norton, 1972.

*———. *Sonata Forms*. New York: Norton, 1980.

Stein, Jack M. *Poem and Music in the German Lied from Gluck to Hugo Wolf*. Cambridge: Harvard Univ. Press, 1971.

*Tovey, Donald Francis. *Essays in Musical Analysis*. London: Oxford Univ. Press, 1946.

Weimer, Eric. *Opera seria and the evolution of classical style, 1755–1772*. Ann Arbor: UMI Research Press, 1984.

Wellesz, Egon and Frederick Sternfeld, eds. *The Age of Enlightenment, 1745–1790*. London, Oxford Univ. Press, 1973.

Yorke-Long, Alan. *Music at Court: four eighteenth-century studies*. London: Weidenfeld and Nicolson, 1954.

5. HAYDN, MOZART, AND BEETHOVEN

Beethoven

Anderson, Emily, ed. and trans. *The Letters of Beethoven*. New York: Norton, 1985.

Arnold, Denis, and Nigel Fortune, eds. *The Beethoven Reader*. New York: Norton, 1971.

Cooper, Barry, ed. *The Beethoven Compendium: a guide to Beethoven's life and music*. London: Thames and Hudson, 1991.

Cooper, Martin. *Beethoven: The Last Decade, 1817–1827*. London: Oxford Univ. Press, 1970.

★Grove, Sir George. *Beethoven's Nine Symphonies*. New York: Dover, 1962.

★Kerman, Joseph. *The Beethoven Quartets*. New York: Norton, 1979.

★——— and Alan Tyson. *The New Grove Beethoven*. New York: Norton, 1983.

Landon, H. C. Robbins, ed. *Beethoven: a Documentary Study*. London: Macmillan, 1970.

★Lang, Paul Henry, ed. *The Creative World of Beethoven*. New York: Norton, 1971.

Mellers, Wilfrid Howard. *Beethoven and the Voice of God*. London: Faber & Faber, 1983.

Riezler, Walter. *Beethoven*. Trans. G. D. H. Pidcock. New York: E. P. Dutton, 1938.

Ringer, Alexander. "Beethoven and the London Piano-Forte School." *Musical Quarterly*, 56 (1970), p. 72.

Scherman, Thomas, and Louis Biancolli, eds. *The Beethoven Companion*. New York: Doubleday, 1972.

★Schindler, Anton Felix. *Beethoven as I knew Him*. Ed. D. W. MacArdle. Trans. Constance S. Jolly. New York: Norton, 1972.

★Solomon, Maynard. *Beethoven*. New York: Schirmer Books, 1977.

★Sonneck, Oscar George, ed. *Beethoven: Impressions of Contemporaries*. New York: Schirmer Books, 1967.

★Sullivan, John William Navin. *Beethoven, his spiritual development*. New York: Alfred A. Knopf, 1964.

★Thayer, Alexander Wheelock. *Thayer's Life of Beethoven*. Rev. E. Forbes. Princeton: Princeton Univ. Press, 1967.

Tovey, Sir Donald Francis. *Beethoven*. London: Oxford Univ. Press, 1951.

Tyson, Alan, ed. *Beethoven Studies*, Vol.I, New York: Norton, 1973
Vol.II, London: Oxford Univ. Press, 1977
Vol.III, Cambridge, Cambridge Univ. Press, 1982.

Wallace, Robin. *Beethoven's critics: aesthetic dilemmas and resolutions during the composer's lifetime*. Cambridge Univ. Press, 1986.

Wegeler, Franz Gerhard. *Beethoven remembered: the biographical notes of Franz Wegeler and Ferdinand Ries*. Arlington, Va: Great Ocean Publishers, 1987.

Haydn

Barrett-Ayres, Reginald. *Joseph Haydn and the string quartet*. London: Barrie and Jenkins, 1974.

Brown, A. Peter. *Joseph Haydn's Keyboard Music: sources and style*. Bloomington: Indiana Univ. Press, 1986.

Geiringer, Karl. *Haydn: a creative life in music*. (3rd ed.). Berkeley: Univ. of California Press, 1982.

Gotwals, Vernon, trans. *Joseph Haydn: eighteenth-century gentleman and genius.* Translations of: G. A. Griesinger. *Biographische Notizen über Joseph Haydn,* and A. C. Dies. *Biographische Nachrichten von Joseph Haydn.* Madison: Univ. of Wisconsin Press, 1963.

*Hughes, Rosemary. *Haydn.* London: Dent, 1974.

Landon, H. C. Robbins. *Haydn: chronicle and works.* Bloomington: Indiana Univ. Press, 1976–1980.

———. *The Symphonies of Joseph Haydn.* London: Barrie and Rockliff, 1961.

*Larsen, Jens Peter and Georg Feder. *The New Grove Haydn.* New York: Norton, 1983.

Schroeder, David. *Haydn and the Enlightenment: the late symphonies and their audience.* Oxford: The Clarendon Press, 1990.

Webster, James Carson. *The bass part in Haydn's early string quartet and in Austrian chamber music 1750–1780.* Princeton: Princeton Univ. Press, 1973.

Mozart

Allanbrook, Wye Jamison. *Rhythmic gesture in Mozart: Le nozze di Figaro and Don Giovanni.* Chicago: Univ. of Chicago Press, 1983.

Anderson, Emily. *The Letters of Mozart and his Family.* (3rd ed.). New York: Norton, 1985.

*Blom, Eric. *Mozart.* London: Dent, 1962.

Deutsch, Otto Erich. *Mozart: a Documentary Biography.* Trans. Jeremy Noble and Peter Branscombe. Stanford: Stanford Univ. Press, 1965.

*Einstein, Alfred. *Mozart: his character, his work.* (6th ed.). Trans. Arthur Mendel and Nathan Broder. New York: Norton, 1945.

Hutchings, Arthur. *Mozart: the man, the musician.* London: Thames and Hudson, 1976.

———. *A Companion to Mozart's Piano Concertos.* London: Oxford Univ. Press, 1948.

King, Alexander Hyatt. *Mozart in Retrospect: studies in criticism and bibliography.* (3rd ed.). London: Oxford Univ. Press, 1970.

Landon, H. C. Robbins. *1791: Mozart's last year.* London: Thames and Hudson, 1988.

———. *Mozart and Vienna.* New York: Schirmer Books, 1991.

———. *Mozart, the golden years, 1781–1791.* London: Thames and Hudson, 1989.

———, ed. *The Mozart compendium: a guide to Mozart's life and music.* London: Thames and Hudson, 1990.

*——— and Donald Mitchell, eds. *The Mozart Companion.* New York: Norton, 1969.

*Lang, Paul Henry. *The Creative World of Mozart.* New York: Norton, 1963.

Liebner, Janos. *Mozart on the Stage.* New York: Praeger, 1972.

*Sadie, Stanley. *The New Grove Mozart.* New York: Norton, 1983.

St. Foix, Georges de. *The Symphonies of Mozart*. Trans. Leslie Orrey. London: Dennis Dobson, 1947.

Schenk, Erich. *Mozart and His Times*. Trans. and ed. Richard and Clara Winston. New York: Alfred A. Knopf, 1959.

Steptoe, Andrew. *The Mozart-Da Ponte operas: Cultural and musical background to Le nozze di Figaro, Don Giovanni, and Così fan Tutte*. Oxford: Clarendon Press, 1988.

Novello, Vincent, *A Mozart Pilgrimage–1829*. Ed. Rosemary Hughes. London: Novello, 1955.

Zaslaw, Neal with William Cowdery. *The Compleat Mozart*. New York: Norton, 1990.

6. SEVERAL OTHER COMPOSERS

C. P. E. Bach

Barford, Philip. *The Keyboard Music of C. P. E. Bach, considered in relation*. New York: October House, 1966.

*Helm, E. Eugene. "Carl Philipp Emanuel Bach." In *The New Grove Bach Family*. New York: Norton, 1983.

Ottenberg, Hans-Günter. *C. P. E. Bach*. Trans. Philip J. Whitmore. Oxford: Oxford Univ. Press, 1987.

J. C Bach

Terry, Charles Sanford. *John Christian Bach*. (2nd ed.). London: Oxford Univ. Press, 1967.

*Warburton, Ernest. "Johann Christian Bach." In *The New Grove Bach Family*. New York: Norton, 1983.

Boccherini

Rothschild, Germaine Halphen, *Luigi Boccherini, his life and work*. Trans. Andreas Mayor. London: Oxford Univ. Press, 1965.

Clementi

Plantinga, Leon. *Clementi: his life and music*. London; New York: Oxford Univ. Press, 1977

Ditters von Dittersdorf

Ditters von Dittersdorf, Karl. *Autobiography*. Trans. A. D. Coleridge. Reprint: New York: Da Capo, 1970.

Gluck

*Einstein, Alfred. *Gluck*. Trans. Eric Blom. New York: Collier Books, 1962.

Gluck, Christoph Willibald. *Collected correspondence and papers*. Ed. Hedwig and E. H. Mueller von Asow. Trans. Stewart Thomson. London: Barrie & Rockliff, 1962.

Howard, Patricia. *Gluck and the birth of modern opera.* London: Barrie & Rockliff, 1963.

Grétry

Charlton, David. *Grétry and the growth of opéra comique.* Cambridge: Cambridge Univ. Press, 1986.

Quantz

Reilly, Edward Ray. *Quantz and his versuch: three studies.* New York: AMS Press, 1971.

Sammartini

*Churgin, Bathia. *The Symphonies of G.B.Sammartini.* Vol. 1. "The Early Symphonies." Cambridge: Harvard Univ. Press, 1968.

D. Scarlatti

*Kirkpatrick, Ralph. *Domenico Scarlatti.* Princeton: Princeton Univ. Press, 1953.

Schubert

Brown, Maurice J. E. *Schubert: a critical biography.* London: Macmillan, 1958.

Deutsch, Otto Erich. *Schubert: a documentary biography.* Trans. Eric Blom. London: Dent, 1946.

Reed, John *Schubert–the final years.* London: Faber & Faber, 1972.

Spohr

Brown, Clive. *Louis Spohr: a critical biography.* Cambridge: Cambridge Univ. Press, 1984.

Spohr, Louis. *Autobiography.* New York: Da Capo, 1969.

Index

Page numbers in **boldface** refer to examples. Those in *italics* refer to illustrations.